KUROSAWA

ASIA-PACIFIC:

CULTURE, POLITICS, AND SOCIETY

Editors: Rey Chow, H. D. Harootunian,

and Masao Miyoshi

Mitsuhiro Yoshimoto

KUROSAWA

Film Studies and Japanese Cinema

Duke University Press 2000

© 2000 Duke University Press   All rights reserved

Printed in the United States of America on acid-free paper ∞

Designed by C. H. Westmoreland

Typeset in Minion with Franklin Gothic display

by Tseng Information Systems, Inc.

Library of Congress Cataloging-in-Publication Data

appear on the last printed page of this book.

To my parents,

Sumio and Sachiko Yoshimoto

CONTENTS

ACKNOWLEDGMENTS

I could never have finished this book without the encouragement and help of my friends and colleagues. First and foremost, I would like to express my deepest thanks to Masao Miyoshi, who has unstintingly supported me since I was his student at the University of California, San Diego. He taught me that expertise in any academic subject does not have much value unless it is accompanied by intellectual integrity and political commitment, and that disciplinary boundaries exist not to be respected blindly but to be crossed and problematized. I am grateful to Fredric Jameson for his encouragement and interest in my work. His own work indelibly influenced the way I approach texts and construct theoretical models. I am also indebted to Karatani Kojin personally and intellectually. "Origins" of this book can be traced back to the research I conducted while staying in his study in Tokyo. I thank him for his hospitality and intellectual stimulation.

During the period of the direst predicament, Philip Lutgendorf and Peggy Timm helped me focus on my work. Without the timely advice and aid by Ruedi Kuenzli and Tom Lewis, I am not sure where I would be right now.

I would like to thank Ted Fowler, who offered detailed comments on the manuscript. Dudley Andrew and Abé Mark Nornes gave me valuable criticism on portions of the manuscript. Satomi Saito's assistance at the final stages of preparing the manuscript was indispensable. I wish to acknowledge Aaron Gerow, who made it possible for me to have access to many indispensable books on Japanese cinema. Tom Rohlich was always there to help me. I also benefited from two anonymous readers' comments and suggestions. At Duke University Press, Reynolds Smith has been wonderfully supportive of the project since I first submitted the manuscript.

Finally, I would like to thank Kana Kitsukawa. Without her support, encouragement, and patience, the book would remain still unfinished. Taiyo and Akali probably still do not understand how much they helped me writing. I dedicate this book to my parents, Sumio Yoshimoto and Sachiko Yoshimoto, who waited for its publication for so long. *Domo osoku narimashita.*

INTRODUCTION

Kurosawa Akira secured his position as a representative Japanese film director in Japan and abroad when his *Rashomon* won a Grand Prix at the Venice Film Festival in 1951. Kurosawa is undoubtedly the most widely known and popular Japanese director—perhaps even the most famous Japanese—outside Japan.[1] It would not be an exaggeration to say that Kurosawa has been almost singularly responsible for the global recognition of Japanese cinema as a viable national cinema worth paying attention to.[2] Without the international success of Kurosawa, it would have taken much longer for Japanese cinema to achieve the status of a recognizable national cinema for the non-Japanese audience and academics. Because of the success of *Rashomon* abroad, the Japanese themselves realized the significance of the international film market. The worldwide acceptance of Kurosawa gave them an opportunity to rearticulate consciously what constituted the national and cultural specificity of Japanese cinema. Both in and outside of Japan, the imagining of Japanese cinema as a national cinema has been intricately intertwined with a critical reception and consumption of Kurosawa's films.

Despite his importance and popularity, however, if we examine the images of Kurosawa more closely, their clarity starts to dissipate. In fact, the position of Kurosawa in various critical discourses on Japanese cinema is even more problematic than that of such directors as Ozu, Mizoguchi, or Oshima. For instance, how Kurosawa is treated by Noël Burch, who reinvigorated an academic study of Japanese cinema in the late 1970s, is emblematic of a certain critical difficulty surrounding not only Kurosawa and his films but also Japanese cinema in general. Even though the prewar films of Mizoguchi and Ozu to a large extent have the greatest "use value" for Burch's avant-garde project, the pivotal figure for the project's overall coherence is neither Mizoguchi nor Ozu, but Kurosawa. Burch claims that "after Kinugasa, [Kurosawa] was only the second film-maker in the history of the Japanese film who, after thoroughly assimilating the Western mode of representation, went on to build upon it."[3] Interestingly, this Westernization of Kurosawa is counterbalanced by a diametrically opposite argument on Kurosawa's fundamental Japaneseness: "Kurosawa, despite the essential singularity of his undertaking, was nonetheless a late avatar of a tradition whose roots . . . are fundamentally Japanese, and even more fundamentally, *non-Western*, whatever the fruitfulness of the encounter with Western aesthetics."[4] Yet in the end, Burch does not satisfactorily explain how these two contradictory images of Kurosawa can be reconciled.

Kurosawa's position as a filmmaker in Japan has not been secure and unambiguous, either. The Japanese images of Kurosawa are at least as complex and contradictory as the Western images. By many Japanese, Kurosawa is regarded as the most Westernized Japanese director. As a testimony to this view, we can point out that Kurosawa's name is often written in katakana, a type of Japanese syllabary usually used to write Japanese words of foreign origin. The non-Japaneseness of Kurosawa's image is reinforced by the adjective "world-famous," which is commonly used with his name written in katakana: "*sekai no Kurosawa*." At the same time, the Japanese media have invented a nickname that is antithetical to his de-Japanized image. Kurosawa is often referred to as *tenno*, "(Japanese) emperor," for his allegedly authoritative behavior. Surprisingly, these two conflicting images are simultaneously present even in a single piece of criticism whose author is oblivious to an inherent contradiction of his or her argument.[5]

In both Japanese and Westerners' construction of images of Kurosawa as a film director, there is a certain sense of anxiety, an apprehension about the validity of the critical concepts and frameworks they employ. I would argue that Kurosawa, who occupies a central position in the study, consumption, and construction of Japanese cinema, arouses the feeling of anxiety in Japanese and Western critics because his films problematize Japan's self-image and the West's image of Japan. To the extent that his films reveal the existence of a geocultural fantasy in a seemingly neutral critical language of film criticism, "Kurosawa" can be understood as a symptom of Japanese cinema as it is perceived as a national cinema. A careful analysis of the films of Kurosawa and discourses surrounding his work will illuminate, among other things, the basic assumptions underlying the critical conceptualization of Japanese cinema as a national cinema. This book tries to reexamine widely circulating clichés about Kurosawa and his films not as nonsensical misconceptions but as discursive reactions to real sociocultural contradictions, institutional dilemmas, and disciplinary formation and constraints in the university.

Thus the choice of Kurosawa as the focus of this study is a strategic one. The book is not just intended for fans or aficionados of Kurosawa's "samurai films" or his gripping contemporary dramas with serious moral messages. Nor is it written for scholars in film studies or Japanese studies who are interested simply in learning more about Kurosawa's films. While it closely examines the specificity of Kurosawa's cinema, this study also tries to shift the basic ground on which the scholarship on Japanese cinema has been built and to problematize this scholarship's dominant interpretive frameworks. No matter how sophisticated it might be, a study of some particular critical or historical problem that can be easily appropriated as another fine addition to the field of Japanese cinema studies would not achieve my goals. The sheer accumulation of empirical evidence and new historical information would not by itself change the image of Japanese cinema exchanged and circulating on the academic market. This study of Kurosawa's cinema is based on the belief that one of the most effective ways to contest the axioms of a particular field of study or discipline is to take up a subject that is not necessarily new but already accepted as a canonical material. Given the central position he occupies in the reception of Japanese cinema, Kurosawa is a logical choice for an intense critical scrutiny and rethinking of the disciplinary formation and configuration of Japanese cinema scholarship.

But why does it have to be Kurosawa instead of equally — if not more, in certain respects — canonical filmmakers such as Mizoguchi and Ozu? There are practical and critical reasons for my avoidance of these two acclaimed filmmakers for this particular project. The most immediate problem with Mizoguchi is that so many of his films are either permanently lost or currently unavailable. As a result, a study of his cinema will be dictated not by our critical choice but by the arbitrariness of the material conditions. In the case of Ozu, it is precisely his canonical status that makes him a problematic choice of the type of critical project this study attempts to pursue. Since the late 1970s, more than any other Japanese director, including Kurosawa, Ozu has enjoyed an enormous popularity critically and perhaps to a limited extent also commercially. The celebration of Ozu's work and its central position in the discussion of Japanese cinema are attested by the numerous books on Ozu and his films published in the last two decades.[6] But new studies of Ozu have not changed the basic framework of the scholarship on Japanese cinema. Instead, they have either merely refashioned Ozu as a modernist or avant-garde auteur or reinforced Ozu's "Japaneseness" in the midst of the neo-nostalgia boom.[7] This prolific industry of Ozu criticism is closely connected to the institutional demands and specific cultural — "postmodern" — conditions of the 1980s; that is, the Ozu criticism since the 1980s tells us more about the cultural myths and social contradictions of postmodern Japan and global formation than about modernity and the Japaneseness of Ozu.

Part 1 of this study deals with large disciplinary and institutional questions. Its focus is the scholarship on Japanese cinema, which is thoroughly scrutinized as a symptomatic manifestation of the current disciplinary crisis. This part critically reassesses three historical phases of the American study of Japanese cinema and contextualizes them in relation to the formation and institutional configuration of film studies as an academic discipline. It then examines how allied disciplines, specifically Japanese studies and comparative literature, have or have not constructed Japanese cinema as a legitimate object of institutionally sanctioned knowledge, and how the generally ephemeral status of Japanese cinema as an object of scholarship has been maintained by the disciplinary politics and institutional imperatives of academia.

Part 2 consists of thirty-one chapters of varying lengths, each of which, except the first, focuses on a specific Kurosawa film. The first chapter briefly goes over the question of auteurism and authorship and discusses the authorship of Kurosawa by using the notion of autobiographical pact. The rest of part 2 is not organized according to some common thematic or stylistic motifs, or a set of critical questions. I will try to simultaneously take into account the specificity of each film and the larger critical questions that cannot be confined within the boundary of any particular film. Ideally, all Kurosawa films should be analyzed as closely as possible; however, this is an impossible task because of the sheer limitation of space. I have to decide which films to discuss extensively and which ones to examine briefly. The amount of space allocated for the discussion of each film obviously reflects a value judgment on my part, although there is not always a direct correlation between the length of the chapter and the aesthetic and other kinds of value accorded to the film under discussion. Some films are discussed extensively not necessarily because of their intrinsic value but because of types of critical questions they raise with regard to Kurosawa's cinema and Japanese cinema in general. The uneven distribution of space is also due to my desire to avoid the repetition of the same argument as much as possible. Thus some chapters are quite short because critical issues which can be raised in relation to the films discussed in those chapters are more extensively treated in the analyses of other films.

I have decided to examine each Kurosawa film in a separate chapter because I do not wish to erase the specificity of each film by assimilating it into the putative grand "project" of Kurosawa as an author. The diversity, as much as the coherence, of Kurosawa's cinema will be emphasized. This does not mean, however, that part 2 is just a collection of textual readings of Kurosawa's films. The specificity of each film is certainly respected, but the larger critical issues that Kurosawa's cinema inevitably raises (although they have been left mostly untouched because of institutional constraint and disciplinary politics) are simultaneously explored. Kurosawa and his cinema are therefore defamiliarized as a way of coming to grips with the disciplinarity of film studies and, however limited it may be, as a first step toward the reinvention of a field of Japanese cinema studies.

Throughout the book, all Japanese names are given in Japanese order: the family name precedes the given name. When the person has published in English, the given name appears first. All translations from Japanese are mine unless otherwise noted.

PART I

JAPANESE CINEMA IN SEARCH

OF A DISCIPLINE

After having experienced two decades of rapid institutional expansion and consolidation, film studies is now facing a new challenge. The specificity and significance of film as a distinct object of scholarly investigation have been problematized by the emergence of new electronic and digital technologies. The current predicament of film studies is also a result of its institutional growth and development. Since the 1970s, the specificity of film studies has been determined largely by its focus on theory and radical interdisciplinarity. Yet when so many other humanities and social science departments claim a share of cultural studies and offer courses on critical theory, the boundaries between film studies and traditional disciplines are increasingly becoming blurred.

The purpose of this part is not, of course, to propose a large-scale solution to the disciplinary impasse of film studies. In what follows, I shall instead reexamine the scholarship on Japanese cinema as a symptomatic manifestation of the current disciplinary crisis. It is important to note that Japanese cinema was not simply added to the canon of film studies some time after the successful legitimation of film as an object of serious academic research; on the contrary, Japanese cinema played a significant role in the establishment of film studies as a discrete discipline. The position of Japanese cinema is inseparable from the question of how film studies has constituted itself, legitimated its existence, and maintained its institutional territoriality through a double process of inclusion and exclusion.

Very schematically, the history of American scholarship on Japanese cinema can be divided into three phases: (1) humanistic celebration of great auteurs and Japanese culture in the 1960s, (2) formalistic and Marxist celebration of Japanese cinema as an alternative to the classical Hollywood cinema in the 1970s, and (3) critical reexamination of the preceding approaches through the introduction of discourse of Otherness and cross-cultural analysis in the 1980s. Instead of being confined within the subfield of Japanese cinema, these stages were an integral part of the expansion and consolidation of film studies as a discrete discipline during the last three decades. To understand how Japanese cinema is constituted as an object of knowledge, it is not enough just to study scholarly books and articles on Japanese films. A critical re-examination of scholarship on Japanese cinema must be accompanied simultaneously by a reassessment of the larger discursive contexts of film studies and Japanese studies, which are constrained and regulated by specific disciplinary structures and rules.

How has Japanese cinema been constructed as a distinct object of knowledge in film studies? How has Japanese cinema been treated by Japan specialists? How has Japanese cinema been studied in the academic context of the United States? How can we study Japanese cinema differently? Is film studies the best institutional site where the research on Japanese cinema is conducted? If not, what discipline is better prepared for, or more congenial to, the study of Japanese cinema? What is necessary to make the scholarship on Japanese cinema more solid, reliable, or exciting? How can we structure the field of Japanese cinema to ensure its continuity and growth? These are some of the questions that the following discussion attempts to grapple with.

Humanism and Essentialism in the Postwar Era

In the 1950s, it was mostly journalists and critics at large who published essays on Japanese films. Japanese cinema burst on the American film scene when Kurosawa's *Rashomon* was unexpectedly awarded a Grand Prix at the Venice Film Festival in 1951. This unique period film was extensively reviewed in the major newspapers and highbrow magazines, and its critical and commercial success aroused American curiosity in other Japanese films. Parallel to Hollywood depictions of Japanese life and culture in the 1950s,[1] many of these journalistic writings relied on stereotyped images of Japan or fixated specific aspects of Japanese culture and social customs as the Japanese essence. For Hollywood and journalistic film criticism, Japan was often nothing more than a land of exoticism and alien culture.[2]

As Japanese cinema began to be treated as a distinct object of knowledge in the 1960s, the production of critical discourses on Japanese cinema was also transformed into a more specialized activity. The first significant text that contributed to this transformation was *The Japanese Film: Art and Industry,* by Joseph L. Anderson and Donald Richie, published in 1960. Intended for a serious yet general audience, *The Japanese Film* is a highly informative overview of Japanese film history combined with separate sections on major film directors and actors, generic types, and industrial structure. The publication of this book did not immediately engender the field of Japanese cinema in academia; however, over the years, Anderson and Richie's pioneering work has firmly established itself as the most basic reference book for film scholars conducting research on Japanese cinema.[3] In addition to *The Japanese Film,* Richie has published, as the most authoritative voice in the West and in Japan, numerous articles and books on Japanese cinema.

The 1960s discourse on Japanese cinema, exemplified by the works of Richie, is a type of humanist criticism, which sees film as a repository of universal values. The best films, humanists argue, can teach audiences, without overtly being didactic, important moral lessons regarding human dignity, freedom, and the unity of the human race. But these universal ideals are most effectively conveyed to audiences when they are represented through the concrete images of a particular nation, history, or culture. According to humanist criticism, what makes a film a great artistic achievement is therefore not the abstract presentation of the universal values but the complex interplay of the universal and the particular, in which the latter embodies the former.

One of the most enduring legacies of the 1960s humanist criticism on Japanese cinema is the use of "national character" as the particular, through which the humanistic ideals of universal significance are said to be represented concretely. This focus on national character as a determinate factor in analysis and interpretation has led to an unfortunate situation, in which stereotypes of the Japanese national character and cultural essence are routinely used to explain thematic motifs, formal features, and contextual backgrounds of Japanese films. Thus, in American scholarship on Japanese cinema, the Japanese are often presented as the homogeneous, ahistorical collective essence called the "Japanese mind." ("To the Japanese mind, the self-sacrificing hero is the most admirable hero of all.")[4] It is argued that "Japanese culture and consciousness are marked by a valuing of the irrational," and this is why "one finds in Japanese culture a deeply embedded notion called *yugen,* which entails the presence of mystery and incomprehensibility in all things."[5] Many sweeping statements on Japanese culture are made without any consideration for its relationship to social practices and history. ("The Buddhist view of the world as transitory and full of pain has suffused the entire culture, inducing a sense of resignation in the presence of political brutality"; "Zen has infiltrated all aspects of Japanese culture, including the cinema"; "Although the codas [the unchar-actered shots that begin and end most sequences of Ozu's films] have narrative significance, Ozu's privileging them over simply following the action of the characters suggests an aesthetic attitude that places the individual as a mere element in the universe, the 'void,' rather than at the center, as in Western, Greco-Roman thought.")[6] Japanese films are said to be worth studying because of "what they reveal of the Japanese character."[7] The ubiquitous presence in Japanese cinema of the tradi-tional aesthetic is simply assumed without any critical analysis of that aesthetic. ("The black and white becomes an aesthetic device, which in this case reflects the Japanese ideal of *wabi* [poverty, the prizing of that which looks simple].")[8]

It is of course not possible to determine precisely where this valoriza-tion of the Japanese national character came from. But two discursive systems from quite different areas, auteurism in film criticism and the legacy of the American military intelligence activity during and after World War II, cannot be ignored. Japanese films' appeal to the audi-ences in and outside of Japan led many critics to conclude that there was some kind of universal value in those films. While the exotic ap-peal of Japanese cultural specificity was acknowledged, the critical ac-claim that certain Japanese films — particularly *gendaigeki,* or films set in contemporary Japan — earned at international film festivals was re-garded as a living proof of Japanese cinema's ability to go beyond the parochial context of Japanese society. The gap between universality and particularity was believed to be filled by "humanity," which was posited as the most common denominator among diverse groups of people transcending national and cultural differences. And it was the role of auteurs to mediate the specificity of cultural tradition and the univer-sality of films' messages. Therefore, in the context of 1960s auteurism, the most important book on Japanese cinema was not Anderson and Richie's *The Japanese Film* but Richie's *The Films of Akira Kurosawa*

(1965), since the latter was not only the first comprehensive study of the work of a Japanese film director but also one of the earliest examples of serious film books devoted to *any* auteur's work.[9]

Auteurism has, according to Janet Staiger, three basic criteria to determine the value of filmmakers as auteurs: "transcendence of time and place, a personal vision of the world, and consistency and coherence of statement." In their pursuit of "universality" and "endurance," the auteurist critics find history transcended in the works of great filmmakers.[10] These basic characteristics of auteurism make it an ideal system of critical discourse that has created a space for Japanese cinema in American academia. Whether explicitly stated or not, the idea of the universality of shared humanity is indispensable for making Japanese films intelligible to the American audience. Because of the great auteurs' putative ability to transcend the specificity of history and cultural context, the seemingly exotic films of Kurosawa, Mizoguchi, and other Japanese directors can easily be incorporated into a canon of the "world cinema." However, to the extent that history and cultural tradition cannot but play a significant role in the formation of a "personal vision," what is supposedly transcended sneaks back into the auteurs' works. The humanist studies of Japanese cinema typically try to resolve this ambivalent relationship of the universal and the particular through recourse to Zen and the idea of religious transcendence.

One of the most revealing examples of the use of Zen is Paul Schrader's study of Ozu in *Transcendental Style in Film: Ozu, Bresson, Dreyer*.[11] Schrader argues that Ozu, Bresson, and to a lesser extent Dreyer created what he calls a "transcendental style," which is a transcultural film form expressing the holy or the transcendent. For our purpose, the viability of the notion of transcendental style is not too important. We shall also refrain from exhaustively enumerating questionable points and obvious factual errors in Schrader's description of Ozu's career and films. Instead, what really concerns us here is Schrader's precarious attempt to reconcile the universal and the particular in his discussion of Ozu's transcendental style.

"To what extent was Ozu's personality unique, and to what extent was it representative of the Zen culture? Did Ozu subjugate his personality in the manner of the traditional Orientalist artist, or were his films actually highly individualistic expressions?" (24). According to Schrader, these auteurist questions are not relevant for the case of Ozu because "considered in the larger context of Zen culture, man and his surroundings are counterenveloping, just as are mind and body, content and form; any distinction between them is arbitrary" (25). Schrader eagerly tries to mold Ozu into a Zen artist of the East whose personality and culture are so steeped in Zen that his films express the Transcendent. Schrader's strategy is to create a holistic space called "Japan," which can be represented as a series of concentric circles: at the center of this space is located Ozu's personality, which is "enveloped by Zen culture, and that Zen culture [is] enveloped by a transcending reality" (24). Once homological relations are established between the author, the text, and the context, it is easy for Schrader to claim that Ozu's films express the Transcendent as Zen art does.

The particularity of Ozu's personality and the universality of the transcendental style are reconciled with each other through the mediating presence of Zen and the transcendental nature of Oriental art in general. In Schrader's argument, "Zen" and "Orient" are magic words that miraculously solve critical dilemmas and contradictions of his theory of auteurism. To assert that Ozu was a commercially successful director and at the same time an auteur of the transcendental style, that is, to reconcile the seemingly impossible combination of the popular and the esoteric, or the commercial and the aesthetic, Schrader appeals to what he perceives as a unique characteristic of Japanese culture. Schrader claims that what initially appears to be the unattainable goal of developing the transcendental style within the context of the commercial film industry is not in the end impossible to achieve because the "concept of transcendental experience is so intrinsic to Japanese (and Oriental) culture, that Ozu was able both to develop the transcendental style and to stay within the popular conventions of Japanese art" (17).

While making a culturalist claim on homology between Ozu's personality, films, and Japanese culture as manifestations of Zen, Schrader is at pains to minimize the role of culture in the formation of Ozu's transcendental style, since the transcendental style, "not determined by the film-makers' personalities, culture, politics, economics, or morality" (3), is by definition a transcultural form. There are two basic steps in Schrader's strategy for resolving this contradiction. First, he tries to discard anything that does not confirm the image of Ozu as a Zen artist.

Schrader recognizes, for instance, how Ozu incorporated into his films the "rote repetition of movement [as] a gag in Japanese silent comedy" (37). However, immediately after acknowledging the significance of a non-Zen aspect of Ozu's films, he concludes that "taken as a whole Ozu's techniques are so similar to traditional Zen methods that the influence is unmistakable" (38). What is ambiguous in Schrader's claim is the phrase "taken as a whole." Since Schrader does not explicitly specify the corpus of Ozu's films examined in his study, what he means by the "whole" remains unclear. According to Schrader, "everyone must return to the evidence; one must analyze the films, scenes, and frames, hoping to extract the universal from the particular" (3). Yet, what is absent in his criticism is precisely the evidence for his claim.

Second, Schrader deliberately confounds the transcendental style as a specific film form with the transcendental experience as a represented content in film. He creates this confusion precisely by calling for the necessity of differentiating the two: "Before one can analyze the transcendental style in Ozu's films, one must make (or attempt to make) the crucial yet elusive distinction between transcendental art and the art of transcendental experience within Ozu's work. Do Ozu's films express the Transcendent, or do they express Ozu, Zen culture, and man's experience of the Transcendent?" (23). The phrase "one must make (or attempt to make) the crucial yet elusive distinction" indicates the extreme difficulty of differentiating Ozu's transcendental style (the universal) and Ozu's personality and Zen culture of Japan (the particular). But according to Schrader, what initially seems an almost impossible task becomes achievable once the question of culturally specific perspectives is introduced. To assert the value of the Western perspective, he first concedes its limitation.

It is very difficult for the average Western viewer to appreciate the *aware* of Ozu's themes or the *wabi* of his technique, much less to distinguish between the moods of the *furyu*. The Japanese-English dictionary itself despairs of any attempt to define or delimit the aesthetic twins of *sabi* and *wabi*. Simply because the Western viewer cannot make the distinction between *sabi*, *wabi*, *aware*, and *yugen* in Ozu's films he should not mistakenly think that Ozu is after a single basic emotion, as is much of Western psychological realism. The codas of

Ozu's films are remarkably complex, and the difference between a still shot of a vase, a *tatami,* and Mount Fuji may mean the difference between *sabi, wabi,* and *aware.* When the still shot of the vase is first shown in *Late Spring* it evokes *wabi,* but by the time that same shot is "repeated" later in the film it also connotes both *aware* and *yugen.* (34)

While acknowledging the disadvantage of the Western viewer, Schrader asserts the necessity of the Western perspective for the discernment of Ozu's transcendental style. According to Schrader, "the point at which Zen style stops and transcendental style begins is almost indiscernible in Ozu's films" (53), and this is particularly the case when the audiences regard his films, as many Japanese do, as a direct extension of Japanese culture. Thus, "it is not possible to extrapolate the transcendental style from within a totally Japanese perspective; one needs several cultural perspectives" (53).

The problem with Schrader's argument lies in his use of the identity of the viewer as the determining factor in a successful or unsuccessful understanding of Ozu's films. For instance, according to Schrader, Western viewers often fail to differentiate the different types of *furyu* (the four basic untranslatable moods of Zen) in Ozu's films, and the Western viewers' failure is attributed to the limitation of their culturally specific perspective. It does not occur to Schrader that the reason for this unsuccessful appreciation of Ozu's films may have more to do with the absence of those subtly differentiated moods in Ozu's films themselves. I am not aware of the existence of any credible study explicating nuances of *wabi, sabi, aware,* and *yugen* in Ozu's films. Nor have I yet met any Japanese who can perceive the subtle change of moods from *wabi* to *aware* and *yugen* evoked by the famous shot of the vase in *Late Spring.* Similarly, if as Schrader argues Japanese viewers usually do not notice the point where the representation of the transcendental experience is transformed into the transcendental style, it may have little to do with the limitation of the Japanese perspective but more to do with the conceptual flaws in Schrader's differentiation of the transcendental style and the transcendental experience.

Did Ozu create the transcendental style of film *because of* Zen's infiltration into Japanese daily life or *in spite of* Japanese culture's affinity to the Transcendent? How did Ozu create a filmic form that successfully expresses the "Transcendent" by transcending Japanese culture when, according to Schrader, Japanese culture, so thoroughly permeated by Zen as a way of life, embodies the "Transcendent"? Is Zen an instance of a particular culture to be transcended, or is it the universal that makes transcendence of a particular culture possible? Instead of trying to resolve the ambivalence articulated by these questions, Schrader exploits it. What remains most precarious in Schrader's argument is the logically impossible status of Zen, and the problem lies in Schrader's confusion of the "transcendental" with the "transcendent."[12] The ambivalence of Zen is never resolved; on the contrary, it is precisely through his ambivalent use of Zen that Schrader tries to reconcile the universal with the particular and constructs Ozu as an auteur of the transcendental style.

Auteurism as a critical discourse enabled critics such as Richie and Schrader to transcend contradiction of universalism and particularism. The field of Japanese cinema was also shaped by another set of discursive practices: the ethnographic study of Japanese national character promoted by the U.S. government during and after World War II.[13] The extensive wartime collaboration of anthropologists, sociologists, and psychologists with the U.S. military intelligence produced a significant body of work on the Japanese national character. The "fundamental premise of the national-character approach was," writes John Dower, " 'the psychic unity of humankind' — the assumption, as Margaret Mead later expressed it, that 'all human beings share in a basic humanity.' "[14] This combination of the universality of a basic humanity and the particularity of national character is not as strange as it might seem at first, since the notion of national character was evoked in part to discredit the racist theories of biological determinism. Researchers engaged in the study of national character argued that instead of race, "integrated cultural patterns, the unconscious logic of sentiments and assumptions, and the processes of 'enculturation' were the keys to understanding all people participating in a common milieu."[15] In other words, the national character study was first promoted as a way of dislodging race from the status of a final determinant in production of differences. However, despite its anti-racist impetus, it is no secret that the national character study was quickly appropriated by, and contributed to, the racist discourse of wartime propaganda.

The most influential work on the Japanese national character is Ruth Benedict's *The Chrysanthemum and the Sword* (1946),[16] which opens with the following sentences: "The Japanese were the most alien enemy the United States had ever fought in an all-out struggle. In no other war with a major foe had it been necessary to take into account such exceedingly different habits of acting and thinking."[17] As her opening remark shows, Benedict approaches Japan as the most complete Other to the United States. Drawing on diverse sources of information including Japanese films, Benedict tries to find deep-seated cultural patterns in seemingly contradictory manifestations of Japanese daily life. Benedict especially focuses on categories of social and moral obligation such as *on, chu, ko,* and *giri* to demonstrate how the cultural patterns of Japanese are fundamentally different not only from those in the Occident but also from those in the Orient. As the Japanese ethnographer Yanagita Kunio points out, Benedict's "theory of culture patterns . . . seems to be concerned with those patterns which are permanently attached to a nation or a race, and which are not modified by changes in environment and by the power of time."[18] Race recedes from the foreground of discussion, yet to the extent that "cultural patterns" are permanently fixed to a particular race without any real possibility for their fundamental changes, Benedict's argument is as problematic as a more overtly racist theory. Benedict's view of Japanese society is too totalizing, and not enough attention is paid to various kinds of differences in class, gender, region, and so on. Her sweeping claim on Japanese patterns of thought and behavior is ahistorical, "guilty of ignoring meaningful temporal distinctions, e.g., using materials of Tokugawa period currency to draw generalizations about present-day behavior."[19]

During World War II, Japanese cinema was studied as part of the military intelligence activities to grasp the Japanese national character, and their thought and behavioral patterns.[20] The final result of this type of research was then used to aid policy makers in deciding how to deal with Japan during and after the war. In the 1950s and 1960s, this relationship between national character and cinema was reversed by film critics. Instead of analyzing Japanese cinema as a key to unlock the mystery of the Japanese national character, they started using the Japanese national character as a means of "correctly" appreciating Japanese cinema. The ideas of *on, giri, ninjo,* and so forth, which Benedict had laboriously analyzed, were blithely used in analyses of Japanese films without being critically scrutinized. The fundamental operative principle of humanist criticism of Japanese cinema is the inversion of question and answer; that is, what should be scrutinized through a careful analysis of films is used precisely as the answer to interpretive questions raised by those films. This inversion corresponds to what Tetsuo Najita calls "Japanese inversion of Benedict." Najita argues that the postwar Japanese social scientists and critics such as Nakane Chie and Doi Takeo "proceed from the presumption that the Japanese are 'unknowable' except to Japanese, and that the role of social science is to mediate and define their self-knowledge in terms accessible to the world of others. . . . The 'scientifically' reduced structural forms and relational axes explained the distinctiveness of a Japanese culture which outsiders could not directly know or participate in, and could at best approach through the mediations of social-scientific interpreters. Just how effective this Japanese 'inversion' of Benedict has been can be appreciated by the consistent use of this perception of Japanese exceptionalism (unknowable but not inscrutable) in terms of group harmony and vertical loyalty to explain Japanese technological and organizational proficiency."[21] In the humanistic study of Japanese cinema, through this process of inversion, the difference of Japanese cinema is attributed to that elusive entity called "Japan."

The axiomatic characteristics of the humanist scholarship on Japanese cinema basically preclude possibilities of political intervention. The fixated notions of national character, the Japanese mind, and the Japanese way of life make an attempt to intervene in the status quo of society simply superfluous. Even when some attempt is made to introduce politics and ideology into criticism, the haunting effect of the essentialized Japaneseness often reinforces the national stereotypes. When, on rare occasion, humanist critics call for a political change, they still end up reaffirming national stereotypes, thus creating adverse political effects. A plethora of claims on the feudal remnants in modern Japanese society, like Benedict's argument, virtually eliminate historical specificity from what is supposed to be a historical study of Japanese cinema.[22]

A Theoretical Turn?

The success of film studies as a newly emerging discipline was inseparable from a certain spirit of contestation in the 1960s against the way knowledge was produced in the traditional humanities. For a younger generation of scholars who were increasingly unsatisfied with the limits of academic disciplines, film was not just another type of art deserving serious scholarly attention. The radical critics of the late 1960s and early 1970s turned to film to question the ideological underpinnings of what was considered as constituting "scholarly seriousness." The study of Japanese cinema did not remain outside this trend of theoretical radicalization. The 1970s saw the rise of the second wave of scholarship, characterized by its oppositional politics of aesthetic and form, on Japanese cinema. The most important work of this radicalized scholarship is Nöel Burch's *To the Distant Observer: Form and Meaning in the Japanese Cinema* (1979),[23] which introduced the ideology of film form as a central question in the study of Japanese cinema.

One of the axiomatic premises of Burch's work is that there is an "essential difference between the dominant modes of Western and Japanese cinema."[24] Throughout his book, Burch constantly contrasts the cinema and culture of Japan with those of the West. For instance, according to Burch, Western cinema is representational, whereas Japanese cinema, following the traditions of Kabuki and Bunraku, is best characterized as presentational. While Western illusionist painting strives to create a sense of depth, Japanese painting deliberately draws the viewer's attention to the surface. The Western bourgeois ideology valorizes originality and individual creativity; in contrast, in traditional Japanese aesthetics, the concept of originality is irrelevant. The process of signification is something that needs to be concealed according to the Western realist convention; by reflexively inscribing the signifying process in the text, the Japanese textual practice foregrounds the constructedness of meaning. As these characterizations of Western and Japanese textual practices show, the operative principle of Burch's theory is very much akin to Benedict's paradigm of "Us/Not-Us,"[25] that is, the absolute dichotomy of the West and Japan. What Burch is ultimately interested in is not the latter but the former, since Burch's study "is intended . . . as a step in the direction of a critical analysis of the ideologically and culturally determined system of representation from which the film industries of Hollywood and elsewhere derive their power and profit."[26] And some critics have confirmed Burch's objective by finding in *To the Distant Observer* one of the most lucid descriptions of the formal system of the classical Hollywood cinema.[27]

Because in his theory the significance of Japanese cinema is completely dependent on the hegemonic system of Western cinema, Burch has been accused of being engaged in an Orientalist project. For Burch, Japanese cinema has a meaning only to the extent that it functions as a model of a new cinema that critiques the bourgeois ideological assumptions of the dominant Western cinema. Or as one critic puts it, Burch uses "Japanese cinema as a rod with which to beat the back of Western bourgeois transparent cinema."[28] Burch's theoretical bias — understanding of the West mediated by a "detour through the East" — is not by itself a fatal flaw. Nor is there anything inherently wrong with an attempt to search for some alternative system of representation and textuality in Japanese cinema (or for that matter in the emerging moment of the cinema in the early-twentieth-century West),[29] provided that "Japanese cinema" used for this purpose is not a mere mirage of the critic's desire. Conversely, the critic can "also . . . isolate somewhere in the world *(faraway)* a certain number of features . . . and out of these features deliberately form a system" and decide to call this system "Japan"[30] as long as this "Japan" always remains an imaginary construct, not a reality. The problem with *To the Distant Observer* is precisely the confounding of Japan as a fictitious construct and as a reality. As Dana Polan argues, there is a fundamental contradiction in Burch's project,[31] a contradictory split between the fictional status of the "Japan" he constructs and his claim that his "approach is . . . historical in every sense."[32] Burch is most misleading when he tries to develop a historical argument because to substantiate his point, he often tailors the modern Japanese history to fit his Orientalist view of Japanese cinema's essential difference. Burch's view of nonsynchronous development of aesthetic form, political ideology, and capitalist economic system may be complex and full of nuances;[33] however, the sheer complexity of a historical model guarantees neither the historical accuracy nor the antiethnocentricity of that model. What makes Burch's Orientalism particularly troubling is his critical stance on the dominant mode of filmic representation in the West. As he indicts the ideology of the dominant Western cinema, Burch falls prey to the Orientalist trap and, despite his avowed intention, ends up affirming the same ideology that he criticizes.

Does Burch deny universal values and examine the "history of film style not in terms of cross-cultural universal values, but of dominant and supplanted practices, of norms and deviations within a social context"?[34] Burch does not seem to be concerned with the interplay and conflict between the normative modes of filmic representation and the deviant or subversive modes in the sociohistorical context of modern Japan. The social context where Burch places "dominant and supplanted practices" is contemporary Western society, in which he is searching for a radical mode of filmmaking as an avant-garde artist-critic. Even though the subject of his study is Japanese cinema, Burch does not show any specific interest in the ideological effect of Japanese and other cinemas in the context of Japanese society. The norm for Burch is not the dominant representational practice in Japanese film history but the abstract model called "institutional mode of representation" exemplified by classical Hollywood cinema. Burch does not accord the value of universality to the dominant mode of representation in the West; however, the West remains the ultimate bearer of universality to the extent that the value of Japanese cinema is always determined through its comparison to the dominant Western cinema. Although the role and specificity of perspective is acknowledged (as we can see in his self-positioning as a "distant observer"), Burch's study never considers the specificity of the institutional site of discourse.

What is "troubling," writes one critic, "is Burch's inability to avoid all the pitfalls of the well-publicized Orientalist syndrome, for he often appears to be constructing a model of Japanese culture that is idealized and arbitrary. Yet despite these failings, Burch's book is ignored at great cost by scholars of Japanese film, in the classroom as well as the study."[35] I sympathize with this attempt to separate positive elements of Burch's study from shortcomings and weaknesses, but I must say that this is a task extremely difficult to accomplish. The two components of Burch's work, Orientalist clichés and theoretical insights, cannot be separated from each other so easily because there is a structural connection between Burch's formal analysis and his Orientalist premises. Theory in Burch's work is not a set of critical premises free of ideology or a neutral tool of analysis, and Orientalist tendency is not mere baggage that can be discarded at will. In fact, *it is precisely because of Burch's Orientalist biases that his theoretically informed work on the Japanese film history is in its own way exciting and thought provoking.*

It is important for us not to simplistically equate Burch's Orientalism to the shortcomings of his project as a historical study. There is no guarantee that other critics who are more interested in historical context and cultural specificity are immune to Orientalist assumptions. Sometimes a false equation is made between the Orientalist tendency and theoretical approach to Japanese cinema exemplified by Burch's work. When the more "contextual" analysis of Japanese cinema is naively valorized over Burch's theoretical imperialism, a critique of Burch can become as problematic as Burch's own study.[36] Moreover, the more detailed historical research — the use of Japanese scholarly works, the analysis of primary materials — does not necessarily eliminate Orientalist tendencies from the field of Japanese cinema, either. The expert knowledge of Japanese film history is not incompatible with Orientalism at all. On the contrary, as Edward Said has definitively demonstrated, Orientalism as an ideology has been produced, maintained, and propagated not by "distant observers" like Burch but by professionally trained experts on things Oriental.

Despite its critical success, Burch's work failed to create a "theoretical turn" in the study of Japanese cinema. Why did the humanistic studies of Japanese cinema continue to thrive even after the publication of Burch's pioneering work? For revitalization of the scholarship on Japanese cinema, it is imperative to recognize that a theoretical study of Japanese cinema initiated by Burch was not simply interrupted or abandoned by scholars more interested in contextualizing Japanese cinema historically and culturally. Despite their apparent differences, there is in the end no absolute disjunction between the humanism of the 1960s and the ideological criticism of the 1970s. Both schools of criticism start from the premise that Japanese cinema is essentially different from Hollywood cinema; what has changed is the system of explanation to account for Japanese cinema's Otherness and how that system breaks down because of internal inconsistency and contradiction. Paul Schrader's argument on Ozu's transcendental style is dependent on his deliberately ambivalent construction of Zen as the particular to be transcended and as the universal that makes transcendence of the particular possible. Whenever the logical impossibility of his formulation comes to the fore, Schrader tries to resolve the contradiction in the name of the ahistorical, holistic "Japaneseness." Similarly, Burch tries to evade the question of history and contextualization by enlarging the notion of text to encompass the entirety of the Japanese cultural history; that is, the text and the context are merged into the unity of the supertext called "*le texte japonais,*" which nullifies the distinction of formal analysis and historical study.

Thus, despite their appearances, there is a complicity between auteur-centered humanism and Burch's radical theorization. Instead of theoretically reexamining the critical premises of humanist criticism, Burch develops his poststructuralist/Marxist approach to Japanese cinema based on those premises. Instead of introducing a theoretical turn in the field of Japanese cinema, because of the inseparability of his theoretical claim and Orientalism, Burch's theoretical intervention ends up authorizing the continuation of more traditional humanistic studies.

Cross-Cultural Analysis and Identity Politics

Burch's book has been extensively reviewed and discussed since its original appearance in 1979. Out of these discussions have grown two types of trends in the field of Japanese cinema. On the one hand, those who see excessive theorization and lack of attention to historical context in Burch's project try to produce more contextualized accounts of auteurs' works, aesthetics, movements, and limited periods of Japanese film history.[37] On the other hand, what is called cross-cultural analysis tries to continue theorization of Japanese cinema and simultaneously construct a new historical narrative of intercultural exchange. What Burch does in his first major theoretical work on the non-Western cinema is symptomatically represented by its title, *To the Distant Observer: Form and Meaning in the Japanese Cinema*. After briefly justifying his critical position as a "distant observer" who is not too familiar with Japanese history, culture, and language, Burch concentrates on his ideological and formalist analysis of "form and meaning in the Japanese cinema." Cross-cultural analysis reverses this hierarchical relationship of the critical premise and the main body of argument in Burch's book; that is, instead of treating the position of the critic as a significant yet ultimately secondary methodological issue, cross-cultural analysis foregrounds it as a central point of contention in the study of Japanese cinema by American academics.

Scott Nygren develops an argument on cross-cultural influence, mis-recognition, and exchange in two articles, "Reconsidering Modernism: Japanese Film and the Postmodern Context" and "Doubleness and Idiosyncrasy in Cross-Cultural Analysis."[38] The former tries to construct a large-scale historical model of cross-cultural exchange between the West and Japan; the latter is more concerned with the role of the critic's identity in cross-cultural analysis. One of Nygren's main theses in both texts is that modern Japan and the West are in a certain sense the inverted mirror image of each other. "Humanism and anti-humanism," writes Nygren, "play inverse roles in the conflict of tradition and modernism in Japan and the West: each culture turns to the other for traditional values which function to deconstruct its own dominant ideology. Japan borrows humanism from the West as a component of Japanese modernism, just as the West borrows anti-humanist elements from Japanese tradition to form Western modernism. At points of cross-cultural exchange between Japan and the West, traditional and modernist values are likely to seem paradoxically intertwined."[39] What makes him realize this inverted relationship is the emergence of postmodernism, which "is conceived in the West as a non-progressivist freeplay of traditionalist and modernist signification without progressivist determinism" (7).

There are a number of problems in what Nygren presents as cross-cultural analysis, but first and foremost is the ambiguity of certain key terms he uses. For instance, although he wavers between different usages of the phrase "Western modernism," what he means by it is fairly clear. The most consistent examples of Western modernism mentioned are various artistic movements of the late nineteenth century and early twentieth century (e.g., impressionism, cubism, surrealism, futurism, etc.). In contrast, it is difficult to pinpoint what he calls Japanese modernism. He neither defines the term clearly nor provides a coherent set of examples of Japanese modernists or modernist works.[40] Strangely, there is no explicit reference to various modernist movements in Japanese literature, art, theater, architecture, and even film.[41] Granted that it is never possible to analyze comprehensively every aspect of Japanese modernism in a single article or book, it is still easy and necessary to specify what kind of modernist movement is examined and what others are excluded from a particular study. Without some kind of delimitation, the word "modernism" remains nothing more than an empty signifier, and the discussion becomes indistinguishable from a mere wordplay.

Why is it the case that while mentioning different kinds of modernism in the West, Nygren fails to differentiate various modernist movements in Japan? It is because any specific examination of Japanese modernism would make it impossible to establish the relationship of inversion between Japan and the West. Nygren's claim that there is a correspondence between what the "modern" meant for the Japanese of the Meiji period and Western humanism and individualism is highly contestable. Even if we accept his claim for argument's sake, it still does not automatically lead to the conclusion that Japanese modernists were most influenced by Western humanism, not modernism, even in the 1920s, 1950s, or 1960s. Despite his insistence that Japanese artists leaned more toward humanism than modernism, it is difficult to understand why Japanese artists' alleged preference of impressionism and postimpressionism over such avant-garde movements as cubism, surrealism, and dadaism can be construed as evidence of the "deconstructive role of the Western humanist tradition in a Japanese context."[42]

To support his argument that the "principles of inversion, paradox and *aporia*" underlie the cross-cultural relations between the West and Japan, Nygren mentions Doi Takeo's psychoanalytic theory of Japaneseness. According to Nygren, Doi's theorization of *amae* as a core of Japanese intersubjective relationship shows curious resemblance to the psychoanalytic theory of Jacques Lacan: "The *amae* subject appears as dispersed among relationships with numerous others, and the other is always bound up in any possible subject position. . . . In these terms, the *amae* model of subject formation parallels the Lacanian model of a split subject which cannot be conceived separate from otherness." This supposed similarity of Doi's and Lacan's theories is presented as further evidence of how "a traditional Japanese formation is linked with a modernist practice in the West" (11) as if Doi's *nihonjinron* discourse were an accurate description of a traditional Japanese subjectivity.[43]

Nygren discusses a mythological function of the notion of feudalism in modern Japan: "Feudalism was conceptualized during the modern era in Japan as a means to categorically discard the established social order. 'Feudalism' itself as a term mythologizes Japanese historical traditions in much the same way that humanism does for the West. 'Feudalism' implicitly positions all of Japanese history as analogous to the medieval stage of Western development, and imagines that history again as unitary, without internal contradictions. As such, the term becomes an extension of humanist ideology open to deconstruction" (10). Again, there is a willful attempt to confound two distinctively different notions. Even if both "feudalism" and "humanism" are sometimes used to create a false sense of the unitary past in Japan and the West, this does not necessarily make "feudalism" "an extension of humanist ideology." What is ignored is that the term "feudalism" is also a historically specific category, and that there is a massive amount of scholarship on Japanese feudalism produced by both Japanese and non-Japanese scholars who do not mythologize the past.

"Cross-cultural reading is always at least double, and articulates both cultural situations, that of the reader and that of the read, unavoidably and simultaneously" (184). Yet instead of presenting "both cultural situations, that of the reader and that of the read," Nygren's reading of Kurosawa's *Ikiru* plays only with the reader's construction of the West and Japan. His description of the cultural situation of the read is full of stereotypes and clichés about Japanese society, institutions, and the "psychoanalytic formation of the Japanese subject," in other words, fixated images of the Japanese essence produced by *nihonjinron* (discourse on Japaneseness). When what is articulated as Japanese "reality" is only a stereotype or cliché constructed by the "Western" reader from the very beginning, how can cross-cultural analysis take place as an event? Can cross-cultural analysis be developed with a false sense of reciprocity? Where exactly can a critical space of cross-cultural analysis be located? How can we genuinely pursue cross-cultural analysis when the ahistorical, decontextualized account of Japanese social dynamics is used as a critical premise? The task of cross-cultural or any engaged analysis is not to see how Kurosawa's *Ikiru* "sustains an irreconcilable conflict between the so-called feudal pejorative view of Western individualism and the Western humanist discounting of traditional Japanese consensus society" (179) but to question for what ideological purposes the idea of "traditional Japanese consensus society" was created in the first place.[44] Moreover, the unreflective use of the term "West" in his essays also ends up reinforcing the identity of the West as something transparent, natural, and self-evident. (John Guillory points out that the "concept of Western culture is itself of relatively recent origin — perhaps no earlier than the eighteenth century — and that it is constructed by suppressing the elements of African and Asian culture it has assimilated, as well as the difficult suturing of the Judaic and the Hellenic.")[45]

Nygren claims: "If we as Westerners can only conceive of the Orient by speaking or writing through the Other of Western ideology, then it is also true that the West appears to the East in terms of its own Other. Japan's view of the West through its Other is as valid, as problematic, and as unavoidable as the West's conception of Japan through its own Other."[46] Yet history shows otherwise. In 1854 Commodore Perry and the shogunate officials signed a diplomatic treaty between the United States and Japan, both of which had vastly different interpretations of the same treaty. The United States, however, immediately took action to enforce its own version of interpretation, and faced by the infinitely superior military power, Japan did not have any other choice but to accept it. H. D. Harootunian finds in this historical event a paradigmatic pattern of the interaction between the United States and Japan in the last century and a half: "It might be argued, on the basis of this inaugural misrecognition, that Japanese/American relations derived from and were set upon their course by an act of interpretation, whereby the United States jumped to occupy the 'enunciative voice' to determine the meaning of a statement before the Japanese were able to press their own claim. On their part, the Japanese appeared to have been assigned to the status of second-term, or silent, interlocutors whose interests, hereafter, were to be represented to themselves by another. Sometimes the interaction has resembled the relationship between ventriloquist and dummy."[47] What is erased in Nygren's equivocal conflation of Japan's and the West's views is precisely the historical specificity of the geopolitical hierarchy and power relationship evident between the United States and Japan since the mid–nineteenth century.

"Burch's text stands as an implicit open critique to all those historians who would pursue historical artifacts as self-defining objects already positioned within the hierarchical organization of linear time and centralized space dictated by humanist ideology. This hierarchy centers the West as ultimate frame of reference and value in order to organize the material, and it is this hierarchization that so frequently goes in the West by the name 'history.'"[48] What remains unclear in this defense of theory against history by Nygren is this: In what way does the "hierarchical organization of linear time" necessarily "[center] the West as ultimate frame of reference and value"? If the type of hierarchization that positions the West as the center "so frequently goes in the West by the name 'history,'" it goes by the name "theory," too.

The cross-cultural analysis's valorization of theory over history is only a veneer, since there is nothing particularly theoretical about cross-cultural analysis. (Dropping theorists' names [Derrida, Lyotard, Lacan, Barthes] or their key terms [différend, méconnaissance, punctum, grand récit] does not make an analysis of Japanese cinema automatically theoretical.) The real dichotomy in cross-cultural analysis is established not between theory and history but between the identity of Japanese and that of Westerners. While trying to decenter the hierarchical relationship of Japan and the West, cross-cultural analysis ends up reaffirming the fixed identities of both. To this extent, cross-cultural analysis is in a complementary relation to monocultural analysis promoted by native Japanese scholars such as Keiko I. McDonald. Because her book on Japanese cinema and classical theater "is not a book on film theory," writes McDonald, "it disavows any absolute theoretical stance or ideological commitment of the sort seen in the second semiology (Marxist-psychoanalytic-semiology)": "My own approach has most to do with that basic question about cultural specificity which I seek time and again as a teacher and scholar of Japanese cinema to answer: How does a person coming from the Japanese tradition see a

Japanese film for what it is?"[49] Thus, in both cross-cultural and mono-cultural analysis, the question of theory's role in interpretation is displaced by identity politics.

Japanese Cinema and the Institutionalization of Film Studies

The critical and methodological problems with the scholarship on Japanese cinema cannot be discussed merely as an internal problem of the field of Japanese cinema. To understand them fully, we must broaden a horizon of our examination to include the larger institutional context. Because the field of Japanese cinema is not an autonomous entity but an integral part of film studies' disciplinary formation, a brief examination of the history of film studies as an academic discipline is in order.

Film has been part of the American university curricula for many years,[50] yet it was only in the late 1950s and early 1960s that film studies finally came into existence as an academic discipline. Many new courses on film were created in the 1960s, and they were gradually consolidated into coherent programs and curricula. The increasing popularity of film as an academic subject meant a great demand for survey books on film. New film history books (e.g., Arthur Knight's *The Liveliest Art* [1957]) were published and widely used in the classroom,[51] and the classical works about film history were also reprinted in a new paperback edition or under a new title.[52] In the late 1960s and throughout the 1970s, film studies experienced an extraordinary period of rapid expansion. As the study of film was firmly established as an academic discipline, the institutional centers of study of film shifted from museums and archives to universities. There was a dramatic increase in not only the number of film courses but also the number of universities offering them.[53] In addition to such established journals as *Film Quarterly* and *Cinema Journal,* new film journals were created for film scholars to publish peer-reviewed articles that were essential for tenure and promotion.[54] As the need for legitimating the study of film as a serious academic endeavor increased, the formation of a professional society became necessary. In 1957 and 1958, the Museum of Modern Art in New York organized meetings of film teachers at American universities. Out of these meetings was born the Society of Cinematologists, which later became the Society for Cinema Studies, the most influential organization of film academics.[55]

What made film studies one of the fastest growing academic disciplines in the late 1960s and the 1970s? The influx of art films in the 1950s and 1960s, mainly from Europe, dramatically changed the image of cinema in the United States. Fellini, Bergman, Antonioni, and others were celebrated as serious artists, and in the eyes of many intellectuals and professors, these directors' films were as important as the canonical works of English literature, music, and fine arts. As the prestigious status of these filmmakers as auteurs was firmly established, Hollywood cinema was reappraised, too. French film critics' enthusiasm over American cinema was brought back to the United States, and through the works of critics like Andrew Sarris, directors such as Ford, Hitchcock, Huston, and Wyler were elevated to the status of auteurs. The romantic conception of filmmakers as serious artists who imprint their films with their unique signatures (e.g., stylistic and thematic motifs consistently found in their oeuvres) became orthodoxy not only in the academia but also in the world of journalistic film criticism.[56]

Another phenomenon that prompted the transformation of film into a legitimate object of serious study was the eclipse of film vis-à-vis the increasing popularity of television. The "respectability of film as academic area was enhanced by the fact that by the 1960s in the United States film no longer functioned as *the* American popular entertainment form, having been recently supplanted by television. With television viewing becoming a daily habit in millions of American households, fewer alarms were raised over the negative social effects of movie-going and more concern was expressed over the effects that televised violence and advertising had on children."[57] Ironically, the status of film as an art form was enhanced in part because the American film industry was in disarray, and the cinema's popularity in a real world was superseded by a new electronic medium of audiovisual entertainment.

Because of the constitutive hybridity of film as a medium, film courses were initially offered by such a wide variety of departments as motion pictures, radio and television, theater, art, English, sociology, political science, and business. But the disciplines that most eagerly appropriated film as a new object of analysis were the humanities. Dudley Andrew observes that the humanities needed new courses to offer in order to accommodate the rapid expansion of university enrollments and to cope with the effects of the 1960s' university reform and democratization of higher education:

> The humanities . . . were primed to profit from the rising interest in the study of film. As the largest academic division within American universities, not only were there excesses of students eternally seeking new (and "relevant") courses, but excesses of faculty eager to teach them. Since the humanities were not experiencing anything like the growth pattern of the social sciences, their faculty were trying to achieve distinction in a crowded arena. The development of film as an extension of this arena gave many English, philosophy, theater, and language professors opportunities to find a new audience to teach, new journals to publish in, and renewed enthusiasm for their professions. When academic requirements in the humanities began to loosen up and even disappear in the late 1960s, film studies became a way to uphold enrollment for many departments, primarily language departments.[58]

Even in the pioneering days of film studies, when education departments offered the largest number of film courses, the "courses dealing with film history, criticism, or appreciation . . . were usually attached to literature or drama departments."[59] The inroad of film into the American university system in the 1960s reinforced this connection between film studies and the humanities, or more specifically, literary studies.

As students became less interested in traditional courses on literature, English and language departments began to teach film and other noncanonical texts to boost enrollments. Besides the pedagogical use of film as a mere illustration of the literary masterpiece, a number of film and literature topics were suggested by literature/film teachers: comparison of films and their original literary sources; comparison of films and literary works that are not directly related to each other yet share similar narrative devices or thematic concerns; study of film scripts as literary works; influences of film on literature, and vice versa; connections between specific films and literary movements; established writers' direct involvement in directing films and writing scripts. To legitimate the inclusion of film in literary curricula, many argued that "film is a branch of literature."[60] Even those who insisted on "the autonomy of both media, their differences and unique potential," found the most viable model of film studies in literary criticism.[61]

The impact of literary criticism on the academic study of film went beyond the institutional affiliations of language departments and film programs. In terms of the sheer number, more universities and colleges offered film courses in speech, communication, and film/television departments than in English and language departments.[62] But even in the nonlanguage departments, the critical paradigm of the study of film was a humanistic, interpretive one. The specific institutional locations of film programs and curricula were less important than the emergence of a new institutional paradigm of film criticism that readily crossed departmental boundaries.

If the combination of auteurism and art cinema launched film studies as a respectable academic field in the 1960s, it was theory that made film studies a cutting-edge discipline in the 1970s. A number of humanities scholars took their cues from European cultural criticism and theoretical thinking. For these radical critics, the study of film was more than just an introduction of a new object of research into the humanities. They saw it as an "opportunity to help shift the ground of the whole realm of humanities."[63] Semiotics, Lacanian psychoanalysis, and Althusserian Marxism were enthusiastically studied and used to theorize subject positions, spectatorship, and textual unconscious; the results of theorization and critical pieces that applied theory to specific films were constantly published in journals on film, literary studies, critical theory, and cultural studies. In the rapidly expanding field of film studies, theory occupied a privileged position; to some extent, theory and methodology were more important than what was being theorized or analyzed.

In the 1970s and early 1980s, film studies experienced a research boom, and there was a genuine sense of newness and excitement. Yet by definition, a boom does not last forever, and there now seems to be a consensus that the field of film studies has reached an impasse. There are probably a number of different ways to discuss the state of the discipline, but I find Robert Ray's and David Bordwell's assessments of the situation particularly illuminating. Although they have very different agendas and solutions to remedy the problem at hand, in general both seem to agree that a major source of the stalemate is the hegemonic status of theory-inspired film criticism in the discipline.

In *Making Meaning,* Bordwell argues that we can construct only four types of meanings out of a film — referential, explicit, implicit, and symptomatic meanings (the first two together constituting so-called literal meanings) — and that film criticism basically falls into either thematic explication (constructing implicit meanings) or symptomatic interpretation (symptomatic meanings).[64] Although these two types of interpretive activity are normally regarded as being very different from each other by film scholars, Bordwell sees otherwise. He examines numerous examples of explicatory and symptomatic criticism to demonstrate that there is no such radical disjunction between the two, not even between auteur criticism as explication and Lacanian and Althusserian ideological critique as symptomatic interpretation. Through a careful analysis of interpretive rhetoric, Bordwell tries to demonstrate that poststructuralist film criticism owes much less to poststructuralist theory than to the set of inferential patterns and rhetorical devices that have been widely used by film critics of various persuasions since World War II. From Bordwell's standpoint, poststructuralist film criticism's emergence in the 1970s and its dominance in the 1980s did not introduce anything particularly new in film studies; on the contrary, its proliferation ensured the continuation of routine interpretive practices to such an extent that film criticism has become totally repetitive and uninteresting. Thus Bordwell proclaims: "Film interpretation is in no crisis; it is in stagnation";[65] "the great days of interpretation-centered criticism are over . . . the basic strategies and tactics have all been tried."[66]

Robert Ray also contests the current state of film studies. He points out the futility of producing interpretive pieces based on the mechanically repeatable procedures and reusable theoretical jargons as follows:

The extraordinary contagiousness of contemporary theory lies precisely in its generalizing power: the old model of scholarship, which relied on a specialized, scrupulous coverage of a field of study, insisted that the right to speak about, for example, fiction or narrative accrued only to those who had read all the major novels in a given literature (hence such books as Wayne Booth's *The Rhetoric of Fiction,* which seems to mention every important English novel). Contemporary theory, on the other hand, finds its representative model in Barthes's *S/Z,* which uses one Balzac novella (and a minor one at that) to make an argument about narrative in general. Having seen that approach in action, academics have ignored its lesson and insisted on using it as a new model for case-by-case analyses. But if you understand Barthes's points about storytelling, you do not need to see them worked out with a hundred other examples: that procedure may be useful for beginning students, as a way of apprehending Barthes's approach, but surely it should not be the model for advanced scholarly work. . . . Having committed itself to a particular way of doing business (which we might call "semiotic," using that term to stand for the amalgam of structuralist, psychoanalytic, ideological, and feminist methodologies), film studies has, since 1970, constructed an enormously powerful theoretical machine for exposing the ideological abuse hidden by the apparently natural stories and images of popular culture. That machine, however, now runs on automatic pilot, producing predictable essays and books on individual cases.[67]

While criticizing, like Bordwell, the mass producibility of theoretical interpretation of particular films, Ray also recognizes the significance of theory's introducing discontinuity into the development of film studies. According to Ray, the impasse of film studies is created not by poststructuralist theory's inherent flaws but by the discrepancy between the radical potential of theory as practice and the sterile thematization of theory in routine, streamlined interpretation.

Film studies' development briefly described earlier has not only shaped the Japanese film scholarship but also used Japanese cinema for its own purposes. As Ray argues, at the early stage of its institutionalization, film studies transgressed both national and disciplinary boundaries: "Because its subject matter was international, [film studies] could never have respected the university's linguistic divisions: the movies, after all, were not just 'French' or 'American' or 'German' or 'Japanese'; they constituted a new language which similarly disregarded the old, neat distinctions between music, dance, painting, and the plastic arts. Inevitably, therefore, film studies found an almost immediate need for interdisciplinarity, and for methods which would guide its activities in the unsponsored, uncharted free zones between official departments."[68] When film studies was struggling to establish itself as a discrete discipline, the international dimension of the cinema was a significant point to emphasize. The international scope of film as a hybrid art form could justify the establishment of a new academic unit because, limited by their focus on either specific nations or artistic media, traditional departments were not particularly suitable for the study of the cinema.

It was in this context of disciplinary power struggle that Japanese cinema played an indispensable role. Film studies as a new intercultural discipline became all the more acceptable with the discovery of other cinemas, such as Japanese cinema, whose unique artistic quality made it simultaneously an instance of particularity and a proof of the cinema's universal appeal. Japanese cinema was an ideal example demonstrating the dialectic of the universal and the particular, and a widely used rhetorical trope to reconcile contradictory aspects of the cinema as high art and popular culture, as universal language and culturally specific practice.[69] Japanese cinema was also valuable to film studies because it boasted two great auteurs, Mizoguchi and Kurosawa. The idea of individual authorship was essential for the self-legitimation of film studies at its early stage of institutionalization. Without the presence of auteurs like Fellini, Antonioni, and Bergman, it would have been much more difficult for humanities professors in the 1960s to incorporate film into their teaching and research. Japanese cinema continued to play a significant role in film studies' disciplinary and canon formation by steadily supplying other auteurs besides Kurosawa and Mizoguchi (e.g., Ozu, Naruse, Kobayashi, Oshima, and Imamura).

Interpretation gained its hegemonic status not only because film studies was most closely aligned with literary criticism but also because it was remarkably international and cosmopolitan. For film critics who were not familiar with the language, history, and cultural context of Japan, Brazil, or Hungary, the easiest way to deal with the cinemas of these countries was to interpret—either explicatively or symptomatically—thematic motifs and stylistic aspects of individual films. For the purpose of interpreting unfamiliar national cinemas, film studies has built a powerful interpretive machine, which, by supplying film critics with stock images of national character, tradition, and fixed cultural traits, makes it possible for them to understand and say something intelligible about those cinemas. Thus, to this extent, the disciplinary structure of film studies demands the concept of national cinema as part of its strategy of containment. Because of this interpretive machine, even those who do not have command of necessary languages can study non-Western national cinemas, and these studies are justified in the name of cross-cultural analysis.[70] However, the final product of this kind of national cinema criticism is often as equally predictable and repetitious as theoretical criticism, the value of which is seriously questioned by Bordwell, Ray, and others.

The national cinemas Ray mentions in the passage previously quoted — French, American, German, and Japanese cinemas — do not coexist side by side in a nonhierarchical relationship. Each of them does not have the same kind of leverage over the formation of film studies' disciplinary structure, in which theory occupies a privileged position. Despite theory's — explicit or implicit — universalist claim, specific examples used and analyzed in theory are often from American, French, and German films.[71] In contrast, Japanese cinema has never been included in the canon of film theory except when, as in Burch's study, theory is used to assert Japanese cinema's essential difference from Western cinema. There is a privileged connection between Western cinema and theory, which is supposed to present a totalized, general view, capable of explaining different aspects of the cinema irrespective of national and cultural differences. This grandiose claim of theory has been criticized by Bordwell, Noël Carroll, and others, who point out theory's internal contradictions and axiomatic claims unsupported by empirical evidence.[72] In addition to these internal critiques, it is also important to note a larger disciplinary context in which the primacy of theory and theoretical criticism has been maintained.

Film studies has constructed a code-switching mechanism that enables theory to legitimate its universal claim by seemingly acknowledging its own limitation. This code-switching mechanism represents theory as "Western" theory, which is, according to theorists, not directly applicable to non-Western cinema without inflicting some kind of critical violence on it. However, when a critical interpretation that "applies" Lacanian psychoanalytic theory to a Japanese, Taiwanese, or Indonesian film turns out to be less than convincing, it does not necessarily show either the difficulty or danger of applying Western theory to a non-Western text. Instead, it merely foregrounds a shaky ground on which theory can be used in the interpretation of any text, whether Western or non-Western. The dichotomy of Western theory and non-Western texts is a rhetorical device, the primary purpose of which is not to be attentive to the specificity of non-Western texts but to hide a problematic relationship of Western theory and Western texts. Another purpose of this dichotomy is to create an alibi for theorists to ignore non-Western cinema on the ground that the former is not applicable to the latter. Thus there is a process of marginalization going on within an interdisciplinary and international discipline that guards itself against the colonizing power of Western theory. On the one hand, by evoking the dichotomy of Western theory and non-Western texts, film studies acknowledges the limitations of theory as a culturally specific discursive activity. On the other hand, by institutionally marginalizing the study of non-Western cinema, film studies in actuality sanctions the universalist claim of theory. And the scholarship on Japanese cinema has been a primary product of this marginalization; at the same time, it has also played a significant role in the promotion and legitimation of the same marginalizing process.

Anxiety of Japanese Studies

In his article "Our Dream Cinema: Western Historiography and the Japanese Film," David Bordwell proposes topics of research that need to be investigated in the field of Japanese cinema. His examples and argumentation are persuasive, and many of his proposed ideas still remain to be put into practice.[73] I refer to this article not to go over Bordwell's suggestions but to point out a certain ambiguity in the following statement: "The reluctance of Japanese-speaking scholars to examine primary data means that the more basic spadework remains to be done. . . . Elementary establishment of dates, events, and chronology can issue only from diligent probing in primary materials."[74] As Bordwell argues, primary materials—studies done by Japanese critics, Japanese magazine and newspaper articles, filmmakers' memos and diaries, internal documents of major and minor film studios and independent production companies—should be more seriously examined and incorporated into the scholarship on Japanese cinema. But what intrigues me in Bordwell's statement is the vagueness of the phrase "Japanese-speaking scholars." Who are these Japanese-speaking scholars of Japanese cinema? In what academic disciplines are they trained and located? Why have Japanese-speaking scholars been so reluctant to do a kind of basic research that is commonly done by scholars of American and to some extent major European cinemas? All these questions lead us back to the problematic of the study of Japanese cinema as an institutional practice.

Far from existing in an institutional vacuum, the Japanese-speaking scholars are a product of specific academic disciplines. If the basic work on primary Japanese materials has not been done, it is not simply because of "the reluctance of Japanese-speaking scholars" but of the specific institutional configuration of the field of Japanese cinema in American academia; and both Japanese-speaking and non-Japanese-speaking scholars are responsible for the construction and maintenance of the field. Judging from the minuscule number of Japanese-speaking film scholars, we can conclude that film studies has been less than a perfect environment in which research on primary materials in Japanese film history is conducted. Since the discipline in which the majority of Japanese-speaking scholars teach and conduct research is Japanese studies, our attention is obviously drawn to this discipline, particularly its literary studies subdivision, as an alternative space for the study of Japanese cinema.

Jonathan Culler points out that "national literature departments have increasingly become sites where a wide range of cultural objects are studied—not just film and popular culture but discourses of sexuality, conduct books, and any discourse that contributes to the construction of cultures and individuals."[75] Yet this observation is applicable mostly to European language and literature departments, not to their Asian counterparts. Unlike English, French, or German departments, East Asian language departments have not been receptive to a general trend of broadening the definition of "text" to include film, popular culture, media, urban space, and so on. Why has film not become part of East

Asian departments? Why do Bordwell's "Japanese-speaking scholars" of Japanese cinema remain phantom entities for the most part? Obviously there are no simple answers to these questions. But we can still think of several possible reasons why film has not become part of Japanese language and literature programs.

The emergence of Japanese studies as an area studies discipline after World War II was closely tied to the U.S. intelligence activity during the war and its postwar attempt to incorporate Japan into the hegemonic sphere of the United States engaged in the Cold War. This original complicity of the objectives of Japanese studies and those of the American government's policy toward Japan and East Asia has continued to influence the subsequent development of the discipline. The specific ideological bent of Japanese studies has been actively maintained through teaching; training of young researchers; standards and priorities for publications, tenure, and promotion; control over distribution of research money and scholarships; selection of conference topics and objectives; and so on. Since its inception as an organized discipline, Japanese studies has produced research helping the State Department and trade negotiators to deal with security questions concerning the protection of American interests in the East Asia region. Another institutional role of Japanese studies has been to provide ideological justification for the American subordination of Japan, which after World War II reached "a new stage of imperialism and colonialism without territorialization."[76] As John Dower reports, "many leading American Japan specialists have at one time or another not only worked for the American Government or spoken on its behalf in support of the United States–Japan military and economic relationship, but have also engaged in a sustained endeavor to discredit that sector of the Japanese intelligentsia which has opposed postwar American actions in Asia and Japan's support of those actions."[77]

It must be clear from this brief sketch of the discipline's history that the study of Japanese literature does not occupy the central position in Japanese studies. In American academia, where Eurocentrism and Orientalism are still at work at multiple levels of institutional standards and practices, Japanese studies is for the most part marginalized in an academic ghetto. The field of Japanese literature is further marginalized in this already marginal discipline, in which literary scholars have less leverage over the direction of the discipline than historians, sociologists, anthropologists, political scientists, or economists. Japanese literature scholars can sometimes gain a lot more by interacting with their counterparts specializing in other national literatures than by simply intermingling with Japanologists; however, the institutional structure of the university, venues of publications, and topics and structures of conferences do not allow this kind of interliterary communication to happen as often as it should.

It is important to note that the doubly marginal status of Japanese literature does not necessarily indicate the ideological innocence of the field of Japanese literature. Even though its hierarchical position is subordinate to social sciences, the study of Japanese literature plays a significant role in the self-legitimation of Japanese studies. As a discipline, Japanese studies is sustained by the division of labor that assigns different functions to social sciences and literary studies: the former is often used as a direct instrument for the American government in determining its foreign policy, whereas the latter creates a facade hiding the discipline's instrumentality. The field of Japanese literature dissociates itself from the worldliness of Japanese culture and tries to mold Japanese literature into an instance of high culture, which is ancient, unique, mysterious, and aesthetically refined. As classical Japanese literature is used to affirm the fixed image of Japaneseness, modern Japanese literature is marginalized and devalued. The hierarchy of classical and modern is firmly entrenched in the disciplinary structure of Japanese studies, and the pristine, authentic classical text is valorized over the contaminated, hybrid modern text. Of course, modern Japanese literature is not ignored completely; however, it is often studied to reaffirm the central significance of classical literature rather than to attend to its historical specificity. By detecting in the modern text the resilient presence of traditional aesthetics and sensibility in spite of the impact of Western influences, the study of modern Japanese literature tends to emphasize the continuity of Japanese literary history and the derivative position of modern literature vis-à-vis classical literature.

At first, it may appear that at a certain level of institutional struggle the hypostatization of Japanese tradition has a certain strategic value. Through the assertion of the classical text's unique value, Japanese literature is made into an instance of major national literature. Yet no matter how effective a strategy it might seem, the essentialization of Japanese literary aesthetics as a different tradition does not change the status of Japanese literature as a minor literature at the margin of the humanities. We must remain wary of the dialectic of fetishism and marginalization, since it is precisely through the fetishism of the classical text as difference that the marginality of Japanese literature is further reinforced. There is nothing inherently liberating about recognition of difference. In fact, Orientalism feeds on it. The fetishism of Japanese tradition makes Japanese literature an object worthy of serious scholarly attention as long as the Eurocentric paradigm recuperates Japanese literature as one term of the East-West dichotomy. Scholars of Japanese literature cannot blame the Eurocentrism of the academia as the only cause for their institutional marginalization. Instead of challenging the hegemony of Eurocentrism, Japan specialists' fetishistic assertion of the value of classical Japanese literature supplements it.

The coherence of Japanese studies is not maintained by shared theoretical assumptions or research methodologies. What gives the discipline of Japanese studies a sense of unity is the putative identity of Japan as a strategically important nation or geographic region for the American national interest. The role assigned to literary studies is to depoliticize Japan as a geopolitical entity and represent it as a sign of unique cultural totality. By equating classical Japanese literature and high culture, Japanese studies tries to hide its political instrumentality and legitimate itself as an ideologically neutral academic discipline.

To the extent that its main purpose is to create a fixed image of Japanese tradition, the field of Japanese literature does not need any rigorous theory or analytical methods. The mastery of language and the training in reading original manuscripts from hundreds of years ago are by themselves valuable without much regard to what kind of purpose they are put to use. Richard Okada describes the methodological poverty of the study of classical Japanese literature as follows:

> Having begun their careers as translators, many among the critics [of Japanese literature] found in philology the "discipline" needed to write "commentary" and in New Criticism the "method" needed to help execute the addendum, usually called "introduction," to a translation that required the supplying of "background" or "criti-

cal" remarks. The actual activity of scholars in the field, however, at times only vaguely resembled the two methodologies. "Philology" too often became yet another act of "translation," not the adaptation of any complex method of philology or text criticism but rather the more mundane (and arbitrary) search for "appropriate" English equivalents to Japanese words. And far from any consistent and rigorous employment of New Critical reading procedures, criticism has meant either summary of Japanese scholarship in terms of historical "background" information and detailed points of descriptive interpretation or an unquestioned (and most often unstated) reliance on the writer's own political and cultural norms for broader interpretive maneuvers.[78]

Although Okada's main target of criticism is the way classical Japanese literature has been studied, what he points out also in general applies to the scholarship on modern Japanese literature, whose dominant topoi include writers' biographies, relationships of sources and influences (e.g., influences of *The Tale of Genji* on the works of Kawabata, influences of Western naturalism on Japanese *shizenshugi*), themes and symbols in the work of a particular writer, and so on.

Given this institutional background of the field of Japanese literature, there is nothing surprising about its unresponsiveness toward Japanese cinema. Undoubtedly the lack of attention to Japanese cinema by Japan specialists is related to the valorization of classical literature over modern literature and to the fetishism of ancient culture. For Japanese studies, film is far more dangerous than modern literature, since as popular culture it poses a direct threat to the institutional legitimation of Japanese literature programs and Japanese studies. As long as they speak from the position of authority on Japanese literature and culture, literary scholars' occasional excursion into film criticism is acceptable. But the wholesale incorporation of film into Japanese studies is out of question because it will erode the luster of Japanese culture as high culture. To the extent that film studies and poststructuralist film theory are inseparable, Japanese studies' refusal to take film seriously is also a sign of its aversion to theory. Furthermore, Japanese studies' indifference or outright hostility toward Japanese film is testimony to complicity between Japanologists in the United States and the official ideology of the Japanese government. Even though there were periods when certain government agencies showed interest in marketing Japanese film abroad, in general, the Japanese government has been reluctant to support Japanese cinema. Despite many filmmakers' and film critics' complaints, the Japanese government has refused to admit the cinema as a significant part of Japanese culture and has kept its condescending attitude toward Japanese film.

At a certain level of research, the language competency of the researcher plays a less crucial role for the study of cinema than for that of literature. In film, language is directly present as spoken dialogue, lyrics, intertitles, and visual images on the screen, and to this extent, it is certainly an important part of the filmic experience. Unlike for literature, however, the role of language is less essential for film because of its audiovisual nature. There is a definite difference in the degree of mediation between a translated Japanese novel and a Japanese film with English subtitles. Whereas in the former almost no aspect of the novel escapes from the effect of translation, in the latter the original sound and image remain intact. This is why it is possible for non-Japanese-speaking scholars to watch and study Japanese films in the academic context of film studies and to produce a significant body of scholarly works. However, precisely for the same reason, film has never been treated as an object worthy of receiving Japan specialists' serious scholarly attention. If anyone can seemingly understand Japanese film without specialized training in Japanese language, history, and culture, why is it necessary for Japanese studies to acknowledge it as a legitimate object of scholarship? The absence of Japanese cinema in Japanese studies is closely related to the discipline's institutional history and the question of what constitutes disciplinary expertise. To the extent that film presumably does not require Japan specialists' expert knowledge to be made into an intelligible object, the study of Japanese cinema questions the notions of professional training and expertise, which are often used as an excuse for protecting the vested interests of so-called specialists and for excluding issues that might challenge the legitimacy of the discipline.

In the humanities, comparative literature seems to be the closest to film studies in terms of its disciplinary structure, expectations, and objectives. Both film studies and comparative literature go beyond the boundary of a single nation. Regardless of their specialization in any particular national cinemas, film scholars are first and foremost expected to be students of film as a medium of art and industry in general; similarly, scholars of comparative literature try to study literature as a human activity unrestricted by national boundaries. It is in part these transnational characteristics that have made both film studies and comparative literature a stronghold of literary and critical theory in academia. This focus on theory has been a major factor in the distinction of film studies and comparative literature from foreign language and national literature departments.

Despite their similarities, comparative literature and film studies have different positions on the question of foreign language competency. Many film scholars are competent in French and German, two languages in which theoretical texts on film and relevant topics are extensively published. Yet, generally speaking, film studies as a discipline does not particularly lay special emphasis on foreign language skill. In contrast, comparative literature strongly stresses the significance of reading literary texts in the original languages. For comparatists and other literary scholars, language is not a research tool. A major purpose of studying literature is precisely to critique an instrumental view of language as a transparent medium of communicating information. For comparative literature, the competency in foreign languages is a core of its disciplinary identity. And this is where comparative literature has more affinities with Japanese studies than with film studies. Whereas in film studies the majority of books and articles on Japanese cinema have been written by those who do not know Japanese, a good command of Japanese is an essential prerequisite for any comparatist who claims to be a Japanese literature specialist.

To the extent that it combines two strong points of film studies and Japanese studies, that is, a focus on theory and language, comparative literature seems like a better discipline in which research on Japanese cinema can be pursued. Once housed in comparative literature, the study of Japanese cinema will not suffer at least from the researchers' lack of facility in the language and critical methodologies. Comparative literature can train students to become "Japanese-speaking scholars" who are also conversant in film theory and critical issues in interpretation, formal analysis, and historiography. But before jumping to these conclusions, we must first examine the current state of comparative literature, the disciplinary identity of which has become no less problematic than that of either film studies or Japanese studies. Comparative literature is not immune from the same institutional forces that has prompted film studies to search for its new disciplinary identity and objective.

As René Wellek reports in his often-quoted statement made in 1958, comparative literature as a discipline has never had a clear and stable identity: "The most serious sign of the precarious state of our study is the fact that it has not been able to establish a distinct subject matter and a specific methodology."[79] Other distinguished comparatists have expressed a similar sense of uncertainty about comparative literature: "Although I hold a Ph.D. in comparative literature, I have never been sure I deserved it, since I've never been sure what the field, or the discipline, is and never sure that I could really claim to be teaching it or working in it";[80] "Let's not kid ourselves: I am not a comparatist. I am not even entirely sure what a comparatist is or does."[81] What makes comparatists particularly nervous now is the emergence of cultural studies as a postdisciplinary discursive activity of academics. Cultural studies has attracted many comparatists as a way of renewing comparative literature as a viable discipline of the present and the future, but it has simultaneously alarmed others who see it not as a solution but as a major cause of comparative literature's crisis. The nervous tension between comparative literature and cultural studies is not a unique phenomenon but part of a sea change in the university, where so many other disciplines and departments are experiencing similar kinds of crisis or going through the intense process of self-examination. The significance of the debate about cultural studies does not always lie in what proponents and opponents say about cultural studies but lies in what they say about other disciplines. According to Fredric Jameson, cultural studies is not really a theory or a "floor plan for a new discipline"; instead, cultural studies, a symptom of the

crisis of the university, "came into the world as the result of dissatisfaction with other disciplines, not merely their contents but also their
very limits as such." [82] Cultural studies is often perceived as an external threat invading the boundaries of existing disciplines; at the same
time, it is also a projection of those disciplines' internal contradictions
and deficiencies. By attacking, embracing, or selectively appropriating
cultural studies, other disciplines reaffirm their legitimacy, test their
coherence, or expand and redraw their limits and boundaries.

Many prominent comparatists defend the literariness of literature
against the onslaught of cultural studies by arguing that "literature
can be taught 'as literature' . . . with its 'invariant features' . . . without worrying about the historical contingency of this category. That
worry belongs with cultural studies, which for these critics constitutes
an approach to literature from without, not a theory of reading but
an ideologization of aesthetic values for the purpose of political critique." [83] Peter Brooks defends the specificity of (comparative) literature against the generality of cultural studies, which in his argument
seems to be equated to "contextualization." [84] Jonathan Culler calls for
the transformation of comparative literature into a "real" comparative
literature department, in which comparatists study the aesthetic features of literariness without being hampered by such nonliterary contingent factors as national differences.[85] Trying to defend the specificity
of literature, some comparatists attack the vagueness of "culture" as an
all-inclusive term.[86]

It does not seem to be particularly interesting to decide whether
the best readers are comparatists or cultural studies critics. Nor does
it seem to be fruitful to discuss which term, literature or culture, is
too all-inclusive to be a viable notion around which to build a discrete discipline. On the one hand, it is ludicrous to deny literature any
specificity or to construe it as a type of textual discourse no different
from a medical treatise, advertising pamphlet, or camcorder manual.
On the other hand, it seems futile to try to stop the erosion of comparative literature's disciplinary identity by espousing the notion of literariness. First, the idea of literature upheld by opponents of cultural
studies is extremely restricted and narrow in its scope. This does not
mean that literature should be studied only "as one discursive practice among many others in a complex, shifting, and often contradictory

field of cultural production."[87] The problem with the narrow definition of literature lies not in its rejection of contemporary cultural theory but in its refusal to acknowledge the historicity of the idea of literature. I am much more sympathetic to the position of Lionel Gossman, whose "allegiance is probably to a far older conception of 'literature' than that current in present-day university departments of literature, comparative or otherwise. . . . That older conception of literature embraced a wide range of discourses, extending from philosophical and political argument, to sermons, eulogies, and works of erudition. . . . It is a conception completely antithetical to the restrictive and purist post-Romantic idea of literature that has become generally accepted in our culture—and in departments of Comparative Literature certainly no less than anywhere else."[88] Second, if what comparatists are supposed to study is the literariness of literature, then it is more appropriate to call this new discipline "literature" rather than "comparative literature." The exclusive focus on the notion of "literature," which is chosen as a strategy to defend comparative literature against cultural studies, cannot but lead to the dissolution of comparative literature as a discipline.

What is not clearly elucidated in the debate about comparative literature is the notion of "comparative." As Rey Chow argues, "the 'comparative' in comparative literature is equally, if not more, crucial a factor in considering the future of comparative literature: exactly what constitutes 'comparison'—what kinds of relations, critical formations, analytical perspectives are relevant?"[89] Regardless of whether comparatists actually compare anything, there is always a hierarchy created among different national literatures, and this hierarchy is either explicitly delineated or implicitly accepted as a natural order. Even when the comparison of literature is carried out by crossing national boundaries, new boundaries are created at a higher level, whereby the imagined unity of the nation is replaced by that of the larger geopolitical entity: "Europe." Like "literature," "comparative" is not an ideologically neutral term. "Comparatists" refer to those who specialize in certain European literatures, whereas those who study Chinese and Japanese are called "Asiatic comparatists."[90] Eurocentrism still guides comparative literature even when it tries to adapt itself to institutional changes in the university and the post–Cold War world of globalization. The displacement of comparison as a central activity merely masks the ingrained Eurocentric bias of the discipline instead of grappling with it.

In the final instance, the identity of comparative literature has never been determined by its emphasis on theory, multilingualism, comparison, or literature as a transnational art form. Instead, at the disciplinary core of comparative literature has always been the idea of Europe. I would even venture to argue that comparative literature is less a discipline of literature than a type of area studies, a counterpart to East Asian studies, Middle Eastern studies, Latin American studies, and so forth. It is therefore no accident that some prominent comparatists find an alternative model of comparative literature in area studies.[91] To this extent, as an alternative institutional space for the study of Japanese cinema, comparative literature is at least as equally problematic as Japanese studies.

Conclusions

Japan has produced one of the most remarkable body of films in the history of the cinema. For this reason alone, Japanese cinema deserves serious scholarly attention in the years to come. But as we have examined in the previous sections, Japanese cinema does not legitimately belong to any established discipline. Film studies, which for many years was the center of Japanese film scholarship, no longer pays much attention to Japanese cinema. It is therefore urgent for us to establish a new institutional space or culture in which Japanese cinema can be studied as a legitimate object of knowledge. We must discuss not only the teaching of Japanese film courses but also the training of future teachers and scholars of Japanese cinema, the formation and expansion of a scholarly community and a forum for serious debates where new ideas are produced and exchanged on a regular basis.

At the same time, in the current climate of disciplinary uncertainty, the lack of Japanese cinema's clear disciplinary affiliation does not necessarily hinder the reconceptualization of Japanese film scholarship. When the institutional identities of well-established disciplines are far from self-evident anymore, the free-floating status of Japanese cinema can be used as an effective means of problematizing the idea of autonomous discipline. Whether Japanese film's formal system, industrial structure, or position in the cultural history of modern Japan is analyzed, the object of study in each case needs to be invented against various kinds of disciplinary constraint. Whatever institutionally recognized discipline we happen to belong to, we cannot study Japanese cinema seriously without simultaneously questioning the basic premises of the discipline. The new study of Japanese cinema in the post-disciplinary age must be political; that is, beyond its specificity, it must be conceived as a tactical intervention in the structures and practices of the established disciplines.

PART II

THE FILMS OF KUROSAWA AKIRA

1. Kurosawa Criticism and the Name of the Author

Why Kurosawa?

Given the institutional history and disciplinary ambiguity of the scholarship on Japanese cinema outlined in part 1, what does it mean to write another book on the cinema of Kurosawa? Why is it necessary to study Kurosawa now? Are there not too many books and essays on Kurosawa's films? And how can we explore institutional and disciplinary issues underlying the elusive field of Japanese cinema studies in a study of one filmmaker's work? Despite the enormous quantity of Kurosawa criticism, there are just a handful of book-length studies of his work. In English, there are only two comprehensive books, covering all Kurosawa films released at the time of their publication: Donald Richie's *The Films of Akira Kurosawa* and Stephen Prince's *The Warrior's Camera: The Cinema of Akira Kurosawa*.[1] I will refrain from discussing these two books in detail here, since they are used as a sounding board for my own argument in the rest of this book. In Japanese there are many books about Kurosawa, but again there are only two critical works that deal with his work as a whole.[2] One is Tsuzuki Masaaki's two-volume study titled *Kurosawa Akira*, the first volume of which examines Kurosawa's life, his working methods, and the dominant thematic motifs of his films, and the second volume consists of "readings" of individual films. Despite its comprehensiveness, Tsuzuki's study is disappointing, since it is mostly a mere combination of plot summary, excerpts from the scripts, and remarks made by Kurosawa and others who were directly involved in the production of his films. The other Japanese book on Kurosawa is Sato Tadao's *Kurosawa Akira no sekai* (The World of Kurosawa Akira), which was originally published in 1969 and revised in 1986. Undoubtedly superior to Tsuzuki's, Sato's book contains a number of insightful comments on Kurosawa films. But Sato's study is somewhat less systematic and consistent than Richie's or Prince's because many parts of the book are essays and film reviews previously published elsewhere. I will also refer to Sato's work throughout the rest of this study.

Despite the critical acclaim and popular support Kurosawa's films have received over the years, there is disproportionately little *serious* critical writing on his work. Kurosawa Akira is arguably the best-known, yet most undervalued, Japanese filmmaker. It is too often the case that critics' feelings toward Kurosawa as a director are unnecessarily intermixed with their interpretations of his films, or that their examination of Kurosawa's work as a uniform totality erases the specificity of individual films. Particularly in Japan, it is not unusual to find what is supposed to be a review or criticism of his films lapsing into a critic's personal commentary, impressions, or attack on Kurosawa as a director or as a person. So much has been written about Kurosawa, but we still do not know much about his films themselves. This discrepancy between the value and critical neglect of Kurosawa by itself justifies a book-length study of his films.

Because of the centrality of Kurosawa in Japanese cinema, a new study of his work can also illuminate the degree to which Japanese cinema scholarship has been shaped by specific kinds of institutional constraint and disciplinary configuration. A close examination of the films of Kurosawa and Kurosawa criticism will tell us what types of critical assumptions and interpretive approaches are dominant in Japanese cinema scholarship and how they contribute to the construction of a particular image of Japanese cinema that impedes discussions of many significant critical issues pertinent to our understanding of Kurosawa's films.

But the question "Why Kurosawa?" has its own specific methodological implications; that is, it raises questions concerning the problematic of auteurism and the viability of writing a book about the work of an individual film director. After auteurism has been discredited critically, why do I write another book on Kurosawa at this point? Am I "turning back the clock in Japanese cinema studies" by studying the films of arguably the most canonical Japanese film director?[3] No matter what I do, am I simply producing another auteurist study of Kurosawa? To answer these questions, it is first necessary to take a quick look at auteurism and its critical legacies.

Auteurism Revisited

One of auteurism's central tenets is that film as a serious art form can be used as a vehicle for a director's personal expression. Auteurism places the utmost importance on the uniqueness of the film director's personal expression and vision. At the same time, the auteur's personal expression is cherished precisely because it goes beyond the sphere of the personal and reveals the condition of humanity in general. Another important aspect of auteurism is its belief in the totality of the auteur's personal vision or "signature." Once film directors are elevated to the pantheon of great auteurs, their lesser works in relation to their masterpieces are regarded more important than the successful films of mere artisans of film.

Where do the institutional aspects of film production or sociocultural contexts fit in auteurism? Andrew Sarris, one of the most influential proponents of auteur criticism, does not deny the influences of economic systems or cultural conditions on a filmmaking practice. But as Edward Buscombe points out, the "acknowledgment of 'conditions' turns out to be mere lip service,"[4] since Sarris admits the effects of the historical contexts to erase them completely from critical writings on an auteur's work. According to Sarris, certain film directors are called auteurs precisely because they overcome economic, cultural, and historical constraints and limitations; therefore, there is no need for auteur critics to pay attention to any of these mere "external" conditions, from which film aesthetics remain autonomous. "If directors and other artists cannot be wrenched from their historical environments," argues Sarris, "aesthetics is reduced to a subordinate branch of ethnography."[5] This definition of auteur leads to his polemical position on the supremacy of American cinema:

After years of tortured revaluation, I am now prepared to stake my critical reputation, such as it is, on the proposition that Alfred Hitch-

cock is artistically superior to Robert Bresson by every criterion of
excellence and, further, that, film for film, director for director, the
American cinema has been consistently superior to that of the rest
of the world from 1915 through 1962. Consequently, I now regard the
auteur theory primarily as a critical device for recording the history
of the American cinema, the only cinema in the world worth exploring in depth beneath the frosting of a few great directors at the top.[6]

What Sarris devalues is any overt presence of a filmmaker's personal
expression as it may be found in the European art film. The auteur's
signature must instead be inscribed in his or her films as recurrent stylistic features, which must be deciphered rather than naively perceived
by connoisseur critics. To the extent that Hollywood is the most highly
developed culture industry, American directors are forced to be more
innovative as auteurs than European directors who may be less constrained by external conditions and be able to express themselves more
freely. In Sarris's eyes, it is precisely the rigid commercial constraints
on American directors that make many of them more authentic auteurs
than directors of foreign cinemas.

The assertion of the supremacy of American cinema as a national
cinema makes Sarris's auteurism highly problematic as a critical endeavor.[7] Poststructuralist film theory further questions the underlying
ideological premises of auteurism with its famous tenet "the death of
the author." Following theorists such as Roland Barthes and Michel
Foucault,[8] a new breed of theoretically minded critics declare that the
author is dead, or that the author does not preexist the text as a unified
intentionality or coherent source of meanings. The poststructuralist response to auteurism by critics such as Raymond Bellour and Stephen
Heath has produced a kind of theoretically informed interpretive work
in which the author—a mere effect of the text—is displaced from a
central position by the structure and textual mechanism of the classical
Hollywood cinema as an ideological apparatus.

One of the practical consequences of the poststructuralist repudia-
tion of auteurism is the proliferation of theory-influenced criticism,
which often falls prey to repetitive reductivism. At the hands of poststructuralist critics, film analysis becomes another occasion to find
a common structure or mechanism of meaning production, and the

specificity of a film turns out to be a mere illusion. "For all the apparent commitment to Barthesian notions of 'plurality,'" asserts Robin Wood, "it seems to me that Heath and Bellour both ultimately close off the texts they 'read': they turn out to be the same old 'classical narrative text' all over again."[9] The equally significant shortcoming of poststructuralist critique is its insufficient engagement with the problematic status of author. If auteurism is questionable as a critical endeavor, the declaration that the author is dead is at least equally problematic. Michel Foucault argues that "it would be false to consider the function of the author as a pure and simple reconstruction after the fact of a text given as passive material, since a text always bears a number of signs that refer to the author."[10] The author is not a mere textual effect but a function of discourse, something that is not reducible to a text's internal structure or productive mechanism.

Another influential mode of response to classical auteurism is to separate the author as a person and the name of the author given to a common structure found in a particular body of work. The best-known proponent of this revisionism is Peter Wollen, who argues that "by a process of comparison with other films [by the same director], it is possible to decipher, not a coherent message or world-view, but a structure which underlies the film and shapes it, gives it a certain pattern of energy cathexis. It is this structure which *auteur* analysis disengages from the film."[11] The deep structure discovered through comparison of Hawks's works is called "Hawks." This distinction between Hawks and "Hawks" is necessary because "*auteur* analysis does not consist of retracing a film to its origins, to its creative source. It consists of tracing a structure (not a message) within the work, which can then *post factum* be assigned to an individual, the director, on empirical grounds."[12] Wollen's distinction between Hawks and "Hawks" corresponds to the descriptivist and antidescriptivist positions on names and their referents. Hawks as a name refers to an actual individual called Hawks who happened to work as a film director in Hollywood. Here, the name Hawks is interpreted in an antidescriptivist manner, so that it "is connected to an object . . . through an act of 'primal baptism,' and this link maintains itself even if the cluster of descriptive features which initially determined the meaning of the word changes completely."[13] In contrast, "Hawks" is a name interpreted descriptively; that is, "it means a cluster of descriptive features . . . and subsequently refers to objects in reality in so far as they possess properties designated by the cluster of descriptions. . . . Intention thus has logical priority over extension: extension (a set of objects referred to by a word) is determined by intention (by universal properties comprised in its meaning)."[14] The problem with this differential use of descriptivist and antidescriptivist interpretations of the name Hawks is that it still does not explain the reason for the choice of the director's name to refer to a particular set of structural features and stylistic markers. Wollen argues that the "structure is associated with a single director, an individual, not because he has played the role of artist, expressing himself or his own vision in the film, but because it is through the force of his preoccupations that an unconscious, unintended meaning can be decoded in the film, usually to the surprise of the individual involved."[15] But this introduction of the director's unconscious does not fundamentally change the basic premises of classical auteurism. Unconscious or not, the film director is still said to imprint his films with his uniquely individuated expressions and worldview. Once again, Foucault's insight illuminates the problem with this type of revisionism. Foucault argues that "the author serves to neutralize the contradictions that are found in a series of texts. Governing this function is the belief that there must be—at a particular level of an author's thought, of his conscious or unconscious desire—a point where contradictions are resolved, where the incompatible elements can be shown to relate to one another or to cohere around a fundamental and originating contradiction."[16] Wollen's attempt to graft semiotics to auteurism still preserves this function of the author described by Foucault, and to that extent, Wollen's revisionist auteurism is not essentially different from classical auteurism.

The Autobiographical Pact

The author as a social institution is very resilient, and its "death" turns out to be mere displacement. Even when criticism concentrates on the formal organization and structure of a work without trying to establish some kind of intrinsic relation between the work and the author's intention, thought, or experience, the author does not necessarily dis-

Kurosawa Akira circa 1950.
Photo courtesy of Photofest.

appear. As Foucault points out, the notion of work as a unity implies the presence of the author, which prevents the unity of a work from disintegrating into a random collection of novels, short stories, diaries, letters, contracts, advertisement copies. Moreover, according to Foucault, even the poststructuralist concept of *écriture*, or text, "has merely transposed the empirical characteristics of an author to a transcendental anonymity."[17]

If the concepts of work, writing, and text are all insufficient to replace the concept of author, how shall we approach the question of Kurosawa's authorship? In Kurosawa criticism, auteurism has not been the focus of any extended debate. Richie's book about Kurosawa is one of the first manifestations of auteurism in Anglo-American film criticism. Desser's work on Kurosawa's "samurai film," published in the early 1980s, is also written within the general framework of auteurism. Even Prince's more formally sensitive study tends to bypass the question of auteurism and reinforce the auteurist image of Kurosawa. On the one hand, Prince's emphasis on the relation between Kurosawa's cinema and postwar Japan's sociopolitical conditions sets his study apart from auteurism. On the other hand, to the extent that he tries to analyze Kurosawa's "project," a search for "a method of constructing a viable political cinema that is, at the same time, popular," and this project's "maturation, and evolution, and its eventual defeat,"[18] it becomes hard to distinguish Prince's study from auteur criticism. As Foucault argues, when "any unevenness of production is ascribed to changes caused by evolution, maturation, or outside influence," it is the author that gives unity and coherence to a body of work.[19] In his "intertextual" study of Kurosawa's films, James Goodwin uses the notion of "author-function" to differentiate his work from auteurist studies. "Conventional belief," argues Goodwin, "treats the author as an autonomous, unified voice, while concepts of the author-function indicate a plurality of voices and subjective relations within a cultural text even while produced by an individual. . . . As elaborated by Michel Foucault, Roland Barthes, and Jacques Derrida, concepts of the author-function bear no resemblance to authorship's fixed, consolidated identity, from which the work issues and to which it in turn conforms."[20] According to Goodwin, the notion of author-function opens up the text as an intersecting site of multiple intertexts. But it is not easy for us to understand the exact mechanism of the author-function by reading his analysis of Kurosawa's films, which is for the most part as conventional as the majority of Kurosawa criticism.[21]

There is no doubt that Kurosawa is one of the few Japanese filmmakers who have successfully maintained artistic autonomy while working in the studio system. Kurosawa started his career at Toho, but never played the role of a mere contract director. Almost all his films were initiated as his own projects, and his personal involvement in every stage of production is legendary: he writes his own scripts by himself or in collaboration with other scriptwriters;[22] he never leaves setting up cameras to his cinematographers by themselves; at the stage of script writing, he often already has particular pieces of music in mind to be used in specific scenes; he sometimes designs costumes and props himself; he rehearses scenes thoroughly before filming; and perhaps most important, he is a superb editor who edits his own films.[23] Given that Kurosawa fiercely tries to protect his control over every aspect of his films, it would be extremely difficult not to discuss such films as *Rashomon, Ikiru, Seven Samurai, Yojimbo,* and *Ran* as the films of Kurosawa Akira as an author. However, this does not necessarily lead to the conclusion that he is therefore an auteur as it is formulated by classical or revisionist auteurism. Nor is it the case that Kurosawa's authorship implies his pursuit of a unified project, either aesthetic, moral, political, or otherwise. Kurosawa's films are too worldly and historical to be appreciated either as mere aesthetic objects where his personal vision is inscribed or as a structure or textual system that reveals his unconscious desire. The sheer diversity of his films, which were made over the span of fifty years, cannot be discussed as a manifestation of a single project without extreme reductionism. What is called for in our study of the cinema of Kurosawa is neither the absolute banishment of the notion of author nor the use of his authorship as a final answer to various interpretive questions that arise when we examine each of his films. Instead, we must come back to Kurosawa's authorship as a question or a site of negotiations. The author "Kurosawa" is a discursive product, the critical meaning and social function of which are constantly negotiated by Kurosawa, critics, and audiences. The reception and interpretation of his films cannot but be influenced by a particular construction of Kurosawa as an author. At the same time, a close analysis of his films may give rise to a more complex, contradictory model of his authorship.

In his study of the cinema of Ozu, David Bordwell introduces a very useful notion that can further elucidate the practical implications of the authorship question. Bordwell asks the question of how to situate Ozu's biographical background in a study of his cinema. Rather than denying the author's biography completely, Bordwell recasts it into a "biographical legend," a notion borrowed from Russian formalist critic Boris Tomashevsky. Bordwell argues that the biographical legend "functions in two ways: to permit works to come into being, as fulfillments of the legend; and to orient perceivers to them, to favor certain construals and to block others." [24] To treat Ozu's biography as a socially mediated discourse means that we must "qualify and contextualize the biographical legend, discounting it when it runs afoul of other evidence while still preserving it as a precious clue to the diverse aesthetic and political roles the work could fulfill." [25]

Although numerous interviews and review essays have contributed to the construction of Kurosawa' biographical legend, the most important text that provides his biographical information is *Something like an Autobiography*, a collection of his autobiographical essays.[26] In the book, Kurosawa recounts his life from his birth in 1910 to the success of *Rashomon* at the Venice Film Festival in 1951. One of the most striking aspects of Kurosawa's autobiographical text is the presence of many descriptions of his childhood experiences that remarkably resemble scenes from his own films. For instance, his experience of being ambushed by a group of schoolchildren echoes the first fight scene in *Sanshiro Sugata*.[27] Kurosawa's relationship with his sister Momoyo and their celebration of the Doll Festival on March 3 cannot but remind us of the episode "The Peach Orchard" in *Dreams* (17–19). In the "Tunnel" episode of the same film, Kurosawa's surrogate figure appears as a platoon leader who lost all of his men during the war; even though he never fought in the war, Kurosawa was trained as a platoon leader in middle school (59). An episode of his experiences in Father's village can be recognized in *Madadayo:* "Also in this village there lived an old man who hated thunder. When a thunderstorm began, he would crawl under a huge shelf he had suspended from the ceiling to block the thunder. He huddled there until the storm ended" (63). Like Kikuchiyo in *Seven Samurai,* the young Kurosawa was forced to catch fish with his hands (65). As Kurosawa explains, he has a personal connection to one of the principal characters of his film *The Men Who Tread on the Tiger's Tail:* "My father's older sister . . . married into the Togashi family in the town of Omagari in Akita. This Togashi household were descendants of the border captain Togashi, who has Benkei read the subscription list in the famous Kabuki play *Kanjincho,* upon which I based my 1945 film *The Men Who Tread on the Tiger's Tail*" (68). And the last moment of this aunt described by Kurosawa resonates with the last days of Kane's long lost brother in *Rhapsody in August* (69). An episode from Kurosawa's leftist activist days reminds us of the scene in *No Regrets for Our Youth* where the protagonist, Noge, is arrested by the detectives: "One snowy day I was on my way to an appointment near Komagome Station. As I opened the door of the coffee shop, I suddenly froze. There were five or six men inside who all stood up simultaneously as they saw me. At one glance I knew they were special police detectives; they all had the same strange reptilian look about them" (77–78). Then, a more explicit confluence of Kurosawa's life experience and creation can be found in the following passage:

Near the main thoroughfare of the village stood a huge rock, and there were always cut flowers on top of it. All the children who passed by it picked wild flowers and laid them atop the stone. When I wondered why they did this and asked, the children said they didn't know. I found out later by asking one of the old men in the village. In the Battle of Boshin, a hundred years ago, someone died at that spot. Feeling sorry for him, the villagers buried him, put the stone over the grave and laid flowers on it. The flowers became a custom of the village, which the children maintained without ever knowing why. (63)

If we erase the proper noun "the Battle of Boshin," this passage is almost exactly repeated in the last episode of *Dreams*, "Village of the Watermills." Moreover, in Father's native village, the young Kurosawa meets an old farmer whose remark we hear from the mouth of Ryu Chishu in the same episode: "You might wonder what could be interesting about living in a hovel like this and eating slop like this. Well, I tell you, it's interesting just to be alive" (63).

Why are there so many similarities between Kurosawa's autobiographical narrative and his films? One possible reason for such conflation of art and life is that the refraction of his memory by his films has made him reconstruct what he experienced in the past to imitate his creative work. Yet this plausible hypothesis cannot explain every instance of resemblance because the publication of his autobiography precedes some of his late films that reproduce autobiographical episodes. To elucidate the relation of art and life further, we must examine Kurosawa's autobiographical text more closely.

Throughout the book, Kurosawa downplays the truth value of his autobiographical essays. He states that human memory is fundamentally unreliable. Even when we think we remember and narrate what really happened in the past, we so often end up distorting our memory for the purpose of self-promotion or aggrandizement. That the distortion is not always a conscious process is attested by our surprising discovery of a gap between our own and others' images of ourselves: "The self I see when I think about my past and the Kurosawa Akira that others remember are so different that I am uncomfortably surprised" (43). If this difference in perception is not a mere mistake or a simple case of self-deception, how can we remember the past as it really was? One possible solution is to introduce a different perspective than our own. For Kurosawa, this second perspective is provided by Uekusa Keinosuke, his childhood friend and collaborator on *One Wonderful Sunday* and *Drunken Angel,* who had already published an autobiographical novel before Kurosawa started serializing his autobiographical essays.[28] To the extent that memory is a manifestation of desire, neither Kurosawa's nor Uekusa's autobiographical account is reliable by itself. But if their memories are superimposed to produce a composite image, we might have an access to a more accurate picture of Kurosawa Akira. ("The details of our life in this era can be found in a novel Uekusa wrote. But Uekusa has his viewpoint and I have mine. And because people want themselves to have been a certain way, they have a disturbing tendency to convince themselves they really were that way. Perhaps if I wrote an account of my childhood with Uekusa to be compared with the account in his novel, we would come very close to the truth.")[29]

Memory of a single person cannot be trusted completely because of a human propensity for using memory as a means of self-justification. The use of multiple perspectives on the past is a way of rectifying this tendency. But as the following example from the autobiography's conclusion shows, the addition of the second perspective does not necessarily make the representation of the past more accurate.

Through *Rashomon* I was compelled to discover yet another unfortunate aspect of the human personality. This occurred when *Rashomon* was shown on television for the first time a few years ago. The broadcast was accompanied by an interview with the president of Daiei. I couldn't believe my ears. This man, after showing so much distaste for the project at the outset of production, after complaining that the finished film was "incomprehensible," and after demoting the company executive and the producer who had facilitated its making, was now proudly taking the full and exclusive credit for its success! . . . Watching the television interview, I had the feeling I was back in *Rashomon* all over again. It was as if the pathetic self-delusions of the ego, those failings I had attempted to portray in the film, were being shown in real life. People indeed have immense difficulty in talking about themselves as they really are. I was reminded once again that the human animal suffers from the trait of instinctive self-aggrandizement. And yet I am in no position to criticize that company president. I have come this far in writing something resembling an autobiography, but I doubt that I have managed to achieve real honesty about myself in its pages. I suspect that I have left out my uglier traits and more or less beautified the rest. In any case, I find myself incapable of continuing to put pen to paper in good faith.[30]

Because of an "unfortunate aspect of human personality," different persons' memories of the same event often only present mutually contradictory versions of the past with no possibility of reconciling them. While he categorically asserts that the president of Daiei, Nagata Masaichi, distorts the facts for self-aggrandizement, Kurosawa says he is not criticizing Nagata's egotism because he cannot suppress his doubt that there are similar kinds of distortion and idealization in his portrayal of himself.[31] Thus, in what appears to be a paradoxical move, Kurosawa concludes his autobiography with the expression of his suspicion about its truthfulness.

Does this mean that according to Kurosawa it is impossible to reveal his true self? Immediately after the passage just quoted, Kurosawa makes the following remark, which is his final word in the autobiography.

I am a maker of films; films are my true medium. I think that to learn what became of me after *Rashomon* the most reasonable procedure would be to look for me in the characters in the films I made after *Rashomon*. Although human beings are incapable of talking about themselves with total honesty, it is much harder to avoid the truth while pretending to be other people. They often reveal much about themselves in a very straightforward way. I am certain that I did. There is nothing that says more about its creator than the work itself.[32]

Kurosawa suggests that his films, fictional works, can reveal his true self more accurately than his autobiography, so that it is the viewers' task to look for truth in his films. Here we have a classical example of what Phillipe Lejeune calls the "autobiographical pact."[33] According to Lejeune, the value of autobiography lies not in its truthfulness per se but in its effect on the readers who read and interpret the author's nonautobiographical works. Autobiography is a textual strategy of the author trying to construct a specific interpretive space or framework within which his or her other texts will be interpreted.[34] And it is precisely through the author's expression of doubt about the value or reliability of autobiography that the autobiographical pact is made.

> Indeed, at the very moment when in *appearance* Gide and Mauriac depreciate the autobiographical genre and glorify the novel, in *reality* they are drawing something very different than drawing a more or less questionable scholarly parallel: they designate the autobiographical space in which they want us to read the whole of their work. Far from being a condemnation of autobiography, these often quoted sentences are in reality an indirect form of the autobiographical pact. . . . If the novel is truer than autobiography, why are Gide, Mauriac, and many others not happy with writing novels? In posing the question in this way, everything becomes clear: if they had not *also* written and published autobiographical texts, even "inadequate" ones, no one would ever have seen the nature of the truth that it was necessary to look for in their novels. Thus these declarations are perhaps involuntary but very effective tricks: we escape accusations of vanity and egocentrism when we seem so aware of the limitations and insufficiencies of our autobiography; and no one notices that, by the same movement, we extend on the contrary the autobiographical pact, in an *indirect* form, to the whole of what we have written.[35]

Thus, how accurately Kurosawa describes his life experiences in his autobiography is not particularly important. What Kurosawa has achieved by writing the autobiography, which is scattered with his own skeptical remarks about its truthfulness and reliability, is the establishment of his authorship. Kurosawa emerges as an author of his films precisely by declaring that he has not been completely successful in writing a genuine autobiography.

The resemblances between Kurosawa's films and his autobiographical episodes are not confined to the level of content. The merger of his films and autobiography is also accomplished by cinematic techniques and principles that underlie his personal memories. Throughout his autobiography, the cinema remains a dominant trope for the work of memory. Kurosawa writes: "The clarity of my memory seems to improve in direct proportion to the intensity of shock I underwent." [36] What his examples of unforgettable events and scenes show is that the shock effect is often created by the contrast and juxtaposition of extreme opposites (e.g., his memory of the aftermath of the Kanto Earthquake in 1923). Although he never explicitly says so, for Kurosawa, memory seems to be generated by the principle of "montage." His effort to remember his childhood days at primary school is compared to shooting figures at extreme long distance with a telephoto lens in an optimal condition: "I have to do something equivalent to removing the wide-angle lens from the camera and replacing it with a telephoto lens, then looking once again through the viewfinder. And even this isn't enough. I need to concentrate all my lights on these two boys and stop down the lens so as to record them clearly" (14).

If his memory is structured like film, Kurosawa's artistic creation is in turn dependent on his memory. Kurosawa was introduced to the world of art by his primary school teacher Tachikawa Seiji, who broke the conventions of art education: instead of instructing students to copy a model painting as faithfully as possible, he told them to draw anything they wanted freely. From Tachikawa *sensei,* Kurosawa learned that art is not the imitation of models but the creation of something new (12–13). To create a work of art, therefore, one must cultivate the faculty of imagination rather than the mere copying skill. However, imagination does not have power to create something new from zero: "I couldn't do it out of nothing" (194). What Kurosawa discovers later in his life is that imagination by itself is not a sufficient condition for artistic creation. For imagination to do its work, it needs raw materials to work on. And it is our memories that play the role of raw materials. Without an ability to tap our memory reservoir, we cannot create a work of art. Of course, an artwork does not simply reproduce a particular piece of memory. Instead, imagination transforms and translates fragments of memory into a new form called art. After being filtered through his imagination, the young Kurosawa's kendo outfit and high wooden clogs became "visual devices showing Sanshiro's new dedication to a life of judo" in his first film, *Sanshiro Sugata* (30). Sometime after the release of *Scandal,* Kurosawa suddenly realized that one of its principal characters, Hiruta, an unscrupulous yet timid lawyer, was not a purely fictional character; Kurosawa had once met somebody like him at a bar. Even though this man made an unforgettable impression on him, Kurosawa did not consciously remember the real-life model during the production of *Scandal*. Instead, it was through his artistic creation that his memory returned.[37] Closely intertwined like "two wisteria vines," memory and imagination for Kurosawa presuppose each other's existence.

Something like an Autobiography and numerous other interviews and essays contribute to the establishment of Kurosawa's authorship. Kurosawa's films and what are presented as fragments of his autobiographical narratives form a closed circuit, in which the two are readily interchangeable. Once this closed circuit is formed, Kurosawa's recollection of his past does not necessarily reveal who he really is. Its principal function is to give the critics and viewers specific ways of interpreting his films. The autobiographical pact Kurosawa proposes is another manifestation of his will to control every aspect of his work; that is, it is his attempt to exercise control over the reception of his films. If we rely on Kurosawa's autobiographical texts as final interpretive answers in our analysis of his films, we are simply falling into the trap he has set. Any serious reexamination of his authorship must therefore open up the autobiographical space by introducing various kinds of context and history that are excluded from this space. And our close textual analysis will show that the autobiographical pact is often betrayed by the specific audiovisual details of his films.

In the remainder of part 2, we will examine Kurosawa's thirty films one by one. The chronologically arranged thirty chapters are not necessarily similar to one another in terms of their length and focus. They do not treat the stylistic and thematic features of all thirty films equally. Nor do they attempt to construct a linear developmental model of Kurosawa's authorship. Instead, each Kurosawa film — not all films are discussed extensively because of the limitation of space — is used as an occasion for exploring various critical issues pertinent to our understanding of Kurosawa's work and Japanese cinema studies as an institutional practice.

2. *Sanshiro Sugata*

Action Film

Kurosawa's first film, *Sanshiro Sugata* (Sugata Sanshiro, 1943), is an entertainment film packed with action spectacles. There is nothing remarkable about the story of *Sanshiro Sugata*. The conventionality of the film's story can be illustrated by comparing it to popular sword fight novels, particularly Yoshikawa Eiji's *Miyamoto Musashi,* to which the film is remarkably similar.[1] In both stories, we are first introduced to a young hero who is talented in martial skills or arts but does not know how to use his strength properly. He is untamed energy that must be controlled to make it socially beneficial. The transformation of the hero from a ruffian to a responsible man is achieved by the intervention of a Buddhist priest, who challenges the hero to face his true self squarely. At first the hero resists, but then after a struggle comes a moment of his enlightenment. The hero realizes that the mere use of physical force or violence is not enough because he will eventually confront a swordsman or judo master who is physically stronger than he is. To defeat the enemy, the hero must not only improve his skills but, more important, cultivate his character and learn to control himself through self-discipline; that is, the most formidable enemy is not others but himself. The enlightened hero decides to travel around the country for further training while refusing to settle down with a young woman who is in love with him.

Even though its basic narrative pattern is quite conventional, *Sanshiro Sugata* is far from an ordinary film. What distinguishes it from other run-of-the-mill genre films using a similar narrative formula is first and foremost its form. In particular, meticulous attention is paid to the formal construction of action scenes. In the original film, there were seven fight scenes, out of which five remain in the surviving version.² Each action scene has distinct formal features, which give the film a sense of variety and contrast. In the first fight scene, Yano Shogoro (Okochi Denjiro), the founder of a new judo school called Shudokan, is attacked by the jujitsu master Monma Saburo and his disciples. The whole scene is organized around the juxtaposition of movement and stasis, which is created by the repetition of slow lateral tracking shots in both directions. In contrast, the vertical movement of crane shots gives a distinct look to the second action scene, a brawl where Sanshiro (Fujita Susumu) confronts a sumo wrestler. The fourth action scene is an exhibition match between Monma and Sanshiro. The key technique used in this scene is slow-motion cinematography. At the conclusion of the match, we see in slow motion a small sliding paper door falling on Monma, who has been thrown against a wooden wall by Sanshiro. The eerie effect of this slow-motion scene is further accentuated by the silent sound track. And then, all of a sudden, the silence is broken by Monma's daughter Osumi's scream. The sixth fight scene, between Sanshiro and Murai Hansuke (Shimura Takashi) at the Metropolitan Police, is similar to the fourth except that it is much longer and contains new camera positions including some high-angle shots toward the end of the scene. Here, the out-of-focus image of Sanshiro is used as the subjective view of Murai whose vision is blurred after he is thrown to the tatami mats by his opponent. Murai's interior psychology is also represented by an auditory flashback, the voice of his daughter Sayo.

At the film's climax, Sanshiro fights with his archrival, Higaki Gennosuke (Tsukigata Ryunosuke). The shot selection here is more varied in terms of camera angle and distance. Particularly notable is the editing that alternates the extreme long shots of Sanshiro and Higaki and the close-ups of their faces. This last fight scene stands in contrast to the first scene of Monma's surprise attack on Yano. The film's first fight occurs in the middle of a town on a serene night with clear skies and a bright moon. The silence of the night is occasionally broken by Yano's voice and the sound of Monma's men being thrown into the water. The physical setting of the last fight consists of dramatically different elements: rolling hills, gusty winds, rapidly moving clouds, tall waving grasses. This strong contrast between the two scenes helps to create the dynamic narrative development that prevents the film from becoming a random collection of isolated action scenes.

It is important to emphasize that before *Sanshiro Sugata,* the action movies in Japanese cinema were almost all sword fight movies *(chanbara eiga).* With *Sanshiro Sugata,* Kurosawa demonstrated that it was possible to make a breathtakingly exciting action film without including a single sword fight scene. This discovery became valuable for Japanese filmmakers a few years later when the Occupation banned sword fight scenes from Japanese cinema because of the American censors' belief that the alleged cruelty of such scenes would encourage feudalistic behavior and antidemocratic sentiment among the Japanese.

Zen and Samurai Values

Sanshiro Sugata is a good film to start our reexamination of Japanese cinema studies and its general culturalist orientation as is manifested in the use of samurai and Zen values as interpretive answers. Because of the close resemblance between *Sanshiro Sugata* and Miyamoto Musashi movies, Sanshiro appears as a modern-day samurai who fights with his bare hands rather than with swords. Together with such popular films as *Seven Samurai, Yojimbo,* and *Sanjuro, Sanshiro Sugata* seems to foreground the centrality of samurai in the world of Kurosawa and, as many critics assert, in the formation of his authorship. Kurosawa criticism has been trying to discover at the core of his authorship a number of widely accepted thematic motifs that are directly tied to the Japanese history and cultural traditions. The symbolic image of samurai is one of these motifs, which is often used as an interpretive answer to the questions raised by Kurosawa's films. What normally justifies the legitimacy of this critical move is Kurosawa's family background and so-called Japanese cultural heritage. In his autobiography and numerous other publications, Kurosawa has told us that his father was a former samurai, whose Spartan character had fundamental influences on his upbringing. Kurosawa criticism tends to accept the public image of Kurosawa as a modern-day samurai without much critical scrutiny and finds the way of the samurai *(Bushido)* and the samurai ethos everywhere in his films and writings. Thus, in the image of a drunken man aimlessly swinging a sword in *Dodeskaden,* Joan Mellen sees a "brief but consummate suggestion of the futility of attempting to invoke the warrior values of

Japan's feudal past in a present more closely approximated by the disintegration shown in [this film]."[3] But in *Dodeskaden,* which is a *gendaigeki* film depicting the everyday life of slum dwellers in Japan around 1970, there is nothing that even remotely suggests a connection between the drunken man's sword and the "warrior values of Japan's feudal past." Stephen Prince refers to a passage in Kurosawa's autobiography describing how courageously Kurosawa's mother grabbed with her bare hands a pot with oil burning inside and calmly carried it out of the house to prevent a fire. Her hands were burned so badly that a doctor peeled away the charred skin, but she never cried or complained about pain. Immediately after mentioning this episode, Prince continues: "In foregrounding such qualities, Kurosawa's films display a warrior ideal, regardless of the historical era in which they are set. For one of the duties of a warrior was the injunction to maintain severe discipline."[4] Remarkable as it is, the self-discipline and endurance demonstrated by Kurosawa's mother has nothing specifically suggesting some kind of samurai quality. It can easily be argued that because of their suffering and oppression, farmers or working-class people would endure a similar kind of pain just as calmly as she did.[5] The reference to Kurosawa's mother as a symbol of warrior values is particularly misleading because in the autobiography, Kurosawa brings up this episode to show how "things were the opposite of what they appeared on the surface"; that is, contrary to their appearances, "[his] father was actually the sentimentalist, and [his] mother the realist."[6] In other words, by bringing up this episode, Kurosawa tries to problematize the image of his father as a self-disciplined samurai who can perfectly control his sentiment and emotion.

The criticism that tries to find samurai values in Kurosawa films makes us suspicious because there is a tradition of "samurai discourse" in the colonial domestication of Japan by the West.[7] The exotic image of Japan as a nation of samurai was invented by the West and Japan to make the Japanese "intelligible" in the modern geopolitical space of imperialism and colonialism. There is no need to further perpetuate this type of cultural essentialism by making use of samurai to explain Kurosawa's films without qualification. Although it is beyond the scope of this study, it would be much more interesting and meaningful to examine how Kurosawa criticism has been contributing to the dissemination of samurai discourse since the 1960s.

One of many subthematic systems that form samurai discourse is Zen Buddhism and its aesthetic principles. It is therefore not surprising that Zen is discussed prominently in the Kurosawa criticism, too. Prince, for instance, argues that there are many similarities between Kurosawa's films and the religious tenets and practices of Zen Buddhism: "A comparison of Kurosawa's narratives and characters with the model of enlightenment posited by Zen Buddhism can be instructive and can help us to understand some of the ways that Kurosawa's work resonates with a Japanese cultural heritage."[8] He draws our attention to the master-disciple relationship and skepticism toward verbal language as basic characteristics commonly found in Zen and Kurosawa's films. Prince regards the latter feature of Zen as a basic characteristic of Eastern religious thinking in general and uses it to explain Kurosawa's distrust of film criticism:

> Responding to modern currents of film criticism, such as structuralism, he has objected to an oververbalization and overintellectualization of the medium. . . . This distrust of verbal language is not unique to Kurosawa. It is typical of many creators who prefer not to analyze what they have done. Given, however, the models of instruction and education that prevail in the films, it might also be seen as analogous to doctrines of enlightenment that are centuries old and which typify practices found not only in Japan. The Chinese Taoist master Lao-Tzu, for example, is said to have remarked, "Those who know do not speak, those who speak do not know." Heinrich Dumoulin observes that the doctrine of enlightenment in Mahayana Buddhism seems to deny the connections between words and their referents in favor of a policy whereby "meditation must avoid language." Zen Buddhism, for example, distrusts verbal language and abstract conceptualization, preferring instead the realities of concrete experience.[9]

As with the case of samurai values, however, Zen and Eastern religions do not in the end adequately explain Kurosawa's films or authorship. Even though Kurosawa dislikes so many film critics and reviewers, this has nothing to do with his distrust of verbal language (otherwise, why does he urge younger generations of filmmakers and students to read literary masterpieces and write film scripts?). Kurosawa is critical of film reviews and essays precisely because he has too much respect for film criticism. Kurosawa sees film criticism as a creative act, so that only a select group of talented people can engage in critical activities. His profound dissatisfaction with Japanese film critics comes from his belief that so few of them take what they do seriously.[10]

What is often overlooked by Kurosawa criticism and Japanese cinema studies is how Zen Buddhism has been reorganized and appropriated by Japanese intellectuals in modern Japan. There is a fundamental categorical mistake in a critical gesture that tries to establish connections between the cinema of Kurosawa and Zen. If we are seriously interested in a possible analogous relation between the two, we need to study what possible similarities and differences exist between Zen Buddhist elements in Kurosawa's films and Zen Buddhism as appropriated by modern Japanese writers and intellectuals (e.g., the followers of Natsume Soseki or the Kyoto School philosophers in prewar Japan). By examining Zen in Kurosawa's films, we do not learn so much about how Kurosawa is influenced by Japanese cultural tradition; instead, we can learn how his films are related to various attempts to appropriate or reinvent Zen for certain ideological purposes in modern Japan. In other words, it tells more about the modernity of Kurosawa's cinema than his inheritance of so-called cultural heritage.

Unnatural Nature

The danger of culturalism and the inadequacy of using Zen as an interpretive answer can be further illustrated by examining the representation of nature in Kurosawa films. Prince explains the connection between Zen's understanding and Kurosawa's treatment of nature as follows:

> Through one's enlightened actions flows the benevolent spirit of the universe, which may bring one into unity with all things. That unity extends especially to the world of nature. Zen is informed by a reverence for nature quite unlike the perspective of the Western world,

wherein nature is something to be conquered and dominated by human beings. For Zen, one does not dominate nature and expect to live in a truly spiritual fashion. *Satori* flows from living in harmony with the natural world. Zen reverence for nature has influenced the traditional arts in Japan, including the tea ceremony. The ideal of the art of tea is to contemplate and draw closer to nature. . . . Like the tea ceremony, other Japanese arts exhibit the reverential attitude of those who seek harmony with the world of snow, moonbeams, and mountain streams. The *haiku* is a seventeen-syllable poem that uses the Eastern conception of emptiness as a positive quality and the glory of nature even in its smallest creatures. Like these arts, Kurosawa's films are filled with representations of the interconnectedness of human life and the natural world. . . . But, beyond the merely descriptive level, the films visualize the natural world as an extension and elaboration of human conflict. . . . These films indicate one of Kurosawa's strengths: a talent for making environments and characters reciprocal units of expression. As in Zen, human life and the natural world interpenetrate.[11]

It is not clear how one can reconcile the image of the harmonious coexistence of nature and human beings with that of a reciprocally interpenetrating relation between the two. And this difficulty of reconciliation indicates that Zen and the traditional Japanese arts are probably not the most relevant context to explain the function of nature in Kurosawa's films. To understand the specificity of Kurosawa's use of nature, it is much more fruitful to compare it to the representation of nature in conventional Japanese films.

In mainstream Japanese films, which are often called "naturalistic" by Japanese critics, the images of nature occupy a central position in their narrative economy and formal system.[12] In Kurosawa films, too, nature, particularly weather and season, plays an extremely significant role. In fact, his films often give us the impression that weather is at least as important as human characters. For instance, in *Stray Dog*, Murakami's desperation and the turmoil of the immediate postwar days are brilliantly conveyed by the depiction of simmering hot summer days. The shots of sweating faces and bodies intensify the sense of tension, which is suddenly broken by heavy rainfall marking a cathartic moment. This rhythmic alternation of the scenes filled with two kinds of liquids—sweat perspired from human bodies under the blazing sun and rain pouring from a dark sky—creates a sharp contrast or sense of dualism.[13] In *High and Low,* the dramatic tension is in part created by the contrast between Gondo's white, comfortably air-conditioned house at the top of a hill and Takeuchi's dark, cramped boarding room without luxury of modern technology. The story of *Record of a Living Being* is set in the rainy season in the summer *(tsuyu),* so that at least in half of the film, the narrative unfolds against the background of a torrential rain and thunderstorm. By showing one raining scene after another, the film reminds us of the radioactive rain, which is so feared by Nakajima, and further reinforces an ominous sense of impending nuclear threat.[14] Because of these raining scenes, a close-up of the sun in the film's penultimate scene becomes all the more shocking as an image of the exploding earth.[15]

What becomes apparent from these examples is that there is a dramatic difference between Kurosawa's work and conventional Japanese films in terms of how they treat nature. The naturalistic tendency of the latter can be characterized by the proximity of humans and nature. The peaceful coexistence of the two is certainly an obvious example of this proximity; however, even when nature is much less cooperative, human characters are not totally alienated from it. In a small island country such as Japan, which lacks an endless desert or the indefinitely extending horizon without any sign of human habitation, nature is not an absolute other to humans and never totally overwhelms human existence. And this already diminished power of nature is further tamed by fetishistic attention to season. The cyclical change of seasons transforms nature into something predictable and manageable, and seasonal changes become a sign of the transitoriness of human life. Therefore, the scenes of nature in naturalistic films have less to do with the idea of objective representation of reality; instead, their realism depends on their capacity to affect the audience through the evocation of atmosphere *(fun'iki)* and emotion *(jocho).* Natural environment in these films is permeated with atmospheric feelings and emotion, which are created by the ambiguity surrounding the relation of humans and nature. Humans do not completely subjugate nature to their will, nor do they remain utterly powerless when confronting the sheer physical power of nature. Instead, humans and nature are believed to fuse into one, so that they do not form the dichotomy of subject and object or of culture and nature. In the context of naturalistic films, the appreciation of nature can easily turn into the state of characters' passivity and their quiet acceptance of the present condition as something natural and beyond human control. The issue of human responsibility can easily evaporate into thin air, and what remains is often the silence of nature encompassing both human life and natural environment.

By contrast, the function of nature in Kurosawa films is radically different from the way nature is used in conventional Japanese films. In Kurosawa films, nature is not accorded a status of immutable existence beyond human intervention. Nor is it a mere symbol of human evanescence because what characterizes humans in the world of Kurosawa is their perfectibility, ability to initiate action, and belief that there is nothing that cannot be changed by human effort. Moreover, nature in Kurosawa films is not just a background against which characters act and react. Nature and humans do not simply exist side by side in a state of mutual indifference or harmony. Far from remaining a silent background or decor, by actively interacting with human characters, nature becomes at least as expressive as human characters without necessarily becoming a predictable symbol. In Kurosawa films, nature does not preexist characters' action; instead, what appears to be natural environment is from the very beginning created by the gargantuan clash of human and natural forces.[16]

True, characters in Kurosawa films do talk about beauty of nature as an object of quiet contemplation. Often, these characters have forgotten about nature's beauty in the midst of daily routine but suddenly remember how beautiful a starlit sky (the pickpocket Ogin in *Stray Dog*) or the setting sun (Watanabe in *Ikiru*) can be. But it is important to note that these characters' remarks are not particularly convincing. Ogin and Watanabe are hardly contemplative aesthetes who appreciate the silent beauty of nature in their everyday lives. They are stirred with emotion not necessarily because they rediscover nature's beauty but because they consciously remember their own past. Through their fresh observation of nature's beauty, a rudimentary sense of who they are resurfaces to consciousness. This is a moment that is similar to the emergence of a new subjectivity or "interiority" in modern Japanese literature, which is analyzed by Karatani Kojin as a product of a complex dialectic of obsession with, and indifference, to natural environment as landscape.[17] However, what we see in Kurosawa's work is not reducible to the discovery of an interiorized subject. What is crucial for Ogin or Watanabe is a connection between the past and the present, and the role of nature is quite restricted to that of a catalyst that facilitates the reestablishment of that temporal connection. To the extent that nature in modern Japanese literature is just an excuse for a subject to celebrate the autonomy of its interiority, there is no surprise in the lack of aestheticized, beautiful images of nature in the scene where Ogin expresses her mild surprise at the charm of the starlit sky. We have to wait until *Dersu Uzala* to see Kurosawa's more straightforward indulgence in depicting the natural beauty of landscapes. But even there, beautiful as they are, the images of Siberian landscapes are quite different from the kind of images shown by the National Geographic specials on television.

Much more than a mere meteorological phenomenon, weather heightens the dramatic tension in Kurosawa films.[18] Because the representation of weather is not naturalistically motivated, the sense of the cyclical season—a symbol of Japanese sensibility in conventional films—is remarkably absent in his work.[19] The season, which supposedly symbolizes the proximity of Japanese life to nature, is denaturalized and, depending on the context, transformed into a Manichaean device *(Rashomon)*, a sign of class conflict *(High and Low)*, or a product of technology running amok *(Record of a Living Being)*. *Stray Dog* is a particularly interesting case because it virtually opens with the voice-over narration "It was a very hot day." This explicit—even crude—establishment of the film's climatic setting leads to the analytic use of weather in the rest of the film. For instance, the unbearable heat is used as a diegetically motivated justification for Kurosawa's graphic experiment; that is, it is used to explain why there are so many electric fans, handheld fans *(uchiwa),* and sunshades, all of which are, however, arguably more important as visual obstacles for characters and the audience. The seasonal setting is also exploited as a formal device for introducing a rhythmic pattern in the narrative. A sudden shower with thunder and lightning marks a cathartic moment, which temporally suspends dramatic tension while signaling a coming narrative resolution. Finally, the extremely accentuated sense of the season and the highly manipulated use of weather problematizes the identity of self. Because of the extreme heat, some characters momentarily lose their mind and behave in such a way that even they cannot comprehend their own actions. This separation of thought and action is further emphasized by the close-up shots of perspiring human bodies, which are presented as if they were mere objects, completely cut off from human consciousness.

Kurosawa's antinaturalist interest in nature is apparent in the essay titled "The Scenery of Tohoku" (Tohoku no fubutsu) published in 1946.[20] In this text, Kurosawa talks about the attraction of the four seasons in the Tohoku region. Yet rather than dwelling on the sense of seasons per se, he concentrates on visual and temporal effects created by natural phenomena. To illustrate his point, he constantly refers to works of art. For instance, in his description of Tohoku's summer, the green color of a pasture at sunset becomes unmixed emerald green colors painted on canvas, and leaves of grass are said to come alive as if painted by van Gogh; the magnificence of a rainbow after a shower is compared to columns of an ancient Greek palace. As these and other examples show, Kurosawa is attracted by landscapes and sceneries of Tohoku not necessarily because they are part of pristine, uncontaminated nature but because they remind him of Beethoven's symphony, Chagall's painting, or *Alice in Wonderland*. Ironically, as Kurosawa earnestly talks about the beauty of seasonal attractions in Tohoku's natural landscape, the primary status of nature as original is eclipsed by nature as representation or copy. In *Dreams,* Kurosawa further problematizes the relationship between nature and representation of nature as a tribute to the art of van Gogh. In the episode titled "Crows," a Japanese painter, who is Kurosawa's surrogate, is transported to Arles, where a bridge, a barn, and roadside grass and flowers are painted to make them resemble van Gogh's paintings. After his brief encounter with van Gogh (played by Martin Scorsese), the painter finds himself inside van Gogh's paintings. By using high-definition video, Kurosawa transforms a represented landscape into a real one, in which the painter can freely wander as he searches for the master painter, the creator of an artificial world, which is more "real" than a real world perceived with our naked eye. Thus, nature in Kurosawa films has almost nothing to do with a traditional Japanese sensibility valorized by culturalist discourse in Japanese cinema studies.

3. *The Most Beautiful*

In 1944 Kurosawa made his second film, *The Most Beautiful* (Ichiban utsukushiku). The narrative of the film focuses on a group of young women working at an optical factory in Hiratsuka. The film's exclusive focus on young women workers was consistent with the government's new policy of enlisting them for various jobs that had been occupied mostly by men. As men were forbidden in 1943 by the government to take up seventeen types of occupation including sales clerk, conductor, and hairstylist, women at the home front were mobilized for the war effort at the full scale. Women's Labor Volunteer Corps (Joshi Kinro Teishintai) were organized, and women under the age of twenty-five were drafted and sent to munition factories and other traditionally male workplaces.[1]

The ongoing war with China and the battle against the United States called for centralization of not only the political system and economic structure but also cultural activities and people's consciousness. The government was therefore more than eager to mobilize the cinema for the war by tightening its control over the content of films and by restructuring the system of film production, distribution, and exhibition. In 1939 the Diet passed the Film Law (Eigaho), which laid a foundation for the wartime control and centralization of the cinema by the government. In 1941 the government's pressure forced the reorganization of the film industry, the effect of which greatly influenced the development of Japanese cinema after the end of the war. The two largest companies in the early 1940s were Toho and Shochiku, and there were eight other majors, some of which were either directly subsidized or partially owned by the former two. The government initially tried to consolidate ten companies into two, but a faction of the film industry under the leadership of Nagata Masaichi convinced the bureaucrats to change their plan in order to prevent Shochiku from monopolizing the film industry. In the end, the government's revised plan gave rise to one brand-new company and two restructured ones. Toho absorbed Nan'o, Daiho, Takarazuka, and Tokyo Hassei, and Shochiku took over Koa. Out of Nikkatsu, Shinko, and Daito was created a new company called Dai Nihon Eiga, or more commonly, Daiei. Meanwhile, the distribution of films was also under the new government control, so that a single company handled the films of all three studios. The industry was forced to go along with the government because it threatened to cut off the supply of raw film stock, which was strategic military supplies. At the same time, the leaders of the film industry did not passively accept the government plan out of patriotism. Kido Shiro, Nagata Masaichi, and other heads of film companies actively tried to exploit the wartime emergency as another business opportunity for consolidating a monopoly structure of the film industry.

As the government controlled the domestic film industry in the name of wartime emergency, Japanese filmmakers were also asked to play a part in Japanese imperial expansionism. Wherever the Japanese army advanced and invaded, the Japanese filmmakers followed. In Japanese colonies of Taiwan and Korea, the Japanese military and film industry established a centralized system of film production and distribution modeled after the Japanese domestic system. In China, new film studios—such as the China Motion Picture Company (Chuka Den'ei)—were established jointly by Japanese and Chinese film companies. In Manchukuo, which was established as a Japanese puppet state in 1932, the Manchurian Motion Picture Association, or Man'ei, employed a number of Japanese filmmakers and produced films for Japanese and Chinese audiences. To promote Japanese films in Southeast Asia, the South Seas Motion Picture Association (Nan'yo Eiga Kyokai) was established in 1940 as a joint venture of Shochiku, Toho, Towa, and the China Motion Picture Company. The association was headed by Kido, who had been actively pursuing Shochiku's coproduction with Japanese-backed Asian film studios, and helped the infiltration of Japanese films into the Greater East Asia Co-prosperity Sphere (Daitoa Kyoeiken).

A number of propaganda films were made during the war, particularly after the beginning of the Pacific War. The Office of Public Information regulated the content of films through censorship and demanded that the industry produce "national-policy films" glorifying war and the self-sacrifice of the Japanese. As a result, the film industry for the first time started systematically producing war films, which had not existed as a respectable film genre before. One of the most spectacular war films was *The War at Sea from Hawaii to Malaya* (Hawai-Marei oki kaisen, 1942), directed by Kurosawa's mentor Yamamoto Kajiro. To celebrate the first anniversary of the Pearl Harbor attack, the Imperial Headquarters' Information Office came up with a plan to produce a film, and the Ministry of the Navy chose Toho to carry out this national project. Even though there are two nominal protagonists, the film mostly depicts the daily training of a corps of young pilots who at the film's climax participate in the Japanese attacks on Pearl Harbor and a British fleet off the Malay Peninsula. The miniature models and special effects to recreate the battle scenes were so detailed and realistic that some American occupation officers after the war believed they were watching documentary footage.[2]

To some extent, regardless of their specific content, all the films from this period must be regarded as propaganda films, since no film could be produced unless it passed the censors first. The existence of strict militaristic censorship seems to lead to the conclusion that any filmmakers who participated in film production in this period could not escape from the accusation of war collaboration. The problem with this argument lies in its assumption that the wartime censorship was carried out by a uniform, coherent program, by which the production of films was systematically regulated to maximize propaganda effect. But the evidence shows that this was hardly the case. The relationship between the military and filmmakers was almost always strained even when the latter were making overtly propagandistic films. During the production of *The War at Sea from Hawaii to Malaya,* the navy, which commissioned the film in the first place, refused the director Yamamoto Kajiro any access not only to real aircraft carriers but also to their photographs for construction of miniature sets. As a result, to make models of Japanese Navy ships, Yamamoto used pictures of the U.S. Navy's *Lexington* and *Saratoga,* which he found in a copy of the *Life* magazine.[3] Without any consistent censorship program or means of implementing censorship codes systematically, the result of censorship seemed at best confused. Under such circumstances, the fact that a particular film was produced did not necessarily make it a propaganda film. Some films were obviously propagandistic, and some others were perhaps obliquely so. What is certain is that the government approval of a particular film did not necessarily make that film a propaganda piece. Conversely, a film that was disapproved by the censors did not automatically qualify as an antigovernment or nonpropaganda film. Unlike the Nazis, the Japanese militarist government did not try to integrate cinema as a crucial means of aestheticizing politics, and its rather haphazard policy on cinema and culture prevented a smooth integration of the film industry into a larger war machine.

The difficulty of systematically exploiting film as a means of propaganda also had something to do with the specificity of the cinema in the cultural landscape of prewar Japan. For instance, why did so many Japanese war films focus on the purity of the Japanese themselves instead of demonizing the Americans to arouse audiences' hatred of the enemy? The relative absence of images of the enemy in the Japanese war films seems particularly puzzling because "in wartime cartoons as well as popular colloquialisms . . . it was commonplace to depict the Americans and British as demons *(oni)*, devils *(akki, akuma)*, and monsters *(kaibutsu)*."[4] But when we think about how enormously popular Hollywood films were among the Japanese audiences before Pearl Harbor, there is nothing strange about this absence. When Charlie Chaplin, Greta Garbo, Marlene Dietrich, and Gary Cooper were at least as popular as Japan's biggest movie stars, when the Japanese were so enamored with the American scenery, commodity culture, and way of life, how could the Japanese film industry have made propaganda films that showed devilish images of Americans in any convincing way?[5] In the discursive field of Japanese film culture, which was so thoroughly infiltrated by Hollywood, the "devilish Anglo-Americans" were simply unrepresentable. Another explanation for the absence of enemies' images is that the film censors were less interested in arousing people's hatred toward the Anglo-American enemies than in creating a myth of pure Japaneseness. The Japanese government was interested in creating the "national cinema" *(kokumin eiga)*, in which, as war collaborator Tsumura Hideo argued, the word *kokumin* should signify something fundamentally different from the English word "nation."[6] Parallel to such a notion as the "national language" *(kokugo)*, the "national cinema" was conceived as a harmonious unity of the Japanese spirit and cinema, and one of the first steps to be taken was to eliminate American influences from Japanese cinema. The ultimate goal of the "national cinema" was to represent the national spirit or pure Japaneseness uncontaminated by any outside influences, and to achieve this goal, the representation of outside enemies was almost irrelevant.

The Japanese war films seem to "contain strains of humanism and even pacifism" despite their status as propaganda,[7] but again there is no contradiction in this apparently incongruent combination. The wartime Japanese films were a field of cultural contestation where contradictory ideologies and values simultaneously coexisted. Moreover, what seems like contradictory coexistence of incongruous messages to us might not have appeared so to the original audiences of those films. We cannot determine from our vantage point whether a particular film is propaganda simply by examining its overt content. By definition, the ultimate purpose of propaganda is to manipulate the audiences' opinions and behavior for a specific ideological purpose. The close reading of a film alone cannot always reveal its propagandistic aspects unless it is contextualized in relation to the reception of that film by its contemporary audiences. To the extent that it demands simultaneous examination of its textual specificity and its actual reception, propaganda film as a genre foregrounds the complexity of film as a cultural text precariously balancing its own material textuality and social construction. In the case of the wartime Japanese films, various personal recollections and records of film-viewing experiences during the war show that contemporary audiences' reactions to the films do not always coincide with professional film critics' assessment of those films. Contrary to what Ruth Benedict asserts, the wartime audiences' reaction to Japanese films cannot be discussed in terms of the simplistic binarism of pro-war and antiwar sentiment.[8]

To what extent did individual filmmakers actively support or passively oppose the military? Some actively collaborated, many passively went along with, and very few tried to resist the government's militarist policy. Some filmmakers did not make war films in a narrow sense because they did not know how to make heroic national policy films (e.g., directors who specialized in women's pictures or melodrama). There were also directors who quietly sabotaged orders from the military. For instance, Ozu was sent by the military to Singapore to make a propaganda film about India's independence movement; however, he delayed the production of the film so long that before he could finish it, the war was already over. On the one hand, many Japanese filmmakers did not become avid advocates of Japanese fascism. On the other hand, the fact still remains that like writers, academics, and artists of various kinds, filmmakers did not actively resist Japanese militarism. Moreover, because of the specificity of the cinema as a medium of art and industry, Japanese filmmakers were much more easily co-opted by the militarist policy of the government than other cultural producers. One of the most important characteristics of the cinema is its collective nature. As long as a pen and paper are available, writers can write. Even when their work might not see the light of the day, the production of the original text (writing) is still possible without being reproduced in mass quantity (printing and distribution). Technically speaking, in the case of the cinema, the production of the original negative and the mass reproduction of positive prints are also two separate processes. However, unlike writing a novel, the original production of a film requires a considerably larger amount of capital and calls for the collaboration of many people, so that unless a sufficient number of copies are made, distributed, and exhibited for profit, the production of the original itself is virtually impossible. For all practical purposes, the production and reproduction phases of filmmaking can be regarded as an integral whole. The cinema is a collective type of art through and through. Because it is produced collectively and consumed by the mass audience, the individual is ultimately submerged in the collective. And it is the collective nature of the cinema that allowed filmmakers to collaborate with the government without being fully conscious of their own action. Perhaps this is also why immediately after the Japanese defeat, the question of filmmakers' war responsibilities was raised but quickly forgotten.

Ambiguous Collaboration

During the war, as a young assistant director who had demonstrated his talent under Yamamoto, Kurosawa desperately wanted to make a film of his own. To be promoted to the rank of director, Kurosawa wrote scripts that won prizes, but none of them was approved for production. They were either criticized by the militarist government censors as inadequate for the purpose of whipping up the Japanese fighting spirit or regarded by Toho as too ambitious for the first film of a novice director. For instance, *The San Paguida Flower* (San Paguita no hana) was attacked by the Home Ministry's censors because a scene of a birthday celebration in the script allegedly showed a bad influence of Americanism, and *Three Hundred Miles through Enemy Lines* (Tekichu odan sanzenri) was rejected by Toho for its large production scale.[9] In 1942 Kurosawa was finally given an opportunity to direct *Sanshiro Sugata*. Although it was a commercial success, this judo film did not make it easier for him to make another film. The absolute number of films produced by the three existing studios was already very small by the time Kurosawa made his debut as film director.[10] As the war dragged on, the material condition of the film industry further deteriorated.

Kurosawa tried to write a script or propose a project that would be approved by his own studio and the Public Information Office's censorship board and at the same time allow him enough latitude in development of narrative motifs and formal experiment. Obviously he was treading a thin line. Despite his hatred of the censors, in his scripts and essays, Kurosawa used words and phrases that were part of the militarist vocabulary. To this extent, whatever his intention, Kurosawa was clearly implicated in the militarist government's propaganda effort. He was never an apologist for militarism and did not purposefully collaborate with the government. However, like many other filmmakers, he did not actively resist militarism. Kurosawa's wartime films contain thematic motifs that could easily be appropriated by the militarist government to legitimize the mass mobilization for the war.

In terms of its narrative and thematic subject, *The Most Beautiful* is not a unique film. A group of similar films were made in late 1943 and 1944, urging Japanese to make further efforts to increase production of key war supplies such as steel, aluminum, and coal. These films, including Kurosawa's, were without any question propaganda promoting the national policy of increasing productivity in war industry.[11] National General Mobilization Law (Kokka Sodoinho) was fully used to mobilize every able civilian, since by this time human labor was the only resource left to continue fighting against enemies. To underline the importance of the collective war effort, instead of focusing on a few individual heroines, Kurosawa's film shows a group of young women mobilized at a lens factory. The sense of collectivity is further enhanced by the absence of recognizable stars in the group of women. But there is nothing special about the use of a collective as a protagonist. From "humanistic" war films (e.g., *Five Scouts* [Gonin no sekkohei, 1939]) to war spectacles like *The War at Sea from Hawaii to Malaya*, Japanese wartime films frequently featured collective heroes to interpellate spectators as members of an imagined community of mutual empathy and homogeneity. Another characteristic of *The Most Beautiful*, its documentary-like feeling, was also consistent with a general trend in Japanese cinema toward the fusion of fiction and documentary, which became prominent after the beginning of the "fifteen-year war" between Japan and China in 1931.

In his autobiography and interviews, Kurosawa admits that he was not necessarily forced to make *The Most Beautiful*, and he rather fondly remembers this wartime creation. It is certainly possible to personalize his remark that "*The Most Beautiful* is not a major picture, but it is the one dearest to me"[12] by pointing out that he married one of the film's actresses, Yaguchi Yoko, right after the film was made.[13] But it is at least equally important to note that some of the narrative motifs in this wartime film reappear in his postwar films as vehicles for the assertion of what are often regarded as humanistic ideals.[14] There is a strong sense of continuity between Kurosawa's wartime and postwar films, and this continuity problematizes any facile differentiation of so-called postwar humanism and the wartime militarism of his films. This sense of continuity is found not only uniquely in Kurosawa's career but also in Japanese cinema and more generally in Japanese history. We will come back to the issue of continuity and discontinuity in chapter 6, where the questions of war collaboration and responsibility are more fully explored.

4. *Sanshiro Sugata, Part 2*

In 1945, as a sequel to the commercially successful *Sanshiro Sugata*, Kurosawa made *Sanshiro Sugata, Part 2* (Zoku Sugata Sanshiro) by order of Toho. It might be said that among Kurosawa's works, this film is least satisfying artistically and perhaps most overtly propagandistic. Almost all the characters are cardboard figures, and if we still find some of them interesting, it is only because of our familiarity with *Sanshiro Sugata*, the original film. Put differently, with so many narrative motifs, characters, and other textual details either not fully developed or unexplained, the sequel does not make much sense unless we see the original first. For instance, there are some vague hints of a romantic relationship between Sanshiro and Sayo, but the representation of Sayo in the film adds nothing to what we already know about her from the original. In fact, rather than a sequel to *Sanshiro Sugata*, *Sanshiro Sugata, Part 2* is more like a bad remake of the former. (As we will see in the following chapters, this rather conventional relationship between a superior original and an inferior copy is very uncharacteristic of Kurosawa's work.) Many scenes are directly borrowed from the original but are presented in an uninspiring manner. The film's opening fight between Sanshiro and an abusive American sailor is, in Richie's words, "a parody of the waterfront fight in the first film, done in middle-shot, long-shot, completely unexciting. It is reminiscent of the original fight only in that someone is thrown into the water."[1] The last fight between Sanshiro and Tesshin also imitates the fight between Sanshiro and Gennosuke in the original; the conventionality of the former cannot but become apparent because the same actor, Tsukigata Ryunosuke, plays the roles of both Tesshin and Gennosuke. As an inferior copy of *Sanshiro Sugata*, the sequel does not provide any compelling explanation for why Sanshiro must fight. The film's melodramatic plot and themes do not clearly articulate his moral dilemma but only reveal his indecisiveness. If in the original Sanshiro's honesty and innocence make us feel refreshed, the sequel ends up belittling Sanshiro as a sentimental, simpleminded character. The deficiencies of the film can be explained by the fact that Kurosawa reportedly complied with Toho's demand for a sequel without much personal enthusiasm. It is also possible to speculate that there simply was not enough time or resources to produce the film according to its script, which includes many details not present in the finished film. The film was released on May 3, 1945, only about three and a half months before the Japanese surrender; and by that time, Tokyo and other urban areas in Japan had been reduced to rubble by a series of American carpet bombings.

Some of the film's few notable moments include two fight scenes, the first between *jujitsu* master Sekine and American boxer William Lister, the second between Sanshiro and Lister. Here, the Japanese spirit, which is obliquely present in the original film, is much more explicitly articulated as a sensational nationalistic discourse of us (Japan) versus them (America). What is propagandistic is not just the content of the film (the Japanese judo master defeating obnoxious Americans) but also the way the fight scenes are constructed formally. The treatment of the fight itself has nothing inspiring about it. In the first fight scene, the boxing ring where Lister is beating Sekine to a pulp is shot by a fixed high-angle camera, and what we see is clearly presented as Sanshiro's point-of-view shot; the second fight scene is very brief and conventionally edited without much analytic precision. There is, in short, nothing particularly exciting about the way the fighting is filmed and edited. The focus of these scenes is not the fights as spectacles (as in *Sanshiro Sugata*) but diegetic spectators' reaction. At a climactic moment of each fight, Kurosawa rapidly intercuts two types of close-ups: the shots of American spectators hysterically laughing, jeering, screaming, drinking, or smoking and those of Lister either beating Sekine or slowly getting up after being thrown to the floor by Sanshiro. The close-ups of Americans are shot and edited very effectively as propaganda reminiscent of Soviet silent cinema and Eisenstein's typified images of the corrupt capitalists and bourgeoisie. In the context of the film's narrative, what makes American spectators uncivilized and depraved is their consumption of the fight as a mere entertainment show. To this extent, the uninspiring representation of the two fights may be justified by the film's ideological imperative of not placing the film's actual spectators in the same position as American spectators in the film.

A more subtle yet equally effective propaganda scene appears before the showdown between Sanshiro and Lister. Sanshiro wants to fight with the American boxer and the Higaki brothers, who injured the Japanese national honor and insulted the spirit of the Shudokan school of judo respectively. But he cannot achieve his objective without violating the school's fundamental rules: no fighting without the master's permission; no fighting for a show; no drinking in the school's sacred training hall, or *dojo*. The school's master, Yano, has forbidden Sanshiro to accept the Higaki brothers' challenge to a duel, and the fight with the American boxer is out of the question because boxing is not regarded as a type of martial arts but as a moneymaking entertainment show. Out of frustration, Sanshiro drinks sake in the *dojo* late at night in violation of the third basic rule. Dan Yoshimaro (Mori Masayuki), one of the leading disciples of the school, sits down next to Sanshiro and tries to find out what is going on. Suddenly Yano enters the *dojo*. Dan quickly puts a cup behind him but does not have a chance to hide a large sake bottle lying in front of him. As if noticing nothing unusual, Yano starts talking about a new judo textbook and asks for their help. As he talks about basic forms of feet movement, Yano picks up the sake bottle and demonstrates those forms by masterfully handling it with his feet. After a while, Yano leaves the hall with the words "It's about time to go to sleep." As Sato Tadao's excellent analysis of this scene shows, what we see here is Yano's superb *haragei,* or nonverbalized attempt to communicate with Sanshiro.[2] On the one hand, Yano uses the sake bottle as a metonymic substitute for Sanshiro, and by throwing the bottle again and again, he silently punishes his disciple. On the other hand, Sanshiro is grateful that his master does not directly scold him; and at the same time, fully aware of what lies beneath the master's silence, he is all the more ashamed of his defiant behavior. (Kurosawa intercuts the close-ups of Yano's foot throwing the bottle and those of Sanshiro looking away with his eyes closed.) Through the silent communication, a certain communal feeling is created between Sanshiro and Yano, and once this silent circuit of communication is established, the master can give an order to the disciple without saying a word. By not directly scolding him, Yano tacitly permits, or even encourages, Sanshiro to fight with the Higaki brothers to restore the school's honor and at the same time creates an impression that it is the disciple who voluntarily sacrifices himself for the benefit of the collective. This kind of silent communication based on the communal feeling is an extremely effective means of controlling people, who misrecognize the coercive forces of the communal as the benevolence of the master.

Finally, *Sanshiro Sugata, Part 2* is notable for its overt use of Noh imagery for the first time in Kurosawa films. With his white makeup, wig, and white robe, the youngest of the Higaki brothers, Genzaburo, appears as a figure straight out of Noh repertoire. Instead of walking normally, he moves with Noh steps and carries a bamboo branch in his hands to signify his insanity. Yet again, like so many other aspects of the film, Noh imagery looks like another parodic moment. It is in the next film, *The Men Who Tread on the Tiger's Tail,* that Kurosawa more seriously confronts the culture and discourse of Noh.

5. *The Men Who Tread on the Tiger's Tail*

Kabuki/Noh/Film

In 1945, when Japan's defeat in the war was increasingly becoming certain, Kurosawa began working on *The Lifted Spear* (Dokkoi kono yari), his first *jidaigeki* (period film) and comedy, featuring the extremely popular and highly talented comedian Enomoto Ken'ichi (Enoken for short). The last scene of the film was supposed to show the Battle of Okehazama (1560), in which the feudal lord Oda Nobunaga defeated his rival Imagawa Yoshimoto. In the last days of the war, however, no horses were available for the battle scene, and Kurosawa was forced to abandon the project at the preproduction stage. It took him thirty-five more years to show Oda Nobunaga engaged in a grand battle in *Kagemusha* (1980), at the climax of which the combined forces of Oda and Tokugawa Ieyasu defeat the army of their archrival, the Takeda clan, in the Battle of Nagashino (1575).

As an alternative to *The Lifted Spear,* Kurosawa immediately proposed to Toho that he make *The Men Who Tread on the Tiger's Tail* (Tora no o o fumu otokotachi, 1945). Like *The Lifted Spear, The Men Who Tread on the Tiger's Tail* is a *jidaigeki,* but its scale of production is much smaller and its narrative much simpler. Basically shot with one simple set, this fifty-eight-minute film has no large crowd scene. The film's narrative is based on the well-known Kabuki repertoire *Kanjincho,* so that it did not take much time for Kurosawa to write a script. The genius of Kurosawa lies in his refusal to passively accept these physical limitations and in his exploitation of the material constraints as a moment for artistic innovation.

The historical setting of the film is Japan of the twelfth century, when two noble clans, the Heike (the Taira clan) and the Genji (the Minamoto clan), were bitterly fighting against each other to rule the country. Initially, the Tairas were triumphant. The warlord Taira no Kiyo-mori (1118–1181) wielded power in the capital Kyoto through military strength, political maneuvering, and intermarriage of his daughter and emperor. While the proud Tairas were increasingly losing touch with the situation in hinterland, the Minamotos, led by the brothers Yori-tomo and Yoshitsune, were looking for a chance to overthrow the hege-mony of the Taira clan. Yoritomo was the patriarch of the family, his younger brother Yoshitsune a brilliant general who never lost a battle. Together, they successfully vanquished the Heike (the last major battle was fought at Dannoura in 1185, which is eerily depicted in Kobayashi Masaki's film *Kwaidan* [Kaidan, 1964]), but the relationship between the two brothers soon went sour. Yoritomo was jealous of Yoshitsune's fame and popularity and believed his retainer Kajiwara Kagetoki's slan-derous accusation that his younger brother was plotting against him. Immediately, Yoritomo ordered his men to hunt down and execute his allegedly treacherous brother. Yoshitsune fled to the safe haven of northern Japan, the domain of Fujiwara no Hidehira, but in the end he was betrayed and committed suicide. Out of these historical events emerged the Yoshitsune legend and the popular sentiment of *hogan-biiki*, or sympathy for the underdog. As Ivan Morris points out, "so faithfully does Yoshitsune conform to the ideal of heroism through fail-ure that the term *hoganbiiki* (which literally meant 'sympathy with the Lieutenant' and came from his rank in the Imperial Police) has be-come fixed in language to describe the traditional sympathy with the losing side."[1] Even though Yoshitsune and his retainers are not cap-tured in Kurosawa's film, the Japanese audience, who are thoroughly familiar with the Yoshitsune legend, know that Yoshitsune is doomed. His tragic end is echoed by the circumstance of many other Kurosawa heroes: the obsolescence of samurai as warriors *(Seven Samurai)*, the end of the samurai class *(Yojimbo)*, the annihilation of a clan *(Throne of Blood, Kagemusha, Ran)*, the protagonist's death by cancer *(Ikiru)* or by torture *(The Bad Sleep Well)*.

The original proposal for the film passed the wartime censors be-cause the film's depiction of feudal loyalty was believed to be consis-tent with the militarist policy of the government. However, far from being spirit-raising war propaganda, the film is first and foremost an entertainment film or a musical comedy. Kurosawa started shooting the film right before the Japanese defeat. When the emperor officially announced Japan's surrender to the Allies on the radio, production of the film momentarily halted. But a few days later, the shooting resumed as if nothing had happened, and the film was completed as originally planned. Even though the wartime censorship ended with the Japanese defeat, the film had to pass the Occupation government's censorship instituted in September 1945. One of the first tasks for the Occupation censors was to obtain the list of films already in production at that time. The Japanese censors willfully neglected to report *The Men Who Tread on the Tiger's Tail* in order to get even with Kurosawa, who had humiliated one of them about his ignorance of Japanese cultural tradition. Because the film was not on the list submitted by the Japanese censors, Kurosawa's film was deemed illegal, and Toho was not allowed to show the film in that year. Three years later, the Occupation censors lifted the ban on the film, but it was only in 1952, after the reestablishment of Japan's sovereignty and the commercial release of Kurosawa's twelfth film, *The Idiot*, that *The Men Who Tread on the Tiger's Tail* was shown to the Japanese public for the first time.

The Men Who Tread on the Tiger's Tail depicts a well-known episode from Yoshitsune's escape journey. Yoshitsune and a small group of his loyal retainers are on their way to Hiraizumi, the capital of the Fujiwaras' territory in northern Japan. They are about to reach a newly built barrier at Ataka, where Yoritomo's vassal and guard Togashi is waiting to capture and execute them. By Kajiwara's messenger Togashi is already alerted that Yoshitsune and his retainers have disguised themselves as itinerant Buddhist monks. The leader of Yoshitsune's retainers, Benkei, tries to trick Togashi, who in turn attempts to expose Yoshitsune's true identity. When Yoshitsune's party is finally allowed to pass the barrier, Kajiwara's messenger spots one of the porters as Yoshitsune. To convince the messenger, Togashi, and guards that Yoshitsune is a mere porter who happens to bear resemblance to the famed brother of the shogun, Benkei resorts to an incredible act: in violation of the feudal code of loyalty, he beats his own lord.

In general a straightforward adaptation of Kabuki's *Kanjincho*, *The Men Who Tread on the Tiger's Tail* includes some crucial changes, the most significant of which is the addition of a new character, the porter played by Enoken. Several times the monks admonish the porter to get out of their sight, but he continues to follow them, successfully passes the barrier as a member of their party, and then has a drinking bout with them. One of the obvious functions of the porter in the film is a narratological one. The interaction of the porter and Yoshitsune's retainers in the first scene performs the task of introducing the necessary background information of the story. It is through the porter's mouth that we learn that Yoritomo is relentlessly pursuing Yoshitsune as a traitor; that Yoshitsune and a small group of his retainers are all disguised as mountain monks; that among the retainers is a warrior monk called Benkei, known for his extraordinary strength and skill in the military arts; and that the messenger sent by Kajiwara has already arrived at the barrier and is waiting for the appearance of Yoshitsune's party. The use of the porter as a new character is a very economical way of laying out the context of the story and immediately creating a moment of crisis at the beginning of the film.[2]

It is sometimes argued that the film subtly criticizes the ideal of feudal loyalty, but the addition of the porter does not necessarily make the film critical of the idealized master-retainer relationship. Instead of portraying the loyalty of Benkei to Yoshitsune negatively, the film's treatment of their relationship is much more ambivalent.[3] Throughout the film, the porter remains an outsider to the world of warlords and warriors. Despite his enthusiasm for helping Yoshitsune, the porter does not in the end influence the outcome of the confrontation between Benkei and Togashi. As in *Kanjincho*, it is clearly Benkei who saves Yoshitsune from a dire predicament. Rather than being the film's real hero, as some critics argue,[4] the porter's role is to observe from a distance events that are fundamentally alien to his own world. As a voice of common sense and a witness from the lower class, the porter introduces a sense of critical distance and to this extent relativizes the ideal of feudal loyalty.[5] At the beginning of the film, without realizing the true identities of the mountain monks, the porter says, "After all, a quarrel between brothers is supposed to be something more innocent. It's usually over after they hit each other once or twice. I really don't like the way Shogun is hunting down his own brother as if he were an animal." When they hear this commonsense remark, Yoshitsune's retainers hang their heads and fall silent. But the commoner's critique of the shogun does not lead to a wholesale denial of the warrior class and feudal system. Instead, the film positively portrays Benkei's extraordinary act of severely beating Yoshitsune as the ultimate manifestation of the retainer's feudal loyalty to the master.

The porter is a mediating figure, speaking for Benkei and Togashi, who cannot afford to directly expose their inner thoughts and feelings to their enemies. He is also an implied spectator, whose reactions to the film's unfolding events anticipate those of the audience. Unable to bear watching Benkei beating the frail Yoshitsune, the porter screams. At first, Togashi is hidden behind the messenger and a crowd of guards. As they move to both sides of the screen, Togashi, seated on a stool, is revealed. A trace of tears on his face makes us realize that the porter's scream is the externalized representation of Togashi's interior state of mind. Through the porter, we also vicariously experience Yoshitsune's and Benkei's pain, neither of which is explicitly represented. In a performance of the original Kabuki play, there is no direct expression of characters' psychology; on the stage there is only the opaque surface of the actor's body. In the Kabuki art of acting called *haragei,* neither words nor facial expression directly states the character's inner thought; instead, it is through the erasure of explicit expression that *haragei* tries to invoke a particular kind of emotional response from the spectators. In Kurosawa's film, the plenitude of silence is replaced by the porter's garrulousness, exaggerated facial expression, and blundering physical movement, which all indirectly reveal the interior psychological state of characters around him.

In his adaptation, Kurosawa creates another new character, Kajiwara's messenger, whose role in the film is to take over part of Togashi's responsibility. During Benkei's recitation of the fake subscription list, which is only a blank scroll, Kajiwara's messenger makes suspicious gestures and tries to peep at the list; Togashi, on the other hand, sits calmly on a folding stool and even pretends to be sleeping. In *Kanjincho,* however, it is Togashi who tries to take a peek at Benkei's scroll. Thus the addition of the messenger makes the character of Togashi more ambiguous. Kurosawa's treatment of the recitation scene does not really parody the Kabuki source[6] but results in the purification of the character of Togashi as a hero; that is, Togashi's role as villain in the Kabuki play is reassigned to the new character, Kajiwara's messenger.[7] It seems from the very beginning that Togashi knows the true identity of the party of mountain monks. As the narrative progresses, Togashi's admiration for Benkei grows. The pureness of Togashi's character is emphasized by the fact that his role is played by actor Fujita Susumu, the youthful star of *Sanshiro Sugata*. At the time of filming, Fujita was thirty-three years old, much younger than his opponent Okochi Denjiro in the role of Benkei. The fact that Okochi appears in *Sanshiro Sugata* as Yano Shogoro, Sanshiro's mentor and spiritual guide, contributes to the transformation of *Kanjincho* from a drama of two hostile warriors to one of two independent-willed men connected to each other through the purity of their spirit. And the pureness and sincerity of Benkei and Togashi are contrasted to the suspicious and manipulative personality of Yoritomo, whose representative in the film is Kajiwara's messenger.[8]

If the use of Okochi and Fujita contributes to Kurosawa's unique transformation of *Kanjincho,* equally if not more important is the casting of Enoken as a porter. Enoken started his career in 1922 as a member of Negishi Kagekidan, a popular Asakusa operetta troupe. After Asakusa was devastated by the Kanto Earthquake in 1923, Enoken worked as a bit actor for film in the Kansai area for a few years without much success. In 1929, back in Asakusa, Enoken joined a new vaudeville theater troupe, Kajino Fori (Casino Folie), based at the Asakusa Suizokukan (aquarium) theater. Despite an initial setback, Kajino Fori was enormously popular, and Enoken quickly rose to stardom. Until the emergence of Enoken, popular comedy had been based on a traditional comic act called *niwaka* and Kabuki conventions. In contrast, Enoken's comedy was a combination of Mack Sennett's Keystone comedies, American-style vaudeville, revue, and jazz.[9] In 1934 Enoken returned to the moviemaking business on a contract with PCL, which later became Toho. The second time around, Enoken had a very successful film career, becoming immensely popular nationwide.

Why was Kurosawa interested in using Enoken, one of the most popular and talented comedians in prewar Japan, in the adaptation of such a serious Kabuki play as *Kanjincho*? Kurosawa knew Enoken from his assistant director days. Many of Enoken's films were directed by Yamamoto Kajiro, Kurosawa's mentor, under whose tutelage he learned the craft of filmmaking. Thus, by using Enoken in his film, Kurosawa was following in the steps of his mentor. Moreover, the idea of parodying such a lofty play as *Kanjincho* was not unique. In the 1930s, when *nansensu mono* (nonsense genre) swept the Japanese popular culture scene, parodies of *Chushingura* and other Kabuki classics were quite common at Asakusa revue theaters and elsewhere.

As interesting as they are, these pieces of information still do not explain the specific nature of Kurosawa's adaptation. Did he want to use the star value of Enoken to boost the film's box office? Because of the presence of two other popular stars, Fujita Susumu and Okochi Denjiro, the addition of Enoken would not have made too much difference to the film's commercial value. Did Kurosawa try to make a comedy to raise people's morale at the time of a dire predicament? In 1945 the Japanese mainland was being reduced to rubble by American air raids day after day, and few theaters were left to show films. Nor were film companies producing many films to distribute to theaters in the first place. Besides, without food and shelter, going to the movies was hardly people's priority in the last days of the war. Did Kurosawa opportunistically try to please the censors' demand for patriotic propaganda? If he did, why did he take the trouble of creating a new character for Enoken, a slapstick comedian? This was precisely the point that so irritated the censors, who censured Kurosawa for his allegedly flippant attitude. To the Japanese censors' accusation that the film ridicules Kabuki's most respected repertoire, Kurosawa answered as follows:

> *Tiger's Tail* is being called a distortion of the Kabuki play *Kanjincho,* but I believe that the Kabuki play itself is already a distortion of the Noh play *Ataka.* [The Kabuki is in fact based on this original Noh play.] Moreover, although my film is being called a mockery of the Kabuki classic, I most certainly had no such intention, nor do I understand what aspects of my film can be said to ridicule the play. I would like you to explain to me in concrete detail exactly where such mockery occurs.[10]

As Kurosawa vehemently insists, *The Men Who Tread on the Tiger's Tail* is hardly a "mockery of the Kabuki classic." A crucial difference between slapstick adaptations of classic plays and *The Men Who Tread on the Tiger's Tail* is that despite the addition of the popular comedian, Kurosawa's film is surprisingly sober and respectful of its Kabuki source.

To understand the seeming contradiction of the film fully, we must first briefly examine the history of Kabuki in modern Japan, and also the relationship of Kabuki and Japanese cinema in general. As we will see in the rest of the chapter, any monolithic notion of Japanese tradition cannot explain what Kurosawa tried to achieve by adapting the Kabuki play *Kanjincho* to film. By scrutinizing the specificity of Noh, Kabuki, and Japanese film, we will see how much the culturalist discourse in Japanese cinema studies has missed the significance of Kurosawa's engagement with Japanese film as an institutional practice.

Kabuki and the Construction of a Modern Nation

The question of whether Kabuki influenced the development of Japanese cinema is to a certain extent not even an issue because so many of the former's conventions were adopted by the latter. Terminologies for film actors' and characters' types are largely derived from Kabuki (e.g., *tachiyaku* [a masculine hero], *nimaime* [a handsome lover], *katakiyaku* [a villain]). Acting is called *shibai,* a term signifying the totality of Kabuki and its multiple facets (e.g., theater, play, spectators' seats, acting); *yakusha,* another Kabuki-derived word, is still widely used to refer to a film actor;[11] a bit film actor is called *obeya* (big room) because low-ranking Kabuki actors were housed in a single large dressing room together. Many film stars came from Kabuki and its derivative forms, and their screen names followed a Kabuki convention (e.g., Onoe Matsunosuke, Ichikawa Utaemon, Kataoka Chiezo, Ichikawa Raizo, Nakamura Kinnosuke).

One of the most intriguing accounts of Kabuki in relation to Japanese cinema is given by Noël Burch. Both Kabuki and Japanese cinema are, according to Burch, based on what he calls presentationalism. Unlike Western realist theater and cinema, they do not erase the materiality of the signifier to create the illusion of reality. In Kabuki, the difference between the actor and his role is foregrounded, the stage (illusion) and the auditorium (reality) are not clearly separated, and stage set emphasizes its flat surface instead of producing the illusion of depth. A profoundly reflexive medium of art, Kabuki even incorporates the spectators' response in the overall design of a stage performance. At specific moments of climax during the Kabuki performance, the spectators call out to the actors, and their reactions "become part of the 'text' of the play, part of its musical rhythm and timbre and its dramatic structure. . . . Audience participation of this sort may be regarded as the acme of presentationalism."[12] Other examples of Kabuki's reflexive practices include the use of *oyama* (female impersonator) and *kurogo* (stage assistant whose black costume signifies his invisibility onstage), "the completely free contraction and dilation of narrative time," and "the polysemy and intertextuality of the actual 'libretto.' "[13] Burch claims that many of these constituent elements of Kabuki's reflexivity and presentationalism are present in Japanese cinema, too.

Burch's explanation of presentationalism is often insightful, making us realize how the anti-illusionist principle of presentationalism can be at work both in Kabuki and in Japanese cinema. However, what is not at all clear is a historical specificity of Kabuki's influences on Japanese cinema. Throughout his account, what Burch constantly emphasizes is the essential similarities between Japanese cinema and a variety of traditional Japanese art. It is quite possible that Kabuki, Noh, the doll theater, ukiyo-e, and linked poetry all share the similar traits of presentationalism. At the same time, it can also be argued that Burch finds formal resemblances between Japanese cinema, traditional theater, literature, and painting because he presupposes the ahistorical unity of Japanese culture manifesting itself in various kinds of art and cultural practice. Even though Burch uses words such as "impact" and "influence," what he is interested in is not how specifically Kabuki influenced the development of Japanese cinema but how the presentationalist principle is shared by Japanese cinema, Kabuki, Noh, and many other types of traditional Japanese art across the board.

In contrast to Burch's emphasis on the shared presentationalist characteristics of Japanese cinema and traditional theater, Donald Richie and Joseph Anderson criticize an undiscriminating conflation of the two in an essay titled "Traditional Theater and the Film in Japan: The Influence of the Kabuki, Noh, and Other Forms on Film Content and Style." To the question whether there is any influence of traditional theater on Japanese cinema, Richie and Anderson answer: "Well, to be brief, there isn't any. All of the parallels, drawn in Japan as carelessly as elsewhere, are forced; all the pigeonholes are wrongly labeled; all the conclusions, so carefully jumped at, are as false as the assumptions

upon which they are based. . . . The truth is that the traditional theater in Japan has given almost nothing to the films."[14] The significance
of Richie and Anderson's argument lies in their refusal to make any
facile connection between Japanese cinema and traditional culture in
general. They also rightly emphasize the important role played in the
formation of Japanese cinema by *kodan,* an art of oral performance in
which the storyteller, or *kodanshi,* narrates didactic stories about heroic
adventures of master swordsmen, vendettas, factional fightings among
samurai bureaucrats, and legendary gamblers and outlaws (2–3). What
looks like a Kabuki-influenced film is often an adaptation of a *kodan*
story, and according to Richie and Anderson, the confusion occurs because both Kabuki and *kodan* share similar themes and stories.

However, Richie and Anderson's categorical denial of traditional theater's influence on Japanese cinema is based on some problematic assumptions. As important as it is, *kodan,* a form of popular oral narrative, could not provide Japanese filmmakers with a model of drama.
Nor could *kodan* teach actors how to act. Richie and Anderson are
aware of this problem but try to avoid it by arguing that because "*kodan,* a story-telling art, has no theatrical style, the Japanese period-
films have always contented themselves with an absence of style" (5).
Without further explanation, it is difficult to know what they mean by
the lack of style in Japanese cinema. A similar kind of ambiguity is
found in their use of the word "realism." *Chushingura* (The Loyal Forty-
Seven Ronin) and many film adaptations of *kodan* are called "rigidly
realistic," but Kabuki is not. According to Richie and Anderson, "the
Kabuki style of acting is simply too big for the film. It incorporates and
depends upon dancing and singing, neither of which are appropriate
to the realism which the Japanese film has from the first insisted upon"
(5). Yet it is not at all clear whether Japanese cinema strove for realism from the very beginning, and throughout the history of Japanese
cinema, the idea of realism has been such a contested issue to be used
so monolithically. Another problematic notion in Richie and Anderson's argument is "influence," which is used in a very limited sense.
When they discuss whether Kabuki influenced Japanese cinema, their
focus is almost exclusively on direct adaptations of Kabuki plays and
the adoption of Kabuki conventions. As rare and successful examples
of such adaptation, they mention Kurosawa's *The Men Who Tread on*

the Tiger's Tail, Yoshimura Kozaburo's *The Beauty and the Dragon* (Bijo to kairyu, 1955), and Kinoshita Keisuke's *The Song of Narayama* (Narayama bushiko, 1958). As an isolated example of Kabuki-style acting in film, Richie and Anderson mention a 1956 version of *Chushingura,* in which a well-known Kabuki actor performs *mie,* during which, with his eyes crossed and his tongue stuck out a little, the actor momentarily arrests the movement of his body to emphasize its pictorial beauty or to signify a dramatic climax. But that the audience do not literally confuse a film version of *Chushingura* with its Kabuki performance onstage is hardly sufficient proof for the lack of Kabuki's influence on Japanese cinema. The idea of influence does not presuppose the simple equivalence of two different cultural practices.

What is neglected in both Burch's and Richie and Anderson's argument is the historical specificity of traditional theater. If we are seriously interested in discussing whether Kabuki influenced Japanese cinema, we must take into consideration the history of Kabuki, which has not remained the same for three hundred years since it first appeared as Okuni Kabuki in the late sixteenth century. Throughout its history, but particularly after the Meiji Restoration, a number of changes were introduced in Kabuki. For instance, the structure of a theater was fundamentally modified in the early Meiji. In 1878 the Shintomiza theater in Tokyo was rebuilt as the first Western-style theater with a proscenium stage *(gakubuchi butai).* Until then, in the Kabuki theater, the stage jutted out into the auditorium, so that the audience, instead of occupying the position of invisible observers, surrounded the three sides of the stage. Moreover, two passageways called *hanamichi* extended perpendicular to the stage, and they were connected to each other by a corridor running parallel to the stage in the rear of the auditorium. Because of this unique structure of the Kabuki theater, there was a strong sense of intimacy between actors and the audience, who actively involved themselves in the creation of a theatrical experience. In a modern Kabuki theater, only one *hanamichi* on the left is used; as a result, the level of audience involvement in the performance is much less intense than before.[15] As the source of lighting changed from candles and oil lamps to gas lamps (1878) and then to electric light (1884),[16] Kabuki costume and makeup began to have a different kind of effect on the audience in the brightly lit auditorium.[17]

At first the Meiji government's attitude toward Kabuki was pure disdain. Along with popular fiction (gesaku) and other types of performing arts, theater was regarded as an entertainment that did not serve the national interests (kokka ni eki naki yugei).[18] The sole interest of the government was to contain the negative impact of frivolous and vulgar entertainment on the people, and if possible, to use it as an ideological instrument for legitimating state power. As early as April 1872, the Ministry of Religious Instruction (Kyobusho) issued a directive, consisting of three prescriptions, to control popular fiction and entertainment.[19] Around the same time, the owners and playwrights of three Kabuki theaters were summoned by the Tokyo prefectural government, where they were instructed to stop showing obscene and cruel scenes and to replace fiction and fantasy with historical facts.[20] These governmental interventions had irreversible effects on Kabuki, the most significant of which was the end of its symbiotic connections to people. During the Edo period, Kabuki was at the center of Edo culture. After the Meiji Restoration, the new government tried to use the popular influence of Kabuki to enlighten people as subjects of the imperial state. But the government's attempt to enlist Kabuki as an instrument of mass education was fundamentally contradictory, since Kabuki enjoyed enormous popularity precisely because it was a product of popular fantasy, to which obscenity and cruelty integrally belonged. Aspects of Kabuki that were singled out as undesirable were precisely what made Kabuki such a popular art. It is also significant that only theater owners and playwrights but no actors were summoned by the authorities. Kabuki was such an actor-centered theater that the initial exclusion of actors from the government's attempt to control the art form further contributed to the severance of the intimate tie between Kabuki and common people. A greater emphasis on written plays influenced the subsequent development of not only Kabuki but also modern Japanese theater in general (e.g., shingeki's fetishistic reverence for the plays of Ibsen and Chekhov as written texts).[21]

The instructions given to Kabuki professionals reveal an important fact about a fundamental motive behind the reform of the performing arts promoted by the government. Obscenity and cruelty must be eliminated because in the early Meiji, the audience of Kabuki included not only commoners but also upper-class dignitaries and foreigners; that is, the government tried to change Kabuki in such a way that it could be appreciated by foreigners without offending or alienating them. In Meiji Japan, the idea of ranking among nations was taken seriously, and for the Japanese elite, the West was the standard for measuring the level of a nation's advancement. The national goal set up by the Restoration government was to catch up with the West as rapidly as possible, and to upgrade Japan to the rank of the first-class nation *(itto koku),* the Meiji elite went to Europe and the United States in pursuit of new knowledge. Through their overseas experiences, they came to think that although the advancement in technology, the creation of a strong national army, and the radical transformation of the economic system, legal structure, and social institutions were unquestionably the highest priority, these changes alone would not help Japan join the ranks of the Western powers. Japan must also compete with the West in culture, and the first step toward competition was to create a high culture of the Meiji elite, comparable to Western high culture. When the Meiji elite toured and studied in the West, they were surprised to learn that theater occupied a central position in the society of their Western counterparts. For many Meiji leaders who were so eager to catch up with the West, the creation of a national theater became imperative. The necessity of a national theater further grew urgent as foreign dignitaries began to visit Japan and saw Kabuki and other performing arts. In 1879 Ulysses Grant, former U.S. president, watched Kabuki performances at the Shintomiza and gave Morita Kan'ya, the owner of the theater, a new stage curtain as a gift. Interestingly, around the time Grant visited Japan, the phrase *"kokka ni eki naki yugei"* began to disappear from official government documents. Through their interaction with Grant, the high government officials came to realize the necessity of inventing a uniquely Japanese national culture.[22]

In the 1880s, the earnest pursuit of modernization or Westernization of culture gave rise to various reform movements *(kairyo undo),* focusing on the writing system, housing, clothing, dating, and so forth.[23] The Theater Reform Association (Engeki Kairyo Kai) was created in 1886 to transform Kabuki into a modern national theater of Japan. The Association drew much public attention because the founding members and associates included members of the government oligarchy and well-known politicians (e.g., Ito Hirobumi, Inoue Kaoru, Okuma Shigenobu, Mori Arinori), bureaucrats, business leaders, scholars, and journalists. In 1886 Suematsu Norizumi, a bureaucrat and a key figure in the theater reform movement, gave a public lecture to publicize and clarify the association's objectives. In his lecture, Suematsu called for the necessity of building a new modern-style theater and eliminating or changing many antiquated practices of Kabuki exhibition and performance.[24]

Theater and other reform movements are often regarded as a direct product of the Rokumeikan era, when the government oligarchs, especially Inoue Kaoru, were promoting an exhibitionistic display of Westernized Japan in the hope of making the Western powers agree to give up the privilege of extraterritoriality for Westerners in Japan and their control over Japanese tariff. But the Japanese critic Kurata Yoshihiro suggests that the theater reform movement was not necessarily a direct by-product of the government's Westernization policy, aiming at the revision of unequal treaties; instead, the movement was promoted by a group of the Meiji elite in an attempt to contain the spread of what they perceived as incorrect images of Japan precipitated by the success of *The Mikado* in Europe and the United States.[25] Gilbert and Sullivan's operetta *The Mikado* premiered in London on March 14, 1885, and because of its popularity continued to be performed until January 19, 1887. A satiric depiction of the despotic ruler Mikado in the town of Titipu, *The Mikado* is a bricolage of Europeans' fantasies about the exotic and barbaric land called Japan.[26] The popularity of *The Mikado* in the West made some Japanese realize that the hegemony of the Western imperialist nations was maintained not just by their strong army and advanced technology but also by their monopolistic control of the international flow of information and image. The theater reformers insisted on the necessity of modernizing Kabuki and showing the West the correct image of Japan as the only way of fighting back against Western cultural imperialism. Far from being the embodiment of an antiquated institution, Kabuki was at the forefront of the Meiji government's modernization policy, deeply implicated in the cultural geopolitics of the age of imperialism.

The significance of *The Men Who Tread on the Tiger's Tail* cannot be appreciated if we see it only as "a straight film version of the historical anecdote (including additions from both the Noh and the Kabuki versions)." [27] The primary focus of the film is not the episode itself but *Kanjincho* as an adaptation of *Ataka*. To understand *The Men Who Tread on the Tiger's Tail*, we must not only consider Kurosawa's reason for adapting a Kabuki play but also ask why he chose *Kanjincho* rather than one of the many other equally well known Kabuki works. *Kanjincho* is one of *Kabuki Juhachiban* (Eighteen Favorite Kabuki Plays), the collection of plays assembled by Ichikawa Danjuro VII (1791–1859) as the best of what Kabuki can offer.[28] Danjuro VII selected eighteen plays originally performed by Danjuro I (1660–1704), Danjuro II (1688–1758), and Danjuro IV (1711–1788) to establish classics and legitimate Kabuki as high art. It was also an attempt by the Ichikawa family to strengthen their authority and monopolistic control over a specific set of Kabuki plays as a canon. Among this canon, *Kanjincho* occupied a privileged position, since it was the only play originally performed by Danjuro VII himself. In his opening speech at the premiere of *Kanjincho* in 1840, Danjuro VII presented it as a revival of the Ichikawa family's tradition traced back to Danjuro I. Yet Danjuro VII's *Kanjincho* was so radically different from any preceding variants that his reference to Danjuro I was the invention, rather than the revival, of a tradition.[29]

What distinguished *Kanjincho* from other Kabuki pieces was its incorporation of Noh. Based on Noh's *Ataka*, *Kanjincho* adopted a number of Noh conventions. The set design was extremely simplified, and nothing but backdrops of an old pine tree and young bamboos *(matsubame)* was used as decor. Some of the costumes were in the Noh style, and singers and musicians were lined up on platforms onstage, directly visible to the spectators. Because of its radical departure from the normal Kabuki practices, the spectators' reactions to this hybrid play were mixed. It was only in the early Meiji that through the effort of Danjuro IX (1838–1903) *Kanjincho* came to enjoy popular acceptance. Danjuro IX tried to make *Kanjincho* much closer to Noh by eliminating Kabuki flavor from costumes and by devising a new acting style; that is, he strove to further elevate the status of *Kanjincho* as a lofty, refined piece of Kabuki repertoire worthy of the name of high art. The canonization of *Kanjincho* as the Kabuki masterpiece received the official seal of approval in 1887 when Danjuro IX performed in the presence of the Meiji emperor at the residence of foreign minister Inoue Kaoru (*Tenran Kabuki*). Among the plays presented, *Kanjincho* was undoubtedly the most significant. In fact, the whole occasion was set up by the theater reformers precisely for the purpose of showing *Kanjincho* to the emperor.[30] From that moment on, Kabuki rapidly followed the path of becoming a national treasure while ceasing to be a theater of the common people.

Given this background of *Kanjincho*, what does it mean to make its film adaptation? How does Kurosawa transform one of the most grand, canonical Kabuki plays into a film? Because he views *Kanjincho* as a bad rewriting of Noh's *Ataka*, it is logical to assume that by adapting *Kanjincho*, Kurosawa tries to rectify Kabuki's mistakes. He challenges Kabuki by changing parts of *Kanjincho* that interfere with the unity of the play. For instance, in *The Men Who Tread on the Tiger's Tail*, the narrative and songs are much more coherently integrated with each other. In the play, a chorus of singers sings the *nagauta* song "With the feeling of stepping on a tiger's tail and escaping from a poisonous snake," from which the film's title is taken, at its conclusion when Yoshitsune and his party are finally leaving the Ataka barrier. In the film, we hear the same song much earlier, right before Kajiwara's messenger spots one of the porters for Yoshitsune. The film's placement of the song does make sense, since it is sung when Yoshitsune's party is about to pass the barrier thanks to Benkei's effort. In contrast, the Kabuki play's use of the song is a little awkward because it appears toward the end of the play when Yoshitsune and his retinue leave the stage after a drinking bout. By this time, it is clearly established that between Benkei and Togashi there is an unstated recognition of each other's situation: Togashi decided to let Yoshitsune pass the barrier because he was so moved by Benkei's extraordinary loyalty to Yoshitsune; at the same time, Benkei knew that Togashi knew the true identity of him and the others disguised as mountain monks. The mutual understanding of Benkei and Togashi is underlined by the fact that in the play it is Togashi himself who catches up with Yoshitsune's party and offers Benkei cups of sake as a gesture of apology. (In the film, only barrier guards appear in the same scene.) Thus the song's lyrics, "With the feeling of stepping on a tiger's tail and escaping from a poisonous snake," contradict how the play portrays the relationship of Benkei and Togashi.[31] Another contradiction appears at the end of *Kanjincho,* which concludes when Benkei exits from the stage by stepping a *roppo,* an exaggerated dancelike step, on the *hanamichi.* Kurosawa's film does not include this grandiose finale. Instead, at the film's conclusion, Enoken, the comic porter, attempts to imitate a *roppo* step but fails to execute it properly. Why is the comic porter substituted for Benkei? Does this make *The Men Who Tread on the Tiger's Tail* a parody of *Kanjincho?* Does the fact that the porter dances in the last scene necessarily make him a hero of the film?[32] If *The Men Who Tread on the Tiger's Tail* is to some extent a parody of *Kanjincho,* the objective of this parody is not to rewrite the lofty Kabuki play about feudal loyalty in a bathetic mode but to foreground the contradictions of *Kanjincho* — specifically, in this case, the unnatural placement of Benkei's heroic *roppo* immediately after the scene where he tacitly acknowledges Togashi's compassion.[33]

The adaptation of *Kanjincho* also gives Kurosawa an opportunity to contest one of the most popular Japanese film sources, *Chushingura.* If any Kurosawa film has a concrete intertextual relation to *Chushingura,* it is not *Kagemusha,* as one critic argues,[34] but *The Men Who Tread on the Tiger's Tail. Kanjincho* and *Chushingura* are arguably the two most popular Kabuki plays, but only the latter has become a staple of popular *jidaigeki* movies. Interestingly, in the process of becoming a popular film genre of its own, *Chushingura* movies have incorporated a crucial scene from *Kanjincho.* One of the climactic scenes in *Chushingura* movies occurs when Oishi Kuranosuke is on his way to Edo to finally carry out his plan to avenge the untimely death of his lord. To evade the watchful eyes of the shogunate and his enemy, Kuranosuke disguises himself as one Tachibana Sakon, a samurai serving the imperial court in Kyoto. A crisis occurs when Kuranosuke is confronted by the real Tachibana Sakon. At the climactic moment of the showdown, Sakon demands that Kuranosuke show him as a proof of identity an official letter from the imperial court to the shogunate. Without showing any sign of perturbation, Kuranosuke hands him what appears to be a letter. Yet when Sakon sees it, he is speechless because it is only a blank piece of paper. This episode apparently rewrites the scene from *Kanjincho* where Benkei pretends to read aloud a subscription list while holding a blank scroll to deceive Togashi.[35] There is, however, a fundamental difference between the two scenes. In *Kanjincho,* Benkei never shows the opponent a blank scroll, because if Togashi finds out it is not a subscription list, Benkei and the rest of his party will be arrested and executed. Togashi finally let them pass the barrier not because they are the famous party of Yoshitsune and Benkei but because he is so moved by Benkei's willingness to violate the conventional feudal codes of behavior to keep his party's true identity secret and thus to save his lord Yoshitsune's life at any cost. In *Chushingura* movies, without any explanation, Kuranosuke directly shows a blank letter to Sakon, who is forced to interpret Kuranosuke's peculiar response. Unlike Benkei, whose sole interest is to keep the disguise undetected, Kuranosuke reveals his true identity and silently asks Sakon to let him pass without making a commotion.[36] As Hashimoto Osamu argues, the reason why Sakon decides to let Kuranosuke continue his journey has less to do with what Kuranosuke does—unlike Benkei, he really does not do anything—and more with who Kuranosuke is. In other words, Sakon realizes that a suspicious samurai who assumes his name must be *that* Oishi Kuranosuke, who was mythologized after the Edo period as a paragon of feudal loyalty.

The Men Who Tread on the Tiger's Tail, an adaptation of *Kanjincho,* rewrites a scene from *Chushingura* movies, which itself is a rewriting of *Kanjincho.* As an implicit critique of *Chushingura,* Kurosawa's film foregrounds the authoritarianism of Kuranosuke and Tachibana Sakon's complicit relationship with him. Kuranosuke behaves as if he has a birth-given right as a famous loyal samurai to finish his journey to Edo and avenge his late lord; instead of relentlessly questioning his peculiar behavior, Sakon acquiesces simply because the man he faces is Oishi Kuranosuke. The silent communication between Kuranosuke and Sakon is a type of Kabuki *haragei,* which has degenerated here into a means of reaffirming a communal unity. In contrast, in Kurosawa's film, Benkei and Togashi face each other as Other; and as a critique of *haragei,* their confrontation demonstrates what a nonverbalized communication between two strong-willed individuals in an extreme situation is really like.

Kurosawa's emphasis on the intertextual relation invites us to interpret *The Men Who Tread on the Tiger's Tail* as a critical commentary on the relationship of Kabuki and Japanese cinema. Given that Kabuki played a constitutive role in the formation of Japanese cinema, any serious attempt to adapt Kabuki to film cannot but be a self-consciously reflexive act of reexamining Japanese cinema and its history. *The Men Who Tread on the Tiger's Tail* is a prime example of such reflexivity. In his subsequent films, Kurosawa further pursues a critique of Japanese cinema's connection to Kabuki by incorporating elements of Noh and its comic corollary Kyogen more directly. For instance, *Kagemusha* includes a scene in which after learning of the death of his rival Takeda Shingen, Oda Nobunaga sings a part of *Atsumori*, a well-known piece of Kowakamai. In *Throne of Blood,* acting style, facial "expression," iconography, set design, and so forth are heavily influenced by Noh. In *Ran,* the role of Tsurumaru is played by a Kyogen actor, and the farcical language and gesture of Kyoami, the Fool, are directly borrowed from Kyogen. By appropriating Noh selectively, Kurosawa attempts to create new film forms and eliminate the remnants of Kabuki conventions from Japanese cinema.

Kurosawa comments: "I like Noh, and have read Zeami's *Kadensho* a number of times. But I don't like Kabuki, particularly *haragei* for its lack of reality." [37] Ironically, Kurosawa's revolt against Kabuki through a return to Noh repeats what Kabuki did with Noh in the nineteenth century; that is, Kurosawa's cinema comes closest to Kabuki precisely when it takes a critical stance toward Kabuki by embracing Noh. Ichikawa Danjuro IX's attempt to create a new Kabuki mainly consisted of two efforts, performance of *matsubame mono* (Kabuki repertoire in the style of Noh) and new historical plays called *katsureki*.[38] When the remnants of Edo culture were regarded obsolete and even harmful to people, Kabuki tried to legitimate itself as high art and to establish itself as a new national theater of modern Japan by using the prestige of Noh as classics and by pursuing realist representation. Kurosawa also uses these two strategies to invent a new kind of Japanese cinema that is less dependent on Kabuki conventions.

If there is any danger involved in the kind of appropriation of Noh Kurosawa pursues, it is not his ironic repetition of what Kabuki did in the late nineteenth century but his tendency to substantialize the differential dichotomy of Noh and Kabuki as absolute opposites. For Kurosawa, Kabuki is a theater of artificiality and unnecessary embellishment, whereas Noh's simplicity and naturalness lead us to the true Japanese spirit. If Kabuki and popular Japanese cinema uncritically assert a communal ethos that reinforces the myth of Japanese homogeneity, the Japan that Kurosawa affirms as a way of criticizing that myth is also another myth. It is no coincidence that Kurosawa's name became known as a promising filmmaker when his script *A German at Daruma Temple* (Daruma-dera no doitsujin) was published in 1941. The protagonist of this light comedy is Lutwig Lange, a German architect modeled after Bruno Taut (1880–1938). Lange comes to stay at a Buddhist temple in a small village to experience Japanese life and write a paper on Japanese culture. Even though he is an avid admirer of Japan, he differentiates two types of Japanese culture: a genuine Japanese tradition exemplified by the Katsura Detached Palace, the Shugakuin Detached Palace, the Horyuji Temple, and the Ise Shrine, and a phony tradition epitomized by the Toshogu Shrine at Nikko. For Lange, the essential characteristic of Japanese culture is the beauty of simplicity, and the flashy exterior and elaborate artifice of the Toshogu Shrine is the opposite of that essence. Although this dichotomous view of Japanese cultural tradition is presented as that of a fictional character, as his films, essays, and interviews amply demonstrate, Kurosawa clearly has a personal stake in it.[39] How Kurosawa's cinema shares similarities with Taut's thinking can be seen in the following passage where Taut contrasts the Toshogu Shrine at Nikko and the Katsura Detached Palace:

> At Nikko, as in many architectural attractions of the world, the effect is gained by quantity—about in the same way that an army of two hundred thousand is larger than one of twenty thousand. At Katsura, on the contrary, each element remains a free individual, much like a member of a good society in which harmony arises from absence of coercion so that everyone may express himself according to his individual nature.[40]

Note how Taut's description of the structural principle of the Katsura Palace is remarkably applicable to Kurosawa's cinema and a type of individualism it valorizes.

In his rebuttal of Taut's position, the Japanese writer Sakaguchi Ango cautions us not to assert the essence of Japaneseness by espousing the notion of tradition.[41] Sakaguchi argues that contrary to what Taut claims, there is no absolutely fixed connection between Japanese tradition and Japaneseness. What was practiced by Japanese in the past is not necessarily part of the Japanese essence. It is also quite possible that Japanese find some "foreign" practices much more suitable for them than an ancient "Japanese" one. To single out limited aspects of Japanese tradition as the essence of Japanese culture is nothing more than an ideological manipulation that reaffirms the Eurocentric worldview at the expense of the subjectivity of Japanese. How Kurosawa thinks about "Japanese culture," "tradition," and "national character" is very close to Sakaguchi's deconstructive stance on Japaneseness. Unlike Taut, Kurosawa does not celebrate certain types of Japanese culture to develop a discourse of anti-Americanism. Yet his taste for Japanese artworks is so much influenced by the Orientalist ideology that his thinking does not embrace. Kurosawa's critique of Kabuki and Kabuki-influenced Japanese film seems valid to the extent that it contests the conceptualization of Japan as a nation where communal dependency suppresses individual wills and autonomy. Yet once he starts asserting Noh as an absolute opposite or alternative to what Kabuki represents, his critique is appropriated by the logic of Orientalism. The culturalist discourse in Japanese cinema studies reduces this paradoxical coexistence of the two opposite tendencies simply to a manifestation of Kurosawa's interest in traditional Japanese arts and as a result fails to recognize it as the possibility and limitation of Kurosawa as an artist, or as a possible reason why many Kurosawa films have elicited the strong ambivalent reaction of simultaneous attraction and aversion from the spectators.

6. *No Regrets for Our Youth*

The Rhetoric of Politics and the Politics of Film

No Regrets for Our Youth (Waga seishun ni kuinashi, 1946), Kurosawa's first film after Japan's defeat in the Pacific War, features a woman, Yagihara Yukie (Hara Setsuko), as its protagonist. The focus of the film's narrative is the transformation of Yukie from a naive bourgeois girl into an independent woman with a strong sense of self. In the first scene, we see college students and their professor's family going for a picnic at Mount Yoshida. Yukie's father, Yagihara (Okochi Denjiro), is a liberal professor of law at Kyoto Imperial University. Among a group of his students, there are two who seem to be competing for Yukie's love. One is Itokawa (Kono Akitake), who is a conventionally good student but a little timid and indecisive. The other is Noge Ryukichi (Fujita Susumu), a man of action and leadership. The bucolic scene of the picnic is suddenly disrupted by the sound of a machine gun and the appearance of a heavily breathing soldier lying on the ground. The subsequent scenes show how the principal characters react to the rise of militarism and the government oppression of those who oppose its expansionist policy. Dismissed from the university because of his liberal beliefs, Yagihara opens a free legal counseling office to help disadvantaged people. Noge is unsatisfied with his mentor's academic liberalism and becomes more deeply involved in an underground leftist movement to prevent a war with the United States. While Noge and to a lesser degree Yagihara remain true to their ideals, Itokawa does not go against the stream. At the pleading of his mother, he quickly drops out of a student movement and becomes a public prosecutor.

Yukie wavers between two choices: a "safe and peaceful, but somewhat boring life" with Itokawa or a "dazzling, exciting life" with Noge. She leaves home and starts living by herself in Tokyo, where she again meets Itokawa, and then Noge. Even though she is simultaneously attracted to, and scared of, Noge's secret political activity, Yukie starts living with him until he is arrested by the special police. Jailed and investigated as Noge's accomplice, Yukie gradually begins to understand the meanings of her father's and Noge's earlier remarks ("Remember that freedom can be achieved only by making sacrifice and taking responsibility"; "The truth will be known ten years from now, and the Japanese people will thank our effort"; "No regrets in my life!"). Yukie does not say a word during questionings and refuses to cooperate with the police. After she hears the news of the Japanese naval attack on Pearl Harbor on the radio, she is finally released and goes back to Kyoto with her father. Meanwhile Noge is falsely indicted as a leader of a spy ring who tried to sabotage the government's war effort. When Yagihara returns to Tokyo to defend Noge in court, he learns from prosecutor Itokawa that Noge already died in prison. Although it is never explained, it is obvious that he was tortured to death.

At this point, Yagihara finally realizes how inadequate his liberalism has been, and he regrets his inability to understand Noge's radical criticism of fascism in the past. When Yukie learns of Noge's untimely death, she decides to go to his parents' place in the countryside as his wife. At first, his parents do not take Yukie seriously. They are ashamed of their son (not completely, of course). Yukie is determined to show the villagers that she has nothing to be ashamed of being the wife of Noge, because more than anybody else, Noge was working so hard to steer Japan away from an impending catastrophe. Noge's mother begins to understand her daughter-in-law and starts working with her in the rice fields despite the villagers' constant harassment. Even Noge's father, who does not utter a word after Yukie arrives, finally decides to stand up to the villagers when Yukie hurries to the ruined rice fields in spite of a high fever. In the last sequence, the war has finally ended. Yukie is temporarily back at her parents' place in Kyoto. Yagihara returns to the university to teach, and Yukie decides to go back to Noge's village and work for its democratization, particularly for the improvement of women's lives.

Released in 1946, *No Regrets for Our Youth* was enthusiastically received as one of the first postwar Japanese films condemning militarism and celebrating democracy. The most powerful embodiment of democratic ideals in the film is without any doubt Yagihara Yukie, played by Hara Setsuko, and many Japanese critics raved about her powerful performance portraying a strong-willed individual who refuses to give in to the militarist government and fascism in everyday life. However, for many others, including those who praise the film in general, the figuration of Yukie is too peculiar and unrealistic. Hara's performance is said to be too exaggerated, distorted, and unbalanced. The critics charge that the depiction of Yukie's psychological state is so muddled and unclear that she appears simply as a hysteric, eccentric, or abnormal *(henshitsuteki)* woman, a monstrous embodiment of an abstract idea *(kannen no bakemono)*.[1] As much as she has dazzled Japanese audiences by her "shining" image of youth, Hara in the role of Yukie as an eccentric woman has been a source of irritation to many others.

In contrast to Japanese critics' ambivalent reaction to Yukie, Donald Richie tries hard to downplay her eccentricity. For instance, the way Yukie plays the piano is said to portray her as a quintessential Japanese girl. ("When they [students] are talking about the dismissal she continues to play the piano, the Mussorgsky *Pictures at an Exhibition,* played with all the mechanical prowess and lack of understanding exhibited by most Japanese girls who have learned how to play hard pieces on the piano.")[2] Her flower arrangement lesson is mentioned as evidence of her typical Japaneseness. Richie construes Japanese critics' dismissal of Yukie as an unbelievable character as a sign of their inability to accept a universal value of self-realization, which he insists is what Kurosawa's film is all about. According to Richie, "What the critics and public alike resented most deeply was" "Kurosawa's daring to state that most fundamental and disturbing of all truths: the road to yourself is the hardest road of all and it is the only road which can justify life, since we humans believe justification necessary; the only road which can vindicate, since we insist upon vindication; the only road which — since we are living beings — allows us to live" (40).

The key to Richie's attempt to transform Kurosawa into a filmmaker of universal human value and truth is his depoliticization of the film and Yukie's character and actions. Both textually and contextually, *No Regrets for Our Youth* is a political film through and through. Yet Richie persistently tries to depoliticize the film and transform Yukie into a naive bourgeois woman in love. See, for instance, his description of a scene that occurs immediately after the prosecutor Itokawa and the "converted" Noge leave Yagihara's house.

> It is her [Yukie's] father who first calls attention to her state. He says to his wife: "I'm worried." She, thinking of the dismissal, of the university, says: "Oh, students! They are—" He interrupts with: "No, I'm talking about her." The glances up-cut-there, in an entirely different part of the house, stands Setsuko [Yukie], not doing anything, just standing, but the abstracted expression, the droop of the shoulders, the caressing touch of her fingers on the banister, the sad, bemused eyes—this, in context, is the very picture of the young girl in love.[3] (37)

If Yukie shows an "abstracted expression," it is not just because she is the "very picture of the young girl in love." Yukie's facial expression and demeanor come from a tension between her attraction to Noge and her uncertainty about his apparent transformation from a militant left-wing activist into a collaborator of the militarist government. Did he really recant his leftist political beliefs and convert to militarism in prison? Does he now lick up to the government for personal gain, or is his conversion only a pretense? Yukie's inner struggle in this scene is inseparable from all these political and ethical questions. A choice she has to make is further clarified in the following scene described by Richie.

> A bit later she is playing the piano again—those hard scales at the end of *The Great Gate of Kiev*—and suddenly she stops and pounds the piano. Her mother comes in. She turns, and almost shouts at her: "I'm going to get married. I'm going to get married." Instantly, she continues and the only change of expression is a smile which might be guilty, might be joyous: "No, it's a lie. It's a lie. I'm not. I was lying." (37)

In this scene, Yukie does not simply say, "I'm going to get married." Instead, she says: "I'm going to get married to *Mr. Itokawa*." Yukie's behavior here clearly shows that she finds herself in a situation where she must make a choice between two diametrically opposite political and ethical positions. Does she remain faithful to her personal conviction and go against the stream by choosing Noge? Or does she decide to follow the pack and pursue what appears to be a socially respected, stable life with Itokawa? Yukie's emotional instability and sudden change of mood emphasize that there is no such thing as a purely personal choice outside of politics.

According to Richie, "Kurosawa's political uninvolvement is nowhere better seen than in these farm sequences. The military, the heroes of the right, are monsters; the peasants, heroes of the left, are also monstrous. The world and both of its extremes are not good enough, and how can simple striving humanity exist in such a place?" (39). But how is it possible that Yukie is mistreated by the Left when the Left is hardly represented in the film? The farmers may be "heroes of the left," but they are not leftists in the film. On the contrary, their ostracization of the Noges as a family of spies indicates that the farmers are an integral part of the wartime militarist system of surveillance and oppression. Moreover, it is uncertain whether the farmers are always heroes of the Left. For instance, in his short story "House in the Village" (Mura no ie), Nakano Shigeharu, one of the most influential leftist writers in Japan, portrays farmers not as the leftists' heroes but as an ambivalent site of ideological contradictions of Japanese modernity.[4]

Among a number of radical changes made by the Occupation, women's liberation was one of the most important and prominent. Women gained the right to vote on December 17, 1945. At the first postwar general election, thirty-nine women were elected to the Diet. In 1946, *No Regrets for Our Youth* was not the only film prominently featuring a woman as a protagonist. Kinoshita Keisuke's antimilitarist maternal film *A Morning with the Osone Family* (Osoneke no asa) was released on February 21, 1946, and the first of Mizoguchi's trilogy about women, *The Victory of Women* (Josei no shori), was shown on April 18.[5] (*No Regrets for Our Youth* was released on October 29.) On February 28, 1946, two American films were commercially released for the first time in postwar Japan. One of them was Mervyn LeRoy's *Madame Curie* (1943), in which Greer Garson played the title role of the noted woman scientist who won two Nobel Prizes.[6] All of these films clearly reflected GHQ's promotion of women's liberation as part of its democratization policy. In fact, the Occupation actively directed the Japanese film industry to produce films featuring strong and independent female protagonists as one of their recommended subjects. In addition to women's liberation, other political imperatives of the immediate postwar period directly influenced the production of Kurosawa's film. On May 3, 1946, the International Military Tribunal for the Far East began the trials of Japanese war criminals. The Occupation was naturally eager to deliver antifascist messages to the Japanese to justify the trials. It was perhaps no coincidence that *Casablanca* was released and enjoyed a commercial success in June of the same year.[7] And *No Regrets for Our Youth* was an ideal vehicle for propagating those messages against militarism and war collaboration. The Occupation's agrarian reform was also a significant political program influencing the narrative of Kurosawa's film, particularly its final part, set in Noge's village. The initial impetus for the production of the film came from CIE or Toho management trying to collaborate with the former. The original script of *No Regrets for Our Youth* was then written by Hisaita Eijiro, a well-known leftist writer of *shingeki* plays and film scripts. Hisaita also wrote the script of *A Morning with the Osone Family,* which was *Kinema junpo*'s number one film of the year (*No Regrets for Our Youth* was voted second best). The film's producer, Matsuzaki Keiji, was also like Hisaita active in the prewar proletarian art movement, and for him *No Regrets for Our Youth* was more than just a "democratization film" dealing with recommended subjects. Matsuzaki was a student of Takigawa Yukitoki, professor of law at Kyoto Imperial University, the model for the film's Yagihara. Matsuzaki had a personal interest in the Takigawa incident, the fictionalized version of which is found in the film's beginning part.[8]

All these immediate political connections cannot but question the depoliticized rewriting of Kurosawa's film's narrative and the image of Kurosawa as a middle-of-the-road humanist. To further problematize the humanist interpretation of *No Regrets for Our Youth,* let us examine closely its two male protagonists, Noge and Yagihara, Yukie's husband and father, both of whom play the decisive roles in the eventual independence of Yukie as an individual. A liberal professor of law at Kyoto Imperial University, Yagihara fights for the freedom of expression and ends up being expelled from the university. One of Yagihara's students, Noge, disagrees with his mentor's liberal stance, actively participates in clandestine activities of subverting the government's militarist policy, and finally dies in prison after the Japanese attack on Pearl Harbor. What is not at all clear in the film are the specific ideological beliefs and political stances of these two characters. In what kind of underground activity is Noge actually engaged? On what specific grounds is Yagihara expelled from the university? What concrete thought or action of Yagihara makes him a liberalist? Why is it just Yagihara but not his liberal colleagues whom the Ministry of Education has decided to expel from the university?

Oshima Nagisa, who confesses how profoundly *No Regrets for Our Youth* affected him when he first saw it as a teenager, argues that the ambiguity surrounding Noge's and Yagihara's motivations and actions makes the film almost incoherent. What gives a sense of coherence to the ambiguous narrative is, contends Oshima, the overall framework of historical contextualization provided by the film's opening title, which reads as follows:

> Taking the Manchuria Incident as a start, militarists, zaibatsu, and bureaucrats condemned as "red" anyone opposing the invasion, thus trying to create a national consensus. The "Kyoto University Incident" was an example: in 1933, Minister of Education Hatoyama, with such an intention, tried to expel the liberal professor Takigawa from Kyoto Imperial University, and met the resistance of the whole university. This became a grave problem unprecedented in the field of education. This film is based on this incident; however, all the characters in the film are creations of the authors, whose intention is to depict the history of the development of the soul of the people who lived according to their principles during the age of persecution and disgrace that followed this incident.[9]

According to Oshima, what makes the audience accept Noge and Yagihara as convincing characters is the presence of this opening title, which enables the audience to identify Yagihara with Takigawa Yukitoki. The character of Noge is also based on a real historical figure, Ozaki Hotsumi. Ozaki was a left-wing intellectual and expert on China. He was arrested in October 1941 for his involvement in the spy ring organized by Richard Sorge. Ozaki and Sorge were both executed as Soviet spies in November 1944. Although nowhere in *No Regrets for Our Youth* is it stated that Noge's model is Ozaki Hotsumi, Oshima argues that the audience would have found enough similarities between the two and therefore used what they knew about Ozaki to supplement the gaps and holes in the characterization of Noge, particularly his political activities. (Ozaki's letters to his wife from prison were collected and published as a book after the war. The book, *Love Is like a Shower of Stars* [Ai wa furuhoshi no gotoku], was a best-seller in 1946 and 1947.) Unlike in the film, there was no connection between Ozaki and Takigawa.

Oshima claims that this initial conflation of fiction and reality leads to the second deception, for which he severely criticizes Kurosawa's film. The ambiguities of Noge and Yagihara are supplemented by the audience's knowledge about Ozaki and Yagihara first, and then the idealized, amalgamated images of these two fictional characters are projected back onto Ozaki and Takigawa. As a result, the two historical figures are transformed into uncompromising defenders of liberalism and resistance, which they never were. (In 1950, when Oshima entered Kyoto University as a freshman, Takigawa gave a speech at an entrance ceremony, forbidding new students to participate in any political activities.)[10] Oshima argues that through this process of double deception, *No Regrets for Our Youth* absolves the Japanese from responsibility for their part in wartime militarism.[11] Oshima points out that contrary to what the opening title says, there was no "resistance of the whole university." From the very beginning, the resistance of the faculty of law was not supported by the rest of the university; moreover, the faculty of law was eventually divided into two factions, one of which left the university while the remaining one severely suppressed the activism of its own students. In Oshima's words, "a history of schisms, submissions, and conversions after conversions, this was the essence of the Kyoto University Incident."[12]

Oshima's analysis of the two male protagonists is perceptive and persuasive. However, as his account of his own viewing experience shows, it does not adequately explain the affective power of the film. *No Regrets for Our Youth* is an important film for Oshima not because of the idealized images of Noge/Ozaki and Yagihara/Takigawa but because of the "shining image" of youth exemplified by Yukie, which has left unforgettable impressions on Oshima and a generation of other Japanese audiences. Why is Yukie such an attractive character? She is an independent individual with a strong ego, who refuses to compromise her principles and give in to social pressures and violence. To this extent, she is not so different from Noge, who is as uncompromisingly idealistic as she is. What makes Yukie a unique character is that unlike Noge, she goes through a process of self-transformation. The film does not present her as an ideal character from the beginning but shows the process of her transformation or conversion from a strong-willed but somewhat capricious woman who does not know where to direct her inner energy to a highly independent responsible individual who fights against wartime militarism and promotes postwar democracy. The attraction of Yukie lies in her ability to convert herself into an uncompromising defender of personal liberty and democracy precisely when she is most threatened by the oppressive power of the militarist government and everyday fascism. As we shall see in the following sections, however, Yukie's conversion is diametrically opposite to the conversion of many Japanese in wartime Japan. And this difference in the directions of conversion gives us insight into the efficacy of the film's narrative.

Conversion/War Responsibility/Japanese Cinema

The word *tenko* (conversion) first began to be used widely to refer to the intellectuals' abandonment of their Marxist and communist beliefs in the 1930s. In 1933 two prominent members of the Japan Communist Party, Sano Manabu and Nabeyama Sadachika, published a statement in which they not only demanded that the Japan Communist Party withdraw from the Third International but also supported the emperor system and Japanese colonial expansionism. This statement had an enormous impact on their fellow communists, and in the following few years, a number of arrested party members and sympathizers followed suit.[13] In literature, this massive defection from Marxism gave rise to "conversion literature" *(tenko bungaku),* literary works dealing with the issue of conversion and written by converted writers.[14] Most conversion literature was written in the form of *shishosetsu,* or confessional narrative, and the crisis of communism as a revolutionary movement was shrewdly replaced by the crisis of characters and writers as weak individuals. There were, however, converted writers who tried to confront the issue of conversion as a matter of political beliefs and ideologies rather than as a pseudoexistential problem. One of the most

significant examples of serious conversion literature is Nakano Shigeharu's "House in the Village," which was published in 1935. In this short
story, written after his own conversion, Nakano tried squarely to face
questions of political beliefs, theory and practice, and intellectuals' responsibility without reaching any facile conclusion. The story focuses
on a confrontation between a converted writer who has recently been
released from prison and his father, who lives in a remote country village. The father asks his son to abandon writing and become a farmer
as a way of remaining consistent in his actions as an intellectual. The
son understands the old farmer's logic but at the same time vaguely
recognizes it as a "trap." The confrontation ends when the son replies:
"I understand very well, but I want to go on writing after all." [15] Here,
there is no simple reconciliation absolving the son's guilty feelings but
the presentation of conversion as an ongoing problem that must be
dealt with in his future actions. The majority of conversion literature
can be regarded as an attempt to dodge the question of conversion,
but Nakano's text is a record of his struggle to understand what really
constitutes conversion in the context of modern Japan.

Since its initial appearance in the 1930s, the notion of conversion has
been used in a much broader sense as apostasy or disavowal of political beliefs in general. The sudden transformation of militarists into
democratic reformers after World War II can obviously be classified as
another example of conversion. In fact, it is possible to see both the prewar Japanese intellectuals' renunciation of communism and the postwar intellectuals' celebration of democracy as a specific manifestation
of the set pattern of behavior that has been present in various forms
at least since the Meiji Restoration. The success of the *bunmei kaika,*
or the Meiji Enlightenment, was dependent on the Japanese willingness to adapt themselves to a new situation as quickly as possible, and
in this sense, conversion is a general symptom of Japanese modernity.
Yoshimoto Takaaki, for instance, argues that conversion occurs as a result of the Japanese intellectuals' inability to comprehend the totality
of social structure in modern Japan. According to Yoshimoto, there are
two types of conversion: conversion as a surrender to the remnants of
feudal systems and customs, and conversion as an avoidance of confronting those feudal remnants by using modernist theories as empty
logic.[16] For Takeuchi Yoshimi, conversion is inseparable from the lack

of subjectivity, which is formed in other Asian countries (particularly China) as a result of resistance against European nations as imperialist powers. Takeuchi argues that in contrast to religious conversion (*kaishin*), the political and intellectual conversion (*tenko*) of the Japanese intelligentsia is a result of their renunciation of individual will and their acceptance of circumstances as naturally given.[17]

In postwar Japan, the question of conversion was debated as two related but separate issues. First, conversion became an issue in the debate about war responsibilities and collaboration. When and how did Japan start taking a wrong course? Why was it impossible for the Japanese to stop the rise of fascism? How could they make sure that Japan would not follow a path leading to a similar historical disaster again? All of these questions haunted the minds of Japanese intellectuals who actively debated the question of war responsibility. Second, the issue of conversion was part of the more general suspicion that any ideological beliefs and theories that were borrowed from foreign countries might have in the end no real relationships to the actual situation of modern Japan. This suspicion led to the wholesale reexamination of Japanese modernity, particularly the position of Japanese as the subject of modernity.

As I pointed out earlier, Japanese filmmakers were not immune to the problem of war crime and collaboration. When the war came to an end with Japan's unconditional surrender, they were faced with a number of difficult questions. What should they do with their wartime films? How should they explain their involvement with the production of militarist films? What kinds of films should they make once Japan was under control by the Allied forces? In other words, Japanese filmmakers were called to account for their past actions during the war and for their reactions to sudden, radical changes in Japanese society after the defeat. More specifically, they must not only make known their positions on democratic reforms, which were imposed on Japanese by the American occupation authorities, but also defend themselves against charges c. war criminality and collaboration with the militarist regime. From the perspective of the American occupation authorities, who had to legitimate their presence on the Japanese soil, one of the urgent tasks was to transform the complexity of the war into an easily comprehensible story with a clear beginning and ending; that is, a story that began with the rise of (Japanese) militarism and ended with the victory of (American) democracy. Moreover, to ensure the governability of defeated Japan, the Occupation needed a simple way of differentiating "good" (democratic) Japanese from "bad" (militarist) Japanese, since any ambiguity concerning the moral character of two groups of Japanese would contradict the SCAP's version of what the war was all about. To ensure the dissemination of the correct story of Japanese militarism and its defeat by the forces of democracy, the Occupation tried to fully use film through a direct censorship and control over the Japanese film industry.

To deal with the question of war responsibilities within the film industry, the Occupation enlisted the All Japan Motion Picture Employees Union (Zen Nihon Eiga Jugyoin Kumiai Domei, or Zen'ei) to draw up a list of war criminals who should be barred from working in the film industry. The initial list of war criminals was too large and impractical for the purpose of actual enforcement. After a series of discussions, the final list was compiled, and thirty-one industry leaders who were designated as most responsible for collaborating with the military regime were purged from the industry. The list of the purged included Kido Shiro, Nagata Masaichi, Mori Iwao, and others who had occupied the rank of executive director *(jomu torishimari yaku)* or higher from July 7, 1937, to December 8, 1941; that is, from the occurrence of the Marco Polo Bridge incident to the Japanese attack on Pearl Harbor.[18] The Occupation also banned 225 out of 554 wartime films because of their "feudal" content, which was regarded as responsible for Japanese militarism.[19] The film companies were ordered to submit all the prints of the banned films to the Occupation, which burned the confiscated prints on the bank of the Tamagawa River. Among various types of Japanese film, the Occupation was particularly critical of *jidaigeki,* which was condemned as an antidemocratic genre encouraging feudal loyalty, cruel violence, and the undemocratic idea of revenge as something desirable. The Occupation's assertion that *jidaigeki* was more responsible for the propagation of militarist ideas than other types of film is only a fiction or a symptomatic manifestation of the contradictions in the Occupation policy. Interestingly, some Japanese also exploited the same fiction for their own purpose; that is, the question of Japanese filmmakers' war responsibility was diluted by positing *jidaigeki* as a main culprit for the collusion of the militarist government and the film industry.[20]

In the midst of the war criminal purge, individual filmmakers' self-questioning was replaced by the public condemnation of selected war criminals by "innocent" filmmakers. What disappeared in the purge was the responsibility of the accusers, who were also in one way or another participants in the militarist government's war mobilization. Who can seriously indict whom as "collaborators" when hardly anyone resisted militarism actively during the war? To what extent did the Japanese filmmakers actively or passively collaborate with the military regime? What did "responsibility" mean for filmmakers working in wartime Japan? The purging of the industry leaders as war criminals could not be an adequate answer to these questions. Instead of leading to filmmakers' serious self-examination, the pursuit of war responsibility in the film industry hindered a critical reevaluation of subjectivity of both the accused and the accusers.

Not all the filmmakers agreed to the purge or the way war responsibility was debated as a problem. Among those who voiced objection, Itami Mansaku most articulately discussed the relevant issues. In 1946 Itami published an essay titled "The Question of People Responsible for the War" (Senso sekininsha no mondai), in which he discussed the questions of public deception and war responsibility.[21] First, Itami describes how the control of the public was actually carried out. According to Itami, "everybody claims he or she was deceived during the Second World War. As far as I know, there isn't anybody who has admitted to deceiving others yet." Yet there cannot be a situation in which there are only the deceived without any deceivers. Moreover, in wartime Japan, the difference between those who were deceived and those who deceived was far from clear. Civilians, for instance, point their fingers to the military and the government as being responsible for the war. Within the hierarchical structure of these institutions, however, everybody lays the blame on the superiors. By this resoning, only one or two persons must have deceived all other Japanese. This is, as Itami points out, obviously absurd. Second, Itami focuses on the idea of deception itself. Itami claims that "to be deceived is itself already a vice": "To be deceived is equal to suffer from others' wrongdoings; however, it has never been written in any dictionary that those who are deceived are right." The general belief that the fact of being deceived can condone the war responsibility is itself another type of deception. Here Itami is concerned with a micropolitics of power and tries to demonstrate how coercion and manipulation are not a simple top-down process. He argues that it was people themselves who ensured the observance of ridiculous orders by the government. It is imperative to pursue the responsibilities of those who deceived others; however, it is also necessary to pursue the responsibilities of those who were deceived. Although Itami does not provide a clear-cut answer to the question of how to deal with war responsibility, he clearly rejects the notion of deception as another way of avoiding that difficult question.

Itami, who died of tuberculosis in 1946 at the age of forty-six, never had a chance to make a film to deal with the recent cataclysmic events and their consequences, including the question of war responsibility. Despite Itami's criticism of deception as an ethically suspicious concept, all too many postwar Japanese films made in the second half of the 1940s and the 1950s use deception and its corollary, victimization, as a core narrative motif.

Shutaisei/*Victim Consciousness/Conversion Narrative*

The way Japanese filmmakers tried to deal with the questions of war responsibility and their own subjective involvement in militarism and the mass-mobilized war effort was part of the larger discussions about subjectivity, or *shutaisei,* called *shutaisei ronso.* In postsurrender Japan, writers, literary critics, philosophers, social scientists, and others extensively and passionately debated the idea of *shutaisei.* The Japanese word *shutaisei* does not precisely correspond to "subjectivity" in English, and what exactly the word can or should signify was one of the points of dispute among postwar Japanese intellectuals.[22]

When faced with the extreme difficulty of establishing a subject position from which their involvement in militarism in the immediate past and reaction to the new reality of democratic Japan in the present can be explained logically without any contradictions, the easiest way out for the Japanese filmmakers was to claim that they were victims of deception by the militarists and war collaborators. Their victim consciousness enabled them to avoid addressing the question of war responsibility seriously, and the fiction of victim consciousness became a dominant narrative motif in the postwar Japanese films themselves. In *No Regrets for Our Youth*, victim consciousness is articulated by the figures of Noge and Yagihara, and this is why Oshima severely criticizes the film. Victim consciousness has been a key term in Oshima's critique of the postwar Japanese cinema in general. He argues that the Japanese filmmakers after the war were not *shutaiteki;* that is, they were not authentic subjects or independent agents of action and thought. According to Oshima, individuals become *shutaiteki* when they are neither completely powerless to change their own fate nor abstractly omnipotent and indifferent to the environment. The *shutaiteki* individuals are engaged in an effort to change a specific social situation in which they find themselves, and to transform themselves in relation to that situation. Besides Oshima, many other postwar intellectuals use the idea of victim consciousness to criticize the contemporary situation of Japanese society or to describe the Japanese national character. Maruyama Masao, one of the most influential political theorists and intellectual historians in postwar Japan, discusses Japanese discursive space in terms of victim consciousness. Maruyama argues that modern Japan is characterized by fragmentation and compartmentalization of social groups and organizations, among which there is no common ground of mutual communication or understanding. As information technology develops more and more, each social group, even when it is hegemonic, perceives itself as powerless and isolated, and everybody feels victimized by the majority, which may not exist in reality.[23] Psychiatrist Doi Takeo sees victim consciousness as a manifestation of *amae,* or dependency, which characterizes the specificity of the Japanese psyche. Doi emphasizes that *amae* is not unique to Japan. It is a psychic phenomenon that can be observed universally. But Doi argues that to the extent that a type of psychic dependency called *amae* is particularly pervasive in Japan, *amae* still becomes a distinctive trait of the Japanese mind.[24]

As suggestive as they are, what is lacking in the discourses about victim consciousness is the attention to the specificity of time and place in which victim consciousness emerged. For instance, Oshima's criticism of the postwar Japanese cinema falls short of explaining how the Japanese filmmakers could have been more *shutaiteki* under the specific sociopolitical conditions of the Occupation period and a newly independent Japan. When we read his critical writings, we get an impression that the problem of victim consciousness is ultimately the question of subjective will; that is, if they had had a strong individual will, the Japanese filmmakers could have produced films without relying on the dominant fiction of victim consciousness. But victim consciousness would not disappear simply by reminding Japanese of their action as victimizers against Asia and various minority groups in Japan. Victim consciousness is not just an alibi for victimization. Nor is victim consciousness a simple example of Japanese forgetfulness. Japan's victimization of Asia and minorities already started as a result of Japanese victim consciousness, so that a mere reminder of their own act of victimization would not fundamentally change the basic mechanism of victim consciousness.

It is important to note that in the specific context of occupied Japan, victim consciousness was not a mere Japanese fantasy. Victim consciousness was, instead, a dominant fiction necessary for *both* Japanese and Americans. In fact, as Masao Miyoshi suggests, without the Occupation's demand for the persecution of Japanese war criminals, *shutaisei* and its various aspects — "responsibility, autonomy, independence, self identity" — would not have arisen as such widely debated topics.[25] If the debate on subjectivity cannot be discussed without taking into account the difference between "subjectivity" and "*shutaisei*," it is because for the Japanese, the establishment of their own new subject position could not be done without taking into account the subject position of the Americans and the Japanese relation to these occupiers. Moreover, if the subjectivity debate did not lead to a satisfying conclusion, it is partly because the Occupation censorship and control played a determinant role in the Japanese rethinking of their subjectivity. For a wholesale reexamination of their subjectivities, the Japanese must first understand the immediate past and the present conditions under which they were trying to accomplish their task. What the Occupation prevented the Japanese from doing was precisely this thorough examination of the war and the Occupation. For instance, the Occupation censorship strictly forbade the Japanese filmmakers to show images of the war, particularly the devastation of Japan by the American forces. The Occupation did not simply suppress the Japanese criticism of the

Occupation. Instead, the Occupation forbid the Japanese filmmakers to mention, let alone concretely represent, the fact of occupation even in a positive manner. Thus, when we watch the Japanese films of the Occupation period, on the surface, nothing in them explicitly shows or indicates the presence of the Occupation forces. The Occupation also tried to make sure that Japanese militarism was responsible for everything negative, including the war devastation and the dire situation of the immediate postwar years.[26] These directives and the general policies of the Occupation led to the situation in which the Japanese filmmakers were forced to concentrate on the images of the Japanese existing in an imaginary space where the villain is always Japanese militarism or more commonly war, and the Japanese are victims of abstract or natural forces beyond their control.

What was missing in the Japanese attempt to establish a responsible, independent subject of postwar Japan, and what was suppressed by the Occupation, is a structural link between the Japanese war experiences and the larger historical context of Western imperialism and colonialism. Miyoshi writes:

> If the objective of this postwar soul-searching was to inquire into the conduct of the Japanese state in relation to its neighboring nations, it might as well have been directed to the larger context of international aggression and colonialism during the last century. Are not aggressive nations equally guilty? All individuals? Should there be distinctions among them in accordance with the severity of the crimes? What is the general war crime above and beyond specific acts of brutality and atrocity condemned by the Geneva Conventions? Is it a moral sin or legal crime? According to whose law? Are the Hiroshima and Nagasaki bombings justified? If the Allies, too, are guilty on specific counts, why are they not being tried? If they are guilty but not to be brought to trial, what is the status of the Tokyo Tribunal? Was the cause of the Allies wholly guiltless? Isn't it perfectly possible to argue, as did Takagi Yasaka earlier and Noam Chomsky later on, that Japan was following the precedent established by Great Britain and the United States, and was exercising its own Monroe Doctrine and realizing its own Manifest Destiny? And if the Japanese version of Manifest Destiny is distinguishable from its act of aggres-

sion and atrocity, how should the two be articulated? This type of fundamental inquiry was not attempted by most Japanese critics and historians either before or after the end of the Occupation in 1951 [sic]. The writers seem simply to have presumed that war crimes had been committed by the Japanese, without asking about the precise charges.[27]

Miyoshi argues that there are several reasons why the Japanese did not seriously examine the connections of Japanese and Western imperialism: fear of the Occupation censorship; fear of being labeled as revisionists or Pan-Asianists; the farcical effect of the Tokyo Tribunal; adoration for the West since the mid–nineteenth century.[28] Regardless of the specific reasons, without asking the kinds of questions Miyoshi formulates in his critical assessment of the debate on *shutaisei*, the Japanese filmmakers were not able to tackle the question of war responsibility in any fundamental way.

So many postwar Japanese films create and propagate the dominant fiction of victim consciousness through sentimentalism and emotionalism. I shall call these sentimental films of the postwar Japanese cinema "conversion narrative," which, as a mode of negotiation rather than as a simple act of negation, helped the Japanese to come to terms with the war, the Occupation, and the aftermath of both by situating themselves in the position of victim.[29] The success of the postwar Japanese cinema as conversion narrative came to a large extent from the seeming naturalness of August 15, 1945, as a radical point of disjunction in modern Japanese history. The prime objective of conversion narrative was to negate the ultimate failure of Japanese modernity, which in the end brought Japan to ruin as a result of imperialist adventurism. However, as a means of collective psychic disavowal, conversion narrative cannot be understood merely as a source of Japanese forgetfulness. Disavowal is inseparable from a psychoanalytic notion of ambivalence, the "simultaneous existence of contradictory tendencies, attitudes or feelings in the relationship to a single object — especially the coexistence of love and hate."[30] In conversion narrative, memory of the past was not simply erased; instead, nostalgia for the prewar and celebration of the postwar as a radical new beginning coexisted simultaneously. What guaranteed this coexistence was "August 15, 1945," which functioned as

a nodal point of fantasy that bound together two mutually contradictory moments of affirmation and denial. In other words, in the dis-
avowing process, "August 15, 1945," was transformed into a fetish.

One of the crucial features of disavowal is that unlike repression, it is
directed toward reality existing outside the subject. Whereas repression
occurs as a result of the conflict between the ego and the id, disavowal
is a defense mechanism of the ego refusing to admit a traumatic perception of external reality.[31] What was that "traumatic perception of external reality" for the Japanese after the defeat? Did that reality consist
of air raids, compulsory physical labor at factories, evacuation to the
countryside, or starvation during the war? Did it also include the Japanese colonialism and the violence and brutality of the Japanese military, colonial administrators, and civilians in Asia? Was it constituted
by the willing or compliant participation of the ordinary Japanese in the
formation and expansion of Japanese fascism? Was the trauma derived
from the first occupation of Japan by any foreign power, which was
accompanied by the overnight change in the systems of value underlying the areas of politics, economy, culture, and morality? Did it also
have something to do with the hypocrisy of the Americans, who promoted democracy by authoritatively forbidding the Japanese to discuss
the reality of the Occupation freely and democratically? What was traumatic is in fact not necessarily any particular isolated incident but the
totality of the Japanese experiences extending from the early 1930s to
the late 1940s and even to the first half of the 1950s. Conversion narrative attempted to give order to this ensemble of fragments of schizophrenic experiences. For the Japanese, one of the major questions was
how to situate themselves in relation to the wartime reality of fascism
and the postwar reality of the Occupation and its legacy. To suture
the schizophrenic split, the structural problem of modernity, to which
Japanese fascism and American imperial expansionism belonged as an
integral part, was rewritten in the form of a linear historical progress.
This particular narrativization of modern Japanese history—the defeat
of fascism followed by the triumph of democracy—became possible because of the fixation on "August 15, 1945," as a fetish. The fetishization
of "August 15, 1945," made a relative discontinuity in modern Japanese
history absolute. By radically severing the tie between prewar and postwar Japan, this fetish divided modern Japanese history simply into the

before and the after; that is, a fundamental rupture in history was created by the myth of the liberation and democratization of Japan by the American occupation forces. What was disavowed was therefore not simply wartime Japanese fascism or the Occupation but the *continuity* of the prewar and the postwar. In the process of disavowal, the problematic of imperialism and colonialism was carefully erased from the postwar Japanese discursive space. To be more precise, it was through the erasure of this problematic that the "postwar," or *sengo,* was constituted as a discursive space. What was willfully forgotten in this discursive space of the postwar was the United States as an imperial power and Asia as an object of Japan's colonial ambition.

As one of the early postwar films made under the watchful eyes of the Occupation, *No Regrets for Our Youth* also uses Japan's unconditional surrender to the Allied powers as the point of historical disjunction separating a militarist Japan and a democratic Japan. At the same time, the film subtly undermines this dichotomy in its epilogue, which starts with the title "The day of judgment—defeat! And the day liberty is restored." Yagihara goes back to the university and gives a speech in an auditorium packed with students. He says he hopes to see more students like Noge, who refused to compromise his principles and sacrificed himself to the future of Japan. Meanwhile Yukie is visiting her parents briefly. Her mother asks her to come home, but Yukie says she is going to stay in the village, which needs her as a "shining" leader of the village culture movement. Yukie becomes an activist for democracy not because of Japan's defeat but because of her belief in Noge's antiwar activism at the height of militarism. To the extent that the end of the war does not really change her subjectivity, Yukie is a symbol of historical continuity. Time, however, does not stand still, and the irreversibility of history is symbolized by Yukie's physical changes, particularly her hands.

Throughout the film, her hands appear as a dominant iconic image that tells us her inner thoughts and psychology, sometimes more eloquently than her words or facial expressions. First we see her gathering flowers with her hands in the field, and playing a Mussorgsky piece on the piano. In the middle of the film, the anxious state of her mind is symbolically represented by her hands destroying the elegantly arranged flowers and throwing them in a basin. (The shot of three flowers floating in the basin is a not so subtle allusion to the triangular relation between Yukie, Noge, and Itokawa.) When Itokawa visits Yukie in Noge's village to take her back to Kyoto, Yukie is washing her muddy hands in a rapidly flowing brook. They are, as she says to her mother in the film's epilogue, rough and bony hands not suitable for playing the piano. Yukie is no longer a capricious bourgeois girl but a hardworking farmer. Then the film underscores the irreversible flow of time by showing the hands of a younger Yukie playing the piano in overlap. Before heading back to the village, Yukie visits Mount Yoshida, the same spot near a stream where Noge and Itokawa extended their hands to Yukie more than ten years ago. Yukie watches young students in uniform crossing the stream while singing the university dormitory's song, which is used at key narrative points in the film. Her face radiates with nostalgia for her shining days of youth and at the same time clouds with melancholic feelings. Instead of celebrating a new beginning, the film nostalgically looks back on the idyllic days before the rise of militarism and Yukie's heroic struggle against everyday fascism.

The ambivalent sentiment is further reinforced in the film's final scene, which is supposed to be celebratory but hardly appears so. The film concludes with Yukie walking with her suitcase on a desolate country road. Two trucks pass Yukie, and a third stops and waits for her. With some help, she climbs into the truck, where villagers nod to her shyly, and she smiles ambiguously. At a signal from one of the villagers, the truck starts to take them back to the village. This is supposed to be a happy moment for Yukie, a leader of the village's culture movement. Yet the last image of her face is so melancholic, and if not disturbing, extremely ambivalent. Contrary to what she has said to her mother, Yukie looks out of place and unhappy among the villagers. More than anything else in the film, I believe this image of Yukie's face registers Kurosawa's resistance to the Occupation's attempt to propagate their version of recent Japanese history. Kurosawa continued to pursue more fully his covert resistance to the Occupation in his subsequent postwar films.

7. *One Wonderful Sunday*

One Wonderful Sunday (Subarashiki nichiyobi, 1947) is remarkably different from the preceding film about the liberal intellectual's resistance against the war and the assertion of woman's subjectivity. Inspired by D. W. Griffith's *Isn't Life Wonderful* (1926), Kurosawa's second postwar film focuses on two young lovers on a date in the midst of the postwar ruin and economic hardship.[1] In the early postwar years, young couples in Tokyo often met at the entrance of a major train station on late Sunday morning. On a typical date, they strolled around in the black market, dropped in at a makeshift coffee shop or restaurant, and went to the movies if tickets were available. At dusk, they headed back to the station to go home. It was not safe to walk around outside after dark because of the lack of streetlights in war-ravaged Tokyo.[2] The film's protagonists, Yuzo and Masako, are one of these typical young couples of the immediate postwar period. On one Sunday, Yuzo and Masako meet at a train station and, even though they have little money to spend, try to enjoy the day together. But contrary to what the title says, their Sunday is far from "wonderful." From the beginning, nothing goes well. They go to see a tacky model house and get depressed because it is still well beyond their budget. When Yuzo joins kids to play baseball on a vacant lot, the ball he hits lands in a nearby concession stand and ruins a few steamed buns. After this minor disaster, they go to a cabaret owned by Yuzo's war buddy. However, mistaken as a hooligan asking for spending money, Yuzo is politely refused entrance. At a zoo, Yuzo and Masako are disappointed to find out that there are neither elephants nor lions, which were killed during the war not only because there was a dire shortage of feed, fuels, and staff members but also because the government officials were afraid of wild animals escaping from zoos after air raids.[3] Instead of cheering up Yuzo and Masako, the zoo painfully reminds them of the war and the current hardship of their life. The most miserable incident happens when they go to a concert featuring Schubert's "Unfinished" symphony. While Yuzo and Masako are waiting in line to get tickets, scalpers buy all the tickets and start selling them at a higher price. Yuzo confronts the scalpers and demands that they sell him tickets at the original price, but they just give him a good beating in the rain.

Slow and ponderous, *One Wonderful Sunday* has a distinctly different feel compared to other Kurosawa films from the same period. To the extent that it deals with the question of fantasy, imagination, and hope for the future, the film shares similar thematic concerns with such later films as *The Lower Depths, Dodeskaden,* and *Dreams.* However, it is in the end different from even these films because of the main characters' passivity and indecisiveness. This is largely because the script was written not by Kurosawa but by Uekusa Keinosuke, Kurosawa's childhood friend and an accomplished writer in his own right. If as Sato Tadao claims, the scene in Yuzo's apartment shows us one of the rare occasions in Japanese cinema where sexuality is so forcefully and beautifully represented,[4] it owes a lot to Uekusa's sensibility. But the film as a whole clearly suffers from the discrepancy between Kurosawa's proclivity for accentuating dramatic tension through the juxtaposition of strong-willed individuals and Uekusa's more subdued poetic lyricism.

Kurosawa's touch can be glimpsed in the use of music and sound effects, but even here the juxtaposition of sound and image tends to be rather mechanical and not well designed (e.g., the comical contrast of Yuzo striding to the concession stand to apologize for ruining the steam buns and the accompanying music, the march from Bizet's *Carmen*). Japanese critic Nishimura Yuichiro argues that the problem with the film's music comes from the rationale behind the selection of various musical pieces: they seem to be selected not for their musical quality but for their titles.[5] The sound effects also often go their own way instead of playing a supportive role in the film's specific audiovisual design. For instance, in the interior scene of Yuzo's apartment, the irregular sound of raindrops dripping into a washbowl is supposed to signal the dejection and inner psychological turmoil of Yuzo. When we actually see this scene, however, we are so irritated by the sound of dripping water that our attention is merely drawn to the artificiality of the sound effect.

The most problematic use of sound appears in the penultimate scene of the film, in which Yuzo pretends to be a conductor in front of an imaginary orchestra performing Schubert's "Unfinished" symphony. At first, we do not hear anything but the sound of a cold wintry wind. Yuzo becomes dejected, but with a big hand, Masako encourages him to try again. Yuzo tries once more, but still nothing happens. Then, violating normal cinematic conventions, Masako directly faces the camera and asks us to clap our hands and help make their dream a reality. Masako's plea is followed by diegetically unmotivated applause, and as Yuzo confidently starts conducting the invisible orchestra, we finally hear the "Unfinished." In the earlier draft of the script written by Uekusa, the same scene is treated much more realistically. Originally, the performance of the "Unfinished" is not a private fantasy of Yuzo and Masako but a shared collective fantasy of many other couples. The sound of clapping hands is diegetically justified by the insertion of images of other young couples sitting on benches at a band shell in the dark. Thus the applauding sound marks a moment of surprise while still maintaining the illusion of diegetic unity and autonomy of this fantasy scene. In the finished film, Kurosawa tries to destroy this illusion by not only attempting to create a participatory form of cinema but also inviting the film's audiences to become part of the fictional characters' fantasy. The contemporary spectators of the film reportedly did not respond to Masako's plea for clapping their hands to make the fantasy happen. This anecdote might tell us something about the prevalent mode of film viewing in Japan of the immediate postwar period. Yet it is also possible that the spectators remained silently sitting in their seats because they did not find Yuzo and Masako attractive enough to actively share the fantasy of these fictional characters.

8. *Drunken Angel*

Drunken Angel (Yoidore tenshi, 1948) is narratively structured around the opposition between two protagonists. Sanada (Shimura Takashi), a drunken doctor, works in the slums to help the socially underprivileged and oppressed; Matsunaga (Mifune Toshiro), a tubercular *yakuza*, tries to get over his illness with the help of Sanada but in the end dies as a result of a meaningless fight with a rival senior yakuza, Okada. In Matsunaga, Sanada sees the image of his younger self, and despite his harsh words, he cannot but identify with this small-time gangster. Matsunaga rebels against Sanada precisely because he knows that what the delinquent doctor tells him is right. What supposedly distinguishes them from each other is that Sanada knows how to control himself based on what he calls reason *(risei)*, while Matsunaga does not.

Stylistically speaking, *Drunken Angel* is a highly self-conscious film. The film's diegetic space consists of the slums and the black market, which surround a polluted, disease-breeding sump. The recurrent appearance of this contaminated sump at key moments in the narrative not only helps to segment the film into distinct sections but also subtly explains the inner psychological states of the principal characters. The symbolic meanings of the sump are further refined and expanded by the use of concrete objects and human figures associated with it (e.g., an abandoned doll, a guitar player, bubbling methane gas, mosquitoes). The nightclub where Matsunaga and Okada compete for the hostess Nanae is called "No. 1—Social Center of Tokyo." As a counterpoint to Matsunaga, Sanada has another patient, a high school girl played by Kuga Yoshiko, who cures her tuberculosis by using the power of reason. The spilled white paint in Matsunaga and Okada's fight scene provides a visual distraction and makes the fight itself ignoble and pathetic. In the same fight scene, the split image of Matsunaga is reflected in the three-paneled mirror as if to show his final psychological breakdown.

One of the most striking images in the film is the contrast between Matsunaga's body and the fluttering white clothes on a small drying platform on the roof of Nanae's apartment building.

Yet despite Kurosawa's sure control over film form and stylistic play evinced in these examples, *Drunken Angel* is surprisingly static and even one-dimensional. It has often been argued that the weakness of *Drunken Angel* lies in the reversal of the hierarchical relation between Sanada and Matsunaga. As the film's title indicates, the hero of the film is the drunken doctor Sanada, played by Shimura. But because of Mifune's powerful performance (his first appearance in a Kurosawa film), Sanada is eclipsed by Matsunaga, who emerges by the end of the film as a tragic hero. Another miscalculation on the part of Kurosawa is that he tries to go beyond the simplistic dichotomy of good and evil by making Sanada a drunkard. But as the finished film shows, despite his bad habit, Sanada remains an idealistic hero without a darker side. The drunken angel is still an angel, an unrealistic figure in the slums of postsurrender Japan.

9. *The Quiet Duel*

Once the most successful Japanese film company, Toho was ravaged by strikes in the late 1940s. During the famed third Toho strike, the American military even sent tanks and fighters to Toho's Kinuta studios to threaten striking workers. To continue making films outside the troubled studios, in March 1948, Toho's contract director Yamamoto Kajiro and producer Motogi Sojiro formed Film Art Association (Eiga Geijutsu Kyokai), with Kurosawa as one of its founding members. As an independent production collective, Film Art Association could not raise capital to produce its own films; instead, it pursued joint film projects with other major companies. During its existence between 1948 and 1951, the association produced fifteen films, and besides Yamamoto, Motogi, and Kurosawa, it boasted such prominent members as Taniguchi Senkichi (director), Mifune Toshiro (actor), Tanaka Tomoyuki (producer), Matsuyama Takashi (set designer), and Naruse Mikio (director). The success of Film Art Association partially owed to the shortage of films on the market. In the late 1940s, the majors could not keep up with the rapid increase in the popular demand for films, and they were all desperate to find any films to fill the weekly bills. In addition to independently produced films, the movie theaters routinely showed prewar Japanese films that passed the Occupation censors, and foreign films that had been imported before the defeat but had never been shown because of Japanese censorship.

Kurosawa's first film as a member of Film Art Association, *The Quiet Duel* (Shizukanaru ketto, 1949, produced for Daiei), is based on Kikuta Kazuo's play *The Abortion Doctor* (Dataii).[1] Kurosawa saw a performance of the play by a little theater group in Tokyo called Baraza, whose leader, Chiaki Minoru, later became an indispensable member of the Kurosawa troupe. The film opens with a field hospital scene, in which Fujisaki (Mifune Toshiro) contracts syphilis while operating on an injured soldier called Nakata. Because of the lack of drugs at the front, his venereal disease reaches a fairly advanced stage by the time he repatriates to Japan after the end of the war. In the remainder of the film, the focus of the narrative is the moral struggle of Fujisaki, torn between his personal desires and his sense of public responsibility as a doctor. Fujisaki has a fiancée, Misao, who has been waiting for him for six years. On his return, however, Fujisaki breaks off their engagement without any explanation. Everybody around him is puzzled by his behavior as he continues to work as a compassionate doctor treating poor patients at the clinic run by his father (Shimura Takashi) in a bombed-out neighborhood. Minegishi Rui, a former dancer who started working at the clinic after having been made pregnant and left by a hooligan, cynically brands Fujisaki as a hypocrite. Minegishi and even Fujisaki's father misunderstand when she witnesses Fujisaki giving himself a salvarsan injection late at night. But as she learns the true reason for his infection with syphilis, she begins to admire Fujisaki for his genuineness and decides to give birth to a baby and become a nurse. Meanwhile Fujisaki chances on Nakata at a police station. In contrast to Fujisaki, Nakata is married and expecting a baby. It turns out that Nakata ignored Fujisaki's sincere advice at the field hospital and never got treated for his syphilis seriously. Although Fujisaki urges Nakata to test his wife and himself for syphilis, he refuses to listen and finally, when he sees the body of his deformed baby, goes insane. Fujisaki continues to treat his own disease patiently, fights off temptation, and after some struggle decides to give up Misao. The film concludes on a hopeful note, showing Fujisaki operating on another patient.

Before Kurosawa could begin production, the entire project first had to be approved by the Occupation government's Civil Information and Education Section (CIE). The censors told Kurosawa that it was commendable for him to educate the film's audience about the seriousness of venereal disease. However, the film should not overemphasize the terror of syphilis; otherwise, according to the CIE officers, people with the disease might simply abandon any treatment. The censors also objected to the portrayal of the doctor, who does not treat his syphilis until it is too late and consequently goes insane. From the CIE's "educational" standpoint, the doctor, who is supposed to cure patients, should not behave so irresponsibly as to leave his syphilis untreated and lapse into insanity. Because of these objections, Kurosawa was forced to introduce major changes to the script, particularly with regard to the portrayal of Fujisaki. In the revised script, it is no longer Fujisaki but Nakata who goes insane. A major change was made with regard to Fujisaki's past, too. In the original play, before he goes to the war, Fujisaki performs an abortion to save a pregnant woman's life. He has a clear conscience, yet his reputation as a doctor is tainted (thus, the title of the original play, *The Abortion Doctor*). In the finished film, this episode is completely dropped.

The changes enforced by the American censors made *The Quiet Duel* a rather uninspiring film. It is often too sentimental and unrealistic, marred by the simplistic representation of moral conflict embodied in the characters of Fujisaki and Nakata. The two characters form a moral dichotomy, with Fujisaki representing a sense of responsibility, humanity, and the innocent victim, and Nakata embodying irresponsibility, impurity, and the social victimizer. The rigidity of this moral dichotomy makes the film rather shallow and uncompelling. Throughout the film, Fujisaki remains a compassionate doctor and an innocent victim of unfortunate circumstances, and his position in the moral dichotomy and the certainty of his subjectivity are never seriously problematized. Nakata appears as the exact opposite or double of Fujisaki, but this recurrent Kurosawa motif, the doubling of hero and villain, is nothing more than a mechanical schema and not sufficiently developed. Instead of questioning a social norm underlying the dichotomy of the two characters, the film merely reaffirms the validity of the norm.

Despite these shortcomings, *The Quiet Duel* contains some compelling images and significant thematic motifs. For instance, Tada Michitaro sees *The Quiet Duel* as a seminal film in which Kurosawa tried to tackle the problem of individual responsibility. After the end of World War II, writes Tada,

> We Japanese unanimously pointed out the evilness of the external condition, but completely remained indifferent to the evil in our own mind. Were we thinking that together with military fascism a thing like our own evilness had been hanged? Then, Kurosawa's *Drunken Angel* (1948) and *The Quiet Duel* (1949) appeared. The story of the latter centers around an ex-military doctor who refuses to get mar-

ried to his fiancée even though she has been waiting for him to come back from the war for six years. The reason for his adamant refusal is that during an operation at a field hospital, he was infected with spirochete pallida through a cut on his fingertip. It is a strange situation in which he is pure yet has lost purity.

What kind of crime did we the Japanese masses *(shomin)* commit by participating in the war? The idea of war responsibility did not quite come home to us. We created some scapegoats, and believed we were still innocent. I also had rather similar feelings inside myself. However, we had actually lost our purity without realizing it. It was never just a sin of society. It was the problem of individuals *(kojin)* who create society. This is the kind of problem presented in *The Quiet Duel.*

Kurosawa Akira was perhaps the first author who tried to introduce the individual into Japanese cinema. But for historical reasons, this individual could not have a kind of naturalness found in the rising bourgeoisie of England and France. Kurosawa tried to construct a still unknown individual by exposing and crushing a wound left by semi-feudal fascism inside us. The one who was killed and the one who did the killing were both ourselves.[2]

If the mechanical dichotomy of good and evil and the unbelievability of the narrative's premises make *The Quiet Duel* an uncompelling film, then where can we find the kinds of affective forces Tada detects in the film? How does the film suggest that Fujisaki's "quiet duel" is more than just a medical struggle to cure his disease?

What saves *The Quiet Duel* from becoming an easily forgettable film is probably the superb first sequence, which is imbued with a sense of futility, desperation, and guilt. Set in a field hospital at an unspecified location — probably somewhere in Southeast Asia or the Pacific — in 1944, this sequence shows how Fujisaki contracts syphilis while operating on Nakata. It is preceded by the opening credits, which are shown against the background images of braided strips of bark, a large leaf of a tropical plant, and the muddy ground in the torrential rain. Throughout the credits, we hear the sound of a drum, which is more than just an embellishing device to create a sense of exoticism. The drum's heavy beat is like *basso continuo,* not only anticipating the intensely charged atmosphere of the first sequence but also ensuring that what happens in that sequence continues to influence the trajectory of the film's narrative. Even though the images of the field hospital never reappear once the locale of the story is moved to Japan after the war, the sense of futility and lost innocence evoked in the opening scene haunts the rest of the film.

The field hospital sequence is permeated with the sense of exhaustion and futility. Inside a makeshift operating room, Fujisaki and his chief assistant, in surgical gowns, are sleeping while sitting on chairs. Fujisaki, whose face is dripping with perspiration, is totally exhausted after having operated on patient after patient. Wounded soldiers are continuously being brought to the hospital, which has neither adequate staff nor necessary medicine. Other than Fujisaki's question, "How many more patients?" and the assistant's reply, "It's endless," there is no verbal description of the current predicament. Instead, the chaotic situation of the field hospital and the war is presented in concrete audiovisual images. The sequence opens with the shot of a red cross and an arrow, which are briefly illuminated by a headlight in the pitch-dark night and the torrential rain. It appears a truck has just brought a new patient to the field hospital. We see the irritated driver of the truck shouting something through the windshield, but we cannot hear what he is saying because his voice is drowned out by the heavy rain. His shouting face without voice, seen through the windshield, makes him look trapped inside the cramped cab. Here, the awkward disjunction of sound and image does not produce a comic effect but raises the intensity of the scene. If the lack of sound (human voice) in the opening is a source of the sense of futility and irritation, during the operation, it is the excess of sound that produces a similar effect. As Fujisaki starts operating on Nakata, the roof starts leaking near the operating table. One of the assistants puts a washbowl under it at once but fails to alleviate the problem. In fact, Fujisaki gets more edgy precisely because of the annoying sound of water dripping into the bowl.

Visually, various obstructions and shadows aggravate the sense of irritation, futility, and entrapment. Fujisaki starts operating on Nakata, who has been shot in the abdominal region. Our view of the operation is partially blocked by a rhythmically moving fan in the foreground. In one shot, we see the upper half of the moving fan at the bottom of the screen, and at the top a part of the tent's fly swaying in a different rhythm. In the foreground of another shot are Nakata's feet, and Fujisaki and his assistants are squeezed into the frame, leaving no visible space empty on the screen. At the conclusion of the operation scene, the camera is placed outside, showing the operation in progress through a window, whose bars form cross-shaped patterns and ostentatiously frame the scene inside. Throughout the sequence, the sense of claustrophobia and entrapment is heightened by decor and shot composition. On the outside deck of the field hospital, patients lie everywhere on the floor, but inside the hospital, the ceiling is so low that it seems it might come down onto Fujisaki and crush him at any moment. Even the air does not seem to be transparent in this sequence. The extreme heat and humidity thicken the air, and although it is invisible, we can feel the presence of the stagnant air as a tactile substance.

A less successful yet equally striking scene is the film's climax, when Fujisaki for the first time loses control and exposes his vulnerability to Minegishi, the converted apprentice nurse. In contrast to the opening scene, it is snowing outside. As Fujisaki's fiancée Misao leaves the clinic, we hear the sound of a train's whistle. Then, inside the clinic's consultation room, Fujisaki starts revealing his frustration, anger, and desire to Minegishi. According to Richie, "The sequence represents all it is supposed to: his renunciation, his agony, his renewed dedication — but the lack of tact, the inordinate length, the atrocious acting, all point to Kurosawa's basic lack of interest."[3] It is true that everything in the scene gives us an impression of clumsiness. The mise-en-scène is quite uninspiring; the camera never crosses the imaginary 180-degree line to disrupt our sense of spatial orientation; and the editing does not even create the rhythmic effect through the shot/reverse shot technique. The conventionality of film form makes this scene rather static and "theatrical." But according to Kurosawa's own account, if the climactic confession of Fujisaki is not a well-crafted scene, it is not because he had no interest in the unfolding drama but because he had too much interest in it.[4] The whole scene consists of seven shots and lasts about ten minutes, but the focus of the scene is a five-minute-long take, in which Fujisaki restlessly walks up and down the room and expresses his inner turmoil with irrepressible bitterness and anger. "Atrocious" is perhaps too strong a word to describe the performance of Mifune, but it is defi-

nitely not what is ordinarily called good acting. Yet it is precisely because of Mifune's "bad" performance that this scene is so memorable.
If Mifune's monologue moves us, it is not because of the believability
of the fictional character Fujisaki played by Mifune but because of that
of Mifune, who plays the role of the fictional character Fujisaki. The
climactic long take has a strange documentary-like quality, which is
produced by the distance between actor Mifune and character Fujisaki.
This scene and the opening sequence are the two most genuine moments in this rather stale film. For a more fully realized treatment of the
problems presented by *The Quiet Duel*, we have to wait for Kurosawa's
next film, *Stray Dog*.[5]

10. *Stray Dog*

Speech/Writing/Image

The story of *Stray Dog* (Nora inu, 1949) centers on a young homicide detective, Murakami (Mifune Toshiro), and his quest to recover his stolen handgun. The film starts with the scene in which Murakami reports to his superior that he had his pistol stolen on a bus. Murakami is immediately sent to Section Three, which specializes in cases of theft and robbery, to go through all the relevant files on pickpockets. With the help of the veteran section chief, Murakami eventually finds a card about the woman pickpocket Ogin, who was standing right next to him on the bus. After failing to get any information out of Ogin, Murakami follows her everywhere. Ogin tries to shake off Murakami by luring him into alleyways and by using hidden exit doors. Every time Murakami loses sight of Ogin, he manages to catch up with her at the last moment. By the end of the day, Ogin gives in to Murakami's zeal and tells him to look for an illicit pistol dealer hanging around in a black market. Disguised as an ex-soldier, Murakami wanders all over Tokyo for a few days without any luck. Totally exhausted from walking and the heat, he finally succeeds in contacting a gun dealer, who tells Murakami to wait for a woman at a nearby coffee shop. Too eager to recover his stolen gun, Murakami arrests her on the spot and ends up letting her boss Honda and Yusa (Kimura Isao), the young man who has Murakami's gun, get away. This second mistake leads to the further intensification of Murakami's frenetic search. To capture Honda, he and his veteran partner Sato (Shimura Takashi) go to a baseball park packed with fifty thousand spectators. To discover Yusa's whereabouts, they visit a revue theater where Yusa's girlfriend works as a dancer. As Murakami continues his search, he brings us to scenes of postwar chaos and confusion punctuated by a burst of energy and mesmerizing visuality. At the film's climax, Sato is shot by Yusa, and Murakami — and the audience — finally confront this criminal face-to-face. After they tussle with each other in the mud, Murakami handcuffs Yusa. In the last scene, we learn that Murakami has been officially commended for his contribution to the arrest of Honda and the seizure of more than ten illegal guns. Despite Sato's congratulating words, however, Murakami does not look terribly happy, since he still cannot forget about Yusa completely. The film ends with a hopeful note, Sato's reassurance that as Murakami arrests more criminals, the image of Yusa will eventually fade from his memory.

Stray Dog opens with the credit image of a dog panting for air. For several reasons, this image has a striking sense of presence. First, the sequence consists of one long shot and another brief shot, in which the camera is not exactly static, but moves only slightly to follow the movement of the dog's head from screen left to right in order to reframe it in the center of the screen. A transition from the first long-lasting shot to the second brief one is almost invisible because of a subtle use of dissolve that optically creates an impression of the dog's head turning back to the original position. Thus the image track of the credit sequence is constructed in such a way that the audience is forced to see the close-up image of the dog's head without being distracted by any drastic changes in shot composition or transition. Second, the physiognomic features and motion of the dog have a strong affective quality: a large, open mouth with sharp teeth, and a long, extended tongue in constant and rhythmic motion. Without a collar, the dog appears to be an ownerless mongrel rather than a pure-blooded pet, and the dog's fierce look has the power of disturbing the spectator emotionally. Third, the sound of the dog's heavy breathing at the beginning and end of the sequence, which is accentuated by the use of dramatic music in between, cannot but direct the spectators' attention to the source of that sound.

Most important, however, the close-up of the dog's head retrospectively sticks to the spectators' mind because there is no other image of a dog in the rest of the film; that is, the opening image stands out from the rest of the film as something superfluous, since what is represented in the shot — the dog — does not seem to exist in the film's diegetic space. This apparent lack of a referential connection between the image of the dog and the diegetic space makes the former look like a metaphoric image. But it is too hasty to see this image only as a visual metaphor, since there are, after all, *verbal* references to a dog in the film's narrative. In the middle of the film, for instance, the seasoned detective Sato refers to the criminal Yusa as a stray dog turning into a mad dog. Does this mean that the opening image of the dog is a metonymic image, an image whose narrative significance is derived from the principle of referential contiguity? The answer to this question can be only a qualified yes because Sato's use of "stray dog" is obviously a metaphoric expression, and the literal translation of this verbal metaphor into a visual image maintains the sense of metaphoricalness very strongly, as is confirmed by our initial impression of its superfluousness. The opening image of the dog is, on the one hand, a metaphor as it is used by characters in the film, and on the other hand, precisely because that metaphor appears as part of the film's diegesis, a metonymy. Moreover, the close-up of the dog breathing hard acquires a different meaning when at the last second of the credits we hear the narration, "It was extremely hot that day," in a male voice. This voice-over introduces the question of representability of nonconcrete verbal descriptions in visual images, and the image of the dog becomes a metaphoric image of scorching heat and humidity, the feeling of hot summer days.

What is ultimately important is, however, not the image's referential type but its discursive status; that is, what makes the opening image of the dog stand out is that the syntagmatic position of this image in *Stray Dog* is arbitrary.[1] The only cue given for us to naturalize the image's syntagmatic position is the credits, which make us conclude that the film's story has not yet started. The arbitrariness of the first image's syntagmatic relation to the rest of the film is put under erasure by placing the image outside the diegetic frame. Even if the opening image is excluded from the film's diegesis, however, it cannot be external to the film as a narrative discourse. If we pay attention to the relationship of the image of the dog and the film's title, "Stray Dog," the opening image becomes a metonymy at the discursive level, a literalization of the film's title. It can be argued that this is the most literal image of the film; that is, the close-up image of the head of a dog panting for breath is a literal rendering of the film's title, "Stray Dog," into an audiovisual image. It is perhaps not too farfetched to say that to a large extent, *Stray Dog* is about the rhetoric of filmic narration.

The opening image of *Stray Dog* is an extradiegetic image of reflexivity, which marks a moment of the film's self-reference, thus foregrounding its discursiveness. Profoundly concerned with the terms of its own constitution as a discourse, *Stray Dog* is full of rhetorical complexity and undecidability and therefore demands us to examine it closely as a text, that is, "as a generative, open-ended, non-referential grammatical system and as a figural system closed off by a transcendental signification that subverts the grammatical code to which the text owes its existence."[2]

All of this analysis so far might seem rather pedantic or inconsequential for understanding and appreciating *Stray Dog*. But if the analysis looks too intellectualized or academic, it tells more about the prevalent image of Kurosawa as a film director and the general critical expectations in Japanese cinema studies than about the seeming triviality of close textual analysis as a mode of criticism. For instance, Kurosawa has often been compared to Eisenstein, and the comparison is almost always focused on the similar visual quality of their works: geometric shot composition, dialectic montage, dynamic motion, visual shock, and other characteristics.[3] This type of comparison often points out significant aspects of Kurosawa's work; however, its inadequacy is also hard to deny, since it tends to end up trivializing not only Kurosawa's but also Eisenstein's work.[4] What is often overlooked is the reason why Eisenstein was so interested in exploring the possibility of dynamic montage and graphic design in the first place. Eisenstein did not theorize montage in his writings and films just to make his films visually enticing or entertaining. Different types of montage are conceived in such a way that they dialectically develop into more complex, sophisticated types, which approximate the inner process of both human thought and affect (e.g., intellectual montage, inner thought, etc.). Likewise, Kurosawa is not interested in graphic composition or dynamic movement per se. The stereotype of Kurosawa as a mere artisan of graphic dynamism has been circulating in criticism of Kurosawa films partly because thematic motifs and stylistic aspects of his films are often examined separately. To make a comparison between Kurosawa and Eisenstein truly relevant, we must abandon the stereotyped image of Kurosawa as a superb artisan of visual dynamism without sophisticated ideas and thoughts.[5] True, Kurosawa's films can be at times thematically too bourgeois and naive. But to the extent that this thematic understanding of Kurosawa's films takes what characters or narrators say in his films at face value, it is as naive as the putative object of thematic criticism.[6] In *Stray Dog,* "thinking" can be found not in characters' speech but in the tension between thought and action, and in the complex intertwining of visuality and signification. One good place to start our examination of the film's textuality is the representation of letters and scripts. As Tom Conley argues, "Writing . . . possesses the virtue of being able to allegorize, that is, to problematize the relation of its part to the whole of the film. In this sense a piece of script can serve as a visual *mise-en-abyme* or interior duplication that sums up the seemingly greater problems of character and intrigue within a given shot."[7] Another significant instance of rhetoric of image can be found in the conjuncture of visual representation and voice-over speech, to which we shall turn our attention first.

According to Donald Richie, one of Kurosawa's technical mistakes in *Stray Dog* is the use of the voice-over narration. Richie finds two major faults in the film's voice-over. First, it creates the sense of inconsistency in the film's narration: "One of the most glaring miscalculations is the use of a narrator in the beginning of the film . . . , an intrusion further unwarranted in that, at the end of the film, the off-screen voice has turned into Mifune's . . . and so there is basic disagreement between narrations."[8] Second, the voice-over at the beginning of the film is redundant, merely representing in verbal discourse what the audience sees on the screen. Without adding anything new to the meaning created by mise-en-scène or editing, "during the flash-back pistol-stealing scene on the bus, [the anonymous narrator] continues, in *benshi* fashion . . . to tell us what we are seeing as we are seeing it: 'Sweat was in his eyes . . . a woman was leaning heavily against him, etc.'"[9] In other words, Richie claims that because of its redundancy and inconsistency, the voice-over in *Stray Dog* is superfluous to the film's overall economy of narration.

Would the sense of redundancy simply disappear if the voice-over is removed from the film? The answer is no, since what appears to be verbal duplication of the visual image is not an aberration but an integral part of the film's textual system, which includes not only the voice-over but also written texts recorded on the film's visual track. For instance, in the credit sequence, the image of a stray dog and the film title "Stray Dog" are presented simultaneously on the screen. (Which is the original? Which is the duplicate? Is the original the phrase "stray dog" rendered in three Chinese characters, or the audiovisual image of a dog?) The semantic redundancy created by the superimposition of the film's title as a striking graphic sign over the image of a dog is very similar to the "technical miscalculation" of the voice-over narrations. Another example of seeming redundancy can be found in the scene in the lobby of the Yayoi Hotel, where Sato is seriously wounded by Yusa's (i.e., Murakami's) gun. Sato has finally located Yusa in this small lodging and tries to get in touch with Murakami, who is at Yusa's girlfriend Harumi's apartment. Sato goes inside a telephone booth and calls the apartment building's custodian, an old man with some hearing difficulty. Sato shouts into the receiver but is increasingly irritated by the old man's off-the-mark responses and by various kinds of noise. In addition to a thunderstorm, the sound of dance music coming from a radio in the lobby makes it almost impossible for both Sato and the custodian to understand each other. What is most striking in this scene, which is already overloaded with information, is three large Chinese characters 電話室 (telephone booth) painted on the telephone booth's glass. Although there is nothing unusual about the booth by itself, when we see the graphic sign "telephone" in the foreground partially blocking our view of Sato, who is shouting into the receiver without his words reaching the film's audience, the effect is almost surreal.

Throughout *Stray Dog*, words and images are consistently juxtaposed in a seemingly redundant way. If we regard the use of the voice-over as a mistake, then we would need to dismiss the entire film as a failure. To avoid this, it is necessary to examine the notion of redundancy more carefully. For the voice-over, superimposed script, or diegetic/nondiegetic writing to redundantly duplicate what is visually present on the screen, there should be the possibility of establishing an equivalent relation between language and the image. Can the verbal description or words exactly duplicate the visual image? As Roland Barthes and other semioticians have demonstrated, what characterizes the image as a sign is its fundamentally polysemic nature and lack of double articulation. As Barthes argues, a verbal text accompanying a photograph functions as an anchor that tries to delimit the image's polysemic tendency and to draw our attention to the image's limited aspects. This does not necessarily mean that the verbal text is less polysemic than the image. The difference lies in how they create meanings. Whereas language can be broken down into distinct units of meaning (morphemes) and sound (phonemes), the image does not consist of comparable minimal units.[10] The digital image may have something similar to phonemes, yet it still cannot be constructed out of autonomous semantic units. Thus, as distinctly different systems of signification, the image and the verbal text cannot exactly duplicate what the other signifies: each always signifies much more or far less than the other does. To the extent that there can never be the exact linguistic equivalent to the image and vice versa, whether a mistake or not, any sense of redundancy created by the juxtaposition of words and images paradoxically marks a privileged moment of textual discord, which foregrounds not the sameness but the fundamental difference of the image and language as signifying systems. A certain combination of the image and the voice-over narration is often rejected as redundant because by exposing the artificiality of both verbal and visual narrations, it destroys the illusion of the unity and consistency of diegesis as an autonomous universe.[11]

Strictly speaking, in *Stray Dog*, the voice-over narration is used only once, at the very beginning. Mifune's voice mentioned before is not a narration but an interior monologue, and the other two instances of voice-over are a variation of asynchronous speech (the whispering voices of Yusa's victim's neighbors) and the verbalization of a written script shown on the screen (a narrator reading aloud Yusa's fragmentary note). What is common among these instances of speech is the sense of distance created between what we see and what we hear. The image loses transparent legibility. We must decipher it consciously as if it is a hieroglyphic inscription. Toward the end of the film, for instance, we are reminded of the tension between image and language by the last instance of the voice-over, the interior monologue of Murakami, who desperately tries to identify Yusa among several possible suspects at a train station. As Murakami scrutinizes every possible suspect and his appearance, we hear the following voice-over: "Damn it! Which one is Yusa? Which one is Yusa? Don't get panicky. Don't get panicky. Take it easy. Calm down. Calm down. Twenty-eight years old. A white linen suit. But he might have changed his clothes. Then, about twenty-eight years old male. About twenty-eight years old male. About twenty-eight years old male. Twenty-eight. Calm down. Don't get panicky. Ah, that's right. He rushed outside when raining heavily last night. Muddy shoes. Muddy shoes. Muddy shoes. Muddy pants. Muddy pants. Muddy pants. Muddy. . . ." Not an articulate expression of his inner thoughts but a reading of his surrounding as an image, Murakami's repetitive speech demonstrates how the meaning of the image changes as different words are attached to it.

What appears to be a redundant juxtaposition of language and the image does not duplicate the two but problematizes their seeming equivalency. To characterize their relation as merely redundant is misleading because it presupposes the transparency of the visual image. What the image so naturally seems to refer to is in fact an effect of information contained in the "redundant" voice-over or graphic sign on the screen. This misrecognition of the image's transparency is produced by what Michel Chion calls "added value."

> By *added value* I mean the expressive and informative value with which a sound enriches a given image so as to create the definite impression, in the immediate or remembered experience one has of it, that this information or expression "naturally" comes from what is seen, and is already contained in the image itself. Added value is what gives the (eminently incorrect) impression that sound is unnecessary, that sound merely duplicates a meaning which in reality it brings about, either all on its own or by discrepancies between it and the image. The phenomenon of added value is especially at work in the case of sound/image synchronism. . . . But first, at the most basic level, added value is that of text, or language, on image.[12]

As Chion argues, the visual image's naturalness, or its transparent signification, is merely an illusion. And the seemingly redundant voice-over in *Stray Dog* makes us realize how a self-evident image is already divided within itself, how we have naturalized our act of reading the visual image to such an extent that our construction of a meaning appears to be the image's literal meaning. Moreover, the impression of redundancy foregrounds the impossibility of fully internalizing the sign as part of the interiority of the mind. When we see Yusa's handwritten note on the screen in close-up, it is read aloud by an anonymous narrator, whose voice sounds muffled and unfamiliar. On the one hand, what we hear is the intimate expression of Yusa's interiority. On the other hand, the voice attached to that expression introduces a discord in the relation of language and interiority, since it belongs to nobody, neither Yusa (author) nor Murakami (reader), not even the omniscient narrator of the film's voice-over narration. The juxtaposition of Yusa's writing and its reading aloud draws our attention to the externality of the sign to consciousness. To the extent that the redundant juxtaposition of image and language problematizes the centered, interiorized subject, the whole film can be regarded as a form of writing (as opposed to speech, in Derrida's sense of the word).

The Madness of Rhetoric

Madness is a recurrent motif in Kurosawa films. In *The Quiet Duel,* Nakata's brain is affected by syphilis; obsessed with the danger of nuclear threat, Nakajima goes mad in *Record of a Living Being;* in *Throne of Blood,* Asaji goes insane; Yoshiko in *The Bad Sleep Well* loses her mind when she learns that her husband was killed by her own father's henchmen; in *Ran,* Hidetora lapses into insanity. How is madness represented in *Stray Dog?* What is madness according to this film? Where is a line drawn between reason and madness?

In *Stray Dog,* madness is represented first of all as a verbal metaphor, "mad dog" *(kyoken).* This metaphorical expression is used by Sato for the first time in the ballpark scene when he stresses the urgency of preventing Yusa from committing another crime: "The first time can be an accident, but from the second time, it's a different story. A stray dog becomes a mad dog." Madness here stands for not only antisocial behavior or criminality but also single-minded obsession or compulsion to repeat the same action. And it is the latter aspect of madness that links Murakami, the pursuer, to Yusa, the pursued. When a popsicle vendor finds the gangster Honda in the baseball stadium, Murakami tries to rush to him immediately even though the game is still in full swing. So eager to arrest Honda, Murakami cannot see the fifty thousand spectators whose life would be endangered by his reckless action. Sato reprimands him for his myopic carelessness: "Can't you see anything but Honda? Honda is probably armed. We must avoid exposing these spectators to danger. You can't handle a bullet like a foul ball." Murakami's single-minded focus on Honda shows that unlike Sato, he cannot see the larger picture of the situation, which is distorted by his warped perspective.

Murakami's irrational obsession with his stolen gun limits his vision and impairs his ability to work as a detective. As if to underline his metaphorical nearsightedness, in one scene, he is literally presented as a myopic person. Murakami and Sato visit Yusa's sister's shabby house, where the criminal has been staying since he was repatriated. In the backyard is Yusa's wretched hovel. Inside this tiny space, they find a crumpled piece of paper, on which Yusa writes about his sadistic killing of a stray cat and his feeling of desperation. Stepping outside, Murakami examines Yusa's note so intensely that his eyes almost touch the paper's surface. Since in the film there is nothing indicating Murakami's literal nearsightedness, with almost no distance between his eyes and the object of his look, realistically speaking, he would not be able to read what is written on the paper. Rather than an example of the intertextual moment in Kurosawa's film, this peculiar use of Yusa's written text is another instance of a verbal metaphor (Murakami's "myopic" view on the situation) being transformed into a visual image through the representation of the literal meaning of that metaphor ("nearsightedness").[13]

The representation of madness does not stop at the level of the rhetorical figure. Rhetoric is found at the heart of madness itself. In *Stray Dog*, madness is not silence or the lack of language. Nor is it manifested as an unintelligible series of words. Instead, madness lies inside language as language's difference from itself. Neither a psychological nor a physiological phenomenon, madness is first and foremost a figural event. After the second holdup, at a police station, a reporter asks Sato, "What about a suspect [*hoshi*]?" Sato rhetorically evades the question by saying, "We can't see any stars [*hoshi*] tonight because of clouds." A wipe leads to the next scene inside a train, where Sato and Murakami are discussing Yusa's next move. Looking outside, Sato says, "It looks like coming tonight." Caught off guard, Murakami responds, "What? Who is coming?" Murakami misunderstands Sato partly because Sato does not say *what* or *who* is coming. In Japanese conversation, the subject of the sentence is often not mentioned. But Sato's following remark, "Who? I meant there's going to be a shower," makes Murakami realize that he confused the literal and figural meanings. Immediately after this mistake by Murakami, we hear the following conversation between them:

Sato:	Cops who are all nerves are no good.
Murakami:	I feel like I'm about to break down.
Sato:	It looks as though you already have.
Murakami:	(silence)
Sato:	I think the most important moment has come. The guy already killed a person. Look, killers are like mad dogs. Do you know how a mad dog acts?
Murakami:	(silence)
Sato:	There is even a *senryu* [satirical seventeen-syllable poem] about them: "For a mad dog's eyes, there is only a straight road."
Murakami:	(silence)
Sato:	Yusa can no longer see anything but a straight road. Yusa is in love with Harumi. Yusa can only see Harumi. He'll certainly come to Harumi's.

The interplay of not only the literal and the figural but also language and image is emphasized by the visual composition of the scene. During this conversation, Sato and Murakami are standing next to the train's front glass window, through which we can see a railroad track stretching out straight in front of the train. By forcing us to see the straight road and thus positioning us as a mad dog, *does the film try to implicate us in the madness of rhetoric?*

If a rational mind properly differentiates literal and rhetorical uses of language, madness leads to a constant confusion of the one for the other. In marked contrast to Murakami's ineptness, Sato can use language freely, correctly, and even playfully. The only time Sato shows his vulnerability is in the scene at his house where he tries to use the phrase *apure geru (après-guerre),* which refers to the Japanese postwar generation. Never comfortable with this expression, every time he tries to pronounce it, he stutters, and Murakami, who can say it smoothly, corrects Sato's pronunciation. According to Sato, there are two types of *apure geru:* genuine (Murakami) and phony (Yusa). Throughout this scene, there is the sound of croaking frogs, which is used by Sato as another occasion for a wordplay to "master" the foreign expression and dismiss Yusa and a phony *apure geru* simultaneously. First, Sato substitutes *gaeru* for *geru* to make a new phrase, *apure gaeru,* whereby *gaeru* or its original form *kaeru* means "frog." Next he transforms this phrase into another one, *akire keru,* which means "dumbfounded." Besides "frog," *kaeru* or its variant *keru* also means "to return," "to turn inside out," "to be reversed," "to change," "to turn," "to substitute," and so on. During the war, Murakami saw so many ordinary people turning literally into "beasts" for simple reasons. In the extreme situation of the war, the cruel, ugly, and despicable side of humans come to the surface, and what is regarded as a metaphorical expression in an ordinary situation becomes a literal description. For Murakami, the word "beast" is a signifier for the ambiguity of difference between normal and abnormal, rationality and insanity, reason and madness. In contrast, Sato uses rhetorical figures of animals to align himself firmly with the first terms of these binary oppositions. He rhetorically plays with the names of animals to domesticate or neutralize what Murakami actually experienced in the war.

The Rhetoric of Visuality

One of the most conspicuous aspects of *Stray Dog* is the excess of visual images. The reflecting surfaces of mirrors, shop windows, and glass divide reality into fragments of images. Often, the camera is deliberately placed in such a way that various objects deny our view of characters. At a shooting gallery, moving targets in the foreground conspicuously block our view of Murakami in the background. At the coffee shop "Conga," Honda's woman stands behind an aquarium with some goldfish. In the scene at Sato's house, a blurred image of trees in the foreground creates frames within the frame, which separates Murakami from Sato. The revue theater's backstage is cluttered with nets and stairways. The characters' views are also obstructed by stairs, pillars, plants, trees, and electric and handheld fans. In almost every scene, there are reed screens, bamboo blinds, or string curtains, which not only function as visual distractions but also create multiple shades and shapes of shadow.

The existence of miscellaneous objects is naturalistically justified by the opening voice-over ("It was a very hot day"), but the use of shadows and distracting objects is simply too excessive to be appropriated by the logic of realism completely. In addition to creating a reality effect, the placement of visual obstacles in the foreground seems to have several different functions. First, since nothing is clearly in view, we are forced to decipher actively what is on the screen. The visual obstacles draw our attention away from the center of narrative action in the background and force us to *read* the scene instead of immersing ourselves in the diegetic illusion. By obstructing our vision, the film makes us conscious of our own act of perception. Second, reality is not transparently present, and the film apparatus cannot mechanically reproduce reality that simply exists out there. In cinema, objects are not mechanically represented; instead, only an illusion of objects is created through manipulation of light and shadow. What seems to be the excessive use of shadows in *Stray Dog* highlights the material condition of cinema's existence; that is, rather than functioning merely as visual obstructions, shadows are foregrounded as the necessary terms for visibility. Third, the proliferation of shadows transforms the screen space from a kind of transparent container into a heterotopic space of competing meanings and functions. When Murakami, Sato, and other detectives are waiting for the result of the crime lab's investigation at the police station, all types of shadows—vertical and horizontal stripes, and lattice patterns of various kinds—are cast over the detectives' faces and bodies and the walls. These shadows divide the screen space into not only foreground and background but also multiple planes, some of which are parallel, some angular to the screen surface. The filmic space here is not a sum of two-dimensional planes located at different distances from the camera; instead, it gives us an illusion of a three-dimensional space consisting of various sizes and shapes of cubical blocks. By creating a sense of volume, the filmic space acquires the dimension of tactility. Finally, the cluttered screen space is part of the film's rhetorical strategy that problematizes the dichotomy of the literal and the figural. The idea of visual obstacles is somewhat misleading because it presupposes the existence of something that is obstructed. Trees, plants, or staircases appear to be obstacles only if we assume that the characters' action is the central focus of a scene. But once we discard this character-centered view of the narrative, visual obstacles start to appear as something else. Just like the case of literal and figurative meanings, the difference between the figure and the ground collapses as they are constantly reversed and conflated with each other.

The excess of visuality is perhaps most conspicuously present in the black market sequence, where mise-en-scène and editing are masterfully combined to create a sheer sense of energy, chaos, and superfluity. Murakami, disguised as a jobless ex-soldier just repatriated from abroad, wanders through the searching for his stolen handgun. Lasting about nine minutes with almost no dialogue, this black market sequence is the result of a complex image-sound editing. Wipes, dissolves, and superimpositions are used with maximum effect to create an impression of fragmentation in fluidity. Close-ups of feet, faces, eyes, and other fragmented body parts dominate the screen space, and the camera movement within each shot and the position and distance of the camera in relation to the filmed objects constantly change. The sense of density and fragmentation is not created by the visual image alone. The sound track is a masterpiece of montage using the natural sounds of the black market—human voices, a loudspeaker, the sounds of trains and cars, and so forth—and discrete segments of contemporary popular songs. As in the editing of the visual image, these diverse types of sound are masterfully superimposed over, and juxtaposed with, one another to form a kind of *musique concrète*. All of these characteristics, which squeeze so much information into each shot and series of shots, contribute to the creation of the sense of disorder and dynamic energy.

Critics have reacted strongly to the black market sequence: for some, this sequence is what makes *Stray Dog* artistically so successful;[14] for others, too muddled and unnecessarily long, it shows Kurosawa's immaturity as an auteur or his technical miscalculation.[15] According to Kurosawa's original plan, this sequence was supposed to be much shorter and constructed very differently: the screen was to be divided into four segments, each showing the seedy sides of Tokyo's major districts, Shinjuku, Asakusa, Shibuya, and Ueno, and at the center of the screen the overlapped image of the detective searching for his gun.

This original plan was abandoned because, with a typhoon approaching Tokyo, Kurosawa thought he did not have enough time to shoot all the necessary scenes in multiple locations.[16] This anecdote tells us that Kurosawa had a much different design for dealing with the narrational problem of how to show Murakami's search for the gun. But we cannot use the anecdote as evidence for Kurosawa's directional mistake in the finished film.

The sequence opens with the appearance of Murakami in the black market in the form of his image reflected in the shop window. At first, because of the composition of the shot, we think Murakami is approaching us, or walking from the screen's background to the foreground. Only when he stops in front of the shop window and sees his reflection in the glass do we realize that we have been watching the reflected image of Murakami. At the very beginning of the sequence, it is clearly registered that in the diegetic world of *Stray Dog*, image and reality are confusingly intertwined, and that it is the task of the film's audience to learn how to distinguish the one from the other. Moreover, the confusion of image and reality produces another effect, the creation of the double or doppelgänger. As the close-up of Murakami's eyes indicates, in the following part of the sequence, Murakami becomes a pure sensory receptor, and his split subjectivity is further fragmented into pieces of perceptual effects. In this montage sequence, where the black market is presented as a milieu of pure perception, we are bombarded with pure sensory stimuli and debris of fragmented subjectivity. Whereas in many other parts of the film, the juxtaposition of word and image problematizes the consistency of the diegesis, here it is the excess of audiovisual fragments that disrupts the diegetic unity. What Murakami must do is to reconstruct audiovisual fragments into some kind of totality that enables him to understand his situation and recover a clear sense of who he is. To remap bits of perceptual information for the purpose of reconstructing the entire view of a situation is necessarily inseparable from the simultaneous reconstruction of subjectivity and what Gilles Deleuze calls the extraction of a question from the situation.[17]

It is important to stress that the black market sequence is not a random aggregate of fragmentary images depicting scenes of postwar chaos and atmosphere or showing Murakami's pain. Instead, through metonymic references to key incidents from Murakami's past, the sequence inscribes the ambivalence of Murakami's subjectivity on its textual surface. The split image of Murakami at the sequence's opening announces the beginning of his journey to the past, and as the sequence progresses, Murakami relives the past and experiences a kind of life that he might have chosen to live.[18] One of the most significant segments occurs in the middle of the sequence as follows:

1. Medium shot of Murakami walking toward the camera diagonally from screen left to the center. In the middle of the screen is a large advertising banner that reads "Kodan Kurabu."
2. Overlap. Long shot of a freight train moving horizontally from right to left.
3. Cut to medium-long shot of a freight train, maintaining the same movement but shot from a low camera position. In the foreground are a man's (presumably Murakami's) legs, partially blocking our view of the train.
4. Dissolve to long shot of a crowded alley, which vertically extends from the screen's background to the foreground. Policemen are running after a group of men.
5. Dissolve to long shot of another crowded alley. Murakami walks from right to left.
6. Dissolve to medium shot of customers wolfing down food at a makeshift food stand. The camera pans right to show Murakami, who simultaneously eats and watches out for his surroundings.
7. Dissolve to medium tracking shot of homeless men sitting by the roadside. The camera is very close to the ground, and the angle is also extremely low. As the camera moves from left to right, we see a shingle on a utility pole saying "Muraki Clinic." The camera finally stops and shows Murakami among the sitting men. A policeman in uniform taps Murakami on the shoulder. Murakami takes his ID out of his bag, and the policeman salutes him and walks away.

As the shot breakdown shows, this short segment is a narrative figure for Murakami's immediate past. The overlapping images of Murakami and the train are a metonymic signifier of his experience of having his knapsack stolen on a train immediately after repatriation. The synecdochic image of shot 3 gives us an illusion that Murakami has just gotten off the train. The dichotomy of the police and criminals is introduced in shot 4, and shot 6 presents Murakami ambiguously in relation to this dichotomy. The ambiguity of Murakami's identity is emphasized in shot 7 by the uniformed policeman questioning him. It is only when Murakami shows the policeman what appears to be his ID that Murakami's identity as a detective is restored. At the same time, however, the sign "Muraki Clinic" in the same shot problematizes Murakami's identity at a different level. The sign belongs to a series of textual details that establish a close connection between Murakami and Yusa's girlfriend, Harumi. The name "Muraki" is written in two Chinese characters, the first of which is identical to the first character of the name "*Mura*kami" and the second to the second character of Harumi's last name, "Nami*ki*."

Name and Textuality

The name of the criminal, Yusa, is rather unusual. The racketeer's mistress says during questioning by the police that she couldn't read the name on a rice ration card because of difficult Chinese characters. What is foregrounded by her remark is the question of legibility of writing as sign and of Yusa as a character. Yusa is a rebus, which needs to be deciphered as a "miniature allegory scripted into the film."[19] His full name is Yusa Shinjiro.[20] "Shinjiro," 新二郎, literally means a "new, second son" or "new, second man." Yusa's first name, therefore, resonates with the film's important motifs: the first character draws our attention to the newness of postwar Japan and, by implication, to the question of historical continuity and discontinuity; the last two characters belong to the chain of signifiers that posit the relationship of double (二) between two (二) male (郎) characters, Yusa and Murakami. If we focus on the pronunciation, "Shinjiro" can also mean "believe," so that the first name becomes part of another important narrative motif, the question of ethical standards and individual choice. The last name "Yusa" consists of two Chinese characters, 遊佐. The first character means "to play," "to wander," or "to float around," and the second signifies "to help." Thus, the name "Yusa" suggests two opposite possibilities of action: to float around without committing oneself to any constructive purpose (Yusa), or to help others realize a better future (Murakami). The difficulty of reading the name 遊佐, as experienced by Honda's mistress, is therefore the difficulty not only of understanding Yusa's character but also of making a right choice. As in the case of the first name, what is equally important is the sound of the characters. If we reverse the order of the two characters, the new combination can be pronounced "sayu," which, if written with different characters (左右), means "left-right." Yusa is left-handed, and this fact plays a pivotal role in Murakami's identification of Yusa in the film's penultimate sequence. Inside a waiting room at a train station, Murakami must identify Yusa, whom he has never seen before, among some dozen young males. The moment of their mutual recognition finally comes when Yusa lights up a cigarette with his left hand.

The last but not the least important aspect of the name "Yusa" lies in its inscription of the historical context. Although *Stray Dog* was made in occupied Japan, there is no overt reference to this sociopolitical situation because of strict censorship by the American Occupation forces. As if to elude the American censorship, the film contains a number of textual details and figures that allude to the shadow of America. The film displaces the dichotomy of Japan and the United States with that of signifiers of Japaneseness and democracy. Instead of directly showing images of the American armed forces, the film foregrounds such words and phrases as *jinken jurin* ("a violation of human rights," Ogin's favorite phrase) and *heiwa* ("peace" as in Heiwa Taxi). Japaneseness is in turn emphasized by the names of hotels: Sakura (cherry blossom) Hotel, which is called Metro Hotel in the original script, Azuma (east) Hotel, and Yayoi Hotel (Yayoi is the name for Japan's prehistoric period, ca. 300 B.C.–A.D. 300).[21] The American censorship is inscribed on the textual surface of the film in the image of Yusa's personal note as a self-reflexive allusion. Yusa's writing is significant not only because it shows his disturbed state of mind but also because it contains a number of blacked-out mistakes, which cannot but remind us of school textbooks in the immediate postwar years. As Carol Gluck writes, the "Americans immediately forbade 'false history,' ordering children to ink out passages about sacred emperors and sacrificing samurai from their textbooks. They suspended historical instruction in the schools and began their censorship of the press."[22] Finally, Yusa himself is strongly marked by the signifiers of America. The anonymous criminal becomes Yusa when his identity is revealed by his rice ration passbook, or *beikoku tsucho:* the word *beikoku,* 米穀, means "rice," but its homonym *beikoku,* 米国, signifies the United States of America. Is the persecution of the criminal (Y)usa an unconscious textual inscription of the imaginary resistance against the U.S.A.?[23]

Fetishism as Intervention

Murakami's obsession with recovering his gun is gently criticized by his superiors as too excessive. From the police's standpoint, the recovery of Murakami's gun is far less important than arresting underground gun dealers and confiscating their guns. From the narratological perspective, too, the central focus on Murakami's gun and the number of bullets left do not enhance the reality effect. Even though Kurosawa's use of the number of bullets is sometimes praised as an effective means of creating suspense,[24] like Japanese film critic Futaba Juzaburo, I believe its artificiality as a narrative device merely draws our attention to the peculiarity of Murakami's obsession and the somewhat ponderous pace of the narrative progression.[25] Marked as unnatural both narratologically and diegetically, Murakami's obsession with his gun is best characterized as fetishism and the gun as a phallic symbol. Banal as it may sound, this interpretation is amply supported by the film's textual details.

The most obvious example of these details can be found in the opening sequence. The first line of the film after the voice-over ("It was a very hot day") is the chief detective Nakajima's exclamation: "What! You had your pistol stolen?" Immediately after this abrupt opening, there is a flashback to the firing-range scene. Murakami has just finished his practice and is talking with his colleagues:

Detective A:	What's your score?
Murakami:	It's really bad. I didn't sleep last night because of a stakeout.
Detective B:	Were all bullets lost? [*Minna dankon fumei ka.*]

Left, Namiki Harumi (Awaji Keiko); *right,* Detective Murakami (Mifune Toshiro). *Photo courtesy of Photofest.*

Murakami:	No, a bullet hit a stump right above that target.
Detective A:	Why don't you go home and sleep? Your eyes are really red.
Murakami:	But everything looks yellow.

The Japanese word for "bullet mark," *dankon,* also means "penis" or "phallus," so that *dankon fumei* (a bullet lost) can be understood as "a phallus lost." Thus, syntactically, a direct connection is made between the loss of a pistol and the loss of *dankon,* that is, a phallus. The connection between the two is further reinforced by the following flashback scene, in which Ogin steals Murakami's Colt on a crowded bus. It is significant that even though gangsters who control the underground gun market are all presumably male, the pickpocket who actually steals Murakami's pistol is a middle-aged woman, Ogin. Wearing heavy makeup and reeking of cheap perfume, Ogin is a castrating woman who emasculates the novice detective.

The entanglement of gun and sexuality is explicitly presented toward the end of the black market sequence when Murakami mistakes a woman at a shooting gallery for an underground gun dealer.

Murakami:	I need your help.
Woman:	Do you have money? It's expensive. We have a good collection of women [*tama*].
Murakami:	How many bullets does it have?
Woman:	Eh?
Murakami:	How much?
Woman:	For a short play . . .
Murakami:	What?
Woman:	Don't you want a woman?
Murakami:	Tut! What I'm looking for is this [showing his right hand imitating the shape of a pistol].
Woman:	You're barking up the wrong tree.
Murakami:	Don't lie to me! My friends told me about this place.
Woman:	Get out of here, or I'll call the police!

Murakami starts the conversation by asking the woman what appears to be a simple question, yet they both interpret it in completely different ways. She thinks Murakami's questions are directed toward her as a manager of prostitutes, not as an attendant at the shooting gallery. A toy rifle for her is only a metaphorical figure standing for sexual intercourse in exchange for money. For Murakami, however, it is a mimetic sign, signifying a real rifle through its iconic verisimilitude. The object of his desire is not a prostitute as metaphorically represented by a toy rifle but a real gun and bullets. Murakami's confusion is further compounded when the woman uses the word *tama*, a pejorative word for women, which also literally means "bullets." Here Murakami again confuses the figural and the literal, and his mental instability or inability to make a correct rhetorical distinction is directly linked to the state of his emasculation.[26]

In the penultimate sequence of the film, Murakami directly confronts

Yusa and, after being shot in the left arm, finally recovers his Colt. Diegetically, the film's treatment of this scene is rather unnatural, but it does unambiguously underline for the last time Murakami's obsession with the gun, whose symbolic significance far exceeds even his duty of capturing the criminal Yusa. Does the successful recovery of the gun mean that Murakami also regains his masculinity? Not really. First of all, we must remember the relationship of Murakami and Yusa as each other's double. To the extent that Yusa is Murakami's alter ego, Murakami's arrest of Yusa by his own hand as a criminal registers the moment of a permanent loss instead of that of a triumphant recovery of his unified self. Even though Murakami regains the phallic symbol, as we will see shortly, Yusa at the same time continues to remind him of lack traversing his subjectivity. Second, the film constantly reminds us of the relationship of identification between Murakami and Harumi, a revue dancer at the Blue Bird theater. The opening voice-over implies that Murakami had his pistol stolen because he was tired; similarly, Sato tells Murakami that Harumi refused to answer Sato's question, broke down suddenly, and cried out loud because she was tired. The outburst of Harumi's "irrationality" (i.e., a frenzied spinning move wearing the expensive dress given to her by Yusa) is closely followed by Murakami's nervous breakdown at the hospital where Sato is brought after having been shot by Yusa. Harumi informs Murakami that Yusa is waiting for her at the local train station in the early morning, and Murakami goes to the station in her place. And as we have already seen, Murakami and Harumi are merged into one identity in the sign "Muraki Clinic" in the black market sequence. To see *Stray Dog* as a narrative of loss and recovery of masculinity does not quite take into account these textual details, which mark Murakami with the value of femininity throughout the film.

If the narrative of *Stray Dog* cannot simply be reduced to that of restoration of masculinity, is there also a need to reexamine the status of Murakami's gun as a phallic symbol? If the gun is not simply a phallic symbol, how exactly does it function in the textual economy of the film? The objective of the police is to apprehend the criminal who committed armed robberies and a murder using Murakami's stolen gun. Moreover, Murakami's superiors Sato and Nakajima are much more interested in arresting a racketeering ring and seizing illegal guns to stop violent crimes than in finding the specific gun that belongs to Mura-kami. For Sato, the theft of Murakami's gun is ultimately not important because Yusa would have used any other gun he could lay his hands on. What is ultimately important for the police, which believes its mis-sion is to protect the safety of the general public, is not to identify the specific gun used by Yusa but to stop the circulation of all illegal guns on the black market. In the last scene of the film, Sato tells Murakami: "Thanks to your Colt, we seized more than a dozen handguns from Honda." Sato sees Murakami's gun as an initial investment that is used to maximize a profit later. Although as a detective Murakami shares the same objective of arresting the criminal, his quest does not exactly coincide with that of the police force as a whole. Whereas the police as a state apparatus is determined to maintain law and order, Murakami is much more eager to recover his own gun at all costs. Murakami's fe-tishistic obsession with his own pistol does not necessarily contribute to the achievement of the police's mission; in fact, instead of solving the case, his careless action ends up producing more victims.

To understand how Murakami's fetishism functions in the overall economy of the film's narrative, we must introduce another type of fe-tishism, the Marxian notion of commodity fetishism. As our discussion so far indicates, what underlies the film's treatment of the gun is a dis-course of economy and the market. Murakami's Colt is, for the police, just a gun, which is interchangeable with any other gun circulating in the underground gun market. But for Murakami, his Colt is a unique gun that is absolutely irreplaceable. To this extent, Murakami is a fe-tishist. But does this make him a commodity fetishist?

It is important to note that somebody who fetishizes a certain com-modity in a psychoanalytic sense is not necessarily a commodity fe-tishist. Slavoj Žižek explains commodity fetishism as follows:

The *value* of a certain commodity, which is effectively an insignia of a network of social relations between producers of diverse com-modities, assumes the form of a quasi-"natural" property of another thing-commodity, money: we say that the value of a certain com-modity is such-and-such amount of money. Consequently, the essen-tial feature of commodity fetishism does not consist of the famous replacement of men with things ("a relation between men assumes the form of a relation between things"); rather, it consists of a certain misrecognition which concerns the relation between a structured network and one of its elements: what is really a structural effect, an effect of the network of relations between elements, appears as an immediate property of one of the elements, as if this property also belongs to it outside its relation with other elements.[27]

Commodity fetishism does not simply present value as a natural property of things. Nor does the mere inversion of the networks of social relations and its effect constitute commodity fetishism. What is fetishized in commodity fetishism is not any thing-commodity but money as the embodiment of value; that is, commodity fetishism arises when value is regarded as a natural property of money. For the social relations and their effect to establish an inverted relation in which the effect appears to be an autonomous thing existing even outside of the social relations, the materiality of money-form, or what Žižek calls money as a "sublime object," is necessary. Money establishes the general equivalency between qualitatively different things. The capitalist money economy incessantly violates the logical distinction of literal and figural. On the one hand, money functions as a mere sign, a token, a label for value. In itself, money does not have any value (literal). On the other hand, money also functions as the embodiment of value (figural). Money is simultaneously a particular commodity (literal) and a general equivalent for all the commodities (figural). Even though in itself it has no value, money is not a mere sign or token for value. Without money, the value-form does not appear. This is the materiality of money-form as a sublime object.

W. J. T. Mitchell argues that

> Commodity fetishism can be understood, then, as a kind of double forgetting: first the capitalist forgets that it is he and his tribe who have projected life and value into commodities in the ritual of exchange. "Exchange-value" comes to seem an attribute of commodities even though "no chemist has ever discovered exchange-value either in a pearl or a diamond." . . . But then, a second phase of amnesia sets in that is quite unknown to primitive fetishism. The commodity veils itself in familiarity and triviality, in the rationality of

purely quantitative relations and "natural, self-understood forms of social life."[28]

But how can we *remember* the underlying social relations among producers of commodities? Here, conscious remembering is not enough, since as Marx said, "it is not the consciousness of men that determines their being, but, on the contrary, their social existence determines their consciousness."[29] One cannot avoid being a commodity fetishist just by recognizing that money is only a sign without any intrinsic value while at the same time constantly being engaged in the act of exchange in everyday life; that is, understanding of commodity fetishism often ends up in fetishistic disavowal ("I know very well, but. . ."), not in "remembering."

It is here that Murakami's fetishism of the gun becomes important. His refusal to admit the interchangeability of guns, and by implication the determination of the value of his gun through the logic of equivalency, is absurd if we understand it naturalistically. But his obstinate denial of interchangeability and exchangeability can be interpreted as a gesture of resistance against commodity fetishism and the logic of the market. As Murakami fetishizes and pursues one specific gun, he encounters resistance at strategic points of social networks, which commodity fetishism refracts and transforms into the object of disavowal. Murakami's fetishism shows us a possibility of real remembering in the system where society forgets the inversion of social relations and its effect precisely through the conscious act of remembering by its constituting members. If Murakami remembers, his memory is not in his thought but in his action.

The Dialectic of Memory

When the detective Murakami visits his superior Sato's house in the middle of the film, his eyes are caught by certificates of award hung on the living-room wall. Sato has been commended a number of times for arresting criminals during his more than twenty years of service as a detective, and Murakami is apparently impressed by his mentor's past distinctions. As a *senpai* who is much more experienced on the job and in the art of living, Sato benignly tells his junior colleague over a bottle of rationed beer not to feel too responsible for the stolen gun and not to lose his temper. Here is another representation of the master-pupil relation so frequently found in Kurosawa films. In this peaceful interlude, Sato is unambiguously presented as a good role model, a surrogate father figure for Murakami to emulate.

But as we examine the scene more closely, our attention is drawn to something else on the wall, the date of one of the certificates: the seventh year of Showa, that is, 1932. We cannot but wonder what it means to be a good cop in 1932, nine years before the beginning of the Pacific War, when Japan was increasingly becoming militaristic, and the special secret service police was arresting, jailing, and persecuting intellectuals and others for their allegedly subversive activities. The date of the certificate makes us rethink Sato's confidence in the absolute difference between good and evil. Without any hesitation, Sato tells Murakami that good is always good while evil is always evil, and that as a good cop, he simply hates evil. As far as Sato is concerned, there is no ambiguity involved in the distinction of good and evil. However, if much of what was called evil in prewar Japan is no longer evil, how can he justify his absolute view on morality? Sato, a model cop during the times of militarism, is still working as a detective after the war. (Let us not forget that Shimura Takashi, who plays the role of Sato, appears in *No Regrets for Our Youth* as a wicked detective nicknamed *dokuichigo,* or "poisonous strawberry.") How can he be a "good cop" in postwar Japan if he really believed that what he was doing for the repressive government was right? How does he justify his act of changing ideological positions or conversion? The only way he can justify his actions, it seems, is to relegate his responsibility as an individual to the social circumstances; that is, he used to be a good detective working for the militarist government, and now he is a defender of democratic society because this is just the way the social circumstances have forced him to act. According to the unspoken logic discernible in his actions, Sato does not act by his own will but lets the circumstances decide what he should do.

In contrast, Murakami at first seems to be a relativist, more ambivalent about making any absolute moral judgment. Murakami, the detective, sees his double in Yusa, the criminal. As ex-soldiers, both were in similar positions in the chaotic situation of the immediate postwar years, and Murakami thinks that by some quirk of fate he could have ended up a criminal like Yusa. The black market sequence in the film starts with the reflection of Murakami in the shop window, which indicates not only the splitting of Murakami's subjectivity but also the presence of his double continuing to haunt Murakami in the rest of the film. Murakami and Yusa are literally presented as a mirror image of each other in the scene in which they directly confront each other for the first time. In the waiting room of a train station, Murakami has to pick out Yusa from among several suspicious men without knowing what he looks like. What connects the two characters in the scene is their behavior. Murakami anxiously surveys the waiting room while holding a cigarette with his left hand. Eventually one of the young men sitting on the opposite bench lights a cigarette with his left hand. At that moment, their eyes meet, and Murakami and Yusa instantaneously recognize each other. The near identity of Murakami and Yusa takes the form of literal indistinguishability in the penultimate scene of the film where they fight each other in the mud, and we cannot tell for a moment which is Murakami and which is Yusa. At the same time, however, the more the similarities between Murakami and Yusa are emphasized, the clearer the difference between them becomes: the existence or absence of a strong individual will defying the imposing forces of the social circumstances. What separates Murakami from Yusa is not his innate goodness but his willingness to confront the new social circumstances squarely and to decide on the course of his action, for which he is ready to take full responsibility. Thus, in the case of Murakami, the question of the absolute standard is displaced by that of the individual as a responsible agent of an independent action.

The question formulated by the film is this: do we act in the way we do because of our individual will or because of social circumstances over which we do not have absolute control? On the one hand, by stressing the fundamental difference between Murakami and Yusa, Sato rejects a theory of the environment creating individuals; however, by implicitly justifying his own conversion as an inescapable result of the changing social circumstances, Sato ends up denying the existence of any absolute, unchanging standard differentiating good from evil. By continuously being a "good cop" in prewar and postwar Japan, Sato acts as a practical relativist in spite of his own theory. On the other hand, Murakami's sympathy for Yusa aligns Murakami with relativists who do not acknowledge any absolute set of moral standards. But he ultimately rejects the relativist theory of morality by introducing the element of individual will. According to Murakami, what needs to be affirmed is not the absolute standard unaffected by the environment but the responsibility of the individual, who should not blame the social circumstances for the result of his or her action. In other words, on the axiomatic level of the narrative, there is a chiasmastic relation of reversal between what Sato says to Murakami and what he actually does in his own life, and what Murakami says to Sato and how he actually acts.

The paradoxical relationship of belief and action is inseparable from the question of memory. In *Stray Dog*, there are two types of memory, and Sato and Murakami appear as representatives of each type. Early in the film, immediately after Murakami reports the loss of his handgun to his superior, he goes to the record-keeping section to look for information about a possible suspect. In this scene, we see towering card cabinets on both sides of aisles. Looking at one card, detective Ichikawa tells an assistant that the pickpocket recorded on that card just died and asks him to dispose of it. The card boxes are the official memory machine, whose functional orientation allows only necessary and useful storage of information about the past. Because many of the criminals whose records are kept in the card boxes were active before the Japanese defeat in 1945, the record room also functions as a memorial to the bygone days. Even when he randomly picks up information cards, what Ichikawa sees there are all familiar faces. As his use of the word *natsukashii* indicates, he is looking back on the past nostalgically. The sense of nostalgia evoked here is further heightened in the following scene, in which Ichikawa and Murakami visit the woman pickpocket Ogin at a loach restaurant in the old downtown section of Tokyo *(shitamachi)*. They cross a river by boat to get to this area, where the war-ravaged city still preserves traditional architecture and the culture of the common people. Even though they are still in modern-day Tokyo, it is almost as if they were making a time trip to the distant past, and the peaceful sound of a small boat's engine reinforces the sense of nostalgia. The nostalgic feelings are heightened not only by the decor and locale but also by the personal history of Ogin, who is spatially and culturally displaced in the postwar Japanese landscape. Before the war, she used to wear a kimono and steal money in the *shitamachi* area. In the midst of the postwar chaos, however, her appearance has completely changed. In tawdry Western-style dress, she has heavy makeup, and her hair is permed; and instead of money, she now steals something that she never touched before, handguns. Yet the film does not present Ogin only as a symbol of negative effects produced by Japanese militarism and defeat. She is also an image of a liberated woman who is no longer bound by patriarchal customs and rules. The whole episode about Ogin ambivalently acknowledges the changing times and articulates the nostalgia for the years before militarism. This kind of complex intertwining of the acceptance of the present and the yearning for the past shares a peculiar resonance with a dramatically different film made in the same year, Ozu's *Late Spring*. And the mixed feeling toward Japan's past and present is much more melodramatically exploited in the films of another Shochiku director, Kinoshita Keisuke, who was regarded as a rival of Kurosawa in the immediate postwar years.

"All kinds of things happened since I received my first salary twenty-five years ago," says Sato. While nostalgically remembering his own past, Sato urges Murakami to forget about Yusa. Sato's behavior demonstrates that the functionality of the official memory and the sense of nostalgia are not contradictory to each other. The official memory urges us to forget certain things in order to grow; otherwise, it says, we would lose our mind or, like Murakami, suffer a nervous breakdown. And nostalgic feelings facilitate a selective process of remembering and forgetting by relegating any disturbing elements to the repressed past securely cut off from the present, that is, by beautifying the past as an object of nostalgic longing. Sato does not feel torn between belief and action because he replaces the dialectic of remembering and overcoming the past with the static system of nostalgic longing and forgetting.[30] For Sato, memory is not really a part of lived experience but the skeletal remains of what once was. Sato reifies the past as the referent and his consciousness as an autonomous existence. The dialectic of temporality is frozen, and the historical process of social transformation is replaced by the natural process of inevitable change. As Richard

Terdiman argues, to the extent that memory is not the work of reproduction but that of representation, by definition, memory is inseparable
from the forces of change, transformation, and intervention. As a form
of representation, memory acknowledges human action's contingency,
that is, its historicity. The loss of memory leads to the acceptance of the
present as a natural state and that of the past as a historical relic. For
Sato, there is a clear separation between sign, referent, and consciousness. His "mastery" of language or ability to differentiate grammar and
rhetoric unambiguously leads to his belief in his existence outside of
historical time as an autonomous consciousness. What is overlooked is
that the relationship of sign to referent is always mediated by subjectivity. In our experience, there is no referent untouched by the forces of
representation; that is, there is no experience without the transformation of the world into signs. At the same time, however, the world is not
a mere text or collection of signs at our disposal, and there is no autonomous consciousness that can freely manipulate and interpret signs
for its own pleasure. By reifying signs and consciousness, Sato creates
an illusion of autonomy from the past and social forces at work in the
present.

In marked contrast, for Murakami, the past is not an object of nostalgia but is vividly alive in the present. A lingering remnant of the past
first appears in his language, in the way he refers to himself as *jibun,*
which is the way he was taught to speak in the army. Murakami disguises himself as a returned soldier and descends into the chaos of the
black market immediately after Ogin's remark "Oh, look. How beautiful. For the last twenty years or so, I've completely forgotten there are
such nice things as stars." Whereas for Ogin remembrance of the past
marks a moment of nostalgia, Murakami is not allowed to indulge in
similar feelings toward the past (see, for instance, Murakami's peculiar
facial expression when Ogin makes this remark; he does not seem to
understand why she is talking about stars so longingly). In the black
market sequence, Murakami disguises himself as a homeless veteran.
Yet because he was a returned soldier, he is not really in disguise but
plays the role of himself. Instead of looking back to the past with a
sense of nostalgia or regret, Murakami must come to terms with the
past by reliving it. For Murakami, who is constantly forced to ask questions about the relationship of the past and the present, the former is

not closed off from the latter and does not exist in complete autonomy; instead, the past is open-ended, acquiring meanings only through his active intervention in the present condition.

Murakami and Yusa are returned soldiers *(fukuinhei)*, who, like the well-known folktale figure Urashima Taro, come back from a distant place to their native land to find the familiar world unfamiliar and thus feel totally alienated.[31] Even though they have made diametrically opposite choices in the midst of the postwar chaos, Murakami's and Yusa's psyches are deeply wounded by their war experiences. Even in the case of those who seem to have adjusted themselves well to the radically changed social condition, the scars left by the war have not completely disappeared. Sei-san is a womanizing bellboy who hangs around with his war buddy Yusa in order to get to know Harumi, Yusa's childhood friend, who works as a revue dancer. But this Americanized ex-soldier has not completely forgotten his military experience. When Murakami and Sato go to Sakura Hotel to question him, Sei-san is in the bathroom, preparing a bath for a customer. Sei-san is obviously frightened by Sato's high-handed manner and, like a soldier in front of a sergeant, stands at attention. Sato sardonically tells Sei-san: "You must have been beaten a lot in the army, but don't worry. This is not the army." While playing with the shower, Sato continues to ask the returned soldier questions about Yusa. Instead of reassuring us that he does not have any intention of hitting Sei-san, Sato's remark and demeanor produce the opposite effect. It looks either as if Sato is capable of hitting or even torturing this delinquent with hot water if necessary or as if he did actually abuse crime suspects in the past. The whole scene of confrontation between Sato and Sei-san is imbued with sinister atmosphere, and the excess of mise-en-scène and acting not only cast doubt on Sato's past and moral integrity but also inscribe on the film's textual surface the wartime experience of returned soldiers.

The repatriated soldier is a familiar figure in Kurosawa films. Yuzo in *One Wonderful Sunday,* Matsunaga in *Drunken Angel,* Fujisaki and Nakata in *The Quiet Duel,* Kamada in *The Idiot,* and the protagonist of the episode "Tunnel" in *Dreams* are all returned soldiers.[32] But these films and *Stray Dog* do not necessarily show what kinds of difficulties returned soldiers face once they try to readapt themselves to a chaotic yet "normal" society. Instead, through the representation of the repatriated soldier, Kurosawa raises the question of memory and its suppression in the construction of democratic society. Noma Hiroshi, one of the leading postwar writers who emerged in the Occupation period, argues that in postwar Japan, returned soldiers were treated as stray dogs, abandoned by both their former master (the emperor) and their new master (the democratic government supported by GHQ).[33] According to the official discourse of the Occupation authorities and the Japanese government, Japan was reborn as a completely new country that absolutely renounced its past militarism and determined to uphold the principles of liberty, democracy, and world peace. In this new society, there was no room for returned soldiers, who were perceived as nothing more than the refuse of the past militarist decade. Caught in the gap between "the Great Japanese Empire" and "Democratic Japan," returned soldiers were social outsiders. Their alienation was further compounded by the fact that those politicians and bureaucrats who had supported and worked for the militarist government were still in power, now preaching the value of freedom and democracy. Despite the visible transformations and changes, deep down, nothing had fundamentally changed in postwar Japan, and the celebration of democracy was often superficial. Moreover, the alienation of returned soldiers occurred not just in the public but also in the private sphere. When released from the army, they were expected to illegally take some military goods home; if they didn't, their families were openly disappointed. Even for their own families, returned soldiers were sometimes unwelcome outsiders who were valuable only as a source of food and material goods.[34]

In *Stray Dog,* Yusa appears as a return of the repressed, something many Japanese simply wanted to forget, and what the official discourse tried to erase. Yusa must be repressed for Japanese to be able to believe in the radical newness of postwar democratic Japan or to continue the incomplete project of imperial Japan as if nothing had happened in the last few decades. At the very end of the film, Sato urges Murakami to forget Yusa, but Murakami is still reluctant to follow Sato's advice wholeheartedly. It is by concluding the film with Murakami's hesitation that Kurosawa urges us to remember the past and use memory as a moment of intervening in the present social condition.

11. *Scandal*

Scandal (Sukyandaru [Shubun], 1950), Kurosawa's first film for Shochiku, is a social protest film indicting the irresponsibility of yellow
journalism. The tabloid magazine *Amour* publishes a faked-up story
titled "The True Love Story of Saijo Miyako." Aoe Ichiro (Mifune Toshiro), a young painter featured in the article as a secret lover of the
popular vocalist Miyako (Yamaguchi Yoshiko, aka Shirley Yamaguchi/
Li Hsian-lan/Ri Koran), decides to sue *Amour* and its owner, Hori,
for libel. When Aoe's decision to fight back against the verbal violence
of irresponsible journalism is publicized in the newspapers, he is ap-
proached by the lawyer Hiruta (Shimura Takashi), who volunteers to
work for him as a defense counsel. Although almost everything indicates Hiruta's incompetency and questionable character as a lawyer,
Aoe in the end decides to hire him after meeting his daughter Masako,
whose pureness convinces the painter that the squalid lawyer is not
really a bad person. However, contrary to Aoe's expectation, Hiruta
easily yields to temptation and accepts a bribe from Hori in exchange
for agreeing to sabotage his own client's defense. When Hori's victory
in court is about to be sealed, Masako dies of tuberculosis, believing
that her father would not do anything wrong and hurt Aoe. Hiruta's
conscience awakens at the last moment, and he changes his mind and
exposes Hori's and his own corruption in front of judges.

The strict control over speech and writing during the war, coupled
with the extreme shortage of printing supplies in the final days preceding the defeat, made it impossible for people to get access to information except the mindless messages of the government propaganda.
Thus, to satisfy Japanese demand for true information and knowledge,
as soon as the war ended with the Japanese defeat, numerous magazines
of all kinds were newly created or restarted.[1] Many of these magazines
seriously investigated Japan's immediate past and examined the prob-

lem of postwar democracy. However, a deluge of short-lived magazines meant that there were also a number of dubious publications that tried to boost their sales by publishing sensational articles and by manufacturing celebrity scandals without any consideration for the rights to privacy. To some extent, Kurosawa's film, which deals with the violence of yellow journalism and rampant commercialism, was ahead of its time. It was not until the late 1950s that Japanese cinema began to analyze the problems of media, image, and consumption seriously (e.g., Masumura Yasuzo's *Giants and Toys* [Kyojin to gangu, 1958]). Yet despite the timeliness of its subject matter, *Scandal* is one of Kurosawa's least convincing films. It is marred by the shift of focus from the violence of tabloid journalism to the conversion of the petty, corrupt lawyer. When Hiruta's daughter Masako appears, the film shifts gears, and the focus of the story from that moment on is Hiruta's moral struggle. Falling short of squarely dealing with the expansion of the media as a social problem, *Scandal* lapses into sentimental melodrama.

One of the recurrent motifs of the film is the question of imitation and the relation of reality and image. In the opening scene, three woodcutters watch Aoe painting a picture of Mount Kumotori, and they comment on the painting's strangeness. When one of the woodcutters says that he has never seen such an eccentric painting, Aoe says that it is his own unique painting, and it is perfectly natural that it does not resemble anybody else's. To another woodcutter's protest that Aoe's Mount Kumotori is too red, he replies that the mountain has reminded him of a red mountain existing in his mind. Immediately following this scene, Aoe tells Miyako that people say he imitates Maurice de Vlaminck by riding a motorcycle; however, they think he imitates Vlaminck because they themselves do nothing but imitate others. The truth cannot be revealed simply by imitating reality; instead, it must be discovered by the sincere effort of an autonomous individual. This critique of imitation is further developed in the treatment of the film's central theme, the manufactured scandal. If Aoe's "unrealistic" painting captures a certain truth about Mount Kumotori, what appears to be a faithful reproduction of reality, a secretly taken photograph of Aoe and Miyako together, gives us a false impression about the true nature of their relationship. The ambiguity of the photographic image is exploited by the tabloid magazine, which publishes the picture of Aoe and Miyako with suggestive captions and concocted stories. Yet *Scandal* does not in the end fully explore the tension between language and image at the textual level. Nor does it sufficiently develop the ambivalent relationship of image and reality as a thematic motif.

12. *Rashomon*

The original script of *Rashomon* (Rashomon, 1950), possibly the best-known Japanese film outside Japan, was written by Hashimoto Shinobu, who first became interested in the art of film script when he was hospitalized for tuberculosis. In his hospital bed, he started writing scripts and sent them to the director Itami Mansaku. After Itami's death in 1946, Hashimoto met one of Itami's disciples, Saeki Kiyoshi, who in turn introduced the writer to Kurosawa. Kurosawa was shown some of Hashimoto's scripts, and one of them caught Kurosawa's attention. It was an adaptation of Akutagawa Ryunosuke's short story "In a Grove" (Yabu no naka, 1921). The script was too short to be made into a feature-length film, and Hashimato was asked to expand the script further. To respond to Kurosawa's request, Hashimoto decided to add to his original script another Akutagawa story, "Rashomon" (Rashomon, 1915), consisting of three confessions by the bandit, the wife, and the husband. It was Kurosawa's idea to create a new character, the woodcutter, as an eyewitness to the crime. The final version of the script was written by Kurosawa alone.

"In a Grove" consists of four testimonies at the police and three confessions by the parties concerned. All of these micronarratives are presented as they are narrated by the individual characters; that is, Akutagawa does not attempt to create a coherent structure out of the testimonies, which are merely juxtaposed to each other as autonomous fragments. The lack of a framing narrative emphasizes all the more each character's egotistic self-defense or aggrandizement, but not necessarily the relativity of truth.[1] "Rashomon" features a samurai's former servant trying to decide whether he should become a thief for his own survival. On top of the Rashomon gate, he sees the eerie scene of an old woman pulling out the hairs of a corpse. The former servant's initial fear and hatred toward the woman's evil evaporate when the woman justifies her own hideous act by pointing out the deception of the dead whose hairs she is collecting in the name of survival. At this point, no longer tormented by the moral dilemma, he robs the old woman of her clothes and disappears into the night.

How does Kurosawa combine these two unrelated stories? Kurosawa's film incorporates the thematic content of "In a Grove" more or less intact (only the testimony of the victim's mother is omitted)[2] but completely rewrites "Rashomon." Gone are the protagonists of the story, the samurai's former servant and the old woman. What the film retains is the story's physical setting, the Rashomon gate, and a general social background of chaos and devastation. The film also borrows the motif of "stealing" from Akutagawa's story. But even these borrowed elements are thoroughly modified or transformed into something completely different. For instance, the social chaos of medieval Japan is clearly presented in the original story. In fact, it is the indispensable background against which the story of the jobless man and the old woman is narrated. In the film, we hear about social chaos and disorder from the priest, but except for the dilapidated Rashomon gate, there is no other concrete image of social collapse and violence that corroborates the priest's remark. The nature of the chaos and devastation is also slightly different in the story and the film. The original story states: "For the past few years the city of Kyoto had been visited by a series of calamities, such as earthquakes, whirlwinds, and fires, and Kyoto had been greatly devastated."[3] The causes of Kyoto's devastation in the original are not man-made but natural disasters. In the film, as is evident in the priest's remark, the world is becoming like a hell not only because of natural disasters but also because of human greed and savagery: "Oh, you're right. Wars, earthquakes, great winds, fires, famines, plague — each new year is full of disaster. And now every night the bandits descend upon us. I, for one, have seen hundreds of men dying, killed like animals. Yet . . . even I have never heard anything as horrible as this before. There was never anything as terrible as this. Never. It is more horrible than fires or wars or epidemics — or bandits."[4]

The film underlines the man-made nature of the social chaos. What leads humans to destroy themselves is egotism. At the same time, what saves humans comes from themselves, too. Egotism must be countered by human compassion, honesty, and altruism. Otherwise, the world would become like the dilapidated Rashomon gate, from which, according to the commoner, even demons have fled because they are horrified by humans. The film is unequivocal about its assertion of this central theme. Even though the appropriateness of the ending, where the woodcutter decides to raise the foundling as his own child, has been the cause of a heated debate among critics in Japan and abroad, it does not at all ruin what is achieved by the rest of the film. Is the sentimentality of the ending too much? Yes. But so is the expression of doubt and fear by the priest and the woodcutter. As many critics have pointed out, there are places in *Rashomon* where the tone of narration is unnaturally serious. The film opens with shots of the Rashomon, under which the woodcutter and the priest are taking shelter from the pouring rain. The first line of the film is the woodcutter's remark, "I can't understand it. I just can't understand it at all," which is repeated several times in the rest of the film. Both the woodcutter and the priest look ponderous and serious. The woodcutter's expression of perplexity and the priest's pronouncement on the sin of human egotism are very unnatural, exaggerated, and theatrical in a bad sense—in short, hardly convincing. Thus what many see as the film's excessively sentimental and contrived ending is not an abrupt shift in, or unnecessary addition to, the narrative; on the contrary, its unnaturalness exactly corresponds to the theatrical artificiality of the film's opening. Hardly a "mistake" by Kurosawa, the ending remains fairly consistent with the rest of the film. In fact, the affirmation of humanity at the final moment as a narrative pattern is similarly found in Kurosawa's other films from the same period. In *Stray Dog,* the temptation to look for easy money and to blame society for one's misfortune is repeatedly denied as the narrative approaches the final resolution. In the last scene, detective Sato unequivocally reasserts the difference between good and evil in his attempt to convince the novice detective Murakami that criminals with egotistic desire are only a minority in society. At the final moment of *Scandal,* the unscrupulous lawyer reforms during the trial by exposing the opponent's and his own corruption.

Audiovisual Abstraction

What makes *Rashomon* such a special film is first and foremost its formal experiment, particularly its audiovisual form and narration. The focus of the film is how the story is presented as much as what it is about. To give the film a sense of formal unity and coherence, Kurosawa extensively relies on the power of geometric abstraction, simplification, and juxtaposition of extreme opposites, which create symphonic rhythm and architectonic beauty. Take, for instance, the use of the number three as a key structural element. The film's narrative unfolds in *three locations* (the Rashomon, the courtyard, the forest); in each location, there appear *three principal characters* (the woodcutter, the priest, and the commoner at the gate, and the bandit, the wife, and the samurai or the medium in the forest and in the courtyard); a *three-day interval* passes between the testimony scenes in the courtyard and the recounting of those scenes at the gate; and on the gate's signboard are carved *three Chinese characters* that read "Rashomon."

A more important feature of the film's formal organization can be found in the juxtaposition of vertical and horizontal compositions as a dominant visual motif. In the scenes at the Rashomon, vertical lines structure the screen space: the vertical movement of the rain from top to bottom, the gate's vertical structure, the vertically tilting camera. In contrast, horizontal lines and bands dominate the superbly composed testimony scenes. What strikes us in these scenes is the contrast of light and shadow. The surface of the screen is divided into six horizontal bands. In front are the witnesses testifying in shadow; behind them is sunlit white gravel, where the woodcutter and the priest remain sitting throughout the testimonies of the bandit, the wife, and the medium; then there is a courtyard wall, which is divided into three horizontal strips of light and shadow; and finally above the wall spreads a sunny sky with columns of clouds. The width of shadow on the ground and on the wall changes, indicating the passing of time. The courtyard scenes are connected to the scenes of the Rashomon not only through the juxtaposition of horizontal with vertical but also through visual rhyming: the courtyard's horizontal bands are rhymed by the close-ups of stone steps in the gate scenes.

And the horizontal and vertical compositions come together in the forest scenes. The vertical lines of trees are juxtaposed with the horizontal movement of Kurosawa's signature shot, a series of swish pans following the bandit and the samurai's wife running in the forest (cf., *No Regrets for Our Youth, Seven Samurai, The Hidden Fortress,* etc.). Light and shadow, which give a compositional stability and variation to the courtyard scenes, are instead used to visually represent the complexity of the human mind. Miyagawa Kazuo's superb cinematography shows the photogenic beauty of human faces crisscrossed by the intricate and ever-changing patterns of light and shadow. And the extraordinary effect of Miyagawa's camera work (e.g., the woodcutter's first flashback, where his simple walk in the woods is transformed into a virtuoso dance by Miyagawa's cinematography) is further multiplied by Hayasaka Fumio's hypnotic musical score.[5]

Narration in Film

How does Kurosawa deal with the problem of narration? Akutagawa's "Rashomon" is a reflexive story, calling attention to the fact that it is not a transparent presentation of what happened at the Rashomon but a narrated story. The story begins as follows:

> One early evening, a samurai's servant stood under the Rashomon, waiting for a break in the rain. No one else was under the wide gate. On the thick column, its crimson lacquer rubbed off here and there, perched a grasshopper. . . . A short while ago, the author wrote, "a samurai's servant stood under the Rashomon, waiting for a break in the rain." But the servant had no particular idea of what to do after the rain stopped. Therefore, rather than saying "a samurai's servant stood under the Rashomon, waiting for a break in the rain," it is more appropriate to say, "Confined by the rain, a samurai's servant was at a loss with no place to go." And the weather also contributed to the Sentimentalisme of this Heian Age servant. The rain, which had started in the late afternoon, seemed unlikely to stop. Thus, he was lost in thoughts of how to make his living tomorrow. While thinking what to do with something that is useless to think about, he had

been aimlessly listening to the pattering of the rain on the Sujaku Avenue.[6]

As is apparent in this passage, Akutagawa's story has a metadiegetic narrator, who intrudes into the story by referring to himself as the author *(sakusha)*. The presence of the metadiegetic narrator is further foregrounded by the phrase "the *Sentimentalisme* of this Heian Age servant." Instead of transliterating the French word *sentimentalisme* into Japanese letters, Akutagawa uses it as is, thus creating a strange contrast between the words "Heian Age" (*Heiancho*) and "Sentimentalisme," ancient Japan and the (modern) West. The presence of this French word also clearly registers the status of the story as a modern reinterpretation, rather than a simple reproduction, of an old tale.

In Kurosawa's film, Akutagawa's anonymous but intrusive narrator is replaced by two diegetic characters, the woodcutter and the priest. Moreover, the film tries to incorporate the reflexivity of the original story by introducing another character, the commoner, whose presence reminds us that the film focuses not only on the question of human egotism and altruism but also on the problem of narration and storytelling. Like Akutagawa's servant, the commoner is a diegetic character, whose self-centeredness must be counteracted by the woodcutter's compassion and altruistic act. But the commoner also functions as a metafilmic character, to whom the priest and the woodcutter narrate their stories. The commoner is a surrogate figure for the film's audience, who are interested not in hearing a sermon but in watching an interesting story (e.g., the commoner's remarks: "Look here now, priest, let's not have any sermons. I asked some questions because it sounded like an interesting story"; "Good heavens! Not another sermon! I don't mind a lie or a trivial story as long as it's interesting"). Moreover, even though the woodcutter and the priest are storytellers, the film's visual composition makes them appear as the audience's surrogate figures, too. In the courtyard scenes, the witnesses' testimonies are presented in two different manners. The less typical of these is found in the scene of the samurai's testimony through the medium's mouth. In this scene, the magistrate's presence off-screen is implied, and the lack of a shot showing his presence does not make us nervous. All the rest of the testimony scenes are, however, constructed quite differently. In these more typical scenes, the witnesses all sit on the ground frontally facing toward us without directly looking at the camera. They are presumably looking at the magistrate, whose presence is assumed only through their reactions. The medium shots of these witnesses cue us to expect a reverse shot showing the object of their look, but the reverse shot never appears in the film. As if to compensate for the lack of the reverse shot, the film shows instead the woodcutter and the priest, who sit silently in the background of the courtyard as witnesses to the testimonies. Because of their position and the direction of their look, the woodcutter and the priest become the mirror image of the film's audience.

Rashomon was regarded as an incomprehensible film during its production and after its release. Nagata Masaichi, the idiosyncratic president of Daiei, which produced the film, and Kurosawa's assistant directors expressed their bewilderment over what the film was about. One of the assistant directors, Kato Tai, who was a nephew of Yamanaka Sadao and later became a significant director in his own right, reportedly clashed with Kurosawa constantly during the shooting. Ironically, the incomprehensibility of a narrated story is precisely a major theme of the film. By saying, "I can't understand it," Nagata, Kato, and others were captured by the film's rhetorical effect, putting themselves in the position of the woodcutter and the priest, the surrogates for the audience. Precisely by performing the role of the bewildered spectators, they "correctly" responded to the film without realizing it.

Some criticize *Rashomon* for its allegedly uninventive use of flashbacks, which do not reflect the characters' biases and subjectivities clearly. Apparently, the bandit, the wife, and the husband are all lying to some extent. There are many discrepancies between their versions of what happened in the woods, yet the film does not include any clearly marked details that enable us to determine the truth value of (segments of) their stories. This kind of criticism misses the point of the film's narration, since what is foregrounded in *Rashomon* is not the question of the characters' reliability as narrators but the question of the reliability of narration in image. It is possible to construct the characters' flashbacks in such a way that by carefully comparing their testimonies, we can determine the extent to which each character falsifies the truth. The logical discrepancy between flashbacks is certainly not difficult to create. What is almost impossible to problematize is the overwhelming reality of visual image as representation. By not constructing any complex logical scheme underlying the testimonies of the defendants and witnesses, Kurosawa foregrounds the fundamental affirmativeness of narration in film image. If *Rashomon* has an optimistic outlook, it is not necessarily because of its affirmation of human compassion and goodness but because of its jubilant celebration of film as a medium of storytelling.

This does not mean that *Rashomon* is devoid of any connections to the immediate sociopolitical context of its production. It was, after all, made in Occupied Japan, only five years after the Japanese defeat in World War II. The tumultuous conditions of wartime and postwar Japan can easily be compared to the chaotic situation depicted in the film set in the late Heian period. Kurosawa said that he wanted to show a large crowd at the film's opening. According to his unrealized plan, there is a black market in front of the Rashomon; the rain starts to fall, and as it becomes a downpour, the crowd run away in all directions; the three characters take shelter under the gate and start telling stories about the rape and murder incident.[7] This unrealized version of the film would have made much more explicit the connection between the film's narrative and the contemporary situation of Japan under the Occupation. In the existing version of the film, the fact of the Occupation is most clearly registered in the absence of the magistrate in the courtyard scenes. Even though all the principal characters seem to be answering the magistrate's questions, we neither see him nor hear his voice. Consistent with the overall design of the film, the censoring eyes of the Occupation are formally inscribed on the film's textual surface as structural absence.

13. *The Idiot*

In 1951, after the lukewarm success of *Rashomon,* Kurosawa ventured on his next ambitious project, the film adaptation of Dostoyevsky's novel *The Idiot* (Hakuchi). It is widely accepted that *The Idiot* is a failure because as an adaptation it is too superficially faithful to Dostoyevsky's original. It is often regarded as a preliminary exercise for a masterpiece to follow, *Ikiru,* a film based on an original script, yet, according to a critical consensus, more faithful to Dostoyevsky's spirit.[1] Time and again, critics have declared that Dostoyevsky's novels are impossible to adapt to film because they do not include many descriptions of physical environment and observable objects; that is, the predominance of dialogues and psychological descriptions makes Dostoyevsky's novels unsuitable for film, which must show characters' inner psychology mostly in concrete visual images. Detractors of the film also argue that there is a fundamental difference between nineteenth-century Russia and contemporary Japan: the lack of deep-rooted Christian traditions in Japan makes it difficult to move the setting of the novel to Japan without destroying the reality effect of the original; the physical landscape of Hokkaido is in the end different from that of Russia despite some resemblance between the two; and Dostoyevsky's characters are so utterly un-Japanese in their psychology and behavior — for instance, many critics insist that in Japan there is no woman like Nasu Taeko (Nastasya Filippovna in the novel, played by Hara Setsuko in the film).

The Idiot was the second film Kurosawa agreed to make for Shochiku, but the relationship between the two was severely damaged because of their dispute over who should have a right to the final cut. Kurosawa originally edited the footage to a four-hour-and-twenty-five-minute version, but Shochiku pressured him to cut the length to two hours and forty-six minutes. The truncated version was regarded still too long for a commercial release, and Kurosawa was pressured to edit more scenes out of the film. On hearing Shochiku's unreasonable demand, Kurosawa finally lost his temper and challenged Shochiku to cut the entire film in half lengthwise. Thus the existing film does not really convey the true sense of what Kurosawa tried to achieve. Although it is not unusual for a finished film to diverge from its original script, in the case of *The Idiot*, the difference between the film and the script is so extensive and artistically unjustified that it is not particularly fair to Kurosawa to discuss the available version of the film as a satisfactory realization of his artistic vision. For instance, the extensive use of intertitles and voice-over in the film, which is construed as evidence for Kurosawa's inability to capture the feeling of Dostoyevsky's novel, was not in the original script. Instead, they were inserted into the existing version by Kurosawa as a result of Shochiku's demand that he cut the film's length drastically.[2]

As important as it is, this production background is not the only reason why most negative judgments about *The Idiot* are problematic. For instance, is Kurosawa's adaptation indeed faithful to the original text by Dostoyevsky? Richie argues that "Kurosawa's faith in his author was so strong, and so blind, that he seemed to feel that the mere act of photographing scenes from the novel would give the same effect on the screen as they do on the page."[3] Similarly, Prince writes: "So strongly dialogue-bound an author seems to have compelled Kurosawa to work at the level of the actors' performances, not of the image. With very few exceptions, the scenes are staged as they appear in the novel."[4] But what exactly is the "mere act of photographing scenes from the novel"? How is it possible to do that in the first place? Is such a transparent translation of the novel into film possible? As my analysis of *Stray Dog* shows, Kurosawa is so well aware of the complex relationships between verbal discourse and visual representation that he would be the last filmmaker to believe naively in the possibility of simply "photographing scenes from the novel." It is certainly possible for us to compare the film and the novel closely by enumerating as many differences and similarities as possible. Yet unless we first establish some criteria by which we can differentiate a simple transposition of words into photographic images from a complex adaptation of the former to the latter, a mere comparison of Kurosawa's film and Dostoyevsky's novel (or to be more precise, its Japanese translation) does not tell us whether Kurosawa in fact photographs the novel's verbally represented scenes faithfully. Kurosawa's adaptation can be used as an occasion to ask some fundamental questions concerning translation between different artistic media, cultures, and historical periods, but critics who slight *The Idiot* avoid addressing these questions. The extremely harsh judgment or simple dismissal of the film confirms prevalent interpretive codes of Japanese cinema criticism. Japanese adaptations of Western texts are often regarded as mere imitations; it is only when some uniquely Japanese codes of traditional culture are mixed with great Western originals that Japanese adaptations become worthy of praise and appreciation (e.g., the Western reception of *Throne of Blood*).

One thing that clearly stands out in *The Idiot* is the extensive use of close-ups showing the actors' faces. Although Kurosawa is blamed for relying so heavily on the close-up,[5] I agree with Sato Tadao that the faces of the principal actors, those of Mori Masayuki and particularly Hara Setsuko, are extremely beautiful and even sublime.[6] Admittedly, Kurosawa does not use Hara's potential as much as Ozu does in his postwar films (e.g., *Late Spring* [Banshun, 1949], *Early Summer* [Bakushu, 1951], and *Tokyo Story* [Tokyo monogatari, 1953]).[7] Ozu in general prevents his actors from showing off their acting skills, and he tries to get rid of any unnecessary expressions and movements from their performances in order to distill their own natural qualities as actors. In his relationship with actors, restraint becomes a dominant mode of direction, so that sometimes it looks as if Ozu prohibited actors from acting at all. Yet the result is truly astonishing when his direction is successful, as in *Tokyo Story,* where Hara Setsuko subtly shows an extraordinary range of complex feelings and emotions. We can recognize on the face of Hara what Béla Balázs calls the "polyphonic play of features," whereby "a variety of feelings, passions and thoughts are synthesized in the play of the features as an adequate expression of the multiplicity of the human soul."[8] Ozu's treatment of Hara is especially remarkable because her physiognomic features tempt Japanese directors to take an opposite approach; that is, her large eyes and clear-cut features for a Japanese — compare her face, for instance, to the face of Tanaka Kinuyo — give directors a misleading cue that the best way to realize her talent is to make her overact rather than underact. Although Ozu remains aloof from this temptation, Kurosawa seems to succumb to it. In marked contrast to Ozu, Kurosawa exaggerates his actors' performances and idiosyncratic mannerisms as much as possible, and his use of Hara in *The Idiot* is no exception. (Let us note here that there is nothing intrinsically "Japanese" about Ozu's formalistic restraint; nor is there anything "Western" about Kurosawa's penchant for dynamic exaggeration.) Kurosawa tries to use Hara's unique physiognomic features through overacting and exaggeration partly to destroy the fixed screen image of Hara as a young lady of good breeding.[9] But instead of increasing the expressive possibilities of Hara's face, Kurosawa's strategy seems to suppress all those possibilities. To this extent, various critiques of Hara's performance in *The Idiot* are not completely unfounded. Yet what is important is that precisely because of the suppression of subtle expressivity, Hara's face is purified, and only a single emotional tone remains on her face. What appears on her face is the sense of noble sublimity that cannot be violated by any external forces. The uniqueness of Hara's performance can be clarified by comparing her to Kyo Machiko, who plays the role of the samurai's wife in *Rashomon*. Kyo Machiko can express as wide a range of feelings and emotions as Hara Setsuko, but there is a fundamental difference between the two as actresses. Even when she plays the role of a noblewoman, Kyo Machiko always has a touch of the common woman. What we see on the face of Kyo is the raw energy of a commoner who never gives up at a time of extreme adversity. In contrast, whether she plays the role of a commoner or a woman in a compromising situation, Hara Setsuko's face expresses a nobility of spirit. What Hara brings to the role of Nasu Taeko in *The Idiot* is this sense of spiritual nobility, which I believe is captured in the close-up images of her face, even though—or sometimes precisely because—her facial expression is strained and exaggerated. Hara Setsuko as an actress will probably not be remembered for her role in *The Idiot*. But the film *The Idiot* will remain unforgettable for, among other things, the performance and close-up face of Hara.

14. *Ikiru*

Point of View and Subjectivity

In 1952, with the international success of *Rashomon* behind him, Kurosawa returned to Toho for the first time since 1948 to make *Ikiru* (Ikiru). The film's protagonist is Watanabe Kanji (Shimura Takashi), head of City Hall's Citizen's Section, who accidentally learns that he has less than six months to live because of stomach cancer. The film follows Watanabe's existential search for meaning in his life, and his coworkers' and immediate family's search for the reason why Watanabe suddenly changed in the last five months of his life. *Ikiru* has attracted the attention of many critics mainly for two reasons. First, the film deals with the existential question of how to confront death squarely and find meaning in one's life. Second, the film presents this story in a complex narrative structure created by flashbacks, voice-over narration, and narrative ellipses.

From the beginning of the film, the point of view as such is foregrounded. The first image of the film immediately following the opening credits is the close-up of an x-ray picture, which is accompanied by the following voice-over narration: "This is an X-ray picture of a stomach; it belongs to the man this story is about. Symptoms of cancer are there but he doesn't yet know anything about it."[1] There is nothing strange about the voice-over itself. It is a kind of omniscient narration routinely used in documentary and conventional fiction films. What is mysterious is the visual image, the x-ray picture of the stomach. What is the rhetorical status of this image? Where does this x-ray come from? Shortly thereafter, Watanabe goes to the hospital and has his stomach x-rayed. But the opening x-ray picture is clearly different from the second one. In the former there is a black shadow only in the pyloric region, but in the latter the shadow spreads over a much larger area of the stomach. When and by whom was the first x-ray picture taken? Although the film does not give us any information about the picture, we see Watanabe taking medicine at his desk in the opening scene. It is therefore possible to speculate that Watanabe went to the hospital before and had his stomach checked by a doctor. But this hypothesis is not too convincing because the first x-ray picture shows that Watanabe's stomach cancer is still treatable, so that if Watanabe had gone to see a doctor and had his stomach x-rayed, his cancer would have been medically treated, very probably surgically removed. We know that this did not happen, and therefore it is difficult to connect the origin of the first x-ray picture to Watanabe's hypothetical prior visit to the hospital. In other words, the opening x-ray image of Watanabe's stomach is an "impossible" image whose origin cannot be accounted for diegetically. By starting with this impossible image, the film immediately calls attention to the problem of point of view. It also shows that the omniscient narration functions differently in sound and image. What the omniscient narrator says in words is relatively easy to accept without scrutinizing where those words come from; in contrast, what the omniscient narrator shows in concrete visual images can be more problematic, especially when it presents an x-ray picture of a character's stomach, which splits the unity of the omniscient camera into the invisible x-ray camera and the camera showing the x-ray picture on the screen.

After the opening x-ray picture, the scene moves to the Citizen's Section of City Hall. A group of women come to ask the city to do something with an unsanitary drainage near their houses. The camera follows the receptionist Sakai, who walks from the reception window to Watanabe's desk to ask what to do with the women's request. Watanabe mechanically replies, "The Public Works Section." The camera moves back a little and shows a quarter view of Watanabe's upper body facing screen right. At this point, the voice-over returns to tell us that it is still boring to talk about Watanabe because he is not really living. Suddenly there is the lively laughter of a young woman. Startled, Watanabe looks up to see the direction from which the laughter is coming (shot 1). The following is a shot breakdown of the rest of this segment.

2. The camera shows the entire Civic Section from the side of the reception window. In the foreground is Sakai, sitting facing screen right, and in the background is Watanabe at his desk, facing toward the camera.
3. The same as shot 1. Watanabe starts taking off his glasses.
4. The same as shot 2. Match on action. In the background, Watanabe takes off his glasses. Assistant Chief Ono stands up in the background right and reprimands Odagiri Toyo for laughing so loudly during working hours. Toyo says somebody in the office is circulating a joke published in the newspaper. Ono orders her to read it aloud. Toyo starts standing up.
5. The camera has moved 90 degrees counterclockwise. Match on action. Toyo stands up. Now facing the camera, she reads the joke and then starts sitting down. The joke itself goes as follows: "You've never had a day off, have you?" "No. Why?" "Are you indispensable?" "No, I just don't want them to find out they can do without me."
6. The camera has again moved 90 degrees counterclockwise, showing the Civic Section from Watanabe's side. In the foreground is Watanabe's back, and Sakai in the background; that is, this is the reverse image of shot 2. Match on action. Toyo sits down.
7. The camera shows Watanabe at his desk frontally. He puts on his glasses and, as if nothing has happened, goes back to work.

The camera shows Watanabe raising his head from the desk to see what all the commotion is about, but the scene is constructed in such a way that the look of Watanabe and the look of the camera do not coincide with each other. Watanabe is consistently denied the subject position of the look; instead, he is placed in the position of the other's look. By displacing Watanabe's reaction to the joke with his subordinates' embarrassed yet curious gaze toward Watanabe in shot 6, the camera rhetorically suggests that the joke is on none other than Section Chief Watanabe. This is confirmed later in the sequence when his subordinates speculate about why he is absent from the office for the first time in thirty years. The absence of Watanabe's point-of-view shot indicates that he is not all that interested in what's going on in the office. The most important thing for him is, according to the voice-over, "to keep busy simply to stay where he is." It also establishes that in the rest of the film, Watanabe will be the object of the look of his coworkers, the omniscient narrator of the voice-over, and the film's spectators.

This does not mean that Watanabe continuously remains only the object of others' observation. One of the first signs of Watanabe's subjectivity appears in the scene right after his visit to the hospital. Watanabe is absentmindedly walking on the street, now firmly convinced that he is dying of cancer. On the wall behind Watanabe are many identical posters, advertisements for "Morinaga Penicillin Ointment." The medical reference reminds us of the immediately preceding scene at the hospital, and the word "penicillin" also emphasizes the incurability of Watanabe's disease. The introduction of penicillin after the war saved numerous Japanese from tuberculosis, but Watanabe is forsaken even by that miracle drug. All of a sudden, the roaring sound of a truck and construction noise rush in, making us realize that this eerie scene has been until this point without any sound. Kurosawa manipulates the sound track in such a way that not only the interior psychological state of Watanabe is figuratively articulated but also the film's spectators are led to identify with Watanabe's interiority.

In the following scene, however, the film deliberately breaks up this emphatic relation of identification between Watanabe and the spectators by presenting a misleading point-of-view shot of Watanabe's house at night. Accompanied by the sound of walking, the camera slowly moves toward the front door of the house, and we assume that the shot represents the point of view of Watanabe coming home. The manipulation of sound in the previous scene has firmly established our identification with Watanabe, and the use of wipe, rather than a simple cut, between the two scenes subtly helps to maintain this identification by deliberately making us conscious of temporal ellipsis as a red herring. Therefore, when we hear the voices of a young man and woman, we are mildly surprised. What we thought was the point-of-view shot of Watanabe turns out to be that of his son, Mitsuo, and his daughter-in-law, Kazue. By deliberately betraying our expectation, the film calls our attention to its rhetoricity and the fragility of Watanabe's subjectivity.[2]

Confession

Watanabe's conviction that he is going to die of stomach cancer leads him to a desperate search for meaning in his life. First he turns toward his son for sympathy and care, but the son's inattentiveness merely disappoints him and throws him into a state of panic and despair. He tries to, but cannot, commit suicide by taking sleeping pills because an empty feeling inside prevents him from taking a final step. What torments Watanabe is not necessarily his fear of death but his feeling that his life has been a total waste of effort. Watanabe desires to desire but does not know exactly what he is looking for. Then, at a shabby drinking stall, he meets a writer and asks him to show him how to enjoy life. The writer jokingly refers to himself as a good Mephistopheles who does not ask for payment. The irony is of course that unlike Faust, Watanabe cannot pay him anyway because he is already destined to die in six months or so. The writer kicks a black stray dog at the stall's entrance, and Watanabe's Walpurgis Night begins. They spend a night together playing pachinko, drinking beer and whisky, dancing, and watching a strip show. In the expressionistic sequence of Tokyo's nightlife, Watanabe is bombarded with all kinds of sensory stimuli including neon, street noise, music, a crowd, and so forth. Mirrors are used to disorient our perception of scenes' spatial unity, and Watanabe and the writer are often filmed through visual obstacles of neon signs, openwork screens, lattice-patterned fences, and short hanging curtains made of strings of beads. This fantastic world of audiovisual overload mesmerizes Watanabe. When he sees the naked body of a stripper on the stage, he roars with joy and stops the traffic by bawling and walking in the middle of the road. Despite the release of his repressed energy, however, Watanabe cannot in the end find solace in drinking and dancing with bar hostesses. The close-up of his ghostly face in the alley and his miserable face on the following morning show that Watanabe's pursuit of carnal pleasure in Tokyo's nightlife has been a futile attempt to find fulfillment in his life.

Why is it that the guide who plays the role of a drunken Mephistopheles is a writer, not a doctor, petty lawyer, yakuza, or *sarariman*? The writer shows a keen interest in Watanabe when he starts talking about his stomach cancer and his feeling of emptiness. The writer offers to help Watanabe enjoy life with the following words:

> You know, you're very interesting. I know I'm being rude, but you're a very interesting person. I'm only a hack writer, I write trashy novels, but you've made me really think tonight. I see that adversity has its virtues — man finds truth in misfortune; having cancer has made you want to taste life. Man is such a fool. It is always just when he is going to leave it that he discovers how beautiful life can be. And even then, people who realize this are rare. Some die without ever once knowing what life is really like. You're a fine man, you're fighting against death — that's what impresses me. Up until now you've been life's slave, but now you're going to be its master. And it is man's duty to enjoy life; it's against nature not to. Man must have a greed for life. We're taught that that's immoral, but it isn't. The greed to live is a virtue. Let's go. Let's find that life you've thrown away. Tonight I'll be your Mephistopheles, but a good one, who won't ask to be paid.[3]

The writer's words, appearance, and demeanor suggest that he is a caricature of a *shishosetsu* writer. For the writer, the meaning of Watanabe's life is not ultimately determined by what Watanabe specifically does in his life. The most important action from the writer's perspective is to confess sincerely and truthfully. By confessing that he will die very soon of stomach cancer, and that he feels his life has been meaningless, Watanabe has, from the writer's perspective, already transcended the futility of life and achieved the privileged status of a martyr or a Christ carrying a cross called cancer ("Ecce homo," says the writer, pointing to Watanabe, to the small bar's hostess).

What is at stake in the sequence and in the film as a whole is the possibility of a truthful confession, and to foreground this motif, Watanabe's guide must be a writer. ("Leave psychological analysis to writers," says Sato to Murakami in *Stray Dog*.) *Shishosetsu*, or the I-novel, is an autobiographical fiction with a strong connection to the writer's own life as a referent. What is valued as a mark of artistic achievement is the writer's willingness to confess his or her authentic self sincerely, to tell the writer's own life as faithfully as possible.[4] Does Watanabe make a confession to the writer? Watanabe states the fact (or to be more precise, his belief) that he will die of cancer very soon, but this is not a confession of his innermost secret. It is not the case that Watanabe carries a dark secret inside himself and in desperation confesses it to the writer. Instead, Watanabe is tormented by the fact that he has nothing to confess, even at the last stage of his life when death is imminent. The writer misunderstands Watanabe and takes Watanabe's painful acknowledgment of his inability to confess as his act of confession. As he spends time with Watanabe, however, the writer begins to realize an unbridgeable gap between his romanticized image of Watanabe as a martyr and Watanabe as he really is. Toward the end of the nightlife sequence, the writer expresses his feeling of repulsion for Watanabe, who appears by this time only as the embodiment of death.

Ikiru much more clearly articulates what *Rashomon* accomplished with its use of multiple threads of narration. *Rashomon* deals with the problem of narration in terms of subjectivity and perspective. It shows that no neutral narration is possible, particularly when the narrators themselves appear in the story that they are narrating. Because of its parallel narrative structure, in which four different characters recount basically the same event in their own flashbacks, *Rashomon* does not thoroughly explore the question of a self-referential narration and can therefore be, and has been, interpreted as a film that examines the question of whether humans are too egotistic and self-centered to tell the truth. *Ikiru* is different from *Rashomon* in that it much more lucidly demonstrates the problematic relation of narration and subjectivity. In *Ikiru*, it is not that the self-centered ego contaminates a self-referential narration or confession to preserve its self-interest. Watanabe's inability to confess his illness to his family does not simply signify that what he wishes to confess is an unspeakable topic, his own death. What *Ikiru* shows is that the self-centered ego or a particular mode of subjectivity does not preexist as a fixed entity; that confession, only a mode of discourse, does not have any privileged connection to truth or the innermost thought and feeling of the subject; and that subjectivity is an effect of the act of a self-referential narration or confession, not the other way around.

Identification

Kurosawa's films are almost always regarded as masculine films. But *Ikiru* shows that this seeming truism does not apply to every Kurosawa film. Throughout *Ikiru,* Watanabe is consistently feminized. His association with femininity is most conspicuously manifested in his muteness. He hesitates, stutters, and often does not complete a sentence. Because he cannot articulate his thoughts most of the time, the close-up of his face becomes as important as what he says. Although he is estranged from everybody including his family, there is one group of people who sincerely appreciate his work and accept him as a member of their group: the women who live on Kuroe Street, where a children's park is being built through Watanabe's extraordinary effort and determination. Watanabe, in fact, becomes one of them, a maternal figure caring for the welfare of children who need a park instead of a stinking drainage. When the women of the Kuroe Street come to Watanabe's wake, they never utter a single word but only cry. In this scene, the identification between Watanabe and the women appears to be complete. Another example of his feminization can be found in the scene in which he requests that the deputy mayor reconsider the proposal for building a children's park. After having told Watanabe to forget about the proposal, the deputy mayor goes back to his conversation with his subordinates and starts talking about a college student who works as a part-time geisha and is ignorant of the protocols and customs of the geisha world. This remark is made precisely when Watanabe breaches bureaucratic protocols and talks back to the deputy mayor, his superior. Thus the film implicitly identifies Watanabe's daring act with the innocence and naïveté of an amateur geisha-student. Watanabe is also feminized through his interaction with Odagiri Toyo. Attracted by her candidness and energy, Watanabe tries to identify himself with Toyo and live a fulfilled life vicariously through this identification.

But it is Watanabe's relationship with Toyo that problematizes the status of identification in the film, for he soon learns that identification with somebody else does not in the end solve his problem. Identification induces a strong emotional response momentarily but does not fundamentally change the identifying subject. (See how Watanabe's co-workers identify themselves with him at the wake but immediately forget their resolve to fight back against bureaucratic inertia.) Watanabe misrecognizes Toyo, who is not a simple, happy-go-lucky girl full of energy and vitality as Watanabe sees her. Watanabe's image of Toyo is put into question mostly through the juxtaposition of Toyo and other young girls and women. For example, in the first coffee shop scene, where Watanabe learns from Toyo the nicknames of his subordinates and himself, she is sitting on screen left, and Watanabe is sitting on screen right. Between them in the background is a young woman who sits near the coffee shop's entrance, facing toward the camera and reading a magazine. Throughout the scene, which is one long fixed shot lasting about two minutes and twenty-five seconds, the young woman occupies the central position of the screen, distracting our attention from the scene's focus, Watanabe and Toyo in the foreground. Considering Toyo's financial situation, she would not be able to come to this coffee shop on her own. The young woman in the background is a subtle yet constant reminder of Toyo's class background that is completely absent in Watanabe's fantasized image of her.[5] (Earlier in the film, when Toyo talks about how tiny her apartment is compared to Watanabe's house, he seems completely oblivious of her remark.) There is another scene of a different coffee shop, which is much larger and fancier. In this last encounter of Watanabe and Toyo, he finally confesses to her that he is dying of cancer. Toyo, who is visibly frightened of Watanabe, does not know what to do with him anymore. In desperation, she takes out a mechanical toy rabbit from her bag and suggests that he make something, too. Watanabe's revelation soon follows, but that is not necessarily the only important moment of the scene, particularly from Toyo's perspective. Before the camera settles on Watanabe and Toyo, it first shows two other adjacent groups of customers. One is a young couple who sit in the foreground and quickly disappear from the scene as the camera moves forward to focus on Watanabe and Toyo. The other is a group of joyous high school girls who are having a birthday party for their friend. They are located in the background across the stairway and a glass wall, which accentuates the separation of their self-enclosed space from the space of Watanabe and Toyo. As in the first coffee shop scene, the details of the mise-en-scène emphasize what Toyo does not have, or cannot be. The couple reminds us that Toyo does not have a boyfriend with whom she can come to a fancy coffee shop. She does not have money, and even time; as she tells Watanabe, she would rather go to sleep early because she is too tired from hard labor during the day. And it is also obvious that she will never be invited to the kind of birthday party she sees across the stairway. Her life has nothing to do with the world of bourgeois girls. As she admits to Watanabe, Toyo enjoys making toy rabbits for babies all over Japan. Yet it is not the case that she is completely satisfied with her economically hard-pressed life. Because he is too preoccupied with his own desperate situation, Watanabe does not see this side of Toyo. Thus Watanabe's identification with Toyo does not solve his problem, not only because he cannot live his life to the fullest extent vicariously through his identification with the other, but also because the object of his identification is not who Toyo really is but who he wants her to be. In this sense, Watanabe repeats the mistake of the writer who romanticizes Watanabe as his object of fantasy, and the film's spectators also end up committing the same mistake by idealizing Watanabe as somebody who finally discovers the meaning of his life. When we recognize our misrecognition, Watanabe begins to reappear as an enigma to us as much as to the film's characters.

Death and Narrative Closure, or the Modality of Not Yet

The first image of *Ikiru* is a close-up of an x-ray photo showing Watanabe's stomach affected by cancer. The accompanying voice-over narration announces the approaching death of the protagonist. Watanabe is obviously stunned when he realizes that he is going to die in less than six months, and that there is nothing he or the doctors can do about it. Literally, there is no hope for Watanabe, whose future is now firmly set, without any possibility of change or the slightest deviation from the fixed course. Watanabe's universe, which seemed infinite and open, all of a sudden collapses. He tries to make sense out of this ruin, to comprehend what the imminent death means for him. In a moving flashback sequence, he remembers various events from his life with his son Mitsuo: Watanabe's wife's funeral, Mitsuo's appendicitis operation, his departure for the war, and so forth. These fragments of memory further accentuate the shadow of death in Watanabe's present situation. In the past, death was something that happened or could have happened to others, but this time, it is different. Watanabe is confronted with his own death, and he realizes that he must deal with his impending death alone.

Moreover, it is not only Watanabe but also the film's audience who are caught off guard by death. Although there is no way of knowing exactly when his death will actually come, we expect Watanabe to die toward the end of the film. Cinematic conventions frequently use a protagonist's death to seal a film's ending, to create a clear sense of narrative closure. Thus when the protagonist of *Ikiru* abruptly disappears about two-thirds of the way through, his death surprises us as something utterly shocking, even though it is totally expected. Death, in the end, comes unexpectedly for everyone. There are elements of anticipation and surprise at the same time. How can the film continue without the protagonist? Both Watanabe and we know that everybody, without exception, will die someday. Yet when he learns his life will be over in six months or so, Watanabe is shocked. We are also shocked when Watanabe dies as predicted. We are shocked not because something unexpected happens but because something expected really happens as expected. We assume that biological death and closure of our lives somehow coincide with each other. What surprises us is that this is hardly the case. It seems that death is always untimely, no matter how well prepared we think we are.[6]

15. *Seven Samurai*

The impetus for the production of *Seven Samurai* (Shichinin no samurai, 1954) came from Kurosawa's interest in making a new type of *jidaigeki* film. Kurosawa's intention was to destroy clichés and dead formulas to renew *jidaigeki* as a film genre that could show the past more accurately and at the same time appeal to the contemporary sensibility of the audience. His effort to break the stalemate of *jidaigeki* as a genre led to a search for accurate historical facts about how samurai actually lived in the Edo period. Originally, the film was supposed to portray one day of a samurai's life: he gets up in the morning, goes to work at a castle, makes some mistake on the job, and goes home to commit *seppuku,* or ritual suicide. With scriptwriter Hashimoto Shinobu and producer Motogi Sojiro, Kurosawa dug into archival materials and talked to historians. But this initial plan stalled quickly because it was almost impossible to find out any specific details of the samurai's daily life (e.g., what kind of food did samurai typically have for breakfast? What was their daily routine like at the castle?). The plan was soon changed to make a film based on famous episodes from the lives of military arts masters. Hashimoto proceeded to write a script based on this new idea and finished it in two months. But this second plan was again abandoned because Kurosawa realized that a narrative film needs more than just a series of climaxes. The third and final idea came from Kurosawa's interest in the details of *mushashugyo,* the samurai's journey to perfect his martial arts skills. As Kurosawa, Hashimoto, and Motogi began research on this subject, they learned that samurai sometimes worked as watchmen for peasants in exchange for meals. Kurosawa decided to expand this historical fact into a film in which peasants hire a group of samurai to defend their village from bandits. Hashimoto wrote the first draft of the script, and Kurosawa and Oguni Hideo later joined in its revision.[1]

One of the most popular Kurosawa films, *Seven Samurai* has been extensively commented on by American and Japanese critics alike. The predominant approach to the film seems to be an allegorical reading. Frederick Kaplan suggests that "Kurosawa uses cinematic technology to explore the dialectic between time and history; he deals cinematically with the past in order to deal ideologically with the present and future, and, more specifically, with class struggle and the role of intellectuals in that struggle."[2] Bert Cardullo argues that *Seven Samurai* "portrays the power of circumstance over its characters' lives. . . . The work of circumstance is interested in what surrounds the human being, and how he reacts to it, under stress. Tragedy is interested in what is immutable . . . in each human being, and the world, and how this leads to man's . . . destruction. . . . The one art looks out, the other in. It is the difference between East and West, self and other."[3] Kida Jun'ichiro finds in *Seven Samurai* a *basso continuo* of Kurosawa films, the absence of civil society and the powerlessness of intellectuals in Japan.[4] For Stephen Prince, "*Seven Samurai* is a film about the modern works, an attempt, by moving farther back into history, to uncover the dialectic between class and the individual, an effort to confront the social construction of self and to see whether this annihilates the basis for individual heroism."[5] Sato Tadao found that *Seven Samurai* justified the Japanese rearmament; in 1954 the National Safety Force and the Maritime Safety Board were reorganized into the Self-Defense Force (Jieitai) in apparent violation of the Article 9 of the 1947 constitution, which "renounces war as a sovereign right of the nation and the threat or use of force as a means of settling international disputes."[6] Another critic suggests that the image of the dead samurai might be a reference to those Japanese who were killed in World War II.[7]

In this chapter, instead of proposing another thematic reading of the film, I will focus on its different aspects, most importantly its generic status as a *jidaigeki* film. I will first examine the history of *jidaigeki* as a dominant genre and then contextualize *Seven Samurai* in relation to that history. What is *jidaigeki*? How did this popular genre come about? What are some of the basic features of *jidaigeki*? What kind of role did it play in the development of Japanese cinema? How has it changed or remained the same since its emergence? And how does Kurosawa situate himself in the history of the *jidaigeki* film?

Genres as institutions are created by the film industry largely to control the mode of film reception and consumption. Along with the star system and other economic practices of the film industry (e.g., the vertical integration of studios, distribution divisions, and theaters), genres serve to minimize financial risks for the industry. The studios strive to achieve the predictability and stability of their business enterprise by repeatedly using in their films similar themes, story patterns, character types, dramatic settings, physical locations, formal devices, visual iconography, and sets and decor. By carefully combining these generic subcomponents to produce infinitesimal differences, the studios try to develop a field of intertexts that restrict the meanings and effects of films and create specific audience expectations. Genres therefore function as a contract between producers and consumers, which facilitates a smooth exchange of money and commodities. However, the total predictability stymies the self-perpetuation of genres. The audience expects certain kinds of products guaranteed by generic conventions but simultaneously demands constant variations within the parameters of those conventions. To satisfy the audience's simultaneous demand for the expected and the new, genres must periodically renew themselves by infusing new elements and creating unexpected variations. The occasional violation of generic conventions is therefore permitted or even welcomed because what is demanded by the audience is not the repetition of the same but the repetition of differences. Another important aspect of genres is that they are not completely autonomous but interdependent on each other. As Fredric Jameson argues, it is impossible to understand fully the significance of any particular genre unless it is related to other contemporaneously existing genres constituting a genre system.[8] The ideological underpinnings of a genre can be decoded only when it is examined as part of the synchronic system of genres existing at a specific historical moment.

For critics interested in the question of genre, Japanese cinema is a fertile object of study. In Japanese cinema there are as many different genres and subgenres as in Hollywood cinema. There are studies of specific Japanese film genres, but surprisingly, the genre system as such has not been examined by film specialists or scholars of modern

Japanese culture. This neglect of the Japanese cinema's genre system is another sign of how Japanese cinema studies has been shaped by the specific agendas of disciplinary politics and border patroling discussed in part 1.

What makes genres in Japanese cinema unique is that they can be classified into two mega-genres, *jidaigeki* (period film) and *gendaigeki* (modern film), the equivalents of which do not exist in Hollywood cinema. The absolute importance of this distinction is reflected in the directorial system, the star system, and even the physical structure of film studios.

Although they are fundamental to the way Japanese cinema is structured, *jidaigeki* and *gendaigeki* did not exist in the early Japanese cinema. The first dominant generic distinction was established between *kyugeki* (or *kyuha*) and *shinpa* (or *shinpageki*), which were later transformed into *jidaigeki* and *gendaigeki* respectively. In principle, *kyugeki* — the word literary means "old drama," and the alternative expression *kyuha* means "old school" — was derived from Kabuki. The early Japanese cinema started with the filming of Kabuki performances (e.g., *Viewing Scarlet Maple Leaves* [Momijigari], *Two People at Dojoji Temple* [Ninin Dojoji], both made in 1899). Instead of trying to hide the stage, these early Kabuki films emphasized the fact that the audience is watching a theatrical performance. To this extent, the Kabuki film was a substitute for a real Kabuki performance and thus was regarded as poor people's theater.[9] *Kyugeki* film took off as a popular entertainment when Makino Shozo started infusing his films with non-Kabuki elements (e.g., stories from a popular oral storytelling form called *ko-dan*, trick photography, etc.). Makino also created the first Japanese film star, Onoe Matsunosuke, who became a children's idol for his appearance in numerous *ninjutsu* (art of the ninja) films. A former itinerant Kabuki actor, Matsunosuke was the most popular star of the early Japanese cinema *(katsudo shashin)*. The height of his popularity was the period between 1912 and 1918, during which he appeared in close to one thousand films. Where *kyugeki* was based on a traditional theater, *shinpa* (new school) was directly derived from a new type of drama that appeared in the early twentieth century. Originally a political drama associated with the Freedom and People's Rights Movement of the 1880s, *shinpa* dealt with contemporary social issues and Western ideas; however, stylistically, it did not completely cut off its ties to native theatrical traditions and made liberal use of many Kabuki conventions including the *oyama,* or female impersonator. Often called *shinpa daihigeki* (a grand tragedy), *shinpa* tended to be a sentimental drama with a tragic ending.

The dichotomy of *kyugeki* and *shinpa* poses a number of crucial questions about the early Japanese cinema, but to pursue those questions fully is beyond the scope of the present study. What I would like to do instead is to speculate about some of the implications of the shift in Japanese cinema from the *kyugeki/shinpa* paradigm to the dualism of *jidaigeki/gendaigeki* as a fundamental classificatory principle. The most obvious aspect of this shift is the emergence of a new historical awareness, a sense of historical distance and perspective. The classificatory categories of dramatic form (*kyugeki* versus *shinpa,* i.e., old versus new) are replaced by the dichotomous categories of historical periodization (*jidaigeki* versus *gendaigeki,* i.e., past versus present), which are a manifestation of the utmost importance of separating the present from the past. Moreover, the dichotomy of *jidaigeki* and *gendaigeki* also foregrounds the fact that the ideas of past and present are not neutral categories. Instead, the new generic distinction shows how historical consciousness is inseparable from the recognition of a larger historical process, that is, the end of feudalism and the rise of capitalism. The differentiation of Japanese films into *jidaigeki* and *gendaigeki* becomes possible by positing the point of the past/present disjunction in history, the point of historical break characterized by the encroachment on Japan by the Western imperial powers posing the threat of colonization. Although modernity, imperialism, and colonialism are sometimes treated as separate issues, the basic distinction between *jidaigeki* and *gendaigeki* in Japanese cinema most clearly shows that questions of modernity can never be answered when they are separated from the other two terms. To the extent that it enables the Japanese to imagine a new Japan radically different from what is perceived as the old world (i.e., pre-Meiji Japan and the rest of Asia), the binarism of *jidaigeki* and *gendaigeki* can play a complicit role in the formation of Japan as a nation-state and even the homegrown imperialism of modern Japan. By instituting the major distinction between *jidaigeki* and *gendaigeki,* Japanese cinema contributed to the ideological imperative of imagining the absolute point of historical disjunction, which was essential for the Japanese national formation.

The replacement of *kyugeki/shinpa* by *jidaigeki/gendaigeki* marked a fundamental shift in the conceptualization of the cinema. When it was first introduced into Japan in the late nineteenth century, the cinema was perceived as another specimen of modern technology from the West. But the early history of Japanese cinema shows that the way this modern technology was appropriated cannot necessarily be called modern. Initially, traveling exhibitors showed films throughout Japan. Even after the first permanent movie theaters were built in 1903, these itinerants did not disappear immediately. The mode of exhibition was also heavily influenced by the tradition of oral storytelling and performance. Even though they are related to each other oppositionally, *kyugeki* and *shinpa* are in the end semiautonomous practices, representing different approaches to the question of how to create a new kind of dramatic and narrative entertainment by using film technology. The distinction of *kyugeki* and *shinpa* does not constitute a coherent structural totality; that is, *kyugeki* and *shinpa* cannot be reduced to species of the genus called cinema. In spite of its fundamentally modern nature as a technological device, the cinema in Japan still had to go through a process of modernization (i.e., the creation of a new mode of representation specific to monopoly capitalism) along with such traditional cultural practices as literature, theater, and fine arts. It is only as a result of this modernization that *jidaigeki* and *gendaigeki* emerged as genres of the cinema as a fully established art form for the masses *(taishu).*

Various attempts to modernize Japanese cinema appeared late in the second decade of the century. Inoue Masao's *The Captain's Daughter* (Taii no musume, 1917) used a moving camera and close-ups *(outsushi)* and tried to do away with *kowairo,* oral performers who imitated the voices of the film's characters. Nikkatsu Mukojima studios' reform movement produced *The Living Corpse* (Ikeru shikabane, 1918), whose innovations included the use of a realistic set instead of a cheap painted backdrop and the inclusion of the name of the director and other main staff members in the credits. The first articulate attempt to modernize Japanese cinema can be found in the effort of Kaeriyama Norimasa and the Pure Film Movement (*Jun Eigageki Undo*). Originally a technical specialist, Kaeriyama tried to replace *shinpa* with *shingeki* by following Hollywood conventions with the intention of exporting Japanese films. Kaeriyama formed the Film Art Association (Eiga Geijutsu Kyokai) and produced *The Glow of Life* (Sei no kagayaki, 1919) and *Maid of the Deep Mountains* (Miyama no otome, 1919). His innovations included the use of a script and actresses rather than oyama, or female impersonators. In 1920 the new film company Taikatsu was established to pursue the production of innovative films. Under the direction of Thomas Kurihara and Tanizaki Jun'ichiro, Taikatsu produced such films as *Amateur Club* (Amachua kurabu, 1920), *The Sands of Katsushika* (Katsushika sunago, 1920), *The Night of the Doll Festival* (Hinamatsuri no yoru, 1921), and *The Lasciviousness of the Viper* (Jasei no in, 1921).[10] In the same year, Shochiku founded a new film company whose goal was to modernize Japanese cinema by importing the system of moviemaking directly from Hollywood. Along with the film production company, Shochiku also established an actor's school and invited Osanai Kaoru, the leader of *shingeki,* to be the school's director. But Shochiku's ambitious plan, which originally included the development of a new modern city around its film studios, suffered a severe setback because of the exhibitors' and audiences' resistance to rapid changes. For a similar reason, Tanaka Eizo's attempt to modernize *shinpa* film at Nikkatsu was also brought to a halt.

One of the most decisive events for the emergence of a new Japanese cinema was the great Kanto earthquake in 1923. Although certainly not a direct cause, the earthquake was a major factor in the accelerated process of modernization in the 1920s. After 1923, *jidaigeki* permanently replaced *kyugeki;* around the same time, *shinpa* lost its ground to the emerging genre of *gendaigeki.* Film studios in Tokyo, which mostly produced *shinpa* films, were virtually all destroyed by the earthquake, and the center of film production was momentarily moved to Kyoto, where film studios had been mainly specialized in the production of *kyugeki* films. As filmmakers moved from Tokyo to Kyoto, a number of innovations were brought to *kyugeki.* At the same time, as Tokyo began to reemerge as a new urban center of Americanism, mass culture, and consumerism, *shinpa* was finally replaced by *gendaigeki.*

The dichotomy of *jidaigeki* and *gendaigeki* does not imply any value judgment on the aesthetic merit of either genre. Yet it is clearly *jidaigeki* that holds as a pivot this dichotomous system together. Although films that depict contemporary social incidents and mores do not necessarily draw the audience's attention to their status as representations, *jidaigeki* by its nature cannot but foreground its own generic conventions. Moreover, the sense of the contemporaneity depicted in *gendaigeki* is reinforced by the existence of *jidaigeki,* which shows a distant past. Thus, to understand the ideological implications of the emergence of the new genre system, we must examine the institution of *jidaigeki* more closely.

What Is Jidaigeki?

Let us start our examination of *jidaigeki* by distinguishing it from what is called the "samurai film." The samurai film as a generic category has commonly been used by American critics, but not much by Japanese.[11] Of course, that the "samurai film" has not been a popular term in the Japanese critical scene does not by itself diminish its critical value. It is possible to propose the samurai film as a new theoretical category to raise different questions and shed light on aspects of Japanese cinema that might have been concealed by *jidaigeki* as a historical category of genre. As long as it has a clear definition, raises new questions, and explains old problems more convincingly than already existing generic terms, a new theoretical category can be invented and used in analysis. However, as Rick Altman argues, since a theoretical category can never be outside of history, it is necessary to scrutinize it as much as the historical category of *jidaigeki.*[12]

Where does the generic category of samurai film come from? The notion of samurai in this category is directly derived from the fact that many *jidaigeki* films feature samurai or sword-carrying warriors as main characters. Another important factor in the determination of the samurai film's generic characteristics is the inclusion of sword-fighting scenes *(chanbara).* Yet these two major characteristics of the samurai film lead to critical contradictions rather than elucidation. If the samurai film is defined solely by the social status and class identity of its protagonists, then regardless of its ultimate utility, it could at least maintain a generic coherence. However, when the spectacular sword fight is regarded a more important core of the samurai film as a genre, its generic coherence collapses. Many sword fight masters in *jidaigeki* are not samurai, either lawfully employed or masterless, but commoners, mostly outlaws and gamblers (*yakuza* or *kyokaku*).[13] David Desser is aware of this contradiction when he claims that "those films which center on non-Samurai heroes yet whose focus is on men (or women) who wield swords in feudal Japan, are also Samurai films."[14] He acknowledges the fundamental contradiction by calling it the samurai film's generic complexity, but he never explains why *jidaigeki* films with non-samurai heroes should still be called samurai films. If the use of swords is the only crucial factor in determining the identity and coherence of the samurai film as a genre, then why not call it, for instance, a sword film? This fundamental contradiction in the definition of the samurai film as a genre cannot but lead us back to our previous examination of the samurai as a sign imbued with colonial ideologies. It is rather ironic to hear that the "great paradox of the Samurai Film is that it has nothing whatsoever to do with history and everything to do with myth."[15] For what is ahistorical is not *jidaigeki* films brought together as samurai films but the notion of the samurai film itself. The samurai film as a generic category tells us less about Japanese cinema and more about a colonialist representation of Japan, which is shared by many Westerners and Japanese.

To understand the specificity of *jidaigeki,* we must examine two developments in popular culture in the early 1920s: the rise of popular literature *(taishu bungaku)* and the emergence of Shinkokugeki (New National Theater) as dominant cultural forces. Shinkokugeki was a new school of popular theater founded in 1917 by Sawada Shojiro (aka Sawasho). Although its dramatic repertoire was rich in variety, Shinkokugeki was best known for its realistic sword fights *(tate)* or swordplay *(kengeki).* And it is this *tate* that *jidaigeki* avidly appropriated and further refined. The most popular repertoire of Shinkokugeki included such plays as *Tsukigata Hanpeita* and *Kunisada Chuji* by Yukitomo Rifu, and *Daibosatsu Pass* (Daibosatsu Toge), an adaptation of the mutivolume popular novel by Nakazato Kaizan. The serialization of this long, unfinished novel started in 1913 and with some interruptions continued until 1941, three years before Nakazato's death. Even though the scope of the novel goes beyond the narrow confinement of popular entertainment, *Daibosatsu Pass* is best known for one of its protagonists, Tsukue Ryunosuke. The epitome of evil and nihilism, Ryunosuke is an extremely skilled swordsman who coldly kills people for no apparent reason. He eventually goes blind, but this does not at all diminish his swordmanship. The popularity of *Daibosatsu Pass* was boosted further when Shinkokugeki performed its adaptation in 1920. Sawada's performance of the role of Ryunosuke made indelible impressions on spectators, and from that time on, the popular image of Tsukue Ryunosuke became inseparable from Sawada's stage performance.[16] *Daibosatsu Pass* was imitated and appropriated in numerous sword plays, popular novels, and *jidaigeki* films, and Tsukue Ryunosuke became a prototype of many well-known *chanbara* heroes from the one-armed, one-eyed ronin Tange Sazen to the blind swordsman Zato Ichi.[17]

Popular literature, or more specifically *taishu bungaku,* began to take shape as a new cultural force in the early 1920s under the strong leadership of writer Shirai Kyoji. In 1924 the inaugural issue of the popular magazine *King* came out,[18] and in the following year, the first little magazine exclusively focused on popular literature, *Taishu bungei,* was started. The popularity of *taishu bungaku* soared in 1926 when Heibonsha launched an *enpon* (one-yen book) series called "The Complete Works of Popular Literature" (Taishu bungaku zenshu). Even though it marginally included detective fiction (most notably the works of Edogawa Ranpo) and other types of popular genres, *taishu bungaku* was overwhelmingly *chanbara* fiction or *jidai shosetsu* (period novel), thus sharing almost the identical narrative world with the *jidaigeki* film. Some *taishu bungaku* writers, most notably Naoki Sanjugo, were actively involved in the moviemaking business. In the mid-1920s, *taishu bungaku* and *jidaigeki* film mutually stimulated each other's development. *Jidaigeki* relied on the mass appeal of *taishu bungaku* as its raw material, and *taishu bungaku* expanded its sphere of influence as *jidaigeki* transformed its heroes into cultural icons.

One of the first filmmakers to recognize the value of Shinkokugeki's realistic sword fighting and *taishu bungaku* was Makino Shozo. Right before Tokyo was reduced to rubble by the powerful earthquake, Makino left Nikkatsu to establish his own company, Makino Educational Film (Makino Kyoiku Eiga).[19] Although he was responsible for the enormous success of *kyugeki* and its biggest star, Matsunosuke, Makino was keenly aware of the limitations of what he had created. *Kyugeki* and its counterpart *shinpa* were usually a mere photographic representation of theatrical performances, and for those who were immersed in Hollywood and European films, those Japanese films (*katsudo shashin*) were less than what they considered a true cinema *(eiga)*. In *kyugeki* films, action scenes were often supplemented by various photographic tricks, but heavily influenced by Kabuki; the actual sword fighting *(tachimawari)* was slow in tempo and less a realistic depiction than a stylized dance. At his studios, Makino Shozo assembled a new generation of such filmmakers and actors as Bando Tsumasaburo, Susukita Rokuhei, Yamagami Itaro, and Makino's son Masahiro,[20] whose works soon eclipsed the films of the old group represented by Matsunosuke.[21] And a golden age of *jidaigeki* came in the late 1920s when Ito Daisuke made a series of films featuring Okochi Denjiro, a former Shinkokugeki actor.[22]

From its beginning, the cinema has been an art of spectacle as much as one of drama and narrative. Even after narrative film became the dominant genre of commercial cinema, the spectacle has remained its indispensable component. The dominance of Hollywood in the world market has been in part because of its success in incorporating spectacle scenes into tightly knit narratives. The well-told stories of Hollywood movies lure the audience into a fantasy world, and the extravagant spectacle scenes not only manipulate the ups and downs of their emotions but also provide them with vicarious experiences of conspicuous consumption. To compete against Hollywood movies, cinemas of other countries have also tried to combine spectacles with narrative without making them too independent from the narrative flow. The significance of *jidaigeki* in the history of Japanese cinema needs to be reexamined in this context.

Although the word *jidai* means "times," "age," or "period," *jidaigeki* is not exactly equivalent to either "period film" or "historical film." The period that *jidaigeki* exploits for dramatic purposes is not just any historical time but mostly the Tokugawa or Edo era, from the early 1600s to 1867. There are a number of *jidaigeki* films set in the pre-Tokugawa era, but they are still exceptions rather than the norm. To understand why *jidaigeki* exploits the Edo period as a fertile field of materials, the complexity of Japanese modernity needs to be noted. It is misleading, for instance, to argue that Japanese modernity abruptly started with the Meiji government's modernization policy articulated in such slogans as *fukoku kyohei* (rich nation, strong army) and *wakon yosai* (Japanese spirit, Western technology). In Japanese, there are three different words that approximately mean "modern": *kinsei, kindai,* and *gendai.* The first term is strictly reserved for the Edo period, and the last one can mean both "modern" and "contemporary." Although the phrase "feudal Japan" is often unproblematically equated with "premodern Japan," as the term *kinsei* indicates, the feudalism of Edo Japan was not incompatible with a specific form of a modern socioeconomic system. The formation of modern Japan had already started in the Edo period, and to understand the specificities of Japanese modernity after the Meiji Restoration and the encounter with the Western imperial powers, it is imperative to put it in this larger historical perspective.[23]

Edo Japan as the most common setting for *jidaigeki* allowed filmmakers to transform sword-fighting scenes into mass entertainment spectacles, which contemporary settings would not easily facilitate.[24] No matter how modernized post-Meiji Japan was, the process of modernization was far from complete, and the fast-paced daily lives of the masses did not irreversibly cut off their ties with the older mode of living, either. When filmmakers turned their attention to contemporary Japan, what they saw was not a fully modernized society but strains and contradictions caused by the ongoing process of modernization. As their daily lives were increasingly transformed by the modernizing forces of monopoly capitalism, the audiences demanded more speed and spectacle; yet because of the incomplete state of modernization, that demand could not always be satisfied by showing contemporary Japanese life. Thus a paradox: the more Japan was modernized, the more there was demand for films set in feudal Japan.

Edo Japan as depicted in *jidaigeki* is not a historically accurate representation but the idealized image of Edo. During the Meiji, the writer Ozaki Koyo and his literary group Ken'yusha tried to keep the Edo *chonin* (townspeople) culture alive in their elegantly stylized writings. Thanks also to the advertising campaign by Mitsukoshi, the first modern department store in Japan, the Edo became an enormously popular commodity after the end of the Russo-Japanese War (1904–1905).[25] Amid the nostalgic Edo boom of the late Meiji, the popular imagination idealized the early years of the Edo period and constructed a fictitious historical narrative in which what happened in later years of the period appeared in the idealized setting of the seventeenth century.[26] *Jidaigeki* owed its existence in part to this popular imagination, and the use of a historically ambiguous word such as *jidai* gave rise to the widely shared sense of imaginary history. To this extent, the emergence of Japanese cinema with its new genre system in the mid-1920s contributed to the formation of the national consciousness and the reconstruction of the national history that was violently disrupted and at the same time engendered by Western imperialism. The dichotomy of *jidaigeki* and *gendaigeki* can be read as a symbolic translation of the larger historical framework within which the issues of modernity, imperialism, and colonialism intersect, while subgenres such as maternal melodrama and gangster films narrativize specific types of sociopolitical contradictions induced by the modernization process. Through the institutional distinction of *jidaigeki* and *gendaigeki,* the cinema functioned as one of the essential means for the Japanese to come to terms with questions of modernity.

The emergence of *jidaigeki* as a new genre had little to do with a return to tradition and more to do with a rebellion against the old forms and conventions of Kabuki and *kyugeki.* If Shinkokugeki provided a model of realistic sword fighting, what compelled innovators of *jidaigeki* to push their experiment to the limit was the impact of Hollywood cinema, particularly action movies, or *katsugeki,* exemplified by Douglas Fairbanks's swashbuckling films and William S. Hart's Westerns.[27] In addition, the slapstick comedies of Chaplin, Keaton, and Lloyd provided them with examples of athletic action and movements.[28] The list of Japanese films that adapted or imitated Hollywood productions by merely changing characters' names and physical settings is endless.[29] But these films cannot be regarded as evidence for either the Americanization of Japanese cinema or the Japanization of American cinema. Particular kinds of shot composition, camera movement, editing techniques, narrative motifs, and characterization in Hollywood cinema were thoroughly assimilated as semiotic codes to such an extent that where those formal devices and thematic motifs originated became irrelevant. And only as a successful result of this assimilation did "Japan" become a meaningful sign in relation to film. In other words, "Japan" did not preexist the translation and assimilation of new semiotic codes; instead, "Japanese cinema" emerged precisely as an effect of intertextual fermentation.

The significance of *jidaigeki* did not simply lie in its status as a new commodified spectacle. Like Shinkokugeki, *jidaigeki* precariously balanced itself between a pure entertainment and an art form with important messages and aesthetic value. The founder of Shinkokugeki, Sawada Shojiro, started his theatrical career when he was still a student at Waseda University as a trainee of the *shingeki* group Bungei Kyokai (Literary Association), which was headed by Tsubouchi Shoyo. A highly idealistic *shingeki* actor, Sawada vehemently refused to compromise his aesthetic standards to please what he considered the vulgar taste of popular audiences. Sawada was unsatisfied with Bungei Kyokai's somewhat unexpected success, since it was to a large extent due to the popularity of one actress, Matsui Sumako.[30] He left Bungei Kyokai right before it was dissolved because of internal conflict, and he reluctantly joined Shimamura Hogetsu's Geijutsuza, which was still centered around Sumako, Hogetsu's lover. In 1914, when Geijutsuza decided to stage a play based on Tolstoy's *Resurrection,* Sawada's exasperation over Geijutsuza's commercialization reached the limit. During the performance of *Resurrection,* Sumako (in the role of Katusha) sang a song, which was so popular that its record sold forty thousand copies. Sumako's Katusha became an idol, and her hairstyle and fashion were avidly imitated and sold as character goods. Geijutsuza traveled throughout Japan and the Japanese colonies to show *Resurrection,* which was performed 444 times.[31] Led by his idealistic zeal for theater as high art, Sawada left Geijutsuza and tried to realize his vision elsewhere. But he encountered enormous financial difficulty and suffered a series of setbacks. After having barnstormed and lived a hand-to-mouth life for a few years, he came to realize a need for a new type of popular theater that is neither Kabuki, *shinpa,* nor translated foreign plays (148). In 1917, to achieve his new goal, Sawada started Shinkokugeki, but without a star actress, the troupe failed to attract the popular audience. The financial trouble forced Sawada's troupe to leave Tokyo and move westward to Kyoto, where their fortune went further downhill. As a last resort, at a theater in Osaka, Sawada and his followers decided to include a sword-fighting scene in the program. Partly because of their lack of skill and also because of their desperate state of mind, their performance was extremely speedy, energetic, and violent, nothing like Kabuki's dancelike *tachimawari.* The audience responded immediately, and Shinkokugeki began to be known as the theater of realistic sword fighting. The direction of Shinkokugeki was finally set, and Sawada came up with "a half-step principle" *(hanpo zenshin shugi)* as Shinkokugeki's motto. On the one hand, if artists take a full step forward, argued Sawada, the masses would be simply left behind. On the other hand, if artists stay with the masses by passively satisfying their demands, there would be no progress in art. Therefore, if artists want to pursue art and simultaneously keep in touch with the desire and sensibility of the masses, they must take only a half step at a time. True to his convictions, Sawada continued to explore the possibilities of sword fighting as spectacle and art, while regularly performing other types of plays, including translated Western plays.

Like Sawada Shojiro, many filmmakers, including those who came to specialize in *jidaigeki,* had been involved in *shingeki* movements before they entered the film world. Tanaka Eizo, Katsumi Yotaro, Iwata Yukichi, Moroguchi Tsuzuya, and Kamiyama Sojin (who later moved to Shoyo's Bungei Kyokai) all studied at Tokyo Acting School (Tokyo Haiyu Yoseisho), which was established to train *shinpa* actors but ended up producing *shingeki* actors (162–73). This new breed of film actors and directors had a kind of training and education decisively different from the background of Onoe Matsunosuke and his generation of filmmakers. Ito Daisuke, the most important *jidaigeki* director in this period, was a student of Osanai Kaoru, a leader of the *shingeki* movement. Ito's initial ambition was literature, but when Osanai assumed the post of the head of Shochiku Cinema Institute (Shochiku Kinema Kenkyusho), Ito, with Osanai's assistance, entered Shochiku's acting school as a trainee. When Shochiku started making films in 1920, Ito moved to its script department and in 1924 directed his first film for Tekoku Kinema. For this new generation of filmmakers, the cinema was not just a spectacle or entertainment. It was a new type of mass medium that could appeal to a large number of people as entertainment and at the same time have aesthetic and political significance. Spectacular sword fighting in *jidaigeki* was not at all incompatible with formal experiment and political radicalism.

In the 1920s, Japanese society was undergoing tremendous changes. The great Kanto earthquake in 1923 destroyed the old Tokyo and precipitated the emergence of mass culture and Americanism. A new urban cultural scene in Tokyo and elsewhere was dominated by radio, film, vaudeville theater, weekly magazines, jazz, and cafés. It was also the age of so-called Taisho democracy and political repression. In 1925 universal male suffrage became reality, and all males over twenty-five were now eligible to vote. In the same year, however, the Peace Preservation Law (Chian Ijiho) was passed to suppress widespread leftist activities and labor movements. In 1930 the Great Depression hit Japan. Many workers lost their jobs in cities, and in the countryside, which was severely ravaged by depression and bad weather, many farmers sold their daughters to brothels to avoid starvation. Labor unrest was widespread all over Japan, and socialism and anarchism were extremely popular among youth. At the same time, the government was rapidly leaning toward militarist expansionism, and the extreme right wing assassinated politicians and business leaders who obstructed their pursuit of radicalism. In the midst of social uncertainty, the age of Americanism shifted to that of the "erotic, grotesque, and nonsense" (ero-gro-nansensu), reflecting the nihilistic desperation of popular sentiment.

Popular culture, including film and taishu bungaku, responded to these radical social changes and uncertainties. For instance, the term taishu bungaku itself was a product of this tumultuous period. The word taishu began to be used in the early 1920s by socialists and anarchists such as Yamakawa Hitoshi and Takabatake Motoyuki to refer to the "people" or the "masses." The choice of the word taishu instead of tsuzoku (popular, common, etc.) indicates that taishu bungaku was marked by a sense of class difference and struggle as much as by a more predictable opposition of high art and low culture.[32] The connection between taishu bungaku and leftist politics can also be discerned in the background of one of the founders of taishu bungaku, Nakazato Kaizan, the author of Daibosatsu Pass. Kaizan was born and grew up in the Tama region, which produced not only late Edo loyalists such as Kondo Isami and Hijikata Toshizo but also young activists of the People's Rights movement in the 1880s. Kaizan, too, was a politically active youth, who was forced to resign from his teaching position at an elementary school because of his missionary work and socialist be-

liefs. He soon became a regular contributor to the Christian socialist weekly *Heimin shinbun* (Commoner's Paper), and opposed to the
Russo-Japanese War. Shortly after the High Treason incident (Taigyaku
Jiken) in 1910, Kaizan began to be drawn to Buddhism and continued
to develop his own utopian vision of society. Kaizan was often regarded
as an extremely opinionated, eccentric writer, but it is worthwhile to
remember that he was one of a few writers during World War II who
refused to join the Society for Patriotism through Literature (Bungaku
Hokokukai), a governmental organization established to control and
mobilize writers for war effort. (Another writer who refused to become
a member of this militarist association was Uchida Hyakken, who is
featured as a protagonist of Kurosawa's last film, *Madadayo*.)[33]

What was called *taishu bungaku* was almost exclusively *jidai shosetsu*
featuring samurai and gamblers. Popular stories and novels whose dramatic settings were contemporary Japan were simply called *tsuzoku
bungaku,* which lacked any class-related connotations.[34] Why did *taishu bungaku* as a new literary genre include only stories set in the Edo
period, particularly its last days? Writers like Nagai Kafu exoticized
the remnants of Edo in contemporary Tokyo by way of passive contestation of the autocratic government and its policy of modernization.
Taishu bungaku, which was implicitly marked by the class consciousness of the politicized masses, used as an imaginary field of experiment
the last days of the Edo period *(bakumatsu),* when loyalists *(kinno-
ha)* and *bakufu* supporters *(sabaku-ha)* engaged in a bloody battle and
fought for hegemony. The transitional years from the Edo to the Restoration became an allegorical image of the contemporary social situation, where the radical left and right activists were both trying to promote their versions of revolution. In the cinema, various adaptations of
Shinkokugeki's *Tsukigata Hanpeita* made the last days of the Tokugawa
shogunate one of the most popular dramatic settings for *jidaigeki* in the
mid-1920s.[35] The emergence of *jidaigeki* was almost simultaneous with
the filmmakers' discovery of the figure of the *ronin,* or masterless samurai, which made it possible for them to represent images of youth un-
constrained by social customs and obligations.[36] The most radicalized
images of youth were found in the leftist tendency films *(keiko eiga)*
of the late 1920s and early 1930s.[37] At the same time, the most innovative *jidaigeki* filmmakers were themselves radical youth, who chiefly

worked at Makino Kinema and other small independent production companies established by film stars.[38] According to Makino Masahiro, even before the leftist tendency film became popular, Makino studio was already a hotbed of anarchists.[39] The vitality of *jidaigeki* in the 1920s and early 1930s was inseparable from young filmmakers' anarchistic rebellion against the establishment and, at an institutional level, small production companies' struggle against large capital.[40] Thus it is not surprising that the golden age of *jidaigeki* came to an end with the government suppression of a leftist movement and the dismantling and absorption of small independent companies by the majors, which were accelerated by the introduction of a new technology, synchronized sound. The end of the *jidaigeki*'s golden age coincided with the replacement of the silent cinema and *benshi*'s narration by the sound cinema in the mid-1930s.[41]

Jidaigeki and the Occupation

If the first setback for *jidaigeki* was created by the suppression of the leftist movement and the transition from silent to sound film, the second major crisis came with Japan's defeat in World War II and the subsequent American occupation. During the Occupation, Japanese cinema was under the watchful eye of the American censors, who immediately started working on the control of the film industry. On September 22, 1945, GHQ's Civil Information and Education Section (CIE) issued to some forty Japanese filmmakers a document that laid out a general policy for film production. The CIE's plan was to make Japanese cinema contribute to the elimination of Japanese militarism and ultranationalism; the fostering of basic human rights including freedom of speech, assembly, and religion; and the transformation of Japan into a country that would never again threaten world peace and security. The American officials also explained to the assembled Japanese filmmakers what they perceived as fundamental problems with Japanese film and theater. "Kabuki theater is," according to the Americans, "based on the principles of feudalistic loyalty and revenge. The present world does not accept this type of theater anymore. The Japanese will never be able to understand the foundation of international society insofar as things such as treason, murder, and deception are openly justified in front of the masses, and personal revenge is permitted in place of law. Of course, serious crimes also occur in Western countries; however, Western morality is based on concepts of good and evil, not on loyalty to feudal clans or blood relatives." [42] Two months later, CIE announced a list of thirteen types of films that were no longer allowed to be produced. The list included any films showing revenge as a central theme, distorting historical facts, portraying feudal loyalty or contempt for life as desirable and honorable, and approving suicide directly or indirectly. [43] Through these orders, directives, and "guidance," the Occupation government tried to destroy *jidaigeki*, which was regarded as a major source of what the Americans considered Japanese feudalistic sentiment, and therefore, as such, responsible for ultranationalism and militarism. In the immediate postwar years, *jidaigeki* was basically banned by the Occupation authorities, except when films did not show any sword-fighting scenes or when they explicitly criticized Bushido, revenge, and other feudal ideals.

As we examined in the previous section, *jidaigeki* is, despite its explicit diegetic content, a modern genre, and it does not affirm or reflect feudalistic values straightforwardly as the American censors believed. Not a simple continuation of traditional popular culture, *jidaigeki* has less to do with a revival of tradition than with an emerging society of the masses and various strains of modernization. Why did the Americans react so strongly against *jidaigeki*? What was really behind the Occupation government's ban on these films? To answer these questions, it is illuminating to compare how they treated another "feudalistic" cultural practice, Kabuki. Initially Kabuki, too, suffered from the Occupation's policy, which immediately banned such popular classics as *Chushingura* and *Kanjincho* because of their glorification of feudal loyalty. But the restriction on Kabuki was gradually relaxed by the efforts of an American official who argued that Kabuki's attraction did not necessarily lie in the particular content of a story but in aesthetic beauty based on stylized form and conventions. Through distantiation and stylization, the themes of loyalty to the great lord or self-sacrifice for revenge were said to be emptied out, and the audience rather enjoyed the formal beauty of Kabuki's flamboyant acting and stage design without being influenced by feudal values idealized by drama. In contrast, film—as an intrinsically more realistic medium—would supposedly have a more direct impact on the way audiences think and act.[44]

There is nothing wrong with pointing out some basic differences between Kabuki and *jidaigeki* film as artistic media. But the way the Occupation censors distinguished Kabuki and *jidaigeki* simply raises more questions about the validity of the logic behind their different treatment of the two. Although *jidaigeki* filmmakers tried to get rid of forms and conventions inherited from Kabuki, the connections between Kabuki and film were not completely eliminated. The majority of the biggest *jidaigeki* stars were originally from the world of Kabuki (e.g., Bando Tsumasaburo, Kataoka Chiezo, Ichikawa Utaemon, and Arashi Kanjuro). The term *jidaigeki* itself was probably derived from Kabuki's *jidai mono* (or *jidai kyogen*). The way *jidaigeki* used the past as a dramatic setting to elude censorship paralleled the way Kabuki's *jidai mono* had used pre-Edo history to portray and comment on contemporary social events to avoid the authorities' repression. These obvious similarities between Kabuki and *jidaigeki* make it difficult for us to accept the Occupation censors' clear-cut distinction between them at face value. Another important point to be stressed is that far from being promoted as a vehicle for propagating feudal ideals, *jidaigeki* was disdained and even suppressed by the militaristic Japanese government as a trivial and ultimately useless entertainment. The assertion that by idealizing feudalistic social relations *jidaigeki* functioned as an ideological apparatus of Japanese militarism is basically a fiction. The Occupation censors argued that Japanese militarism was a direct product of feudalism, and that *jidaigeki* shamelessly indoctrinated Japanese audiences by feudal ideas. But if this had really been the case, why did the militarist government during the war try to suppress *jidaigeki*? We can more aptly regard the *jidaigeki* film as a scapegoat, doubly suppressed by the Japanese government during the war and by the Occupation government after the Japanese defeat.

Thus there is a fundamental contradiction in the Occupation censors' characterization of *jidaigeki*, which reveals less about the specificity of this genre than about their ideological agenda and stratagem. The sharp differentiation of Kabuki from *jidaigeki* enabled the Occupation censors to reinforce the status of the former as a national treasure and to replace the specificity of history with the notion of aestheticized

Japaneseness as fetish. The dichotomy of Kabuki and *jidaigeki* also enabled the Americans to differentiate Japanese history into two parts, a good tradition, which is nonviolent and apolitical and shared by the majority of the ordinary Japanese, and a premodern feudalistic tradition, which is deemed largely responsible for Japanese militarism and sadistic atrocities committed by Japanese military officers and soldiers. Behind the Occupation government's ban on *jidaigeki* lies a faith in modernization theory, which asserts a linear, progressive movement of history from feudalism to modernity. By imposing this progressivist view of history on the Japanese, the Americans tried to disguise their Occupation as the liberation and democratization of Japan.

The Occupation censors did not pay much attention to the specific narrative content of *jidaigeki* films. Instead, they were reacting to the immediate images on the screen, particularly the images of swords. There is something absurd about the Americans' excessive obsession with, and fear of, the Japanese sword, which as an iconic image epitomizes for them feudal loyalty, revenge, and the irrational energy and brutality of the Japanese. I shall not venture any possible psychoanalytic connection of the Americans' fear of the Japanese sword, castration complex, and uncertainty about their own national identity. I shall only note how frequently the wartime American films include the images of swords to represent the Japanese as incomprehensible aliens. Frank Capra's propaganda film *Know Your Enemy: Japan* (1944), for instance, shows Japanese swords to categorically assert the brutality of the Japanese as a race (67). *The Purple Heart* (Lewis Milestone, 1944), the first Hollywood film to explicitly show the Japanese torture of American prisoners of war, is another example of the films that associate Japanese fanaticism with the sword. There is a bizarre scene in the film where Japanese soldiers frenetically dance and swing their swords around in a courtroom when they hear the news of MacArthur's retreat from the Philippines. The Occupation feared so much the power of the sword as a symbolically charged iconic sign that the censors cut excessive swordplay scenes even in foreign films (69). When Japanese filmmakers protested against the Occupation's apparently irrational reaction, the American censors defended their decision by saying that the sword is an instrument of feudal revenge, but the gun is a weapon of self-defense and individualism.

The effect of the Occupation censorship on *jidaigeki* was already visible in the films of the immediate postsurrender days. *A Baby Given by a Fox* (Kitsune no kureta akanbo), a *jidaigeki* film directed by Marune Santaro and released on November 8, 1945, does not include any sword fighting scenes. The film's protagonist is Tora (Bando Tsumasaburo), a laborer who carries people and baggage across the Oi River. One day he finds an abandoned baby boy in the woods and decides to bring him up by himself. The boy, named Zenta, is a natural leader. He tells his father that he wants to become a samurai someday. When Tora promises him a reward for his rapid progress in learning writing, Zenta asks for a sword. At first Tora scolds Zenta for his unreasonable request and tries to explain that a sword is only for samurai, not for commoners like themselves. But in the end Tora gives in to Zenta and buys him a small sword. With his new sword, Zenta plays the role of a noble lord, carried by his friends as retainers on a causeway. From the opposite side comes the procession of a real daimyo. Zenta, who is too proud and stubborn, refuses to make way for the daimyo's procession, and the children are captured and incarcerated by the angry samurai. Considering the historical context of the Occupation and its censorship, it is hard not to interpret this episode without reference to the Occupation's fear and condemnation of the sword as a symbol of everything negative about Japanese tradition. The introduction of the sword as a significant narrative motif is too abrupt in this film about the life and feelings of common people. This unnatural turn of events cannot but draw the audience's attention to the sword as an object inviting misfortune. And perhaps the film's peculiar underscoring of the sword is an implicit critique of the Occupation censors' irrational suppression of the images of sword and sword fighting.

The Occupation censorship nearly killed *jidaigeki.* Only seven *jidaigeki* films were made in 1946,[45] and the Occupation censors' relaxation of their control over *jidaigeki* occurred very slowly. Even when the Occupation officially ended its censorship of Japanese films in October 1949, Eirin, the Japanese censorship board established in June 1949 to replace the Occupation censors, continued to limit the number of *jidaigeki* films. In 1950 the film industry agreed to a policy of self-restraint regarding the production of *jidaigeki,* whereby each company was allowed to make only one *jidaigeki* film per month. Under such circumstances, studios, directors, and actors who specialized in *jidaigeki* were forced to make different kinds of *jidaigeki* or even venture into the unfamiliar territory of *gendaigeki*. In *jidaigeki*, there was a boom of *torimonocho*, a type of detective story whose protagonist is not a sword-carrying samurai but a Tokugawa-period detective or *meakashi*, a commoner with some not too serious criminal background. Because *meakashi* used an iron bar called *jitte* rather than a sword, *torimonocho* films could show spectacle scenes without sword fighting. Some *jidaigeki* stars, most notably Kataoka Chiezo, found a new home in *gendaigeki*'s detective genre. In the *Tarao Bannai* series, Chiezo exchanges a sword for a pistol and solves mysterious cases with his brain rather than with his physical strength.

As decisive as it was, the Occupation censorship was not the only reason for the decline of *jidaigeki* as a genre. *Jidaigeki* was also gradually losing its fundamental source of energy and vitality with the radical reconceptualization of modern Japanese history. Until the end of the war, the pivotal point of historical disjunction had been the end of the Edo and the beginning of the Meiji. After the defeat, however, it was August 15, 1945, that became at least as significant as the Meiji Restoration in marking a historical discontinuity. For the postwar Japanese cinema, what was more important was how to deal with the immediate past and contemporary chaos, war and its disastrous consequences. Japanese cinema responded to the necessity of asserting the radical newness of postwar Japan, even if it turned out to be only imaginary, and to a lesser degree, the necessity of repressing the fact of Occupation.

Jidaigeki in the 1950s

One of the most important developments for *jidaigeki* during the 1950s was the founding of a new film company, Toei. In April 1951, Tokyo Eiga Haikyu, a distribution company established two years earlier, was reorganized as Toei after absorbing two production companies, Toyoko and Oizumi studios. Even after the merger, however, Toei was still on the verge of bankruptcy. In Kyoto, stars such as Kataoka Chiezo and Ichikawa Utaemon were forced to round up money to cover the cost of location shootings. The financially desperate situation was so well known that many inns and restaurants refused to serve Toei actors and crews.[46] In 1952, with the end of the Occupation and the resurgence of *jidaigeki* as a popular film genre, Toei's financial situation slowly started improving.[47] Although it produced many *gendaigeki* films at its studios in Tokyo, Toei was predominantly known for its *jidaigeki* films featuring such big stars as Chiezo and Utaemon. When the industry's self-restriction on the distribution of *jidaigeki* films was finally lifted in August 1951, all major studios took advantage of the abolition of the quota. Yet it was clearly Toei that most benefited from the new situation. In 1946 Toei hired Makino Mitsuo, a son of Makino Shozo and a younger brother of Makino Masahiro, as the head of its Kyoto studios when he repatriated from Manchuria, where he had worked as a producer at the Manchurian Motion Picture Association. In the early days of the Occupation, because of the near impossibility of making *jidaigeki* films, Daiei released its biggest *jidaigeki* stars, Bando Tsumasaburo, Arashi Kanjuro, Kataoka Chiezo, and Ichikawa Utaemon. Toei signed exclusive contracts with Chiezo and Utaemon in 1949. In addition to these newly acquired superstars, Toei also had *jidaigeki* stars such as Tsukigata Ryunosuke and Otomo Ryutaro, *jidaigeki* directors Makino Masahiro and his half brother Matsuda Sadatsugu, and scriptwriters Hisa Yoshitake and Yahiro Fuji.[48] In other words, unlike other studios, Toei was fully prepared to mass-produce *jidaigeki* films. In 1952, for instance, ninety *jidaigeki* films were made by the Japanese film industry. Among the five majors, Toei produced the largest number of *jidaigeki* films (twenty-six, or 28 percent of the total output), and it was also the only company that made more *jidaigeki* films than *gendaigeki* films.[49] In 1954 Toei started a weekly double feature, leading the way in the mass production of films. The shorter film of the double feature was called *Toei gorakuhen* (Toei entertainment edition), which, featuring young rising stars such as Nakamura Kinnosuke and Azuma Chiyonosuke, successfully opened up a new market for movies aimed at children under high school age.[50] Kinnosuke grew into one of the biggest movie stars of the 1950s, and his popularity was eclipsed only by Nikkatsu's action star Ishihara Yujiro. In 1957 Toei became the first Japanese film company to adopt CinemaScope, and at the box office, it was number one among the six majors.[51] The height of Toei *jidaigeki*'s popularity and Toei's success lasted from the mid-1950s to the early 1960s, right before Japan experienced the miracle of high-growth economy; in 1961, more than 32 percent of all the films made by the industry were Toei films.[52]

What are some of the basic characteristics of Toei *jidaigeki* films?[53] Based on set patterns and formulas, the story of a typical Toei *jidaigeki* film is simple and predictable. Frequently, the same materials were literally used again and again (e.g., *Chushingura, Shimizu no Jirocho,* etc.). The narrative is organized around the simple opposition of good and evil and predictably leads to a happy ending: the hero always triumphs; the villain is killed or punished. Being so sure of the difference between justice and injustice, the hero never wavers in his judgment and determination.[54] The villain, in contrast, tests the boundary separating justice and injustice, or good and evil. This is why in the world of Toei *chanbara* films, anybody who "thinks" falls into the category of a villain.[55] The anti-intellectual sentiment of Toei *jidaigeki* manifests itself most clearly in the casting. The role of the hero is always played by a former Kabuki actor or somebody who is familiar with Kabuki's milieu; in contrast, the villain's role is played by an actor who comes from the world of *shingeki*. The hero does not have any psychological depth or interiority, and the villain is punished precisely for his "thinking" as much as for his evil deed. Predictably, the hero is a superior swordsman, but this does not necessarily mean that Toei *jidaigeki* includes spectacular swordplay or scenes of excessive violence. The major attraction of Toei *jidaigeki* is a sword fight scene (thus Toei *jidaigeki* is called *chanbara*), yet the sword fighting is not as athletic or realistic as it was in prewar *chanbara* films. Instead, it is a highly stylized and carefully choreographed dance. The absence of realistically violent sword fighting, coupled with the avoidance of any sexually explicit scenes, means that Toei *jidaigeki* is remarkably wholesome, the kind of films the Ministry of Education would conceivably be willing to recommend (in reality, of course, the ministry never endorsed Toei *jidaigeki* because it was regarded as nothing more than a mindless entertainment). The source materials of Toei *jidaigeki* include not only canonical *jidaigeki* texts but also NHK's serial radio dramas resembling *kodan* stories. By adapting these serials, Toei made *ninjutsu*, the art of the ninja, a popular subject again. (In the early 1960s, the ninja film became more than just an entertainment at the hands of directors such as Yamamoto Satsuo, who used this genre as a means of social critique in *A Band of Assassins* [Shinobi no mono, 1962].) Toei *jidaigeki* is to some extent an atavistic return to *kyugeki* and the world of Tachikawa bunko;[56] that is, it is a more technologically advanced version of the primitive cinema exemplified by the films of the *kyugeki* superstar Onoe Matsunosuke.

Toei *jidaigeki* is a star-oriented cinema. The film's plot is not necessarily determined by the inner logic of the narrative but often by the balance of stars appearing in the film. According to the generic rules of Toei *jidaigeki*, the stars should not play the role of villain, and they should also not fight against each other in the film. When there are many stars in one film, a direct fight among them is difficult to avoid, but the star system demands the observance of the rules even if as a result the film becomes utterly artificial and unrealistic. The establishment of a rigid star system and strict hierarchy among actors and staff at Toei was geared toward the mass production of *jidaigeki* films. The use of the leading stars in a weekly rotation enabled the studio to produce two films a week with enough variations in the casting and subtle permutations of stories. Many excellent supporting actors added depth to Toei's offerings. The hierarchical organization of the studio gave actors and other employees the sense of their own proper places and functions, so that it greatly increased the efficiency of production. At the studios, the leading stars were treated like small feudal lords, and this anachronistic treatment ironically gave the actors presence when they appeared as great lords, master swordsmen, or other heroic figures in films.[57]

As dominant as it was, Toei did not completely monopolize the genre of *jidaigeki* in the 1950s. There were alternatives to Toei's formulaic entertainment movies. During the Occupation, there were already some attempts to innovate the genre of *jidaigeki* by such non-*jidaigeki* filmmakers as Kinoshita Keisuke (*The Yotsuya Ghost Story* [Yotsuya kaidan, 1949]) and Yoshimura Kozaburo (*Ishimatsu of the Forest* [Mori no Ishimatsu, 1949]). These new *jidaigeki* films were artistically ambitious but commercially not so successful. In the 1950s, Mizoguchi made a series of unique *jidaigeki* films based on well-known literary sources (*The Life of Oharu* [Saikaku ichidai onna, 1952], *Ugetsu* [Ugetsu monogatari, 1953], *Sansho the Bailiff* [Sansho dayu, 1954], *A Story from Chikamatsu* [Chikamatsu monogatari, 1954], *New Tales of* the Taira Clan [Shin Heike monogatari, 1955]). Imai Tadashi, a leftist director of *gendaigeki,* made his first *jidaigeki* film, *Night Drum* (Yoru no tsuzumi, 1958), an adaptation of a Chikamatsu play. And even at Toei there was an exception. Uchida Tomu, a prewar master of *gendaigeki* films, made some remarkable *jidaigeki* films including *Bloody Spear at Mount Fuji* (Chiyari Fuji, 1955). It is to this list of film directors that Kurosawa Akira belongs.

Western and Jidaigeki

Jidaigeki has often been compared to the American Western. Both genres, set in important periods of Japanese and American national histories, feature armed heroes — samurai and gamblers, cowboys and gunmen — whose violence plays the essential role in the narrative development and resolution. The Western and *jidaigeki* heroes are often social outsiders who restore order or help people fighting against the villains while fully being aware that their virtuous action does not allow them to reintegrate themselves in a renewed social order. These and other similarities between the Western and *jidaigeki* are more than just coincidental. As I noted earlier, *jidaigeki* is not a pure Japanese genre. The Hollywood cinema, including the Western, strongly influenced the formation of *jidaigeki* conventions. For instance, Kurama Tengu, one of the most beloved heroes of *jidaigeki,* is played by Arashi Kanjuro (or Arakan) wearing black headgear to hide his identity. Sato Tadao speculates that Kurama Tengu and other masked heroes of *jidaigeki* were in part a product of influences of Hollywood movies such as *The Mark of Zorro* (Fred Niblo, 1920), featuring Douglas Fairbanks as a swashbuckling hero. The Japanese release of *The Mark of Zorro* in 1921 was in fact soon followed by its direct *jidaigeki* imitations.[58] By emulating Buster Keaton, Arakan created another favorite *jidaigeki* character, Muttsuri Umon, who rarely shows his emotion on his face. As Sato Tadao points out, there are remarkable parallels between William S. Hart's Westerns and a subgenre of *jidaigeki* called *matatabi mono,* films featuring wandering kyokaku or yakuza. The key figure in the proliferation of *matatabi* films was the writer of *taishu bungaku* Hasegawa Shin, whose popularity is attested by the fact that between 1929 and 1940, seventy-six films were made based on his novels.[59] As in William S. Hart's films, the hero of Hasegawa's stories is a "good-bad man": a bad man who is converted into a good man through his encounter with the purity and innocence of a virginal woman. The narrative in which the woman plays such a role did not exist in traditional Japanese fiction and drama. Kawatake Mokuami's plays, particularly *shiranami mono,* which features thieves as protagonists, do share certain similarities with the films of William S. Hart, but the encounter between a woman and a good-bad man in Mokuami's plays does not lead to the purification of the man's soul.[60]

Borrowing narrative motifs from a remarkably different cultural tradition is easy to do. But it is rather difficult to appropriate them so thoroughly that the end result does not show the fact of borrowing. Why could the Japanese *jidaigeki* film so successfully incorporate Hollywood motifs and become popular to such an extent that the spectators believed the films they were watching were based on Japanese cultural traditions? Sato Tadao proposes to explain this remarkable success by the similarity between Japanese and American social changes in the 1920s and 1930s. "It is possible," writes John Belton, "to locate the origins of the Western in the disturbance of an agrarian-pastoral order introduced by the Industrial Revolution, technological innovation, urbanization, and in the transformation of small-town America into a modern, mass society." The Western can thus be regarded as "a conservative reaction to a growing dependence upon technology and to the impersonality of the consumer-oriented mass culture that accomplishes the modernization of America in the 1920s and later."[61] This view is shared by Sato Tadao, who argues that because of a similar process of transition in Japan from an agrarian society to a modern and urban-oriented society, *jidaigeki* as a popular genre has an affinity with the Western.[62]

The transformation of *kyugeki* into *jidaigeki* was without a doubt facilitated by the appropriation of Hollywood conventions. At the same time, *jidaigeki* was not perceived as a simple imitation of the Western and other Hollywood genres. Heroes of Hasegawa Shin's works are as remarkably "Japanese" as the loyal forty-seven ronin of *Chushingura.* Despite his admiration, Arakan was not interested in becoming Japan's Buster Keaton; instead, he interpreted Keaton's performance as a sign and recoded it to suit his own purposes. In short, despite their affinities, the Western and *jidaigeki* differ from each other in some crucial aspects.

The most obvious difference is the meanings of the names of the two genres: "*jidaigeki*" is, as we have already discussed, a temporal term, and "Western" is a spatial one. The term "Western" is directly related to America's western expansion in the nineteenth century and the idea of Manifest Destiny, "a providentially or historically sanctioned right to continental expansionism."[63] To the extent that its historical setting is roughly the period of 1865 to 1890, the Western is a historical genre. Nevertheless, the name of the genre itself emphasizes a geographic location and spatial expansion rather than a historical period. In marked contrast, for *jidaigeki*, history is far more crucial for its generic identity than spatiality. As Joseph Anderson writes, "few *jidai-geki* present the wide open spaces of the old-style Western."[64] The smallness of the Japanese land, of course, partly explains why the images of expansive space are rare in *jidaigeki*. The relative spatial confinement in *jidaigeki* is also due to the different nature of the Japanese historical situation in the nineteenth century, which is neither encapsulated by the idea of Manifest Destiny nor characterized by the constant westward movement of the frontier, but best described in terms of the acute sense of encroachment by the imperial powers including the United States. If the Western hero is associated with the untamed wilderness, for the hero of the *jidaigeki* film, such culturally unmarked landscape is rarely available. Traditionally places in Japan have symbolic meanings and historical associations, as one can see in numerous *makura kotoba* and other poetic references. If American imagination spatializes time, its Japanese counterpart temporalizes space.

Also called "horse opera," the Western requires the iconographic image of horses. The horse in the Western is an important means of transportation and movement and often emphasizes the vast expanse of desolate landscape to be traversed. The images of cowboys on horseback and covered wagons alert us to the enormity of wilderness and the vulnerability of humans. To the extent that it makes it possible for Westerners to go into "uncharted" territories freely, the horse also symbolizes freedom. For *jidaigeki*, on the other hand, the horse is not a crucial narrative or iconographic component. There is no new territory to be conquered, no wilderness to be tamed in the world of *jidaigeki*. In

Kurosawa on the set of *Seven Samurai. Photo courtesy of Photofest.*

fact, in the majority of *jidaigeki,* people's lives are so rigidly stratified based on various kinds of differences that the ideas of movement and mobility are antithetical to the normal functioning of society. Whereas characters in Westerns have the option of leaving a community and joining a new one, characters in *jidaigeki* are so rigidly constrained by, or torn between, *giri* and *ninjo* that the only available form of freedom left to them is often to kill themselves. "The final image of the solitary swordsman walking into the distance indicates that he is an exile from the familiar world and an outcast from the social situations which give him stature as a man. . . . Roads in *jidai-geki* lead to nowhere."[65]

Kurosawa and Reinvention of Jidaigeki

Kurosawa, whose emergence as a filmmaker more or less coincided with the demise of the prewar *jidaigeki,* was never part of the *jidaigeki* establishment.[66] Among the eleven *jidaigeki* films he made, four are based on original scripts *(Seven Samurai, The Hidden Fortress, Yojimbo,*

Kagemusha); one is an adaptation of a Kabuki play *(The Men Who Tread on the Tiger's Tail);* three are adaptations of modern Japanese literary works *(Rashomon, Sanjuro, Red Beard);* and three are adaptations of foreign works *(Throne of Blood, The Lower Depths, Ran).* Except *Kagemusha,* Kurosawa's *jidaigeki* films do not rely on specifically historical facts. Nor do they use canonical *jidaigeki* materials—for example, *Chushingura, Tange Sazen, Kunisada Chuji, Miyamoto Musashi*—to satisfy the audience's demand for the same or the predictable. When Kurosawa does incorporate popular *jidaigeki* elements, he transposes them to a dramatically different setting to foreground their generic conventions. Kurosawa's first film, *Sanshiro Sugata,* is based on the popular novel with the same title by Tomita Tsuneo, which itself is a judo version of the popular novel *Musashi,* by Yoshikawa Eiji. Instead of remaking *Daibosatsu Pass,* Kurosawa wrote a script, *A Sword Fighting Master Danpei* (Tateshi Danpei), a story of Danpei, who worked for Sawada Shojiro's Shinkokugeki and invented a realistic sword-fighting style as opposed to Kabuki's stylized dance.[67] By making films that deviate from the generic conventions of *jidaigeki,* Kurosawa maintains a metacritical relationship to this popular genre.

Kurosawa is not, however, the first director to innovate *jidaigeki* as a genre. In the 1930s there were two remarkable filmmakers, Yamanaka Sadao and Itami Mansaku, whose *jidaigeki* films explored the genre's possibilities and showed new directions. What distinguishes the films of Yamanaka and Itami from the mainstream *jidaigeki* is a contemporary sensibility. Both do not present the samurai as a heroic figure but take a satiric view of *Bushido.* They reject *chanbara* only for the sake of *chanbara,* focus on social outcasts and people on the margins of society, and prefer humor to irony as a trope of narration. The settings and characters of their *jidaigeki* films are often straight out of *gendaigeki* and foreign films, yet there is nothing tacky about their attempt at hybridization. They maintain a sense of critical distance from the *jidaigeki* materials but never look down on them. Unfortunately, Itami's and Yamanaka's careers were interrupted by their untimely deaths before they could realize the full potential of their abilities and artistic visions. Yamanaka died in 1938 from a disease he had caught at the front in China; Itami died of tuberculosis in 1946.

Despite these similarities, Yamanaka and Itami have remarkably different temperaments as filmmakers. Itami Mansaku is essentially a man of letters, one of the best scriptwriters and a conscience of the prewar cinema. In his teenage years in Matsuyama, Itami immersed himself in literature and art with his friends Ito Daisuke and Nakamura Kusatao. Itami studied Western-style painting by himself and like Kurosawa tried to pursue a career as an artist in his twenties. Even though Kurosawa was ten years younger than Itami,[68] there was an overlapping period during which they were both trying to pursue the same goal. In 1928 Kurosawa's paintings were selected for Nikaten; in 1927 Itami's painting caught an eye of the leading modernist painter Kishida Ryusei, who praised Itami's work and invited him to become his student. Itami was deeply moved by Kishida's words but declined the invitation, saying that he did not have enough confidence in his work and feared he could not live up to Kishida's expectations. Instead of moving to Kishida's place, in the same year, Itami moved to Kyoto to stay with Ito Daisuke and, on Ito's advice, started writing film scripts. After finishing a brief stint as actor and assistant director, Itami directed his first film in 1928. His unique *jidaigeki* films and scripts are filled with intelligent humor and critical sensibility. Among twenty-six films he directed or codirected, only three have survived more or less intact.[69] *Akanishi Kakita* (Akanishi Kakita, 1936), one of the currently available films, is based on Itami's own script, which is the adaptation of a short story by Shiga Naoya. The general setting of the story is very well known, the disturbance and power struggle within the Date clan in the mid-seventeenth century, which was first popularized by Kabuki's *Meiboku Sendai hagi* (1777). Kataoka Chiezo stars in the film, playing two different roles: Akanishi Kakita, an ugly spy trying to expose the plot against the Date clan, and Harada Kai, the leader of the discontented group framing the plot. Chiezo does not simply portray two characters with different social status and personalities but demonstrates two different modes of acting. When he appears as Akanishi, he acts naturally without wearing any heavy white makeup; as Harada Kai, his acting is in the style of a conventional *jidaigeki,* which is heavily influenced by Kabuki, and his face is covered with white powder. Itami pretends to showcase Chiezo's star value by casting him in the two leading roles but in fact develops a metacriticism of *jidaigeki*'s obsolete generic conventions by contrasting the naturalistic look of Akanishi and the utterly artificial, antique-looking appearance of Kai.[70] The new sensibility of the film is apparent in the opening raining scene, which is accompanied by Itami's favorite artist Chopin's piano piece "Raindrop" (which Kurosawa uses in *Dreams*, in episode 5, on van Gogh). And the humorous moments are abundant (Kamiyama Sojin's blind masseur, fish-related names of many characters, etc.). Shimura Takashi, who appears as Tsunomata Hirenoshin, a neighbor of Akanishi, and plays the role of Kanbei in *Seven Samurai*, admits that Itami's *Akanishi Kakita* made him understand for the first time what the cinema can do as an art form.[71]

If Itami Mansaku kept a critical distance from *jidaigeki*, Yamanaka Sadao immersed himself in it. Yamanaka is a man of cinema with a highly developed cinematic sensibility. He directed his first film in 1932 at the age of twenty-three and between 1932 and 1937 became one of the most innovative filmmakers whose work has left an indelible mark on the subsequent development of Japanese cinema. Of all his films, only three sound films still exist: *Tange Sazen and the Pot Worth a Million Ryo* (Tange Sazen hyakuman ryo no tsubo, 1935), *Kochiyama Soshun* (Kochiyama Soshun, 1936), and *Humanity and Paper Balloons* (Ninjo kamifusen, 1937). The first one is a parodic retelling of the Tange Sazen story, and the latter two are loose adaptations of Kawatake Mokuami's Kabuki plays. In all cases, what is impressive is Yamanaka's ability to digest and transform popular materials into radically new works. Tange Sazen, the one-armed, one-eyed ronin, first became a pathetic symbol of anarchic energy and rebellion when Ito Daisuke made his *Ooka's Trials* (Ooka seidan) series. Yamanaka completely rewrites this image of Sazen by changing him into a child-loving, openhearted, and good-natured ronin living in a tenement house with his wife. Yamanaka's parody is so convincing that since his film his lovable Sazen has become a standard image.[72] Yamanaka's ability to create his unique style out of diverse materials, both Japanese and foreign, *jidaigeki* and *gendaigeki*, is quite impressive. It seems that for Yamanaka there is only one cinema, and national and generic distinctions are in the end not particularly relevant. Yamanaka is a master of cinematic language, and his films are smooth and flawless. The rhythmic lyricism of his films is in part created by various transitional devices, some of which remind us of the cinema of Ozu. Another feature of Yamanaka's films is the creative ellipsis of sword fight and bloody scenes.[73] There are scenes of violence in *Humanity and Paper Balloons,* but none of them are directly shown on screen except one. At the end of the film, the ronin Unno Matajuro is killed by his wife, who then kills herself. We never see the scene of this double suicide. With a dagger in her hand, the wife approaches the husband lying on the floor, presumably drunk and sleeping. As she blows out a lamp, the screen darkens. In the next shot, it is the following morning, and neighbors are looking inside the couple's tenement from the alley. We learn from them that the couple has committed a double suicide. The camera is positioned inside the tenement in such a way that the samurai couple's bodies completely remain in off-screen space. The fate of the couple is symbolically represented by the film's last shots (one of the most celebrated last shots of Japanese cinema), a paper balloon in a ditch flowing away from the camera. At the climax of *Kochiyama Soshun,* there is a rare sword fight scene. But even here, what is impressive is not the sword fight itself but the protagonists' willingness to die to save an innocent girl or to stick to their principles, and the lateral tracking shot of Kochiyama and Hirotaro running through a narrow sewer between tenement houses.

Kurosawa's attempt to create a new type of *jidaigeki* film is a further extension of what Itami and Yamanaka accomplished in the 1930s, with a new twist. Unlike his two predecessors, Kurosawa does not reject *chanbara.* His *jidaigeki* combine a radically different type of sword fight and spectacle with a strong allegorical narrative and serious thematic motifs. In the early 1950s, when the Occupation was not yet over, Kurosawa was searching for a new kind of *jidaigeki.* In addition to *A Sword Fighting Master Danpei,* Kurosawa wrote another *jidaigeki* script, *The Duel at the Kagiya's Corner* (Ketto Kagiya no tsuji, 1952), and asked Mori Kazuo to direct it. Mori speculates that Kurosawa, who was experimenting with ideas about how to make an innovative *jidaigeki* film, was perhaps not ready to direct it himself and used Mori to see whether his ideas would work or not.[74] *The Duel at the Kagiya's Corner* is an unusual film at least in two senses. First, it is a film about one of the best-known *jidaigeki* episodes, the legendary revenge of Araki Mataemon, the kind of material Kurosawa was never willing to use for his own films. Second, even though the film's story is well known, the specific treatment of that story is radically different from other preceding Mataemon films. Kurosawa's approach is a demythologization of the legend in search of realism. According to the widely known story, which was first popularized by *kodan* storytellers, Araki Mataemon slew thirty-two *hatamoto,* or shogun's vassals; in reality, he killed only two helpers of the enemy. In the myth, Kazuma avenges the murder of his father; actually it was not his father but his younger brother who was killed. Kurosawa's script narrates a historicized story of the duel at the Kagiya's Corner instead of repeating the popular, mythicized version. Kurosawa's desire to demythologize the legend is so strong that he opens the script with a legendary version of the duel scene and then immediately undercuts the reality effect of the scene by adding a voice-over narration that explains the difference between myth and history. The voice-over claims that a true record is far more exciting than an exaggerated fiction and declares that the film will represent the actual duel as faithfully as possible based on authentic historical records. As if to make sure that this is not a conventional remake of the Mataemon story, the next scene shows the contemporary image of the Kagiya's Corner, still accompanied by the voice-over explaining what this famous scenery used to look like in the seventeenth century. Then, finally, the narrative flashes back to the actual day of the duel. According to Mori, Kurosawa gave him specific instructions regarding the production of the film. Kurosawa, for instance, showed Mori pre-Meiji photographs of Japanese wearing their hair up in topknots as models. Kurosawa also advised Mori how to direct a realistic sword fight scene (188). The reception of Mori's *Duel at the Kagiya's Corner* was mixed. Many praised an unconventional style of sword fighting at the film's climax. But the film did not do well at the box office. Mori himself finds the film's unnecessarily artificial beginning largely responsible for the film's failure (191–92). Kurosawa reportedly did not appreciate Mori's direction; considering the perfectionist tendencies of Kurosawa, who insisted on getting involved in every facet of film production, there is nothing surprising about his reaction. Regardless, the result of this "experiment" was used as a stepping stone for the production of Kurosawa's first real *jidaigeki, Seven Samurai.*[75]

For Kurosawa, who was so eager to make a different kind of *jidaigeki,* it was fortunate that he did not work at Toei, Daiei, or Shochiku. The company he worked for was Toho, which was known not for *jidaigeki* but for lighthearted comedies and other *gendaigeki* genres featuring urban office workers and petite bourgeoisie. Toho never had, unlike the three majors just mentioned, either separate studios for the production of *jidaigeki* in Kyoto or corps of actors specialized in *jidaigeki*. It is therefore not surprising that the first *jidaigeki* film produced by Toho, when it was still called PCL, was a parody of *jidaigeki*, *Enoken's Kondo Isami* (Enoken no Kondo Isami, 1935), featuring the comedian Enomoto Ken'ichi. After the war, Toho's reticent attitude toward *jidaigeki* did not change much. But after Inagaki Hiroshi joined Toho in the early 1950s, this *gendaigeki* studio started producing a small number of *jidaigeki* films on a consistent basis. Kurosawa was able to make *Seven Samurai* and a few other innovative *jidaigeki* films in this unique environment. His singular *jidaigeki* films could not have been made at any other major studio where old *jidaigeki* conventions were still alive and dominant.[76]

In the original pamphlet for *Seven Samurai*, Kurosawa says: "An action film is often an action film only for the sake of action. But what a wonderful thing if one can construct a grand action film without sacrificing the portrayal of humans. This has been my dream since the time I was an assistant director. For the last ten years I have also been wanting to reexamine *jidaigeki* from a completely new angle. *Seven Samurai* has started with these two ambitions of mine."[77] To realize the first objective, he constructs the narrative of *Seven Samurai* around delicately balanced depictions of distinctly individual characters and the group to which they belong. There are three major groups in the film: seven masterless samurai, peasants, and bandits. Each of these groups has its own identity and particular way of establishing relationships among its members. Each member of the samurai's group has his own clear individual identity, whereas only some members of the peasants' group are portrayed as individuals. The least individuated group is the bandits, who more or less appear as one undifferentiated mass. One of the focal points of the film is the formation and eventual dissolution of an alliance between the first two groups, samurai and peasants.

The seven samurai are simultaneously types and individuals whose distinct personalities exceed the character traits of mere types. Kanbei, who does everything with aplomb, is an ideal leader figure. Katsushiro (Kimura Isao) is an idealistic youth who has yet to experience the world. Gorobei is a skilled swordsman who can detect Katsushiro's ambush immediately. Even though Heihachi is not as strong as other samurai, he has a great sense of humor that can lift the spirits of people around him. Kanbei's right-hand man, Shichiroji (Kato Daisuke), is a survivor, who can become, if necessary, even a vendor. Kyuzo, a laconic sword master or killing machine, is also a samurai with compassion. And there is the lovable farmer-samurai Kikuchiyo (Mifune Toshiro), without whom the alliance of the samurai and the peasants would perhaps be impossible. All these personal qualities are not verbally explained in the film; instead, they are vividly revealed when the seven samurai react to concrete problems or situations. The personality of each samurai is not an abstract idea determining what he says and does. On the contrary, it is the concrete details of his actions that enable other characters and us to see who he is.

As individuated as they are, the samurai and the village leaders are not completely autonomous individuals. They belong to different groups and communities but decide to form a temporary alliance to fight against the bandits. It is therefore certainly possible to debate to what extent individuals in the film are forced to subordinate their personal desire and necessity to specific goals of groups. Stephen Prince, for instance, argues that individuals are ultimately subsumed under the group, both thematically and compositionally. He refers to a scene in the beginning part of the film, in which the peasants gather in a village square to discuss how to deal with the bandits. The peasants are distraught and do not believe they can resist the bandits' demand for rice, barley, and women. One of the villagers, Rikichi, refuses to bow down to the bandits and urges the others to take up arms against the bandits: either kill or be killed by them. Nobody agrees to his plan, and Rikichi, angered and frustrated, leaves the villagers' circle and sits alone. As Prince perceptively points out, when Rikichi isolates himself in diegetic space, the composition of the following shot immediately reintegrates him into the community. In the new composition, Rikichi is in the foreground, and the rest of the villagers are in the background. The spatial distance between the two is almost eliminated by Kurosawa's trademark use of the telephoto lens, which flattens the image.[78] In the rest of the film, spatial relations between characters in diegetic space and in on-screen space often tell us different stories. And until the last scene after the battle, whenever there is a discord in the samurai-peasants alliance, the composition of the shot frequently tries to integrate dissenting members into the group. But this tension between diegesis and narration can happen and become significant only because *Seven Samurai* shows us the images of distinct individuals, which are unique in the genre of *jidaigeki*.

Another conspicuous formal trait that foregrounds the individuality of key characters is an extreme close-up of their faces. For instance, in the village scene just described is inserted a close-up of Rikichi's desperate face. When the village elder appears on-screen, we see his wrinkled face in close-up. When Katsushiro learns that he is allowed to accompany Kanbei and the others to the village, his joyous face is shown in close-up. These instances of close-ups are not a part of the classical shot/reverse shot pattern that creates spatial and narrative unity by carefully manipulating the direction of characters' looks, graphic composition, sound cues, and so forth. The close-up face is not distinctly registered either as an object of the other's look or as a subject of the look. Its appearance is often abrupt and abstract. The spatial isolation of the actor's face on the screen is presented as a mark of the individuality of the character he or she plays. The close-up makes us confront the face as a window to the character's interiority. While the close-up of the human face isolates an individual from a group, a close-up of an inanimate object reestablishes the relation between the two. For instance, when Kanbei holds a bowl of rice and agrees to defend the village from the bandits, the foreground of the shot is occupied by the extreme close-up image of the bowl, while in the background are Rikichi, Manzo, Mosuke, and Yohei. Here, the bowl of rice functions as a pivotal sign that unifies the peasants in the background and the samurai who are in the off-screen space.

It is important to reiterate that *jidaigeki* is not a history film,[79] and *Seven Samurai* is certainly no exception. Kurosawa's interest in the past as it really was is not necessarily the same as an attempt to reproduce the past as faithfully as possible. We should never forget that the period of civil wars (Sengoku jidai) on the screen is in the end only a representation, no matter how "accurate" it might seem. This elementary distinction seems to get lost very often in Kurosawa criticism in the United States. (The tendency in Japan is the opposite: Kurosawa's films have often been accused of being historically inaccurate.) Thus the relationship of individual and group in *Seven Samurai* does not necessarily reflect the historical reality of sixteenth-century Japan. If "Kambei tells the [farmers] that everyone must work together as a group and that those who think only of themselves will destroy themselves and all others," it is not because "the material of the past discloses no spaces in which the individual can move, no spaces not already inhabited by groups and their demands."[80] Considering that *Seven Samurai* is a film about a military battle between bandits and peasants led by a group of samurai, there is nothing surprising about Kanbei's speech to the villagers. The essentialist notion of an "interactionist self" — "The self must be an interactionist self or cease to exist"[81] — cannot explain the dynamic of human interactions in the film. Because *jidaigeki* can be only a fictitious representation of the historical past, it is not impossible to make a *jidaigeki* film set in the Sengoku period featuring individual heroism. As Kuwabara Takeo reminds us, the peasants in the fifteenth and sixteenth centuries were not as cowardly as they are portrayed in the film. It was probably not unusual for a village like the one in the film to have a few peasants who participated in military battles as common foot soldiers. Kuwabara further speculates that in reality Kanbei would have become a lord of the village, and Katsushiro would have kept Shino as his mistress.[82] I am not suggesting that *Seven Samurai* is pure fantasy; on the contrary, the film's scriptwriters, Kurosawa, Hashimoto, and Oguni, dug into historical documents and used some of what they found to construct the story, characters, and other narrative details. The point I am trying to make is that the film's reality effect cannot be equated to its historical accuracy. Instead of substantializing the historical past represented in the film, we must try to locate exactly where the film's overwhelming sense of reality comes from.

If *Seven Samurai* successfully elevates the level of *jidaigeki*'s realism a notch, it is not by representing historical facts accurately. Instead, the film creates a heightened sense of realism by meticulously showing all kinds of details that are normally ignored in conventional *jidaigeki* films. These small details include plot and story, character traits, sets and props, costumes, and acting style. The art director and his staff went to Shirakawago to sketch old farmhouses and farming tools, many of which were used as models. Clothes for principal characters and even extras were newly made and then naturally made to look old. The actors' hairstyles were not conventionally handled by using a Kabuki-style wig but realistically done by carefully matching each actor's physical idiosyncrasies and the characteristics of the role he or she played. Kurosawa even wanted Mosuke's wig to look like an uneven head he saw in an old picture scroll. To create the feel of an antique house, Kurosawa and his staff endlessly polished wooden boards.[83] The preparation for the bandits' attack by the samurai and the villagers is shown meticulously. Men in the village are divided into different groups and trained by the samurai. To block the bandits' access to the village, new fences are built at the village's western entrance; the bridge at the other end is destroyed; and on the south side, a rice field is irrigated. Kanbei draws a map of the village, and each bandit is represented by a circle on the map's margin. Every time a bandit is killed, Kanbei crosses out a circle. The map therefore emphasizes not only the strategic significance of geography and the village's spatial configuration but also the necessity of killing the bandits one by one in hand-to-hand fighting. About the battle sequences there is nothing conventional, either. What we see there is not a stylized dance as in Toei *jidaigeki*. Nor is it just an athletic display of kinetic movement. It does not matter if one uses his sword properly. When necessary, even farming tools become deadly weapons. The last battle sequence is particularly brutal. It is raining heavily, and the samurai and villagers must fight not only the bandits but also the mud, which drags them to the ground. The fighting is now clearly a matter not of style but of survival. But even in the midst of this fiercely realistic battle for survival, there are moments of poetic beauty. In this sequence, we see one of the most striking images of the film: Kanbei, standing straight in the downpour, slowly draws a bow and then quickly releases it to shoot an arrow at a bandit on a horse. Or see the last image of Kikuchiyo, which Andrey Tarkovsky mentions as an example of the cinematic image—specific, unique, and factual, that is, everything he thinks symbols are not: "The samurai wear an ancient Japanese garment which leaves most of the leg bare, and their legs are plastered with mud. And when one samurai falls down dead we see the rain washing away the mud and his leg becoming white, as white as marble. A man is dead; that is an image which is a fact. It is innocent of symbolism, and that is an image."[84] "The beauty and cleverness of story arise from a certain harmony between the simplicity of the plot and the wealth of details that slowly delineate it," writes André Bazin. "Obviously this kind of narrative reminds one of Ford's *Stagecoach* (1939) and *Lost Patrol* (1934) but with a more romantic complexity and more volume and variety in the fresco." [85]

Did *Seven Samurai* change the state of *jidaigeki* as a popular genre in the mid-1950s? The answer to this question is no. *Seven Samurai* is in many ways an exceptional film. From the start of shooting, it took eleven months to finish the film, and the total cost was ¥210 million, which was seven times as much as the budget for a typical film around that time. Its scale of production was simply too large to become a model for conventional *jidaigeki* films. More important, other studios, particularly Toei, did not see any need to take such a financial risk to produce a film like *Seven Samurai*. When *Seven Samurai* was released, it was the height of Toei *jidaigeki*. Enjoying a huge commercial success, Toei did not see any necessity for changing their popular formula. Even in the early 1960s when filmgoers were apparently getting tired of Toei *jidaigeki*, Toei continued producing the same old formula films. The fatal blow to Toei's crumbling kingdom came suddenly in 1961 when Kurosawa's *Yojimbo* enjoyed great success at the box office. At select theaters, *Seven Samurai* was shown together with *Yojimbo*.[86] (The Hollywood remake of *Seven Samurai*, *The Magnificent Seven* [John Sturges, 1960], which was the most commercially successful foreign film that year, was also released simultaneously.) [87] The end of Toei *jidaigeki* was sealed in 1962 with the success of Kurosawa's *Sanjuro*. Finally, in 1963 and 1964, Toei departed from its outworn formula and produced a series of *jidaigeki* films called *shudan koso jidaigeki* (collective struggle *jidaigeki*). As this label suggests, like *Seven Samurai*, instead of a single hero, these films focus on a group of protagonists who fight against corrupt officials or the system in a bloody battle. But it was already too late to salvage the declining state of *jidaigeki* by this time. Toei soon abandoned *jidaigeki* completely and switched to yakuza movies.[88]

16. *Record of a Living Being*

Record of a Living Being (Ikimono no kiroku, 1955) is about a man who fears the possibility of nuclear extermination so much that he eventually goes insane. The protagonist Nakajima (Mifune Toshiro), the owner of a foundry, tries to emigrate to Brazil with every member of his extended family to avoid the effect of nuclear fallout. The film's narrative is remarkably simple in its single-minded focus on Nakajima's struggle for survival and his family's resistance to his quixotic plan. Stylistically, *Record of a Living Being* is a typical Kurosawa film. The shot is often cluttered with people and objects; objects are placed in front of characters to partially obstruct our view (e.g., Nakajima's face filmed through a mosquito net looks like the face of a man dying of "ashes of death"). But unlike many other Kurosawa films, there is not much movement within each shot. The static shot packed with objects and human figures creates an oppressive atmosphere appropriate for the film's subject. Another conspicuous feature is the sparse use of music. Film music can be heard only during the opening credits and after the film's main narrative is completely over.[1] The composer Hayasaka Fumio, who was arguably Kurosawa's most important collaborator since *Drunken Angel,* died of tuberculosis during the filming of *Record of a Living Being.* Hayasaka left only a few sketches of music for the film, and they were completed by his disciple Sato Masaru, who composed music for every Kurosawa film from *Throne of Blood* to *Red Beard. Record of a Living Being* is also notable for the first systematic use of multicamera shooting by Kurosawa. In his preceding film, *Seven Samurai,* he had simultaneously used several cameras with telephoto lens to shoot the final battle sequence. The complex action scenes with peasants, bandits, samurai, and galloping horses moving in different directions in rain and mud at multiple planes of the shot could not be repeated twice in exactly the same manner. The multicamera technique was therefore employed to capture the dynamic action of the scenes without breaking them down into disjunctive segments. Kurosawa applied the same technique to *Record of a Living Being,* an incomparably more static film with no action scenes in a conventional sense. In multicamera shooting, actors do not face the camera as an invisible observer. They are simultaneously filmed by several—typically three—cameras, which, moreover, do not necessarily remain stationary. Therefore, it becomes extremely difficult for actors to completely control their bodies and become fictional characters vis-à-vis every camera present during the filming. When the technique is used masterfully, multicamera shooting can create an unexpected effect by capturing a dimension or moment of actors' bodies that eludes their conscious control. It can also decenter the represented space on the screen by showing us the montage of images that cannot be captured from the orthodox camera positions. Kurosawa continues to refine this technique in the rest of his career to create stunning visual and thematic effects.

Thematically, the fundamental point of *Record of a Living Being* comes down to this: how can we really feel the threat of nuclear warfare and the possible extinction of the human race not as an abstract issue handled and manipulated by career politicians and bureaucrats but as a concrete problem seriously menacing all of us? In the film, Nakajima is the only character who can actually feel the threat, and he tries to do everything he can to avoid the possibility of being killed by the nuclear fallout. The solutions Nakajima pursues, however, are not realistic at all. During arbitration at the Family Court, we learn that Nakajima has tried to build an underground nuclear shelter in the northern region of Japan. But when he hears that the radioactive fallout from the Soviet nuclear tests would reach that region, he leaves construction of the shelter unfinished. For some reason, Nakajima then becomes convinced that South America is the only safe place on earth, and since then, he has been trying to emigrate to Brazil with all the members of his family including his mistresses and illegitimate children. There is of course no basis for his belief that Brazil is somehow safe from the nuclear fallout. As Sato Tadao points out, Nakajima is definitely not the most sympathetic character in the film.² It is quite possible that the film's viewers more easily identify themselves with some of his family members, whose everyday life is threatened by the obsessive patriarch. He excessively shows unwanted kindness to his family, and forces his views on others regardless of their opinions and feelings. Nakajima lives in his own monologic world and does not really communicate with any other persons. The limitations of Nakajima's action become acutely apparent when he sets fire to his own foundry to force his children to emigrate to Brazil with him. What he has not thought about is the lives of his workers and their families, who are now out of work. If Nakajima does not in the end appear egotistic despite all his shortcomings, it is because his absurd action is motivated not by rational calculation but by the primal fear of a "living being" or animal that is desperately trying to survive.

The unrealistic solutions Nakajima earnestly pursues do not reveal the limitation of Kurosawa's unrealistic "psychological" approach to the sociopolitical problem.³ There is no ready-made solution to the threat of nuclear extinction, and it is unreasonable to expect from Kurosawa some kind of political plan that can be implemented to eliminate nuclear bombs and the possibility of nuclear warfare. In fact, any facile proposal of a political solution to the escalating nuclear race would appear phony and unconvincing and make *Record of a Living Being* a simple message film or propaganda. Some critics also argue that the film is a failure because it tackles the problem of nuclear extinction too seriously and thereby alienates the average film viewer. Kurosawa objects to this criticism by saying that a satiric treatment of the nuclear problem is not possible when he himself is no different from Nakajima's family, who indirectly drive him insane. Kurosawa admits that among the film's characters, he is closest to the snobbish instructor of French literature Yamazaki (Shimizu Masao), whose rational approach to the threat of nuclear warfare seems motivated less by his realistic assessment of the contemporary political situation than by his desire to get his share of Nakajima's money. In other words, it is not possible for Kurosawa to treat the subject of nuclear extinction satirically when he himself can be nothing more than an object of satire.⁴

The ominous threat of nuclear weapons is real, yet it is totally invisible. Instead of telling us what to do, by showing us the sheer intensity of Nakajima's fear of the bomb and radioactive fallout, *Record of a Living Being* helps us to see the situation clearly. As a filmmaker, Kurosawa has done his part of the job. What to do with the situation, which is defamiliarized by the work of Kurosawa's imagination, is up to the film's viewers.[5]

17. *Throne of Blood*

The Search for Japaneseness

Throne of Blood (Kumonosujo, 1957) is one of the most frequently discussed Kurosawa films. This is not particularly surprising when we think about the film's remarkable beauty and formal precision. Almost every aspect of the film (e.g., sets, acting, camera work, editing) demonstrates the originality and superb craftsmanship of Kurosawa as a filmmaker. In other words, the film has a number of intrinsic merits that justify the kind of attention it has received critically. Yet they are not the only reasons why *Throne of Blood* has been regarded as a unique film among Kurosawa's work. The popularity of *Throne of Blood* as an object of critical analysis is inseparable from the fact that it is an adaptation of Shakespeare's *Macbeth,* and it is precisely this relation that has gotten the most attention. Kurosawa criticism has meticulously noted and enumerated the similarities and differences between Kurosawa's film and Shakespeare's play partly because of the following "paradox": *Throne of Blood* is regarded by many as the best adaptation of Shakespeare's work into film, yet at the same time among many Shakespeare adaptations it departs from Shakespeare's text most radically. In this chapter, I will not detail specific similarities and differences between the film and the play unless the comparison becomes absolutely necessary. Instead, I will discuss *Throne of Blood* by asking the following questions. Why did Kurosawa decide to make a film based on Shakespeare's *Macbeth*? What does it mean for a Japanese filmmaker to use Shakespeare's text as the basis for a *jidaigeki* film set in medieval Japan? Why are so many Japanese critics disappointed with *Throne of Blood,* unlike their Western counterparts? Why have so many critics been obsessed with *Throne of Blood*'s connection to *Macbeth* at the expense of almost everything else? Why is it necessary to list the similarities and

Kurosawa and Yamada Isuzu (Asaji) on the set of *Throne of Blood*.
Photo courtesy of Photofest.

differences of *Throne of Blood* and *Macbeth* every time the film is discussed? What is in the end achieved by a detailed comparison of the
film and the play? In other words, the purpose of this chapter is not to
compare Kurosawa's film to Shakespeare's play but to scrutinize comparison as a mode of cross-media and cross-cultural criticism. Critical
writings on *Throne of Blood* amply demonstrate the difficulty of genuine comparative studies, as I pointed out in part 1. Specifically, I will
discuss adaptation as a particular mode of comparative discourse that
foregrounds some of the problematic aspects of comparative studies in
cultural criticism.

To avoid any misunderstanding, I would like to say at the outset that
when it is done skillfully, the enumeration of various textual details
where Kurosawa departs from Shakespeare's text can help us better appreciate *Throne of Blood*. There is nothing inherently wrong with the
act of comparison, which is a useful and often necessary mode of criticism. Comparison becomes problematic when it is used as a means of
establishing or reinforcing a hierarchical relation between the original

and the adaptation regardless of the specific value accorded to each term of the hierarchical dichotomy. And we can find many examples in the critical writings about *Throne of Blood* that show the danger of value judgment disguised as comparative approach. For instance, John Gerlach makes some interesting points by analyzing *Throne of Blood* in relation to *Macbeth,* but his overall argument remains unconvincing because his comparison does not lead to an analysis of Kurosawa's film on its own terms. The ultimate objective of Gerlach's essay is to prove that Kurosawa's film is an unsatisfactory adaptation because it does not faithfully translate Shakespeare's tragedy into a new medium.[1] Frank Kermode simply refuses to consider *Throne of Blood* in his review of Shakespearean films because he sees it as "an allusion to, rather than a version of, *Macbeth.*"[2] Even when Kurosawa's adaptation is granted a much greater sense of autonomy, frequently it is still subordinated to the original's "essence." Thus Robert Hapgood asks what distinguishes *Throne of Blood,* Verdi's operas *Otello* and *Falstaff,* or Prokofiev's *Romeo and Juliet* from run-of-the-mill adaptations of Shakespeare's work. "On the one hand," writes Hapgood, "they have their own integrity and can be enjoyed on their own terms without reference to Shakespeare. . . . On the other hand, although they may take considerable liberties with the original, they are faithful in their own ways to some essence in it."[3]

Macbeth is not the only original source to which *Throne of Blood* is compared. Another source that is mentioned frequently by critics is Noh. In fact, the study of the film's connection to Shakespeare's text and the study of the film's borrowing of Noh conventions are often pursued simultaneously. For many critics, the influence of Noh in the film is precisely what makes it unique and successful. They agree that Kurosawa's superb use of Noh successfully Japanizes Shakespeare. For others, the imprint of Noh makes *Throne of Blood* an aesthetically complete yet, unlike other Kurosawa films from the same period, anti-humanistic film. Donald Richie, for instance, sees Noh as static, the opposite of human freedom: "In equating Asaji with both the witch . . . and with the Noh, Kurosawa suggests that the rite, the ritual, man's idea of the world, the rigid, the formal, the pattern of life endlessly the same—that this is the opposite of the free, the human. The static, the full-formed, is negative. The only positive is that which chooses faith, which chooses to believe and does so in the face of reason, history, experience and the world as it seems."[4] David Desser also finds the limitation of the film in its appropriation of Noh: "The narrative mode employed by *Throne of Blood* combined with its presentational mode of action points up what is, at heart, the problem with the film. If No is an abstract form, a form of symbols which substitute for action, the cinema is concrete. . . . No tries to remove the concrete from its presentation through a variety of formal means. Although No uses human actors, these actors are abstracted by the wearing of symbolic masks. No relies on specific dance movements to substitute for action. . . . Kurosawa tries to use the concrete nature of the cinema in similarly abstract ways."[5] Again, it is absurd to say that the discussion of Noh is irrelevant for our understanding of *Throne of Blood*. That the witch in the woods first looks like the mask called *yaseonna* (old lady) and later appears with the face of the mountain witch *yamauba* is an important piece of information.[6] However, it is hardly enough to point out how Kurosawa uses a particular Noh mask as a model for the face of a particular character in the film, for it does not really say anything specific about the film itself. Moreover, some of the connections pointed out by critics have already been explained explicitly by Kurosawa. For instance, Kurosawa reports to Sato Tadao that he showed Mifune (who plays the role of Washizu/Macbeth) the Noh mask called *heida,* a mask of a warrior, and to Yamada Isuzu (Asaji/Lady Macbeth) the *shakumi* mask, a face of a beautiful middle-aged woman on the verge of madness.[7] I do not think that the task of the critic is to repeat merely what the film's director has already said; rather, we must scrutinize and test his remark in relation to the film.

One of the prevalent objectives of Kurosawa criticism has been to assert the Japaneseness of *Throne of Blood*. For this purpose, Robert Hapgood tries to locate the sources for Kurosawa's alterations of *Macbeth* in Japanese history. According to Hapgood, the historical setting of the film is the earlier part of the civil war period (1392–1568) because in the film's diegesis, muskets are absent and the codes of feudal loyalty are not yet completely discarded. He suggests that the model for Lady Asaji can be found in such historical figures as Hino Tomiko, Ike no Zenni, and Hojo Masako.[8] He might be right about these references, which are all historically specific pieces of information. But this hodgepodge of alleged historical allusions does not necessarily lead to the conclusion that in *Throne of Blood* Kurosawa strives to achieve historical authenticity. Perhaps it is more accurate to say that historical allusions are discovered in the film to give a seal of approval to the film's authentic Japaneseness even though it is an adaptation of a Western play. The correlative reason why the determination of the film's sources is so important for many critics is that it can fix a horizon of interpretation within which the film's meanings and worldviews are unambiguously deciphered. Stephen Prince, for example, connects the use of Noh conventions in *Throne of Blood* to Buddhist tenets and principles:

> The transposition of Shakespeare's themes into a Buddhistic frame is enforced by Kurosawa's aesthetic choices, specifically his decision to call upon traditions of art influenced by Buddhist principles. We have already noted how Kurosawa dispenses with the play's introspective passages where the characters reflect upon the meaning of their actions. In place of this, he offers a presentation of character informed by the traditions of the Noh theater, which was a theater of the aristocratic and warrior classes contemporaneous with the age the film depicts. Noh plays typically presented the confrontation of a wandering priest with a ghost or spirit drawn back to this world by longing and regret and were intended to dramatize Buddhist ethics.[9]

What is problematic is not the reference to the connection of Noh and Buddhism; instead, it is the absence of an explanation of the specific ways Kurosawa successfully transposes Buddhist principles underlying Noh to *Throne of Blood*. Anybody can use formal features of Noh for a variety of purposes, so that the presence of Noh conventions in film, modern theater, or literature by itself does not — and in most cases cannot — simply reproduce the specific religious worldview of Noh without any modifications or transformations. "Much use is made in the film of mist and rain — a tradition in both Chinese and Japanese art, where fog symbolizes what is hidden and mysterious," writes another critic.[10] But again, what specifically fog may or may not symbolize cannot be determined by a reference to traditional Japanese art but only through a careful textual analysis of the film itself. In short, the film's possible sources, whether Shakespeare's *Macbeth*, Noh, traditional Japanese ink painting, or Japanese history, do not solve interpretive questions arising when we see the film but raise more questions that need to be dealt with in our interpretation of the film.

"When Shakespeare was first introduced to Japan in the nineteenth century, Tsubouchi Shoyo, the translator, later felt free to recast the characters of Lady Macbeth and Ophelia into their Japanese counterparts Lady Yodogimi and Kagero in his play *Kiri hitoha*. Kurosawa is following this tradition, allowing himself freedom to render Shakespeare not in western terms, but rather in the style of Japanese battle literature and art of the Middle Ages."[11] This argument by Ana Laura Zambrano is interesting because she does not simply discover traditional Japanese arts in *Throne of Blood* but situates Kurosawa's film in the history of Japanese reception of Shakespeare. The problem with her argument is that Shoyo's *Kiri hitoha* is a so-called *Shin kabuki* (new Kabuki), which became popular in the early twentieth century when Kabuki more or less abandoned its attempt to be a modern theater that directly responded to the rapidly changing conditions of contemporary society. Unlike the Kabuki of the theater reform movement in the 1880s, *Shin kabuki* was not an attempt to reform Kabuki fundamentally or to create a new type of modern theater; instead, it tried to present new materials in a classical Kabuki style.[12] As we shall see, *Throne of Blood* is another attempt by Kurosawa to create a radically new type of *jidaigeki* film. To this extent, it is misleading to see Kurosawa's film as part of a particular tradition represented by Shoyo's play.

Whereas Zambrano makes a cursory reference to an earlier example of Japanese appropriation of Shakespeare, John Collick tries to situate *Throne of Blood* and Kurosawa's other Shakespearean film *Ran* in the specific sociocultural situation of modern Japan and in the history of Japanese reception of Shakespeare in order to challenge the hegemony of text-centered New Critical versions of Shakespeare propagated by the Anglo-American cultural industry. "A materialist analysis of Kurosawa's *Macbeth* necessitates a greater awareness of the cultural position of the film. Most critiques have searched for similarities between Western readings of the play and Kurosawa's. Yet they fail to acknowledge how the Japanese have absorbed and appropriated Shakespeare into their own culture."[13] As Collick argues, there is no question about the significance of the history of the Japanese appropriation of Shakespeare for our understanding of *Throne of Blood*. What does Shakespeare mean in the Japanese context? Why did Kurosawa decide to adapt Shakespeare's play to film? Is there something peculiar about Kurosawa's decision? Collick argues that the Shakespeare Kurosawa appropriates is part of "Japanese tradition":

> Most importantly Shakespeare signified the apex of an era of cultural development in European history. His works were emblematic for many Japanese who sought to create a parallel renaissance in their own country. The plays were transmitted by the British as a cultured expression of civilised patriotism. The emphasis on individualism and sentiment in the writings of contemporary Western critics made the plays appear especially pertinent to those Japanese scholars trying to locate their own identities in a rapidly changing world. They read Shakespeare as a writer who expressed the complexities of motivation and who shattered the simplistic moral equations of traditional Confucian learning. Hence they used the medium of translation to try and formulate a new code of ethics. *In all cases the Japanese intellectuals were able to "read" Western culture according to their own codes of meaning with little interference from colonial ideology.* Once we recognize this then Tsubouchi's, Asano's and Tozana's [*sic*] claims that Shakespeare translation was a patriotic activity are understandable. Furthermore it underlines the crucial fact we must bear in mind when dealing with Kurosawa's films: Shakespeare in Japan is, and always has been, an essentially Japanese tradition. (161; italics mine)

There are at least two problems with Collick's argument. First, what Collick calls "Japanese tradition" is rather ambiguous, and its critical value dubious. "In the cultural revolution of the late nineteenth and early twentieth centuries," argues Collick, "the foundations of Japanese Shakespeare as a cultural, dramatic and literary tradition were firmly established. Recreated from the components of the traditional Japanese theaters, plays like *Julius Caesar, Hamlet* and *King Lear* provided many Japanese people with a medium for expressing the problems of cultural identity" (160–61). What exactly does it mean to say that Shakespeare was firmly established as a Japanese tradition? Does it mean that Japanese so thoroughly digested Shakespeare's work that they were able to use this alien form to express the specific problems of Japanese modernity? Or does it suggest that the use of the conventions of traditional Japanese theaters successfully Japanized Shakespeare? Second, the assertion that Shakespeare was read by Japanese "with little interference from colonial ideology" is highly questionable. One of the earliest examples of Japanese translations and adaptations of Shakespeare's work is *Sakuradoki zeni no yononaka* (1885), based on *The Merchant of Venice*.[14] In the published version of the play, the play proper is preceded by a discussion of Western and Japanese literature among the three fictional characters, each of whom represents a different ideological position. One of them, Wada, promotes and celebrates the Westernization of Japan; Nakamura opposes Westernization; and Toriyama pursues a hybrid combination of West and Japan. In their fictional conversation, Japan's inferior position vis-à-vis Western imperial powers is clearly registered (e.g., Wada refers to Japan as a "half-civilized" country), and three characters represent different reactions to Japan's geopolitical position in the age of imperialism and colonialism. It turns out that the play itself is written by Toriyama, who tries to construct a new Japanese subject — internationally at least equal to the Western imperials nations, and domestically obedient to the imperial dictates of the Japanese nation — by combining Shakespeare (or his popularized version by Charles Lamb) and the popular literary forms of Edo. What underlies Collick's assertion is a problematic periodization of modern Japanese history. Collick writes that "Japan was fortunate enough to escape invasion during the mid nineteenth century and, despite the rapid progamme of 'Westernization' at the beginning of this century, managed to preserve its developing culture from political or ideological interference until after 1945."[15] As I pointed out earlier, the use of 1945 as a fundamental point of disjunction in modern Japanese history is an ideological maneuver carried out by both Western and Japanese critics for their own political purposes. Collick's assertion of a pristine Japan uncontaminated by Western colonial ideology is no different from Noël Burch's discovery of pure Japaneseness in prewar Japanese cinema. The contextualization of Kurosawa's cinema without questioning the illusion of autonomous, self-enclosed prewar Japan is bound to be problematic. But this pristine Japan is essential for Collick's argument because without it he cannot assert the essential Japaneseness of a Shakespeare interpreted by the Japanese at least until the end of World War II.

Collick's idea of radical interpretation of Shakespeare appears particularly questionable in the following passage: "[During the American Occupation of Japan, MacArthur] encouraged the transformation of the education system so that it followed the style of American campuses. More university places were made available for Japanese students, re-absorbing the intellectual into the mainstream of society. It also narrowed the gap between English, American and Japanese approaches to Shakespeare. One sign that the Anglocentric concept of the plays had a far greater hold on intellectual circles after 1945 was the numerous attempts to translate the texts into idiomatic Japanese. It would seem reasonable to assume that the less precise a rendition the more 'open' it is to radical appropriation" (164). But if this is really the case, why would anybody bother to translate Shakespeare's texts into Japanese in the first place? If "the less precise a rendition the more 'open' it is to radical appropriation," where and how can we draw a line separating appropriation from creation? What maintains a connection between original and translation when the latter so radically departs from the former? Is it the former's "essence" as Hapgood suggests? Again, Collick's dismissal of postwar Japanese translations of Shakespeare as too idiomatic reveals his romanticization of a pure, exotic Japan that never existed.

The Discourse of Adaptation and Cultural Capital

Adaptation is one of the least-explored topics in contemporary film theory. As a critical topic, it is mostly ignored, and sometimes even stigmatized, as an obsolete issue. What makes adaptation a questionable topic is, as I have briefly touched on in the preceding section, the implied notion of fidelity; that is, whenever adaptation is discussed, the adaptation's fidelity to the original almost inevitably comes up. Yet fidelity is a misleading and unproductive notion because it establishes a hierarchical relation between original and adaptation, and also because it assumes that there is some uniform set of standards for comparing two artworks in different media. What is ignored in both is not only the specificity of the adaptation but also that of the original. The neglect of adaptation has also perhaps something to do with the institutional history of film studies, its desire to distance itself as much as possible from the memory of the 1960s, when film was smuggled into the American university system in the form of "literature-and-film" courses in which serious theoretical questions on the specificity of film were rarely raised. Although film studies does not need to take up this old topic again as a significant part of research and teaching, as long as a certain type of discourse about adaptation continues to be used in film criticism, we cannot avoid dealing with the question of adaptation in a critically engaged fashion.[16]

"Adaptation" is not a neutral term simply signifying a cross-media, cross-historical, or cross-cultural translation (e.g., from play to film, from a Renaissance text to a contemporary one, from a French novel to an American film). There is always value judgment involved in the use of the term "adaptation." On the one hand, when the original is less important than the adaptation, the film may customarily be called adaptation, but the original and its film adaptation would not be laboriously compared. On the other hand, if the original is regarded as a great piece of artwork, no matter how good the film is, the value of the film adaptation would be measured against that of the original work of art. In what I shall call the discourse of adaptation, the original is always valorized over the adaptation, which is never granted autonomy regardless of its aesthetic value. The discourse of adaptation is therefore less the discourse of aesthetics than that of power. Even when it ostensibly focuses on the merits and shortcomings of different aesthetic forms and media, the discourse of adaptation has more to do with the question of power, cultural capital, and the politics of cultural traffic.

Pierre Bourdieu argues that cultural capital can take three different forms: the embodied state, the objectified state, and the institutionalized state.[17] Cultural capital in its embodied state—"in the form of long-lasting dispositions of the mind and body," or more simply, culture, *Bildung*, or *kyoyo*—is something that cannot be transmitted or purchased instantaneously. Embodied cultural capital can be acquired only with the investment of time, effort, and even sacrifice. Cultural capital in its objectified state can exist as paintings, manuscripts,

monuments, artifacts, machines, and so forth and because of its materiality can be easily transferred from one owner to another. As Bourdieu points out, however, "what is transmissible is legal ownership and
not (or not necessarily) what constitutes the precondition for specific
appropriation, namely, the possession of the means of 'consuming' a
painting or using a machine, which, being nothing other than embodied capital, are subject to the same laws of transmission." [18] Cultural
capital in the institutionalized state is produced by academic institutions that certify the qualifications of those who go through an accred-
ited course of study, and in the specific fields of study issue the legally
guaranteed certifications.

Bourdieu's theory of cultural capital helps us to understand the discourse of adaptation and the way it operates in the critical writings
about *Throne of Blood*. The original play by Shakespeare functions as
the objectified cultural capital, which is appropriated by Kurosawa to
make a new cultural product. What is transferred in this transaction is
of course not any specific manuscript of Shakespeare as a material object but the text of Shakespeare titled *Macbeth* (or to be more precise,
a Japanese translation of that text). But this does not fundamentally
change the status of Shakespeare's text as the objectified cultural capital. It merely foregrounds the fact that the acquisition of cultural capital in the objectified state is not just the question of legal ownership
but that of the ability to use that capital, that is, the embodied cultural
capital. *Throne of Blood* as an adaptation is a product of Kurosawa's appropriation of Shakespeare's *Macbeth* as the objectified cultural capital;
moreover, the film demonstrates how much cultural capital in the embodied state Kurosawa possesses. What the discourse of adaptation tries
to control is the specific distribution of cultural capital in the process of
adaptation. In the specific relation of original and adaptation valorized
by the discourse of adaptation, the adaptation is regarded as a means
of capitalizing on the prestige of the original as cultural capital. The
value of the adaptation here can never be independent of the original,
and the quantity of cultural capital objectified in the adaptation never
exceeds that of the cultural capital objectified in the original. Another
factor that plays a significant role in the distribution of cultural capital
by the critical writings about *Throne of Blood* is that the original in this
case is not only perceived as a great work of art but also categorized as a

Western text. The question raised by the discourse of adaptation is not just how Shakespeare's text can be transposed into another aesthetic medium, film, but also how a Western artwork can be translated into a non-Western text. Thus, in the relationship of *Macbeth* and *Throne of Blood*, the distribution of cultural capital and the control over the convertibility of cultural capital into money are not just an instrument by which class division is statically affirmed and reinforced within the boundary of a nation-state; instead, they are directly connected to the questions of imperialism and colonialism, and of the global dynamic of cultural hegemony and struggle. In the discursive field established by the discourse of adaptation, the flow of cultural capital between the West and the non-West is unequal. On the one hand, for the West, non-Western culture exists, if it is regarded valuable, mostly as objectified cultural capital, which can be plundered or cheaply purchased from the non-West as concrete material objects. Therefore, when the West acquires non-Western culture in the form of cultural capital material-ized in specific cultural objects, the subjectivity of the West does not go through any fundamental change or transformation. The acquisi-tion in this case is strictly the process of changing the ownership. On the other hand, for the non-West, Western culture functions as the em-bodied cultural capital. The acquisition of cultural capital in this case cannot but bring about the transformation of the subject of acquisition, the most brutal form of which is called cultural imperialism. The dis-course of adaptation employed in the critical writings about *Throne of Blood* ensures the hegemony of Eurocentrism by asserting the value of Shakespearean essence as cultural capital, whose uniqueness can only perpetuate the reproduction of itself. *Throne of Blood*, regardless of the degree of its success or failure asserted by a particular critic, is recog-nized as cultural capital only to the extent that it contributes to the self-reproduction of Shakespeare's play as a great canonical work.

Specificity of Form and Mode of Production

Why did Kurosawa decide to adapt *Macbeth* to film? What made Ku-rosawa use Noh in his adaptation of Shakespeare's play? What kind of effect is created by the appropriation of Noh conventions? How does the presence of iconographic conventions of traditional scroll paintings change our interpretation of the film? Does the incorporation of traditional pictorial and theatrical conventions in the film indicate that Kurosawa tries to Japanize Shakespeare? Is the film, as Iwasaki Akira claims, a manifestation of Kurosawa's attempt to create a new style of national cinema?[19] To enumerate formal and thematic aspects of *Throne of Blood* that resemble traditional Japanese arts without answering these questions does not in the end adequately illuminate the specificity and critical significance of the film. When critics point out the presence of Noh and other conventions of traditional Japanese arts in *Throne of Blood,* they merely establish the relation of the source and the adaptation and stop short of analyzing how those conventions function in the specific context of the film's textual system. Whether it is a classical theater, historical anecdote, pictorial motif, or religious belief, the search for the film's sources in Japanese traditions as an explanation for formal or thematic aspects of the film often ends up merely asserting the film's alleged Japaneseness.

As I pointed out in the preceding section, the reception of Shakespeare in modern Japan is inseparable from the questions of Western imperialism and hegemony maintained by the unequal production and distribution of cultural capital. But this ideological critique of cultural hegemony does not exhaustively account for all aspects of the Japanese appropriation of Shakespeare. It is also necessary to shift our attention to the formal dimensions of Japanese and Shakespearean theaters. Tsubouchi Shoyo, the most influential figure in the transposition of Shakespeare in Japan, saw the closest equivalent of Kabuki in Elizabethan theater, particularly Shakespeare's, and Spanish drama of the Golden Age.[20] Kawatake Toshio further develops Tsubouchi's argument by claiming that Kabuki and Shakespearean theater share many similarities because both are examples of baroque theater as opposed to classical theater. According to Kawatake, classical theater maintains the three unities (of time, place, and action); it is representational and static; bloody scenes and erotic scenes are not shown onstage but only reported by characters; spoken words are far more important than audiovisual spectacles; genres — tragedy and comedy — are clearly separated; the spectators are encouraged to identify themselves with characters on stage. Baroque theater is basically the opposite of classical

theater: the three unities are freely violated; the identification of spectators and characters can be momentarily broken by defamiliarizing devices; the mode of performance tends to be presentational, and its effect
more dynamic; spectacles of violence and erotic scenes are shown on
the stage as attractions; supernatural entities defy the rules of realism.[21]
Kawatake argues that these two theatrical traditions are not found exclusively in the history of Western theater but also in that of Japanese
theater. For example, Chikamatsu's *shinju mono* and *sewa joruri* can be
regarded as examples of classical tradition because of their observance
of the three unities. Even though Noh has some baroque characteristics (e.g., use of ghosts and the supernatural, audiovisual presentation of a character's illusion and recollection), it is still closer to classical tradition because of its aristocratic sensibility and the three unities
maintained by its centripetal, convergent, and cohesive tendencies. The
baroque tradition in Japanese theater is best represented by Kabuki,
whose identity is formed by dynamic changes and hybridity constantly
violating the classical sense of order and unity. (The word "Kabuki,"
"the noun form of the adjective *kabuku,* tilted or off-centre, meant the
unorthodox, the strange, the new.")[22] A Japanese tradition represented
by Kabuki is therefore quite different from a Japanese tradition represented by Noh. In certain respects, Kabuki shares more common features with Western baroque theater than with Noh.[23] Here is another
indication that the dichotomy of East and West is more a problem to
be scrutinized than an answer to interpretive questions arising when
we study Japanese theater, cinema, literature, and other art forms.[24]

In *Throne of Blood* there are many shots that remind us of traditional
Japanese ink paintings. Are these images simple imitations of specific
visual styles found in the history of Japanese art? Are they used to Japanize the pictorial look of the film? To answer these questions, we must
take into consideration the development of fine arts in modern Japan.
In the world of art, the binarism of Japan and the West reigns supreme.
Since the early Meiji, art has been divided into two distinct categories,
the product of native Japanese traditions and that of modernity influenced by the West.[25] Often, the binarism appears explicitly in generic
distinctions such as *nihonga* versus *yoga* (Japanese-style painting versus Western-style painting) and *hogaku* versus *yogaku* (Japanese-style
music versus Western-style music). In literature, it takes the form of

tanka/haiku versus *shi*. Although the dichotomy of Japan and the West played a fundamental role in institutionalization of art, it did not create simple homologies between different art forms. For instance, *nihonga* was established as a distinctive genre much more firmly and earlier than *hogaku*. Moreover, as cultural institutions, *nihonga* and *hogaku* stood for markedly different values and ideologies.

Nihonga as an artistic genre was invented and promoted by Ernest Fenollosa and Okakura Tenshin. With Fenollosa, Okakura participated in the founding of Tokyo Art School (Tokyo Bijutsu Gakko) in 1889 and tried to set a unique direction of official art education in modern Japan. Initially, the art school did not teach Western-style painting to students. It was not until 1896 that a department of Western-style painting and design was added to the school's structure. By the time Tokyo Art School was established, however, Western-style painting was on the rise. Influenced by *rangaku,* or Dutch studies, Japanese artists—for instance, Takahashi Yuichi—had been struggling to master the newly discovered art of Western-style painting. The government also supported *yoga* because of its usefulness for military and scientific purposes. Okakura reacted against the Meiji Enlightenment and the mindless modernization promoted by technocrats. Okakura in this sense was not a straightforward traditionalist or ultranationalist as he was depicted by the Nihon Roman-ha (Japanese romanticists) during the 1930s, and his promotion of *nihonga* was not a simple return to Japanese tradition. Instead, Okakura tried to establish a new national art without succumbing to the utilitarian desire to catch up with the West by simply imitating it.[26]

If *nihonga* was a symbol of resistance against the Meiji Enlightenment and Westernization in the name of modernization, *hogaku* was part of the remainder of Japan's feudal past that needed to be preserved as a historical record. Okakura's counterpart in the field of music was Izawa Shuji, who as the first president of Tokyo Music School (Tokyo Ongaku Gakko) tried to modernize Japanese music. Izawa was a rationalist and believed in the goal of the Meiji Enlightenment. In his scheme, traditional Japanese music was something that needed to be modernized and improved through a gradual fusion of Japanese and Western musical scales. Izawa's position was reflected in the curriculum of Tokyo Music School, where only Western-style music was taught. It was in the late Meiji that the Ministry of Education finally decided to get involved in the preservation of traditional Japanese music. But the official effort to keep a permanent record of traditional music by using the Western notational system was not successful. Because Western and Japanese music have very different musical scales, the notational system of Western music as a system of signs cannot accurately transcribe the sound of traditional Japanese music. The promoters of modernization believed this to be a necessary loss to give Japanese music a universal language.[27]

The markedly different positions of Japanese-style painting and Japanese-style music were also inseparable from the question of market value. The establishment of *nihonga* as an autonomous genre distinctively different from Western art was possible partly because of the acceptance and consumption of Japanese art by the West. Without the impressionists' "discovery" of Japanese art and a large demand for Japanese woodblock prints and other traditional artworks, Okakura would not have been able to resist the pressure from the government and ideologues of *bunmei kaika*. The native Japaneseness, which was so dear to ultranationalists, was in the end constructed in the nineteenth century by the dynamic of the international art market and the desires of Western consumers.

This brief examination of music and painting in the Meiji period shows how protean the dichotomy of Japan and the West can be. The art of the novel presents another different relationship of these two categories. Unlike painting or music, the novel does not allow such a distinction as the Western-style novel and the Japanese-style novel. A painter can choose to be an artist of Western- or Japanese-style painting, but a writer can only be a writer of the novel. Any novels written by Japanese writers are simply novels regardless of their stylistic features and forms; in contrast, styles, techniques, and raw materials clearly differentiate Japanese-style paintings from Western ones. There are writers who are influenced by, or actively try to appropriate, traditional literary genres such as *gesaku bungaku* and *monogatari*. But unlike traditional forms of poetry such as *tanka* or *haiku*, *gesaku bungaku* as such did not survive modernization, and no writer can claim to be a *gesaku sakka,* or writer of *gesaku bungaku,* today except as a symbolic gesture.

Why is it that modern Japanese writers could not establish something like *"Nihon shosetsu,"* or the Japanese-style novel? There is first of all the question of language. Language is not an external material whose form one can manipulate freely. The inseparability of language and consciousness does not allow a transcendental position from which one can switch back and forth between "Japanese-style subjectivity" and "Western-style subjectivity." Another reason why the modern Japanese novel did not follow the pattern of other art forms is that the novel defies formal constraint. In other art forms, formal rules and material constraint make it possible to construct a generic distinction of Japanese and Western styles. As a literary genre, the novel cannibalizes other genres and conventions, so that the differentiation of the Japanese- and Western-style novel as two distinct subgenres of the modern Japanese novel simply does not make any sense. As an art form whose existence is very much dependent on contemporary social structure, economic system, and modes of communication, the novel has been affected by modernization most brutally since the Japanese encounter with the West in the mid–nineteenth century.

Among the three types of art just discussed, cinema is closest to the novel. The instruments or machines used to produce films are standardized throughout the world, and film stocks are also basically the same. Film, a quintessential art of the age of industrial capitalism, is a supple and omnivorous medium that can incorporate almost any artistic forms, traditions, and media by freely crossing national boundaries. Therefore, what appears to be the most specifically Japanese features of the film does not guarantee its Japaneseness. Instead of confirming the idea of national cinema with unique film form, the self-conscious appropriation of traditional arts problematizes it. Woodblock prints, traditional music, or classical theaters do not have any fixed meanings when they are appropriated or quoted in films. Their significance and function can be determined only by examining how they are specifically used in a particular film.

We examined earlier *The Men Who Tread on the Tiger's Tail* as a complex intertextual reworking of Kabuki and Noh originals. *Throne of Blood* approaches similar historical and formal problems with another intertextual twist. Instead of directly adapting a Kabuki play, Kurosawa chooses to translate Shakespeare's play. Because of formal affinities between Kabuki and Shakespearean theater, the adaptation of

Shakespeare's play becomes a mediated commentary on Kabuki conventions and their influences on Japanese cinema. Whereas in *The Men Who Tread on the Tiger's Tail,* Noh is present mostly as an intertext in the literal sense, *Throne of Blood* appropriates Noh more specifically as a performing art. The masks, makeup, body movement, and symbolic conventions of Noh are fully incorporated in the film. In the specific context of the Japanese reception of Shakespeare, Kurosawa's use of Noh can be regarded an act of experiment. It is also a contestation of the dominant conventions of *jidaigeki,* which is, as I pointed out earlier, so much influenced by Kabuki. The most conspicuous—and notorious—example of Kurosawa's attempt to get rid of Kabuki style from *jidaigeki* is the way the actors deliver their lines.[28] Instead of pronouncing words articulately, they loudly yell so fast that it is often impossible to understand what they are saying. One critic, who is extremely upset by Kurosawa's alleged disrespect for the sound quality of the actors' pronunciation, demands that he add subtitles to the film. The critic even sarcastically adds that *Rashomon* was internationally recognized as a masterpiece because the foreign audiences could see it with subtitles, while the Japanese audiences had to struggle with the incomprehensible lines of the actors.[29] Another possible explanation for the use of Noh in *Throne of Blood* comes from theory of cultural capital. Noh has been used as a device of legitimating popular culture as a type of serious art in the modern cultural history of Japan. *Throne of Blood* can be seen as Kurosawa's conscious attempt to create "art cinema" within the Japanese studio system. In conjunction with this institutional use of Noh, it is also important to remember that there is a tradition of appropriation of Noh by Western modernists and Orientalists (e.g., William Butler Yeats and Ezra Pound, via the work of Ernest Fenollosa). The 1950s was the period when international—European—film festivals began to play a large role in the production and distribution of films as cultural capital on an international scale. The incorporation of Noh, which was perceived as the imprint of unique Japaneseness, responded to the emerging international film culture regardless of Kurosawa's intention.

It is also important to examine Noh conventions in *Throne of Blood* from the perspective of cross-media translation. Noh provides an interesting solution to the problem of adapting theater to film. One of the striking aspects of *Throne of Blood* is that unlike *Macbeth* it is far less dependent on language. Critics almost unanimously agree that Shakespeare's poetry is replaced by visual imagery in *Throne of Blood*. What is crucial here is that the replacement of Shakespeare's poetry with visual image has little to do with the film's "Japaneseness." As André Bazin points out, in theater, the verbal text plays the essential role, and the decor is, no matter how realistic it may look, fundamentally artificial. The film adaptation of theater must find a way of transposing the verbal text into realistic sets and decor while creating the sense of what Bazin calls "dramatic opaqueness" that is produced by the original's artificial or exaggerated sets.[30] The visual details of *Throne of Blood* that remind us of traditional ink and scroll paintings achieve precisely this goal of creating dramatic opaqueness in the realistic images of the world (e.g., the white mist, the fortress and the black mountain castle with its low ceiling, Noh stage–like rooms, the forest where there is a thundershower while the sun is shining). Noh conventions in the film successfully translate the original's dramatic energy and intensity without having recourse to the verbal language. I therefore respectfully disagree with those who laud *Throne of Blood* as a great artistic achievement yet refuse to discuss it as a genuine Shakespearean adaptation ("The great masterpiece, of course, is the Kurosawa film, *Throne of Blood*, which doesn't really come into the Shakespeare question at all because it doesn't have the text.")[31] As Bazin argues, the cross-media translation or adaptation is always a transformative process, in which there is no place for the fetishistic attempt to reproduce the original's formal features (e.g., Shakespeare's text).

> It's true that everything in the film [*The Pastoral Symphony* (Jean Delannoy, 1949)] isn't a success, but this is certainly not due to what some consider to be the ineffable aspect of the original. I don't care much for Pierre Blanchar's acting, but I do think that Michèle Morgan's beautiful eyes—which are able to communicate the blind Gertrude's innermost thoughts—and the omnipresent motif of the ironically serene snow are acceptable substitutes for Gide's simple pasts. All it takes is for the filmmakers to have enough visual imagination to create the cinematic equivalent of the style of the original, and for the critic to have the eyes to see it.

To be sure, this theory of adaptation comes with the following warning: that one not confuse prose style with grammatical idiosyncrasies or, more generally still, with formal constants. Such confusion is widespread—and unfortunately, not merely among French teachers. "Form" is at most a sign, a visible manifestation, of style, which is absolutely inseparable from the narrative content, of which it is, in a manner of speaking and according to Sartre's use of the word, the metaphysics. Under these circumstances, faithfulness to a form, literary or otherwise, is illusory: what matters is the *equivalence in meaning of the forms.*[32]

Bazin's theory of adaptation makes us see *Throne of Blood* not as an anomaly but as an exemplary case of film adaptation.

Despite its use of Noh and other types of traditional Japanese art, *Throne of Blood* has little to do with the affirmation of Japaneseness. Nor is it an attempt to create a new national film style. Instead, Kurosawa simultaneously tries to expand the possibility of film form and reexamine the specific history and genre conventions of Japanese cinema. *Throne of Blood* is a unique film made by a true innovator of cinema.

18. *The Lower Depths*

The Lower Depths (Donzoko, 1957) is an adaptation of Maxim Gorky's famous play of the same title. Except the transposition of the story's setting to the Edo period, Kurosawa's film is quite faithful to Gorky's text. Because Gorky's *The Lower Depths* was a major repertoire piece of a type of modern Japanese theater called *shingeki,* the film can be discussed as another attempt by Kurosawa to reexamine the modern history of Japanese theater and its interrelationship with the formation of Japanese cinema.[1]

There is nothing artificially theatrical about the film's sets and decor. As usual, they are designed and built with tremendous care under the direction of art director Muraki Yoshiro. The physical setting of the film is confined to a dark pit surrounded by a stone wall. In the pit are two buildings, a squalid tenement house and the landlord's house, which is in slightly better condition. Inside the tenement house, which is tilted to one side, everything is dirty and broken. Posts and crosspieces are warped and rotten, and walls and sliding doors are blackened with soot and dust. The dilapidated tenement looks very real. Along the long wall are bunk beds with curtains, which, by functioning as framed "stages" within the screen space, open up interesting formal possibilities. But even these theatrical devices do not appear to be artificial, since they are fully integrated into the overall architectural design of the tenement. The filth is matched by grimy costumes that are again realistically faded and torn. According to Yamada Isuzu, who plays the role of Osugi (Vassilissa in Gorky's play), the rehearsal for shooting in the open set lasted for sixty days. Everything was carefully prepared for the rehearsal as if it had been an actual take; the only thing missing was the camera. Yamada reports that Kurosawa wanted the actors' costumes to be worn ragged naturally at the end of the unusually long period of rehearsal.[2]

While the sets and costumes are made to intensify the effect of cinematic realism, the actors' performances are highly theatrical. *The Lower Depths* shows us a brilliant example of ensemble acting in film: the actors are all unnaturally talkative and articulate, and the interactions between them are rhythmic and well timed. As Donald Richie suggests, instead of a realistic representation of characters, the film seems to present the virtuoso performance of the actors, who maintain distance from the roles they play. Thus, by superbly integrating cinematic realism and theatrical presentationalism, *The Lower Depths* presents another innovative model for the adaptation of theater to film.

19. *The Hidden Fortress*

Kurosawa's first wide-screen film, *The Hidden Fortress* (Kakushi toride no san akunin, 1958) is a typical formula *jidaigeki,* an adventure movie set in the sixteenth-century civil war period. The princess Yukihime's family Akizuki is destroyed by its rival clan, Yamana. Yukihime must travel to the domain of a friendly feudal lord, Hayakawa, with clan treasure to reestablish the Akizuki clan. Yukihime's loyal retainer and general Makabe Rokurota (Mifune Toshiro) deceives two peasants, Tahei (Chiaki Minoru) and Matashichi (Fujiwara Kamatari), into carrying gold bars hidden inside sticks. The duo of greedy, cowardly, and comical peasants are constantly quarreling with each other but cannot go their separate ways. Yukihime, who talks and acts like a man, yearns for life outside the rigid social hierarchy of the feudal system. Rokurota understands Yukihime's feeling but sacrifices everything, including his own sister's life, for the sake of the Akizuki clan. The film introduces a series of what appear to be insurmountable obstacles, and our interest lies in watching how the film's principal characters overcome those obstacles one by one to finally escape from the enemy's territory.

The simplicity of the formula narrative is juxtaposed with some breathtaking audiovisual composition and spectacles, which exploit the potentialities of the wide-screen format. Yet *The Hidden Fortress* is in the end too formulaic and shallow, lacking a kind of textual density found in Kurosawa's other *jidaigeki* entertainment such as *Seven Samurai* or *Yojimbo*. It has been pointed out that *The Hidden Fortress* shares some similarities with *The Men Who Tread on the Tiger's Tail*.[1] In both films, the powerless lord is helped by the devoted retainer; the protagonists are pursued by the overwhelmingly powerful enemy; to survive, they must pass the enemy's barrier; and there are comic commoner(s) who end up helping the protagonists escape. Some critics emphasize the similarities between these two films so much that they claim *The*

Hidden Fortress is a big-budget remake of *The Men Who Tread on the Tiger's Tail*. But despite the obvious similarities, the two films are fundamentally different. *The Men Who Tread on the Tiger's Tail* is among other things a brilliant commentary on Noh's influences on Kabuki and Kabuki's influences on Japanese cinema, but *The Hidden Fortress* lacks any such intertextual complexity.

The film's original title is *Kakushi toride no san akunin* (Three Bad Men in a Hidden Fortress).² "Three bad men" apparently refers to the general and the two peasants. What remains unclear is in what specific ways they are bad. They may appear bad in the eyes of the two peasants, who believe the general is a bandit trying to smuggle gold bars out of enemy territory and see themselves as his accomplices trying to outsmart him. But from early on, we know that none of them are really bad. Rokurota is a person of high integrity in the context of feudal society, and as greedy as they are, Tahei and Matashichi are in the end comically lovable characters. This ambiguity of badness or difference between good and evil is further reinforced by the absence of clear images of the enemy, who remain anonymous throughout the film. The only individuated character among the enemy is Tadokoro Hyoe (Fujita Susumu), who in the end betrays his lord and helps Rokurota and the princess. The film therefore lacks a by now familiar Manichaean moral dichotomy, which is simultaneously asserted and problematized in many of Kurosawa's successful films. What we find in this technically superb yet trite film is instead the "sparkle of an imitation jewel" (Hanada Kiyoteru) and cardboard figures who are "inhabitants of Disneyland" (Masumura Yasuzo).³

20. *The Bad Sleep Well*

Political Corruption and Theatrical Performance

After *Seven Samurai,* the budget for Kurosawa films continued to be larger than that for an average film produced by Toho. Therefore, Toho asked Kurosawa to establish his own production company to reduce Toho's financial risk and to appease disgruntled employees who complained of the studio's favoritism. As the first film coproduced by Toho and Kurosawa Production, *The Bad Sleep Well* (Warui yatsu hodo yoku nemuru, 1960) was a somewhat risky project because of its subject matter, political corruption at a high level of bureaucracy and big business. Kurosawa's personal commitment to make a socially relevant film certainly played a large part in the realization of the project. The socio-political situation of contemporary Japan is also relevant for our understanding of this ambitious film. *The Bad Sleep Well* was made in 1960, the year of a great political upheaval. A mass protest was launched against a revision and renewal of the U.S.-Japan security treaty (Anpo). The target of the so-called Anpo struggle was the continuous incorporation of Japan into the Cold War system as a shield against the advancement of communism in East Asia. People from different social backgrounds from all over Japan participated in political demonstrations in fear that postwar democracy might be killed by the return of authoritarian militarism. They detested the heavy-handed style of prime minister Kishi Nobusuke, who had held various important ministerial positions during World War II and had been imprisoned as a class A war criminal during the Occupation. Japanese cinema, which had been reluctant to get involved directly in radical political activism, could not completely ignore the immediate political concerns of so many Japanese. The political climate of 1960 cast its shadow over not only the films of a short-lived New Wave movement represented by

Oshima Nagisa and a few other Shochiku directors but also the more mainstream films.

The Bad Sleep Well does not contain any direct reference to key political events of 1960, except that the behind-the-scenes kingpin whom Iwabuchi (Mori Masayuki) talks to on the phone several times might remind the viewers of Kishi Nobusuke. Kurosawa's film belongs to a subgenre of films dealing with political conspiracy and corruption among politicians, bureaucrats, and corporate executives, the best-known practitioners of which include such filmmakers as Yamamoto Satsuo and Kumai Kei. What distinguishes *The Bad Sleep Well* from the films of Yamamoto or Kumai is that Kurosawa is not particularly interested in portraying the specificities of a corruption case. *The Bad Sleep Well* never concretely shows how a bid system works, how a secret price arrangement is made, or what political parties or politicians are involved in an illegal price-fixing agreement to raise election campaign money or to line their own pockets. Instead of depicting the mechanism of corruption in concrete detail, the film merely refers to the corruption as an established fact. In contrast, in Yamamoto's *Annular Eclipse* (Kinkanshoku, 1975), which also deals with the collusion of a leading conservative party, public corporation, and construction companies, the development of a political scandal is painstakingly delineated, and the film's detailed representation of the corrupt relationships between bureaucrats, politicians, and the business elite functions by itself as a form of indictment. In *The Bad Sleep Well,* the evil of the establishment and corporate powers does not necessarily lie in the corruption per se but lies in the personal sacrifices imposed on those who are less powerful. When we watch Yamamoto's films, we learn about the concrete mechanism of corruption in contemporary Japan. *The Bad Sleep Well,* in contrast, tells us almost nothing about the specific details of collusive bidding. Each type of film has its own advantages and disadvantages. In the rest of this chapter, instead of discussing which is the more politically effective, I shall mostly focus on some of the specific strategies used by Kurosawa to deal with the difficult subject of corruption.

From the beginning, it is clear that the operative mode of narration in *The Bad Sleep Well* is not realism. In fact, the film's first scene is paradigmatic to the extent that it demonstrates the utmost importance of a staged performance in the film. Almost everything in *The Bad Sleep Well* is a carefully orchestrated spectacle, and the sense of theatricalness is emphasized throughout. The film opens with Nishi Koichi (Mifune Toshiro) and Iwabuchi Yoshiko's wedding reception, which is, as a social ritual, already theatrical by nature. The inherent theatricalness of the diegetic content is further reinforced by the way it is presented. The first shot after the credits shows the elevator's doors. As the doors open, the guests for the wedding reception leisurely get off the elevator and proceed to a reception desk. The elevator arrives again, but this time it is not the guests but a group of newspaper reporters and cameramen who rush to the reception desk. The opening of the elevator's doors functions as a visual punctuation mark, announcing the start of a theatrical performance to follow.[1] As if to emphasize the stagedness of the whole scene, the film constantly draws our attention to the scene's spatial arrangement, especially the existence of a boundary separating the reception hall and the waiting area. Only certain kinds of people — the formally invited guests and waiters — are allowed to cross this boundary, which is graphically represented as a frame or proscenium arch on the screen, whereas the detectives and reporters must stop at the threshold of the reception hall as a stage. Moreover, as we see in the conversation between newspaper reporters, the film's characters themselves see the wedding reception as a staged performance: "This is the best one-act play I've ever seen"; "What do you mean — one act? This is only the prelude." Iwabuchi, Moriyama (Shimura Takashi), and Shirai — the corrupt bureaucrats at a semipublic corporation called Japan Unused Land Development Public Corporation — are referred to by these reporters as "oshoku no kurin appu torio" [a cleanup trio of corruption].[2] This use of a baseball metaphor is another indication that what will unfold subsequently is not a natural event but a spectacle, which is meant for the reporters, who are surrogate figures for the film's viewers. The identification of the viewers with the reporters is encouraged by the fact that in the first scene, it is not yet clear who the film's hero is. We guess that Nishi will probably emerge as a protagonist in the rest of the film because Mifune Toshiro is cast in this role, but the significance of his character is not coded clearly in the opening sequence. All the major characters are presented rather evenhandedly, and this deliberate diffusion of the narrative focus prevents us from identifying with any single character and directs us instead to place ourselves in the position of the reporters watching the performance.

The establishment of a clear boundary between the reception hall and the waiting area creates a distance between staged events and spectators. In the rest of the film, Kurosawa reinforces this sense of distance through the stunning manipulation of mise-en-scène and juxtaposition of sound and image. The observers watch the unfolding of events from a safe distance without directly being threatened by those events. At the same time, they do not have a direct influence on the course of events, either. The most extreme case of the distant observer is Wada (Fujiwara Kamatari), a lower-ranking bureaucrat, who is arrested by the detectives at the wedding reception and later, under the instructions of his superiors Moriyama and Shirai, tries to kill himself by jumping into a volcano. He is saved at the last moment by Nishi, who uses him for his revenge plan. Since Nishi leaves Wada's personal belongings at the edge of a crater, Wada is pronounced dead. Thus Wada occupies the impossible spectatorial position, that is, the position of the dead. He can see everything (his look is almost like an x ray penetrating the opaque surface of things) but cannot take action except as a ghost because he is legally a dead person. The case of Wada shows how the total access to visibility inhibits him from acting on the world to change it. The opposite case is found in Nishi. After his father Furuya, another lower-ranking bureaucrat, commits suicide, Nishi goes to the funeral and observes it from a distance by hiding behind a utility pole. He believes that he is watching the funeral without being seen by anybody. In reality, however, he is the object of the look of the other who takes a picture of him watching the funeral without being noticed by him. At the moment when Nishi believes he is an invisible observer, he ends up being transformed into a photographic image, a key piece of evidence that eventually reveals his true identity to Moriyama and Iwabuchi. Whereas Wada has a privileged access to visibility because he is "dead," Nishi's complete subjection to the look of the other ultimately leads to his own death.

It is important to note that the word "theatricalness" does not have any negative connotation such as the "anticinematic." Instead, it refers to a particular setup of the scene by which the diegetic space is divided into two clearly demarcated areas of performance and observation. As in the wedding reception scene, the performers can be aware of the presence of the observers and therefore adjust their actions accordingly. There are also situations in which the observers see the performers without being recognized by them. In the latter case, the setup resembles the film-viewing experience. For example, Nishi and Wada observe Wada's funeral service, which, as the script describes, "looks like a wide-screen image through the windshield of Nishi's car."[3]

The reception hall scene is remarkable for its analytic precision and narrative economy. The details of the story are so effectively presented in the scene's staged performance, yet unlike more conventional films, the efficient progression of the narrative does not give us the sense of simple linearity. The film's opening anticipates constructed dissonance in the rest of the film, in which what we see and what we hear are thrown into a maelstrom of dialectic interaction. If the film constantly transforms the world into a series of staged performances, it is because reality is hidden beneath what is immediately visible and audible. In *The Bad Sleep Well,* theatricality is a double-edged sword. Depending on how it is used, it can either make the invisible visible or ensure the invisibility of the structure of corruption. On the one hand, theatrical setup is used as a device through which those who hide their corruption cannot but reveal who they really are in spite of themselves. For example, the president of Dairyu Construction Company, which has paid an illegal rebate to Iwabuchi's group, gives a speech at the wedding reception. Jolted by the arrest of Wada and his company's executive, the president apologetically repeats in his speech that he does not know anybody in the Public Corporation. Through his persistent denial, he ends up admitting that he does know some of the top bureaucrats of the corporation rather intimately. What leads to this revelation of truth through denial is the theatrical setting of the reception scene. On the other hand, theatricality is also used by the corrupt bureaucrats to make the system of corruption invisible to others. Iwabuchi is like a seasoned actor performing onstage when he faces newspaper reporters and photographers in front of his office door. The backstage is his office, shut off from the outside by the doors, yet connected to the invisible Boss through the telephone line. Throughout the film, the door appears as a recurrent visual motif separating onstage and off-stage areas.

The construction of theatrical space is also facilitated by the fact that the film's drama occurs at a limited number of mutually isolated locations. Although the film includes some exterior scenes and references to real geographic sites, no realistic sense of unified diegetic space emerges because spatial relations between different locations are not clearly established. Spatial fragmentation is underlined by the lack of exterior views of the office buildings and private homes where the actions occur. For instance, in the opening sequence, there is no establishing shot showing the exterior appearance of the building in which the wedding reception is held. The only exceptions are the "N-I Motazu," a garage owned by Nishi and his close friend Itakura, and the office building from which Nishi's father jumped to death. The film shows the exterior views of these buildings, both of which are closely related to Nishi's past and revenge plot.

Duplicitous Identity and Deadly Knowledge

When Nishi comes home with a bouquet of flowers for the second "bridal night," his true identity has just been exposed. Tatsuo, his brother-in-law, calls Nishi by his real name, "Itakura." Unprepared, Nishi turns around. He barely escapes when Tatsuo tries to kill him with a shotgun. After this incident, Nishi and Itakura move to their new hideout, the remains of a munitions factory. Together, they reminisce about the wartime and postwar days: how they became good friends while working at the munitions factory, and how they survived the postwar chaos together. Back then, they were innocent and hopeful, but the promise of a new Japan that they saw in the immediate postwar years has been mercilessly broken in the corrupt world of the present, which is symbolized by Iwabuchi and his group. The insertion of this nostalgic scene right after the exposure of Nishi's true identity indicates that Nishi, even though some of his tactics may seem dangerously close to his enemy's, is fundamentally different from Iwabuchi and what he represents. Unlike the characters in many other Kurosawa films, Nishi and Iwabuchi are merely hero and villain, between which there is no relationship of doubling to render their identities ambivalent.[4]

The absence of ambivalent opposition between hero and villain in *The Bad Sleep Well* does not necessarily mean that the film simply lacks any kind of uncertainty. On the contrary, almost everything in the film is duplicitous, including verbal utterances, images, and characters. Take, for instance, the film's original title, *Waruiyatsu hodo yoku nemuru* (The Worse They Are, the Better They Sleep). At first, its meaning seems rather simplistic. As ironic as it is, it merely inverts a common-sensical understanding of bad guys' psychology: those who commit a crime would be tormented by their conscience, so that they would not be able to sleep well. But once we examine the implications of the key term "to sleep" *(nemuru),* the meaning of the title becomes far more ambiguous. The word *nemuru* and its related phrases are used in the film's key scenes. *Nemuru* means "to sleep" literally and "to die" meta-phorically. The film deliberately plays with these two different mean-ings of the word. When Nishi closes in on the corrupt bureaucrats, Iwa-buchi receives a bottle of sleeping drugs from the Boss. Ostensibly it is a "gift" to Iwabuchi, who cannot sleep well because Nishi is increasingly gaining the upper hand. The implicit message is, however, that Iwa-buchi must commit suicide before the investigation of the corruption scandal starts implicating the Boss, who does not hesitate to sacrifice Iwabuchi or anybody else to stay in power. In his office at home, Iwa-buchi adds a few drops of the sleeping medicine to a glass of wine. Is he going to commit suicide or just going to sleep? If he takes a little dose of the medicine, he can refresh himself by a good night's sleep. If he takes too much, however, he will never wake up. When we watch this scene, we cannot tell Iwabuchi's intention. The moment of suspense is interrupted by the return of Yoshiko from Nishi's secret hideout. He tries to pump the information out of her about Nishi's whereabouts by blatantly putting on a show of repentance. Then he urges her to drink a glass of wine with the sleeping medicine to make her susceptible to his words. At this point, we realize that earlier Iwabuchi was not about to kill himself but only trying to sleep well.

Another sleep-related phrase repeated in the film is "Good night." Iwabuchi's son Tatsuo comes to see Nishi to find out what he is up to every night. He asks Yoshiko to get more crushed ice for whisky. She comes back but falls down on her hands in a corridor. Unlike in the film's opening scene of the wedding reception, this time, it is not Tatsuo but Nishi who rushes to help her, showing Nishi's growing affection toward his wife, which he probably did not have when he married her. When he sees Nishi's affectionate treatment of Yoshiko, Tatsuo looks apparently relieved and happy and leaves their living quarters while loudly saying "Good night" to them. Tatsuo's words are ironic because Nishi and Yoshiko have never slept together. And yet those words are in the end uncannily appropriate because toward the end of the film, Nishi is put to sleep by Iwabuchi's killers. The almost identical phrase is uttered by Iwabuchi in the last scene during his telephone conversation with the Boss. Before he hangs up the phone, Iwabuchi says, "Good night, sir," even though it is still morning. He immediately apologizes to the Boss for his mistake. He explains that he did not sleep the preceding night to take care of Nishi, so that he mistook day for night. Is this a simple slip of the tongue? Is it the unconscious manifestation of Iwabuchi's resentment toward the Boss, who indirectly ordered Iwabuchi to kill himself? Or is it a figurative speech reflecting the film's title, "the worse they are, the better they sleep"? Throughout the film, "to sleep" is a dominant rhetorical trope whose meaning remains ambiguous because of its constant shift between literal and figural.

Even though they do not form a relationship of doubling between them, Nishi and Iwabuchi are contradictory characters by themselves. The most extreme case of the characters' duplicity is found in Nishi. On the one hand, to hide his identity, Nishi has exchanged his family register with his friend Itakura. Thus Nishi is actually not Nishi but Itakura, and Itakura is Nishi. To pursue his revenge against Iwabuchi, Nishi in a way commits suicide first. As I have just pointed out, Nishi's figural death is literalized by the hands of Iwabuchi and his gang at the film's end. On the other hand, Nishi's scheme of hiding his identity is counteracted by his desire to recover his authentic self. If he really wants to conceal who he is, why does he so obsessively try to remind the corrupt bureaucrats of his father's suicide? What Nishi wants is not a simple revenge but social recognition. He desires to be recognized by others, not only by those responsible for his father's death but also by society *(seken)*. Symbolically, Nishi's identity is from the very start a false one. He is the illegitimate son of a bureaucrat, who was forced to commit suicide by the Iwabuchi gang. By exposing the hideous crime of Iwabuchi, his father-in-law, Nishi can simultaneously kill a symbolic father who has robbed him of an authentic self and atone for his insensitive treatment of his real father.

On the surface, Iwabuchi is at least as contradictory as Nishi. The film presents him as a good-natured father and a cold-blooded killer at the same time. A similar kind of contradiction is present in *Ikiru,* another Kurosawa film featuring a bureaucrat. As a civil servant working at the city hall, Watanabe is almost nonexistent. Watanabe's career in bureaucracy spans thirty years, during which he has not taken even one day off. He buries himself in piles of papers, mechanically stamps them with his seal, and eats noodles for lunch every day. Following the same routine like clockwork and rarely showing any sign of emotion, Watanabe is like a mechanical doll, or as his nickname says, a "mummy." Watanabe's lack of interest in others at the office is quite a contrast to his strong attachment to his son, Mitsuo. While bureaucracy robs him of humanity, the family seems to give him back the sense of who he is. As a bureaucrat, Watanabe has not accomplished anything, but as a father, he has at least achieved the goal of raising his son by himself. Watanabe's identity is almost completely dependent on his role as father and his desire to become dependent on his son once he retires. Yet when he finds out he has stomach cancer and less than six months to live, Watanabe finally comes to realize how meaningless his daily routine at the office and his sentimental attachment to his son are. In *Ikiru,* Watanabe's love for his son is clearly portrayed as compensation for his suppression of human feelings and desire in the bureaucratic environment.[5] How strongly Watanabe feels attached to his son is inversely proportional to how worthy he feels as a social being. What appears to be contradiction in Watanabe's character is in fact not a contradiction at all; instead, the manifestation of his human emotion in the familial realm is a direct result of his alienation in the public one.

Unlike Watanabe, Iwabuchi does not act as a caring father as compensation for his loss of humanity in the public realm. In fact, Iwabuchi's identity in the familial setting has no direct connection to what he does as a remorseless bureaucrat. In the world portrayed by *The Bad Sleep Well,* the public and the private are so clearly separated from each other that the same person can simultaneously be an affectionate father and a self-serving bureaucrat without any apparent inner conflict. Powerful as he is, Iwabuchi is in the end a replaceable cog of the gigantic bureaucratic machine, and if there is any contradiction, it is not in Iwabuchi's interiority but in the system itself. What constitutes people like Iwabuchi is the reification of society, through which the relationality of social life is occluded. Iwabuchi simultaneously occupies two contradictory social positions without experiencing any inner turmoil because there exists no position from which the totality of the system can be grasped. In the world in which Iwabuchi lives, the public and the private are so clearly fragmented and compartmentalized that a logical contradiction does not turn into a contradiction in lived human experiences.

What distinguishes Nishi and Iwabuchi is that the former is tormented by his contradictory identity, whereas the latter is not. Although it has been argued that the film's social criticism is ultimately marred by a melodramatic twist in the plot, the film's real structural flaw lies in Nishi's weak motivation. As an illegitimate son, Nishi was never close to his father. It was only after the father's untimely death that Nishi tried to reconcile himself with his past and fulfill his filial obligations. The unnaturalness of his revenge is suggested by the photograph of his father's dead body. Whenever Nishi's avenging spirit begins to fail, he gazes at this picture, which he always carries with him, and its gruesomeness reminds him of the wickedness of Iwabuchi and other bureaucrats at the Public Corporation and spurs him again to pursue his plan to its end. Nishi's need for this horrifying picture as an artificial stimulus belies his motivation for carrying out a plan to avenge his father, and the technical brilliance of Nishi's maneuver merely ends up accentuating the absence of an urgent cause that motivates him to act. As he starts reflecting seriously on the meanings of his action, he is tormented by his doubt that he is using innocent Yoshiko as a mere means for his personal vendetta. Nishi finally resolves his inner conflict by admitting his love for Yoshiko and by transforming what started as personal revenge into an act of indicting the corruption of bureaucracy and big business. "Take good care of Yoshiko. Otherwise, I'll kill you," Tatsuo says to Nishi at the wedding reception. Tatsuo feels responsible for his sister's physical handicap because she injured her leg while riding a bicycle with him when they were children. Tatsuo's threat is of course only a figure of speech, a mixed expression of his guilt, his challenge to the world that sees his friend Nishi as an opportunist, and his plea to Nishi to protect his sister from the gossip of scandalmongers. Ironically, however, Nishi is killed toward the end of the film precisely when he decides to take care of Yoshiko as a loving husband. It is because of the successful justification of his own action that Nishi finally falls short of realizing what he sets out to achieve and suffers a deadly consequence.

Nishi is not the only one who is punished for his self-understanding and awareness of the invisible system of corruption. There are also others who end up knowing what they should not. In the preceding section, I pointed out that the film's diegetic space consists of a limited number of mutually isolated, autonomous places. The mechanism of corruption and the true identities of the corrupt officials are protected by spatial fragmentation, staged performances, and fragmentary subject positions. The revelation of truth becomes possible when the fragments of social relations are connected in such a way that the structure underlying them can be rendered in the form of narrative. More specifically, the invisible mechanism of corruption comes to the surface when the film shows the characters' movement from one location to another in transitional shots. Three scenes of movement are particularly important: Shirai's complicated route to get to the safe-deposit box at the bank where his share of kickback money is stored; Nishi's rescue of Shirai from an assassin; and Tatsuo and Yoshiko's drive to Nishi's hideout. What is common in these scenes is that when Shirai and Iwabuchi's children reach their respective destinations, they encounter startling truths that are unbearable to them. When Shirai finally opens the safe-deposit box, his kickback money, ¥5 million, is missing; what is left instead is a picture of the office building where Nishi's father, Furuya, killed himself. To remind Shirai of this incident, there is a X mark put on the seventh-floor window from which Furuya jumped to his death. When he is about to be murdered by Iwabuchi's killer, Shirai is saved and taken by Nishi to that office building's seventh-floor room with the X-marked window. In the room, Shirai finally learns that Wada is still alive, and that Nishi is the son of Furuya, whom Shirai forced to commit suicide five years ago. At the end of the third transitional scene, Tatsuo and Yoshiko learn from Itakura that Iwabuchi's henchmen have already murdered Nishi, whose death is cleverly disguised as a drunk driving accident. These rare transitional scenes are included not to enhance the sense of realism but to mark the eventual revelation of shocking facts, which drive the two characters appearing in these scenes insane: because of Nishi's psychological torture, Shirai ends up suffering from acute schizophrenia; Yoshiko mentally breaks down when she finally understands what kind of person her father really is.

To render the invisible structure visible does not necessarily mean that what is hidden must be represented visually. The film also tries to deconstruct the naturalistic illusion by exploring the contradictory relation of sound and image. In the scene of Wada's funeral, he watches his superiors, Moriyama and Shirai, paying their respects to the soul of the deceased (i.e., Wada) while Nishi's tape recorder plays back Moriyama and Shirai's conversation previously recorded at a nightclub. The two bureaucrats talk about how they successfully tricked Wada into committing suicide. As Nishi starts the tape recorder, the solemn sound of *mokugyo* (a wooden drum used at a Buddhist ceremony) and the priests' chanting of a sutra is replaced by the lively sound of mambo music at the nightclub, which further widens a gap between the outward appearance and the interior psychology of Moriyama and Shirai and transforms the funeral as a sacred ritual into a farcical performance. Through this juxtaposition of sound and image, Nishi tries to make Wada see what he believes as reality is only a field of (mis)representation. However, it is important to remember that Wada has access to the truth of who Moriyama and Shirai really are through Nishi's defamiliarizing technique only because of his figurally dead status. And like Nishi, Wada is literally killed by Iwabuchi's henchmen toward the end of the film.

One character who survives the battle unscathed is Iwabuchi. There is, however, a moment when Iwabuchi, too, seems to glimpse an opportunity for recognizing a fundamental rift between his public and private selves. Right before he learns the location of Nishi's hideout from Yoshiko, whom he has just drugged, Iwabuchi seems a little startled by his own image reflected in a mirror in the upstairs corridor of his house. This is a rare moment of self-reflection when he becomes conscious of himself. Because of the particular way in which the shot is composed, we get a strange feeling that what we see in the mirror is not Iwabuchi's reflection but another person who looks like Iwabuchi looking back at himself. Iwabuchi's hesitation in front of the mirror creates a moment of suspension. Then Yoshiko comes out of the room to run after Iwabuchi. At first, only her reflection in the mirror is visible on the screen, while she remains in the off-screen space. When we see Yoshiko entrapped in the mirror, we realize that Iwabuchi has lost his chance of self-recognition and will continue his fight even by exploiting his own daughter as a means for self-preservation.

Memory and Repetition

In the film's penultimate scene, Itakura hysterically cries out, "All Japan will be fooled again." What does "again" refer to? The corruption scandal that Nishi tries to expose is not the only one in which Iwabuchi, Moriyama, and Shirai are involved. It is a repetition of what happened five years ago. Nishi's father, Furuya, was forced to commit suicide to protect his superiors; this time, it is Wada's turn to play the sacrificial lamb. When Shirai begins to believe that Wada is still alive through Nishi's psychological manipulation, Moriyama and Iwabuchi try to calm him down by entertaining him at a geisha restaurant, the exact same place where they tried to persuade Furuya to commit suicide. Shirai recognizes the repetition of what happened five years ago, and when Nishi forces him to reenact Furuya's action till the end, he finally loses his mind. Far from being an isolated incident, the collusion of Dairyu and the Public Corporation is an integral part of the larger system that rules Japanese society.

The physical setting of the scene, the ruins of a munitions factory, gives another dimension to Itakura's desperate cry. The desolate landscape cannot but suggest that the first time all Japan was fooled was either during or after the war: the wartime Japanese government's propaganda that continued to hide the disastrous results of Japanese military campaigns in euphemistic language, or the Occupation's reversal of the initial democratization process as a result of the U.S. government's Cold War policy. In this case, the repetition of deception does not simply refer to the specific corruption case for which Nishi is killed but points more broadly to the joint effort by the American and Japanese governments to renew the mutual security treaty in spite of a massive protest by the Japanese people.

During the war, when they were higher school students, Nishi and Itakura were mobilized at the munitions factory. In the middle of the desolate remains of the factory is a smokestack, under which they had a big fight and as a result became good friends. Itakura and Nishi say they were a good pair because Itakura's family were all killed by the American air raid in Muroran, Hokkaido, and Nishi is an illegitimate son. Nishi and Itakura, two *apure geru* who could have been killed during the Americans' carpet bombing of the factory, survived the war and the postwar years together. A decade and a half later, they come back to the same location to expose the underside of the Japanese power structure that is directly responsible for the cycle of political corruption. They confine Moriyama in the bomb shelter and do not give him any food until he tells them where he hides kickback money. During the war, it was Nishi, Itakura, and other mobilized students who were starved; this time, it is Moriyama, who belongs to the generation of Japanese who mobilized young students for the war effort, who is forced to starve by the two former students. Thus Nishi's effort to expose the corruption of bureaucrats and corporate executives has a symbolic dimension.

However, Nishi is again defeated by the system of domination. It is not Iwabuchi but Nishi who is tortured in one of the remaining bomb shelters of the ruined munitions factory and killed at a nearby railroad crossing. What could have happened fifteen years ago finally happens at the hands of those who were responsible for the Japanese military aggression and its disastrous consequences. To this extent, the final elimination of Nishi at the remains of the munitions factory creates a certain sense of ending or closure. The legacy of postwar democratization is suppressed by those who most profited from militarism (e.g., the invisible Boss, who, for many contemporary viewers, stood for prime minister Kishi Nobusuke). Itakura tells Tatsuo and Yoshiko that he can never go back to his real self, "Nishi," since Nishi died in the car that is registered under the name of Nishi. Now there is a permanent split in the identity of Itakura, who can no longer reclaim his own past. This fundamental break in Itakura's personal history metonymically signifies the similar disjunction in the history of Japan. After Kishi resigned from his office in the midst of the Anpo turmoil, Ikeda Hayato became prime minister and promoted the "income-doubling plan." The annual double-digit economic growth in the 1960s led to the so-called Japanese economic miracle. For many Japanese, the immediate postwar years were rapidly becoming a distant memory.

21. *Yojimbo*

Yojimbo (Yojinbo, 1961), the second film produced by Kurosawa Production, was an enormous commercial success, one of the most profitable films distributed by Toho in 1961. As briefly noted earlier, the release of *Yojimbo* had a devastating effect on Toei *jidaigeki*, whose popularity had already began to eclipse slowly but irreversibly. What was so new about this film that shows a masterless samurai's involvement in a vicious gang rivalry? Why did it deliver a fatal blow to the once dominant kingdom of Toei *jidaigeki?* Instead of rejecting genre cinema outright, Kurosawa fully embraced a popular formula of *jidaigeki.* Far from an art film that criticizes the popular cinema aloofly from a safe distance, *Yojimbo* is first and foremost an entertainment film, only it is incomparably more exciting than the average product of Toei *jidaigeki.* In other words, the release of *Yojimbo* had such enormous repercussions because this time Kurosawa beat Toei *jidaigeki* filmmakers on their own game.

As in such films as *Seven Samurai* and *Throne of Blood,* Kurosawa systematically ignores all Kabuki-derived conventions of Toei *jidaigeki.* Sato Masaru's extraordinarily powerful and often comical musical score violates the conventions of film music by deliberately using "wrong" instruments in the orchestration.[1] Another innovation Kurosawa introduces in *Yojimbo* is realistic sound effects, particularly the sound of slashing human flesh with a sword. In Toei *jidaigeki,* the sword fight is a ritualistic dance, in which the hero demonstrates his elegant handling of the sword in carefully choreographed movement. So many villains can be slaughtered without making the spectators sick because instead of accentuating the consequences of violence, they only act to supplement the hero's graceful action. By introducing the realistic sound of human flesh being cut, Kurosawa made the viewers realize how artificial Toei *jidaigeki* was. And in addition to sound effects, the graphically explicit depiction of violence also contributes to the new level of realism in *Yojimbo.* When he comes to the town of Manome, Sanjuro (Mifune Toshiro) is greeted by a stray dog holding in its mouth a severed human hand. As he hears from Gonji about the rival gangs' bloody battle, Sanjuro decides to stay and clean up the town. To sell himself as a bodyguard to the gang boss Seibei, Sanjuro demonstrates his martial skills by cutting off the left arm of a ruffian who works for the rival gang led by Ushitora. To underline the gore of the scene, Kurosawa does not forget to insert a shot of the severed arm falling to the ground. In the middle of the film, Ushitora's brothers Inokichi (Kato Daisuke) and Unosuke (Nakadai Tatsuya) attack Seibei's son Yoichiro and one of his lead henchmen, Magotaro. When Inokichi kills Magotaro with his sword, blood gushes from the victim's neck. As Hashimoto Osamu points out, traditionally there was no direct representation of blood in the conventional *chanbara* film. No matter how many enemies the hero kills, the sword fighting in Toei *jidaigeki* is therefore absolutely bloodless. Only the horror film *(kaidan eiga)* explicitly showed blood on the screen.[2] *Yojimbo* destroyed this convention once and for all.

Toei and other film studios were swift to pick up and imitate these bloody images of realistic sword fighting from *Yojimbo.* A new genre of film called "cruel film" *(zankoku eiga)* emerged in the wake of the commercial success of *Yojimbo* and its "sequel" *Sanjuro.* In 1963, for instance, Toei's most successful film at the box office was no longer a formulaic *jidaigeki* film but Imai Tadashi's *Cruel Stories of Bushido* (Bushido zankoku monogatari), an omnibus film that graphically depicts the masochistic sufferings of the protagonists over seven generations.[3] By this time, Toei *jidaigeki* as it had existed in the 1950s was already over, and for a brief period of time, *jidaigeki* as a genre tried to survive by providing the spectators with escalating depictions of physical violence. Kurosawa deeply regretted having inadvertently initiated this new trend of excessively gory films. To show that violence is not a prerequisite for *jidaigeki,* he made *Red Beard,* which does not include a sword fight scene.

Although it was largely responsible for the rise of cruel films, many of which can be classified as art cinema, *Yojimbo* is fundamentally different from the majority of films that belong to this subgenre of *jidaigeki.* What distinguishes *Yojimbo* from other graphically violent films is its humor. The protagonists of Imai's *Cruel Stories of Bushido* or Koba-yashi Masaki's *Harakiri* (Seppuku, 1962) are serious figures who endure or indict the cruelty of the feudal system and its customs. In contrast, Sanjuro never presents himself as a defender of social justice; he is a self-consciously humorous character who always maintains a critical distance from himself. The humorous aspect of Sanjuro becomes apparent, for instance, when he reveals or invents his name. The nameless protagonist makes up his name, "Kuwabatake Sanjuro" (mulberry field thirty years old), when he sees the open expanse of a mulberry field next to Seibei's house. This scene reminds us of a famous scene from Itami Mansaku's masterpiece *Akanishi Kakita* where the protagonist Kakita names a merchant's daughter "Sazanami" when he sees the rippling surface of a pond *(sazanami)*. This kind of humor is markedly absent in the cinema of cruelty and in Toei *jidaigeki*: in the former, the hero often takes himself too seriously, and in the latter the hero's personality is ultimately insignificant because it is completely subordinate to the public persona of the star. Moreover, in *Yojimbo*, the villains are also grotesquely humorous and unique; they look like caricature figures straight out of comic books, yet each is not a mere stock character but carefully individuated and distinguishable from the others. This strange combination of exaggerated distortion and unique individuality in the figuration of villains is something that is simply absent in Toei's popular *jidaigeki* and artistically acclaimed cruel films.

What makes *Yojimbo* more than just a popular genre film is its superb use of wide-screen format. Along with 3-D, CinemaScope was introduced in Japan in 1953. The first CinemaScope film exhibited in Japan was *The Robe* (Henry Koster, 1953). In December 1953, before the film was shown to the general public, Twentieth-Century Fox held a gala screening attended by Japanese princes, foreign diplomats, and other dignitaries. The screening opened with a short film about the coronation of Queen Elizabeth II, followed by the main feature. Although *The Robe* was commercially shown only at two theaters (one in Tokyo and the other in Osaka), CinemaScope was so popular that by the following August, twenty-four theaters equipped with anamorphic lenses and new sound systems had already been built throughout Japan.[4] In 1957 Toei released the first Japanese film in CinemaScope, *Bride of Otori Castle* (Otori-jo no hanayome), a *jidaigeki* directed by Matsuda Sadatsugu. Whereas the popularity of 3-D movies faded rather quickly as soon as they were shown as a novelty in urban centers, CinemaScope and its variants became a de facto standard format in the 1960s.

Kurosawa was quick to adopt this new technological innovation. In 1958 he made his first wide-screen film, *The Hidden Fortress*, and continued to explore the possibilities of the 'Scope screen until returning to the standard format in *Dodeskaden* (1970). In *Yojimbo*, with the master cinematographer Miyagawa Kazuo, Kurosawa fully exploits the compositional possibilities of the wide-screen format. In the early part of the film, the camera follows Sanjuro closely. One of the recurrent images here is the low-angle medium close-up of Sanjuro's body from the chest up. Because the screen is jam-packed with Sanjuro's upper body, the upper portions of the houses, and the skies, the low-angle composition on the 'Scope frame creates the feeling of claustrophobia and abstraction. Even though Sanjuro walks from one location to another to explore the town's main street, the audience does not get a clear sense of how the diegetic space is organized yet. Only after Sanjuro decides to destroy the rival gangs does the camera show the town's physical environment in the straight-on angle composition. A diametrically opposite type of composition is used in the scene where the two rival gangs confront each other at the town's crossroads. Kurosawa foregrounds the rectangular shape of the 'Scope frame by placing each group of gangsters at the edges of the screen, leaving the large middle space empty (except that in the background is Sanjuro, who is on top of the watchtower, enjoying the confrontation of the cowardly gangsters below). Kurosawa uses diegetic objects on the screen as framing devices to divide the 'Scope frame into distinct spaces of voyeuristic observers and images observed, thus freely changing the shape of a frame within the 'Scope frame. These kinds of formal experiment and precision distinguish *Yojimbo* from other run-of-the-mill entertainment films.

22. *Sanjuro*

The setting of *Sanjuro* (Tsubaki Sanjuro, 1962) is a feudal castle town during the Edo period. The chamberlain's nephew Izaka Iori (Kayama Yuzo) and his friends gather at an abandoned shrine for a secret meeting. They are worried about the corruption of the junior chamberlain Kurofuji (Shimura Takashi) and the clan elder Takebayashi (Fujiwara Kamatari). Iori reports to his friends that he saw the chamberlain to request an official investigation of the two corrupt officials, but the chamberlain said that he might be the real bad one behind them. He advised Iori not to judge people only by their appearances and then tore up the young samurai's petition with a smirk on his face. Disappointed, Iori met the superintendent Kikui next. At first Kikui was hesitant to take any action, but when he heard the chamberlain's reaction to the petition, his attitude changed, and he became supportive. Nine young samurai, including Iori, have come to the shrine at the request of the superintendent, who agreed to discuss with them how to clean up the clan politics. As the young men are rejoicing at Kikui's positive reaction, from the inner sanctuary appears a grubby ronin, Sanjuro (Mifune Toshiro). Yawning and scratching himself, Sanjuro does not even look at the young men directly, but the tone of his voice reveals that he is apparently amazed by their naïveté. Iori and his friends are naturally suspicious of Sanjuro, who explains why he thinks that the chamberlain is genuine, and the superintendent phony. Sanjuro asks them how the chamberlain and the superintendent look. It turns out that the superintendent is a good-looking man, and the chamberlain has an ugly face. Even though they refuse to admit it, the young samurai are judging the two senior administrators by their appearances, thus acting contrary to the chamberlain's advice. Sanjuro's intuition turns out to be correct: the chamberlain is a good guy;

the superintendent, whom the young samurai thought genuine, is the behind-the-scenes kingpin. By this time, the main hall of the shrine where the young men and Sanjuro are hiding is already surrounded by the superintendent's men. Only Sanjuro's tact and masterful swordsmanship save their lives. Unable to watch the young samurai's clumsy actions quietly, Sanjuro decides to help them clean up the corruption among the senior clan officials. Throughout the rest of the film, the youths are saved by Sanjuro time and again but never really understand the discrepancy between appearance and reality and continue judging the character of Sanjuro by his shabby appearance and indifferent attitude toward samurai decorum.

Yojimbo's commercial success prompted Toho to ask Korosawa for a sequel. He had a script based on Yamamoto Shugoro's novel Nichinichi heian (Peaceful Everyday), featuring as a protagonist the hungry, unheroic samurai Sugata Hirano.[1] The script was for Kurosawa's disciple Horikawa Hiromichi, but Kurosawa decided to use it himself after revising it extensively to transform the protagonist into Yojimbo's Sanjuro character. Although the studio's commercial interest played a large part in the origination of the film, it is not the case that Sanjuro, "compared with its predecessor, is considerably more static, and the humor, while more subtle, is also far less radical in intent."[2] Sanjuro, which is not another Sanshiro Sugata, Part 2, is more than just a sequel to Yojimbo.

Despite the presence of the almost identical superhero as a protagonist, Yojimbo and Sanjuro are two quite different films. The most conspicuous difference is that unlike Yojimbo, Sanjuro does not have a close relation with either the Western or hard-boiled fiction. If there are any connections between this film and the Western, it is only to the extent that jidaigeki in general has incorporated some Western structures and motifs.[3] Among Kurosawa's films, Sanjuro is the one that comes closest to a conventional jidaigeki film. It focuses on the internal conflict and power struggle of a feudal clan in the Edo period. Although the film's protagonist, Tsubaki (camellia) Sanjuro, is a ronin, every other principal male character is a real samurai except one, Muroto Hanbei (Nakadai Tatsuya), a henchman of the corrupt superintendent Kikui. The setting of the story is a castle town, and the sense of confinement is accentuated by the fact that most of the action occurs inside samurai residences. In the self-enclosed, civilized space of Sanjuro, there are no galloping horses, no cloud of dust in a desolate town square, no mass of slaves dashing down the enormous stone steps.

The setting of *Sanjuro* is conventional, but the film itself is not necessarily so. The director Kato Tai points out that the conventional *jidaigeki* film starts from an incident or conflictual situation. Individual characters have only secondary importance because they are assigned to the prescribed roles that the given situation requires. That situations and incidents are often derived from the canonical tales and rigidly codified patterns makes the conventional *jidaigeki* doubly predictable. *Sanjuro*, on the other hand, reverses the hierarchical order of situation and individual. The focus of the drama is the conflict and interaction between individual characters, not the conflictual situation. The course of the narrative is not predetermined by any conventional patterns; instead, it changes depending on how the principal characters interact to resolve conflicts among themselves.[4]

As is usually the case with Kurosawa *jidaigeki,* most of the cast of *Sanjuro* do not specifically specialize in *jidaigeki.* What distinguishes *Sanjuro* from *Yojimbo, Throne of Blood,* or *Seven Samurai* is that the film uses a group of young stars who frequently appear in Toho's sarariman comedies and other popular genre movies.[5] The leader of the young samurai group who tries to fight against corruption is played by Kayama Yuzo. In the early 1960s, Kayama became a star by playing the leading role in the Wakadaisho (A Young Master) series. Between 1961 and 1971, Toho produced seventeen Wakadaisho films, staring Kayama as Tanuma Yuichi, a handsome, smart, athletic college student.[6] In every film, Yuichi tries a different sport and sings songs composed by Kayama himself. Yuichi is called "young master" because he is not only the son of an old sukiyaki restaurant owner but also a born leader. Mostly a harmless entertainment, the Wakadaisho films celebrate the economic miracle of the 1960s and the sanitized image of youth culture. Among the young samurai of *Sanjuro,* there are two actors who are also regulars of the Wakadaisho series. Ehara Tatsuyoshi (Sekiguchi in *Sanjuro*) is Wakadaisho's friend, and Tanaka Kunie (Yasukawa) is Wakadaisho's rival, Aodaisho ("a Japanese rat snake," but literally "a blue master"). Hirata Akihiko (Terada) is an indispensable actor in Toho's other popular genre, monster movies (in the original *Godzilla,* Hirata plays Dr. Serizawa, who invents the "oxygen destroyer" and dies with Godzilla). While these young actors play the roles of naive, ineffective heroes, the villains in *Sanjuro* are all played by Kurosawa actors or members of the so-called Kurosawa-gumi: Nakadai Tatsuya, Shimura Takashi, Fujiwara Kamatari, and Shimizu Masao. It is possible to conjecture that *Sanjuro* reflexively criticizes Toho's mass-produced genre movies by using for the roles of naive samurai Toho's young stars, whose acting skill is clearly inferior to that of the veteran Kurosawa actors.

Whereas *Yojimbo* is a black comedy of excess and the grotesque, *Sanjuro* is much more straightforwardly humorous. The film's humor often comes from the incongruity of action and situation. In the film's second sequence, Sanjuro and the young samurai try to rescue the chamberlain's wife and daughter, who are shut up in their own residence by Kikui's underlings. It is already night, and they are all on the premises of the chamberlain's mansion, which is occupied by the enemies. The young samurai are obviously grateful to Sanjuro, who has just saved their lives. At the same time, they are still offended by his casual manners and treatment of them as greenhorns. They protest against Sanjuro and try to act independently. But the film shows how the young samurai constantly misjudge situations and often mimic Sanjuro's behavior without being aware of it. Here, humor is generated by the discrepancy between the young samurai's self-image and their actual behavior, which undercuts that image. When they believe that they are mature samurai in their own right, they act in such a way that they are nothing but imitators of Sanjuro, whom they look down on. To avoid being detected by the enemies, Sanjuro stoops and stealthily moves through the shrubbery. The nine young samurai tag along behind him in the same manner ("like goldfish's feces," in Sanjuro's words). They not only imitate Sanjuro without knowing it but also defeat the very goal they try to achieve by "hiding" in such a conspicuous manner.

Another humorous scene in the same sequence occurs when the chamberlain's wife and daughter Chidori are saved and brought to a barn. It is the first time the chamberlain's wife comes to the barn, but Chidori tells her that she and Iori often come to this hiding place and lie down on a pile of hay together. The mother and the daughter talk about the nice smell of hay and gently lean on a pile of hay as if taking a rest. Chidori's innocent demeanor and her mother's dignified yet carefree manner are completely out of place at this moment when their lives are in danger. Their humorously inappropriate behavior continues in the following scene at the back of the mansion. The young samurai are on the wall, extending their hands to pull up Chidori and her mother, but the two properly dressed ladies refuse to climb the wall. Sanjuro, irritated by their behavior, kneels on the ground and asks them to use him as a stool. The chamberlain's wife still hesitates because it is impolite to put her feet on the samurai's back. Her adherence to proper manner and decorum is absurdly inappropriate under the circumstances. Only when Sanjuro warns her that he will have to kill more people unless she hurries does she finally step on his back while apologizing for breaching propriety. At this point, the film cuts to the next shot showing the grimacing face of Sanjuro feeling her weight.

Sanjuro's threat refers back to a conversation between him and the chamberlain's wife in the barn. Two of the young samurai have captured Kikui's watchman, who refuses to tell where the chamberlain is. Sanjuro suggests that the young samurai kill the watchman because he knows who they are. Immediately the chamberlain's wife objects to Sanjuro and gently admonishes him not to kill people unnecessarily ("Don't kill people so easily—it's a bad habit"). She tells him that he is too "glaring," like a naked sword that cuts well. But according to her, a really good sword is in a sheath. Always with a smile on her face, she does not seem to be perturbed by the immediate danger. Sanjuro is amazed by her out-of-place remark, but he is not angry at her. Although Sanjuro treats the nine young samurai as hopelessly naive greenhorns, he does not react to the chamberlain's wife in the same way. She provides a different perspective, which even Sanjuro cannot dismiss outright. He tries to solve problems by confronting them directly and using the most immediate solution (i.e., violence). He succeeds in achieving his goal because of his masterful swordsmanship, but his method looks immature from society's standpoint. Despite his frustration over the naïveté of the young samurai, Sanjuro is not completely different from them. He has not, socially speaking, grown up yet, though biologically he is no longer young (e.g., Sanjuro's remark "My name? My name is . . . Tsubaki . . . Sanjuro, but I'm nearly Shijuro [forty years old]"). Without his own immaturity or youth, Sanjuro might not have decided to help the young samurai in the first place.[7]

It is worth pointing out that the chamberlain's wife is played by Irie Takako, one of the biggest stars of the prewar Japanese cinema. Irie was born to a declining aristocratic family and in 1927 joined Nikkatsu when acting was regarded as a socially despicable profession, particularly for somebody with her class background. She soon became a star by playing the roles of a modern woman and appearing in such films as Uchida Tomu's *A Living Doll* (Ikeru ningyo, 1929) and Mizoguchi's *Tokyo March* (Tokyo koshinkyoku, 1929). In 1932 Irie left Nikkatsu and started Irie Production, the first production company established by a female film star. In 1933 she starred in Mizoguchi's *White Threads of the Cascades* (Taki no shiraito). After the war, her professional career rapidly declined, and she suffered a series of health problems and humiliating experiences both personally and professionally. In the 1950s, Irie even appeared in many B horror movies as a goblin cat to support her family. The final blow to her career came in 1955 when Mizoguchi forced her to quit *The Princess Yang* (Yokihi). When Kurosawa earnestly asked her to appear in *Sanjuro,* she was retired from the film world and was managing a club in Ginza.[8] When we see in *Sanjuro* Irie Takako playing the role of the chamberlain's wife with a serene air, we cannot but think of her professional career, moments of both glory and humiliation, and her perseverance throughout without becoming too embittered and resentful. If the chamberlain's wife commands the attention of Sanjuro and the film's viewers, it is because of the genuine performance of Irie Takako, who herself embodies the sword in the sheath.[9]

The most talked-about scene in the film is the last scene, the duel between Sanjuro and Muroto Hanbei. The two master swordsmen face each other in an extreme state of concentration without any movement for about thirty seconds. The moment Hanbei and Sanjuro finally draw their swords, the fight is already over: the spout of blood immediately bursts forth into midair from Hanbei's chest.[10] The sudden explosion of violence is shocking, and the gore of the scene unprecedented. After *Sanjuro* and *Yojimbo,* the depictions of violence both in B pictures and in critically acclaimed films escalated increasingly. In so-called *zan-koku eiga,* the cinema of cruelty, severed arms and heads are routinely shown; eyes are gouged out; ears are cut off; a spear pierces the mouth and comes out from the neck; and a samurai is forced to commit seppuku with a bamboo sword.[11] Kurosawa's films were largely responsible for the celebratory images of gruesome violence in *zankoku eiga*. But what many imitators of Kurosawa did not understand was that the sudden burst of violence at the climax of *Sanjuro* was not the primary reason for the film's popular appeal. More than just a gratuitous depiction of violence, the duel of Hanbei and Sanjuro is justified by the careful development of a dramatic conflict underlying the relationship of the two characters.

Why does Hanbei challenge Sanjuro to a duel when everything is clearly over? Why is he so outraged by Sanjuro? And why is Sanjuro reluctant to fight Hanbei? Hanbei is after all a henchman of the corrupt officials whom Sanjuro single-handedly destroys. Does Sanjuro try not to fight with Hanbei because of his great admiration for his opponent? Does he respect Hanbei as a real samurai like himself? If he does, what personal quality of his opponent commands his respect?

Sanjuro:	Do you insist that we should fight?
Hanbei:	I do. I've never seen a man as terrible as you. You've made a fool out of me!
Sanjuro:	Don't be so angry. It couldn't be helped. I gave you the edge on me, that's why. . . .
Hanbei:	What's the use of all that now? Draw your sword!
Sanjuro:	I don't want to fight. If we draw our swords, one of us would just die. It's not worth it.
Hanbei:	It is to me. Anyway, I just can't take your insult lying down!
Sanjuro:	Well, then, let's do it.

Hanbei cannot control his rage not just because Sanjuro fooled him. As Hashimoto Osamu argues, if Sanjuro, a hungry ronin, had outsmarted him to secure employment with the chamberlain, then Hanbei would at least understand Sanjuro's motivation and probably accept his own defeat. But Sanjuro did not force Hanbei to leave the domain unemployed for his own personal gain. Instead of settling down in the castle town as the clan's retainer, like Hanbei, Sanjuro is leaving for nowhere as a masterless samurai. From Hanbei's perspective, Sanjuro's action is totally absurd, and it looks as though Sanjuro has fought with Kikui's group for no apparent reason, except perhaps for amusement.[12] This is probably why Hanbei is so enraged and challenges Sanjuro for a duel. Yet there is more to their relationship.

Hanbei has worked for the superintendent Kikui as a henchman but has never trusted or respected his employer. In fact, he has never thought much of his boss. The film does not give us too much background on Hanbei, but it is clear that he is a drifter hired by Kikui because of his intelligence and masterful skill with the sword. An outsider to the stifling feudal system of the Edo, Hanbei seems to be motivated less by personal greed than by hatred of the system.

Sanjuro: I saw the bulletin board. It seems this clan is in an uproar.

Hanbei: Ha, ha, ha, ha.

Sanjuro: Quite a few men left here a while ago. Where did they go?

Hanbei: I'll take you there now. By the way, what that bulletin board says is outright lies. The bad one is superintendent Kikui.

Sanjuro: But you are Kikui's . . .

Hanbei: Retainer. Birds of a feather flock together. I'm very bad. [With a meaningful smile on his face.] But chamberlain Mutsuta is a fine character. He is difficult to fool. But once he is removed, this clan will be an easy prey. Kikui is crafty but small-minded. If Kikui gets rid of the chamberlain and seizes control of the clan . . .

Sanjuro: You and I can easily manipulate . . .

Hanbei: Him. Well, I'll immediately introduce you to Kikui. Look now, Kikui fancies himself smart. That's why . . .

Sanjuro: He'll be in a good mood if I tickle his pride.

Hanbei: Yes, you listen to me well. A good boy.

Hanbei thinks Sanjuro can be his friend and ally in his revenge against the system. They are both outsiders to the Edo system because they are men of obscure origin and because they are too smart and strong. Sanjuro understands Hanbei's thinking so well that he can finish the henchman's sentences without any difficulty. As Sanjuro sees himself in Hanbei, so Hanbei sees himself in Sanjuro. There is clearly a mutual understanding and recognition. Hanbei has understood who Sanjuro is, and Sanjuro has not only understood who Hanbei is but also recog-

Left to right: Nakadai Tatsuya (Muroto Hanbei), Kurosawa, and Mifune Toshiro (Tsubaki Sanjuro). *Photo courtesy of Photofest.*

nized Hanbei's understanding of who Sanjuro is. In many ways, their relationship is comparable to the relationship of Benkei and Togashi in *The Men Who Tread on the Tiger's Tail.*

Then why does Sanjuro not go along with Hanbei's plan? Is it because he respects chamberlain Mutsuta? It is important to remember that Sanjuro does not help the chamberlain but helps the young samurai who are clumsily trying to wipe out corruption in the upper strata of the clan government. In fact, to the extent that like Hanbei he is an outsider to the rigid hierarchical system of Edo society, Sanjuro opposes what the chamberlain represents. The chamberlain understands who Sanjuro is and therefore feels relieved when he finds out that the grubby ronin has already left town without saying a word. From the beginning, Sanjuro is drawn to the young samurai because of their immaturity and naïveté, that is, their *youth.* Superintendent Kikui tries to capture the young samurai through deception: he has told the group's leader, Iori, that he will join the young people and with them take action against the corrupt clan elders. Sanjuro does exactly what Kikui has promised but failed to do, that is, join the young samurai's group as its tenth member to defeat the corrupt elders' plan. Despite his sarcastic remarks, Sanjuro is attracted to the youth, but not to the mature chamberlain. And as I briefly mentioned earlier, this is partly because Sanjuro himself is not quite grown up despite his age. Even though Sanjuro treats the young samurai as boys, he is himself called "a good boy." The same line, "Yes, you listen to me well—a good boy," is repeated twice in the film: the first time as Sanjuro's remark to the leader of the young samurai, Iori, and the second time as Hanbei's to Sanjuro. As he approaches forty, Sanjuro must grow up. The question is how. He decides not to join Hanbei's revenge against the system; at the same time, he is not interested in obediently working under the chamberlain. He orders the young samurai not to follow him and to stay in sheaths. As Hashimoto points out, the film ends abruptly,[13] as if to signify the film's inability to present a convincing alternative to Hanbei and the chamberlain; rebellion against, and obedience to, the system. In *Yojimbo,* Sanjuro can make the rival yakuza groups fight with each other and kill virtually everybody in the small yakuza-infested town for amusement. Those Sanjuro slays are all good-for-nothing gamblers and criminals, so that he has no remorse whatsoever for his killing spree. In *Sanjuro* the situation is different. Muroto Hanbei is not a yakuza. As Sanjuro says after the duel, *Hanbei is exactly like him.* In the final duel, Sanjuro faces and kills his own double without finding any compelling reason for doing so. Does Sanjuro remain a naked sword? Can he find his own sheath? Is he even interested in finding a sheath? What does he do next after having decided not to challenge the system by working with either Hanbei or the young samurai? What can he do when he has no collectively shared ideal, unlike Benkei and Togashi in *The Men Who Tread on the Tiger's Tail?* These questions remain unanswered as Sanjuro abruptly disappears in front of our eyes.

23. *High and Low*

Form and Content

Part 1. Gondo (Mifune Toshiro), an executive director managing the production division of a large shoe-making company, and the three other executives gather in his living room. The purpose of the three executives' visit is to drag Gondo into their conspiracy to oust the company's president from his post. After a heated discussion, Gondo refuses to participate in their plan. The executives threaten to kick out Gondo from the company and angrily leave his house. On the driveway, Baba, the leader of the conspiracy, promises Gondo's secretary Kawanishi a promotion to the rank of senior vice president if he helps them sabotage Gondo's secret plan. Kawanishi dodges Baba's proposal ambiguously and returns to the living room. Kawanishi is naturally curious about what Gondo is up to, and a vague sense of foreboding makes Gondo's wife, Reiko (Kagawa Kyoko), anxious. Then the telephone rings to break the silence. It is a call from Gondo's associate in Osaka, who informs him of the successful outcome of the negotiation to buy the company's shares. Gondo for the first time tells Reiko and Kawanishi what he has been doing for the last few years. Gondo has secretly been buying the company's shares, so that unbeknownst to his enemies, he is already the largest shareholder. The acquisition of the Osaka shares will enable Gondo to control the company without allying himself with the three executives or the president. To raise money to buy up the shares, Gondo has borrowed against everything he owns, including the house, but his gamble in the end seems to have paid off. Gondo orders Kawanishi to fly to Osaka immediately with a ¥50 million check as a deposit for the shares. When Kawanishi is about to leave for the airport, the telephone rings again. The call is from a young man who claims he has just kidnapped Gondo's son Jun and demands a ransom. Gondo and Reiko are visibly upset and flustered. A moment later, Jun comes into the living room from outside. Was the phone call only a malicious prank? No. Gondo realizes that his chauffeur Aoki's son, Shin'ichi, is missing. The kidnapper has mistakenly abducted Gondo's chauffeur's son, whom he threatens to kill unless Gondo pays him ¥30 million, an exorbitant ransom by any standard. The kidnapper says he made a lucky mistake; Gondo angrily screams that the kidnapper's demand is simply absurd. At first Gondo shows no sign that he will pay the ransom in spite of the plea made by the chauffeur Aoki and Reiko and in spite of the police detectives' request to "borrow money for a while." The choice is very clear: Gondo can refuse to meet the kidnapper's demand, buy the Osaka shares, and successfully take over the company's management; or Gondo can pay the ransom to save his employee's son, but as a result he will not only fail in his scheme but also lose everything, his position at the company and his entire property. After spending an agonizing night, Gondo explains to the detectives why he has decided not to pay the ransom. Inspector Tokura (Nakadai Tatsuya) asks Gondo at least to pretend to accept the kidnapper's demand so that the police will have more time to track down the whereabouts of Shin'ichi and the kidnapper. When the kidnapper calls again, Gondo says he will pay the ransom. He then calls the Bank of Tokyo and asks the president of the bank to bring ¥30 million in cash to his house in the afternoon. As instructed by the kidnapper, Gondo drops bags stuffed with ransom money from a rest room window of an express train and safely recovers Shin'ichi, who has been left alone on the riverbank. Headed by the overly enthusiastic Tokura, the police immediately start the frenetic pursuit of the kidnapper.

Part 2. The kidnapper, who remains invisible throughout part 1, is shown to us in his miserable environment down below Gondo's house. Meanwhile Tokura and the senior detective called "Bo'sn" ask for the Gondos' and their household employees' assistance to capture the kidnapper by showing visual information about the kidnapper's associates. In Gondo's living room, the detectives project an eight-millimeter film and show photos taken from the express train. Gondo is now celebrated by the media as a popular hero. People from all over Japan send him letters of encouragement and support. Creditors are, however, not as generous as the general public. They refuse to accept advance payment of interests and demand the full payment of debt by the deadline. After a painstaking investigation of every possible lead, the police locate the kidnappers' hideout, where they find the bodies of two accomplices. Despite this major setback, the police finally identify the kidnapper as a young medical intern, Takeuchi (Yamazaki Tsutomu), and decide to let him remain free until they can get hold of decisive evidence to convict him of murder. To make Takeuchi reenact the murder of his accomplices, the police give him a forged letter, in which the accomplices threaten to use the ransom money unless he brings them more drugs.

Part 3. The disguised detectives closely shadow Takeuchi all over Yokohama. He seems to stroll aimlessly downtown, where he sees Gondo looking at shoes in a shop window. Takeuchi quickly approaches Gondo and asks for a light. While Takeuchi talks to his victim, Gondo obviously does not recognize the perpetrator. Tokura and his men are watching this bizarre encounter from their car, and they grind their teeth with vexation. After purchasing heroin at a seedy restaurant, Takeuchi goes to a dope alley to test its purity. He chooses a drug addict woman as a guinea pig and kills her by injecting pure heroin into a vein. Thus Inspector Tokura's fanaticism unnecessarily creates another victim, yet instead of regretting his decision to let the kidnapper remain free, Tokura triumphantly declares that because of this murder, Takeuchi cannot escape the death penalty. When he finally shows up at the hideout, Takeuchi is arrested by Tokura and his men. When he handcuffs Takeuchi, Tokura does not forget to say, "Takeuchi, you'll be executed!" In the last scene of the film, at the request of Takeuchi, who is to be executed soon, Gondo visits him in prison. Separated by the glass and wire, Gondo and Takeuchi talk to each other face to face. Gondo asks Takeuchi, "Why are you so convinced that it is right that we hate each other?" Yet no real communication seems to happen between them, and they remain an enigma to each other. Takeuchi bluffs at first, but as he talks he begins to shiver and then cries, shouts, and shakes the wire. As Takeuchi is quickly taken away by the prison guards, the shutter is pulled down over the wire and glass. The echo of the falling shutter is followed by the sound of solemn music. Gondo is now left alone, facing his reflection in the glass. The end title.

Schematic as it is, this brief synopsis nonetheless tells us why there are two predominant interpretations of the film *High and Low* (Tengoku to jigoku, 1963). By many, it has often been regarded a stylistically brilliant yet ideologically reactionary film. Noël Burch calls the tour de force of the film's formal organization a "rough-hewn geometry." Opposite to the illusionist tenet of organic or natural form, Kurosawa's geometric strategy foregrounds the artificiality and constructedness of the cinema at multiple levels of the film's textual system. For instance, the linear narrative development is frequently disrupted and reversed; extreme opposites — close-up and long shot, moving and fixed shots — are abruptly juxtaposed to dislocate the spectator's expectation; the 180-degree rule is routinely violated by the systematic use of the 180-degree reverse-angle shot; and the hard-edged wipe amplifies the sense of jaggedness by showing the frame line moving across the screen. According to Burch, in contrast to these instances of radical experimentation with film form, the thematic content of the film is rather naive and conservative. The credo of Inspector Tokura and the way the police orchestrate the arrest of Takeuchi seem to suggest the existence of political naïveté and conservatism framing the film's ideological space. In *High and Low,* anything seems to be permitted as long as "humanism and democracy" are protected. Nowhere in the film can we find any expression of remorse for the victims — except the rich victim, Gondo — or doubt about capital punishment, which is inherently class biased yet so unreflectively affirmed by the film. Thus Burch writes: "Faithful to the ideology that had dominated Kurosawa's films since the very start, [*High and Low*] tells us that 'there is much misery among us but our police force is excellent' and that 'a chauffeur may earn less than a capitalist but class difference can succumb to good will and human solidarity.'"[1] Another predominant interpretation of the film focuses on Gondo's dilemma rather than on Takeuchi's action and the police's reaction. Although it does not hesitate to acknowledge the stylistic brilliance of the film, this type of criticism focuses more on the film's thematic side. It transforms *High and Low* into a highly charged morality play, the main focus of which is centered on the question of whether Gondo should save the child or himself. By paying the ransom, Gondo "accepts his own actions and accepts those of others as though they were his own,"[2] so that Gondo elevates himself to an ethically higher level of the humanistic ideal. Both of these readings —

straightforward politicization and simple psychologization—point out important aspects of *High and Low* but still fall short of explaining the sheer power of this film and the sense of awkwardness felt by the film's audience. A schematic division of form and content underlying a politicized reading is as suspect as Inspector Tokura's dualistic view of society, and a humanistic reading ignores the film's second part, where Gondo hardly plays any role as a character.[3]

One of the purposes of this chapter is to question these predominant interpretations of the film. I shall not necessarily suggest that Kurosawa is not as politically conservative as Burch argues. Nor shall I try to demonstrate that Kurosawa is not a "humanist." If the object of our inquiry is Kurosawa's intention, then there is no need to psychoanalyze his mind, or to develop a lengthy discussion about his interior psychology. Always, Kurosawa's intention is clear and simple. Kurosawa made *High and Low* "to show the audience how detestable a kidnapping is." Interestingly, whether they admit it or not, the formal and thematic interpretations are finally not much different from each other, since they both end up accepting Kurosawa's publicly stated intention as the film's message. The only difference between the formal and thematic readings is that the former sees the film's message as an evasion of class conflict as a sociopolitical issue, and the latter sees it as an affirmation of humanity as a universal value. Even though his intention is not something we can simply ignore, it needs to be bracketed for a moment and treated as another textual element that is no less or no more important than the film itself. As our examination of Kurosawa's films so far shows, it is sometimes the case that they are artistically successful precisely when Kurosawa fails to achieve what he originally intended to do; that is, it is not unusual to find an inverse relationship between what Kurosawa intends to do and what he actually ends up doing. This is partly the reason why we cannot understand the geometric precision of Kurosawa's formal construction unless we take the content of the film more seriously. What seems like Kurosawa's humanistic cliché for the formalistic critics is not some contingent factor that can be ignored; on the contrary, without this cliché, there might be no rigorous formal experiment in the first place. The critics in the thematic camp also fall short of convincingly demonstrating how concretely humanistic messages are articulated by the film's textual system. What appears to be

an obviously humanistic message in *High and Low* is much more rigor-
ously integrated with the film's formal aspects, and on critical scrutiny,
it may turn out that the film's formal structure problematizes, rather
than reinforces, humanistic leitmotivs.

Like many other films by Kurosawa, *High and Low* is full of overt
binary oppositions and juxtapositions, which are created both thematically and formally. Take, for instance, the characters' clothing. When
she first appears in the film, Reiko wears a Japanese kimono, a traditional Japanese dress. But on the day when Gondo agrees to pay the
ransom and thereafter, she is dressed only in Western-style clothes. In
another instance, what is mobilized for a symbolic effect is the color of
clothes. Kawanishi initially wears a gray suit; after seeing off the guests,
he takes off his gray jacket and wears a white short-sleeved shirt and a
tie; the following morning, he appears in a black suit with a bow tie and
admits that he betrayed Gondo's secret scheme to the rival executives.
The color of Kawanishi's clothes therefore changes from gray and white
to black, symbolically representing his proselytism. The juxtaposition
of the thematic opposites is perhaps most apparent in the film's title,
Tengoku to jigoku, or "heaven and hell." The sense of extreme dualism
on the thematic level is further reinforced by various kinds of formal
juxtaposition. When Tokura and Bos'n try to implant capsules filled
with chemicals into leather bags, Gondo unexpectedly volunteers to
do the job himself. As Gondo calmly talks about his apprentice days
as a shoemaker and starting his new life from scratch, the other characters suddenly stop whatever they were doing up to this point and
maintain their stationary positions. The detectives and Aoki intensely
and/or suspiciously stare at Gondo, and Reiko stands and slightly bows
the head as if she is at prayer. There is nothing unusual about a sudden
break in the kinetic movement of the characters, since it is thematically
motivated; that is, the characters stop moving and maintain their postures in their admiration for, and surprise at, Gondo's calmness at the
moment of possibly the largest crisis in his life. Yet the carefully orchestrated way in which the characters simultaneously take their stationary
postures and their relative positions to each other on the screen makes
a thematic reading only partially acceptable. As they assume the stationary postures, the characters in the scene become part of a graphic
tableau, the stasis of which is juxtaposed to the kinetic energy and flu-

idity in the preceding scenes. This sharp contrast between movement and stasis is further amplified in a shot transition. From the graphic tableau, Kurosawa directly cuts to the inside of the express train running at full speed. The abruptness of this cut from stasis to movement, and from silence to the roaring sound of the express train, shocks the unprepared spectator. Similarly, the single use of color — pink smoke from a tall factory chimney — in this black-and-white film is exemplary for its effect of total unexpectedness.

The formal juxtaposition of binary opposites initially produces a perceptual shock effect, defamiliarizing what seems mundane and normal. At the same time, the lack of subtlety makes the extreme formal dualism rather simplistically Manichaean and predictable. This sense of predictability is further reinforced by such overt symbolism as the number of Takeuchi's prison cell, "four," or *shi*, whose homonym means "death" in Japanese. The compounding effect of explicit thematic and formal oppositions is that *High and Low* starts to look like a film that confirms the prevalent critical view: Kurosawa's films are formally interesting yet lack serious thought in conformity to the taste and mentality of the masses. On critical scrutiny, however, *High and Low* turns out to be a film that proves the simplicity of the dominant critical consensus. To go beyond stereotyped interpretations, the relationship between the formal organization and thematic motifs of the film must be examined more closely.

Despite his formalist position, Noël Burch does not completely ignore his problematic separation of film form from content. For instance, he tries to reconnect the two by recognizing the "stubbornness" of the Kurosawa hero as a key motif.

One feature . . . common to many of these [Kurosawa] films . . . is both thematic and formal; it provides, in most of the mature masterpieces, the key articulation between the two levels. This is the characteristic stubbornness of Kurosawa's protagonists. Indeed, "perseverance in the teeth of adversity" is a phrase that describes nearly every one of Kurosawa's main characters. Instances of this are: the absurd single-mindedness with which Mifune, as the policeman in *Stray Dog*, pursues his stolen revolver; in *Quiet Duel* the surgeon's refusal to tell his fiancée the horrible truth and his headstrong wallowing in private misery; the stubbornness of the drunken doctor pursuing the equally pig-headed hoodlum in *Drunken Angel*. They shed some light on Kurosawa's proclivity for stubborn fantasizers in Western literature, such as Prince Mishkin or the outcasts of *The Lower Depths*. And we shall see that in at least one film, *Living*, this theme provides the entire structural support.[4]

It is not too difficult to see this stubbornness as a consistent thematic motif in Kurosawa's films. As for its formal function, Burch does not fully demonstrate how this character trait is concretely related to the formal organization of any specific film. He evades the question of how formal and thematic concerns are interrelated by adopting the authoritative voice of an ethnographer à la Ruth Benedict: "I should add that this stubbornness syndrome is not merely a personal form; masochistic perseverance in the fulfillment of complex social obligations is a basic cultural trait of Japan, and no doubt contributed to Japan's military successes in the Chinese and Pacific Wars."[5]

To reintegrate the form and content of Kurosawa's films, we need to look at the deceptive obviousness of both formal and thematic dichotomies. The sense of explicit dualism is not created by a random collection of binary oppositions; instead, the binary pairs themselves are systematically juxtaposed to each other. The analysis must focus on how the binary opposite pairs are interrelated to each other in the totality of the film, since their meanings and significance are structurally determined. In Kurosawa's films, a limited set of simple motifs are presented first, and then they go through a series of transformations. Every time basic motifs are repeated, they are slightly displaced and changed. The film as a whole consists of their variations and permutations, which are tightly interconnected in fuguelike construction. Through the process of variation and permutation, parallel relationships are established between two apparently antithetical thematic terms, and two similar motifs often turn out to be the opposite of each other. Rather than being an empty stylistic exercise, Kurosawa's rigorous formalism is crucial to this systematic process of introducing the difference into the same, or the similarity into the difference. This problematization of difference and identity is a twofold process. Kurosawa first introduces a limited number of dichotomies without any ambiguity; then he systematically problematizes the identities of extreme opposites. The problematization occurs both at the levels of form and content, and it is because of this twofold process that form and content are so tightly integrated. Architectonics rather than geometry is probably a more appropriate term to convey the sense of systematicity permeating the totality of Kurosawa's film.

Self and Double

Many Kurosawa films are profound meditations on difference and identity, and *High and Low* is exemplary for its articulate presentation of this axiomatic motif. For instance, the film's protagonists, Gondo and Takeuchi, are presented as the exact opposite of each other. Gondo is a humanitarian and self-made man who has worked hard to attain his aims yet is compassionate enough to abandon his ambition if it interferes with the well-being of innocent others. Takeuchi, in contrast, is portrayed as a cold-blooded, calculating kidnapper-murderer, whose hatred of Gondo is misdirected. Whereas Gondo is called a humanitarian in a newspaper article, Takeuchi is variously called a madman, maniac, and brute. The difference between Gondo and Takeuchi is further underlined when Inspector Tokura explains the psychology of the kidnapper. When the irritated Gondo tells the detectives to ask the kidnapper to return the child at once, Tokura replies that that kind of action would endanger the child's life because the kidnapper has threatened to kill the child if Gondo reports the kidnapping to the police. Gondo becomes more agitated and insists that once the kidnapper realizes his mistake, he will return the child safely to the parent, since he can never extort ¥30 million from a mere chauffeur. Tokura calmly continues to argue that that is only what Gondo thinks the kidnapper would think, and that judging by the maniac characteristics of his action, the kidnapper will probably follow through with his original plan and kill the child. This episode emphasizes that the ways Gondo and Takeuchi think are fundamentally different, so that a line of communication cannot be established between the two. Positioned at the opposite ends of a moral spectrum, Gondo and Takeuchi seem to represent the diametrically antithetical values of a Manichaean universe.

As the preceding chapters have shown, the presence of the Manichaean moral system is not unique to *High and Low*. *Stray Dog* focuses on Murakami's relation to Sato, a veteran detective who guides him as a mentor, and Yusa, a jobless ex-soldier who uses Murakami's gun to commit armed robberies and murders. What is at stake in *Stray Dog*, which was made four years after Japan's defeat in the Pacific War, is how to reconstruct in the chaos of postwar Japan a moral universe in which good (ordinary citizens and the police as their protectors) and evil (criminals like Yusa) are unambiguously separated from each other. In *Rashomon*, skepticism toward humanity is firmly countered by the film's final episode, in which the repentant woodcutter decides to raise an abandoned baby as his own child. This affirmative episode is taken up and developed further by *Red Beard*, where the free medical clinic as a sanctuary for the poor is opposed to a brutal, morally corrupt outside world. The explicit moral Manichaeism underlying these and many other films by Kurosawa is one of the basic characteristics of melodrama. However, the Manichaean perspective of his films does not necessarily make Kurosawa a typical director of this popular film genre. The axiomatic dichotomy of *giri* (obligation or debt) and *ninjo* (human feeling), which is so important for Japanese film melodrama, plays a markedly minimal role in Kurosawa's films.[6] In fact, *giri* and *ninjo* are antithetical to the world of Kurosawa. Kurosawa's aversion to *giri* and *ninjo* comes from the fact that their intelligibility and binding power stem from the overwhelming presence of an organic community as a primary social unit. In the social system governed by the principle of *giri* and *ninjo*, human feeling is not the inner feeling of an autonomous individual but the communally shared feeling. Irreducible to the duality of the public and the private, the opposition of *giri* and *ninjo* articulates the contradiction of the communal system, in which there is no place for an autonomous, individuated self. And it is precisely this logic of communalism based on the differential use of *giri* and *ninjo* that is rejected by the Kurosawa hero. Before the outburst of intense action, the Kurosawa hero falls into a momentary impasse not because he — very rarely she — is torn between *giri* and *ninjo* but because he tries to see through a communal dilemma as an independent individual. Rather than the absolution of the contradictions of the communal system, in the narrative trajectory of the Kurosawa hero is laid out a much more fundamental form of questioning that system. This is why Gilles Deleuze claims that

> Kurosawa is . . . in his own way a metaphysician . . . he goes beyond the situation towards a question and raises the givens to the status of givens of the question, no longer of the situation. Hence it matters little that the question sometimes appears disappointing, bourgeois, born of an empty humanism. What counts is this form of the extraction of an any-question-whatever, its intensity rather than its content, its givens rather than its object, which make it, in any event, into a sphinx's question, a sorceress's question.[7]

Thus, as I pointed out earlier, despite its detective story narrative, the focus of *Stray Dog* is not just whether Murakami is able to recover his stolen gun; instead, it is also the question of how moral judgment can still be made in the chaotic situation of occupied Japan. In *Seven Samurai,* as Deleuze notes, "there is a higher question which can only be extracted gradually from all the situations. This question is not 'Can the village be defended?' but 'What is a samurai today, at this particular moment of History?'"[8]

In Kurosawa films, the manner of presenting two opposite moral values might be absolute, but the way those values are finally related to each other is far more ambiguous. Even though good and evil are fairly obvious by themselves, the boundary between the two is constantly tested, questioned, and problematized. This is why the Kurosawa hero must almost always wrestle a moral question out of the given situations instead of knowing the right answer from the very beginning. The critical moment of transformation comes when the Kurosawa hero is confronted and tried by the ambivalence of a Manichaean system. As we have already examined, this ambivalence of the moral dichotomy is often represented as the similarities between the hero and the villain in spite of their apparent differences. This is also true in the case of *High and Low,* where the similarities between humanitarian Gondo and murderous Takeuchi are strongly emphasized. Despite the absolute difference in what they morally represent, the film establishes a parallel relationship between the two characters. Gondo initially appears as an arrogant businessman. Like Takeuchi, confident and aggressive, Gondo knows exactly what he wants and how to achieve his objective. The negative image of Gondo is only gradually corrected by a revelation of his humble origin, and ultimately by his decision to sacrifice his own life to save somebody else's child. Gondo and Takeuchi are also similar in their refusal of melodramatic sentimentality. Gondo's resistance to sentimental emotion is revealed in his reaction when the chauffeur Aoki prostrates himself before Gondo and promises to pay back the money even if it takes all his life. The sincere expression of gratitude by the chauffeur immediately puts Gondo in a bad mood, and he irritatingly asks Aoki to leave him alone. Takeuchi tries to prove his immunity from sentimentalism by inviting Gondo to the prison right before his execution. Unlike Takeuchi, Gondo does not actually murder anybody, yet his aggressiveness is still expressed in a remark such as "I'll kill them,"[9] which he utters right after the executives leave his house. This remark is followed by the sound of the toy gun and Reiko's murmur: "I'm afraid of Jun taking after you. He also likes killing."[10]

The film opens with the moment of a great change in Gondo's life. The conspiring executives ask Gondo to join them in their plan to oust the president from his post. If Gondo becomes a member of the group, he will be promoted one rank higher; if he refuses, he might be kicked out from the company by the joint forces of the executives and the president. Undaunted by the possibility of losing his job, Gondo flatly refuses their proposal. Gondo's self-confidence comes from his aggressive philosophy of life, which is most succinctly summarized in his advice to his son Jun: "Don't run away from the sheriff all the time. Hide yourself somewhere, and watch for a chance to attack the sheriff. Men either beat or are beaten by others." Following his father's advice, Jun tries to meet Shin'ichi with a surprise attack. But Shin'ichi never shows up, so that Jun's plan to ambush the sheriff fails. This does not mean that Gondo's advice is simply wasted; on the contrary, what he tells his son is so useful that somebody else puts it into practice before Jun and Gondo can finish their respective plans. Jun, the outlaw, misses his opportunity to ambush Shin'ichi, the sheriff, because Takeuchi, the real outlaw, kidnaps Shin'ichi first. The real target of Takeuchi's ambush is, of course, Gondo, who too, as a result of the kidnapping, is ultimately forced to abandon his chance to ambush his enemy. What Gondo tells the kids is exactly what he and Takeuchi both try to do, so that the moral opposition between Gondo and Takeuchi is already undermined from the start. To some extent, Gondo's frustration comes from the fact that he confronts his own double, who has outsmarted him at his own game. Takeuchi's appearance at a crucial moment of Gondo's takeover scheme is not a pure accident. Takeuchi is the repressed side of Gondo's desire, which Gondo must confront as his own problem. That Takeuchi does not appear in the film's first part is important, since his invisibility cannot but force Gondo to look at himself closely. At the beginning of the film, what remains invisible to Gondo is not only Takeuchi but also his own self. Forced to confront himself through the mediation of the invisible kidnapper as his double, Gondo starts reexamining his sense of identity and figuratively returns to the early days of his career as an apprentice shoemaker. And once he starts seeing himself more clearly, whether the police capture the kidnapper or not is no longer a main issue. This partially explains why Gondo is displaced from the central position in the middle and last part of the film's narrative.

The Anxiety of Urban Space

Two crucial questions arise when we examine the relation of Gondo and Takeuchi: (1) Why does Gondo decide to pay the exorbitant ransom to save somebody else's child? (2) Why does Takeuchi hate Gondo so much? Let us put aside the first question for a moment and concentrate on the second. In the film's last sequence, Takeuchi tells Gondo that his shabby boarding room is too hot and humid in summer, and too cold in winter. When Takeuchi is suffering miserably in his room, he can see directly from the window Gondo's luxurious, perfectly air-conditioned mansion, which constantly reminds Takeuchi of his meager existence. For Takeuchi, Gondo's house is nothing but an arrogant display of wealth, an embodiment of the economically privileged's condescending attitude toward the less unfortunate. Thus, an image — how Gondo's mansion appears to Takeuchi — plays a fundamental role in the formation of Takeuchi's hatred toward Gondo. And that image is produced largely because of a spatial relationship between Gondo's residence and Takeuchi's boarding room. If, for instance, Takeuchi could not see Gondo's white mansion directly from the window of his room, he might not have borne ill feelings toward Gondo so strongly. In other words, the particular configuration of urban space and the image created by that configuration are responsible for the occurrence of the kidnapping as much as the economic inequality and class difference.

If the spatial organization of the city partially accounts for Takeuchi's criminal act, the complexity of the urban landscape and geography misleads the police's search for Takeuchi. During the police briefing, what is emphasized is the systematic mapping of space around Gondo's house. On the large map on the wall in the briefing room, directions and spatial relations are clearly marked, and the position of the sun at a different time of a day at a different location is precisely calculated to pinpoint the kidnapper's dwelling. As the film's narrative progresses, however, the sense of order is gradually displaced by that of chaos. After the police briefing scene, the confusion of geography and spatial directions dominates as a significant narrative motif. The spatial relationships and directions mislead and surprise almost everybody. Shin'ichi's drawing of the setting sun confuses the police detectives and his father precisely because it is an accurate image. In downtown Yokohama, Tokura and his men inside the unmarked police car are momentarily disoriented and surprised by the sudden appearance of Takeuchi, who approaches the unsuspecting Gondo to ask for a light. To understand these instances of spatial articulation and their ideological implications further, besides closely analyzing the textual organization of the film, it is necessary to examine such topics as the specific conditions of the Japanese urban landscape in the 1960s, their representations in Japanese cinema, and a theoretical question about the relationship between city and cinema in general.

Space and Cinema

With its tour de force stylistic plays, *Tokyo Drifter* (Tokyo nagaremono, 1966) by Suzuki Seijun is one of the most hyperbolic films of the 1960s. In this highly stylized film, the architectural structure of the sets and the urban landscape play crucial roles. The film's concern with space and the built environment is already apparent in the credit title sequence, which shows various architectural objects of the new Tokyo's cityscape. The title of the film first appears against the background image of the Tokyo Tower, whose height is stressed by the camera's low angle. This image of the imitation of the Eiffel Tower is followed by a high-angle shot of the elevated railroad tracks on which commuter and bullet trains are moving slowly in opposite directions; an image of the complex, winding urban highway system; the Olympic Stadium designed by Tange Kenzo; a large steel-frame bridge over a river; a small outside music hall in a park; and a familiar image of a Ginza street illuminated by neon lights.

This fascination with the city is not unique to *Tokyo Drifter* but quite common among the 1960s Japanese films in general.[11] The comedian Ueki Hitoshi's *The Man Who Flatters Most in Japan* (Nippon ichi no gomasuri otoko, 1965) has a similar credit title sequence showing aerial views of the bullet train, the highway, the Olympic Stadium, the Tokyo Tower, and a Tokyo waterfront. Almost all these images of the city are connected to a radical spatial transformation occurring in the late 1950s and 1960s. The economic recovery and the so-called end of the postwar period were the first important driving forces that initiated the change of the city's outlook. The Tokyo Tower, which was built in 1958, was one of the new architectural structures embodying the end of the postwar period and symbolizing Japan's aspiration to rejoin a club of "advanced nations." But without any doubt, it was the 1964 Tokyo Olympics that radically changed Tokyo's urban landscape. To accommodate the enormous number of spectators and to showcase the recovery and redevelopment of a defeated Japan to foreign visitors, Tokyo must be "modernized." In more concrete terms, money and energy were invested in the modernization of transportation and communication networks. The bullet train (Shinkansen) between Tokyo and Osaka was opened in 1964. Inside Tokyo, the most conspicuous change in the shape of the city was caused by the appearance of the highway system. The filling in of canals, which had started immediately after the end of the war in 1945, continued throughout the 1950s and early 1960s. The widening of streets and the construction of new subway lines meant that there were diggings and constructions all over Tokyo (e.g., the opening scene of Ichikawa Kon's *Tokyo Olympiad* [Tokyo Orinpikku, 1965]). The facelifting of the city continued as vagrants were cleared away from the major train stations and ragpickers were expelled from the new suburbs (e.g., Hani Susumu's *She and He* [Kanojo to kare, 1963]). The emergence of a new urban topography meant that the old map of Tokyo was no longer useful. While developing the new communication networks, the government also tried to modernize the mapping of the urban space. Boundary lines inside metropolitan Tokyo were redrawn, and some of the old wards were integrated into new larger wards. To improve the locatability of places, new street names and numbering systems were gradually introduced without much result. Far from being simplified, the mapping system was further complicated by the coexistence of old and new place names.

One of the effects of this historical shift in the spatial organization of the city was the erasure of collective memory or the dehistoricization of the built environment. All through history, the features of the built environment have been used as powerful mnemonic devices.[12] Names and information that need to be memorized are first attached to particular sections of distinct architectural models or structures so that necessary information can later be retrieved by visualizing those structures and by scanning their relevant sections. This close connection between memory and the spatial organization of the built environment is not an isolated phenomenon observed only in the specialized field of the art of memory. On the contrary, the art of memory exploits an architectural organization of space precisely because in any society space is never an empty container for objects but a social construct whose coherence is maintained by meanings attached by the members of that society to its specific structural aspects. Space has symbolic meanings, and the names attached to places function as a memory bank for people.[13] As a result, not only the actual transformation of the built environment but also the alterations of place names cut off the space's historical ties to the past and accelerate the popular memory's fading-away process.

Since the 1970s, formalist film theory has been instrumental in our understanding of different modes of spatial articulation in film. In his classic study of film form, Noël Burch tries to enumerate all the logical possibilities of constructing filmic space.[14] David Bordwell has further refined Burch's formalist project by reformulating it in terms of cognitive psychology.[15] What is common in various formalist approaches to the question of filmic space is their assumption that the construction of space in film is mainly an aesthetic question. As a result, not much has been done so far on how the filmic construction of space is related to people's experience of social space. Space is not a meaningless, neutral form that makes our experience possible; on the contrary, it is constructed according to formal patterns and rules necessitated by specific ideological requirements. The interpellation of the spectator as a subject is dependent on how people cognitively map the physical environment as social space as much as how film constructs imaginary space through various perceptual cues provided by the image on the screen.

Depending on particular ways in which buildings and objects are constructed and organized in relation to each other, people have different experiences of space, or as Kevin Lynch has it, different images of space. According to Lynch, our experience of space is never direct but highly mediated. The relation of the specific structure of the physical environment to the observer produces the image, through which we can experience the space. Obviously, different constellations of objects produce different images of space, so that any analysis of space needs to be able to decode the space's "imageability." According to Lynch, imageability is "that quality in a physical object which gives it a high probability of evoking a strong image in any given observer." When the imageability of a particular environment is weak, we experience spatial disorientation; or worse, space simply eludes our perception, and the stability of subjectivity itself is in danger. However, when the imageability is too firmly established, it impairs any practical use of that highly visible space. Lynch writes: "A landscape loaded with magical meanings may inhibit practical activities. . . . Exploitation is more easily accomplished where there is no sentiment about the land. Even conservative use of resources may be impaired where habitual orientation does not allow easy adaptation to new techniques and needs."[16] The imageability of the built environment therefore plays a vital role in the transformation of society and, more fundamentally, in the organism's struggle for survival. While the highly imageable space could dissolve subjectivity into a preestablished web of meanings, the space's low imageability might leave the subject in a state of schizophrenia. The absolute disorientation or dissemination of subjectivity inhibits a society from adjusting to new historical circumstances.

Far from simply reflecting the way people cognitively map the pre-given physical environment, film, as what Benjamin calls a collective art of distracted subjectivity, excites the perceiving drive and actively participates in the construction of social space and the formation of subjectivity articulated by that space.[17] Film as a representation can change and negotiate the imageability of the urban landscape and at the same time can also give to the city a new kind of imageability that did not exist before. The Japanese cinema of the 1960s registers its fascination with, and anxiety over, the spatial transformations in the midst of the high-growth economy. Highways, the bullet train, and the Olympic Stadium are shown as signs of Japan's successful reconstruction and economic development; that is, as in the Meiji period, the city is conceived as a showcase for foreigners and for Japanese who are acutely aware of the gaze of foreigners.[18] At the same time, the persistent appearance of these symbols of economic recovery and technological advancement in Japanese films of the 1960s is also a sign of anxiety and uncertainty. Ironically, the ultramodern structures are some of the few legible landmarks that can give a sense of direction to the rapidly changing cityscape.

Subject, Space, and Nation

High and Low is an allegorical text of the spatial transformation brought about by the radical socioeconomic changes of the 1960s. From the opening credit sequence, spatiality is foregrounded in a series of panoramic views of the cityscape. Unlike in popular films of the same period, no obviously recognizable buildings or landmarks are shown. What is presented looks like an arbitrary collection of images of the city that do not have any symbolic meanings associated with famous landmarks. The images in the credits seem like point-of-view shots of somebody looking out from Gondo's salon, but the scale of images tell us that they are probably not. (For instance, compare the shot of two neon billboards and the first shot of the sequence immediately following the credits. In the latter, the identical billboards can be seen through the glass door of the salon, but their size is incomparably smaller than the way they appear in the former.) However, the construction of the sequence strongly suggests the presence of a controlling agent of narration that invites us to decipher the images of the city as a meaningful text. In fact, a closer look at the images reveals that there are many details that anticipate the film's narrative development. Some of the film's crucial thematic motifs and spatial markers are already in the panoramic images of the city, so that the credit sequence as a whole becomes a spatialized outline of the film's narrative. What is further remarkable about the sequence is that not only visual images but also sound is employed to construct the sense of space (e.g., sounds of the city, the port, the traffic, trains, etc.).

In the rest of the film, the principal characters, particularly police detectives, must read the surface of the cityscape as a text. One of the lessons they learn quickly is that naked human perception is inadequate to the task of deciphering the city. The image and representation unmediated by mechanical means of reproduction are not always helpful. In fact, they are sometimes outright deceptive. One of the pictures drawn by Shin'ichi does not look like an island, and it is only after some legwork that detectives finally discover that the Enoshima island does look like Shin'ichi's picture if viewed from a specific geographic location near Takeuchi's accomplices' hideout. This episode is one example showing how unmediated human perception can easily be deceived by reality, that is, how reality is often different from what our naked eyes and ears directly perceive.

The radical transformation of space and the social relations underlying it requires technology of audiovisual images as an interpretive tool. Thus various types of audiovisual technology appear in *High and Low:* an eight-millimeter camera and a projector, still cameras, binoculars, tape recorders, and so forth. First, on the diegetic level, these technological devices of sound and image are essential tools for locating and apprehending the kidnapper. Second, they also mark self-reflexive moments in the film. To give just one example, the tape recorder is used as a formal means of articulating spatial relationship and manipulating temporal flow. In the scene where Kawanishi is finally leaving for the airport, the telephone rings. Gondo picks up the phone and says,

"Hello. Gondo speaking." Then the film's second wipe leads to the next shot, where the detectives are playing back the tape-recorded conversation of Gondo and the kidnapper, which starts with Gondo's words, "Hello. Gondo speaking." In this brief transition from one scene to another, the artificiality of film as a system of representation is doubly marked. The wipe is a conspicuously visible graphic marker that cannot but draw our attention to the screen as a two-dimensional flat surface with clearly marked boundaries. Through the repetition of Gondo's remark, the temporal complexity is created without recourse to auditory flashback. Moreover, technology of sound reproduction demonstrates that film sound is not real but, like filmed image, only a representation. By repeating Gondo's recorded voice immediately after his "original" utterance, these two shots joined by a wipe remind us that film is an audiovisual representation through and through. Here *High and Low* becomes reflexive of its own conditions of production. And finally, technology of sound and vision is extensively employed as a means of cognitively mapping the social relations and history underlying the radically changing surface of the cityscape. One of the key pieces of information for locating the kidnapper's accomplices' hideout is the recorded sound of a specific type of train (Enoden). A veteran train operator can identify the sound because of the train's distinct mechanical structure, which is no longer used by the modern railroad system. The sedimented history in the train's sound is deciphered by the train operator because that sound is despatialized and becomes a fragmented, portable piece of the reproducible sound unit by the tape recorder, and that historical sediment in turn contributes to the mapping of radically changing space.

The film's division into distinct parts also emphasizes the transformation of cityscape and spatial relations. Particularly significant is the spatial organization of part 1. Gondo's salon is a kind of experimental chamber where Kurosawa uses cinematic technology (e.g., multicamera shooting, 'Scope frame, telephoto lens, etc.) to construct a complex permutational social space. The salon is a carefully controlled environment marked by a strong sense of theatricality. Immediately after the credits sequence, a man (Gondo) intrudes into the screen space from the lower right corner as he stands up in the dark. The camera follows him walking to the left to turn on the light; at the same time, another man (Kawanishi) carrying an ice bucket enters the same space from screen left. Until this moment, almost nothing is visible except the glass doors, through which the outside cityscape at dusk is visible. The sudden illumination by the artificial light shows that the dark interior space is a large salon, and more important, it functions as a punctuation device, announcing the beginning of a new dramatic sequence to follow. The transformation of the salon into a highly artificial dramatic space is further supported by Kurosawa's decision not to show any other parts of Gondo's house. The only other parts of the house shown to the spectator are auxiliary spaces such as the entrance hall, the stairs, and the shower stall, which are all contiguous to the salon. Isolated from the rest of the house, the salon is sparsely furnished, and there is nothing overtly conspicuous in the room. But precisely because of the simplicity of the set, almost everything there plays a significant role in the filmic construction of space. The slight displacement of objects transforms the meaning of the screen space; that is, the salon as a diegetic space remains unchanged, but the represented space on the screen changes throughout the sequence. Characters constantly come into and go out of the frame; their relative positions to each other are also carefully controlled and permutated by editing and camera positions.

When he learns the success of a negotiation in Osaka, Gondo tells Kawanishi to fly to Osaka immediately. Kawanishi tries to use the telephone in the salon to book a flight, but Gondo tells his secretary to use the second phone upstairs because he is waiting for a return call from Osaka. Gondo unplugs the phone from a wall, plugs it into a different outlet, and then places it on the table. The phone rings again, and for the first time Gondo shows Reiko and Kawanishi a ¥50 million check, which is about to be used to make Gondo the largest shareholder of National Shoes. Then Gondo's chauffeur Aoki comes into the room, asking them whether Shin'ichi is there. As Reiko looks toward a glass door to see whether Shin'ichi and her son Jun are playing in the yard, the camera shows a beautifully illuminated view of the cityscape. This night scene of the city below marks a dramatic turn in the following segment, where Gondo receives the first phone call from the kidnapper. In part 1, we are keenly aware of the presence and power of the camera, which plays a pivotal role in the systematic construction and permutation of the spatiotemporal continuum. In contrast, in the rest of the film, space becomes opaque and chaotic, and audiovisual technology and theatrical disguise become a means of deciphering space and identities of characters.

To understand the connection between the cognitive mapping of space and the formation of subjectivity, it is important to note that space in *High and Low* is not just the changing landscape of the city but also the space of the Japanese nation. Throughout the film, nation-related images are conspicuously present. The most obvious instance is the name of the shoe-making company, "*National* Shoes," a site of sly ruses and a power struggle. The opening line of the film is a remark by one of the executives in Gondo's salon: "Look, National Shoes is a commercial enterprise. It's business." In the credit sequence, as I mentioned earlier, there is a shot of two neon billboards, one of which on screen left says *Nashonaru*, "National," a domestic brand name of Matsushita. The national symbol Mount Fuji plays a crucial role in the discovery of the kidnappers' hideout. Another nation-related image is "the rising sun": Shin'ichi draws a picture of Mount Fuji with the sun on the horizon.

All these verbal and visual references to national images and symbols cannot but make us think about how the film tries to construct the sense of Japanese nationhood. At the same time, the specificities of those references foreground the problematic status of Japan's national identity. Instead of presenting a coherent image of Japan as a nation, *High and Low* problematizes the identity of the Japanese nation as divided, fragmentary, illusive, corroded by turning national symbols into clichés. Mount Fuji appears as a majestic mountain symbolizing the Japanese nation and at the same time as a kitch picture painted on the tile wall of a chaotic restaurant where Takeuchi buys heroin. The Japanese nation is represented as people who send letters of encouragement to Gondo from all over Japan; it is also figuratively represented as a neon sign reading "National," a brand name for mass-produced commodities. It is no coincidence that right next to the National's neon sign in the credit sequence is another neon advertisement for the Takashimaya department store. (The detectives arrive at Gondo's house disguised as Takashimaya's deliverymen.) In Shin'ichi's picture, it turns out that the sun is not rising but setting. Ironically, the "Rising

Sun" is the name of the kidnapper Takeuchi's squalid apartment building (Hinode Apato). Far from reassuring us of the sublime unity and stability of Japan as a nation-state, *High and Low* presents shattered images of the nation divided by confusion, ambiguity, and the reversal of values.

The film's original title, "Heaven and Hell," articulates the dichotomy of order and chaos, but this dichotomous relationship is somewhat undermined by the spatial proximity of the two. The credit sequence shows a panoramic view of the city of Yokohama accompanied by film music and the sounds of the city. The noise from the outside is completely cut off as Gondo shuts a glass door. Gondo's house (heaven) overlooks the dingy city (hell), and what separates the two is only the transparent glass door in Gondo's salon. Similarly, in the last scene of the prison's visiting room, only glass and wire separate Gondo and Takeuchi. What is important is not necessarily heaven or hell by itself but the contiguity of the two and the various kinds of boundaries — spatial, ethical, class — between them. In this respect, the choice of Yokohama, instead of Tokyo, as the setting is crucial. Yokohama, one of the premier port cities in Japan, has developed as an international trading port since the mid–nineteenth century. Along with another port city, Kobe, Yokohama has a sizable number of foreign businessmen and residents. Open to foreign countries through its port, Yokohama is a border city whose existence is dependent on a complex interaction between the inside and outside of a nation-state. The seedy restaurant where Takeuchi buys heroin is an epitome of Yokohama. There are black, white, and Asian customers; their nationalities are also diverse; there are American GIs, Japanese and foreign sailors, day laborers, and possibly some prostitutes; the menus on the wall are written in Japanese, English, Chinese, and Korean; customers are drinking beer, whisky, and sake and eating all kinds of food; and for some reason, there is a *torii* (Shinto shrine gate) at the entrance. It is an exotic, chaotic, and hybrid space full of energy and vitality. It is situated at the margin of society, where the nation-state cannot completely exercise its power of surveillance and control. By juxtaposing the Japanese national symbols and their inflections with the images of foreigners and foreign culture, *High and Low* tests the national identity of Japan as an ideological construct.

The driving force behind the actions of postwar Kurosawa heroes is not the sacred purpose of the Japanese empire anymore but the ideologies of humanism and democracy. However, as I pointed out in earlier chapters, in terms of the basic narratological structure, we find great similarities among many of Kurosawa's films. For instance, the persistent and self-determined character of Yukie in *No Regrets for Our Youth* is very similar to that of the leader of the female high school students working at the lens factory in *The Most Beautiful*. (It is perhaps no coincidence that she has the same last name as the hero of *Ikiru*, Watanabe, another stubborn Kurosawa hero.) Yet it is also true that Kurosawa's prewar and postwar films are not exactly identical. In *The Most Beautiful*, there is a perfect match between a group and its members' allegiance to it, and this group solidarity is rendered essentially in a melodramatic fashion. In contrast, in the postwar films, the melodramatic sentimentality is internalized by the protagonists, so that melodramatic conflicts are transformed into characters' existential dilemmas; that is, these existential characters loathe melodramatic situations not because they are nonmelodramatic but precisely because they are the most melodramatically sentimental characters but do not want to be recognized by others as such. Thus, in spite of some apparent differences, we can see a strong sense of continuity between Kurosawa's prewar and postwar films.

Yet this continuity in Kurosawa's career does not necessarily lead to the conclusion that he has always been either an authoritarian militarist or a liberal democrat throughout his career. Instead, what his films show is his obsession with the problematic of Japanese modernity. Even when his films deal with the more topical issues and themes of the day, he examines them within the larger framework of the Japanese modern. And it is in relation to this obsession that we should understand one of the dominant motifs of Kurosawa's films: the ethic of professionalism and perfectionism. To some extent, this ethic, which often takes the form of the valorization of a thorough planning and perfect execution of a plan, functions as a reflexive device reminding us of the work ethic of the perfectionist director Kurosawa himself. It is also a nostalgic longing for a bygone era when individual artisans could perfect their own skills without being obsessed with the idea of making a profit. But more important, it manifests a fear of instability and fluidity threatening the secure identity of the self and nationhood.

It has been argued by both Kurosawa and critics that the assertion of the self is a by-product of Japan's postwar reform. But characters' single-minded devotion to their roles, tasks, or professions is found in any Kurosawa film—from his first, *Sanshiro Sugata* (1943), up to the last one, *Madadayo* (1993)—regardless of the date of its production.[19] Contrary to Kurosawa's claim, there is no essential incompatibility between what he sees as the assertion of the self and the oppression by the militarist regime. It becomes quite doubtful, therefore, whether we can find in the Kurosawa hero merely the autonomy and independence of the centered self. More than just a representational illustration of postwar individualism, Kurosawa's films are an attempt to come to terms with the fluidity of modernity as it is evinced in his fondness for choosing as his films' historical settings transitional periods of radical social transformations: the period of the civil wars *(Seven Samurai, Throne of Blood, The Hidden Fortress),* the late Tokugawa era *(Yojimbo, Sanjuro),* and the immediate postwar years *(Drunken Angel, The Quiet Duel, Stray Dog).* Similarly, Kurosawa likes to deal with the aftermath of a great historical event—for instance, *Ikiru, The Bad Sleep Well,* and *High and Low* all try to come to terms with the legacy of the war and the postwar. And Kurosawa's commitment to professional perfectionism articulates his ambivalence toward modernity as the never-ending process of transformation. The transmission of technical skills needs to be constantly perfected by the Kurosawa heroes, yet any deviation from the norm is strictly prohibited in the name of professional ethics. Although the dynamic movement of modernity is affirmed by the Kurosawa heroes' constant effort to improve their own technical skills to perfection or to overcome their own weakness, the ethic of professionalism ensures that sense of the unchanging stability of the self, which is on the blink of extinction in the modern age.

Important as it is, and as often as it has been commented on, the master-disciple relation is only one type of male bonding found in Kurosawa's films. As we have already seen, the metaphysical nature of his films in part comes from the existential proximity of the hero and the villain. A near complicity of the hero and the villain is also a major reason why *High and Low* is such a powerful film despite its reactionary message about class antagonism. At the end of the film, Takeuchi and Gondo confront not only each other but also their own images reflected on the safety glass dividing them in the prison's visiting room. Here, the motif of the double becomes so explicit that the hero and the villain can be interpreted as two conflicting aspects of the split subject instead of two autonomous individuals. The self that Kurosawa is so eager to affirm cannot be found in any single character but lies in the relationality of the never-resolving tension between the hero and the villain.

In the existential ambivalence of the Kurosawa hero can be discerned a critique of what might be called postwar Japan's economism. It is not surprising to see a villain who is as attractive as much as, if not more than, the hero, because in the "evil" capitalist society, an antisocial act can easily become a form of protest against, or resistance, to the system. However, we also need to remember Sanjuro: the superhero of *Yojimbo* destroys protocapitalist thugs but cannot escape the underlying mechanism of capitalism himself. When he throws a stick to decide which road to take at the opening of the film, he inadvertently plays the game of chance or wager. To the extent that the existential dilemma of the Kurosawa hero is in part created by the internalization of the melodramatic, he can never quite escape from the sentimentalism of commodified culture that Kurosawa abhors.[20] Yet Kurosawa is in a sense "aware" of his own contradictions, since he is not reluctant to admit that he is a mere sentimentalist.[21] To this extent, we can say that Kurosawa does not simply reject but disavows the emerging society of mass consumption and the masses.

The ethical paradox of Kurosawa films is the following: the more a contrast between good and evil is emphasized, the more a difference between the two becomes ambiguous. Put differently, in Kurosawa films, the melodramatic structure is foregrounded by the strong sense of moral Manichaeism but is at the same time deconstructed by the ambiguity of the hero-villain relationship. When Manichaeism does not rule the diegetic world, however, Kurosawa's films lose a deconstructive edge and fall prey to sentimentalism.[22] If the strong sense of Manichaeism gives cohesion to the male bonding of the master-disciple or hero-villain relation, it is the woman who functions as a catalyst of sentimentalism by neutralizing, instead of deconstructing, binarism. Kurosawa films often marginalize the woman by transforming her into either a consumer with insatiable desire or a mere commodity or spectacle.[23] But the woman is marginalized in a much more fundamental way by Kurosawa's films, in which good and evil form a Möbius strip of male bonding. The woman, who is excluded from this closed circuit of moral chiasma, cannot in the end even become a personification of evil. Without being able to produce any value by herself, the woman in Kurosawa's films is often the embodiment of passivity threatening the solipsism of the split male subject.

At this point in our discussion, we need to go back to one of the two questions raised earlier. The first half of *High and Low* focuses on the question of whether Gondo should pay the ransom to save his chauffeur's son or use his money to take control of the shoe company. The film's narrative presents in a tightly orchestrated manner the conflict of interests, which leads to moral dilemmas for Gondo and other principal characters. But is Gondo really in such a position that he is forced to make a clear-cut moral choice? Aggressive as he is, Gondo is very different from Iwabuchi in *The Bad Sleep Well*. Gondo is not presented as a morally despicable person or somebody who is interested in taking advantage of his position to line his own pocket. He does try to stage a little coup, but his takeover attempt is devised not to merely make more profit but to produce better shoes. As we can see in his words of encouragement to Jun and Shin'ichi ("Try your best, both of you!") and in the testimony of a worker at the factory, Gondo is a fair and even-handed man. The choice he is forced to make is therefore not simply between pure personal greed and humanitarian sentiment. The situation in which he inadvertently finds himself is, as he says, just an absurd one. Gondo's agony is represented by Kurosawa and Mifune in such a subtle way that we cannot but probe into his moral dilemma. Yet the fundamental absurdity of the situation does not allow us to find out what in the end makes Gondo decide to ruin himself financially. This absence of a clear motivation is further foregrounded by Reiko's remark "Shikata ga nai" [it can't be helped]; that is, Reiko and the boy's father can't help asking Gondo to save the kid, and Gondo can't help paying the ransom even if as a result the Gondos lose everything they own. Reiko's remark is not refuted by any character including Gondo. This is particularly surprising because the idea of *shikata ga nai* is exactly what the Kurosawa hero rejects time and again.

Herein lies another paradox of *High and Low*. It is precisely when Gondo withdraws into the intense moment of contemplation that his interiority seems to dissipate. No rational explanation mediates a period of intense contemplation and a sudden outburst of action. When Gondo makes up his mind to pay the ransom, he jumps into the darkness without knowing whether he will land safely at the far side of an abyss. Significantly, what emerges through Gondo's blind leap is a certain sense of collectivity, which the hero of the previous film, *Sanjuro,* does not seem to be able to find. This collectivity is different from a family or some kind of community valorized by the sentimental melodrama of mainstream Japanese cinema. Because Gondo does not save his own son Jun but saves his chauffeur's son Shin'ichi, his most important action takes place outside the familial space of blood relation. It must also be distinguished from a mere interest group such as the group of capitalist investors who demand full repayment of a loan from the financially ruined Gondo. On the one hand, the strong affirmation of individualism found in the figuration of Gondo and even in Takeuchi clearly differentiates *High and Low* from the films of sentimentalism. On the other hand, as I pointed out, Gondo and Takeuchi are not free from sentimental emotion; they have simply internalized it through repression.

Far from being a completely autonomous individual, Gondo seems to belong to a collective and through his action ends up taking responsibility for its well-being. What exactly is this collective, which is neither a family, community, interest group, nor a mere aggregate of individuals? By now, it must be clear that the collectivity that is reinforced by Gondo's action is Japan's nationhood. Takeuchi is a necessary evil or a sacrificial lamb, which is essential for the reaffirmation of Japanese national identity. At the same time, because of Takeuchi, Gondo, an innocent man, also ends up sacrificing himself for the well-being of the nation-collective without fully understanding exactly why and for what purpose his sacrifice is called for. But this noncomprehension of the meaning of the sacrifice is not important as long as that sacrifice maintains an intimate relation with sentimentality of one kind or another. The nation-collective can emerge precisely because of the "meaningless sacrifice" that resists interiorization or internalization by individual psychology. The presence of the sacrifice and repressed sentimentality at the heart of *High and Low* confirms what Ernest Renan argued about the foundational features of a nation: "A community of interest is assuredly a powerful bond between men. Do interests, however, suffice to make a nation? I do not think so. Community of interest brings about trade agreements, but nationality has a sentimental side to it; it is soul and body at once. . . . A nation is therefore a large-scale solidarity, constituted by the feeling of the sacrifices that one has made in the past and of those that one is prepared to make in the future." Thus Gondo's action is a means of reconstructing the identity and unity of the Japanese nation, which was increasingly being problematized by spatial transformation and the intrusion of a foreign body (e.g., popular and consumer culture and, most obviously, heroin smuggled from abroad).

The question is, does the film *High and Low* successfully renew the sense of Japanese nationhood? My answer is no. As I have discussed so far, there are simply too many textual details or excess that cannot be assimilated into the normative narrative of national identity. Gondo's sacrifice or audiovisual technology is in the end not enough to reassemble shattered images of Japanese nationhood.

24. *Red Beard*

Red Beard (Akahige, 1965) is Kurosawa's second *jidaigeki* based on Yamamoto Shugoro's story. The film's protagonists are Niide Kyojo (Mifune Toshiro), or "Red Beard," the director of the publicly funded clinic
for the poor, and Yasumoto Noboru (Kayama Yuzo), a young doctor
who is assigned to the clinic against his wish. The film is more than
three hours long, and loosely organized around many discrete episodes.
What gives it the sense of coherence is the main narrative thread that
follows the progressive growth of Yasumoto as a morally responsible
doctor under the tutelage of Niide. Critics' reactions to this overtly
pedagogical and technically superb film have been starkly divided. On
the one hand, there are those who see the film as the culmination of
Kurosawa's career, the ultimate statement of Kurosawa as an auteur:
the celebration of, and the ultimate faith in, human compassion, goodness, and altruism. On the other hand, there are others who express
disappointment or even anger. For them, *Red Beard* is what is left after
all positive aspects of Kurosawa's films are removed: the blind affirmation of patriarchal authoritarianism. What both groups of critics find
in *Red Beard* is not new to Kurosawa's cinema. What is missing in *Red
Beard* is a dialectic movement that mediates the opposing values discerned by critics. The film's formal perfectionism is remarkable even
among Kurosawa's works (e.g., large-scale sets of the clinic and rows
of stores and houses, props including a medicine cabinet with numerous drawers containing real medicines that never appear on-screen,
authentic-looking costumes, actors' natural performances). In fact, the
film is so perfectly crafted that it exorcises from itself any kind of genuine conflict and disharmony, either among characters or between characters and environments. Even the scores of Sato Masaru, whose contribution to the rough-hewn geometric feel of *Yojimbo* is immeasurable,
reinforce the extreme sense of stability. At the film's conclusion, the

main theme of *Red Beard,* which reminds us of Brahms's Symphony no. 1 in C Minor and Beethoven's Ninth (Choral) Symphony,[1] and the dominating image of the clinic's gate in a perfectly balanced composition seal the film in the final state of stasis. This ending perhaps announces the end of an era, for *Red Beard* is the last Kurosawa film in which Mifune Toshiro appears, marking the conclusion of a remarkable collaboration of two illustrious artists.

25. *Dodeskaden*

The End of an Era

During the 1960s, Japan experienced phenomenal economic growth. The annual double-digit growth of the GNP made Japan by the early 1970s the second largest economy among capitalist nations. As the spectacular rise of the Japanese economy continued, people with more disposable income started spending money for a variety of leisure activities. The once dominant position of the cinema as popular entertainment was quickly replaced by television. Despite its struggle to survive the turbulent decade of socioeconomic transformation, the Japanese film industry steadily disintegrated. Oshima and other filmmakers of the younger generation were forced to establish their own independent production companies and make low-budget films not just to preserve their artistic integrity but also to adjust to the new economic reality of filmmaking in the 1960s. The financial limitations were not necessarily bad for these filmmakers because the limited budget sometimes created an artistically positive effect, forcing them to experiment with film form in a way that they might not have thought about if more money had been available. Yet in general, it is undeniable that the lack of capital had a demoralizing effect. The Japanese cinema was also losing its human resources as many leading filmmakers passed away. In 1963, Ozu Yasujiro lost his battle with cancer on his sixtieth birthday. Shimizu Hiroshi, Uchida Tomu, Tasaka Tomotaka, Yamamoto Kajiro, and such pioneers as Kaeriyama Norimasa, Henry Kotani, and Sessue Hayakawa all died in the 1960s and early 1970s.

Every Japanese filmmaker was affected by the decline of the film industry, but it hit Kurosawa particularly hard. Among the established directors, Kurosawa was left virtually alone and was forced to find a way to cope with the changing socioeconomic situation by himself.

His special status as the most acclaimed Japanese director abroad *(sekai no Kurosawa)* further isolated him within the Japanese film industry. The financially troubled film companies were no longer willing to take the risk of producing Kurosawa's ever more expensive projects after *Red Beard*. As a result, Kurosawa sought financing outside Japan. *The Runaway Train* (Boso kikansha) was prepared as his first non-Japanese wide-screen color film, but the project was never realized because of miscommunication between Kurosawa's representatives and the American studio that conceived the film as a black-and-white film in standard size. (Kurosawa's script was later adapted and made into film in 1985 by Andrei Konchalovsky.) And then followed Kurosawa's ill-fated involvement in *Tora! Tora! Tora!* (1970), a film about the Japanese attack on Pearl Harbor, coproduced by Twentieth Century Fox and Kurosawa Production.[1] Kurosawa was supposed to direct the Japanese part, and Richard Fleischer was responsible for the American part. After the production started, however, it soon became clear that Kurosawa was not given the kind of environment in which he could pursue his perfectionist style of filmmaking. In January 1969, Twentieth Century Fox fired him on the grounds that his mental illness would not allow him to complete the project as specified by the contract. Kurosawa, on the other hand, vehemently denied his illness at press conferences. What was actually going on behind the scenes still remains unclear.[2] In July 1969 Kurosawa was ready to move on to the next project. He actively organized an artists' collective called Yonki no Kai (The Four Musketeers) with Kinoshita Keisuke, Kobayashi Masaki, and Ichikawa Kon. Kurosawa's *Dodeskaden* (Dodesukaden, 1970) turned out to be the first and only film produced by this collective.

Art/Imagination/Life

Dodeskaden is based on the collection of short stories titled *A Town without Seasons* (Kisetsu no nai machi) by Yamamoto Shugoro, the author of the original stories for *Sanjuro* and *Red Beard*.[3] The setting of *A Town without Seasons* is a nameless shantytown, which is separated from the rest of the city by a river with filthy stagnant water. The contaminated river is the boundary line that neither the residents of the shantytown nor those of the city normally cross. The town exists at the margin of society, and for the city dwellers, it is invisible or exists only as an imaginary space outside of time and the seasonal changes. In the film, the lack of seasons is emphasized by the artificial materials, mostly industrial waste and consumer garbage, that form the slum's physical environment.

Dodeskaden departs from the earlier films of Kurosawa in its use of a semiomnibus narrative structure. Out of the original fifteen episodes, the film uses eight, whose narrative details are mostly preserved. One major adjustment made in the film is that Kurosawa further segments the eight episodes into smaller units and rearranges them to create a new narrative flow. As a result, the film becomes simultaneously episodic and more firmly integrated into a coherent unity. As Sato Tadao argues, each episode is divided into distinct phases of narrative development and then the similar phases from all the episodes are more or less bundled together to give coherency to the film's dramatic development.[4] Thus from scene 1 to scene 17 is the opening part introducing the film's principal characters and their situations. The next part, from scene 18 to scene 68, portrays the slum residents' lives neutrally or sometimes even comically. The film's tone changes quickly in scene 69, in which the good-for-nothing pseudointellectual drunkard Kyota rapes his adopted daughter Katsuko. In the rest of this third part, which ends in scene 96, the film reveals the ghastly sides of the slum residents' lives. The film's final part, from scene 97 to scene 103, is a short coda showing that things return to "normal" in the shantytown, a forgotten space in the middle of the modern industrial world.[5]

The film's sense of unity is also strengthened by the presence of Rokuchan, a "trolley fool."[6] The film opens and ends with Rokuchan's imaginary streetcar scenes, between which the film's other episodes are embedded. Even though he does not interact with the town dwellers except the wise old man, Tanba, Rokuchan's itinerant movement in the shantytown introduces new characters and helps create spatial and narrative connections between different characters and episodes. Rokuchan leaves his trolley garage in the first part and comes back to the garage at the film's end. Diegetically, the last scene just shows Rokuchan's everyday routine, and since various incidents in the film happen over a long period of time, it does not have any special connection to the first garage scene. Formally, however, Rokuchan's trolley scenes at the beginning and end of the film function as a framing device, which gives the film the sense of narrative resolution and unity. Moreover, Rokuchan also contributes to the segmentation of the film into distinct parts. Rokuchan's imaginary trolley scenes are inserted in the film's first and second parts as if to emphasize the illusionary existence of the slum. But he disappears in the third part where what looks like a carefree, even utopic, life in the shantytown reveals its darker, brutal side.

There is one subtle yet major change in the film's treatment of Rokuchan's episode. In the original story, Rokuchan is forced to brake suddenly because of an inattentive passerby, but in the film he is obstructed by a painter. About halfway into the film, there is a scene in which the painter sits and sketches in front of an easel. The painter is in the middle of the street and does not see Rokuchan's imaginary trolley coming directly toward him. To avoid an accident, Rokuchan puts on the brakes to stop the trolley and starts yelling at the painter furiously. For Rokuchan, the painter is a bumpkin who does not understand how dangerous it is to sit on a railroad track. For the painter, Rokuchan is a strange boy who talks about an invisible trolley. Our attention is drawn to the painter because even in the context of a semi-omnibus film, his appearance is not only too brief but also peculiarly out of context. He is best understood as a metadiegetic character intruding into the film. The brief encounter of Rokuchan and the painter can be interpreted as Kurosawa's cautionary reminder for us and himself that the cinema should not merely reproduce what is visible to the naked eye, that reality for the cinema is actively created by the power of imagination. In an interview conducted in the early 1950s, Kurosawa explains that the sense of reality is not created by merely reproducing what already exists in society. Kurosawa argues that cinematic reality does not exist as it is in our everyday world. Because of its sheer constructive power, the cinema can give rise to something that did not exist before its own creation.[7] When the cinema successfully creates a reality, the real world begins to imitate the cinema. For Kurosawa, the cinema is an art of creative construction, not one of mimetic reproduction.

The brief appearance of the anonymous painter can also be interpreted as Kurosawa's autobiographical reference. When he was young, Kurosawa was a promising painter, having his work accepted for the prestigious annual exhibition called Nikaten at the age of eighteen.[8] But he gradually gave up his dream of becoming a professional painter after his disappointing involvement in a proletarian art movement. Kurosawa recalls how he began to lose confidence in his talent as follows:

> I had begun to have doubts about my own talent as a painter. After looking at a monograph on Cézanne, I would step outside and the houses, streets and trees looked like a Cézanne painting. The same thing would happen when I looked at a book of van Gogh's paintings or Utrillo's paintings—everything appeared as if seen with van Gogh or Utrillo's eyes, but never with my own eyes. In other words, I was not able to see things with my own uniquely personal vision.[9]

Years later, when asked whether he ever regretted not having pursued his career in the art world, Kurosawa's answer was no. According to Kurosawa, he knew he was not gifted enough to become a good painter because he was sketching only what he could see with his eyes. In contrast, a real artist has an ability to see something beyond the mere visible surface of the world.[10] Like the young Kurosawa, the painter in *Dodeskaden* can observe the shantytown as it appears to his perceptual organ but fails to see Rokuchan's imaginary streetcar and tracks on the ground.[11] To this extent, the film's painter is a surrogate for the young Kurosawa or somebody he could have become; that is, it is a figural inscription of his personal history.

As the example of the painter shows, *Dodeskaden* is one of the most personal films Kurosawa has ever made. Compared to his previous films, it seems to express much more openly his own feelings and thoughts, and he is not afraid of putting his signature to the film.[12] In the film's opening credit sequence, various parts of a yellow trolley car are successively shown with the names of the staff and actors. The last shot of the credits is a trolley's front plate, on which "Director Kurosawa Akira" is written. Thus from the very beginning there is an explicit connection made between the trolley car and Kurosawa. Because the trolley is visible only to Rokuchan, he becomes Kurosawa's other surrogate figure in the film. At Rokuchan's house, almost all the windows and walls are covered with his drawings of trolleys. Is this, as Stephen Prince argues, the image of a "weird, private world," totally cut off from the outside world? To answer this question, we need to look at how the house is represented on the screen. What strikes us most about Roku-chan's house is the bright colors of his drawings. When it is lighted from outside in the film's last scene, the room looks like a magic lantern. Because the outside light sources constantly move and light up the paper doors that are covered with the drawings, they create an illusion that Rokuchan's drawings of trolleys are somehow in motion. Thus Roku-chan is more than just an imaginative artist; he is a filmmaker who can express his inner vision by using light and moving image.

Rokuchan is called a "trolley fool" by a group of schoolchildren who live in the city, but the film deliberately leaves ambiguous whether Rokuchan is really mentally handicapped or just a little eccentric (Yama-moto Shugoro is explicit about the mental status of Rokuchan: "It has been repeatedly demonstrated by doctors that he is neither imbecile nor mentally deficient").[13] The ambiguity about Rokuchan's mental state is suggested, for instance, by the inclusion of images of a real trolley in the opening and final scenes of the film. Is what appears to be a real trolley only a product of Rokuchan's imagination? Or is Roku-chan's house actually located near a trolley line? The film does not give us any explicit cues — either spatial or diegetic — that would resolve the ambiguity of the status of the trolley just mentioned and therefore of the state of Rokuchan's mind. And the ambiguity of Rokuchan's mental state is quite important considering that he is the surrogate for Kuro-sawa as film director. The difference between imagination and reality is deliberately left ambiguous because the cinema as an art form exists *between* reality and imagination. For Kurosawa, what makes a film a film is precisely the indeterminate nature of the cinematic image, which maintains an ambivalent relation to the representation and construction of reality.

What strikes us most about Rokuchan's driving of a streetcar is his meticulous attention to detail. Rokuchan's imagination is not some personal whimsy or daydream. An imaginary trolley requires as much care and attention as a real one. In fact, to some extent, an imaginary trolley requires more attention precisely because it is imaginary and not visible to the naked eye. When someone is driving a real trolley, every operation is almost routine. For Rokuchan, however, no proce-dure can be taken for granted. Every step of driving must be precise and consciously followed; otherwise, the imagined presence of a trolley dissipates into thin air. For Rokuchan, the imaginary trolley is not a mere object of daydreaming but a result of his hard work. Without a strong will to construct, there would be no trolley as a product of imagination. Rokuchan's attention to detail is shared by the film's other characters, too. Sawagami Ryotaro, a comb maker, has five children, all of whom were conceived by his flirtatious wife Misao and her different lovers. Always irritated, Misao pays no attention to her family and treats Ryotaro with contempt. One of the causes of Misao's irritation is Ryotaro's attention to detail: he always counts the number of bristles and uses exactly thirty bristles for one bundle. Even though it might not seem so significant whether a bundle consists of twenty-nine or thirty hairs, Ryotaro just does not feel right unless he uses precisely thirty hairs for every bundle. From his perspective, too, what looks like an insignificant detail can make a big difference, as it certainly did for Kurosawa, in the quality of his creation.

When Rokuchan comes to a train depot with an oilcan and maintenance tools in hand, he meticulously examines the invisible trolley. He moves around it, touches and observes its imaginary body, and checks the wheels and connector. Rokuchan's painstaking preparation starts to resemble the act of sculpting, so that even if the trolley remains invisible, after a while, we begin to feel its presence. When he tightens a screw, kicks a bearing, or puts the trolley in low gear, we hear an appropriate synchronized sound. The effect is almost a reversal of silent film: whereas in silent film, a visual image is shown without a synchronized sound, in this scene, what is present is a synchronized sound without its visual counterpart. What is defamilialized in this reversal of the sound-image relationship is the seeming naturalness of the visual image. Kurosawa demonstrates how the transparency of the visual image is in fact constructed by music and sound effects, which are normally regarded as supplementary additions. In other words, the visual image does not have any fixed meanings, either referential or figural, and what appears to be self-evident about the visual image is only what Michel Chion calls "added value." But Kurosawa's ingenuity lies in his refusal to stop here. He does not simply reverse the relationship of sound and image whereby image, rather than sound, plays a supplementary role for producing a reality effect. While driving a trolley, Rokuchan mimics its sound, "dodesukaden, dodesukaden," which is a very unusual onomatopoeic word for the sound of wheels moving over rail joints. The sound, which denaturalizes the seeming transparency of the visual image, is in turn shown as a semiotic construct.

Dodeskaden is Kurosawa's first color film. For a long time, he refused to make a color film because he did not know how to deal with the technical possibilities and limitations of color film stock. But is it not rather superfluous for a filmmaker to say that he does not know how to use color when color films have been made for many years? In his hesitation, we can see another manifestation of his perfectionist tendency. For Kurosawa, as noted earlier, no aspect of filmmaking can be taken for granted, and every detail of the production process should be attended to with utmost care. He insists that a seemingly small compromise can easily lead to another compromise, so that in the end there will be no reason to make a film at all. Therefore, Kurosawa's late adoption of color in his career is consistent with his general approach to the art of filmmaking.

During the filming of *Dodeskaden,* Kurosawa showed his staff books of paintings by Goya, Daumier, and Klee to make them understand what kind of effect he was trying to achieve by using colors.[14] The idiosyncratic color scheme of the film—the extensive use of primary colors in symbolic and abstract fashions that transform even nature into a primitive painting—is his attempt to create an overtly painterly effect, which would become a prominent feature of his films from *Kagemusha* to *Madadayo.* For Kurosawa, colors are not an additional formal element that enables him to make a more realistic film. As André Bazin argues, the impression of reality cannot be enhanced just by incorporating another aspect of the world that the film tries to represent realistically because of the synthetic role of human perception.

> It would be . . . naive to think that the filmic image tends toward total identification with the universe that it copies, through the successive addition of supplementary properties from that universe. Perception, on the part of the artist as well as the audience of art, is a synthesis—an artificial process—each of whose elements acts on all the others. And, for example, it is not true that color, in the way that we are able to reproduce it—as an addition to the image framed by the narrow window of the screen—is an aspect of pure realism. On the contrary,

color brings with it a whole set of new conventions that, all things considered, may make film look more like painting than reality.[15]

Rather than simply reinforcing the reality effect, Kurosawa uses colors to defamiliarize the relationship of image and referent. Just like sound and image, colors form another type of semiotic system that has no more privileged relation to reality than the semiotic system consisting of black, gray, and white. There seems, however, to be a fundamental difference between black-and-white and color films. The black-and-white film gives us the overwhelming sense of the past presence; that is, it gives us an impression that what is projected on the screen is something that really took place or existed in the past. When we watch a black-and-white film, the temporal difference between the past of the recorded event and the present of our viewing seems absolutely unbridgeable. It is this impression of temporal disjunction that creates the reality or documentary effect of the black-and-white film. In contrast, the color film overwhelms us with the sense of presence. The present of filming and the present of projection are merged into one and create the illusion of the perpetual present. Interestingly, the overwhelming sense of presence in the color film does not necessarily increase its documentary value. The heightened sense of presence collapses the temporal difference between past and present and to this extent, despite the impression of increased fidelity of image, makes what is depicted in the color film look like a fictional event. Color problematizes the objectivity of image and the value of image as a historical document. Thus Kurosawa's antinaturalistic use of colors in *Dodeskaden* cannot simply be regarded as the expression of his personal vision. True, the expressive possibility of color film stock is undeniably relevant, and the technical feasibility of faithfully reproducing various colors as they exist in Kurosawa's imagination can never be ignored. Yet what is more important is the ontological status of color image. By constantly drawing the viewers' attention to the artificiality of colors, Kurosawa tries to break the spell of color image as atemporal plenitude.

In *Dodeskaden,* an old man visits and begs Tanba to teach him a painless method of committing suicide. "Life is nothing but pain," the old man laments. Everyday life for him is nothing more than a series of routines to sustain his life, and he sees no reason to go on living anymore. His only desire is to die and disappear from the world. As expected, Tanba is sympathetic toward the unhappy old man and out of kindness gives him a powdered poison that can quietly kill him within an hour or so. The old man thanks Tanba and quickly takes the poison. Then, instead of leaving Tanba's house, he starts talking about his family. His sons were killed on the continent during the war, his wife died of an illness soon after, and his house was completely destroyed by an air raid. He became penniless and alone in the world. But every night in his dreams, he sees his wife and sons, who laugh and talk as if they were still alive. At this point, Tanba asks the old man: "Then, in your dreams, you must be quite happy." The old man replies: "Yes, now that you mention it, that's true." Tanba continues: "And it's only because you are alive. In other words, while you are alive, those people are alive, too. Do you really want to kill those people by killing yourself?" After hearing Tanba's words, the old man suddenly wants to live and realizes his fatal mistake. When the old man reachs the peak of his panic, Tanba tells him that the powder he took was not a poison but a stomach medicine.

Despite his affirmation of life and the power of human imagination in *Dodeskaden,* about a year after its commercial release, Kurosawa attempted to take his own life. Fortunately, his self-inflicted wound was not fatal, and he was able to go back to filmmaking in 1973 with his next film, *Dersu Uzala.* It is possible to speculate about why he tried to commit suicide, but the true reason for his action will probably never be known. Suffice it to say that in almost every Kurosawa film, the darker side of human existence is always present, ready to overwhelm the compassionate, morally upright hero with its power.

26. *Dersu Uzala*

After having experienced a series of personal and professional setbacks in the late 1960s and early 1970s, Kurosawa was invited by Mosfilm to make a film in the Soviet Union. In response, he submitted a proposal based on the memoirs of the Russian explorer Vladimir Arseniev. Kurosawa's choice of material was not at all arbitrary; as early as in his assistant director days he was already interested in adapting Arseniev's narrative of exploration to film. During the Occupation, Kurosawa even asked the playwright and scriptwriter Hisaita Eijiro to draft a scenario based on Arseniev's texts by changing the story's setting to Hokkaido in the early Meiji.[1] At that time, however, the project was abandoned in part because of the irreplaceability of Siberia as a physical location. This background information serves as another reminder that we should not succumb to the temptation to construct an evolutionary pattern out of Kurosawa's career.

Dersu Uzala (Derusu Uzara, 1975), Kurosawa's only film shot outside Japan, strikes us as nostalgic and elegiac because of its protagonist, Dersu Uzala, who is doubly marked by the sense of loss and passing time. Dersu has been living a solitary life in the forest since he lost his wife and children to chicken pox and his house and personal possessions were all burned to ashes to protect other community members from the disease. But with the migration of more settlers, a kind of symbiotic relationship between Dersu and the forest is also increasingly becoming a thing of the past. In other words, Dersu, who lives with a memory of the past, is in turn becoming a memory of the bygone era. The pervading emotional tone of the film is further reinforced by the structure of the narrative. The film mostly consists of two long flashback sequences, both of which are presented as Arseniev's memories of his friendship with the Goldi hunter Dersu, and almost nothing happens except Arseniev's act of remembering in the film's diegetic present. The film is divided into two parts, the first of which starts in the year 1910, three years after the death of Dersu. Arseniev comes to visit Dersu's grave but cannot find it because the trees that marked its location have been cut down as a new settlement is being built. Now, with no material sign left, only Arseniev's memory can memorialize the life of Dersu. With grief-stricken Arseniev's murmur "Dersu!" the narrative returns to his first encounter with this Goldi hunter in 1902 and then shows the gradual development of their friendship. After a climactic storm scene where Dersu saves Arseniev's life, part 1 concludes with the end of their exploration. With the title "1907" opens part 2, which follows Arseniev's second exploration of the Ussuri region with Dersu as a guide. Significantly, even at the end of the film, the narrative never comes back to the opening scene of Arseniev's visit to Dersu's grave site in 1910; instead, it concludes with the scene of the burial of Dersu in 1907, when he is murdered by a robber for his expensive rifle, a parting gift from Arseniev. Thus, never reaching a resolution, the film is permanently suspended between the two moments of grief over Dersu's death.

Although temporal displacement and spatial dislocation are familiar motifs of Kurosawa's cinema, *Dersu Uzala* looks distinctively different from his earlier films because of its use of naturalistic imagery and acting style without much stylistic exaggeration or embellishment. As we discussed earlier, Kurosawa frequently uses nature in such an exaggerated way that it becomes one of the film's most "unnatural" elements. Yet in *Dersu Uzala,* Kurosawa refrains from treating nature as a raw material to be transformed into pure kinetic movement or a narratively charged graphic design. The "natural" look of nature scenes has perhaps something to do with the film's physical setting. It can also be explained by the relative lack of overtly self-reflexive moments in the film; in fact, with few exceptions, the shot composition, camera movement, acting, and editing do not deliberately draw our attention to themselves. Some outdoor scenes were shot in studios, but not for the purpose of creating an artificial or stylized look. Instead, the Siberian forest was recreated in soundstages only because location shooting became impossible owing to unfavorable weather or the change of the seasons. Needless to say, the natural look of the film does not at all mean that Kurosawa spent less energy and time for its production. Kurosawa's meticulous production notes on direction, shooting, the personality of each character, the explorers' clothes, outfit, and so forth show how he was obsessed with creating the authentic look of images on the screen.[2] Probably the only unrealistic scene is Arseniev's home in Khabarovsk, which, compared to the rest of the film, looks a little shallow and artificial.[3]

It is important to note that despite its difference from Kurosawa's previous films, *Dersu Uzala*'s nature is still quite different from the kind of nature represented in either conventional Japanese films or generic Hollywood movies. Far from being the mere object of quiet contemplation as in the former, nature in this Kurosawa film exists first and foremost as a pure physical force, whose overwhelming power commands human respect. As Dersu's reverential remarks about the power of the sun, fire, water, and wind suggest, without proper respect, one would not be able to survive in the wilderness of the Siberian forest. The images of nature, which is simultaneously the source of our life and death, evoke not only our admiration for their beauty but also a feeling of awe and dignity. At the same time, in a marked contrast to a typical Hollywood production, *Dersu Uzala* contains neither panoramic views of vast natural landscapes nor moving aerial images of the Siberian forest shot from a helicopter. Instead of these commodified Kodacolor images, the film shows the forest and other natural landscapes as they are actually experienced by Dersu, Arseniev, and other characters.[4]

The significance of the lack of an objectified landscape in the film can be further elucidated by focusing on the question of map. In *Dersu Uzala* there are two different types of map and space. On the one hand, Arseniev and his soldiers basically believe that even though there are indigenous people living in the region, they are treading and surveying an unexplored land, which remains unreadable for them until they transform its physical contours into a two-dimensional map.[5] Arseniev's modern map exists as an autonomous text, which can be read by anybody who has knowledge of its basic semiotic codes. On the other hand, Dersu's map is not a text existing independently from the land. The actual forest is marked by many meaningful signs, which Dersu can recognize and correctly interpret, but Arseniev and his soldiers cannot. To the extent that it is inseparable from his personal experience of living in the forest, Dersu's map cannot be shared with those who do not have an extensive experience in the forest. The map Arseniev is drawing does not have much utility for Dersu because even if he learns how to decode it by mastering its basic coding system, it hardly says anything about how to read real material signs scattered around in the forest. Arseniev's art of modern cartography is not just a simple process of recording the spatial configuration of the Siberian forest; instead, it helps Russian settlers to develop the forest by cutting down trees, building new towns and villages, and constructing a railroad. Far from being just a transparent image of geographic space, the modern map is an instrument through which a space is transformed, and precisely as a result of this transformation, it becomes useful as a sign system. The discovery of nature as an objectified landscape is inseparable from the invention of technologies of mapping, surveying, and representation. And by refraining from showing the Siberian forest as an expansive landscape, *Dersu Uzala* implicitly problematizes its own status as a representation.

27. *Kagemusha*

The opening scene of *Kagemusha* (Kagemusha, 1980), which is rendered in one long take lasting more than six minutes without interruption, shows us three seemingly identical samurai sitting frontally on the wood floor. Sitting on a dais in the center is Takeda Shingen (Nakadai Tatsuya), a Japanese warlord who lived in the sixteenth century, the period of civil war. To his left sits Takeda Nobukado (Yamazaki Tsutomu), Shingen's younger brother and double (*kagemusha,* or shadow warrior). And in foreground screen right is another man who looks identical to Shingen (also played by Nakadai). Through conversation between Shingen and Nobukado, we learn that the man is a thief whom Nobukado saved when he was about to be crucified. Nobukado suggests that they use the thief as Shingen's second double, but Shingen seems skeptical about the idea. The thief looks uncannily like Shingen, but his physical resemblance to the lord is betrayed by his manner of speaking and carrying himself, which cannot but reveal his lowly class origin. When Shingen gently dismisses Nobukado's idea of using the thief as a double, the thief finally speaks up. Apparently intimidated by Shingen, the thief stumbles over his words but manages to say that he, who stole only a few coins, is nothing compared to Shingen, a real scoundrel who slaughtered hundreds and stole others' territories. After hearing this accusation, Shingen seems to show some interest in the thief for the first time. With great composure, Shingen admits that he is in fact a worse thief, a truly heinous, wicked man. But he calmly continues to say that when chaos rules the world, somebody has to step up and unify the country; otherwise, there will be endless rivers of blood and mountains of dead.

This scene seems to give a new twist to some of the basic thematic motifs of Kurosawa's films. Take, for instance, the question of individual autonomy and identity. It is often said that Kurosawa is distinguished from other Japanese directors for his assertion of the principle of individualism. Yet in *Kagemusha* an autonomous individual does not seem to exist. The thief loses his identity as he tries to remold himself into the image of Shingen. During this process of transformation, he seems to identify himself completely with the late lord and lose his original identity. The model of the self presented in *Kagemusha* seems a far cry from the image of an autonomous individual present in Kurosawa's early postwar films. How *Kagemusha* revises Kurosawa's earlier films is described by Stephen Prince as follows:

> The dialectic between self and society is extinguished, along with the prospects for human freedom. These had always been rooted in the autonomous personality, which Kurosawa had valorized over the interactionist self and the socio-economic environment, but this was an ideological move of a deeply problematical nature. Kurosawa's construction of personality, which once embodied the optimism of the postwar years, collided with the institutional nature of political and economic power in the modern world. Buffeted by internal contradictions, troubled by interactionist linkages to normative groups, divorced from the kind of genuinely social perceptions that might renew it, Kurosawa's construction of personality steadily broke apart. Now, in its wake, *Kagemusha* projects it as an empty form by elaborating a world in which illusion and image replace enlightenment and in which personality is hollowed out and becomes a role, to be performed with great artifice, as human will and free choice are crushed beneath the weight of destiny.[1]

There are, however, problems with the critical view that sees *Kagemusha* as a sign of a new pessimistic stage in Kurosawa's development as an artist. The idea of the self, which is so important for Kurosawa, is often "hollowed out and becomes a role, to be performed with great artifice," even in his earlier films. If there is one word that can characterize Kurosawa's films made during the American occupation, it is not optimism but darkness, which makes those films so powerful, disturbing, and poignant. In Kurosawa's early postwar films, the autonomy of the individual is never optimistically celebrated; instead, the status of the individual self is intensely questioned by the dark images of the postwar chaos and the aftermath of the war.

Left to right: Nakadai Tatsuya (Kagemusha), Kurosawa, and Yamazaki Tsutomu (Nobukado). *Photo courtesy of Photofest.*

The status of image in *Kagemusha* and Kurosawa films in general is also much more ambivalent. Instead of forming a simple dichotomy, illusion and reality are often mutually implicated. *Kagemusha* highlights the ambivalent interaction of reality and image by refusing to reduce the relationship of Shingen and the thief to that of original and copy. Whenever the original and the copy are ready to be absorbed into a binary schema, Kurosawa introduces a third term to problematize that specular relationship. In the opening scene, it is Nobukado, an active agent of interpretation, who as a third term prevents the formation of a dichotomy. Even though there is an uncanny physical resemblance between Shingen and the thief on the screen, we learn from Nobukado that nobody except him at the scene of crucifixion noticed the resemblance. This anecdote reverses the usual relationship between reality and image: what is hidden beneath the thief's appearance is not a reality or who he really is; instead, it is an image, the thief's iconic resemblance to the warlord Takeda Shingen. Moreover, this visual resemblance can be discovered only by somebody who has a special ability to discern not so obvious resemblances, and who himself resembles his object of decipherment. The binarism of original and copy is further deconstructed by the fact that even before he becomes Shingen's shadow as a double, the thief is already a shadow of himself. Like Kameda in *The Idiot,* the thief was rescued when he was about to be executed publicly, so that to some extent, when he meets Shingen, he is not really alive. Symbolically, the thief is already dead. If the thief's identity is problematic, it is not necessarily because he so cleverly impersonates Shingen but because he is already a copy of himself even before he accepts the role of Shingen's copy. When the thief finally takes it upon himself to become a double, Shingen, whom the thief is supposed to impersonate, is already dead; that is, the thief, who is a copy of himself, must copy Shingen, who no longer exists. At this point, the binarism of original and copy cannot explain the vertiginous play of image and reality, in which both the thief and Shingen are trapped. Thus, instead of being evidence for the failure of Kurosawa's "political project," *Kagemusha* is a film whose complexity calls for reexamination of the prevalent discourse about Kurosawa's individualism supposedly articulated in his earlier work.

What are mentioned as the unique features that distinguish *Kagemusha* from Kurosawa's earlier works are not particularly new. In fact, it is not difficult to find in *Kagemusha* and other Kurosawa films shared thematic and formal motifs besides the motif of double. In *Kagemusha,* shadow is prominently shown to emphasize the problematic identity of Shingen and the thief. In the opening scene, candlelight casts the large shadow of Shingen on the back wall of the meeting room. As the thief stands up to leave the concubine's quarters, we see his elongated shadow on the wall and the ceiling. Similarly, in *Sanshiro Sugata, Part 2,* the shadow of Higaki Genzaburo ominously threatens Sanshiro in their first encounter in Shudokan's dojo. In *No Regrets for Our Youth,* the shadow of Noge in his office suggests his involvement in clandestine antiwar activities. The thief's dream scene reminds us of Matsunaga's nightmare in *Drunken Angel.* The discord between father and son (Shingen and Katsuyori) is another dominant Kurosawa motif explored in many other films (e.g., *Ikiru, Record of a Living Being, The Bad*

Sleep Well, Yojimbo). Noh-related images are also common in Kurosawa films. As Itami Juzo and Hasumi Shigehiko point out, the images of fluttering ensigns, banners, and flags give a distinct look to *Kagemusha, Seven Samurai,* and *The Hidden Fortress.*[2]

The problem with *Kagemusha* is not that it marks a radical turning point in Kurosawa's career but that it resembles Kurosawa's earlier works too much. *Kagemusha* is a virtual catalog of Kurosawa motifs, which, however, are not integrated into a new whole but exist as mere fragments. What is integrated into the overall design of the earlier films is now used as an autonomous component, a commodified image of Kurosawa's authorial signature. Take, for instance, the use of Noh. In films such as *The Men Who Tread on the Tiger's Tail* and *Throne of Blood,* the formal aspects of Noh are actively interpreted and appropriated as a way of problematizing the dominant genre conventions of Japanese cinema in search of a new film form. These films do not use Noh as an ossified embodiment of tradition. Instead of interpreting or translating Noh, *Kagemusha,* on the other hand, literally shows a Noh performance. Noh is only a represented image, and as only a represented content, it does not have any fundamental connection to the form of *Kagemusha.* It seems the presence of Noh in *Kagemusha* has less to do with Noh itself and more to do with Kurosawa's previous films that actively incorporate Noh into their formal systems. The use of Noh and other motifs that refer back to Kurosawa's other films do not necessarily make *Kagemusha* a self-reflexive film, since Kurosawa does not quote himself to intensify an intertextual dynamic among his films. Instead, Kurosawa seems to imitate his own motifs and style, so that *Kagemusha* looks like a pastiche, rather than a critical appropriation, of his own films.

It is possible to attribute the self-imitative aspects of *Kagemusha* to the decline of Kurosawa as an artist. I shall, however, focus more on the changing conditions of the Japanese film industry and image culture in which *Kagemusha* was produced. In the 1970s, the basic infrastructure of the Japanese studio system, on which Kurosawa had relied to make his magnificent films, was largely gone. Daiei and Shintoho were bankrupt; Nikkatsu was making only soft porn films called *roman poruno;* Toho, Shochiku, and Toei downsized their own production divisions and became increasingly reluctant to get involved directly in film production. Technical specialists who maintained the quality of Japanese films were retired or moved to television and other kinds of entertainment industry because the film companies could no longer sustain in-house staff trained in a hierarchical system of apprenticeship. In the 1940s and 1950s, Kurosawa could criticize the Japanese film industry while using the know-how of filmmaking accumulated by that industry; in the 1970s, the industry as he knew it no longer existed. The task for Kurosawa after the collapse of the studio system was not to criticize the film industry but to find a new way of making films. The formation of Yonki no Kai in 1969 was one such attempt; *Dersu Uzala* was another example of an alternative mode of filmmaking, seeking financial support abroad; and to make *Kagemusha*, Kurosawa again relied on the backup of foreign supporters for finance (Francis Ford Coppola and George Lucas, whose association with the film definitely enhanced its chance of box office success on the domestic market) and moreover tried to rebuild a foundation for Japanese cinema by training a new breed of actors. Excepting the few principal actors, everybody else was chosen by auditions, and some major roles were given to true amateurs or actors with little experience.

Did Kurosawa succeed in laying the foundation of a new Japanese cinema? The film itself shows that his attempt yielded an uneven result. The actors' performances are sometimes flat and unnatural. For instance, the actor who plays the role of Tokugawa Ieyasu, a rival lord of Shingen who ultimately triumphed and became the first shogun of the Tokugawa era, consistently looks amateurish and lacks presence. There is a serious problem with the performance of Nakadai Tatsuya in the roles of Shingen and his double. He tends to overact and exaggerate, and his comical interludes are not humorous but overindulgent. (This does not necessarily mean that Katsu Shintaro, who was originally cast for Nakadai's roles but forced to quit after quarreling with Kurosawa on the first day of shooting, would have been a better choice.) The acting of Hagiwara Ken'ichi (Katsuyori) is surprisingly monotonous and exaggerated enough to make us wonder whether Kurosawa intentionally directed him to act in that way to emphasize how unfit Katsuyori was to lead the Takeda clan. Throughout the film, color is rather subdued and monotonous even when primary colors are used (e.g., red, yellow, green) and often unrealistically stands out from the surrounding environment. The problem with color is particularly conspicuous in the actor's costumes. It is hard to suppress our impression that the actors wear some ready-made clothes rather than costumes specifically made for the film. The limitation of the film's color scheme might be in part due to Kurosawa's own color paintings of *Kagemusha*, a product of his desire to show his vision to the public when he was unable to find any companies to underwrite the project. When we look at these paintings, which were published as a book before the release of the film, we are struck by how closely the film's visual look resembles them.[3] It seems that during the shooting of the film Kurosawa consciously or unconsciously tried to recreate what he had already realized in the paintings, which constrained, rather than opened up, his filmic imagination. Ironically, *Kagemusha* the film looks like a "remake" or a "double" of *Kagemusha* the collection of paintings.

In the 1970s, the *jidaigeki* film as a genre was virtually dead. On television, however, *jidaigeki* remained more popular than ever. One of the most popular *jidaigeki* series was so-called *taiga dorama,* NHK's prime-time historical drama featuring well-known figures in Japanese history. *Kagemusha* reminds us of *taiga dorama* rather than *jidaigeki* films of grand battles between rival warlords. Technically speaking, Kurosawa's film is of course incomparably superior to historical drama on television. But its choice of material, visual look, narrative structure, and acting all make *Kagemusha* look like a superior version of *taiga dorama.* This does not necessarily signify the film's simple failure, Kurosawa's decline, or his old-age style. Instead, *Kagemusha* can best be seen as an experimental film, a result of Kurosawa's search for a new way of making films in the radically different sociocultural conditions where the classical studio system was all gone. By the early 1980s, Kurosawa was a legendary figure, and the name "Kurosawa" was a brand name with commercial value. Thus the presence of his signature motifs in *Kagemusha* reassured the spectators about the "authenticity" of this commodity-spectacle. *Kagemusha* and the following films show that even Kurosawa cannot ignore the "cultural logic of late capitalism" to survive as an active filmmaker.

28. *Ran*

The original idea for *Ran* (Ran, 1985) was formulated in the mid-1970s when Kurosawa became interested in the well-known legend of the medieval warlord Moori Motonari's three arrows. Motonari gave a single arrow to each of his three sons and ordered them to break it; they easily accomplished the task. Next, Motonari challenged them to break a bundle of three arrows; none of them was able to break three arrows together. The moral of the lesson is that alone, they might be weak, but if they help each other and work together, they become much more powerful than the mere sum of the three, and the prosperity of the Moori family will be ensured for years to come. Kurosawa started with the hypothetical question "What if Moori's sons had not listened to his father?" In the process of developing his idea into a script, Kurosawa used and incorporated Shakespeare's *King Lear* as an intertext. Various versions of the script were written by him and his regular collaborators, Oguni Hideo and Ide Masato, but unable to find Japanese film companies willing to underwrite the project, Kurosawa was forced to put it aside for a while. In 1983, after having made the smaller-scale period film *Kagemusha* with the help of George Lucas and Francis Ford Coppola, Kurosawa finally found an overseas investor for the project. A French film company expressed interest in financing the production of *Ran,* and even though the French government's restriction on the transfer of capital out of France nearly aborted the project, the shooting started in June of the same year.

Despite numerous changes and adjustments made by Kurosawa, the similarities between his film and Shakespeare's play are unmistakable. The film opens with a ceremonial hunting, followed by a council where the great lord Ichimonji Hidetora (Lear) cedes power to his eldest son, Taro (Goneril). Although Taro and the second son, Jiro (Regan), behave as dutiful sons and express their resolve to obey their father's

order, the third son, Saburo (Cordelia), characterizes Hidetora's decision to retire in the ruthless times of bloodshed and treachery as fool-
ish behavior. Like Moori Motonari, Hidetora hands his sons a single
arrow and a bundle of three arrows. However, Saburo tries to expose
the spuriousness of idealized filial piety by breaking the three arrows
with his knees. Outraged by Saburo's seemingly defiant behavior, in
which he sees treacherous designs, Hidetora banishes Saburo and his
chief retainer Hirayama Tango (Kent), who defends the outspoken son
as more honest and caring. Hidetora's rivals Ayabe (Cornwall) and Fujimaki (France) witness the whole scene and withdraw their request for a
marriage arrangement between Saburo and their daughters. But on his
way back to his domain, Fujimaki changes his mind and takes Saburo
as his son-in-law. The rest of the film shows, somewhat predictably,
the downfall of the Ichimonji clan. As is expected, Taro, whom his wife
Lady Kaede manipulates at will, betrays Hidetora; he is in turn assassinated by Jiro's chief adviser Kurogane. When Jiro is about to exert
his newly acquired authority of the Ichimonji's lordship, Lady Kaede
quickly assumes control over him through the combination of sexual
seduction and violent threat. By the end of the film, almost all the principal characters associated with the Ichimonji clan are dead or about
to die: Saburo is killed by Jiro's sniper; with the body of Saburo in his
arms, Hidetora dies of grief; Jiro is probably going to commit suicide
in the donjon of First Castle, which is surrounded by the Ayabe's army.

Is *Ran* as pessimistic as many critics claim? Is it more metaphysical than Kurosawa's earlier postwar films? Is it a sign of his withdrawal
from the worldly matters? Does it articulate "aesthetics of extinction"
by positively aestheticizing human destruction and death?[1] Does it
show the "power that Kurosawa now accords to karma and the environment"?[2] Despite its bleak outlook, like *Kagemusha, Ran* shares a
number of similarities with Kurosawa's earlier films. Both *Record of a
Living Being* and *Ran* depict the downfall of authoritative patriarchs,
who are driven to insanity after a bitter legal fight or military battle
with their own children. Lady Kaede reminds us of Asaji in *Throne of
Blood,* another Kurosawa film based on a play by Shakespeare. Kaede's
sudden ferocious attack on Jiro has its precedent in *Red Beard*, where
Yasumoto is almost killed by a madwoman.[3] As is often the case in Kurosawa films, some of the remarks by the principal characters of *Ran*

sound naive, didactic, or overstated (e.g., Tango's reproval of Kyoami at the film's close: "Do not blaspheme! It is the gods who weep. They see us killing each other over and over since time began. They can't save us from ourselves"). The rationality and professionalism of Kurogane reminds us of many other Kurosawa heroes and villains. This list of resemblances between *Ran* and Kurosawa's earlier films can go on and on. Interestingly, we do not get an impression that these recurrent motifs and icons of Kurosawa films are organically reintegrated into a new totality. Again, as in *Kagemusha,* they seem to exist side by side autonomously on the surface of the screen, thus making *Ran* a virtual catalog of thematic and iconographic motifs of Kurosawa films.[4]

In *Ran,* Kurosawa creates a series of magnificent visual tableaux by transforming reality into symbols and abstract patterns. The names of the three sons, Taro, Jiro, and Saburo, mean "first son," "second son," and "third son." These names, therefore, transform the individuality of each son into his hierarchical position in the family system. In a similar vein, the film uses color schematically. Taro, Jiro, and Saburo are respectively clothed in yellow, red, and blue, and their soldiers also carry yellow, red, and blue banners and pennants. The number of horizontal lines on the soldiers' pennants — one, two, and three — corresponds to their leaders' names and familial positions. The troops of Fujimaki, Saburo's father-in-law, are in white, and those of Ayabe, who attacks First Castle at the film's end, are in black. The scarcity of close-ups and the extensive use of long shots render even principal characters abstract figures and, by preventing the spectators' identification with them, create the sense of detachment that positions the spectators as distant observers of a drama of massive destruction. Sue, Jiro's wife, is supposedly beautiful, yet without a close-up of her face, the spectators are not allowed to judge whether there is any validity in the statement asserting her beauty. In fact, the notion of character does not adequately describe the function of human figures here. Without any illusion of psychological depth, they are mere types, used only as part of the pattern of a magnificent tapestry (e.g., the bodies of Sue and her attendant outside Tsurumaru's shack). These abstract signs and designs tend to flatten and transform the film into a transparent surface without any depth.

What really stands out in *Ran* is the allure of visual imagery, and it is often not humans but sets and decor (e.g., castles and monumental gates that either coldly reject or trap Hidetora and his retinue in a hell on earth) that play major roles in the development of the narrative. However, even the impressive sets and decor are in the end images without depth; that is, unlike the castle, the forest, and the mist in *Throne of Blood*, the gates, hills, and expansive fields in *Ran* do not have what Bazin called "dramatic opaqueness." Instead of carrying the dramatic intensity and characters' inner turmoil, the sets and decor are mere visual surface, only part of the film's painterly design. The extreme generalization and abstraction make the film's story, which is already too predictable without any twists, ultimately not significant. The film's pessimistic outlook has in the end only secondary importance compared to the perfectly composed visual tableaux. Among Kurosawa's work, *Ran* is probably the best example supporting Masumura Yasuzo's characterization of Kurosawa as a "magnificent yet tragic genius" who makes a gargantuan effort to present dynamic and perfect images on the screen.[5]

29. *Dreams*

Dreams (Yume, 1990) is different from other Kurosawa films in several respects. First, it is his first omnibus film. *Dodeskaden,* a collection of vignettes about people in the shantytown, uses to some extent a similar type of narrative organization but still retains the spatiotemporal unity of the single diegesis. In contrast, *Dreams* consists of autonomous episodes that are not tied to the same diegetic space and time. It is, however, not a random collection of mutually unrelated episodes. For instance, thematic threads loosely connect some of the episodes. The appearance of the same actor in all the episodes except the first two helps to create a certain sense of narrative coherence. And the use of the identical intertitle at the beginning of each episode functions as a narratological marker unifying the film as a single narrated entity. Second, *Dreams* is unique among Kurosawa's work because it is much more overtly personal than any of his other films, including *Dodeskaden.* For the first time since *The Men Who Tread on the Tiger's Tail,* the script was written by Kurosawa alone. All his postwar films except *Dreams, Rhapsody in August,* and *Madadayo* are based on the scripts collaboratively written by Kurosawa and his close associates or, as in the cases of *One Wonderful Sunday* and *No Regrets for Our Youth,* by other scriptwriters. Each episode in *Dreams* is supposedly based on an actual dream Kurosawa had. It is therefore not surprising to see in the film a number of references to his biography and career. This personal aspect of the film is expressed by the intertitle preceding each episode. The title says: "Konna yume o mita" [I had a dream like this].[1] Thus the title not only clearly marks each episode as a dream but also introduces the implied subject of the dream, "I." And it is strongly suggested that this "I" is the director himself from the very beginning of the film: in the first episode, the nameplate on the gate reads "Kurosawa." Both textually and extratextually, *Dreams* encourages us to see it as Kurosawa's personal film.

The film consists of eight episodes, which are roughly arranged in chronological order. One of the common thematic threads in the film is the feeling of humble respect for the unknown. A little boy in the first episode, "Sunshine through the Rain," is taught that there is something in the world that one should not see. In the second episode, "The Peach Orchard," the boy, who has grown a little, resolves to revere and protect nature after watching an elegant dance of the spirits of the peach trees that were cut down by his family. (This episode ends with the close-up of the boy's face in freeze-frame, probably the only freeze-frame shot in all Kurosawa's films.) Nature comes back with a vengeance as a deadly force in the following episode, "The Blizzard." In the fourth episode, "The Tunnel," death is man-made, or a result of war. The young man (Terao Akira), who survives the blizzard in the preceding episode, returns from war as a former platoon leader. He must confront the ghosts of his soldiers and his responsibility as their superior. Next, in "Crows," he is a young painter who enters the imaginary world of van Gogh's paintings and encounters van Gogh himself (played by Martin Scorsese). The following two episodes, "Mount Fuji in Red" and "The Weeping Demon," deal with the human follies of blindly trusting technological progress. In the former, nuclear reactors explode near Mount Fuji, and a mass of people die from radiation, and in the latter the protagonist finds himself in a desolate postholocaust landscape where humans have turned into demons and eat one another to survive. The last episode, "Village of the Watermills," shows an idyllic image of a village where people live naturally. In this utopian village, death is not something people are afraid of. When people live in harmony with nature, death becomes part of their lives and therefore an occasion for communal celebration.

It is tempting to interpret the film psychologically or psychoanalytically to probe into Kurosawa's psyche. But that the film is marked as his personal film does not necessarily mean that everything in the film faithfully reproduces Kurosawa's personal dreams, or that the best way to approach the film is to find corresponding relationships between the film's narrative details and episodes from his life. Like any other Kurosawa film, *Dreams* is a constructed text and does not provide us with any privileged access to the director's mind. What *Dreams* does instead is to propose an "autobiographical pact" to the viewers; that is, it invites us to sign a contract that stipulates that we read the text as autobiographical. The specific content of each episode is probably less important than the film's attempt to create an autobiographical space in which not only *Dreams* but also Kurosawa's entire work is interpreted autobiographically. As I have argued, in the 1980s, the auteur status of Kurosawa was increasingly being consolidated despite his difficulty in financing his film projects. By recontextualizing Kurosawa's work in the autobiographical space of reception and interpretation, *Dreams* helped this neo-auteurist celebration of Kurosawa as the only genuine Japanese film artist who was still alive.

If there is one thing whose formal brilliance particularly strikes us in the film, it is Kurosawa's superb use of Dolby sound. The clarity and wide range of sound in the film is rather remarkable. Kurosawa's use of silence, a single source of sound, and collage of distinct sound effects articulates a kind of cinematic space that cannot be constructed by shot composition and editing alone. In "Sunshine through the Rain," the young boy defies his mother's prohibition and goes into the forest. As in *Throne of Blood*'s Cobweb Forest, the sun is shining, but it is raining. His transgression and entrance into a liminal space are signified by the sound of rustling leaves and then by that of the rain, so crystal clear that it is as if we can hear the sound of each raindrop. "The Blizzard" is a brilliant episode, both in terms of sound and visual image. We hear the mountain climbers gasping, grunting, and breathing heavily, their mountain gears cranking, and the sound of avalanches and snowslides near and far. The dense fog and blizzard create an incredible variation in the visual look on the level of film's grain, again reminding us of *Throne of Blood*.[2] The only problem with the episode is the music added at the end, which almost ruins the emotional intensity built up by the pure manipulation of audiovisual images until that point. In "The Tunnel," too, sound is most responsible for the episode's success. The sound of dead soldiers' footsteps inside and outside of the tunnel is voices of the past, which still haunts the present. Michel Chion summarizes Kurosawa's unique master of Dolby technology as follows:

Toward the end of the twenties most of the prestigious filmmakers like Eisenstein, Epstein, and Murnau were interested in sensations; having a physical and sensory approach to film, they were partial to technical experimentation. Very few of their counterparts today are innovators ready to meet challenges of new technical possibilities, especially concerning Dolby sound. A symptom, perhaps, of a new stage in the eternal "crisis" of the cinema. Frankly, many European directors have simply ignored the amazing mutation brought on by the standardization of Dolby. Fellini . . . makes use of Dolby in *Interview* in order to fashion a soundtrack exactly like the ones he made before. In Kubrick's latest films there is no particularly imaginative use of Dolby either. With *Wings of Desire,* Wenders puts Dolby to a kind of radiophonic use. . . . As for Godard, . . . he has not fundamentally revitalized his approach to sound in his two films with Dolby. . . . We could continue down the list and note that from the oldest (Bresson) to the youngest (Carax), there seems to be a contest of who can show the least enthusiasm for the new sound resources: just about everyone either neglects them or uses them without inventing anything new. To end on a positive note we should point out Kurosawa's purity and sure hand in mastering Dolby in his *Dreams.* . . . Just what does Dolby stereo offer to a director? Nothing less than the equivalent of an eight-octave grand piano, when what she or he had before was an upright spanning only five octaves, less powerful and less capable of nuance. In short, Dolby offers a gain in resources on the level of sound space and sound dynamics that, of course, no one is obliged to use all the time but that is nevertheless available. . . . Dolby stereo increases the possibility of emptiness in film sound at the same time that it enlarges the space that can be filled. It's this capacity for emptiness and not just fullness that offers possibilities yet to be explored. Kurosawa has magnificently exploited this dimension in *Dreams:* sometimes the sonic universe is reduced to a single point — the sound of the rain, an echo that disappears, a simple voice.[3]

In the 1950s, Kurosawa was repeatedly accused of being indifferent to film sound. He defended himself by saying that if the quality of his film's sound was not so good, it was because he tried to push the capacity of sound technology to its limit. That is, according to Kurosawa, with regard to the sound, he was not less but more daring and experimental than other Japanese directors. Whose story should we believe, the critics' or Kurosawa's, to explain the unintelligible delivery of lines by actors in some of his films from this period? *Dreams* settles this dispute once and for all. It is not a film made by someone who was completely indifferent to the problem of film sound for many years and then all of a sudden decided to turn his attention to it. What *Dreams* shows is that Kurosawa has been a serious experimenter with film sound and continues to explore the possibilities of film form opened up by the development of new technology.

30. *Rhapsody in August*

Four children spend their summer vacation at the house of their grandmother Kane in a village outside Nagasaki. Their parents—Kane's son Tadao and daughter Yoshie—have gone to Hawaii to see her long lost elder brother Suzujiro, who is seriously ill. Kane's place is a traditional farmhouse, and she maintains a simple lifestyle. She does not have a television, washing machine, and other modern electric appliances except a refrigerator, which the grandchildren begged her to buy. She grows vegetables and fruits in the garden for her own consumption. Despite their differences, it is clear that Kane really enjoys the company of the grandchildren, and the grandchildren like Kane very much. Kane receives a letter from her son and daughter, who talk about how they have been welcomed by Suzujiro's family and urge Kane to come to Hawaii with their children. The excited grandchildren try to persuade Kane to go to Hawaii, but she stubbornly refuses to visit her brother, saying that she does not remember him. One day, three of the grandchildren—Tami, Minako, and Shinjiro—go to Nagasaki for grocery shopping. In Nagasaki, they visit the memorial for atomic bomb victims, and the elementary school where their grandfather died of the atomic bomb. They become convinced that the grandmother is reluctant to visit her elder brother in Hawaii because of her bitterness toward the United States, which dropped the atomic bomb and killed her husband. The grandchildren begin to see the grandmother differently and feel much closer to her. Tadao and Yoshie come back from Hawaii. They talk only about how wealthy Suzujiro is and the possibility of working for his pineapple company. The grandmother and the grandchildren are all dismayed by the callous behavior of Tadao and Yoshie and are particularly disgusted when they are accused of having made a mistake by mentioning in their telegram to Suzujiro that Kane's husband died of the atomic blast in Nagasaki. The parents say it is a sensitive issue

Kurosawa on the set of *Rhapsody in August,* with actors Igawa Hisashi, center right, and Richard Gere, far right. Photo courtesy of Photofest.

many Americans do not want to be reminded of. Thus when Tadao and Yoshie find out that Suzujiro's son Clark is coming to visit Kane, they are convinced that the purpose of his trip is to break off a "business partnership." However, it turns out that Clark comes to see Kane to pay respects to her dead husband. A mutual understanding develops between the two, and Tadao and Yoshie regret their greed and egotism. After the village's memorial services for those killed by the atomic bomb is over, Clark receives a telegram announcing his father's death and immediately flies back to Hawaii. Thus Kane has forever missed her opportunity to see her long lost brother. Then something happens to her mind. She starts reliving her past, the day of the atomic attack on Nagasaki. The film concludes with the scene in which the grandchildren and their parents run after Kane, who walks toward Nagasaki in a heavy rainstorm, believing that she is looking for her husband.

The reception of *Rhapsody in August* (Hachigatsu no rapusodi [kyo-shikyoku], 1991) has been predominantly negative and more important, politically charged. There have been some strong reactions against the film by foreign critics, particularly Americans, many of whom are highly critical of the way the bombing of Nagasaki is treated by the film. The film is criticized for its portrayal of the Japanese as mere victims. It is said that it ignores the fact that World War II in Asia was primarily the Japanese aggression against Asia. But the film's controversial reception mostly focuses on one point: that is, its alleged attack on the United States of America as the country that dropped the atomic bombs over Nagasaki and Hiroshima. There are two scenes in the film that have particularly drawn the critics' attention: the scene of Nagasaki's atomic bomb memorial park and its sculpture garden and that of the American nephew Clark's apology to the grandmother Kane. The following are examples of reactions to the first scene:

> The grandchildren notice that unlike Cuba, Bulgaria, and the People's Republic of China, America failed to send a memorial to Nagasaki's memorial park, because, they reason, it was the Americans who dropped the Bomb. The film is so focused on Japanese-American relations that it ignores the complex political motivations for the other countries to send memorials to victims of an American nuclear weapon. The Bomb exists outside of history.[1]

> The camera follows their [the grandchildren's] reverent gazes around the monuments dedicated by various countries to the victims of the bomb, and they remark that of course there is no monument from the United States "because America dropped the bomb." (America's complete responsibility for nurturing and protecting Japan in the postwar era is never acknowledged, nor is the fact that Japan forced America into the war.)[2]

There are two separate issues to be discussed here. The remark that the United States did not send a memorial to the bomb victims because it dropped the bomb is made by the older granddaughter, Tami, whose opinion seems to be shared by two other grandchildren visiting the memorial park together. At this point, what Tami says is not necessarily something endorsed by the film itself as true. To see how her viewpoint is used can be decided only after thoroughly contextualizing it in relation to the rest of the film. On the surface, the film does not seem to explicitly challenge the grandchildren's understanding of why Americans did not send a memorial to the park. There is still, however, some room for interpretive ambiguity because not every pronouncement by the grandchildren is unequivocally endorsed by the film. For instance, the grandchildren are convinced that Kane does not want to visit her only surviving brother because of her hatred toward the United States, which killed her husband with the atomic bomb. But the grandmother blames the war for the death of her husband, not the United States, which she neither likes nor dislikes anymore. It is impossible to know whether the grandmother expresses her true feelings. But at least it is clear that not everything the grandchildren say in the film is unambiguously accepted by the film as a statement of truth.

In addition to the question of who makes the utterance, it is also necessary to discuss what is asserted by that utterance. Is what the grandchildren say about the absence of an American memorial totally untrue? Does it radically distort history as many critics of the film contend? As is argued in the first quote, the film perhaps "ignores the complex political motivations for the other countries to send memorials to victims of an American nuclear weapon." Even if this is in fact the case, it does not at all explain why the United States did not send its memorial to Nagasaki. (Note also that the monuments and sculptures are not only from "Cuba, Bulgaria, and the People's Republic of China," or according to another critic, from "Czechoslovakia, Poland, Bulgaria, China, Cuba, and USSR";[3] the film shows memorials from other countries including Italy, Holland, Brazil, and Portugal.) The objection in the second quote is equally difficult to comprehend. "America's complete responsibility for nurturing and protecting Japan in the postwar era is never acknowledged" simply because what the critic claims never happened. After the defeat, Japan was occupied by the Americans. No matter how "beneficial" the Occupation was for Japan in some respects, the Americans' purposes were never to "nurture" or "protect" Japan. Therefore there is nothing to acknowledge here, except perhaps the relevant fact that the Occupation, which encouraged democracy, never allowed any reference to the atomic bomb in Japanese films through its strict censorship.

The second point of critical controversy is the meaning of Clark's apology to Kane. But for what exactly does the American nephew apologize to his Japanese aunt? Does he apologize for America's dropping of the atomic bomb on Nagasaki, as asserted in major reviews? ("The children are initially anxious about his visit, but he charms them all, as well as the old lady, and apologizes for the atomic attack 45 years ago"; "The old woman forgives all when he apologizes to her for the bombing.")[4] As ambiguous as his broken Japanese is, Clark clearly speaks as an extended family member, not as an American. He admits his family's and his own failure to realize what kind of pain the grandmother has been suffering from her husband's death by the atomic blast. They didn't make a connection between the death of Kane's husband and the location of her home, Nagasaki. Instead, they talked only about themselves without paying attention to Kane's circumstances. By urging her to come to Hawaii as soon as possible, they were even unintentionally asking her to miss the anniversary of the Nagasaki bombing and memorial services for her dead husband.[5] This is the reason why Clark apologizes to Kane; it is not at all the case that he apologizes for the American attack on Nagasaki with the atomic bomb. Thus the misconstrued description of the apology scene reveals more about the critics' understanding of the dropping of the atomic bomb over Nagasaki as a historical fact than the film's representation of this historical fact. Critics who are surprised by what they perceive as Kurosawa's unjustifiable criticism of the United States in *Rhapsody in August* have probably never understood his films, including such postwar masterpieces as *Stray Dog, No Regrets for Our Youth,* and *Rashomon.*

Rhapsody in August has also been criticized for dehistoricizing the dropping of the atomic bomb by treating it as some kind of transcendental event or a natural disaster. ("In *Rhapsody* we are simply told that everything bad that happened was the fault of the war, as if the war was not something that resulted from the actions of individual human beings"; "Kurosawa's central concern is with the legacy of ambivalent feelings created by the war. But having divorced the Bomb from human history, Kurosawa interprets it as a natural and evil force, as unyielding to human reason as a water imp.")[6] However, this criticism again does not accurately grasp what the film actually says about the nuclear attack on Nagasaki. It is hardly the case that Kane abstractly blames the war for the death of her husband and the suffering of numerous others. While she deplores the stupidity of the human race, she never hesitates to say to anybody, including Americans, that it was the United States that dropped the atomic bomb over Nagasaki.[7]

Rhapsody in August is about the possibility of talking about and re-membering as much as the fact of the Americans' atomic destruction of Nagasaki on August 9, 1945. The film does not re-create the scenes of the atomic explosion and its aftermath. Instead, the dropping of the bomb is only indirectly represented by a melted jungle gym in the schoolyard where Kane's husband presumably died and some stone statues of angels damaged by the radioactive blast. Human witnesses to the atrocity remain silent about their experiences, which no words can describe adequately. The elderly people who survived the bomb as schoolchildren come to the melted jungle gym, which is preserved as a memorial, and silently clean and decorate it with young plants. One of Kane's friends, who also lost her husband to the atomic bomb, comes to see her once a month. According to Kane, the friend comes to talk about her atomic bomb experience, yet the film shows them just sitting on the wood floor without saying a word to each other. To the doubt-ful grandchildren, Kane says that people can talk to each other silently, too. Without uttering any words, the two elderly women can under-stand each other's feelings and pain and together mourn for the dead.

In *Rhapsody in August,* the present is haunted by the past. At night after dinner, Kane tells the grandchildren a story of her family. She re-members the names of her eleven brothers and sisters, but Suzujiro is not one of them. She can recall brothers Natakichi and Suzukichi par-ticularly well. According to Kane, her elder brother Natakichi was an apprentice at a shoe shop in Nagasaki but eventually eloped with the master's wife. As they hurried along in the woods behind Kane's house, they came across two cedar trees that had been struck by lightning and burned and twisted together. When the woman saw those trees, she said they looked as if they had committed double suicide. The eloped couple decided to build a hut next to the charred trees and led a quiet life together. The morning after Tateo and Tami hear this story from their grandmother, they go to look for the same trees, which are sup-posed to be still standing in the woods. At first they are skeptical, but they eventually find the leafless trees twisted together in a contorted, grotesque shape. They are a little afraid and observe the trees from a distance. As if they are momentarily taken over by the spirit of the past, Tateo and Tami, sitting side by side, absentmindedly recite what the lovers in the story said to each other. When Tateo, in a half trance, reaches for Tami, she jumps out of her skin. She springs to her feet and runs away from him. Tateo starts running after her, apologizing that he was not himself for a moment. This eerie scene in the woods is immediately followed by the memorable scene of Kane and her friend's silent conversation, which is also haunted by the past.

Another sibling Kane fondly remembers is Suzukichi, her mentally handicapped younger brother. He used to sneak out of the house at night to swim in the pond with a waterfall. One night, a small skinny boy who looked unusually green came to the house to tell Kane that he had rescued Suzukichi, who had almost drowned in the river. Surprised, Kane rushed outside and found Suzukichi, soaked to the skin, lying on the grass. The village people and her father later wondered who the small boy was and finally came to the conclusion that he was a water imp (*kappa*). Shinjiro, the youngest of the grandchildren, has been teased by Tateo since Kane told him that he really looks like Suzukichi. Thus, after he hears Kane's story, he decides to get back at Tateo, his sister, and his cousin. Made up as a water imp, Shinjiro sneaks up to the window and slowly shows his green arms and head. His elder sister and cousins, who are inside the house, are so startled by the appearance of a legendary creature that when Shinjiro finally reveals who he is, Tami and Minako start chasing after him around the house while Tateo plays a comical musical piece with the pedal organ.

Kane is an unpretentious storyteller, who, drawing on her memories, vividly tells strange and gripping tales. The grandchildren are so captivated by her stories that as we have just seen, they end up reenacting those stories. Kane maintains a critical distance from her memories until the last sequence when she finally remembers who Suzujiro is. Kane's recognition of her elder brother is traumatic because the missing memory returns to her only when it is too late for her to see him. The untimely recovery of the memory is so shocking that she becomes delusional and mistakes the death of Suzujiro for that of her husband. As Tateo says, Kane's mental clock starts moving backward to the day when her husband was killed by the atomic bomb. It is not clear whether she suffers from just a temporary mental lapse or from a more permanent illness. What is clear is that the final sequence is consistent with the rest of the film. Kane's medical status is in the end not important because the film's last scene is not at all a realistic scene. Kane is no longer a character but an allegorical figure ("a painfully tragic poem"),[8] whose quixotic march in the storm looks as if she is fighting against the atomic blast. As Kane forces her way in the heavy rainstorm, a gust of wind turns her umbrella inside out, making it look like a rose. At this point, all realistic sound effects are replaced by a children's choir singing the Schubert song "*Heidenröselein,*" reminding us of Tateo's successful repair of the grandmother's out-of-tune pedal organ, with which he plays the Schubert song several times in the preceding scenes, and a swarm of ants climbing up the petals of a brilliantly red rose that captivated the gaze of Shinjiro and Clark during the memorial services. Kane is now not a mentally confused woman but a brave warrior whose struggle against the rain and wind transforms her into an allegorical icon affirming the dignity and preciousness of life.

31. *Madadayo*

Madadayo (Madadayo, 1993) follows the life of the writer Uchida Hyak-ken (1889–1971) from the spring of 1943 when he leaves his teaching position to concentrate on his own writing to 1962 when he celebrates his seventy-seventh birthday. The film's episodes are mostly taken from Hyakken's biography and published essays, yet specific details are freely modified by Kurosawa (e.g., the chronology of Hyakken's life). Un-like most of Kurosawa's films, *Madadayo* presents neither a tightly knit dramatic narrative nor a collection of discrete episodes. Instead, it is organized more like an essay depicting Hyakken's everyday life with his wife, whose name is not given, and a stray cat named Nora, and Hyak-ken's relationship with his former students, who respect their teacher very much. Throughout the film, Hyakken continuously talks, and his wife and students listen to humorous tales and anecdotes narrated by this storyteller. Many details of the film can be interpreted as self-referential allusions to Kurosawa's own life or to his other films.[1] As in many other Kurosawa films, one of the core motifs in *Madadayo* is the teacher-student relationship. The film's specific treatment of this Kurosawa motif is unique because Hyakken is not presented as an in-fallible master and his students as obedient disciples. If Hyakken is presented as an ideal teacher, it is because he does not authoritatively impose anything on his students. Hyakken tries to have his own way, thus sometimes appearing childish (e.g., his despair over the disappear-ance of Nora); it is his students who seem more mature and wise. The students greatly respect their sensei because of who he is, not neces-sarily because of what he knows. Instead of overtly preaching what the ideal relationship of teacher and students should be, *Madadayo* shows a utopian image of the pedagogical relationship, in which teacher and students mutually trust and respect each other. Throughout the film, Hyakken and his students strengthen and reaffirm their close bond by singing songs together. Although film music is sparsely used, there are many scenes where characters sing various kinds of songs: songs for schoolchildren, songs for students, satiric songs, and so forth. None of these songs are sentimental, nostalgic, or rueful. They are all simple and uncontrived, naturally expressing human feelings. Even when they are critical of contemporary sociopolitical situations, their tone is positive and affirmative, not resentful or pessimistic. "Old songs are wonderful, aren't they?" says Hyakken. "They are innocent and natural like Henri Rousseau's paintings. I love old songs!"

After Hyakken's house is destroyed by an air raid, he borrows a tiny shack from a baron in a ruined neighborhood and lives there with his wife for about three years. The film shows successive images of Hyakken and his wife in their shack in different seasons. They are a remarkably beautiful depiction of nature and seasonal changes shot on location, something that rarely exists in other films by Kurosawa. As we have examined earlier, what distinguishes Kurosawa's cinema from conventional Japanese films is his antinaturalistic treatment of nature. The seasonal markers, which are used in conventional Japanese films to evoke sentimental emotion and atmosphere, are transformed in Kurosawa films into pure kinetic signs, narrative elements introducing conflict and disharmony, dramatic devices agitating characters. The title of *Dodeskaden*'s original story is after all "A Town without Seasons" (Kisetsu no nai machi). Even when nature is prominently featured, as in *Dersu Uzala*, it appears not as an object of passive contemplation but as a brutal force that can both annihilate and nourish humans. In *Madadayo*, Kurosawa treats the beauty of the four seasons straightforwardly perhaps for the first time. This does not mean, however, that the seasons are represented sentimentally or naturalistically. Nature in conventional Japanese cinema evokes sentimental emotion by establishing a connection between natural scenes and characters' interior psychological states. In *Madadayo*, nature is not overtly psychologized. In the scenes of Hyakken's shack, Kurosawa abruptly cuts from one shot to another and does not attempt to smooth out the shot transition by inserting the shot of a tree branch covered with snow or a pile of burning leaves; that is, a transitional shot of nature and environment so typically used in Japanese films. Instead, the camera observes the shack in fall, winter, and spring from a detached distance, and the images of nature are not subjectivized by using point-of-view shots or by making Hyakken and his wife comment on the beautiful scenery. Because Kurosawa splices together two shots of almost identical images that are different only in the shot size, the shot transition is sometimes perceptually disturbing and thus subtly prevents the spectators' identification with nature.

The scene of nature returns at the film's conclusion. It is Hyakken's dream, in which he appears as a little boy, playing hide-and-seek with his friends in a large field. As he hides behind a pile of straw while saying "madadayo" [not yet], he looks up at the sky at sunset. The clouds of various shapes beautifully change their colors moment by moment. This time, Kurosawa does not film the clouds on location. Instead, the clouds are painted on a large screen inside a studio and shot with a high-definition video camera. As radically different as they are, these clouds remind us of the swiftly moving clouds above Sanshiro and Higaki in the climactic fight scene from Kurosawa's first film, *Sanshiro Sugata.* What is common in the high-definition video image of painted clouds and the photographic image of natural clouds is a sense of artificiality and excess, that is, something antithetical to a stereotyped notion of Japanese sensibility toward natural beauty valorized by the culturalist discourse of the Japanese cinema studies. Thus, in the last scene of *Madadayo,* the colorful clouds painted on the screen appear as an emblematic sign of Kurosawa's will to construct a world of his imagination, and also implicitly as a sign of his profoundly mediated and ambivalent relationship to the idea of Japaneseness.

EPILOGUE

As I was making the final revisions to the manuscript, Kurosawa Akira passed away on September 6, 1998, at his home in Tokyo. Japanese newspapers reported comments and reminiscences of his friends, staff, actors, and critics. What these brief remarks show is the enormity of Kurosawa's presence in Japanese cinema since the 1940s. They are also a significant reminder that no matter how perfectionist he was as an artist, Kurosawa's films were made collectively. We should not forget the contributions made by actors (Mifune Toshiro, Shimura Takashi, Yamada Isuzu), scriptwriters (Hashimoto Shinobu, Hisaita Eijiro, Kikushima Ryuzo, Oguni Hideo), set designers (Matsuyama Takashi, Muraki Yoshiro), composers (Hayasaka Fumio, Sato Masaru, Takemitsu Toru), cinematographers (Miyagawa Kazuo, Nakai Asakazu), and numerous others, without whose efforts Kurosawa would never have been able to make any of his films.

As a way of concluding my study of Kurosawa, I would like to reiterate some of its basic points and reflect on the future of Japanese cinema studies briefly. It is perhaps worth pointing out one more time that this study is neither an example of auteur criticism nor a subspecies of national cinema studies. Kurosawa is not an auteur who singlemindedly pursued throughout his career, which spanned more than fifty years, a single project, whether artistic, political, or otherwise. Nor is he a representative Japanese filmmaker who, despite his interests in Western art, literature, and film, relied on traditional Japanese aesthetics and sensibility as a foundation for his films' style and worldview. For Kurosawa, "Japan" is not an answer but a problem to be scrutinized. Nothing in his films gives us any privileged access to Japanese aesthetics, sensibility, cultural heritage, or Japaneseness. The complexity, contradiction, and openness of Kurosawa's work cannot be reduced to

either the intention and subjectivity of an auteur or the cultural traditions and patterns of a particular nation called Japan.

There is simply no single approach that fully explains the significance, meanings, or relevance of Kurosawa's films. To explain where the
powerful impact of his films comes from, their style and formal aspects
must be analyzed closely. Yet it is senseless to construe him merely as a
filmmaker of formal innovation at the expense of the richness of thematic matrices in his films. Because he did not work in a vacuum, it
is also necessary to discuss the institutional history of Japanese cinema
and the specific sociopolitical conditions against which his films were
made. The films of Kurosawa are after all not a self-enclosed, autonomous entity where everything can be explained in relation to an inter-
nally consistent structural principle.

In this study, I have tried to discuss as many critical problems and
issues as possible. Some of them are specific to Kurosawa's films, and
others have much broader historical and theoretical implications.
Whether they are about the genre system in Japanese cinema, war responsibility of filmmakers, textual inscription of the Occupation and
aftermath of the war in films, or postwar Japanese cinema and the
manufacturing of popular memory, questions are formulated and
tackled without much regard for their direct relevance and significance
for the agenda and expectations of academic disciplines that have a
stake in Japanese cinema studies. For what is important is not how
much a study of Kurosawa's work can contribute to the continuance
and expansion of any existing discipline. On the contrary, a study of
Kurosawa and Japanese cinema in general must be conducted in such
a way that it reveals how the institutional limits of established disciplines make them unable to deal with fundamental questions of Japanese cinema productively. This does not mean that Japanese cinema
studies should become more interdisciplinary. To the extent that it does
not fundamentally question the identity and autonomy of established
disciplines, interdisciplinary studies is often a mere supplement to the
existing academic structure. What the idea of interdisciplinary studies
tends to efface is a vicious circle of ideological dependency, through
which Eurocentrism and Japanese cultural nationalism mutually reinforce each other to legitimate the existence of established disciplines.

The institutional conditions surrounding the studies of Japanese cinema have changed a little since I started working on this project. While the relative importance of Japanese cinema in the discipline of film studies seems to be diminishing steadily, there is a visible increase in Japanese literary studies' interest in film. It is not uncommon to see doctorate students in literary studies including a chapter about Japanese film in their dissertations. There are more job openings in language and literature departments that expect candidates to have some knowledge of Japanese cinema. This is a welcome new development. But there is also a new danger. Throughout this study, I have tried to show how the way Japanese cinema has been invented or objectified by the discipline of film studies is problematic. However, I do believe that the study of Japanese film requires more than just training in literary studies, since film is after all not a variant of literature and has its own specificity as an audiovisual medium. A challenge is therefore to create a new institutional base that enables us to study Japanese film without erasing its sociohistorical specificity and at the same time without assimilating its formal specificity into culturalist argument. Can the field of Japanese literary studies and its most common institutional base, area studies departments, meet this challenge? Is a new trend of incorporating Japanese film in literary studies more detrimental than beneficial to the development of Japanese cinema studies? Does the shift of the institutional base mean a loss of critical attention to the specificity of film as a medium? Job candidates for tenure-track positions in Japanese literature are now often asked to demonstrate their ability to teach film. But what exactly constitutes a competency to teach courses about Japanese cinema? Will the field of Japanese literary studies and the discipline of Japanese studies change through their embracement of Japanese film as a newly discovered object of knowledge? It is still too early to tell how long this new trend will continue. Nor is it possible to predict whether it will lead to a radical reconfiguration of Japanese cinema studies or end up as an occasion in which Japanese film is appropriated as a mere variant of literature by Japanese studies.

Another challenge to Japanese cinema studies comes from the discourse of globalization. Every day we hear that ours is the age of globalization. Regardless of where we are located geographically, it is hardly possible to find ourselves outside of international and transnational flows of money, goods, information, and people. Boundaries of all kinds are violated, ignored, and destroyed; new connections are made between noncontiguous geographic regions, countries, and communities; space and time are compressed into the global instantaneity of computer networks and satellite-transmitted images. The autonomy of nation-states, which has been a foundation for the constitution of the modern world, is challenged and eroded while new groups and communities are formed based on ethnic and religious identities.

As the concept of national cinema has become not a solution but a problem to be grappled with, the discourse of globalization is an attractive alternative for film studies to latch onto. It also seems to be quite useful for Japanese cinema studies to discuss the recent resurgence of Japanese cinema, which is most evidently shown by the number of Japanese films winning prizes at international film festivals. Yet unless the ideological underpinnings and historical validity of the idea of globalization are scrutinized, the discourse of globalization may simply end up reaffirming film studies' aspiration for cosmopolitan universalism without questioning its Eurocentric bias. Similarly, the discourse of globalization may turn out to be just a new ploy to keep Japanese cinema studies in the orbit of film studies rather than an alternative mode of criticism that thoroughly problematizes the basic methodological assumptions of the former.

Any attempt to reconfigure Japanese cinema studies cannot ignore the cinema of Kurosawa Akira. This is not just because of the central position he occupies in the scholarship on Japanese cinema but, more important, because of the powerful impact of his films. Their thematic richness and formal complexity defy various types of formulaic explanation circulating in Japanese cinema studies. By watching and analyzing the films closely, we cannot but come up with questions that challenge methodological clichés propagated by Japanese cinema studies and reinforced by institutional politics and disciplinary boundaries in the academy. The films of Kurosawa will continue to challenge us to rethink Japanese cinema, modern Japanese history, and film as the art of the twentieth century.

NOTES

Introduction

1 Bungei Shunju, ed., *Isetsu Kurosawa Akira* (Tokyo: Bungei Shunju, 1994), 112–14.

2 In an essay on his personal involvement in the study of Japanese cinema, Donald Richie reports that among many Japanese films he saw in the immediate postwar days, the first film he can definitely identify is Kurosawa's *Drunken Angel*. Richie's friend composer Hayasaka Fumio took him to the film's open set of a sump, where he was introduced to Kurosawa and Mifune for the first time. Richie writes: "Whenever I now see this film and we reach that scene by the sump, I look to the right of the screen — there I am, just a few feet off the edge, twenty-four now, mouth open, watching a movie being made." Thus he tries to inscribe himself permanently in the inaugural space of postwar Japanese cinema while creating an impression that Kurosawa played a central role in that space. See Donald Richie, "The Japanese Film: A Personal View — 1947–1995," *Asian Cinema* 7, no. 2 (winter 1995): 6.

3 Noël Burch, *To the Distant Observer: Form and Meaning in the Japanese Cinema* (Berkeley: University of California Press, 1979), 291.

4 Ibid., 322.

5 Kurosawa's nickname, *tenno* (emperor), or Kurosawa *tenno*, has complex symbolic meanings. As already mentioned, the nickname obviously connotes the site and possession of power, and Kurosawa's alleged authoritarian behavior during production accounts for this use of the nickname. The word *tenno* is also used to point out what is perceived as an increasing gap between Kurosawa's cinema and contemporary social conditions. Like *tenno*, Kurosawa is said to cloister himself in his own small world, which is completely cut off from the everyday reality of the majority of Japanese. The nickname *tenno* is used in this sense to create an image of Kurosawa as a director who abuses his power solely for the purpose of self-indulgence. The phrase "Kurosawa *tenno*" itself is a wordplay; that is, it loosely rhymes with "Kumazawa *tenno*" (Aochi Shin, "Kurosawa Akira," *Chuo koron* [March 1957]: 245). Kuma-

zawa *tenno,* or Kumazawa Hiromichi, a shopkeeper in Nagoya, publicly claimed in January 1946, about two weeks after Emperor Hirohito had denied his own divinity, that he was the true emperor of Japan. According to Kumazawa, his genealogy directly traced back to Emperor Go-Kameyama, who was a descendant of Emperor Go-Daigo. In 1333 Go-Daigo attempted to take back the power from the Kamakura shogunate to exercise his direct political control. The failure of his coup led to the establishment of two separate imperial courts, in Kyoto and in the southern mountains of Yoshino. Hirohito was a descendant of the imperial family in Kyoto, which unified the imperial court in 1392. Kumazawa petitioned General Headquarters GHQ to restore him to the throne as the true emperor of Japan. He also took his case to the court, but his suit was dismissed. While Kumazawa drew the attention of Japanese and foreign mass media, other self-proclaimed emperors appeared all over Japan. Given this historical background, the nickname "Kurosawa *tenno*" belittles Kurosawa as a delusional upstart whose self-important image of himself is as ridiculous as that of Kumazawa Hiromichi.

6 Some of these works on Ozu include Donald Richie, *Ozu Yasujiro no bigaku: Eiga no naka no Nihon,* trans. Yamamoto Kikuo (Tokyo: Firumu Atosha, 1978), originally published as *Ozu* (Berkeley: University of California Press, 1974); Paul Schrader, *Sei naru eiga: Ozu/Bresson/Dreyer,* trans. Yamamoto Kikuo (Tokyo: Firumu Atosha, 1981), originally published as *Transcendental Style in Film: Ozu, Bresson, Dreyer* (Berkeley: University of California Press, 1972); Firumu Atosha, ed., *Ozu Yasujiro o yomu: Furuki mono no utsukushii fukken* (Tokyo: Firumu Atosha, 1982); Hasumi Shigehiko, *Kantoku Ozu Yasujiro* (Tokyo: Chikuma Shobo, 1983); Ozu Yasujiro, *Ozu Yasujiro zen hatsugen, 1933–1945* (Tokyo: Tairyusha, 1987); Atsuta Yuharu, *Ozu Yasujiro monogatari* (Tokyo: Chikuma Shobo, 1989); Tanaka Masasumi, ed., *Ozu Yasujiro sengo goroku shusei* (Tokyo: Firumu Atosha, 1989); Kinema Junposha, ed., *Ozu Yasujiro shusei* (Tokyo: Kinema Junposha, 1989–1993); Hamano Yasuki, *Ozu Yasujiro* (Tokyo: Iwanami Shoten, 1993); Maeda Hideki, *Ozu Yasujiro no ie: Jizoku to shinto* (Tokyo: Shoshi Yamada, 1993); Tsuzuki Masaaki, *Ozu Yasujiro nikki: Mujo to tawamureta kyosho* (Tokyo: Kodansha, 1993); Shochiku Kabushiki Kaisha, ed., *Ozu Yasujiro shinhakken* (Tokyo: Kodansha, 1993); Firumu Atosha, ed., *Tokushu Ozu Yasujiro 30–90* (Tokyo: Firumu Atosha, 1993); Ishizaka Shozo, *Ozu Yasujiro to Chigasakikan* (Tokyo: Shinchosha, 1995).

7 For a study of the recent nostalgia boom in Japan, see Marilyn Ivy, *Discourses of the Vanishing: Modernity, Phantasm, Japan* (Chicago: University of Chicago Press, 1995).

1 The list of the 1950s Hollywood films in which Japan is featured prominently includes *Japanese War Bride* (King Vidor, 1952); *House of Bamboo* (Samuel Fuller, 1955); *Teahouse of the August Moon* (Daniel Mann, 1956); *Sayonara* (Joshua Logan, 1957); *The Barbarian and the Geisha* (John Huston, 1958); *Geisha Boy* (Frank Tashlin, 1958); *The Crimson Kimono* (Samuel Fuller, 1959); and others. For detailed analyses of these films, see Gina Marchetti, *Romance and the "Yellow Peril": Race, Sex, and Discursive Strategies in Hollywood Fiction* (Berkeley: University of California Press, 1993); and Murakami Yumiko, *Iero feisu: Hariuddo eiga ni miru Ajiajin no shozo* (Tokyo: Asahi Shinbunsha, 1993).

2 See, for instance, newspaper and magazine reviews of *Rashomon* published when the film was originally released in the United States and the United Kingdom. Some of these reviews are reprinted in Donald Richie, ed., *Rashomon* (New Brunswick, N.J.: Rutgers University Press, 1987). Yet not all writings on Japanese cinema in the 1950s were so blatantly ethnocentric or reductive. There were a number of articles and reviews whose main purpose was to introduce Japanese cinema to American audiences. Written by both Japanese film critics and American specialists on Japan, these texts discussed not only specific Japanese films but also the history and current condition of Japanese cinema, major directors, genres, stars, the state of Japanese film criticism, and so on. Some of these informative articles on Japanese cinema are Masayoshi Iwabutchi, "1954 in Japan," *Sight and Sound* (spring 1955): 202–5; Akira Iwasaki, "Japan's New Screen Art: More Real than 'Rashomon,' " *Nation*, 12 May 1956, 398–401; Earl Miner, "Japanese Film Art in Modern Dress," *Quarterly of Film, Radio, and Television* 10, no. 4 (1956); Donald Richie, "The Unexceptional Japanese Films Are More Preferred in Japan than Those That Intrigue the West," *Films in Review* (June–July 1955): 273–77.

3 Other books on Japanese cinema published in the 1960s include the following two works by Donald Richie, *The Japanese Movies: An Illustrated History* (Tokyo: Kodansha International, 1966) and *Japanese Movies* (Tokyo: Japan Travel Bureau, 1961). Neither particularly academic nor comprehensive, unlike *The Japanese Film*, these books have hardly been mentioned in American scholarship on Japanese cinema.

4 David Desser, "Toward a Structural Analysis of the Postwar Samurai Film," in *Reframing Japanese Cinema: Authorship, Genre, History*, ed. Arthur Nollett, Jr. and David Desser (Bloomington: Indiana University Press, 1992), 147.

5 Allan Casebier, "Images of Irrationality in Modern Japan: The Films of Shohei Imamura," *Film Criticism* 7, no. 1 (fall 1983): 42–43.

6 Joan Mellen, *The Waves at Genji's Door: Japan through Its Cinema* (New York: Pantheon Books, 1976), 396–97; Desser, "Toward a Structural Analysis," 155; Kathe Geist, "Buddhism in *Tokyo Story*," in *Ozu's "Tokyo Story*," ed. David Desser (Cambridge: Cambridge University Press, 1997), 110.

7 Desser, "Toward a Structural Analysis," 156.

8 Ibid., 149.

9 Another pioneering auteurist study, *Hitchcock's Films* by Robin Wood, was also published in 1965.

10 Janet Staiger, "The Politics of Film Canons," *Cinema Journal* 24, no. 3 (1985): 12.

11 Paul Schrader, *Transcendental Style in Film: Ozu, Bresson, Dreyer* (Berkeley: University of California Press, 1972).

12 "Paul Schrader has spoken of a 'transcendental style' in certain cinema-authors. But he uses this word to indicate the sudden arrival of the transcendent, as he thinks he sees it in Ozu, Dreyer, or Bresson. . . . It is thus not the Kantian sense, which in contrast opposes the transcendental and the metaphysical or transcendent" (Gilles Deleuze, *Cinema 2: The Time-Image*, trans. Hugh Tomlinson and Robert Galeta [Minneapolis: University of Minnesota Press, 1989], 332–33).

13 For instance, to justify the use of Zen as the most pertinent cultural context for his study of Ozu's films, Paul Schrader refers to a report prepared by the Allied Powers' Religious and Cultural Division during the occupation of Japan: "The type of conduct usually expressed by the words 'Japanese spirit' is essentially Zen in nature." And he does not forget to add that this characterization of Japanese culture is "echoed by both Alan Watts and Langdon Warner," Western authorities on Zen and Japanese art respectively (Schrader, *Transcendental Style in Film*, 27).

14 John Dower, *War without Mercy: Race and Power in the Pacific War* (New York: Pantheon, 1986), 119.

15 Ibid., 121.

16 On Benedict's relation to the wartime collaboration of the military and social scientists, see, for instance, Clifford Geertz, *Works and Lives: The Anthropologist as Author* (Stanford, Calif.: Stanford University Press, 1988), 123–26.

17 Ruth Benedict, *The Chrysanthemum and the Sword: Patterns of Japanese Culture* (Boston: Houghton Mifflin, 1946), 1.

18 Yanagita Kunio, "Jinjojin no jinseikan," *Minzokugaku Kenkyu* 14, no. 4 (1949): 290, quoted in John W. Bennett and Michio Nagai, "The Japa-

nese Critique of the Methodology of Benedict's *Chrysanthemum and the Sword,*" *American Anthropologist* 55, no. 3 (August 1953): 407–8.

19 Bennett and Nagai, "The Japanese Critique of the Methodology of Benedict's *Chrysanthemum and the Sword,*" 408. For a deconstructive reading of Benedict's book, see Geertz, *Works and Lives.*

20 Donald Keene reports that in 1942 at the U.S. Navy Japanese Language School in Boulder, Colorado, he and other students were required to watch Japanese films every week to improve their spoken Japanese. The films he saw were all so dreadful that he did not see a single Japanese film for nine years until *Rashomon* won the Grand Prize at the Venice Film Festival (Donald Keene, "Kurosawa," *Grand Street* 1, no. 4 [summer 1982]: 140–41). Is the U.S. military's instrumental use of Japanese films during World War II partially responsible for the neglect of film by Japanese studies, whose founding members were mostly trained by the military and worked for the Occupation government?

21 Tetsuo Najita, "On Culture and Technology in Postmodern Japan," in *Postmodernism and Japan,* ed. Masao Miyoshi and H. D. Harootunian (Durham, N.C.: Duke University Press, 1989), 14.

22 For instance, see Mellen, *The Waves at Genji's Door.* Her seemingly historical argument is sometimes nothing more than the simple imposition of two essentialized stereotypes onto Japanese history, traditional Japan ("feudalism") and the modern West ("modernity").

23 Prior to the publication of the book, Burch published an article outlining the basic theoretical premises of his Japanese cinema project. Noël Burch, "To the Distant Observer: Towards a Theory of Japanese Film," *October* 1 (spring 1976): 32–46.

24 Burch, *To the Distant Observer,* 11.

25 This is the title of the chapter on Benedict in Geertz's *Work and Lives.*

26 Burch, *To the Distant Observer,* 11.

27 "Of most general value . . . are his insights into Western filmmaking. Like Debussy and other avant-garde artists, Burch returns from his contemplation of Eastern art with a critical vision of our own traditions. . . . *To the Distant Observer* succeeds in imposing a sense of a unified representational scheme at work in Western film style" (David Bordwell, review of *To the Distant Observer,* by Noël Burch, *Wide Angle* 3, no. 4 [1985]: 73). Phil Rosen also develops a similar argument: "Burch compares Japanese practices to patterns of editing, camerawork, narrative articulation, etc. common in dominant western practices, the IMR [institutional mode of representation]. The compulsive return to such comparisons is as central to Burch's method of film-textual description as the sensitivity to intertextual vicissitudes of motifs is to Kracauer's.

Indeed, a carefully chosen collection of excerpts from Burch's book on Japanese cinema could supply us with one of his fullest descriptions of the IMR" (Phil Rosen, "History, Textuality, Nation: Kracauer, Burch, and Some Problems in the Study of National Cinemas," Iris 2, no. 2 [1984]: 75–76).

28 Sheila Whitaker, review of To the Distant Observer, by Noël Burch, Framework 11 (autumn 1979): 48.

29 Noël Burch, Life to Those Shadows (Berkeley: University of California Press, 1990).

30 Roland Barthes, Empire of Signs, trans. Richard Howard (New York: Hill and Wang, 1982), 3. After quoting the same passage, Burch asserts that he does "share the basic premises of this opening statement of L'Empire des signes" (To the Distant Observer, 16).

31 Dana Polan, "Formalism and Its Discontents," Jump Cut 26 (1981): 64–65.

32 Burch, To the Distant Observer, 11.

33 "Because his view of the history of class dynamics in Japan is more complex than his view of that history in the west, there is less linearity and teleology in Burch's descriptions of the development of Japanese filmic representation" (Rosen, "History, Textuality, Nation," 79).

34 Donald Kirihara, "Critical Polarities and the Study of Japanese Film Style," Journal of Film and Video 39, no. 1 (winter 1987): 17, 24.

35 Brett de Bary, review of To the Distant Observer, by Noël Burch, Journal of Japanese Studies 8, no. 2 (summer 1982): 410.

36 For instance, Scott Malcomson mentions "David Desser's excellent article, 'Kurosawa's Eastern "Western": Sanjuro and the Influence of Shane,'" as an example of a contextual approach to Japanese cinema in his critique of Burch's project (Scott Malcomson, "The Pure Land beyond the Seas: Barthes, Burch, and the Uses of Japan," Screen 26, nos. 3–4 [1985]: 31). But as my present study will show, this particular article and other studies on Kurosawa by Desser are at least as problematic as Burch's formalist treatise.

37 Examples of this type include Nolletti and Desser, Reframing Japanese Cinema; Linda C. Ehrlich and David Desser, eds., Cinematic Landscapes: Observations on the Visual Arts and Cinema of China and Japan (Austin: University of Texas Press, 1994); David Desser, Eros plus Massacre: An Introduction to the Japanese New Wave Cinema (Bloomington: Indiana University Press, 1988); Kyoko Hirano, Mr. Smith Goes to Tokyo: Japanese Cinema under the American Occupation, 1945–1952 (Washington, D.C.: Smithsonian Institution Press, 1992).

38 Scott Nygren, "Reconsidering Modernism: Japanese Film and the Post-

modern Context," *Wide Angle* 11, no. 3 (July 1989): 6–15; "Doubleness and Idiosyncrasy in Cross-Cultural Analysis," *Quarterly Review of Film and Video* 13, nos. 1–3 (1991): 173–87.

39 Nygren, "Reconsidering Modernism," 14.

40 Nygren refers to the painter Saeki Yuzo and the I-novel as two exemplary cases showing how Japanese modernism aligned itself with Western humanist tradition. But it is far from clear why the case of Saeki is mentioned, since the only significant information given is the fact of Saeki's suicide in 1928. The misleading characterization of the I-novel as a "Japanese response to Western naturalism" also does not tell us much about Japanese modernism (Nygren, "Reconsidering Modernism," 10).

41 There are a number of modernist groups, trends, and movements in modern Japan: the Shin kankakuha (New Sensibility school) writers of the 1920s, dadaism, the Jun eigageki undo (Pure Film movement), the Shochiku Kamata modanizumu, the 1950s' kindaishugi led by the director Masumura Yasuzo, and others. In architecture, various modernist movements existed contemporaneously in Japan and in the West, and there is nothing that suggests Japanese modernist architects somehow "misunderstood" modernism as an extension of Western humanism.

42 Nygren, "Reconsidering Modernism," 13.

43 Nygren writes: "Within the framework of *giri*, obligations to larger social groups 'naturally' precede those of smaller social units. As a result, obligation to the Emperor was paramount, since the Emperor represented in his body or person the entirety of Japanese culture. After the Emperor, any position of social authority follows along the same principle, so that feudal lord or corporate/*zaibatsu* director become interchangeable, and the patriarch within the family is owed duty as the person responsible for that social group" (Nygren, "Doubleness and Idiosyncrasy," 179–80). The explanation of giri in this passage is very misleading. For instance, the size of the social unit does not directly correspond to the degree of obligation. In fact, one's *giri* to a single individual can easily force him or her to reject the demand of a larger social unit such as family, school, or nation. It is also problematic to use the concept of *giri* when we talk about Japanese "obligation to the Emperor." Rather than a general principle of the Japanese social system from time immemorial, the "obligation to the Emperor" was manufactured at different historical moments for specific ideological purposes that cannot be reduced to the idea of *giri*. In short, the image of Japanese social structure presented by Nygren is nothing more than a caricature.

44 The idea of Japanese consensus society is a by-product of so-called modernization theory, which was promoted by conservative American

Japan specialists or Japanologists in the 1960s. Modernization theorists, in collaboration with the U.S. Cold War policy, tried to transform Japan into a positive model of the developing nation on the way to the natural destination of the modernization process, the United States as the embodiment of capitalism. One of the major features of modernization theory is its emphasis on the Japanese value system "as a causative as well as derivative phenomenon." And this focus on the Japanese value system "has resulted in a strong strain of interpretation, in some cases bordering on a cult, which seeks to explain problems as diverse as industrial and agrarian relations, economic oligopoly and economic dualism, authoritarianism, bureaucratism, paternalism and class hierarchy, alienation, factionalism and parliamentary venality, patriotism, right-wing radicalism, agrarian utopianism, anarchism, fascism, conversion to Christianity, recantation from communism, and war itself largely in terms of indigenous and unique Japanese cultural values" (John W. Dower, "E. H. Norman, Japan, and the Uses of History," in *Origins of the Modern Japanese State: Selected Writings of E. H. Norman,* ed. John W. Dower [New York: Pantheon Books, 1975], 61).

45 John Guillory, *Cultural Capital: The Problem of Literary Canon Formation* (Chicago: University of Chicago Press, 1993), 33. Guillory also argues that the "continuity [extending from the pre-Socratics to the present] was always the historical support for *nationalist* agendas. The schools in the early modern nation-states provided an instrument by means of which the state could dissolve the residually feudal bonds of local sovereignty and reattach personal loyalty to itself. . . . In the early modern period, the great vernacular literary works of the nation-states were taught in such a way as to constitute retroactively a pre-national 'West' . . . a continuity intended to cover over the traumatic break of early modern societies with traditional feudal cultures. The 'West' was always the creation of nationalism, and that is why one observes that the assertion of the continuity of Western tradition exactly corresponds in its intensity to the assertion of nationalism itself" (42).

46 Nygren, "Doubleness and Idiosyncrasy," 179.

47 H. D. Harootunian, "America's Japan/Japan's Japan," in *Japan in the World,* ed. Masao Miyoshi and H. D. Harootunian (Durham, N.C.: Duke University Press, 1993), 197–98.

48 Nygren, "Doubleness and Idiosyncrasy," 178.

49 Keiko I. McDonald, *Japanese Classical Theater in Films* (Rutherford, N.J.: Fairleigh Dickinson University Press, 1994), 12–13.

50 For instance, in 1929 the Department of Cinema was established at the University of Southern California, and in 1932 it granted the B.A. in

cinema for the first time in the United States ("University Film Teaching in the United States," *Film Quarterly* 16, no. 3 [spring 1963]: 45).

51 Besides Knight's book, other popular survey books include Richard Griffith and Arthur Mayer, *The Movies* (1957); A. R. Fulton, *Motion Pictures: The Development of an Art* (1960); and Kenneth MacGowan, *Behind the Screen* (1965).

52 These refurbished books on film history include Terry Ramsay, *A Million and One Nights* (1926; reprint, 1965); Lewis Jacobs, *The Rise of the American Film* (1939; reprint, 1968); and Benjamin Hampton, *History of the American Film Industry* (1970), which was first published as *A History of the Movies* in 1931 (Robert C. Allen and Douglas Gomery, *Film History: Theory and Practice* [New York: Knopf, 1985], 28).

53 A dramatic growth of film studies in the 1960s and 1970s can be glimpsed in the following statistics. According to Jack C. Ellis, in the catalogs of the hundred largest American universities for the school year of 1952 to 1953 there were 575 film-related courses. In 1964 to 1965, the number of film courses at the same hundred schools increased to 846, an increase of 47 percent (Ellis, "Ruminations of an Ex-Cinematologist," 48). "In 1967 some 200 colleges offered courses in film. Ten years later the number had passed 1,000, an increase of more than 500 percent. In 1978 the American Film Institute counted nearly 4,200 separate courses in film studies being offered in American colleges and nearly 150 schools offered degrees in film" (Allen and Gomery, *Film History,* 27–28).

54 For example, such leading film journals as *Camera Obscura, Film Criticism, Quarterly Review of Film Studies,* and *Wide Angle* were all established in 1976.

55 Jack C. Ellis, "Ruminations of an Ex-Cinematologist," *Cinema Journal* 24, no. 2 (winter 1985): 49.

56 Robert E. Kapsis, *Hitchcock: The Making of a Reputation* (Chicago: University of Chicago Press, 1992), 101.

57 Allen and Gomery, *Film History,* 27.

58 Dudley Andrew, *Concepts in Film Theory* (Oxford: Oxford University Press, 1984), 5.

59 Ellis, "Ruminations of an Ex-Cinematologist," 48.

60 Robert Richardson, *Literature and Film* (Bloomington: Indiana University Press, 1969), 15. Robert Ray also reports: "A recent chair's letter, recommending one of my colleagues for tenure, describes cinema studies as 'a subdivision of literary studies,' an analogy designed to justify a field which retains an air of illegitimacy" (Robert B. Ray, "Film Studies/Crisis/Experimentation," *Film Criticism* 17, nos. 2–3 [winter-spring 1993]: 57).

61 Marsha Kinder, "Establishing a Discipline for the Teaching of Film: Criticism and the Literary Analogue," *Quarterly Review of Film Studies* 1, no. 4 (November 1976): 424–29.

62 According to Harold W. Schneider, in the early 1970s, about 20 to 25 percent of college film courses were taught in literature and language departments (Harold W. Schneider, "Literature and Film: Marking Out Some Boundaries," *Literature/Film Quarterly* 3, no. 1 [winter 1975]: 30).

63 Andrew, *Concepts in Film Theory*, 6.

64 David Bordwell, *Making Meaning: Inference and Rhetoric in the Interpretation of Cinema* (Cambridge: Harvard University Press, 1989).

65 David Bordwell, "Film Interpretation Revisited," *Film Criticism* 17, nos. 2–3 (winter–spring 1993): 113.

66 Bordwell, *Making Meaning*, xiii.

67 Robert B. Ray, *The Avant-Garde Finds Andy Hardy* (Cambridge: Harvard University Press, 1995), 6–7.

68 Ray, "Film Studies/Crisis/Experimentation," 57.

69 See, for instance, the following passage from the editor's foreword to the 1968 reprint of Lewis Jacobs's classic *The Rise of the American Film*: "Here must surely be one more confrontation of an essential paradox of art: that its potential universality and timeliness grow out of immersion in its own place and time. The truest universals are details of particular existences; the deliberate universals, confected of generalities of whatever grandeur of purpose, dwindle to unfleshed symbols, without roots in life except in slogans and theories. In the cinema, as in all art, the paradox may be observed as a truly Heraclitean mutuality of opposites: particular and universal having an essential unity, being phases in the experiences of audiences. In the process of experience, in a dynamic obeying mysterious laws, the organic tension of particular and universal drives the works of cultures towards Culture" (Martin S. Dworkin, "General Editor's Foreword," in *The Rise of the American Film: A Critical History*, by Lewis Jacobs [New York: Teachers College Press, 1968], x–xi).

70 However, the reverse is hardly accepted as a legitimate academic practice; that is, no reciprocal privilege is granted to non-Western scholars in the United States studying German or French cinema without a good command of German or French. This asymmetrical relationship between Western scholars' study of non-Western cinemas and non-Western scholars' study of Western cinemas reminds us of "unequal treaties" in the age of imperialism.

71 The Soviet and Italian cinemas are also part of the canon of film theory.

Their significance in the canon is heavily dependent on the presence of specific theorists (Eisenstein, Kuleshov, Pudovkin, etc.) and schools or movements (Soviet montage school, Italian neorealism, etc.).

72 See, for instance, David Bordwell and Noël Carroll, eds., *Post-theory: Reconstructing Film Studies* (Madison: University of Wisconsin Press, 1996).

73 David Bordwell, "Our Dream Cinema: Western Historiography and the Japanese Film," *Film Reader*, no. 4 (1979): 45–62.

74 Ibid., 57–58.

75 Jonathan Culler, "Comparative Literature, at Last!" in *Comparative Literature in the Age of Multiculturalism*, ed. Charles Bernheimer (Baltimore, Md.: Johns Hopkins University Press, 1995), 119.

76 Harootunian, "America's Japan/Japan's Japan," 200.

77 Dower, "E. H. Norman, Japan, and the Uses of History," 33.

78 H. Richard Okada, *Figures of Resistance: Language, Poetry, and Narrating in "The Tale of Genji" and Other Mid-Heian Texts* (Durham, N.C.: Duke University Press, 1991), 9–10. Because film cannot be either "translated" or "annotated," traditionally trained literary scholars probably do not know what to do with Japanese cinema. The best they can do is to deal with film scripts or to transcribe films; however, there is little analogy between these activities and the translation of literary texts.

79 René Wellek, "The Crisis of Comparative Literature," in *Concepts of Criticism*, ed. Stephen Nichols (New Haven, Conn.: Yale University Press, 1963), 282.

80 Peter Brooks, "Must We Apologize?" in Bernheimer, *Comparative Literature in the Age of Multiculturalism*, 97.

81 Thomas G. Rosenmeyer, "Am I a Comparatist?" in *Building a Profession: Autobiographical Perspectives on the History of Comparative Literature in the United States*, ed. Lionel Gossman and Mihai I. Spariosu (Albany: State University of New York Press, 1994), 49.

82 Fredric Jameson, "On *Cultural Studies*," in *The Identity in Question*, ed. John Rajchman (New York: Routledge, 1995), 251–53.

83 Charles Bernheimer, "Introduction: The Anxieties of Comparison," in Bernheimer, *Comparative Literature in the Age of Multiculturalism*, 10–11.

84 Brooks, "Must We Apologize?" 97–106.

85 Jonathan Culler, "Comparative Literature, at Last!" in Bernheimer, *Comparative Literature in the Age of Multiculturalism*, 117–21.

86 Marjorie Perloff, " 'Literature' in the Expanded Field," in Bernheimer, *Comparative Literature in the Age of Multiculturalism*, 175–86.

87 Charles Bernheimer et al., "The Bernheimer Report, 1993: Comparative Literature at the Turn of the Century," in Bernheimer, *Comparative Literature in the Age of Multiculturalism,* 42.

88 Lionel Gossman, "Out of a Gothic North," in Gossman and Spariosu, *Building a Profession,* 203.

89 Rey Chow, "In the Name of Comparative Literature," in Bernheimer, *Comparative Literature in the Age of Multiculturalism,* 107.

90 Harry Levin, *Grounds for Comparison* (Cambridge: Harvard University Press, 1972), 84.

91 "It may be . . . that the Ph.D. in comparative literature will be replaced by a Ph.D. in one of many area studies — European studies, Latin American studies, Asian studies, and so on — as well as in different time frames: medieval studies, Renaissance studies, eighteenth-century studies, modernism, postmodernism" (Perloff, " 'Literature' in the Expanded Field," 183). Perhaps following Perloff's suggestions, Charles Bernheimer also proposes period studies and area studies as two possible "new disciplinary configurations with a multicultural comparative outlook" (Bernheimer, "Introduction: The Anxieties of Comparison," 14). In his scenario, studies of non-Western literatures and cultures are valorized as useful supplements to research projects in medieval studies, Renaissance studies, and eighteenth-century studies. In this newly configured period studies, the non-West is still only a supplement, an aid that facilitates a deeper understanding of Western cultures. Bernheimer writes: "If the research groups were to explore the dynamics of the elliptical approach, their comparative work could intersect with that of scholars of non-Western cultures in the same or similar periods, and the result could be a broadened and revitalized conception of literary and cultural history, still centered in Europe but also crucially decentered." "Still, the area studies model could be reconceptualized to foreground literature and to undo, via an elliptical bifocus, the notion of a stable geographical area" (14). But it is not clear how literature can be foregrounded suddenly when it has never been a primary focus of area studies dominated by social scientists.

PART II   The Films of Kurosawa Akira

1.   Kurosawa Criticism and the Name of the Author

1 David Desser's *The Samurai Films of Akira Kurosawa* (Ann Arbor, Mich.: UMI Research Press, 1983) and Goodwin's *Akira Kurosawa and*

Intertextual Cinema (Baltimore, Md.: Johns Hopkins University Press, 1994) do mention the majority of Kurosawa films but mostly focus on limited aspects of his cinema.

2 The majority of publications about Kurosawa are either collections of interviews with Kurosawa and his staff or collections of previously published film reviews and short essays by different critics. Some critical books about Kurosawa deal with only specific aspects of his films. For instance, Nishimura Yuichiro, *Kurosawa Akira oto to eizo* (Tokyo: Rippu Shobo, 1990), focuses on the use of sound and music in Kurosawa's cinema. Ogata Toshiro, *Kyojin to shonen: Kurosawa Akira no joseitachi* (Tokyo: Bungei Shunju, 1992), is a rather simplistic treatment of the images of women in all of Kurosawa's films.

3 Allan Casebier, "Turning Back the Clock in Japanese Cinema Studies: Kurosawa, Keiko McDonald, and Tadao Sato," *Quarterly Review of Film Studies* 10, no. 2 (spring 1985): 166–69.

4 Edward Buscombe, "Ideas of Authorship," *Screen* 14, no. 3 (autumn 1973): 81.

5 Andrew Sarris, "Notes on the Auteur Theory in 1962," in *Film Theory and Criticism: Introductory Readings*, 3d ed., eds. Gerald Mast and Marshall Cohen (New York: Oxford University Press, 1985), 534.

6 Ibid., 535.

7 The original version of auteurism, *Cahier du Cinéma*'s *la politique des auteurs*, valorizes "not so much the director's ability to express his personality, as usually has been claimed, but rather his desire and ability to express a certain world view. An *auteur* was a film director who expressed an optimistic image of human potentialities within an utterly corrupt society. By reaching out both emotionally and spiritually to other human beings and/or to God, one could transcend the isolation imposed on one by a corrupt world" (John Hess, "*La Politique des auteurs*, Part Two: Truffaut's Manifesto," *Jump Cut*, no. 2 [July–August 1974]: 20). According to Hess, this particular worldview was part of a politically conservative trend in France in the 1950s where art was dissociated from concrete sociopolitical concerns of the day (Hess, "*La Politique des auteurs*, Part One: World View as Aesthetic," *Jump Cut*, no. 1 [May–June 1974]: 19).

8 Roland Barthes, "The Death of the Author," in *Image-Music-Text* (New York: Hill and Wang, 1977), 142–48; Michel Foucault, "What Is an Author?" in *Language, Counter-Memory, Practice*, ed. Donald F. Bouchard, trans. Donald R. Bouchard and Sherry Simon (Ithaca, N.Y.: Cornell University Press, 1977), 113–38.

9 Wood, *Hitchcock's Films Revisited*, 19.

10 Foucault, "What Is an Author?" 129.

11 Peter Wollen, *Signs and Meaning in the Cinema* (Bloomington: Indiana University Press, 1972), 167.

12 Ibid., 168.

13 Slavoj Žižek, *The Sublime Object of Ideology* (London: Verso, 1989), 90.

14 Ibid., 89–90.

15 Wollen, *Signs and Meaning in the Cinema*, 167–68.

16 Foucault, "What Is an Author?" 128.

17 Ibid., 118–20.

18 Prince, *The Warrior's Camera*, xvii, xix.

19 Foucault, "What Is an Author?" 128.

20 James Goodwin, *Akira Kurosawa and Intertextual Cinema*, 21–22.

21 Unfortunately, even if we expand the scope of discussion to include the general field of Japanese cinema studies, a serious engagement with the legacy of auteurism is still rarely found. For example, *Reframing Japanese Cinema: Authorship, Genre, History,* edited by David Desser and Arthur Nolletti Jr., is one of the more recent collections of essays on Japanese cinema. As its subtitle indicates, the first part of this anthology focuses on the issues of authorship. Yet none of the essays included in this section engage authorship as a critical question. Instead, they all simply proceed with analyses of specific films directed by Ozu, Kurosawa, Oshima, and Gosho, all widely recognized filmmakers or "authors."

22 From *Drunken Angel* on, the scripts for all Kurosawa films except the last three are cowritten by Kurosawa and his close associates (e.g., Hashimoto Shinobu, Oguni Hideo, Ide Masato, Kikushima Ryuzo, Hisaita Eijiro). In the history of Japanese cinema, Kurosawa's collaborative group is as important as such prewar collectives as Kyoto's Narutaki-gumi (Yamanaka Sadao, Inagaki Hiroshi, and six other directors and scriptwriters who wrote scripts together using the pseudonym "Kajiwara Kinpachi") and Shochiku's "James Maki" (the pseudonym used by Ozu and three other scriptwriters).

23 Uraoka Keiichi, a film editor best known for his collaboration with Oshima in the 1960s, acknowledges Kurosawa as an influential figure in the world of film editing. See Uraoka Keiichi, *Eiga henshu to wa nanika: Uraoka Keiichi no giho* (Tokyo: Heibonsha, 1994), 206–36.

24 Bordwell, *Ozu and the Poetics of Cinema*, 5.

25 Ibid., 7.

26 Akira Kurosawa, *Something like an Autobiography,* trans. Audie E. Bock (New York: Vintage, 1983). Kurosawa's autobiographical essays were

first serialized in the Japanese weekly magazine *Shukan Yomiuri* in 1978 and then published as a book, *Gama no abura: Jiden no yona mono,* in 1984. Interestingly enough, the English translation of the book came out from Alfred A. Knopf in 1982, two years before the appearance of the Japanese original. Without any concrete information on their publication background, I can only speculate on why the publication of the translation preceded that of the original. Is this another sign of Japanese indifference to Kurosawa? Or is it the case that the English translation was published first to reinforce the Japanese image of Kurosawa as an internationally famous film director?

27 Kurosawa, *Something like an Autobiography,* 28–30.

28 Uekusa Keinosuke, *Waga seishun no Kurosawa Akira* (Tokyo: Bungei Shunju, 1985).

29 Kurosawa, *Something like an Autobiography,* 14.

30 Ibid., 188.

31 Contrary to Kurosawa's claim, Suzuki Akinari, a former executive at Daei, reports that no executives or producers were demoted because of their involvement in the making of *Rashomon.* See Suzuki Akinari, *Rappa to yobareta otoko: Eiga purodyusa Nagata Masaichi* (Tokyo: Kinema Junposha, 1990), 6–7.

32 Kurosawa, *Something like an Autobiography,* 188–89.

33 Philippe Lejeune, *On Autobiography,* trans. Katherine Leary (Minneapolis: University of Minnesota Press, 1989).

34 "Perhaps one is an author only with his second book, when the proper name inscribed on the cover becomes the 'common factor' of at least two different texts and thus gives the idea of a person who cannot be reduced to any of his texts in particular, and who, capable of producing others, surpasses them all. This, we will see, is very important for the reading of autobiographies: if the autobiography is a first book, its author is thus unknown, even if he relates his own story in the book. He lacks, in the eyes of the reader, that sign of reality which is the previous production *of other texts* (nonautobiographical), indispensable to that which we will call 'the autobiographical space'" (Lejeune, *On Autobiography,* 11–12).

35 Lejeune, *On Autobiography,* 27.

36 Kurosawa, *Something like an Autobiography,* 5.

37 Ibid., 178–80; Kurosawa Akira, Takemitsu Toru, and Yodogawa Nagaharu, "Kurosawa Akira no sekai," *Sekai* (January 1984): 294.

2. Sanshiro Sugata

1   Oi Hirosuke, *Chanbara geijutsushi* (Tokyo: Jitsugyo no Nihonsha, 1959), 220; Sato Tadao, *Kurosawa Akira no sekai* (Tokyo: Asahi Shinbunsha, 1986), 42–46; Yamamoto Kikuo, "Senji taiseika no eiga sakka tachi," in *Nihon eigashi* (Tokyo: Kinema Junposha, 1976), 120. Yoshikawa Eiji's *Miyamoto Musashi* is available in English as *Musashi*, trans. Charles S. Terry (New York: Harper and Row, 1981).

2   When *Sanshiro Sugata* was released in 1944, Toho cut a number of scenes without Kurosawa's consent. As a result, in the currently available version of the film, the fifth action scene (Sanshiro's intense practice with Yano) is completely missing, and the third action scene starts with the end of a fight.

3   Richie, *The Films of Akira Kurosawa*, 188.

4   Prince, *The Warrior's Camera*, 115–16.

5   Although Kurosawa's father came from a samurai family, his mother was in fact born in a merchant family in Osaka. See Kurosawa, *Something like an Autobiography*, 35.

6   Ibid., 21.

7   Yoshioka Hiroshi, "Samurai and Self-Colonization in Japan," in *The Decolonization of Imagination: Culture, Knowledge, and Power*, ed. Jan Nederveen Pieterse and Bhikhu Parekh (London: Zed Books, 1995), 99–112.

8   Prince, *The Warrior's Camera*, 119.

9   Ibid., 35.

10 Kurosawa Akira, Kinoshita Keisuke, and Takeda Taijun, "Ningenzo sei-sakuho," *Chuo koron* (February 1956): 247; Kurosawa Akira, "Eiga hihyo ni tsuite," *Zenshu Kurosawa Akira*, vol. 2, 272–76 (originally published in *Kinema junpo* [September 1946]).

11 Stephen Prince, "Zen and Selfhood: Patterns of Eastern Thought in Kurosawa's Films," in *Perspectives on Akira Kurosawa*, ed. James Goodwin (New York: G. K. Hall, 1994), 229–31.

12 The phrase "naturalistic film" is widely used in Japanese film criticism. As a critical concept, it is not explicitly defined but probably derived from the name of an early-twentieth-century Japanese literary movement, "naturalism" (Shizenshugi). Although its specific meanings vary depending on who uses it, it does have a commonly shared connotation. Films are often called naturalistic when they look uniquely Japanese as opposed to Western. Naturalistic films—either melodrama, domestic drama, or war movies—supposedly show the uniquely Japanese sentiment and sensibilities in their styles and themes. As such, for many (e.g.,

Masumura Yasuzo, Oshima Nagisa), naturalistic films must be rejected or overcome, while for others they must be encouraged as a representation of Japanese national identity.

13 "Kurosawa is one of the greatest film-makers of rain: in *The Seven Samurai* a dense rain falls while the bandits, caught in a trap, gallop on horseback from one end of the village to the other and back again. The camera angle often forms a flattened image, which brings out the constant lateral movements. We can understand this great breath-space—whether expanded or contracted—if we refer to a Japanese topology" (Gilles Deleuze, *Cinema 1: The Movement-Image,* trans. Hugh Tomlinson and Barbara Habberjam [Minneapolis: University of Minnesota Press, 1986], 188).

14 Richie, *The Films of Akira Kurosawa,* 111.

15 Kurosawa is not completely satisfied with this shot. In an interview with Ogi Masahiro, Kurosawa admits that the close-up of the sun does not have even one-tenth of the impact he originally wanted. He attributes the lack of power to the untimely death of Hayasaka Fumio, a composer and possibly Kurosawa's most important collaborator, who died during the shooting of *Record of a Living Being* (*Kurosawa Akira shusei,* vol. 2 [Tokyo: Kinema Junposha, 1991], 98).

16 Aochi Shin, "Kurosawa Akira," *Chuo koron* (March 1957): 246–47.

17 Kojin Karatani, *Origins of Modern Japanese Literature,* trans. Brett de Bary (Durham, N.C.: Duke University Press, 1993), 11–44.

18 Togawa Naoki, "Kurosawa Akira no shikaku gengo," in *Kurosawa Akira shusei,* vol. 3, 15.

19 Kurosawa's first color film, *Dodeskaden,* is based on the collection of short stories titled *A Town without Seasons* (Kisetsu no nai machi) by Yamamoto Shugoro.

20 *Zenshu Kurosawa Akira,* vol. 2, 257–61.

3. *The Most Beautiful*

1 Sato Tadao, *Zenshu Kurosawa Akira,* vol. 1, 410.

2 For a detailed study of Japanese wartime films, see Peter B. High, *Teikoku no ginmaku: Jugonen Senso to Nihon eiga* (Nagoya: Nagoya Daigaku Shuppankai, 1995).

3 Yamamoto Kajiro, *Katsudoya suiro* (Tokyo: Chikuma Shobo, 1965), 195–224.

4 John Dower, ed., *Japan in War and Peace: Selected Essays* (New York: New Press, 1993), 39.

5 Iwasaki Akira, *Eiga ni miru sengo sesoshi* (Tokyo: Shin Nihon Shuppan-sha, 1973), 27–29.

6 Sakuramoto Tomio, *Dai Toa senso to Nihon eiga: Tachimi no senchu eigaron* (Tokyo: Aoki Shoten, 1993), 39.

7 Dower, *Japan in War and Peace*, 35.

8 Yamamoto Akira, "Jugonen senso ka, Nihon no senso eiga," in *Koza Nihon eiga*, vol. 4, 83.

9 Kurosawa, *Something like an Autobiography*, 118, 120–21.

10 In the 1930s, on average, around 500 films were made every year. After 1941, in which 232 films were produced, the number of films released dramatically decreased. Eighty-seven films were released in 1942; 61 in 1943; 46 in 1944; and a mere 26 in 1945 (*Nihon eigashi* [Tokyo: Kinema Junposha, 1976], 70–71).

11 Shimizu Akira, "Nihon ni okeru senso to eiga," in *Nichi-Bei eigasen: Paru Haba 50-shunen*, by Shimizu Akira et al. (Tokyo: Seikyusha, 1991), 67–70.

12 Kurosawa, *Something like an Autobiography*, 135.

13 High, *Teikoku no ginmaku*, 382.

14 One of the film's principal characters is Watanabe Tsuru (played by Yaguchi Yoko), who looks for one defective lens among thousands by herself; another stubborn Kurosawa character who is determined to accomplish his objective is also called Watanabe (Shimura Takashi) in *Ikiru*. The final shot of the film is a close-up of Watanabe's crying face, which cannot but remind us of the last image of *The Idiot*, a similar close-up of the crying face of a woman (Ayako) who realizes the existence of the pure human soul too late.

4. *Sanshiro Sugata, Part 2*

1 Richie, *The Films of Akira Kurosawa*, 24.

2 Sato, *Kurosawa Akira no sekai*, 58–61.

5. *The Men Who Tread on the Tiger's Tail*

1 Ivan Morris, *The Nobility of Failure: Tragic Heroes in the History of Japan* (New York: Noonday, 1975), 67–68.

2 In *Kanjincho*, the opening scene is at the Ataka barrier, where Toga-shi first introduces himself as Yoritomo's vassal and orders guards to capture and question relentlessly any mountain monks who try to pass

(Gunji Masakatsu, ed., *Kabuki juhachibanshu* [Tokyo: Iwanami Shoten, 1965], 176–77).

3 Richie, *The Films of Akira Kurosawa,* 34; Prince, *The Warrior's Camera,* 62.

4 McDonald, *Japanese Classical Theater in Films,* 177.

5 Enoken's role is further developed into such characters as Kikuchiyo in *Seven Samurai* and Shingen's double in *Kagemusha.*

6 McDonald, *Japanese Classical Theater in Films,* 179.

7 Watanabe Tamotsu, *Kanjincho: Nihonjinron no genzo* (Tokyo: Chikuma Shobo, 1995), 177–78; Kurosawa, Takemitsu, and Yodogawa, "Kurosawa Akira no sekai," 227.

8 The film starts with the following titles: "In 1185, the proud and arrogant Heikes perished in the western sea. Having distinguished himself through brilliant feats of war, Genkuro Yoshitsune should be able to triumphantly parade on the capital's main street. But Shogun Yoritomo, who was known for his distrustfulness, believed his favorite retainer Kajiwara no Kagetoki's slanderous accusation against Yoshitsune, and decided to kill his own brother. Thus, nowhere to hide in Japan, Yoshitsune and six of his retainers disguised themselves as mountain monks, and tried to escape safely to Oshu, the domain of Fujiwara no Hidehira, their sole sympathizer. On their way, they are about to reach a new barrier at Ataka in Kaga. They attempt to pass this barrier, as if stepping on a tiger's tail."

9 Mukai Soya, *Nihon no taishu engeki* (Tokyo: Toho Shuppan, 1962), 120–26.

10 Kurosawa, *Something like an Autobiography,* 143.

11 Hattori Yukio, *Kabuki no ki wado* (Tokyo: Iwanami Shoten, 1989), 2–5, 88–97.

12 Burch, *To the Distant Observer,* 70–71.

13 Ibid., 71.

14 Donald Richie and Joseph L. Anderson, "Traditional Theater and the Film in Japan: The Influence of the Kabuki, Noh, and Other Forms on Film Content and Style," *Film Quarterly* 12, no. 1 (1958): 2.

15 Kawatake Shigetoshi, *Kabuki: Japanese Drama* (Tokyo: Foreign Affairs Association of Japan, 1958), 53–54.

16 Annotation to Suematsu Norizumi, "Engeki kairyo enzetsu," in *Geino,* ed. Kurata Yoshihiro, vol. 18 of *Nihon kindai shiso taikei* (Tokyo: Iwanami Shoten, 1988), 47.

17 Tanizaki Jun'ichiro has this to say about the negative effect of electric lighting on the Kabuki performance: "It is inconceivable that the beautiful women of old — to say nothing of the men — bore any resemblance

to those we see on the Kabuki stage. The women of the No, portrayed by masked actors, are far from realistic; but the Kabuki actor in the part of a woman inspires not the slightest sense of reality. The failure is the fault of excessive lighting. When there were no modern floodlamps, when the Kabuki stage was lit by the meager light of candles and lanterns, actors must have been somewhat more convincing in women's roles. People complain that Kabuki actors are no longer really feminine, but this is hardly the fault of their talents or looks. If actors of old had had to appear on the bright stage of today, they would doubtless have stood out with a certain masculine harshness, which in the past was discreetly hidden by darkness. This was brought home to me vividly when I saw the aging Baiko in the role of the young Okaru. A senseless and extravagant use of lights, I thought, has destroyed the beauty of Kabuki" (Jun'ichiro Tanizaki, *In Praise of Shadows* [In'ei raisan], trans. Thomas J. Harper and Edward G. Seidensticker [New Haven, Conn.: Leete's Island Books, 1977], 27).

18 Kurata Yoshihiro, "Kaisetsu," in Kurata, *Geino,* 381–90.

19 These three prescriptions are (1) respect for the gods and love of country should be embodied; (2) the ways of Heaven, Earth, and Man are to be elucidated; (3) obedience to the emperor and his will should be inculcated (Donald Keene, *Dawn to the West: Japanese Literature of the Modern Era (Fiction)* [New York: Holt, Rinehart and Winston, 1984], 21).

20 Kurata, "Kaisetsu," 392–93.

21 Suzuki Tadashi, *Engeki to wa nanika* (Tokyo: Iwanami Shoten, 1988), 2–26.

22 Kurata, "Kaisetsu," 413–17.

23 Nakamura Mitsuo, "Meiji bungakushi," in *Nakamura Mitsuo zenshu,* vol. 11 (Tokyo: Chikuma Shobo, 1973), 190–92.

24 Suematsu Norizumi, "Engeki kairyo enzetsu," *Jiji shinpo,* 6–12 October 1886. Reprinted in Kurata, *Geino,* 35–61. Immediately after his public lecture on theater reform, with the financial support of the business leaders, Suematsu tried to start a new company to build a modern theater. But the objective situations around that time soon forced him to abandon his plan. It was not until 1911 that the first multipurpose modern theater in Japan, Teikoku Gekijo ("Imperial Theater"), or Teigeki, was opened and became a center of cosmopolitan consumer culture of the Taisho period. For more information on Teigeki, see Mine Takashi, *Teikoku Gekijo kaimaku* (Tokyo: Chuo Koronsha, 1996).

25 Kurata, "Kaisetsu," 435–36.

26 When *The Mikado* premiered in 1885, the Japanese elite's national pride was already wounded by the opening in London of the Japanese village,

which they severely condemned as a national shame. In this combination of exhibition and fairground, Japanese products (e.g., ceramics, bamboo works, food) were sold, and *sumo*, martial arts, dance, and so forth were demonstrated by amateur artisans and performers, many of who were illegally brought to London by the exhibitors. The impact of the Japanese village as a source of (mis)information about Japan was attested by the number of visitors: from January 10 to May 1, 1885, 250,000 people visited the Japanese village. For more information on the Japanese village, see Kurata, "Kaisetsu," 429; and Yano Ryukei's series of newspaper articles published in *Yubin hochi shinbun* in 1885, reprinted in Kurata, *Geino*, 319–36.

27 Richie, *The Films of Akira Kurosawa*, 30. Following Richie, David Desser also observes that "Kurosawa's 1945 film *They Who Tread on the Tiger's Tail* was an adaptation of the story which forms the basis of the No play *Ataka* and the Kabuki classic *Kanjincho*" (Desser, *The Samurai Films of Akira Kurosawa*, 64).

28 *Kabuki Juhachiban* consists of the following eighteen plays: *Fuwa, Narukami* (Thunder God), *Shibaraku* (Just a Moment), *Fudo* (God of Fire), *Uwanari* (Mistress), *Zobiki* (Robbing of an Elephant), *Kanjincho* (The Subscription List), *Sukeroku, Oshimodoshi* (Repulsion), *Uirouri* (Vendor of Uiro), *Yanone* (Arrowhead), *Kan-u, Kagekiyo, Nanatsumen* (Seven Masks), *Kenuki* (Tweezers), *Gedatsu* (Deliverance), *Jayanagi* (Snake Willow Tree), and *Kamahige* (Beard Shaving with a Scythe). For short commentaries on each of the plays see Kawatake Shigetoshi, *Kabuki: Japanese Drama* (Tokyo: Foreign Affairs Association of Japan, 1958), 26–29; Earl Miner, Hiroko Odagiri, and Robert E. Morrell, *The Princeton Companion to Classical Japanese Literature* (Princeton, N.J.: Princeton University Press, 1985), 329–30.

29 Nishiyama Matsunosuke, *Ichikawa Danjuro* (Tokyo: Yoshikawa Kobunkan, 1960), 184–91.

30 Gunji Masakatsu, "Kaisetsu," in Gunji, *Kabuki juhachibanshu*, 40.

31 Hashimoto Osamu, *Kanpon chanbara jidaigeki koza* (Tokyo: Tokuma Shoten, 1986), 176.

32 McDonald, *Japanese Classical Theater in Films*, 177–78.

33 Hashimoto, *Kanpon chanbara jidaigeki koza*, 177.

34 Joseph S. Chang, "*Kagemusha* and the *Chushingura* Motif," *East-West Film Journal* 3, no. 2 (June 1989): 14–38.

35 Director Makino Masahiro reports that during the shooting of his father Makino Shozo's *Chushingura* (1927), Ii Yoho, a leading *shingeki* actor playing the role of Kuranosuke, suddenly started stepping a *roppo* at the end of the showdown between Kuranosuke and Sakon. Makino says

the *roppo* step in the middle of a realistic scene was simply unbearable to watch (Makino Masahiro, *Eiga tosei: ten no maki* [Tokyo: Chikuma Shobo, 1995], 113–15).

36 Hashimoto, *Kanpon chanbara jidaigeki koza,* 165–70. My analysis of *Kanjincho* and *Chushingura* owes a great deal to Hashimoto's somewhat idiosyncratic yet excellent book on *chanbara* and *jidaigeki*.

37 Quoted by Sato, *Zenshu Kurosawa Akira,* vol. 6, 239. Kurosawa's remark was originally published in *Heibon panchi* (7 January 1980).

38 Nishiyama, *Ichikawa Danjuro,* 273–84.

39 Lange's juxtaposition of the Katsura Detached Palace and the Toshogu Shrine is directly taken out of what is widely accepted as the personal view of Bruno Taut. However, what Taut actually said and what he supposedly said do not exactly correspond. Taut was invited to Japan in 1933 by a group of Japanese modernist architects, who clearly manipulated the image and words of Taut and transformed him into a world-renowned architect of high modernism, which he was not. Having started his career as an expressionist, Taut was critical of the rising popularity of the Le Corbusier school. Whereas the Japanese modernists championed the Katsura Detached Palace as a prototypical modernist architectural structure in the Japanese tradition, Taut celebrated the Katsura's classical beauty, which could not be explained by modernist principles of functionality and utility. But Taut's expressions of anti-modernist sentiment were carefully censored from the published versions of his lectures and interviews. Thus, to a great extent, the Bruno Taut celebrated by the Japanese intellectuals was a Bruno Taut whom they needed to promote their political agenda. On the myth of Taut and the Katsura Detached Palace, see Inoue Shoichi, *Tsukurareta Katsura Rikyu shinwa* (Tokyo: Kobundo, 1986).

40 Bruno Taut, *Fundamentals of Japanese Architecture* (Tokyo: Society for International Cultural Relations, 1936), quoted by Paul Varley, *Japanese Culture* (Honolulu: University of Hawaii Press, 1984), 3d ed., 291.

41 Sakaguchi Ango, "Nihon bunka shikan" (1942), reprinted in *Sakaguchi Ango zenshu,* vol. 14 (Tokyo: Chikuma Shobo, 1990), 352–84.

6. *No Regrets for Our Youth*

1 Uryu Tadao, *Eigateki seishin no keifu* (Tokyo: Getsuyo Shobo, 1947), 130–31; *Zenshu Kurosawa Akira,* vol. 2, 345–46.

2 Richie, *The Films of Akira Kurosawa,* 37.

3 In this description of the scene, Richie switches the father's lines with

the mother's; that is, it is not Yukie's father, Yagihara, but the mother who first notices Yukie's restlessness.

4 Nakano's "Mura no ie" is translated into English as "The House in the Village." See *Three Works by Nakano Shigeharu*, trans. Brett de Bary (Ithaca, N.Y.: Cornell University East Asia Papers, 1979), 19–73.

5 The other films of Mizoguchi's trilogy are *The Love of Actress Sumako* (*Joyu Sumako no koi*, 1947) and *My Love Has Been Burning* (*Waga koi wa moenu*, 1949).

6 *Madame Curie* made a strong impression on Japanese audiences, particularly women. Takano Etsuko, who has brought a number of art films to Japan as head of Iwanami Hall in Tokyo, describes how much she was inspired by this film when she saw it at the age of sixteen (Takano Etsuko, *Watashi no shinema raifu* [Tokyo: Shufu to Seikatsusha, 1983], 35–38). Japanese anthropologist Emiko Ohnuki-Tierney reports that her elementary schoolteacher (Fujita Sensei) one day took his students to a movie, *Madame Curie:* "Her image, always clothed in black, and her singular dedication to her science impressed me so vividly that I could scarcely contain myself. I slept very little that night. The next morning I went to Fujita Sensei and declared that I wanted to be a Madame Curie and laid out my plan for a scientific experiment" (Emiko Ohnuki-Tierney, *Rice as Self: Japanese Identities through Time* [Princeton, N.J.: Princeton University Press, 1993], x–xi). Oshima Nagisa remembers how enthusiastically girls around him talked about *Madame Curie* as if every one of them was going to become Madame Curie (Oshima Nagisa, *Taikenteki sengo eizoron* [Tokyo: Asahi Shinbunsha, 1975], 62).

7 Iwasaki, *Eiga ni miru sengo sesoshi*, 31–33.

8 Hirano, *Mr. Smith Goes to Tokyo*, 184.

9 Quoted by Hirano, *Mr. Smith Goes to Tokyo*, 187. Translation slightly modified. The original passage in Japanese can be found in *Zenshu Kurosawa Akira*, vol. 2, 2.

10 Oshima, *Taikenteki sengo eizoron*, 56.

11 A few more notes on the opening title are in order. Another important reference in the title is the name of Hatoyama Ichiro. At the time of the film's production, Hatoyama was the leader of the Liberal Party, about to be appointed prime minister. On May 3, 1946, Hatoyama was expelled from public office by GHQ for his antidemocratic actions as minister of education between December 1931 and March 1934. *No Regrets for Our Youth* directly reflects this action by GHQ. In the currently circulating version of *No Regrets for Our Youth*, this opening title Oshima refers to is replaced by a shorter one, which does not mention both

Hatoyama and Takigawa. In 1955 Hatoyama finally became prime minister. As a result of either direct political pressure from the government or Toho's self-censorship, the opening title was replaced by a far less politically explicit one. In *Zenshu Kurosawa Akira,* the note on the film's script says that the title was made shorter but does not give us any specific information on when this change was made. Hirano Kyoko's informative account of the film's production background is also vague about when the substitution of the original and revised titles occurred. See Hirano, *Mr. Smith Goes to Tokyo,* 189.

12   Oshima, *Taikenteki sengo eizoron,* 54–55.

13   Hirano Ken, *Showa bungakushi* (Tokyo: Chikuma Shobo, 1963), 136–37.

14   Ibid., 208.

15   Nakano Shigeharu, *Mura no ie; Ojisan no hanashi; Uta no wakare* (Tokyo: Kodansha, 1994), 81; *Three Works by Nakano Shigeharu,* 72.

16   Yoshimoto Takaaki, *Yoshimoto Takaaki zen chosakushu,* vol. 13 (Tokyo: Keiso Shobo, 1969), 5–27.

17   Takeuchi Yoshimi, *Nihon to Ajia* (Tokyo: Chikuma Shobo, 1993), 11–57.

18   Tanaka Jun'ichiro, *Nihon eiga hattatsushi,* vol. 3 (Tokyo: Chuo Koronsha, 1976), 221–22.

19   Anderson and Richie, *The Japanese Film,* 161. The number of banned films varies according to the sources. Hirano Kyoko says that 236 out of 455 were banned (Hirano, *Mr. Smith Goes to Tokyo,* 42).

20   Takenaka Tsutomu, *Kikigaki Arakan ichidai: Kurama Tengu no ojisan wa* (Kyoto: Shirakawa Shoin, 1976), 201–4.

21   Itami Mansaku, "Senso sekininsha no mondai," originally published in *Eiga shunju* in 1946, reprinted in *Itami Mansaku zenshu,* vol. 1 (Tokyo: Chikuma Shobo, 1961), 205–14, and *Itami Mansaku esseishu* (Tokyo: Chikuma Shobo, 1971), 75–85. Ogawa Toru et al., eds., *Gendai Nihon eigaron taikei,* vol. 1 (Tokyo: Tojusha, 1971), 1, "Sengo eiga no shupattsu" includes Itami's essay and a few other representative documents dealing with the question of filmmakers' war responsibility. These texts are Jiyu eigajin shudan, "Eiga senso sekininsha no kaimei" (originally published in *Eiga seisaku* [July 1946]); Ieki Miyoji, "Eiga geijutsuka no hansei to jiko kakushin ni tsuite" (originally in *Eiga seisaku* [September 1946]); Iwasaki Akira, "Mazu shutoshite watashi jishin ni tsuite: Eiga no kiroku II" (originally in *Kinema junpo* [August 1946]); and Okuma Nobuyuki, "Kono eigajin o miyo: Itami Mansaku to sono senso sekinin ni tsuite" (originally in *Eiga shunju* [November 1947]).

22   Masao Miyoshi mentions "subjectivity," "subjecthood," "independence," and "identity" as English translations of *shutaisei* found in a Japanese-English dictionary (Masao Miyoshi, *Off Center: Power and*

Culture Relations between Japan and the United States [Cambridge: Harvard University Press, 1991], 97). J. Victor Koschmann, in his study of shutaisei ronso, refers to Miyagi Otoya's 1948 article where he explains seven different usages of the term *shutaisei* (J. Victor Koschmann, *Revolution and Subjectivity in Postwar Japan* [Chicago: University of Chicago Press, 1996], 2–3).

23 Maruyama Masao, *Nihon no shiso* (Tokyo: Iwanami Shoten, 1961), 141–44.

24 This is a very common argument in *nihonjinron*, simultaneously emphasizing the uniqueness and the universality of Japanese culture. It is interesting to analyze not only how Doi theorizes victim consciousness as a variation of *amae* but also how Doi's theory of *amae* as a type of *nihonjinron* can be regarded as a manifestation of victim consciousness. Doi tries to find examples of *amae* not only in the everyday life of contemporary Japanese but also in Japanese cultural history. He thus tries to establish a link between *amae* and a Japanese national character. A kind of etymological explanation of the notion of *amae* he provides must be taken with caution. The presence of the same word at two different historical moments does not necessarily lead to a conclusion that that word has the transhistorically identical meaning or function, or that there is an unproblematic historical continuity between those two moments. *Amae* is in the end another example of an invented tradition.

25 Miyoshi, *Off Center*, 104–5.

26 Hirano, *Mr. Smith Goes to Tokyo*, 54.

27 Miyoshi, *Off Center*, 110–11.

28 Ibid., 111–14.

29 "When I talk of *negotiation* rather than *negation*, it is to convey a temporality that makes it possible to conceive of the articulation of antagonistic or contradictory elements: a dialectic without the emergence of a teleological or transcendent History, and beyond the prescriptive form of symptomatic reading where the nervous tics on the surface of ideology reveal the 'real materialist contradiction' that History embodies. . . . By negotiation I attempt to draw attention to the structure of *iteration* which informs political movements that attempt to articulate antagonistic and oppositional elements without the redemptive rationality of sublation or transcendence" (Homi K. Bhabha, *The Location of Culture* [New York: Routledge, 1994], 25–26).

30 J. Laplanche and J. B. Pontalis, *The Language of Psycho-Analysis*, trans. Donald Nicholson-Smith (New York: Norton, 1973), 26.

31 Ibid., 118–21.

7. One Wonderful Sunday

1 To refer to a severe shortage of food, some people used the phrase *Waga seishun wa kuenashi* (No food in my youth), which is of course a parody of *Waga seishun ni kuinashi* (No regrets for my youth), the title of Kurosawa's preceding film (the film's widely accepted English title is *No Regrets for Our Youth*. But a more literal translation of the original title *Waga seishun ni kuinashi* is *No Regrets for My Youth*). See Endo, *Eirin: Rekishi to jiken* (Tokyo: Perikansha, 1973), 19.

2 Hirosawa Ei, *Kurokami to kesho no Showa shi* (Tokyo: Iwanami Shoten, 1993), 200–219.

3 Sasaki Tokio, *Dobutsuen no rekishi: Nihon ni okeru dobutsuen no seiritsu* (Tokyo: Kodansha, 1987), 316–18.

4 Sato, *Kurosawa Akira no sekai*, 140–41.

5 Nishimura, *Kurosawa Akira oto to eizo*, 45.

9. The Quiet Duel

1 Besides *The Quiet Duel*, for Film Art Association, Kurosawa directed the following four films: *Stray Dog* (for Shintoho, 1949), *Scandal* (Shochiku, 1950), *Rashomon* (Daiei, 1950), and *The Idiot* (Shochiku, 1951). This was a period of experiment for Kurosawa, who made a lighthearted film *(Scandal)* and a more daring and experimental one *(Rashomon)*, sometimes with little consideration for a film's commercial value *(The Idiot)*.

2 Tada Michitaro, *Fukusei geijutsu ron* (Tokyo: Keiso Shobo, 1962), 342–43.

3 Richie, *The Films of Akira Kurosawa*, 57.

4 Kurosawa, *Something like an Autobiography*, 169–70.

5 Kurosawa writes: "I don't really like talking about my films. Everything I want to say is in the film itself. . . . If what I have said in my film is true, someone will understand. That is the way it was with the *The Quiet Duel*. Apparently most people did not grasp what I most fervently wished them to, but a small number did understand very well. In order to make my point more clearly, I decided to make *Nora inu* (*Stray Dog*, 1949). I think the problem with *The Quiet Duel* was that I myself had not thoroughly digested my ideas, nor did I express them in the best possible way. Maupassant instructed aspiring writers to extend their vision into realms where no one else could see, and to keep it up until the hitherto invisible became visible to everyone. Acting on this principle, I decided to take up the problem of *The Quiet Duel* one more time in

Stray Dog, pressing my vision to the point where everyone would see what I saw" (Kurosawa, *Something like an Autobiography*, 172–73).

10. Stray Dog

1 For the referential and discursive classification of figures, see Christian Metz, *The Imaginary Signifier: Psychoanalysis and the Cinema*, trans. Ben Brewster, Celia Britton, Alfred Guzzetti, and Annwyl Williams (Bloomington: Indiana University Press, 1982), 186–91.

2 Paul de Man, *Allegories of Reading: Figural Language in Rousseau, Nietzsche, Rilke, and Proust* (New Haven, Conn.: Yale University Press, 1979), 270.

3 Prince: "Like Eisenstein, Kurosawa conceives of cinematic structure in terms of explosion and strife, and he orders his visual materials to produce a maximum of dialectical shock. Relations of camera and object placement and movement and of image and soundtrack are conceived not in terms of smooth continuity, as in the American model developed by the Hollywood cinema, but in terms of clash, contradiction, reversal" (*The Warrior's Camera*, 45). Richie: "Like the Russians (Eisenstein, Dovshenko) to whose epics *Seven Samurai* has often been compared, Kurosawa — here perhaps more than in any other single film — insisted that the motion-picture be composed entirely of *motion*" (*The Films of Akira Kurosawa*, 103).

4 The only exception is perhaps Noël Burch. See his analysis of Kurosawa in *To the Distant Observer*, especially pp. 292–93. Meanwhile, Kurosawa consistently denies any influences of Eisenstein on his films. Kurosawa's denial seems to have less to do with his analytical assessment of Eisenstein's work — because Kurosawa is merely reacting to those critics, both Japanese and non-Japanese, who find similarities between Kurosawa and Eisenstein without convincingly developing their argument based on an extensive analysis of the works of these two filmmakers — and more to do with his concern with his public image. From Kurosawa's standpoint, the association with Eisenstein would make him appear an excessively verbose intellectual filmmaker, the opposite of his ideal, an artisanal craftsman whose artistic vision manifests itself only in the concrete materiality of what he creates, not in the abstract metadiscourse on his own work.

5 This is the view on Kurosawa held by Masumura Yasuzo, a leading filmmaker of the late 1950s and 1960s, who throughout his career wrote extremely perceptive essays on Kurosawa's films. Masumura's position

regarding Kurosawa is ambivalent. On the one hand, this self-articulate modernist (*kindai shugisha*) does not see anything intellectually inspiring in Kurosawa's work. On the other hand, he is clearly overwhelmed by the power of audiovisual dynamism in Kurosawa's films and even concedes that Kurosawa is superior to those intellectually enlightened filmmakers whose films tend to ignore the fact that the cinema is a type of industrial art for the masses. Whereas Oshima Nagisa without any hesitation defends his own role in the development of Japanese cinema to a right direction, Masumura is unsure about the legacy of *kindai shugi* (modernism) and the New Wave that rejected the filmmakers like Kurosawa. See Masumura Yasuzo and Oshima Nagisa, "Nihon eiga ni tsuite kataro," *Kinema junpo,* part 2 (January 1972): 78–79.

6 Even Gilles Deleuze is no exception here. This, of course, does not diminish the value of Deleuze's insight into Kurosawa's films.

7 Tom Conley, *Film Hieroglyphs: Ruptures in Classical Cinema* (Minneapolis: University of Minnesota Press, 1991), xvi.

8 Richie, *The Films of Akira Kurosawa,* 63.

9 Ibid.

10 Robert Stam et al., *New Vocabularies in Film Semiotics: Structuralism, Post-structuralism and Beyond* (London: Routledge, 1992), 28–33.

11 Michel Chion, *Audio-Vision: Sound on Screen* (New York: Columbia University Press, 1994), 173.

12 Ibid., 5.

13 James Goodwin tries to present a new perspective on Kurosawa's work by finding "intertextuality" at the core of Kurosawa's films. But his interpretations of specific Kurosawa films often remain ambiguous because of the imprecise use of this critical concept. See, for instance, the following analysis of intertextuality in *Stray Dog* by Goodwin: "After the two police officers trace the gun to a holdup man living with his sister in a burned-out area of Tokyo, they search through his meager belongings in a shed he occupied. A crumpled journal entry, in which is recorded his mood of worthlessness and slaughterous rage, fascinates Murakami. The camera gradually scans inked characters written in the criminal's hand. Moments later we watch Murakami pore over the page, his face pressed so close that his eyes consume each character. This textual evidence of a criminal's passionate despair is juxtaposed with the commendations for police work Murakami later admires in Sato's home. The official documents are framed and hang in a place of pride on the wall; Murakami regards them from a respectful distance. Murakami's psychological position is thus again dramatized as intertextual, as at a crossroads traversed by polar values and discourses" (*Akira Kurosawa*

and Intertextual Cinema, 64). After reading this passage several times, I still do not understand what is so "intertextual" about "Murakami's psychological position."

14 Sato Tadao: "Regardless of the author's intention, similar to *Drunken Angel*, which celebrated the roughness of postwar black market scenes, this film [*Stray Dog*] is also a song of praise dedicated to the chaotic social conditions of postwar Tokyo, where scoundrels could swagger as if they were masters of the place. Therefore, one of the most memorable sequences of this film is, for instance, that in which the detective Murakami, looking for an illicit dealer of pistols, wanders around various amusement quarters and black markets all over Tokyo. This sequence consists of about seventy shots over eleven minutes or so. Immediately preceding this sequence, there is another one—twenty-two shots in about five minutes—where the detective Murakami follows a woman pickpocket, and wanders around Tokyo's *shitamachi* district. Both sequences, sixteen minutes put together, are a splendid symphony of postwar scenes in visual images. Each shot is not particularly short, since on average it lasts for ten seconds. But each shot of the sequences is jam-packed with the hustle and bustle, eeriness, chaos, poverty, and desire of those days' black market, the heat of midsummer, and the sense of fatigue" (*Kurosawa Akira no sekai*, 168–69).

15 Richie: "*Stray Dog* is full of temporal miscalculations. One of them is the endless montage sequence of Mifune disguised and searching Asakusa and Ueno for his gun. It is a full ten minutes of double-exposure, dissolves, fades, multiple images. The atmosphere is caught, to be sure (which was the reason for the montage), but it is so long that one expects summer to be over and autumn begun by the time it finally stops" (*The Films of Akira Kurosawa*, 63). Shigeno Tatsuhiko: "In the scene where the detective Murakami, disguised as a war veteran, looks for a 'pistol dealer,' Kurosawa uses images shot on location and real sound, both of which have ended up, however, as an explanatory addition from the outside. To show Murakami's effort, the use of these real scenes is not necessarily required; that is, the script as a whole is not written in such a way that it needs a location shooting. The real scenes shot on location are merely inserted into a plan that can be realized by using a set" (review of *Stray Dog*, *Kinema junpo*, part 1 [December 1949], reprinted in *Kurosawa Akira shusei*, vol. 3, 274).

16 Ogi Masahiro, "Kurosawa Akira jisaku o kataru," in *Kurosawa Akira shusei*, vol. 3, 92.

17 Gilles Deleuze, *Cinema 1: The Movement-Image* (Minneapolis: University of Minnesota Press, 1986), 189.

18 The Japanese critic Shigeno Tatsuhiko argues that because of Mifune's deficiency in acting skill, he looks like a real criminal rather than a disguised detective (Shigeno, review of *Stray Dog*, 276). But to see the transformation of Murakami from a disguised detective into a jobless veteran as a sign of Mifune's poor acting skill completely misses the point. According to the logic of the textual system, Murakami must become a jobless veteran to reexperience the past in search of his identity.

19 Conley, *Film Hieroglyphs*, xvi.

20 Yusa's full name is used twice in the film. First, we see his name written on his rice ration card. Second, Sato uses the full name when he and Murakami talk to Yusa's sister.

21 Eirin (the Film Ethics Regulatory Committee) objected to the use of the name "Metro Hotel" because the association of this name and its employee Sei-san, who is a delinquent and friend of the criminal Yusa, would violate the human rights of employees of the really existing Metro Hotel. See Endo, *Eirin*, 78.

22 Carol Gluck, "The Past in the Present," in *Postwar Japan as History*, ed. Andrew Gordon (Berkeley: University of California Press, 1993), 66.

23 We need a study of how the Japanese films of the Occupation years inscribe on their textual surface the Japanese sentiment toward the United States. My preliminary speculation is that despite the strict American censorship, the Occupation cinema is full of cryptic images of America, many of which are ambivalent toward, or even critical of, the occupiers. As for the Japanese audiences' reactions to the United States, they were as ambivalent as the Japanese cinema's during this period. While enthusiastically receiving many Hollywood movies, the audiences also cruelly rejected, for instance, the Americanized refashioning of the actress Tanaka Kinuyo. One of the leading stars of Japanese cinema since the late 1920s, Tanaka Kinuyo went to the United States on a goodwill mission in October 1949. Dressed in kimono, she visited Hawaii, Hollywood, and several other major cities including San Francisco, Chicago, and New York. When she came back to Japan in January of the following year, however, her appearance and demeanor were completely Americanized. Wearing showy Western clothes and green sunglasses, Tanaka dashingly emerged from the plane's exit door and went down the landing steps. The first word she uttered was not Japanese but English, "Hello!" She then paraded in an open car on the street of Ginza while throwing kisses to the gathered crowd. The media and public saw Tanaka Kinuyo's transformation as betrayal and immediately attacked her as *ameshon joyu* (*ameshon* actress). The neologic word *ameshon* (pissing in the U.S.) is a combination of *ame*rika (America)

and *shon*ben (piss), a play on the expression *tachishon* (pissing on the street). The word was used to refer to a person who has stayed in the United States for a brief period of time (i.e., just enough time to "piss") yet pretends to know everything about America after coming back to Japan. When *Engagement Ring* (Kon'yaku yubiwa, directed by Kinoshita Keisuke, 1950), her first film after her return from the United States, was released, critics derogatorily called her *roshu* (old and ugly). Tanaka Kinuyo was devastated by the vicious public attack and even contemplated committing suicide.

24 Richie, *The Films of Akira Kurosawa*, 64.

25 Futaba Juzaburo, *Nihon eiga hihan: 1932–1956* (Tokyo: Topazu Puresu, 1992), 136–37.

26 In Yusa's case, the first sign of his mental sickness is presented with his interest in pornography. When Sato and Murakami visit his shack, they find a wrinkled letter paper where he writes about his sadistic killing of a stray cat together with some cheap magazines *(kasutori zasshi)* with naked woman's pictures on the cover.

27 Žižek, *The Sublime Object of Ideology*, 23–24.

28 W. J. T. Mitchell, *Iconology: Image, Text, Ideology* (Chicago: University of Chicago Press, 1986), 193.

29 Karl Marx, *A Contribution to the Critique of Political Economy*, trans. N. I. Stone (New York: International Library, 1904), 11–12.

30 The dialectic model of memory presented here derives from Richard Terdiman's work on modernity and memory. See Richard Terdiman, *Present Past: Modernity and the Memory Crisis* (Ithaca, N.Y.: Cornell University Press, 1993).

31 The comparison between Murakami, Yusa, and Urashima Taro is not an arbitrary association but suggested by the film's textual detail. Just before Murakami leaves Sato's house, Sato asks him to take a look at his three children sleeping on the futon. One of Sato's children sleeps with an illustrated book for children in her hand, *Urashima Taro*, which is prominently featured by the shot composition. "Urashima Taro" is an old Japanese folktale. There are many variants, but the basic story is this: Urashima Taro, a young man in a small fishing village, rescues a turtle, which takes him to the Dragon Palace under the sea. At the palace, he is welcomed and entertained by the beautiful princess Otohime. After three days, he becomes homesick and starts worrying about his aged mother. Even though Otohime asks him to stay, he goes home with a farewell gift from her, a precious casket that she forbids him to open unless he is absolutely at a loss. Back in the village, everything looks familiar to him, yet something is wrong. He learns that all the people

he knew are already dead, including his own mother. Three days under the sea turn out to be three hundred years in his village. Completely alone and in despair, he opens the casket. When the white smoke from the casket recedes, he finds himself changed into an old man.

32 Yuzo calls himself a stray dog in *One Wonderful Sunday*. In the "Tunnel" episode in *Dreams*, the protagonist is followed by a vicious stray dog. For a discussion of the image of the repatriated soldier in Kurosawa films, see Kawamoto Saburo, *Ima hitotabi no sengo Nihon eiga* (Tokyo: Iwanami Shoten, 1994), 36–52.

33 Noma Hiroshi, "Eiga *Norainu* no mondai," *Chuo koron* (December 1949): 87–89.

34 Kawamoto, *Ima hitotabi no sengo Nihon eiga*, 40–42.

11. *Scandal*

1 On postwar Japanese magazines, see Kimoto Itaru, *Zasshi de yomu sengoshi* (Tokyo: Shinchosha, 1985).

12. *Rashomon*

1 Nakamura Mitsuo, " 'Yabu no naka' kara," and "Futatabi 'Yabu no naka' o megutte," in *Nakamura Mitsuo zenshu*, vol. 5 (Tokyo: Chikuma Shobo, 1972), 22–49; Karatani Kojin, "Yabu no naka," in *Imi to iu yamai* (Tokyo: Kodansha, 1989), 222–31.

2 The film changes minor details of the original to make the story more realistic and coherent. For instance, in "Yabu no naka," the bandit is thrown by the horse that he has stolen from the samurai and his wife. But as Nakamura Mitsuo points out, it is extremely unlikely that the bandit, who must be a good rider, falls off the horse on which a gentle woman can ride without any problem (Nakamura, " 'Yabu no naka' kara," 26). To make this episode more realistic, the film slightly modifies the situation; that is, according to the bandit, the water he drank in a small stream was probably poisoned by snake venom, so that he was forced to get off the horse and lie down on a riverbank.

3 Akutagawa Ryunosuke, "Rashomon," in *Rashomon and Other Stories*, trans. Takashi Kojima (New York: Liveright, 1952). It is reprinted in Donald Richie, ed., *Rashomon* (New Brunswick, N.J.: Rutgers University Press, 1987), 97. Translation slightly modified.

4 Richie, *Rashomon*, 37–38.

5 For a detailed description of each shot in the sequence, see Richie, *Rashomon*, 39–41.
6 Akutagawa, "Rashomon," in Richie, *Rashomon*, 97–98. Translation modified.
7 *Zenshu Kurosawa Akira*, vol. 3, 307.

13. *The Idiot*

1 For instance, Innami Takaichi mentions *The Idiot* as an example of both commercially and artistically unsuccessful films because of film directors' self-indulgence. According to Innami, Kurosawa realized his mistake and after *The Idiot* made *Ikiru* and *Seven Samurai*, which were critically acclaimed and commercially popular. However, Innami does not particularly find even the latter two films artistically outstanding (Innami Takaichi, *Eiga shakaigaku* [Tokyo: Waseda Daigaku Shuppanbu, 1955], 59–61).
2 Therefore, Donald Richie's following comment is somewhat misdirected: "Kurosawa's refusal to tamper with Dostoevsky gave him endless problems. By insisting upon a complete respect for his author, he found that he had a lot of explaining to do. The first reel is almost entirely compounded of explanatory titles and a very verbal commentator, feverishly filling in the spectator, trying to give the past history of the main characters and their mutual relations. Naturally, this is done in terms of a précis and so the richness and perception of the original disappears" (Richie, *The Films of Akira Kurosawa*, 82).
3 Richie, *The Films of Akira Kurosawa*, 82.
4 Prince, *The Warrior's Camera*, 141.
5 Richie and Prince mention the close-up as a major reason for the film's failure (Richie, *The Films of Akira Kurosawa*, 82; Prince, *The Warrior's Camera*, 141).
6 Sato, *Kurosawa Akira no sekai*, 202–3.
7 For an analysis of Hara's acting in these films of Ozu, see Kataoka Yoshio, *Kanojo ga enjita yaku: Hara Setsuko no sengo shuensaku o mite kangaeru* (Tokyo: Hayakawa Shobo, 1994).
8 Béla Balázs, "The Face of Man," in *Film Theory and Criticism: Introductory Readings*, ed. Gerald Mast and Marshall Cohen, 3d ed. (New York: Oxford University Press, 1985), 260.
9 For Kurosawa's view of Hara Setsuko as an actress, see Kurosawa Akira, "Hara Setsuko no miryoku," *Zenshu Kurosawa Akira*, vol. 2, 281–84; "Secchan ni tsuite," *Zenshu Kurosawa Akira*, vol. 2, 284–85.

14. *Ikiru*

1 Akira Kurosawa, *"Seven Samurai" and Other Screenplays* (London: Faber and Faber, 1992), 9. From now on, dialogues are quoted from this edition of the film's script unless indicated otherwise.

2 As experimental as he is, Kurosawa never completely deviates from the realist conventions of the classical cinema. In addition to the sound of walking, we also hear that of somebody humming the popular song "Too Young." The humming is not particularly noticeable, and its diegetic status is undecidable at first. Only when Mitsuo and Kazue start talking does it become possible to relate the source of the humming to Kazue. This association is later reinforced when "Too Young" comes from the radio as Kazue turns it on. But this attribution of the subject to the humming becomes possible only retrospectively, so that the initial effect of the scene is uncanny.

3 Kurosawa, *"Seven Samurai" and Other Screenplays,* 20–21.

4 This extremely schematic description of *shishosetsu* hardly does justice to the complexity of this influential mode of modern Japanese fiction and literary institution. For thorough studies of *shishosetsu* in English, see the following works: Iremla Hijiya-Kirschnereit, *Rituals of Self-Revelation: Shishosetsu as Literary Genre and Socio-cultural Phenomenon* (Cambridge: Harvard University Press, 1996); Edward Fowler, *The Rhetoric of Confession: Shishosetsu in Early Twentieth-Century Japanese Fiction* (Berkeley: University of California Press, 1988); Tomi Suzuki, *Narrating the Self: Fictions of Japanese Modernity* (Stanford, Calif.: Stanford University Press, 1996).

5 It is significant that in this scene Toyo apologizes for misunderstanding Watanabe. Toyo's nickname for Watanabe is "Mummy," which she admits does not accurately represent who Watanabe really is. Does he ever come to realize the discrepancy between Toyo as his fantasy and Toyo as a real person?

6 Slavoj Žižek, "In His Bold Gaze My Ruin Is Writ Large," in *Everything You Always Wanted to Know about Lacan (but Were Afraid to Ask Hitchcock),* ed. Slavoj Žižek (London: Verso, 1992), 242–43.

15. *Seven Samurai*

1 Sato Tadao, "Sakuhin kaidai," in *Zenshu Kurosawa Akira,* vol. 4, 343–44.

2 Frederick Kaplan, "A Second Look: Akira Kurosawa's *Seven Samurai,*" *Cineaste* 10 (winter 1979–1980): 42.

3 Bert Cardullo, "The Circumstance of the East, the Fate of the West: Notes, Mostly on *The Seven Samurai," Literature/Film Quarterly* 13, no. 2 (1985): 112–14.

4 *Kurosawa Akira shusei,* vol. 1, 232–33. Originally published in *Kinema junpo,* part 1 (November 1983).

5 Prince, *The Warrior's Camera,* 206.

6 Sato, *Kurosawa Akira no sekai,* 236–37.

7 A newspaper review of the film published in *Tokyo shinbun,* 29 April 1954, reprinted in *Zenshu Kurosawa Akira,* vol. 4, 366.

8 Fredric Jameson, *Signatures of the Visible* (New York: Routledge, 1990), 175–77.

9 See, for instance, Komatsu Hiroshi, "Some Characteristics of Japanese Cinema before World War I," in Nolletti and Desser, *Reframing Japanese Cinema,* 234–35.

10 On Tanizaki's involvement in filmmaking, see Chiba Nobuo, *Eiga to Tanizaki* (Tokyo: Seiabo, 1989).

11 Besides Desser's work (*The Samurai Films of Akira Kurosawa* and "Toward a Structural Analysis of the Postwar Samurai Film"), see also Alain Silver, *The Samurai Film* (New York: Barnes, 1977).

12 Rick Altman, *The American Film Musical* (Bloomington: Indiana University Press, 1989), 6–7.

13 Joseph Anderson, "Second and Third Thoughts about the Japanese Film," in Anderson and Richie, *The Japanese Film,* 444.

14 Desser, *The Samurai Films of Akira Kurosawa,* 21.

15 Desser, "Toward a Structural Analysis of the Postwar Samurai Film," 163.

16 The name of *jidaigeki* star Tsukigata Ryunosuke, who played Higaki Gennosuke in Kurosawa's *Sanshiro Sugata,* is a combination of the names of two *jidaigeki* heroes, for which Sawada was best known: *Tsukigata* Hanpeita and Tsukue *Ryunosuke.*

17 Oi, *Chanbara geijutsushi,* 43–45, 123–44.

18 *King* was so commercially successful that its circulation quickly increased from 740,000 to 1,400,000 by 1928 (Ozaki Hotsuki, *Taishu bungaku* [Tokyo: Kinokuniya Shoten, 1980], 31–32).

19 According to Makino Masahiro, director and Makino Shozo's son, the new company name reflected Shozo's regret over *kyugeki*'s bad influence on children (Makino Masahiro, *Eiga tosei: Ten no maki* [Tokyo: Chikuma Shobo, 1995], 36–40). Only a year after its establishment, Makino Kyoiku Eiga was reorganized as Makino Eiga in 1923 and then developed into Makino Kinema.

20 These filmmakers were really young. For instance, Makino's son Masa-

hiro became a director at the age of eighteen and made the highly acclaimed *jidaigeki* film *Roningai* when he was only twenty years old.

21 Onoe Matsunosuke died in 1925 at the age of fifty-one.

22 Okochi Denjiro appeared in four Kurosawa films: *Sanshiro Sugata; Sanshiro Sugata, Part 2; The Men Who Tread on the Tiger's Tail;* and *No
Regrets for Our Youth.*

23 See Tetsuo Najita, *Japan: The Intellectual Foundations of Modern Japanese Politics* (Chicago: University of Chicago Press, 1974), in which
he analyzes ideological underpinnings of the modern Japanese social
system.

24 Hashimoto, *Kanpon chanbara jidaigeki koza,* 222.

25 Jinno Yuki, *Shumi no tanjo: Hyakkaten ga tsukutta teisuto* (Tokyo: Keiso
Shobo, 1994), 124–29.

26 Hashimoto, *Kanpon chanbara jidaigeki koza,* 59–60.

27 Sato Tadao, *Kimi wa jidaigeki o mita ka* (Tokyo: Jakometei Shuppan,
1977), 37–38.

28 Thomas Kurihara and Tanizaki Jun'ichiro's *Amachua kurabu* (Amateur
Club, 1920) is an interesting example showing a connection between
the slapstick comedies of Mack Sennett and a revolt against Kabuki.
A *gendaigeki* film imitating Keystone comedies, *Amachua kurabu* ridicules Kabuki by presenting a group of young amateur Kabuki actors in
a slapstick situation (Iijima Tadashi, "Nihon eiga no reimei: Jun eigageki no shuhen," *Koza Nihon eiga,* eds. Imamura Shohei et al. [Tokyo:
Iwanami Shoten, 1985), vol. 1, 114–17].

29 For a detailed study of Japanese appropriation of foreign films, see
Yamamoto Kikuo, *Nihon eiga ni okeru gaikoku eiga no eikyo: Hikaku
eigashi kenkyu* (Tokyo: Waseda Daigaku Shuppanbu, 1983). In his short
essay "Taishu bunka to shite no eiga no seiritsu," Yamamoto gives us
an overview of his argument more fully developed in his book. Unfortunately, he briefly discusses *jidaigeki* only as a purveyor of tradition
(*Koza Nihon eiga,* vol. 1, 84–85).

30 In 1947 Mizoguchi Kenji made a film based on the life of Matsui Sumako, *The Love of Sumako the Actress* (Joyu Sumako no koi). In the
same year, Kinugasa Teinosuke made a film, *Actress* (Joyu), which also
focuses on Matsui Sumako's career. For a brief biographical account
of Matsui Sumako, see Brian Powell, "Matsui Sumako: Actress and
Woman," in *Modern Japan: Aspects of History, Literature, and Society,*
ed. W. G. Beasley (London: Allen and Unwin, 1975), 135–46.

31 Matsumoto Kappei, *Nihon shingekishi: Shigeki binbo monogatari*
(Tokyo: Chikuma Shobo, 1966), 91–92.

32 Suzuki Sadami, *Nihon no "bungaku" o kangaeru* (Tokyo: Kadokawa Shoten, 1994), 192–94.

33 Hirano Ken, *Showa bungakushi*, 242.

34 Ozaki, *Taishu bungaku*, 45–47.

35 Sato, *Kimi wa jidaigeki o mita ka*, 142–44.

36 Hashimoto, *Kanpon chanbara jidaigeki koza*, 62–63.

37 The tendency film denounced class oppression and exploitation and became popular in both *jidaigeki* and *gendaigeki* (e.g., in *jidaigeki*, Ito Daisuke's *Servant* [Gero, 1927], *Man-Slashing, Horse-Piercing Sword* [Zanjin zanba ken, 1929]; in *gendaigeki*, Mizoguchi's *Metropolitan Symphony* [Tokai kokyogaku, 1929], Uchida Tomu's *A Living Doll* [Ikeru ningyo, 1929], Suzuki Shigeyoshi's *What Made Her Do It?* [Nani ga kanojo o so saseta ka, 1930]).

38 These independent companies of film stars include Bantsuma Puro (established in 1925), Ichikawa Utaemon Puro (1927), Takagi Shinpei Puro (1927), Tanizaki Juro Puro (1927), Arakan Puro (1928), Kataoka Chiezo Puro (1928), and others (Yoshida Chieo, *Mo hitotsu no eigashi: Katsuben no jidai* [Tokyo: Jiji Tsushinsha, 1978], 117). Arashi Kanjuro (Arakan), one of the biggest *jidaigeki* stars, comments that Makino Kinema was not necessarily leftist oriented but definitely a trendsetter (Takenaka, *Kikigaki Arakan ichidai*, 75).

39 Makino Masahiro recalls that when he was still in his early teens, he met Osugi Sakae and showed him around Kyoto. Osugi was a leading anarchist theorist and activist who was murdered by the police in the confusion of the great Kanto earthquake in 1923. Takenaka Tsutomu, *Yamagami Itaro no sekai* (Kyoto: Shirakawa Shoin, 1976), 25–26.

40 Makino Masahiro was summoned by the special police more than once as a film director of "anarchist films." Takenaka, *Yamagami Itaro no sekai*, 35–36.

41 The end of *benshi* meant not only the triumph of large capital but also the disappearance of regional difference. *Benshi* normally used the standard Japanese in their narration, but according to Inagaki Hiroshi, with comedies (e.g., Chaplin, Keaton, Lloyd), they narrated in the specific dialect of the region where a film was exhibited. Takenaka, *Yamagami Itaro no sekai*, 57.

42 Sato, "Kokka ni kanri sareta eiga," *Koza Nihon eiga*, vol. 4, 51.

43 Ibid., 52–53.

44 Hirano, *Mr. Smith Goes to Tokyo*, 66–67.

45 Endo, *Eirin*, 19; Anderson and Richie, *The Japanese Film: Art and Industry*, expanded ed. (Princeton: Princeton University Press, 1982), 174.

Further research is necessary to determine exactly how many *jidaigeki* films were produced in 1946. Kyoko Hirano, for instance, reports that only four *jidaigeki* films were made in 1946 (*Mr. Smith Goes to Tokyo*, 68). According to another source, the number increases to eight (*Toei junenshi* [Tokyo: Toei, 1962], 75).

46 Kato Koichi, *Sukyandaru no Showa shi* (Tokyo: Hanashi no Tokushu, 1985), 78; *Toei junenshi*, 83.

47 Tanaka, *Nihon eiga hattatsushi*, vol. 3, 339–43.

48 *Toei junenshi*, 84.

49 In 1952, 56.5 percent of Toei's total output was *jidaigeki* films, while the percentage of *jidaigeki* films for Daiei, Toho, Shintoho, and Shochiku were 35.3, 28.6, 27.1, and 22.9 respectively (*Toei junenshi*, 92). Toei continued to make more *jidaigeki* films throughout the 1950s. In 1961, out of ninety-six films it produced, seventy-four (or 77.1 percent) were *jidaigeki;* in contrast, Toho made only five *jidaigeki* films, Shochiku three, and Nikkatsu zero (Tsusho Sangyosho [MITI], ed., *Eiga sangyo hakusho: Waga kuni eiga sangyo no genjo to shomondai* [Tokyo: Shobundo, 1963], 8).

50 With their incredible plots, cheap-looking sets, and bad acting, these Toei entertainment edition films were definitely not intended for adult audiences.

51 Toei's adoption of the 'Scope size was much quicker than its conversion to the color film. For instance, in 1958, out of Toei's 105 films, 103 were in 'Scope, and only 53 were in color (Tanaka, *Nihon eiga hattatsushi,* vol. 4, 269).

52 Tanaka, *Nihon eiga hattatsushi,* vol. 4, 373. This number includes films made by Toei and its subsidiary New Toei, which was established as Daini Toei in 1960 to produce and distribute more *gendaigeki* films.

53 I draw on Ogura Shinbi's concise description of some of the major features of Toei *jidaigeki.* See his "Masupuro seisaku no kiseki: Toei," in *Besuto obu Kinema junpo: 1950–1966*, 807–9; originally published in *Kinema Junpo*, no. 231 (April 1959).

54 Hashimoto Osamu claims that Japanese audiences could easily identify themselves with the heroes of Toei *chanbara* films who fight against corruption and injustice because of a number of sociopolitical incidents that cast a dark shadow over the future of postwar Japan (e.g., the Matsukawa and Shimoyama incidents, Zosen *gigoku* and other political corruptions, the Cold War and the Korean War, nuclear and hydrogen bomb experiments, the Shunagawa incident, and the 1960 Anpo). See Hashimoto, *Kanpon chanbara jidaigeki koza*, 71.

55 Hashimoto, *Kanpon chanbara jidaigeki koza,* 73.

56 Tachikawa bunko, or to be exact, Tatsukawa bunko, was a series of popular fiction that was enormously popular among children from the late Meiji to the end of Taisho period. Based on *kodan* stories, it featured well-known historical and fictitious heroes, most importantly Sarutobi Sasuke, a superhero ninja. The *kyugeki* film fed on stories provided by Tachikawa bunko and its imitations, and the popularity of the latter soared as their heroes were played by such film stars as Matsunosuke. For more information about Tachikawa bunko, see Adachi Ken'ichi, *Tachikawa bunko no eiyutachi* (Tokyo: Chuo Koronsha, 1987).

57 Sato, *Kimi wa jidaigeki eiga o mita ka,* 94–101.

58 Ibid., 32–35.

59 Sato Tadao, *Hasegawa Shin ron* (Tokyo: Chuo Koronsha, 1975), 276.

60 Sato, *Kimi wa jidaigeki eiga o mita ka,* 45–48.

61 John Belton, *American Cinema/American Culture* (New York: McGraw-Hill, 1994), 225.

62 Sato, *Hasegawa Shin ron,* 136–41.

63 Anders Stephanson, *Manifest Destiny: American Expansion and the Empire of Right* (New York: Hill and Wang, 1995), xii.

64 Anderson, "Japanese Swordfighters and American Gunfighters," *Cinema Journal* 12, no. 2 (spring 1973): 9.

65 Ibid., 10.

66 Michitaro Tada, "The Destiny of Samurai Films," *East-West Film Journal* 1, no. 1 (December 1986): 48.

67 This script was made into a film by Makino Masahiro at Toyoko Eiga in 1950. It is said that Kurosawa wrote the script in his spare time while preparing for the production of *Rashomon.*

68 Kurosawa was born in 1910, Itami in 1900.

69 Yoneda Yoshikazu, *Itami Mansaku* (Tokyo: Musashino Shobo, 1985), 11.

70 It is ironic that while Itami obviously enjoyed filming Chiezo's superb performance as Akanishi Kakita, Chiezo himself was dissatisfied with his non-*jidaigeki*-like performance as Kakita. The director Saeki Kiyoshi, who worked under Itami as assistant director for *Akanishi Kakita,* reports that Chiezo was able to release his frustration finally when he played the role of Harada Kai in the climactic swordfight scene à la grand Kabuki style. Itami, on the other hand, was turned off by Chiezo's white face and grandiose performance (Saeki Kiyoshi, "Itami-san no enshutsu," *Koza Nihon eiga,* vol. 3, 162–63).

71 Sawachi Hisae, *Otoko arite: Shimura Takashi no sekai* (Tokyo: Bungei Shunju, 1994), 56. There are other connections between Itami and Ku-

rosawa. For instance, Itami wrote a few favorable reviews of Kurosawa's wartime scripts. And Hashimoto Shinobu, a scriptwriter and regular contributor to Kurosawa's films since *Rashomon,* was Itami's disciple.

72 Kato Tai, *Kato Tai eiga o kataru* (Tokyo: Chikuma Shobo, 1994), 98–99.

73 Shigeno Tatsuhiko, "Yamanaka Sadao," *Koza Nihon eiga,* vol. 3, 174–75.

74 Mori Kazuo, Yamada Koichi, and Yamane Sadao, *Mori Kazuo eigatabi* (Tokyo: Soshisha, 1989), 187–88.

75 Nagata Tetsuro, *Tate: Chanbara eigashi* (Tokyo: Shakai Shisosha, 1993), 205–7.

76 Izawa Jun, "Jidaigeki no kindaiha," *Besuto obu Kinema Junpo: 1950–1966,* 805. Originally published in *Kinema Junpo,* no. 231 (1959).

77 Kurosaw Akira, "Katsugeki no yume to genjitsu: *Seven Samurai* kansei ni saishite," in *Zenshu Kurosawa Akira,* vol. 4, 311.

78 Prince, *The Warrior's Camera,* 209.

79 Sometimes even the most important detail of the *jidaigeki* film can be fictitious. For instance, some say that there was no paper balloon around the time depicted in Yamanaka's *Humanity and Paper Balloons* (Imai Tadashi, *Imai Tadashi "zenshigoto": Sukurin no aru jinsei* [Tokyo: ACT, 1990], 88).

80 Prince, *The Warrior's Camera,* 210.

81 Ibid.

82 Kuwabara Takeo, "*Shichinin* no samurai," *Kaizo* (June 1954): 134.

83 Hirosawa Ei, "*Shichinin no samurai* no shigoto," *Koza Nihon eiga,* vol. 5, 268–69; Sato Tadao, "Muraki Yoshiro, Muraki Shinobu ni kiku: Sochi no kiseigainen o uchikowashi shin no genjitsu o sekkei suru," in *Kurosawa Akira shusei,* vol. 2, 131; Tajitsu Tairyo, "Sutaffu zein nikai wa kubi o kakugoshita *Shichinin no samurai,*" in *Kurosawa Akira shusei,* vol. 3, 67–68.

84 Andrey Tarkovsky, *Sculpting in Time: Reflections on the Cinema,* trans. Kitty Hunter-Blair (New York: Knopf, 1987), 73.

85 André Bazin, "*Seven Samurai,*" in *Perspectives on Akira Kurosawa,* ed. James Goodwin (New York: G. K. Hall, 1994), 114.

86 Tanaka, *Nihon eiga hattatsushi,* vol. 4, 391.

87 Ibid., 437.

88 Some of the notable examples of this subgenre of *jidaigeki* include *Thirteen Assassins* (Jusannin no shikaku, directed by Kudo Eichi, 1963), *Seventeen Ninja* (Jushichinin no ninja, by Hasagawa Yasuto, 1963), *Ninja Hunt* (Ninja gari, by Yamauchi Tetsuya, 1963). For *shudan koso jidaigeki,* see Ueno Koshi, *Nikutai no jidai: Taikenteki '60-nendai bunkaron* (Tokyo: Gendai Shokan, 1989), 41–49.

16. Record of a Living Being

1   There are two scenes in the middle of the film where diegetic music is used briefly. After Nakajima is adjudged quasi incompetent (*jun kinchisansha*), the dentist Harada (Shimura Takashi), a volunteer worker at the Family Court, is reading the book titled *Ashes of Death* in his clinic late at night. We hear a languid sound of guitar, the precise source of which is at first unclear. As the sound of guitar becomes smaller when Harada walks to the window and shuts it, we realize that it is not extradiegetic film music. In another scene, Nakajima comes to the tiny boarding room of Ryoichi, his illegitimate son, to borrow some money. For Ryoichi, Nakajima, who has no control over his money as a quasi incompetent, is no longer useful, and Ryoichi refuses to lend any money to his father. Instead of directly saying no, Ryoichi nonchalantly starts playing a record of dance music, which irritates Nakajima and us.

2   Sato, *Kurosawa Akira no sekai,* 220–22.

3   Uryu Tadao, "Ikimono no kiroku: Kyomi bukai hasso," *Eiga geijutsu* (February 1956): 43–45.

4   Kurosawa Akira, Kinoshita Keisuke, and Takeda Taijun, "Ningenzo seisakuho," *Chuo koron* (February 1956): 244.

5   If there is a miscalculation on the part of Kurosawa, as the director Kinoshita Keisuke argues, it is his underestimation of the human capacity not to think about death. Thus, contrary to Kurosawa's intention, many film viewers may simply use *Record of a Living Being* to reinforce their belief that only a madman feels threatened by the nuclear fallout. See Kurosawa et al., "Ningenzo seisakuho," 245.

17. Throne of Blood

1   John Gerlach, "Shakespeare, Kurosawa, and *Macbeth:* A Response to J. Blumenthal," *Literature/Film Quarterly* 1, no. 4 (fall 1973): 352–59.

2   Frank Kermode, "Shakespeare in the Movies," in Mast and Cohen, *Film Theory and Criticism,* 328.

3   Robert Hapgood, "Kurosawa's Shakespeare Films: *Throne of Blood, The Bad Sleep Well,* and *Ran,*" in Davies and Wells, *Shakespeare and the Moving Image: The Plays on Film and Television,* 234.

4   Richie, *The Films of Akira Kurosawa,* 119.

5   Desser, *The Samurai Films of Akira Kurosawa,* 72.

6   McDonald, *Japanese Classical Theater in Films,* 129, 131. See also Mc-

Donald's description of how Noh conventions influence the acting of Yamada Isuzu, who plays the role of Asaji, or Lady Washizu: "Lady Washizu is also closely associated with Noh drama. She does not create her own movement voluntarily. Instead, she follows the formalistic practice of 'prescribed pattern of bodily movement.' She walks like a Noh performer: her feet are not lifted from the floor but slide along it, the toes raised at each step. Her speech is measured, like a Noh soliloquy. In the banquet scene, while Washizu's features work in expressions of horror and dismay, her face is a study in absolute control: static, cold, and impassive, like a female blank Noh mask" (132).

7 Kurosawa, interview by Sato Tadao, *Zenshu Kurosawa Akira,* vol. 4, 353–54. Originally published in Roger Manvell, *Shakespeare and the Film* (New York: Praeger, 1971), 103.

8 Hino Tomiko (1440–1496) was a wife of the eighth shogun, Ashikaga Yoshimasa, in the Muromachi period. Her scheme to make her own son an heir to the shogun was partially responsible for the Onin War (1467–1477). Ike no Zenni was mother of Taira no Yorimori (1132–1186). She saved the life of Minamoto no Yoritomo (1147–1196), who later defeated the Taira clan and established the first shogunate in Kamakura. Hojo Masako (1157–1225) controlled the Kamakura shogunate after the death of her husband Yoritomo.

9 Prince, *The Warrior's Camera,* 144.

10 Manvell, *Shakespeare and the Film,* 105.

11 Ana Laura Zambrano, "*Throne of Blood:* Kurosawa's *Macbeth,*" *Literature/Film Quarterly* 2 (summer 1974): 262–74.

12 Kawatake Toshio, *Nihon no Hamuretto* (Tokyo: Nansosha, 1972), 254–66.

13 John Collick, *Shakespeare, Cinema, and Society* (Manchester: Manchester University Press, 1989), 151.

14 For information about *Sakuradoki zeni no yononaka,* I rely on the following essay: Yoshihara Yukari, " 'Hankai' Nihon: 'Venisu no shonin' Meijiki hon'an," *Gendai Shiso* 24, no. 3 (March 1996): 21–33.

15 Collick, *Shakespeare, Cinema, and Society,* 150.

16 One possible reason why contemporary film theory—structuralist and poststructuralist—has not taken up adaptation as a serious issue is that film studies has not yet completely given up the auteurist paradigm. As André Bazin reminds us, adaptation puts into question the notion of the author and the unity of the work: "The ferocious defense of literary works is, to a certain extent, aesthetically justified; but we must also be aware that it rests on a rather recent, individualistic conception of the 'author' and of the 'work,' a conception that was far from being ethically

rigorous in the seventeenth century and that started to become legally defined only at the end of the eighteenth. . . . the standard differentiation among the arts in the nineteenth century and the relatively recent, subjectivist notion of the author as identified with the work no longer fit in with an aesthetic sociology of the masses, in which the cinema runs a relay race with drama and the novel and doesn't eliminate them, but rather reinforces them. . . . All things considered, it's possible to imagine that we are moving toward a reign of the adaptation in which the notion of the unity of the work of art, if not the very notion of the author himself, will be destroyed" (André Bazin, "Adaptation, or The Cinema as Digest," in *Bazin at Work: Major Essays and Reviews from the Forties and Fifties*, trans. Alain Piette and Bert Cardullo [New York: Routledge, 1997], 46, 49).

17 Pierre Bourdieu, "The Form of Capital," in *Handbook of Theory and Research for the Sociology of Education,* ed. John G. Richardson (New York: Greenwood Press, 1986), 241–58.

18 Ibid., 246–47.

19 Iwasaki Akira and Kurosawa Akira, "*Kumonosujo* o megutte," in *Zenshu Kurosawa Akira,* vol. 4, 312–30.

20 Kawatake Toshio, *Kabuki biron* (Tokyo: Tokyo Daigaku Shuppankai, 1989), 78–79.

21 Kawatake Toshio, *Engeki gairon* (Tokyo: Tokyo Daigaku Shuppankai, 1978), 64–78.

22 Martin Banham, ed., *The Cambridge Guide to Theatre* (Cambridge: Cambridge University Press, 1995), 583.

23 Kawakita Toshio reports that there were concrete connections between Jesuit missionaries' festival plays and pageants and the early Kabuki of the late sixteenth century and early seventeenth century. See Kawatake, *Kabuki biron,* 17–21.

24 Kawatake, *Kabuki biron,* 99.

25 Nakamura Mitsuo, *Nihon no kindai shosetsu* (Tokyo: Iwanami Shinsho, 1962), 5.

26 Takeuchi Yoshimi, *Nihon to Ajia,* 401–3.

27 Ibid., 404–5.

28 Toida Michizo, "Jidaimono to engi no dento," *Eiga geijutsu,* no. 129 (July 1958): 47.

29 Kitagawa Fuyuhiko, review of *Throne of Blood,* in *Shusei Kurosawa Akira,* vol. 3, 284. Originally published in *Kinema junpo,* part 2 (February 1955).

30 André Bazin, "Theater and Cinema," in *What Is Cinema?* vol. 1 (Berkeley: University of California Press, 1967), 76–124.

31 Peter Brook, "Shakespeare on the Screens," *Sight and Sound* 34, no. 2 (spring 1965): 68.

32 Bazin, "Adaptation, or The Cinema as Digest," in *Bazin at Work,* 42.

18. *The Lower Depths*

1 For a comparison of Kurosawa's film and Gorky's play, see James Goodwin, *Akira Kurosawa and Intertextual Cinema,* 86–112. Sumie Jones's essay on *The Lower Depths* is quite informative about the significance of Gorky's *The Lower Depths* in the *shingeki* movement and how Kurosawa reacts to the *shingeki*'s appropriation of the play. See her "*The Lower Depths:* Gorky, Stanislavsky, and Kurosawa," in *Explorations: Essays in Comparative Literature,* ed. Makoto Ueda (Lanham, Md.: University Press of America, 1986), 174–208.

2 Kawamoto Saburo, *Kimi uruwashiku: Sengo Nihon eiga joyu san* (Tokyo: Bungei Shunju, 1996), 292.

19. *The Hidden Fortress*

1 Richie, *The Films of Akira Kurosawa,* 135–37; Desser, *The Samurai Films of Akira Kurosawa,* 92–93; Prince, *The Warrior's Camera,* 220.

2 In 1947, for his friend Taniguchi Senkichi, Kurosawa wrote a script with a similar title, *Yamagoya no san akunin* (Three Bad Men in a Mountain Hut). But when Taniguchi's film, which featured Mifune as one of the bad men (bank robbers), was released, its title was changed to *Ginrei no hate* (To the End of the Silver-Capped Mountains).

3 Hanada Kiyoteru, "Ganzo hoseki no kirameki," *Kinema junpo,* part 2 (January 1959), reprinted in *Besuto obu Kinema junpo jo 1950–1966* (Tokyo: Kinema Junposha, 1994), 777–78; Masumura Yasuzo, " 'Kakushitoride no san akunin' to Kurosawa Akira," *Eiga hyoron* (February 1959), reprinted in *Gendai Nihon eigaron taikei,* vol. 2 (Tokyo: Tojusha, 1970), 137.

20. *The Bad Sleep Well*

1 Chion, *Audio-Vision,* 48.

2 In the climactic scene of his *Rising Sun,* Michael Crichton "quotes" the opening scene of *The Bad Sleep Well.* The setting is similarly theatrical,

and exactly the same names are given to three executives of the Naka-moto America Company: Iwabuchi, Moriyama, and Shirai. See Michael Crichton, *Rising Sun* (New York: Ballantine Books, 1993), 376–77.

3 *Zenshu Kurosawa Akira,* vol. 5, 22.

4 The absence of twisted moral Manichaeism is perhaps not unrelated to the conspicuous lack of severe wether in *The Bad Sleep Well.* There is no heavy rain, scorching summer heat, or strong wind, which plays a dramatically essential role in Kurosawa films at least as much as human characters.

5 Tada Michitaro, *Fukusei geijutsu ron* (Tokyo: Keiso Shobo, 1962), 350–51.

21. *Yojimbo*

1 Akiyama Kuniharu, "Kurosawa eiga no ongaku to sakkyokusha no sho-gen," in *Kurosawa Akira shusei,* vol. 2, 254–56; Nishimura Yuichiro, *Kurosawa Akira: Oto to eizo* (Tokyo: Rippu Shobo, 1990), 178–83.

2 Hashimoto, *Kanpon chanbara jidai geki koza,* 202–3.

3 Tanaka, *Nihon eiga hattatsushi,* vol. 4, 379.

4 Ibid., 124–28.

22. *Sanjuro*

1 Yamamoto Shugoro, *Nichinichi heian* (Tokyo: Shinchosha, 1965).

2 Prince, *The Warrior's Camera,* 233.

3 In "Kurosawa's Eastern 'Western': Sanjuro and the Influence of *Shane*" (*Film Criticism* 8, no. 1 [fall 1983]), David Desser asserts that *Sanjuro* "is basically a remake of George Stevens' *Shane*" (59). But the similari-ties Desser finds between Kurosawa's *jidaigeki* film and Stevens's 1953 Western seem rather arbitrary. First, there is a problem with his "struc-tural analysis." "By a kind of oral telling, or a written plot synopsis," writes Desser, "the two films are almost indistinguishable." Any simple plot summary of the two films, I think, would prove otherwise. Second, Desser argues that both films "utilize children's point of view in their narrative, thereby imbuing the films with something of the nature of a folk tale. *Sanjuro* and *Shane* use children (or youths) as structuring principles to create heroic/mythic images out of their main characters" (56). But *Sanjuro* is not organized around the point of view of the young samurai; moreover, the young samurai are certainly not comparable to

the little boy Joey Starrett in *Shane*. They are direct participants in the scheme against the corrupt clan officials, whereas Joey as a child remains strictly an observer. Instead of being narrated from the young samurai's point of view, *Sanjuro* consistently emphasizes their inability to observe the surrounding situations correctly. They occupy the position of the observed; it is Sanjuro and the film's spectators that observe their naïveté. Third, Desser uses the dichotomy of wilderness and civilization to analyze symbolic meanings of *Shane*'s thematic system. He then superimposes the same dichotomy onto *Sanjuro*, but it is quickly replaced by that of nature and culture. He claims that Sanjuro is situated outside of culture: "Considering the importance of names in Japanese society, Sanjuro, in making up a name for himself, already positions himself outside of culture" (61). But it is easily possible to draw the opposite conclusion from the example Desser uses here. Traditionally, the ability to make up interesting names is prized by writers and poets as a sign of their culturedness. To this extent, the arbitrariness of Sanjuro's name can be interpreted as evidence for Sanjuro's association with culture rather than with nature. (This does not mean that I find the dichotomy of nature and culture particularly useful in discussing *Sanjuro*.) The easy replacement of the opposition of wilderness and civilization with that of nature and culture also obscures the specificities of the notions of wilderness and nature. The association of Sanjuro with the nature/culture dichotomy is at best arbitrary. Finally, as we can see in the following assertion by Desser, what he means by "remake" is rather ambiguous: "*Sanjuro* is something of a remake of *Shane*, a transposition of it in much the same way that *The Magnificent Seven* transposes *Seven Samurai* or *A Fistful of Dollars* is a remake of *Yojimbo*" (59). Sergio Leone's *A Fistful of Dollars* is a literal transposition of *Yojimbo* to a (spaghetti) Western setting; John Sturges's *Magnificent Seven* is a freer adaptation of *Seven Samurai;* and there is hardly any concrete relation between *Sanjuro* and *Shane*.

4 Nagata, *Tate*, 197.

5 Hashimoto, *Kanpon chanbara jidai geki koza*, 189.

6 Kayama starred in all Wakadaisho films except the seventh one. From the thirteenth film, *Furesshuman Wakadaisho* (1969) on, he appeared as a sarariman instead of as a college student. In 1981 another Wakadaisho film featuring Kayama was made to celebrate his thirty-year acting career. In the mid-1970s, Toho tried to launch a new Wakadaisho series by using Kusakari Masao as its star, but the studio's attempt failed after only two films were made.

7 Hashimoto, *Kanpon chanbara jidaigeki koza*, 199–201.

8   *Nihon eiga haiyu zenshu: Joyu hen* (Tokyo: Kinema Junposha, 1980), 92–99.

9   Actually this was not the first time Kurosawa used Irie in his film. She had appeared in his second film, *The Most Beautiful,* in the role of the matron of the girls' dormitory. In her autobiography, Irie talks about how she tried to settle a squabble between discontent groups of actresses during the shooting of the film. She also fondly remembers that one day in 1944 Kurosawa and the film's main actress, Yaguchi Yoko, visited her house to report their plan to get married. See Irie Takako, *Eiga joyu* (Tokyo: Gakufu Shoin, 1957), 165–69.

10 For an illustrated analysis of Mifune's technique, see Abe Yoshinori, *Eiga o aishita futari: Kurosaw Akira, Mifune Toshiro* (Tokyo: Hochi Shinbunsha, 1995), 130–35.

11 Hashimoto, *Kanpon chanbara jidaigeki koza,* 202–10; Nagata, *Tate,* 246–48.

12 Hashimoto, *Kanpon chanbara jidaigeki koza,* 196–97.

13 Ibid., 200.

23. *High and Low*

1   Burch, *To the Distant Observer,* 320.

2   Richie, *The Films of Akira Kurosawa,* 170.

3   Although Kurosawa's films are often discussed as films of humanism, what this ambiguous notion means is not always clear. And his films themselves do not necessarily use the expression "humanism" or "humanity." In *High and Low,* one of Reiko's remarks is translated in the English subtitle as follows: "Success isn't worth losing your humanity." Yet what Reiko actually says to Gondo is *"Kore ijo hito o keotoshite made shusseshite itadakitaku nai wa"* [I don't want you to get ahead more at the expense of others]. In the original, there is no reference to "humanity," and most of the other overtly humanistic references in the English subtitles cannot be attributed to Kurosawa directly.

4   Burch, *To the Distant Observer,* 296.

5   Ibid.

6   On *giri* and *ninjo,* see, for instance, Minamoto Ryoen, *Giri to ninjo: Nihonteki shinjo no ichikosatsu* (Tokyo: Chuo Koronsha, 1969).

7   Deleuze, *Cinema 1,* 189.

8   Ibid., 191.

9   *"Yatsura no ikinone o tometeyaru,"* which is translated as "I'll kick them out" in the English subtitle.

10 "*Jun mo anata ni sokkuri. Koroshiai ga suki de komaru wa,*" which is translated in the English subtitle as "He takes after you. He likes violent games."

11 It can be argued that the seed of the 1980s' *Tokyo bumu* (Tokyo boom) dates back to the early 1960s when Tokyo went through the third wave of radical transformation of landscape in the twentieth century. (The first one is the reconstruction of Tokyo after the great Kanto earthquake in 1923, and the second moment is the postsurrender years.)

12 Kevin Lynch, *What Time Is This Place?* (Cambridge: MIT Press, 1972), 54–55.

13 Ibid., 41.

14 Noël Burch, *Theory of Film Practice,* trans. Helen R. Lane (Princeton, N.J.: Princeton University Press, 1981).

15 David Bordwell, *Narration in the Fiction Film* (Madison: University of Wisconsin Press, 1985).

16 Kevin Lynch, *The Image of the City* (Cambridge: MIT Press, 1960), 138.

17 Walter Benjamin, "The Work of Art in the Age of Mechanical Reproduction," in *Illuminations* (New York: Schocken Books, 1969), 217–51.

18 Henry D. Smith II, "Tokyo as an Idea: An Exploration of Japanese Urban Thought until 1945," *Journal of Japanese Studies* 4, no. 1 (winter 1978): 53–57.

19 The Japanese writer Osabe Hideo also sees a similar consistency in Kurosawa's career. See his "Kurosawa Akira no sekai," originally published in *Eiga hyoron* (July 1965), and reprinted in *Gendai Nihon eigaron taikei,* vol. 4 (Tokyo: Tojusha, 1971), 271.

20 Although it has been repeatedly pointed out that Kurosawa's films are too "Western" (or *batakusai,* which literally means "smells of butter"), this aspect of his films is rather a reflection of Kurosawa's stereotypically sentimental "girlish" taste (e.g., the extremely awkward treatment of heterosexual romantic relationships). And it is worth remembering here that Toho, the film company where Kurosawa started as an assistant director in 1936 and for which most of his films were made, was founded by Kobayashi Ichizo, the founder of the famous Takarazuka Girls Opera Company.

21 Nishimura, *Kurosawa Akira: Oto to eizo,* 40. In one interview, Kurosawa refers to himself as a "crybaby called humanist" (*Esquire,* Japanese edition, September 1990, 100).

22 Tada Michitaro, *Fukusei geijutsuron* (Tokyo: Keiso Shobo, 1962), 346.

23 In light of this section's discussion, it is worthwhile to reexamine the chronotopic dichotomy of Kurosawa's and Mizoguchi's films based on sexual difference as a dichotomy of two different systems of the econ-

omy: Mizoguchi's milieu of merchants, prostitutes, and actors and actresses or commodity exchange versus Kurosawa's world of samurai and heroes or lone wolves trying to situate themselves outside of social relations based on commodity exchange.

24. *Red Beard*

1 Nishimura, *Kurosawa Akira: Oto to eizo,* 213–18.

25. *Dodeskaden*

1 Kurosawa's other major aborted project in the 1960s was a film about the Tokyo Olympics. The preliminary preparation for the film had already started in 1960, when Kurosawa visited the Olympic Games in Rome and met the director of its documentary film. Because of his disagreement with the film's producers over the budget, however, he was eventually replaced by Ichikawa Kon, who completed a highly acclaimed yet controversial documentary, *Tokyo Olympiad* (Tokyo Orinpikku, 1965).

2 On Kurosawa's involvement in the production of *Tora! Tora! Tora!* see a series of excellent investigative reports by Shirai Yoshio, "*Tora, Tora, Tora!* to Kurosawa Akira mondai rupo," *Kurosawa Akira shusei,* vol. 3, 114–210.

3 Yamamoto Shugoro, *Kisetsu no nai machi* (Tokyo: Shinchosha, 1970).

4 Sato, *Kurosawa Akira no sekai,* 350–54.

5 These scene numbers refer to the script published in *Zenshu Kurosawa Akira.* In *Kurosawa Akira eiga taikei,* the first part is from scene 1 to 16, the second part from 17 to 64, the third part from 65 to 90, and the fourth part from 91 to 98. I generally follow Sato's segmentation, but he seems to miss some scenes in parts 3 and 4.

6 I must disagree with Joan Mellen's assertion that the "whole group [of the shantytown residents] is presided over by Tamba, an old craftsman and beneficent spirit who understands and forgives all, a Kurosawa-surrogate who is able to assume sufficient distance to impart the wisdom of empathy" (Richie, *The Films of Akira Kurosawa,* 186). If there is a surrogate for Kurosawa, it is clearly Rokuchan, a daydreamer and artist, not Tamba, whom Mellen sees as the "only fully realized character in *Dodeskaden*" (188).

7 *Kurosawa Akira shusei,* vol. 2, 112.

8 Kurosawa Akira, *Gama no abura: Jiden no yona mono* (Tokyo: Iwanami

Shoten, 1984), 148. In the English translation of this book, "Nika-ten" is for some reason replaced by "Nitten," another national exhibition. But according to all other Japanese sources I consulted, it is Nika-ten, rather than Nitten, that accepted Kurosawa's painting in 1928.

9 Kurosawa, *Something like an Autobiography*, 88. Translation modified.

10 Catherine Cadou, "Kassai no hibiki," *Esquire*, Japanese edition, September 1990, 107.

11 This treatment of the painter in *Dodeskaden* is different from the earlier representation of a painter in another Kurosawa film, *Scandal*. There, the film's protagonist, Aoe, is much more positively portrayed as an artist. His bold use of color and dynamic design are commented on in the opening scene. Aoe is an idealized image of what a young Kurosawa wanted to become. In *Dreams*, a film that is even more overtly personal than *Dodeskaden*, a painter, who is explicitly presented as Kurosawa's surrogate figure, literally "enters" van Gogh's paintings and meets the old master whom he reveres.

12 Tezuka Makoto, a filmmaker and son of a great manga artist Tezuka Osamu, makes a similar point in his interview (*Kurosawa Akira shusei*, vol. 2, 293).

13 Yamamoto, *Kisetsu no nai machi*, 12.

14 Nogami Teruyo, "*Dodeskaden* no Kurosawa enshutsu," in *Kurosawa Akira no eiga taikei*, vol. 1, 109.

15 Bazin, *Bazin at Work*, 88.

26. *Dersu Uzala*

1 Sato, *Kurosawa Akira no sekai*, 373.

2 *Zenshu Kurosawa Akira*, vol. 6, 210–16.

3 We wonder whether the artificial look of Arseniev's home is intentional on the part of Kurosawa. My guess is that it is not. Kurosawa is not a kind of filmmaker who lackadaisically creates an artificial-looking image on the screen. He is always interested in pursuing realistic appearance or otherwise reflexively exaggerates the sense of constructedness. Here, the shallow appearance of the set could be attributed to the difficulty of creating the realistic feel of a foreign domestic space, with which Kurosawa was not thoroughly familiar.

4 Sato, *Kurosawa Akira no sekai*, 364–65.

5 Walter Ong finds an essential connection between the idea of "exploration" and the invention of the printed map: "Only after print and the extensive experience with maps that print implemented would human

beings, when they thought about the cosmos or universe or 'world,' think primarily of something laid out before their eyes, as in a modern printed atlas, a vast surface or assemblage of surfaces (vision presents surfaces) ready to be 'explored.' The ancient oral world knew few 'explorers,' though it did know many itinerants, travelers, voyagers, adventurers, and pilgrims" (Walter J. Ong, *Orality and Literacy: The Technologizing of the Word* [London: Routledge, 1989], 73).

27. *Kagemusha*

1 Prince, *The Warrior's Camera*, 274–75.
2 Itami Juzo, Hasumi Shigehiko, and Nogami Teruyo, "Kurosawa Akira aruiwa hata e no hen'ai," in *Jibuntachi yo!* by Itami Juzo (Tokyo: Bungei Shunju, 1988), 152–84.
3 Kurosawa Akira, *Kagemusha* (Tokyo: Kodansha, 1979).

28. *Ran*

1 Sato, *Kurosawa Akira no sekai*, 390–99.
2 Prince, *The Warrior's Camera*, 285–86.
3 Sato, *Kurosawa Akira no sekai*, 395.
4 What is conspicuously absent in *Ran* is Kurosawa's signature image, the rain. There is a storm scene in which Hidetora, Tango, and Kyoami ask for shelter at Tsurumaru's thatched hut, but even in this scene it does not rain. It is the blazing sun that leads Hidetora to madness and the Ichimonjis to its self-destruction.
5 Masumura Yasuzo, "Sodai ni shite hiso na tensai," in *Kurosawa Akira shusei*, vol. 1, 6–26. Originally published in *Kinema junpo*, part 2 (May 1974).

29. *Dreams*

1 David Desser mistakenly transcribes the title as "*Kono yume o mita* (I had this dream)"—admittedly a minor mistake, but its implication is far from insignificant. In Desser' version, each episode of *Dreams* becomes the dream the implied narrator Kurosawa actually had. But the ambiguity of the word *konna* in the original title makes it undecidable whether the dreams in the film are exact reproductions of, or are simply

based on, Kurosawa's dreams. See David Desser, "Narrating the Human Condition: *High and Low* and Story-Telling in Kurosawa's Cinema," in Goodwin, *Perspectives on Akira Kurosawa*, 169.

2 Another connection to *Throne of Blood* is the appearance of the snow woman and her paradoxical utterance, "The snow is warm. The ice is hot."

3 Chion, *Audio-Vision*, 152–54.

30. *Rhapsody in August*

1 Matthew Bernstein and Mark Ravina, review of *Rhapsody in August*, *American Historical Review* 98, no. 4 (October 1993): 1163.

2 Audie Bock, "The Moralistic Cinema of Kurosawa," in *Kurosawa: Perceptions on Life, an Anthology of Essays*, ed. Kevin K. W. Chang (Honolulu: Honolulu Academy of Arts, 1991), 23.

3 Richie, *The Films of Akira Kurosawa*, 224.

4 Review of *Rhapsody in August*, *Variety*, 20 May 1991, 36; Richie, *The Films of Akira Kurosawa*, 224.

5 Matthew Bernstein and Mark Ravina interpret the scene in their review of the film as follows: "Clark knew that his family was from Nagasaki. He had never considered, however, that his relatives might have been killed by the bomb. In pressuring his aunt to come to Hawaii, he had been unwittingly demanding that she miss her husband's memorial service. His apology is distinctly 'Japanese,' in that it is concerned less with guilt and moral abstraction than with shame and a concern for human sentiment" (Bernstein and Ravina, review of *Rhapsody in August*, 1162). It is, however, difficult to understand why Clark's apology must be regarded as "distinctly 'Japanese.'" Does it mean that if Americans find themselves in a similar situation, they would not apologize? Do Americans apologize only when they are guilty according to some highly abstract moral standard without any regard to human sentiment? I just do not see any need for perpetuating the questionable dichotomy of two "cultural patterns" based on the notions of guilt and shame.

6 Bock, "The Moralistic Cinema of Kurosawa," 23; Bernstein and Ravina, review of *Rhapsody in August*, 1163.

7 *Rhapsody in August* does not deal with the Japanese military campaigns in Asia and the Pacific, and to this extent, the film is vulnerable to the criticism that it fails to contextualize the atomic destruction of Nagasaki in the history of Japanese colonialism and imperialistic expansionism. However, nothing in the film can lead to the speculation that "none of

her [Kane's] eight brothers seems to have left Japan to fight in China or Southeast Asia, a statistical improbability" (Bernstein and Ravina, review of *Rhapsody in August*, 1163). On the contrary, Kane says that some of her siblings died in "faraway places," thus hinting that they might have died as colonial settlers or soldiers during the war.

8 Kurosawa Akira, "*Hachigatsu no rapusodi* kansei daihon," *Kinema junpo*, part 1 (January 1992): 43.

31. *Madadayo*

1 For instance, one of Hyakken's students, Amaki (Tokoro Joji), says: "Sensei, during the war we forgot how beautiful the moon is, didn't we?" As I already pointed out, similar remarks are made by characters in *Stray Dog* and *Ikiru*. During the American air raid that destroys his house, Hyakken is able to take only one book with him: *Hojoki* (1212) by Kamo no Chomei (1153–1216). Like Chomei, who observed the collapse of the aristocratic world from his "ten foot square hut," Hyakken and his wife move into a tiny shack. Bruno Taut, the model for Ludwig Lange, the protagonist of Kurosawa's unfilmed script *A German at Daruma Temple* (1941), lived in a tiny Japanese style cottage with his wife from 1934 to 1936. One of Taut's favorite books was also Chomei's *Hojoki* (Miyamoto Kenji, *Katsura Rikyu: Bruno Tauto wa shogensuru* [Tokyo: Kashima shuppankai, 1995], 145–46). For a meticulous comparison between the fictional biography of Hyakken in the film and the biography of Kurosawa, see Ogata Toshiro, "Kyojin no ripurei," in *Isetsu Kurosawa Akira*, ed. Bungei Shunju (Tokyo: Bungei Shunju, 1994), 178–213.

FILMOGRAPHY

This filmography is largely based on information found in the following
sources: *Zenshu Kurosawa Akira; Kurosawa Akira shusei II; Toho 40 nen
eiga engeki terebi sakuhin risuto; Kinema junpo: eiga video iyabukku;*
various issues of *Kinema junpo;* Stuart Galbraith, *The Japanese Filmography;* Tad Bentley Hammer, *International Film Prizes: An Encyclopedia;*
Peter C. Mowrey, *Award Winning Films: A Viewer's Reference to 2,700
Acclaimed Motion Pictures;* Michael Gebert, *The Encyclopedia of Movie
Awards;* Roy Pickard, *The Award Movies: A Complete Guide from A to
Z.* The other Kurosawa filmographies previously published in English
are also consulted, and inaccurate information and mistakes contained
in them are corrected as much as possible. Unless otherwise noted, all
films are in black-and-white and the standard size with the aspect ratio
of 1.33:1.

Sanshiro Sugata (Sugata Sanshiro, 1943)

Production and distribution: Toho. 77 minutes. 6,929 feet. Released
25 March 1943.

Scenario: Kurosawa Akira, based on the novel by Tomita Tsuneo. Photography: Mimura Akira. Lighting: Onuma Masayoshi. Art direction: Totsuka
Masao. Editing: Goto Toshio and Kurosawa Akira. Music: Suzuki Seichi. Sound: Higuchi Tomohisa. Assistant directors: Sugie Toshio and
Nakamura Tsutomu. Producer: Matsuzaki Keiji.

Cast: Fujita Susumu (Sugata Sanshiro), Okochi Denjiro (Yano Shogoro),
Tsukigata Ryunosuke (Higaki Gennosuke), Shimura Takashi (Murai
Hansuke), Todoroki Yukiko (Sayo), Kosugi Yoshio (Monma Saburo),
Hanai Ranko (Osumi), Kono Akitake (Dan Yoshimaro), Kiyokawa Soji
(Toda Yujiro), Aoyama Sugisaku (Iinuma Tsunetami), Kodo Kokuten
(Priest), Sugai Ichiro (Superintendent-General Mishima).

Award: Kokumin Eiga [national film] Encouragement Award (Japan).

The Most Beautiful (Ichiban utsukushiku, 1944)

Production: Toho. Distribution: Eiga Haikyusha. 85 minutes. 3,061 feet (16 mm print). Released 13 April 1944.
Scenario: Kurosawa Akira. Photography: Ohara Joji. Lighting: Onuma Masayoshi. Art direction: Abe Teruaki. Music: Suzuki Seichi. Sound recording: Shimonaga Hisashi. Assistant directors: Usami Hitoshi and Horikawa Hiromichi. Producer: Ito Motohiko.
Cast: Shimura Takashi (factory head), Kiyokawa Soji (chief of general affairs section), Sugai Ichiro (chief of labor section), Irie Takako (Mizushima Tokuko), Yaguchi Yoko (Watanabe Tsuru), Kono Akitake (music coach), Yokoyama Unpei (janitor).

Sanshiro Sugata, Part 2 (Zoku Sugata Sanshiro, 1945)

Production: Toho. Distribution: Eiga Haikyusha. 82 minutes. 7,366 feet. Released 3 May 1945.
Scenario: Kurosawa Akira. Photography: Suzuki Hiroshi. Lighting: Ishii Choshiro. Art direction: Kubo Kazuo. Editing: Yaguchi Yoshie. Music: Suzuki Seichi. Sound recording: Kameyama Shoji. Assistant directors: Usami Hitoshi and Horikawa Hiromichi. Producer: Ito Motohiko.
Cast: Fujita Susumu (Sugata Sanshiro), Okochi Denjiro (Yano Shogoro), Tsukigata Ryunosuke (Higaki Gennosuke and Tesshin), Kono Akitake (Higaki Genzaburo), Todoroki Yukiko (Sayo), Kiyokawa Soji (Toda Yujiro), Mori Masayuki (Dan Yoshimaro), Miyaguchi Seiji (Tsuzaki Kohei), Sugai Ichiro (Nunobiki Kozo).

The Men Who Tread on the Tiger's Tail
(Tora no o o fumu otokotachi, 1945)

Production and distribution: Toho. 58 minutes. 7,366 feet. Released 24 April 1952. (The film was completed in September 1945.)
Scenario: Kurosawa Akira, based on the Kabuki play *Kanjincho.* Photography: Ito Takeo. Lighting: Hiraoka Ganji. Art direction: Kubo Kazuo. Editing: Goto Toshio. Music: Hattori Tadashi. Sound recording: Hasebe Keiji. Sound effects: Minawa Ichiro. Producer: Ito Motohiko.
Cast: Okochi Denjiro (Benkei), Fujita Susumu (Togashi), Enomoto Ken'ichi (Porter), Mori Masayuki (Kamei), Shimura Takashi (Kataoka), Kono

Akitake (Ise), Kosugi Yoshio (Suruga), Yokoo Dekao (Hitachibo), Iwai Hanshiro (Yoshitsune), Kiyokawa Soji (Togashi's messenger), Kubo Yasuo (Kajiwara's messenger).

No Regrets for Our Youth (Waga seishun ni kuinashi, 1946)

Production and distribution: Toho. 110 minutes. 9,913 feet. Released 29 October 1946. (Because of the labor dispute, the film was shown at Nikkatsu theaters.)

Scenario: Hisaita Eijiro. Photography: Nakai Asakazu. Lighting: Ishii Choshiro. Art direction: Kitagawa Keiji. Editing: Goto Toshio. Music: Hattori Tadashi. Sound recording: Suzuki Isamu. Sound effects: Minawa Ichiro. Assistant directors: Horikawa Hiromichi, Maeda Akitoshi, and Horiuchi Masaru. Producer: Matsuzaki Keiji.

Cast: Hara Setsuko (Yagihara Yukie), Okochi Denjiro (Professor Yagihara), Miyoshi Eiko (his wife), Fujita Susumu (Noge Ryukichi), Kodo Kokuten (Noge's father), Sugimura Haruko (Noge's mother), Kono Akitake (Itokawa), Shimura Takashi ("Dokuichigo"), Shimizu Masao (Professor Hakozaki), Tanaka Haruo (student).

Award: *Kinema junpo,* number two film of the year.

One Wonderful Sunday (Subarashiki nichiyobi, 1947)

Production and distribution: Toho. 109 minutes. 9,801 feet. released: 1 July 1947.

Scenario: Uekusa Keinosuke. Photography: Nakai Asakazu. Lighting: Kishida Kuichiro. Art direction: Kubo Kazuo. Editing: Imaizumi Zenju. Music: Hattori Tadashi. Sound recording: Yasue Juen. Sound effects: Minawa Ichiro. Assistant directors: Kobayashi Tsuneo and Imaizumi Zenju. Producer: Motogi Sojiro.

Cast: Numasaki Isao (Yuzo), Nakakita Chieko (Masako), Watanabe Atsushi (hooligan), Nakamura Zeko (steamed bun vendor), Sugai Ichiro (black marketeer), Shimizu Masao (dance hall manager).

Awards: Mainichi Eiga Concourse (Mainichi eiga konkuru, Japan), Best Director, and Best Scenario (Uekusa Keinosuke); *Kinema junpo,* number six film of the year.

Drunken Angel (Yoidore tenshi, 1948)

Production and distribution: Toho. 98 minutes. 8,815 feet. Released 27 April 1948.

Scenario: Uekusa Keinosuke and Kurosawa Akira. Photography: Ito Takeo. Lighting: Yoshizawa Kinzo. Art direction: Matsuyama Takashi. Editing: Kono Akikazu. Music: Hayasaka Fumio. Song: "Janguru bugi" by Kurosawa Akira (lyrics) and Hattori Ryoichi (music). Sound recording: Konuma Wataru. Sound effects: Minawa Ichiro. Assistant director: Kobayashi Tsuneo. Producer: Motogi Sojiro.

Cast: Shimura Takashi (Sanada), Mifune Toshiro (Matsunaga), Yamamoto Reizaburo (Okada), Nakakita Chieko (Miyo), Kogure Michiyo (Nanae), Sengoku Noriko (Gin), Shindo Eitaro (Takahama), Iida Choko (old wet nurse), Tonoyama Taiji (shop owner), Kuga Yoshiko (girl), Kasagi Shizuko (singer), Shimizu Masao (boss).

Awards: Mainichi Eiga Concourse, Best Film, Best Photography (Ito Takeo), and Best Music (Hayasaka Fumio); *Kinema junpo*, number one film of the year.

The Quiet Duel (Shizukanaru ketto, 1949)

Production and distribution: Daiei. 95 minutes. 8,508 feet. Released 13 March 1949.

Scenario: Kurosawa Akira and Taniguchi Senkichi, based on the play *Dataii* (The Abortion Doctor), by Kikuta Kazuo. Photography: Aisaka Soichi. Lighting: Shibata Tsunekichi. Art direction: Imai Koichi. Editing: Tsujii Masanori. Music: Ifukube Akira. Sound recording: Hasegawa Mitsuo. Sound effects: Hanaoka Katsujiro. Assistant directors: Nakamura Masunari, Furukawa Takumi, Saijo Fumiyoshi, and Yuge Taro. Producers: Motogi Sojiro and Ichikawa Hisao.

Cast: Mifune Toshiro (Fujisaki Kyoji), Shimura Takashi (Fujisaki Konosuke), Sanjo Miki (Matsumoto Misao), Uemura Kenjiro (Nakada Tatsuo), Nakakita Chieko (Nakada Takiko), Sengoku Noriko (Minegishi Rui).

Award: *Kinema junpo*, number seven film of the year.

Stray Dog (Nora inu, 1949)

Production: Shintoho/Eiga Geijutsu Kyokai. Distribution: Toho. 122 minutes. 10,985 feet. Released 17 October 1949.

Scenario: Kurosawa Akira and Kikushima Ryuzo. Photography: Nakai Asakazu. Lighting: Ishii Choshiro. Art direction: Matsuyama Takashi. Editing: Goto Toshio. Music: Hayasaka Fumio. Sound recording: Yanoguchi Fumio. Sound effects: Minawa Ichiro. Assistant directors: Honda Ishiro and Imaizumi Zenju. Producer: Motogi Sojiro.

Cast: Mifune Toshiro (Detective Murakami), Shimura Takashi (Detective Sato), Kimura Isao (Yusa), Awaji Keiko (Namiki Harumi), Miyoshi Eiko (her mother), Yamamoto Reizaburo (Honda), Sengoku Noriko (his mistress), Kawamura Reikichi (Detective Ichikawa), Ito Yunosuke (theater manager), Chiaki Minoru (stage director), Shimizu Masao (Nakamura), Honma Noriko (Yusa's sister), Tono Eijiro (her husband), Matsumoto Kappei (drinking-stall owner), Iiida Choko (proprietor of Kogetsu), Kishi Teruko (Ogin), Sugai Ichiro (Hotel Yayoi's manager), Kodo Kokuten (custodian).

Awards: Mainichi Eiga Concourse, Best Actor (Shimura Takashi), Best Photography (Nakai Asakazu), Best Music (Hayasaka Fumio), and Best Art Direction (Matsuyama Takashi); National Art Festival (Geijutsusai, Japan), Minister of Education Prize; *Kinema junpo,* number three film of the year.

Scandal (Sukyandaru [Shubun], 1950)

Production: Shochiku/Eiga Geijutsu Kyokai. Distribution: Shochiku. 105 minutes. 9,420 feet. Released 30 April 1950.

Scenario: Kurosawa Akira and Kikushima Ryuzo. Photography: Ubukata Toshio. Lighting: Kato Masao. Art direction: Hamada Tatsuo. Editing: Sugihara Yoshi. Music: Hayasaka Fumio. Assistant directors: Hagiyama Teruo, Kobayashi Keizaburo, Nomura Yoshitaro, Nihonmatsu Yoshimizu, Nakahira Ko. Producers: Koide Takashi and Motogi Sojiro.

Cast: Mifune Toshiro (Aoe Ichiro), Yamaguchi Toshiko (Saijo Miyako), Shimura Takashi (Hiruta), Katsuragi Yoko (Masako), Sengoku Noriko (Sumie), Ozawa Sakae [Eitaro] (Hori), Himori Shin'ichi (editorial staff), Mitsui Koji (cameraman), Shimizu Masao (judge), Aoyama Sugisaku (Dr. Kataoka), Hidari Bokuzen (drunk), Kodo Kokuten (woodcutter), Ueda Kichijiro (woodcutter), Tonoyama Taiji (Aoe's friend), Chiaki Minoru (Aoe's friend).

Award: *Kinema junpo,* number six film of the year.

Rashomon (Rashomon, 1950)

Production and distribution: Daiei. 87 minutes. 7,899 feet. Released 26 August 1950.

Scenario: Kurosawa Akira and Hashimoto Shinobu, based on the stories "In a Grove" and "Rashomon," by Akutagawa Ryunosuke. Photography: Miyagawa Kazuo. Lighting: Okamoto Ken'ichi. Art direction: Matsuyama Takashi. Editing: Nishida Shigeo. Music: Hayasaka Fumio. Sound recording: Otani Iwao. Sound effects: Yamane Shoichi. Assistant directors: Kato Tai, Wakasugi Mitsuo, and Tanaka Tokuzo. Producer: Minoura Jingo and Motogi Sojiro.

Cast: Mifune Toshiro (Tajomaru), Mori Masayuki (Takehiro), Kyo Machiko (Masago), Shimura Takashi (woodcutter), Chiaki Minoru (priest), Ueda Kichijiro (commoner), Kato Daisuke (police agent), Honma Fumiko (medium).

Awards: Venice International Film Festival, Golden Lion, and Italian Critics Prize for Best Foreign Film (1951); American Academy Awards, Best Foreign Language Film (1951); National Board of Review (United States), Best Foreign Film, and Best Director (1951); Mainichi Eiga Concourse, Best Actress (Kyo Machiko); Tokyo Blue Ribbon Prizes, Best Scenario (Kurosawa Akira and Hashimoto); *Kinema junpo,* number five film of the year.

The Idiot (Hakuchi, 1951)

Production and distribution: Shochiku. 166 minutes. 14,942 feet. Released 23 May 1951.

Scenario: Hisaita Eijiro and Kurosawa Akira, based on the novel by Fyodor Dostoyevsky. Photography: Ubukata Toshio. Lighting: Tamura Akio. Art direction: Matsuyama Takashi. Editing: Sugihara Yoshi. Music: Hayasaka Fumio. Sound recording: Senoo Yoshisaburo. Assistant directors: Hagiyama Teruo, Kobayashi Keizaburo, Nomura Yoshitaro, Nihonmatsu Yoshimizu, Nakahira Ko, and Ikoma Senri. Producers: Koide Takashi and Motogi Sojiro.

Cast: Mori Masayuki (Kameda Kinji), Mifune Toshiro (Akama Denkichi), Hara Setsuko (Nasu Taeko), Shimura Takashi (Ono), Higashiyama Chieko (Ono Satoko), Kuga Yoshiko (Ono Ayako), Kodo Kokuten (Kayama Junpei), Miyoshi Eiko (his wife), Chiaki Minoru (Kayama Mutsuo), Sengoku Noriko (Kayama Takako), Hidari Bokuzen (Karube).

Ikiru (Ikiru, 1952)

Production and distribution: Toho. 143 minutes. 12,845 feet. Released
9 October 1952.

Scenario: Kurosawa Akira, Hashimoto Shinobu, and Oguni Hideo. Photography: Nakai Asakazu. Lighting: Mori Shigeru. Art direction: Matsuyama Takashi. Editing: Iwashita Koichi. Music: Hayasaka Fumio. Sound
recording: Yanoguchi Fumio. Sound effects: Minawa Ichiro. Assistant directors: Horikawa Hiromichi, Marubayashi Sadanobu, and Maru Teruo.
Producer: Motogi Sojiro.

Cast: Shimura Takashi (Watanabe Kanji), Kaneko Nobuo (his son Mitsuo),
Odagiri Miki (Odagiri Toyo), Fujiwara Kamatari (Ono), Tanaka Haruo
(Sakai), Hidari Bokuzen (Ohara), Himori Shin'ichi (Kimura), Chiaki
Minoru (Noguchi), Honma Noriko, Miyoshi Eiko, Sugai Kin (house-
wives), Watanabe Atsushi (patient), Shimizu Masao (doctor), Kimura
Ko (his assistant), Ito Yunosuke (writer), Nakamura Nobuo (deputy
mayor), Miyaguchi Seiji (gang boss), Kato Daisuke (gang member),
Kobori Makoto (Watanabe Kiichi), Urabe Kumeko (his wife Tatsu).

Awards: Berlin International Film Festival, Prize of the Berlin Senate (1954);
Mainichi Eiga Concourse, Best Film, Best Scenario (Kurosawa Akira,
Hashimoto Shinobu, and Oguni Hideo), and Best Sound (Yanoguchi Fumio); National Art Festival, Minister of Education Award; *Kinema junpo*,
number one film of the year.

Seven Samurai (Shichinin no samurai, 1954)

Production and distribution: Toho. 207 minutes. 18,589 feet. (Part 1, 107
minutes, 9,580 feet; intermission, 5 minutes, 472 feet; part 2, 95 minutes,
8,537 feet.) Released 26 April 1954.

Scenario: Kurosawa Akira, Hashimoto Shinobu, and Oguni Hideo. Photography: Nakai Asakazu. Lighting: Mori Shigeru. Art direction: Matsuyama Takashi. Editing: Iwashita Koichi. Music: Hayasaka Fumio. Sound
recording: Yanoguchi Fumio. Sound effects: Minawa Ichiro. Assistant
directors: Horikawa Hiromichi, Shimizu Katsuya, Hirosawa Ei, Tajitsu
Tairyo, and Kaneko Satoshi. Producer: Motogi Sojiro.

Cast: Shimura Takashi (Shimada Kanbei), Mifune Toshiro (Kikuchiyo),
Inaba Yoshio (Gorobei), Miyaguchi Seiji (Kyuzo), Chiaki Minoru (Hei-
hachi), Kato Daisuke (Shichiroji), Kimura Isao (Katsushiro), Kodo
Kokuten (Gisaku), Fujiwara Kamatari (Manzo), Tsushima Keiko (Shino),

Hidari Bokuzen (Yohei), Kosugi Yoshio (Mosuke), Tsuchiya Yoshio (Rikichi), Shimazaki Yukiko (his wife), Takagi Shinpei (boss), Ueda Kichijiro (bandit), Tono Eijiro (thief), Watanabe Atsushi (steamed bun vendor), Kamiyama Sojin (blind lute player), Nakadai Tatsuya (samurai).

Awards: Venice International Film Festival, Silver Prize; Mainichi Eiga Concourse, Best Supporting Actor (Miyaguchi Seiji); Tokyo Blue Ribbon Prizes, Best Music (Hayasaka Fumio); *Kinema junpo*, number three film of the year.

Record of a Living Being (Ikimono no kiroku, 1955)

Production and distribution: Toho. 103 minutes. 9,250 feet. Released 22 November 1955.

Scenario: Hashimoto Shinobu, Oguni Hideo, and Kurosawa Akira. Photography: Nakai Asakazu. Lighting: Kishida Kuichiro. Art direction: Muraki Yoshiro. Editing: Obata Chozo. Music: Hayasaka Fumio, completed by Sato Masaru. Sound recording: Yanoguchi Fumio. Sound effects: Minawa Ichiro. Assistant directors: Marubayashi Sadanobu, Nonagase Samaji, Tajitsu Tairyo, Sano Takeshi, and Nakamura Takao. Producer: Motogi Sojiro.

Cast: Mifune Toshiro (Nakajima Kiichi), Miyoshi Eiko (his wife Toyo), Sada Yutaka (Nakajima Ichiro), Sengoku Noriko (his wife Kimie), Chiaki Minoru (Nakajima Jiro), Aoyama Kyoko (Nakajima Sue), Shimizu Masao (Yamazaki Takao), Togo Haruko (his wife Yoshi), Negishi Akemi (Kuribayashi Asako), Ueda Kichijiro (her father), Tono Eijiro (the landowner from Brazil), Fujiwara Kamatari (Okamoto), Mitsuda Ken (Araki), Watanabe Atsushi (Ishida), Ogawa Toranosuke (Hori), Hidari Bokuzen (landowner), Kodo Kokuten (employee's family), Honma Noriko (employee's family), Nakamura Nobuo (psychiatrist), Shimura Takashi (Harada), Kato Kazuo (his son Susumu).

Award: *Kinema junpo*, number four film of the year.

Throne of Blood (Kumonosujo, 1957)

Production and distribution: Toho. 110 minutes. 9,852 feet. Released 15 January 1957.

Scenario: Hashimoto Shinobu, Kikushima Ryuzo, Oguni Hideo, and Kurosawa Akira, based on the play *Macbeth,* by William Shakespeare. Photography: Nakai Asakazu. Lighting: Kishida Kuichiro. Art direction: Muraki Yoshiro. Editing: Obata Chozo. Music: Sato Masaru. Sound recording: Yanoguchi Fumio. Sound effects: Minawa Ichiro. Assistant directors: Nonagase Samaji, Shimizu Katsuya, Tajitsu Tairyo, Kaneko Satoshi, Sano Takeshi, and Sakano Yoshimitsu. Producers: Kurosawa Akira and Motogi Sojiro.

Cast: Mifune Toshiro (Washizu Taketoki), Yamada Isuzu (his wife Asaji), Chiaki Minoru (Miki Yoshiaki), Kubo Akira (Miki Yoshiteru), Sasaki Takamaru (Tsuzuki Kuniharu), Tachikawa Yoichi (Tsuzuki Kunimaru), Shimura Takashi (Odagura Noriyasu), Naniwa Chieko (witch), Kodo Kokuten (commanding officer), Kimura Isao (ghost), Miyaguchi Seiji (ghost), Nakamura Nobuo (ghost).

Awards: Mainichi Eiga Concourse, Best Actor (Mifune Toshiro), and Art Direction (Muraki Yoshiro); Tokyo Blue Ribbon Prizes, Best Art Direction (Muraki Yoshiro); *Kinema junpo,* Best Actress (Yamada Isuzu), number four film of the year.

The Lower Depths (Donzoko, 1957)

Production and distribution: Toho. 125 minutes. 11,224 feet. Released 17 September 1957.

Scenario: Oguni Hideo and Kurosawa Akira, based on the play by Maxim Gorky. Photography: Yamasaki Ichio. Lighting: Mori Shigeru. Art direction: Muraki Yoshiro. Editing: Obata Chozo. Music: Sato Masaru. Sound recording: Yanoguchi Fumio. Sound effects: Minawa Ichiro. Assistant directors: Nonagase Samaji, Tajitsu Tairyo, Sakano Yoshimitsu, and Kaneko Satoshi. Producer: Kurosawa Akira.

Cast: Mifune Toshiro (Sutekichi), Nakamura Ganjiro (Rokubei), Yamada Isuzu (Osugi), Kagawa Kyoko (Okayo), Hidari Bokuzen (Kahei), Chiaki Minoru ("Lord"), Fujiwara Kamatari ("Actor"), Tono Eijiro (Tomekichi), Miyoshi Eiko (Asa), Negishi Akemi (Osen), Kiyokawa Nijiko (Otaki), Tanaka Haruo (Tatsu), Mitsui Koji (Yoshisaburo), Ueda Kichijiro (Shimazo), Fujiki Yu (Unokichi), Fujitayama (Tsugaru), Watanabe Atsushi (Kuma).

Awards: Mainichi Eiga Concourse, Best Supporting Actor (Mitsui Koji); Tokyo Blue Ribbon Prizes, Best Supporting Actor (Mitsui Koji); *Kinema junpo,* number ten film of the year.

The Hidden Fortress (Kakushi toride no san akunin, 1958)

Production and distribution: Toho. 126 minutes. 11,311 feet. Tohoscope
(2.35:1). Released 28 December 1958.

Scenario: Kikushima Ryuzo, Oguni Hideo, Hashimoto Shinobu, and Kurosawa Akira. Photography: Yamasaki Ichio. Art direction: Muraki Yoshiro.
Editing: Obata Chozo. Music: Sato Masaru. Sound recording: Yanoguchi Fumio. Sound effects: Minawa Ichiro. Assistant directors: Nonagase
Samaji, Tajitsu Tairyo, Sakano Yoshimitsu, Sano Takashi, Matsue Yoichi,
and Takase Masahiro. Producers: Fujimoto Masumi and Kurosawa Akira.

Cast: Mifune Toshiro (Makabe Rokurota), Chiaki Minoru (Tahei), Fujiwara Kamatari (Matashichi), Fujita Susumu (Tadokoro Hyoe), Shimura
Takashi (Nagakura Izumi), Uehara Misa (Princess Yuki), Miyoshi Eiko
(lady-in-waiting), Higuchi Toshiko (peasant girl), Fujiki Yu (barrier
guard), Tsuchiya Yoshio (Hayakawa's cavalryman), Kodo Kokuten (man
at the signboard), Kato Takeshi (stray soldier), Mitsui Koji (Yamana's
soldier), Ogawa Toranosuke (barrier magistrate), Ueda Kichijiro (slave
trader), Sawamura Ikio (gambler), Kosugi Yoshio (Akizuki's common
soldier), Sada Yutaka (barrier guard), Kuze Ryu (Akizuki's common
soldier).

Awards: Berlin International Film Festival, Best Direction (Kurosawa), and
International Film Critics Prize (1959); Tokyo Blue Ribbon Prizes, Best
Picture; *Kinema junpo,* number two film of the year.

The Bad Sleep Well (Warui yatsu hodo yoku nemuru, 1960)

Production: Toho/Kurosawa Production. Distribution: Toho. 133 minutes.
11,959 feet. Tohoscope (2.35:1). Released 4 September 1960.

Scenario: Oguni Hideo, Hisaita Eijiro, Kurosawa Akira, Kikushima Ryuzo,
and Hashimoto Shinobu. Photography: Aizawa Yuzuru. Lighting: Inohara Ichiro. Art direction: Muraki Yoshiro. Editing assistant: Kaneko
Reiko. Music: Sato Masaru. Sound recording: Yanoguchi Fumio. Sound
effects: Minawa Ichiro. Assistant directors: Moritani Shiro, Sakano
Yoshimitsu, Nishimura Kiyoshi, Matsue Yoichi, and Kawakita Kazuko.
Producers: Tanaka Tomoyuki and Kurosawa Akira.

Cast: Mifune Toshiro (Nishi Koichi), Kato Takeshi (Itakura), Mori Ma-
sayuki (Iwabuchi), Kagawa Kyoko (his daughter Yoshiko), Mihashi
Tatsuya (his son Tatsuo), Shimura Takashi (Moriyama), Nishimura Akira
(Shirai), Fujiwara Kamatari (Wada), Sugai Kin (his wife), Ryu Chishu
(Nonaka), Miyaguchi Seiji (Okakura), Mitsui Koji (journalist), Mitsuda

Ken (Arimura), Nakamura Nobuo (lawyer), Fujita Susumu (detective), Sazanka Kyu (Kaneko), Tsuchiya Yoshio (secretary), Sada Yutaka (weddings receptionist), Sawamura Ikio (taxi driver), Tanaka Kunie (assassin).
Awards: Mainichi Eiga Concourse, Best Supporting Actor (Mori Masayuki), and Best Music (Sato Masaru); *Kinema junpo*, Best Scenario (Hashimoto Shinobu), number three film of the year.

Yojimbo (Yojinbo, 1961)

Production: Toho/Kurosawa Production. Distribution: Toho. 110 minutes. 9,930 feet. CinemaScope (2.35:1). Released 25 April 1961.
Scenario: Kikushima Ryuzo and Kurosawa Akira. Photography: Miyagawa Kazuo. Lighting: Ishii Choshiro. Art direction: Muraki Yoshiro. Editing assistant: Kaneko Reiko. Music: Sato Masaru. Sound recording: Mikami Choshichiro. Sound effects: Minawa Ichiro. Assistant directors: Moritani Shiro, Deme Masanobu, Yoshimatsu Yasuhiro, and Wada Kakun. Producers: Tanaka Tomoyuki and Kikushima Ryuzo.
Cast: Mifune Toshiro (Kuwabatake Sanjuro), Tono Eijiro (Gonji), Fujiwara Kamatari (Tazaemon), Shimura Takashi (Tokuemon), Kawazu Seizaburo (Seibei), Yamada Isuzu (Orin), Tachikawa Hiroshi (Yoichiro), Sazanka Kyu (Ushitora), Nakadai Tatsuya (Unosuke), Kato Daisuke (Inokichi), Sawamura Ikio (Hansuke), Nishimura Akira (Kuma), Kato Takeshi (Kobuhachi), Tsuchiya Yoshio (Kohei), Tsukasa Yoko (Nui), Fujita Susumu (Honma), Rashomon Tsunagoro (Kannuki), Sada Yutaka (Matsukichi), Honma Noriko (farmer's wife), Natsuki Yosuke (her son).
Awards: Venice International Film Festival, Best Actor (Mifune Toshiro); Tokyo Blue Ribbon Prizes, Best Actor (Mifune Toshiro), and Best Music (Sato Masaru); *Kinema junpo*, Best Actor (Mifune Toshiro), number two film of the year.

Sanjuro (Tsubaki Sanjuro, 1962)

Production: Toho/Kurosawa Production. Distribution: Toho. 95 minutes. 8,590 feet. CinemaScope. Released 1 January 1962.
Scenario: Kikushima Ryuzo, Oguni Hideo, and Kurosawa Akira. Photography: Koizumi Fukuzo and Saito Takao. Lighting: Inohara Ichiro. Art direction: Muraki Yoshiro. Editing assistant: Kaneko Reiko. Music: Sato Masaru. Sound recording: Konuma Wataru. Sound effects: Minawa Ichiro. Assistant directors: Moritani Shiro, Deme Masanobu, Matsue

Yoichi, and Wada Kakun. Producers: Tanaka Tomoyuki and Kikushima Ryuzo.

Cast: Mifune Toshiro (Tsubaki Sanjuro), Nakadai Tatsuya (Muroto Hanbei), Kayama Yuzo (Izaka Iori), Shimura Takashi (Kurofuji), Fujiwara Kamatari (Takebayashi), Shimizu Masao (Kikui), Ito Yunosuke (Mutsuta), Irie Takako (his wife), Dan Reiko (Chidori), Kobayashi Keiju (Kimura), Hirata Akihiko (Terada), Tanaka Kunie (Yasukawa), Tachikawa Hiroshi (Kahara), Ehara Tatsuyoshi (Sekiguchi), Tsuchiya Yoshio (Hirose), Kubo Akira (elder Morishima), Hari Tatsuhiko (younger Morishima), Ogawa Toranosuke (Kurofuji's steward), Sada Yutaka (Kikui's subordinate).

Awards: *Kinema junpo*, Best Actor (Nakadai Tatsuya), number 5 film of the year.

High and Low (Tengoku to jigoku, 1963)

Production: Toho/Kurosawa Production. Distribution: Toho. 143 minutes. 12,882 feet. CinemaScope. Released 1 March 1963.

Scenario: Oguni Hideo, Kikushima Ryuzo, Hisaita Eijiro, and Kurosawa Akira, from the novel *King's Ransom*, by Ed McBain. Photography: Nakai Asakazu and Saito Takao. Lighting: Mori Hiromitsu. Art direction: Muraki Yoshiro. Editing assistant: Kaneko Reiko. Music: Sato Masaru. Sound recording: Yanoguchi Fumio. Sound effects: Minawa Ichiro. Assistant directors: Moritani Shiro, Deme Masanobu, Matsue Yoichi, and Omori Kenjiro. Producers: Tanaka Tomoyuki and Kikushima Ryuzo.

Cast: Mifune Toshiro (Gondo Kingo), Kagawa Kyoko (his wife Reiko), Mihashi Tatsuya (Kawanishi), Sada Yutaka (Aoki), Yamazaki Tsutomu (Takeuchi Ginji), Nakadai Tatsuya (Inspector Tokura), Shimura Takashi (chief of investigation headquarters), Fujita Susumu (head of investigation section), Ishiyama Kenjiro (Detective Taguchi), Kimura Isao (Detective Arai), Kato Takeshi (Detective Nakao), Tsuchiya Yoshio (Detective Murata), Mitsui Koji (journalist), Chiaki Minoru (journalist), Tazaki Jun (Kamitani), Nakamura Nobuo (Ishimaru), Ito Yunosuke (Baba), Tono Eijiro (factory worker), Shimizu Masao (warden), Sazanka Kyu (creditor), Hamamura Jun (creditor), Nishimura Akira (creditor), Kato Kazuo (crime lab investigator), Sawamura Ikio (trainman), Sugai Kin (drug addict).

Awards: Mainichi Eiga Concourse, Best Film, and Best Scenario (Oguni Hideo, Kikushima Ryuzo, Hisaita Eijiro, and Kurosawa Akira); *Kinema junpo*, number two film of the year.

Red Beard (Akahige, 1965)

Production: Toho/Kurosawa Production. Distribution: Toho. 185 minutes. 16,654 feet. CinemaScope. Released 3 April 1965.
Scenario: Ide Masato, Oguni Hideo, Kikushima Ryuzo, and Kurosawa Akira, based on *Akahige shinryo tan,* by Yamamoto Shugoro. Photography: Nakai Asakazu and Saito Takao. Lighting: Mori Hiromitsu. Art direction: Muraki Yoshiro. Editing assistant: Kaneko Reiko. Music: Sato Masaru. Sound recording: Watarai Shin. Sound effects: Minawa Ichiro. Assistant directors: Moritani Shiro, Deme Masanobu, Matsue Yoichi, and Omori Kenjiro. Producers: Tanaka Tomoyuki and Kikushima Ryuzo.
Cast: Mifune Toshiro (Niide Kyojo, "Red Beard"), Kayama Yuzo (Yasumoto Noboru), Ryu Chishu (his father), Tanaka Kinuyo (his mother), Yamazaki Tsutomu (Sahachi), Dan Reiko (Osugi), Kuwano Miyuki (Onaka), Kagawa Kyoko (the madwoman), Yanagi Eijiro (her father), Ehara Tatsuyoshi (Tsugawa Genzo), Niki Terumi (Otoyo), Negishi Akemi (Okuni), Zushi Yoshitaka (Choji), Sugai Kin (his mother), Tsuchiya Yoshio (Mori Handayu), Fujiwara Kamatari (Rokusuke), Tono Eijiro (Goheiji), Shimura Takashi (Izumiya Tokubei), Sugimura Haruko (Kin), Naito Yoko (Masae), Mitsuda Ken (her father), Mitsui Koji (Heikichi), Nishimura Akira (chief retainer), Hidari Bokuzen (patient), Watanabe Atsushi (patient), Sada Yutaka (tenement resident), Sawamura Ikio (tenement resident), Honma Noriko (tenement resident), Kuze Ryu (thug).
Awards: Venice International Film Festival, Best Actor (Mifune Toshiro), and Catholic Film Office award; Mainichi Eiga Concourse, Best Film; Tokyo Blue Ribbon Prizes, Best Film, Best Actor (Mifune Toshiro), and Best Supporting Actress (Niki Terumi); *Kinema junpo,* Best Film, and Best Director, number one film of the year.

Dodeskaden (Dodesukaden, 1970)

Production: Yonki no Kai/Toho. Distribution: Toho. 140 minutes. 12,566 feet. Color. Released 31 October 1970.
Scenario: Kurosawa Akira, Oguni Hideo, and Hashimoto Shinobu, based on the story collection *Kisetsu no nai machi* (The Town without Seasons), by Yamamoto Shugoro. Photography: Saito Takao and Fukuzawa Yasumichi. Lighting: Mori Hiromitsu. Art direction: Muraki Yoshiro and Muraki Shinobu. Editing assistant: Kaneko Reiko. Music: Takemitsu Toru. Sound recording: Yanoguchi Fumio. Sound effects: Minawa Ichiro. Assistant directors: Omori Kenjiro, Kawasaki Yoshisuke, Hashimoto

Koji, and Takizawa Nobumitsu. Producers: Kurosawa Akira and Matsue Yoichi.

Cast: Zushi Yoshitaka (Rokuchan), Sugai Kin (his mother Okuni), Ban Junzaburo (Shima Yukichi), Tange Kiyoko (his wife), Igawa Hisashi (Masuda Masuo), Okiyama Hideko (his wife Tatsu), Tanaka Kunie (Kawaguchi Hatsutaro), Yoshimura Jitsuko (his wife Yoshie), Mitani Noboru (beggar), Kawase Hiroyuki (his son), Akutagawa Hiroshi (Hei), Naraoka Tomoko (his wife Ocho), Watanabe Atsushi (Tanba), Minami Shinsuke (Sawamura Ryotaro), Kusunoki Yuko (his wife Misao), Matsumura Tatsuo (Kyota), Tsuji Imari (his wife Otane), Yamazaki Tomoko (his stepdaughter), Kametani Masahiko (Okabe), Kojima Sanji (thief), Kato Kazuo (painter), Fujiwara Kamatari (old man), Jerry Fujio ("Kumanbachi"), Mitsui Koji (stall owner).

Awards: Mainichi Eiga Concourse, Best Supporting Actress (Naraoka Tomoko); National Art Festival, Best Award for Yonki no Kai; *Kinema junpo,* Best Actor (Igawa Hisashi), number three film of the year.

Dersu Uzala (Derusu Uzara, 1975)

Production: Mosfilm. Distribution: Nihon Herald Eiga. 142 minutes. 12,743 feet. 70 mm widescreen. Color. Released 2 August 1975.

Scenario: Kurosawa Akira and Yuri Nagibin, based on the book by Vladimir Arseniev. Photography: Nakai Asakazu, Yuri Gantman, and Feodor Dobronravov. Art direction: Yuri Raksha. Music: Isaac Swartz. Associate directors: Kawasaki Tamotsu and Nogami Teruyo. Assistant directors: Vladimir Vasiliev and Minoshima Norio. Producers: Nikolai Sizov and Matsue Yoichi.

Cast: Maxim Munzuk (Dersu Uzala), Yuri Salomin (Valdimir Arseniev), Svetlana Danielchenko (his wife), Schemeikl Chokmorov (Jan Bao), Piyatokov, Purohanov, Valdimir Bururakov, Alexander Filipenko, Yuri Chernov, and Alexander Alexandrov (members of the 1902 expedition team).

Awards: Moscow International Film Festival, Grand Prix; American Academy Awards, Best Foreign Language Film; Nastri d'Argento (Silver Ribbons, Italy), Best Foreign Director (1976); David Di Donatello Prizes (Italy), Best Foreign Director (1976); *Kinema junpo,* number five foreign film of the year (1975).

Kagemusha (Kagemusha, 1980)

Production: Toho/Kurosawa Production. Distribution: Toho. 180 minutes, 16,201 feet (first domestic version); 159 minutes, 14,296 feet (international/revised version). VistaVision (1.85:1). Color. Released 26 April 1980.

Scenario: Kurosawa Akira and Ide Masato. Photography: Saito Takao and Ueda Masaharu, with the collaboration of Nakai Asakazu and Miyagawa Kazuo. Lighting: Sano Takeji. Art direction: Muraki Yoshiro. Editing assistants: Iwatani Keisuke and Minami Tome. Music: Ikebe Shin'ichiro. Sound recording: Yanoguchi Fumio. Sound effects: Minawa Ichiro. Associate director: Honda Ishiro. Assistant directors: Okada Bunsuke, Inoue Hideyuki, Okawara Takao, Koizumi Takashi, and Yoneda Okihiro. Producers: Kurosawa Akira and Tanaka Tomoyuki; Francis Coppola and George Lucas (international version).

Cast: Nakadai Tatsuya (Takeda Shingen and Kagemusha), Yamazaki Tsutomu (Takeda Nobukado), Hagiwara Ken'ichi (Takeda Katsuyori), Yui Kota (Takeda Takemaru), Otaki Shuji (Yamagata Masakage), Murota Hideo (Baba Nobuharu), Shiho Takayuki (Naito Masatoyo), Sugimori Shuhei (Kosaka Tadamasa), Shimizu Noboru (Hara Masatane), Shimizu Koji (Atobe Katsusuke), Baisho Mitsuko (Oyu no kata), Momoi Kaori (Otsuya no kata), Yui Masayuki (Tokugawa Ieyasu), Ryu Daisuke (Oda Nobunaga), Nezu Jinpachi (Tsuchiya Sohachiro).

Awards: Cannes International Film Festival, Palme d'Or; British Academy Awards, Best Director (Kurosawa), and Best Costume Design (Momosawa Seiichiro); The Césars (France), Best Foreign Film; Nastri d'Argento, Best Foreign Director; David Di Donatello prizes, Best Foreign Director; Mainichi Eiga Concourse, Best Film, Grand Prize, Best Director, Best Actor (Nakadai Tatsuya), Best Art Direction (Muraki Yoshiro), and Best Music (Ikebe Shin'ichiro); Tokyo Blue Ribbon Prizes, Best Film, Best Actor (Nakadai tatsuya), and New Actor/Actress (Ryu Daisuke); *Kinema junpo,* Best Supporting Actor (Yamazaki Tsutomu), number two film of the year.

Ran (Ran, 1985)

Production: Herald Ace/Greenwich Film. Distribution: Toho/Nippon Herald. 158.5 minutes. 14,265 feet. VistaVision. Color. Released 1 June 1985.

Scenario: Kurosawa Akira, Oguni Hideo, and Ide Masato. Photography:

Saito Takao and Ueda Masaharu, with the collaboration of Nakai Asa-kazu. Lighting: Sano Takeji. Art direction: Muraki Yoshiro and Muraki Shinobu. Editing assistants: Otsubo Ryusuke and Minami Tome. Music: Takemitsu Toru. Sound recording: Yanoguchi Fumio and Yoshida Sho-shichiro. Sound effects: Minawa Ichiro. Costumes: Wada Emi. Associate director: Honda Ishiro. Assistant directors: Okada Bunsuke, Koizumi Takashi, Yoneda Okihiro, Yamamoto Ichiro, and Nozaki Kunio. Pro-ducers: Furukawa Katsumi, Serge Silberman, and Hara Masato.

Cast: Nakadai Tatsuya (Ichimonji Hidetora), Terao Akira (Taro), Nezu Jinpachi (Jiro), Ryu Daisuke (Saburo), Harada Mieko (Lady Kaede), Miyazaki Yoshiko (Lady Sue), Nomura Takeshi (Tsurumaru), Peter (Kyoami), Yui Masayuki (Hirayama Tango), Kato Kazuo (Ikoma), Tazaki Jun (Ayabe Seiji), Ueki Hitoshi (Fujimaki Nobuhiro), Matsui Norio (Ogura), Igawa Hisashi (Kurogane), Kodama Kenji (Shirane), Ito Toshiya (Naganuma), Kato Takeshi (Hatakeyama).

Awards: American Academy Awards, Best Costume Design (Wada Emi); Los Angeles Film Critics' Awards, Best Foreign Film, Best Music (Take-mitsu Toru); National Board of Review (United States), Best Foreign Language Film, and Best Director; National Society of Film Critics (United States), Best Picture, and Best Cinematography (Saito Takao, Ueda Masaharu, Nakai Asakazu); New York Film Critics Circle, Best Foreign Film; British Academy Awards, Best Foreign Film, Best Make-Up (Uede Shoichiro, Aimi Tameyuki, Naito Chihako, and Takamizawa Noriko) (1986); British Film Critics' Circle, Best Foreign Film, and Best Director (1986); Mainichi Eiga Concourse, Grand Prize, Best Director, and Best Supporting Actor (Igawa Hisashi); Tokyo Blue Ribbon Prizes, Best Film, and Best Director; *Kinema junpo,* number two film of the year.

Dreams (Yume, 1990)

Production: Kurosawa Production. Distribution: Toho. 120 minutes. Pana-vision. Color. Released 25 May 1990.

Scenario: Kurosawa Akira. Photography: Saito Takao and Ueda Masaharu. Art direction: Muraki Yoshiro and Sakuragi Akira. Editing assistants: Ot-subo Ryusuke, Aga Hideto, and Yafune Yosuke. Music: Ikebe Shin'ichiro. Sound recording: Benitani Sen'ichi. Sound effects: Minawa Ichiro and Saito Masatoshi. Assistant directors: Koizumi Takashi, Yoneda Oki-hiro, Sakai Naohito, Sugino Tsuyoshi, and Vitorio Dalle Ore. Producers: Kurosawa Hisao and Inoue Yoshio.

Cast: Terao Akira ("I," the dreamer), Isaki Mitsunori ("I," the young dreamer), Baisho Mitsuko (his mother), Martin Scorsese (Vincent van Gogh), Ryu Chishu (old man), Harada Mieko (the snow spirit), Zushi Yoshitaka (Private Noguchi), Negishi Toshie (woman with child), Igawa Hisashi (nuclear engineer), Ikariya Chosuke (the demon).

Awards: Mainichi Eiga Concourse, Merits of Excellence, Best Music (Ikebe Shin'ichiro), and Best Cinematography (Saito Takao and Ueda Masaharu); *Kinema junpo,* number four film of the year.

Rhapsody in August (Hachigatsu no rapusodi [kyoshikyoku], 1991)

Production: Kurosawa Production/Shochiku. Distribution: Shochiku. 97 minutes, 30 seconds. 2,674 meters. Panavision. Color. Released 25 May 1991.

Scenario: Kurosawa Akira, based on the novel *Nabe no naka* (In the Cauldron), by Murata Kiyoko. Photography: Saito Takao and Ueda Masaharu. Lighting: Sano Takeji. Art direction: Muraki Yoshiro. Editing assistants: Otsubo Ryusuke, Muramoto Masaru, and Minami Tome. Music: Ikebe Shin'ichiro. Sound recording: Benitani Sen'ichi. Assistant directors: Honda Ishiro, Koizumi Takashi, Yoneda Okihiro, Sakai Naoto, Tanaka Toru, and Vitorio Dalle Ore. Producers: Okuyama Toru and Kurosawa Hisao.

Cast: Murase Sachiko (Kane), Igawa Hisashi (Tadao), Kayashima Narumi (Machiko), Otakara Tomoko (Tami), Isaki Mitsunori (Shinjiro), Negishi Toshie (Yoshie), Kawarazaki Choichiro (Noboru), Yoshioka Hidetaka (Tateo), Suzuki Mie (Minako), Richard Gere (Clark).

Awards: Director's Guild of America, D. W. Griffith Award; Mainichi Eiga Concourse, Merits of Excellence; *Kinema junpo,* number three film of the year.

Madadayo (Madadayo, 1993)

Production: Daiei/Dentsu/Kurosawa Production. Distribution: Toho. 134 minutes. Panavision. Color. Released 17 April 1993.

Scenario: Kurosawa Akira, based on works by Uchida Hyakken. Photography: Saito Takao and Ueda Masaharu. Lighting: Sano Takeji. Art direction: Muraki Yoshiro. Music: Ikebe Shin'ichiro. Sound recording: Nishizaki Hideo. Assistant director: Koizumi Takashi. Producer: Kurosawa Hisao.

Cast: Matsumura Tatsuo (Uchida Hyakken), Kagawa Kyoko (his wife),

Igawa Hisashi (Takayama), Tokoro Joji (Amaki), Yui Masayuki (Kiri-yama), Terao Akira (Sawamura), Kobayashi Asei (Priest Kameyama), Kusaka Takeshi (Doctor Kobayashi).

Awards: Tokyo Blue Ribbon Prizes, Best Supporting Actor (Tokoro Joji), and Best Supporting Actress (Kagawa Kyoko); *Kinema junpo,* number ten film of the year.

BIBLIOGRAPHY

Abe Yoshinori. *Eiga o aishita futari: Kurosawa Akira, Mifune Toshiro.* Tokyo: Hochi Shinbunsha, 1995.

Adachi Ken'ichi. *Tachikawa bunko no eiyutachi.* Tokyo: Chuo Koronsha, 1987.

Affron, Charles, and Mirella Jona Affron. *Sets in Motion: Art Direction and Film Narrative.* New Brunswick, N.J.: Rutgers University Press, 1995.

Akiyama Kuniharu. *Nihon no eiga ongakushi 1.* Tokyo: Tabata Shoten, 1974.

Allen, Robert C., and Douglas Gomery. *Film History: Theory and Practice.* New York: Knopf, 1985.

Altman, Rick. *The American Film Musical* (Bloomington: Indiana University Press, 1989).

———. "Film Studies, Inc.: Lessons from the Past about the Current Institutionalization of Film Studies." *Film Criticism* 17, nos. 2–3 (winter–spring 1993).

Anderson, Joseph L. "When the Twain Meet: Hollywood's Remake of *The Seven Samurai*." *Film Quarterly* 15, no. 3 (spring 1962): 55–58.

———. "Japanese Swordfighters and American Gunfighters." *Cinema Journal* 17, no. 2 (spring 1973).

Anderson, Joseph L., and Donald Richie. *The Japanese Film: Art and Industry.* Expanded edition. Princeton, N.J.: Princeton University Press, 1982.

Andrew, Dudley. *Concepts in Film Theory.* Oxford: Oxford University Press, 1984.

———. "1954 January: On Certain Tendencies of the French Cinema." In *A New History of French Literature,* ed. Denis Hollier. Cambridge: Harvard University Press, 1989.

Annan, Gabriele. "Bomb Culture." *Times Literary Supplement,* 4 October 1991.

Aochi Shin. "Kurosawa Akira." *Chuo koron* (March 1957): 240–47.

Banham, Martin, ed. *The Cambridge Guide to Theatre.* Cambridge: Cambridge University Press, 1995.

Bardsley, Jan, and David P. Phillips. "Teaching and Interpreting the Works of Kurosawa Akira." *Education about Asia* 1, no. 2 (fall 1996).

Barthes, Roland. *Image-Music-Text.* New York: Hill and Wang, 1977.

————. *Empire of Signs.* Trans. Richard Howard. New York: Hill and Wang, 1982.

Bazin, André. *What Is Cinema?* vol. 1. Trans. Hugh Gray. Berkeley: University of California Press, 1967.

————. *Bazin at Work: Major Essays and Reviews from the Forties and Fifties.* Trans. Alain Piette and Bert Cardullo. New York: Routledge, 1997.

Belton, John. *American Cinema/American Culture.* New York: McGraw-Hill, 1994.

Benedict, Ruth. *The Chrysanthemum and the Sword: Patterns of Japanese Culture.* Boston: Houghton Mifflin, 1946.

Benett, John W., and Michio Nagai. "The Japanese Critique of the Methodology of Benedict's *Chrysanthemum and the Sword.*" *American Anthropologist* 55, no. 3 (August 1953).

Bernheimer, Charles. "Introduction: The Anxieties of Comparison." In Bernheimer, *Comparative Literature in the Age of Multiculturalism.*

————, ed. *Comparative Literature in the Age of Multiculturalism.* Baltimore, Md.: Johns Hopkins University Press, 1995.

Bernheimer, Charles, et al. "The Bernheimer Report, 1993: Comparative Literature at the Turn of the Century." In Bernheimer, *Comparative Literature in the Age of Multiculturalism.*

Bernstein, Matthew, and Mark Ravina. Review of *Rhapsody in August. American Historical Review* 98, no. 4 (October 1993).

Blumenthal, J. "*Macbeth* into *Throne of Blood.*" *Sight and Sound* 34, no. 4 (autumn 1965): 190–95.

Bock, Audie. *Japanese Film Directors.* Tokyo: Kodansha International, 1978.

————. "The Moralistic Cinema of Kurosawa." In K. Chang, *Kurosawa: Perceptions on Life, an Anthology of Essays.*

Bordwell, David. "Our Dream Cinema: Western Historiography and the Japanese Film." *Film Reader* 4 (1979): 45–62.

————. Review of *To the Distant Observer: Form and Meaning in the Japanese Cinema,* by Noël Burch. *Wide Angle* 3, no. 4 (1985).

————. *Ozu and the Poetics of Cinema.* Princeton, N.J.: Princeton University Press, 1988.

————. *Making Meaning: Inference and Rhetoric in the Interpretation of Cinema.* Cambridge: Harvard University Press, 1989.

————. "Film Interpretation Revisited." *Film Criticism* 17, nos. 2–3 (winter-spring 1993).

Bordwell, David, and Noël Carroll, eds. *Post-Theory: Reconstructing Film Studies.* Madison: University of Wisconsin Press, 1996.

Bourdieu, Pierre. "The Form of Capital." In *Handbook of Theory and Re-*

search for the Sociology of Education, ed. John G. Richardson. New York: Greenwood Press, 1986.

Brook, Peter. "Shakespeare on the Screens." Sight and Sound 34, no. 2 (spring 1965): 66–70.

Brooks, Peter. "Must We Apologize?" In Bernheimer, Comparative Literature in the Age of Multiculturalism.

Brown, Georgia. "Her Way." Village Voice, 24 December 1991.

Brunette, Peter, and David Wills. Screen/Play: Derrida and Film Theory. Princeton, N.J.: Princeton University Press, 1989.

Bungei Shunju, ed. Isetsu Kurosawa Akira. Tokyo: Bungei Shunju, 1994.

Burch, Noël. "To the Distant Observer: Towards a Theory of Japanese Film." October 1 (spring 1976): 32–46.

———. To the Distant Observer: Form and Meaning in the Japanese Cinema. Berkeley: University of California Press, 1979.

———. "Akira Kurosawa." In Roud, Cinema: A Critical Dictionary, vol. 2.

———. Theory of Film Practice. Trans. Helen R. Lane. Princeton, N.J.: Princeton University Press, 1981.

———. Life to Those Shadows. Berkeley: University of California Press, 1990.

Buscombe, Edward. "Ideas of Authorship." Screen 14, no. 3 (autumn 1973).

Cardullo, Bert. "The Circumstance of the East, the Fate of the West: Notes, Mostly on The Seven Samurai." Literature/Film Quarterly 13, no. 2 (1985): 112–17.

Casebier, Allan. "Images of Irrationality in Modern Japan: The Films of Shohei Imamura." Film Criticism 7, no. 1 (fall 1983).

———. "Turning Back the Clock in Japanese Cinema Studies: Kurosawa, Keiko McDonald, and Tadao Sato." Quarterly Review of Film Studies 10, no. 2 (spring 1985): 166–69.

Chang, Joseph S. "Kagemusha and the Chushingura Motif." East-West Film Journal 3, no. 2 (June 1989).

Chang, Kevin K. W., ed. Kurosawa: Perceptions on Life, an Anthology of Essays. Honolulu: Honolulu Academy of Arts, 1991.

Chiba Nobuo. Eiga to Tanizaki. Tokyo: Seiabo, 1989.

Chion, Michel. Audio-Vision: Sound on Screen. Trans. Claudia Gorbman. New York: Columbia University Press, 1994.

Chow, Rey. "In the Name of Comparative Literature." In Bernheimer, Comparative Literature in the Age of Multiculturalism.

———. Primitive Passions: Visuality, Sexuality, Ethnography, and Contemporary Chinese Cinema. New York: Columbia University Press, 1995.

Chuko Satoshi and Hasumi Shigehiko. Naruse Mikio no sekkei. Tokyo: Chikuma Shobo, 1990.

Collick, John. *Shakespeare, Cinema, and Society.* Manchester: Manchester University Press, 1989.

Conley, Tom. *Film Hieroglyphs: Ruptures in Classical Cinema.* Minneapolis: University of Minnesota Press, 1991.

Cook, Pam, ed. *The Cinema Book.* New York: Pantheon, 1985.

Crichton, Michael. *Rising Sun.* New York: Ballantine Books, 1993.

Crowl, Samuel. "The Bow Is Bent and Drawn: Kurosawa's *Ran* and the Shakespearean Arrow of Desire." *Literature/Film Quarterly* 22, no. 2 (1994): 109–16.

Culler, Jonathan. "Comparative Literature, at Last!" In Bernheimer, *Comparative Literature in the Age of Multiculturalism.*

Cumings, Bruce. "Boundary Displacement: Area Studies and International Studies during and after the Cold War." *Bulletin of Concerned Asian Studies* 29, no. 1 (1997): 6–26.

Davies, Anthony, and Stanley Wells, eds. *Shakespeare and the Moving Image: The Plays on Film and Television.* Cambridge: Cambridge University Press, 1994.

Davis, Darrell William. *Picturing Japaneseness: Monumental Style, National Identity, Japanese Film.* New York: Columbia University Press, 1996.

de Bary, Brett. Review of *To the Distant Observer: Form and Meaning in the Japanese Cinema,* by Noël Burch. *Journal of Japanese Studies* 8, no. 2 (summer 1982).

Deleuze, Gilles. *Cinema 1: The Movement-Image.* Trans. Hugh Tomlinson and Robert Galeta. Minneapolis: University of Minnesota Press, 1986.

———. *Cinema 2: The Time-Image.* Trans. Hugh Tomlinson and Robert Galeta. Minneapolis: University of Minnesota Press, 1989.

de Man, Paul. *Allegories of Reading: Figural Language in Rousseau, Nietzsche, Rilke and Proust.* New Haven, Conn.: Yale University Press, 1979.

Desser, David. *The Samurai Films of Akira Kurosawa.* Ann Arbor: UMI Research Press, 1983.

———. "Kurosawa's Eastern 'Western': *Sanjuro* and the Influence of *Shane.*" *Film Criticism* 8, no. 1 (fall 1983).

———. "*Ikiru:* Narration as a Moral Act." In Nolletti and Desser, *Reframing Japanese Cinema.*

———. "Toward a Structural Analysis of the Postwar Samurai Film." In Nolletti and Desser, *Reframing Japanese Cinema.*

———. "Narrating the Human Condition: *High and Low* and Story-Telling in Kurosawa's Cinema." In Goodwin, *Perspectives on Akira Kurosawa.*

———, ed. *Ozu's "Tokyo Story."* Cambridge: Cambridge University Press, 1997.

Dibble, Lewis. "Crimes of Meaning: Kurosawa and Allegory." In Kawamoto Koji, Heh-Hsian Yuan, and Ohsawa Yoshihiro, *The Force of Vision*.

Dower, John. *War without Mercy: Race and Power in the Pacific War*. New York: Pantheon, 1986.

————. *Japan in War and Peace: Selected Essays*. New York: New Press, 1993.

————, ed. *Origins of the Modern Japanese State: Selected Writings of E. H. Norman*. New York: Pantheon Books, 1975.

Ehrlich, Linda. "Kurosawa's Fragile Heroes: Another Look at the *Tateyaku*." In K. Chang, *Kurosawa: Perceptions on Life, an Anthology of Essays*.

————. Review of *The Warrior's Camera: The Cinema of Akira Kurosawa*, by Stephen Prince. *East-West Film Journal* 6, no. 2 (July 1992): 134–37.

Ehrlich, Linda C., and David Desser, eds. *Cinematic Landscapes: Observations on the Visual Arts and Cinema of China and Japan*. Austin: University of Texas Press, 1994.

Elisonas, Jurgis. "The Warrior in the Shadows." In Kawamoto Koji, Heh-Hsian Yuan, and Ohsawa Yoshihiro, *The Force of Vision*.

Ellis, Jack C. "Ruminations of an Ex-Cinematologist." *Cinema Journal* 24, no. 2 (winter 1985): 47–52.

Elsaesser, Thomas. "Film Studies in Search of the Object." *Film Criticism* 17, no.s 2–3 (winter-spring 1993).

Endo Tatsuo. *Eirin: Rekishi to jiken*. Tokyo: Perikansha, 1973.

Erens, Patricia. *Akira Kurosawa: A Guide to References and Resources*. Boston: G. K. Hall, 1979.

————. "Post-war Japanese Cinema: *The Waves at Genji's Door*." *Quarterly Review of Film Studies* 4, no. 2 (spring 1979).

Felman, Shoshana. *Writing and Madness: Literature/Philosophy/Psychoanalysis*. Ithaca, N.Y.: Cornell University Press, 1985.

Forgens, Jack F. *Shakespeare on Film*. Bloomington: Indiana University Press, 1977.

Fowler, Edward. "Reflections on Hegemony, Japanology, and Oppositional Criticism." *Journal of Japanese Studies* 22, no. 2 (summer 1996): 401–12.

Frayling, Christopher. *Spaghetti Westerns: Cowboys and Europeans from Karl May to Sergio Leone*. London: Routledge and Kegan Paul, 1981.

Futaba Juzaburo. *Nihon eiga hihan: 1932–1956*. Tokyo: Topazu Puresu, 1992.

Gebert, Michael. *The Encyclopedia of Movie Awards*. New York: St. Martin's Paperbacks, 1996.

Geertz, Clifford. *Works and Lives: The Anthropologist as Author*. Stanford, Calif.: Stanford University Press, 1988.

Geist, Kathe. "Late Kurosawa: *Kagemusha* and *Ran*." *Post Script* 12, no. 1 (fall 1992): 26–36.

———. "Buddhism in *Tokyo Story*." In Desser, *Ozu's "Tokyo Story."*

Gerlach, John. "Shakespeare, Kurosawa, and *Macbeth*: A Response to J. Blumenthal." *Literature/Film Quarterly* 1, no. 4 (fall 1973): 352–59.

Gluck, Carol. "The Past in the Present." In Gordon, *Postwar Japan as History.*

Goodwin, James. *Akira Kurosawa and Intertextual Cinema.* Baltimore, Md.: Johns Hopkins University Press, 1994.

———. "Akira Kurosawa and the Atomic Age." In Goodwin, *Perspectives on Akira Kurosawa.*

———, ed. *Perspectives on Akira Kurosawa.* New York: G. K. Hall, 1994.

Gorbman, Claudia. "*Ikiru*'s Soundtrack." In Kawamoto Koji, Heh-Hsian Yuan, and Ohsawa Yoshihiro, *The Force of Vision.*

Gordon, Andrew, ed. *Postwar Japan as History.* Berkeley: University of California Press, 1993.

Gossman, Lionel. "Out of a Gothic North." In Gossman and Spariosu, *Building a Profession.*

Gossman, Lionel, and Mihai I. Spariosu, eds. *Building a Profession: Autobiographical Perspectives on the History of Comparative Literature in the United States.* Albany: State University of New York Press, 1994.

Guillory, John. *Cultural Capital: The Problem of Literary Canon Formation.* Chicago: University of Chicago Press, 1993.

Gunji Masakatsu, ed. *Kabuki juhachibanshu.* Tokyo: Iwanami Shoten, 1965.

Hammer, Tad Bentley. *International Film Prizes: An Encyclopedia.* New York: Garland, 1991.

Hanada Kiyoteru. "Ganzo hoseki no kirameki." *Kinema junpo,* part 2 (January 1959). Reprinted in *Besuto obu Kinema junpo jo, 1950–1966.* Tokyo: Kinema Junposha, 1994.

Hapgood, Robert. "Kurosawa's Shakespeare Films: *Throne of Blood, The Bad Sleep Well,* and *Ran.*" In Davies and Wells, *Shakespeare and the Moving Image.*

Harootunian, H. D. "America's Japan/Japan's Japan." In Miyoshi and Harootunian, *Japan in the World.*

Hashimoto Osamu. *Kanpon chanbara jidaigeki koza.* Tokyo: Tokuma Shoten, 1986.

Hattori Yukio. *Kabuki no kozo.* Tokyo: Chuo Koronsha, 1970.

———. *Kabuki no ki wado.* Tokyo: Iwanami Shoten, 1989.

Havens, Thomas R. *Valley of Darkness: The Japanese People and World War Two.* New York: W. W. Norton, 1978.

Hayase Haruo. *Nancho koboshi: Gonancho to Kumazawa-ke ryakki.* Tokyo: Kindai Bungeisha, 1996.

Hess, John. "*La Politique des auteurs:* Part One: World View as Aesthetic." *Jump Cut* 1 (May–June 1974): 19–22.

———. "*La Politique des auteurs:* Part Two: Truffaut's Manifesto." *Jump Cut* 2 (July–August 1974): 20–22.

High, Peter B. *Teikoku no ginmaku: Jugonen Senso to Nihon eiga.* Nagoya: Nagoya Daigaku Shuppankai, 1995.

Higham, Charles. "Kurosawa's Humanism." *Kenyon Review* 27, no. 4 (autumn 1965): 737–42.

Higuchi Naofumi. *Kurosawa Akira no eigajutsu.* Tokyo: Chikuma Shobo, 1999.

Hijikata Teiichi. *Nihon no kindai bijutsu.* Tokyo: Iwanami Shoten, 1966.

Hirano Ken. *Showa bungakushi.* Tokyo: Chikuma Shobo, 1963.

Hirano, Kyoko. *Mr. Smith Goes to Tokyo: Japanese Cinema under the American Occupation, 1945–1952.* Washington, D.C.: Smithsonian Institution Press, 1992.

Howlett, Kathy. "Are You Trying to Make Me Commit Suicide? Gender, Identity, and Spatial Arrangement in Kurosawa's *Ran.*" *Literature/Film Quarterly* 24, no. 4 (1996): 360–66.

Hunter, Janet E. *Concise Dictionary of Modern Japanese History.* Berkeley: University of California Press, 1984.

Ichikawa Kon and Mori Yuki. *Ichikawa Kon no eigatachi.* Tokyo: Waizu Shuppan, 1994.

Iijima Tadashi. *Senchu eigashi: Shiki.* Tokyo: MG Shuppan, 1984.

Imai Tadashi. *Imai Tadashi "zenshigoto": Sukurin no aru jinsei.* Tokyo: ACT, 1990.

Imamura Shohei et al., eds. *Koza Nihon eiga.* Tokyo: Iwanami Shoten, 1985–1988, 8 vols.

"Imperial Pretender." *Newsweek,* 4 November 1946, 48, 50.

Innami Takaichi. *Eiga shakaigaku.* Tokyo: Wasada Daigaku Shuppanbu, 1955.

Inoue Shoichi. *Tsukurareta Katsura Rikyu shinwa.* Tokyo: Kobundo, 1986.

Irie Takako. *Eiga joyu.* Tokyo: Gakufu Shoin, 1957.

Itami Juzo. *Jibuntachi yo!* Tokyo: Bungei Shunju, 1988.

Itami Mansaku. *Itami Mansaku zenshu.* Vols. 1–3. Tokyo: Chikuma Shobo, 1961.

———. *Itami Mansaku essei shu.* Tokyo: Chikuma Shobo, 1971.

Ito Daisuke. *Jidaigeki eiga no shi to shinjitsu.* Ed. Kato Tai. Tokyo: Kinema Junposha, 1976.

Ivy, Marilyn. *Discourses of the Vanishing: Modernity, Phantasm, Japan.* Chicago: University of Chicago Press, 1995.

Iwabutchi, Masayoshi. "1954 in Japan." *Sight and Sound* (spring 1955): 202–5.

Iwasaki Akira. "Japan's New Screen Art: More Real than *Rashomon.*" *Nation,* 12 May 1956, 398–401.

———. "Kurosawa Akira no sekai." *Chuo koron* (November 1957): 223–28.

———. *Eiga ni miru sengo sesoshi.* Tokyo: Shin Nihon Shuppansha, 1973.

———. *Nihon eiga shishi.* Tokyo: Asahi Shinbunsha, 1977.

———. *Eiga no maesetsu.* Tokyo: Godo Shuppan, 1981.

Jacobs, Lewis. *The Rise of the American Film: A Critical History.* New York: Teachers College Press, 1968.

Jameson, Fredric. *Signatures of the Visible.* New York: Routledge, 1990.

———. *Postmodernism, or The Cultural Logic of Late Capitalism.* Durham, N.C.: Duke University Press, 1991.

———. "On *Cultural Studies.*" In *The Identity in Question,* ed. John Raichman. New York: Routledge, 1995.

Jinno Yuki. *Shumi no tanjo: Hyakkaten ga tsukutta teisuto.* Tokyo: Keiso Shobo, 1994.

Jones, Sumie. "*The Lower Depths*: Gorky, Stanislavsky, and Kurosawa." In *Explorations: Essays in Comparative Literature,* ed. Makoto Ueda. Lanham, Md.: University Press of America, 1986.

Jorgens, Jack J. *Shakespeare on Film.* Bloomington: Indiana University Press, 1977.

Kaplan, Frederick. "A Second Look: Akira Kurosawa's *Seven Samurai.*" *Cineaste* 10 (winter 1979–1980): 42–43, 47.

Kapsis, Robert E. *Hitchcock: The Making of a Reputation.* Chicago: University of Chicago Press, 1992.

Karatani, Kojin. *Imi to iu yamai.* Tokyo: Kodansha, 1989.

———. *Origins of Modern Japanese Literature.* Trans. Brett de Bary. Durham, N.C.: Duke University Press, 1993.

Kata Koji, et al. *Nihon no taishu geijutsu.* Tokyo: Shakai Shisosha, 1962.

Kataoka Yoshio. *Kanojo ga enjita yaku: Hara Setsuko no sengo shuensaku o mite kangaeru.* Tokyo: Hayakawa Shobo, 1994.

Kato Koichi. *Sukyandaru no Showashi.* Tokyo: Hanashi no Tokushu, 1985.

Kato Tai. *Kato Tai eiga o kataru.* Tokyo: Chikuma Shobo, 1994.

Kawamoto Koji, Heh-Hsian Yuan, and Ohsawa Yoshihiro, eds. *The Force of Vision.* Vol. 6. Tokyo: University of Tokyo Press, 1995.

Kawamoto Saburo. *Ima hitotabi no sengo Nihon eiga.* Tokyo: Iwanami Shoten, 1994.

———. *Kimi uruwashiku: Sengo Nihon eiga joyu san.* Tokyo: Bungei Shunju, 1996.

Kawatake Shigetoshi. *Kabuki: Japanese Drama.* Tokyo: Foreign Affairs Association of Japan, 1958.

———. *Gaisetsu Nihon engekishi.* Tokyo: Iwanami Shoten, 1966.

Kawatake Toshio. *Nihon no Hamuretto.* Tokyo: Nansosha, 1972.

———. *Engeki gairon.* Tokyo: Tokyo Daigaku Shuppankai, 1978.

————. *Kabuki biron.* Tokyo: Tokyo Daigaku Shuppankai, 1989.

Keene, Donald. "Kurosawa." *Grand Street* 1, no. 4 (summer 1982): 140–45.

————. *Dawn to the West: Japanese Literature of the Modern Era (Fiction).* New York: Holt, Rinehart and Winston, 1984.

Kermode, Frank. "Shakespeare in the Movies." In *Film Theory and Criticism.* New York: Oxford University Press, 1974.

Kikushima Ryuzo. "Atarashii jidaigeki." *Eiga geijutsu,* no. 129 (July 1958): 36–37.

Kimoto Itaru. *Zasshi de yomu sengoshi.* Tokyo: Shinchosha, 1985.

Kimura Ki. *Taishu bungaku jurokko.* Tokyo: Chuo Koronsha, 1993.

Kinder, Marsha. "Establishing a Discipline for the Teaching of Film: Criticism and the Literary Analogue." *Quarterly Review of Film Studies* 1, no. 4 (November 1976).

————. "*Throne of Blood:* A Morality Play." *Literature/Film Quarterly* 5 (fall 1977).

————. "*Kagemusha.*" *Film Quarterly* 34 (winter 1980–1981): 44–48.

Kirihara, Donald. "Critical Polarities and the Study of Japanese Film Style." *Journal of Film and Video* 39, no. 1 (winter 1987).

————. *Patterns of Time: Mizoguchi and the 1930s.* Madison: University of Wisconsin Press, 1992.

Kitagawa Fuyuhiko. Review of *Throne of Blood. Kurosawa Akira Shusei,* vol. 3.

Komatsu Hiroshi. "Some Characteristics of Japanese Cinema before World War I." In Nolletti and Desser, *Reframing Japanese Cinema.*

Koschmann, J. Victor. *Revolution and Subjectivity in Postwar Japan.* Chicago: University of Chicago Press, 1996.

Kozloff, Sarah. *Invisible Storytellers: Voice-Over Narration in American Fiction Film.* Berkeley: University of California Press, 1988.

Kurata Yoshihiro, ed. *Geino.* Vol. 18 of *Nihon kindai shiso taikei.* Tokyo: Iwanami Shoten, 1988.

Kurosawa Akira. *Kurosawa Akira eiga taikei.* Vols. 1, 2, 3, 4, 6, and 9. Tokyo: Kinema Junposha, 1970–1971. Other volumes were never published.

————. *Akuma no yo ni saishin ni! Tenshi no yo ni daitan ni!* Tokyo: Toho, 1975.

————. *Kagemusha.* Tokyo: Kodansha, 1979.

————. *Something like an Autobiography.* Trans. Audie E. Bock. New York: Vintage, 1983.

————. *Gama no abura: Jiden no yona mono.* Tokyo: Iwanami Shoten, 1984.

————. *Zenshu Kurosawa Akira.* 6 vols. Tokyo: Iwanami Shoten, 1987–1988.

————. "*Seven Samurai*" *and Other Screenplays.* London: Faber and Faber, 1992.

———. "*Hachigatsu no rapusodi* kansei daihon." *Kinema junpo,* part 1 (January 1992).

———. *Madadayo.* Tokyo: Tokuma Shoten, 1993.

———. *Yume wa tensai de aru.* Tokyo: Bungei Shunju, 1999.

Kurosawa Akira, Kinoshita Keisuke, and Takeda Taijun. "Ningenzo seisakuho." *Chuo koron* (February 1956): 240–47.

Kurosawa Akira, Takemitsu Toru, and Yodogawa Nagaharu. "Kurosawa Akira no sekai." *Sekai* (January 1984): 269–95.

Kurosawa Akira no zenbo. Tokyo: Gendai Engeki Kyokai, 1985.

Kurosawa Akira shusei. Vol. 1. Tokyo: Kinema Junposha, 1989.

Kurosawa Akira shusei. Vol. 2. Tokyo: Kinema Junposha, 1991.

Kurosawa Akira shusei. Vol. 3. Tokyo: Kinema Junposha, 1993.

Kusayanagi Daizo. "Za man Kurosawa Akira." *Bungei shunju* (October 1971): 188–200.

Kuwabara Takeo. "Shichinin no samurai." *Kaizo* (June 1954): 132–34.

Lauterbach, Richard E. "The True Emperor of Japan?" *Life,* 21 January 1946, 32–33.

Lejeune, Philippe. *On Autobiography.* Trans. Katherine Leary. Minneapolis: University of Minnesota Press, 1989.

Lévi-Strauss, Claude. *Structural Anthropology.* Trans. Claire Jacobson and Brooke Grundfest Schoepf. New York: Basic Books, 1963.

Levin, Harry. *Grounds for Comparison.* Cambridge: Harvard University Press, 1972.

Leyda, Jay. "Modesty and Pretension in Two New Films." *Film Culture* 2, no. 4 (October 1965): 3–7, 27.

Lynch, Kevin. *The Image of the City.* Cambridge: MIT Press, 1960.

———. *What Time Is This Place?* Cambridge: MIT Press, 1972.

Makino Masahiro. *Eiga tosei: Ten no maki.* Tokyo: Heibonsha, 1977; reprint, Tokyo: Chikuma Shobo, 1995.

Malcomson, Scott. "The Pure Land beyond the Seas: Barthes, Burch, and the Uses of Japan." *Screen* 26, nos. 3–4 (1985).

Malpezzi, Frances M., and William M. Clements. "The Double and the Theme of Selflessness in *Kagemusha.*" *Literature/Film Quarterly* 17, no. 3 (1989): 202–6.

Manheim, Michael. "The Function of Battle Imagery in Kurosawa's Histories and *Henry V* Films." *Literature/Film Quarterly* 22, no. 2 (1994): 129–35.

Manvell, Roger. *Shakespeare and the Film.* New York: Praeger, 1971.

Marchetti, Gina. *Romance and the "Yellow Peril": Race, Sex, and Discursive Strategies in Hollywood Fiction.* Berkeley: University of California Press, 1993.

Marx, Karl. *A Contribution to the Critique of Political Economy.* Trans. N. I. Stone. New York: International Library, 1904.

Mast, Gerald, and Marshall Cohen, eds. *Film Theory and Criticism: Introductory Readings.* 3d ed. New York: Oxford University Press, 1985.

Masumura Yasuzo. "'Kakushitoride no san akunin' to Kurosawa Akira." In Ogawa Toru et al., *Gendai Nihon eigaron taikei* (Tokyo: Tokisha, 1970), vol. 2.

———. "Sodai ni shite hiso na tensai." In *Kurosawa Akira shusei,* vol. 1.

Masumura Yasuzo and Oshima Nagisa. "Nihon eiga ni tsuite kataro." *Kinema junpo,* part 2 (January 1972): 70–79.

Matsumoto Kappei. *Nihon shingekishi: Shingeki binbo monogatari.* Tokyo: Chikuma Shobo, 1966.

Maxfield, James. "The Moral Ambiguity of Kurosawa's Early Thrillers." *Film Criticism* 18, no. 1 (fall 1993).

McDonald, Keiko I. *Japanese Classical Theater in Films.* Rutland, N.J.: Fairleigh Dickinson University Press, 1994.

Mellen, Joan. *The Waves at Genji's Door: Japan through Its Cinema.* New York: Pantheon Books, 1976.

Metz, Christian. *The Imaginary Signifier: Psychoanalysis and the Cinema.* Trans. Ben Brewster, Celia Britton, Alfred Guzzetti, and Annwyl Williams. Bloomington: Indiana University Press, 1982.

Minamoto Ryoen. *Giri to ninjo.* Tokyo: Chuo Koronsha, 1969.

Mine Takashi. *Teikoku Gekijo kaimaku.* Tokyo: Chuo Koronsha, 1996.

Miner, Earl. "Japanese Film Art in Modern Dress." *Quarterly Review of Film, Radio, and Television* 10, no. 4 (1956).

Miner, Earl, Hiroko Odagiri, and Robert E. Morrell, eds. *The Princeton Companion to Classical Japanese Literature.* Princeton, N.J.: Princeton University Press, 1985.

Mitchell, Lee Clark. *Westerns: Making the Man in Fiction and Film.* Chicago: University of Chicago Press, 1996.

Mitchell, W. J. T. *Iconology: Image, Text, Ideology.* Chicago: University of Chicago Press, 1986.

Miyamoto Kenji. *Katsura Rikyu: Bruno Tauto wa shogensuru.* Tokyo: Kashima Shuppankai, 1995.

Miyoshi, Masao. *Off Center: Power and Culture Relations between Japan and the United States.* Cambridge: Harvard University Press, 1991.

———. *As We Saw Them: The First Japanese Embassy to the United States.* New York: Kodansha International, 1994.

Miyoshi, Masao, and H. D. Harootunian, eds. *Postmodernism and Japan.* Durham, N.C.: Duke University Press, 1989.

———. *Japan in the World.* Durham, N.C.: Duke University Press, 1993.

Mori Iwao. "Jidaigeki eiga no unmei ni tsuite." *Eiga geijutsu* 5, no. 3 (March 1950): 2–5.

Mori Kazuo, Yamada Koichi, and Yamane Sadao. *Mori Kazuo eigatabi.* Tokyo: Soshisha, 1989.

Morris, Ivan. *The Nobility of Failure: Tragic Heroes in the History of Japan.* New York: Noonday, 1975.

Mowrey, Peter C. *Award Winning Films: A Viewer's Reference to 2,700 Acclaimed Motion Pictures.* Jefferson, N.C.: McFarland, 1994.

Mukai Soya. *Nihon no taishu engeki.* Tokyo: Toho Shuppan, 1962.

Murakami Yumiko. *Iero feisu: Hariuddo eiga ni miru Ajiajin no shozo.* Tokyo: Asahi Shinbunsha, 1993.

Muraki Yoshiro and Tanno Tatsuya. *Muraki Yoshiro no eiga bijutsu: Kurosawa eiga no dezain.* Tokyo: Firumu Atosha, 1998.

Murata Kiyoko. "In the Pot." In *Japanese Women Writers: Twentieth Century Short Fiction,* ed. Noriko Mizuta Lippit and Kyoko Iriye Selden. Armonk, N.Y.: M. E. Sharp, 1991.

Nagata Tetsuro. *Tate: Chanbara eigashi.* Tokyo: Shakai Shisosha, 1993.

Najita, Tetsuo. *Japan: The Intellectual Foundations of Modern Japanese Politics.* Chicago: University of Chicago Press, 1974.

———. "On Culture and Technology in Postmodern Japan." In Miyoshi and Harootunian, *Postmodernism and Japan.*

Nakamura Mitsuo. "'Yabu no naka' kara." In *Nakamura Mitsuo zenshu.* Vol. 5. Tokyo: Chikuma Shobo, 1972.

———. "Futatabi 'Yabu no naka' o megutte." In *Nakamura Mitsuo zenshu.* Vol. 5. Tokyo: Chikuma Shobo, 1972.

———. "Meiji bungakushi." In *Nakamura Mitsuo zenshu.* Vol. 11. Tokyo: Chikuma Shobo, 1973.

Neal, Stephen. *Genre.* London: British Film Institute, 1980.

Neumeyer, David. "Hayasaka's Music for *Rashomon.*" In Kawamoto Koji, Heh-Hsian Yuan, and Ohsawa Yoshihiro, *The Force of Vision.*

Nichols, Stephen, ed. *Concepts of Criticism.* New Haven, Conn.: Yale University Press, 1963.

Nihon eigashi. Tokyo: Kinema Junposha, 1976.

Nihon eiga haiyu zenshu: Danyu hen. Tokyo: Kinema Junposha, 1979.

Nihon eiga haiyu zenshu: Joyu hen. Tokyo: Kinema Junposha, 1980.

Nihon eiga terebi kantoku zenshu. Tokyo: Kinema Junposha, 1988.

Nishimura Yuichiro. *Kyosho no mechie: Kurosawa Akira to sutaffutachi.* Tokyo: Firumu Atosha, 1987.

———. *Kurosawa Akira: Oto to eizo.* Tokyo: Rippu Shobo, 1990.

Nishiyama Matsunosuke. *Ichikawa Danjuro.* Tokyo: Yoshikawa Kobunkan, 1960.

Nolletti, Arthur, Jr., and David Desser, eds. *Reframing Japanese Cinema: Authorship, Genre, History.* Bloomington: Indiana University Press, 1992.

Nolley, Kenneth S. "The Western as *Jidai-Geki.*" *Western American Literature* 11, no. 3 (November 1976): 231–38.

Noma Hiroshi. "Norainu no mondai." *Chuo koron* (December 1949).

Nosaka Akiyuki. "Kurosawa Akira ron." *Eiga geijutsu* (March 1967): 23–24.

Nygren, Scott. "Reconsidering Modernism: Japanese Film and the Postmodern Context." *Wide Angle* 11, no. 3 (July 1989): 6–15.

———. "Doubleness and Idiosyncrasy in Cross-Cultural Analysis." *Quarterly Review of Film and Video* 13, nos. 1–3 (1991): 173–87.

Ogata Toshiro. *Kyojin to shonen: Kurosawa Akira no joseitachi.* Tokyo: Bungei Shunju, 1992.

Ogawa Toru et al., eds. *Gendai Nihon eigaron taikei.* Vols. 1–3. Tokyo: Tokisha, 1970–1971.

Ogi Masahiro. "Taishu jidaigeki ron." *Eiga geijutsu,* no. 129 (July 1958): 28–33.

Oi Hirosuke. *Chanbara geijutsushi.* Tokyo: Jitsugyo no Nihonsha, 1959.

Okada, Richard. *Figures of Resistance: Language, Poetry, and Narrating in "The Tale of Genji" and Other Mid-Heian Texts.* Durham, N.C.: Duke University Press, 1991.

Okada Susumu. "Kurosawa Akira no dorama kozo o bunseki suru." *Eiga geijutsu* (May 1963): 57–59.

Ong, Walter J. *Orality and Literacy: The Technologizing of the Word.* London: Routledge, 1989.

Oshima Nagisa. *Taikenteki sengo eizoron.* Tokyo: Asahi Shinbunsha, 1975.

———. *Sengo 50 nen eiga 100 nen.* Nagoya: Fubaisha, 1995.

Otis, Paul. "Japanese Folklore and Kurosawa's *Dreams.*" *Education about Asia* 2, no. 1 (spring 1997).

Ozaki Hotsuki. *Taishu bungaku.* Tokyo: Kinokuniya Shoten, 1980.

Parker, Brian. "*Ran* and the Tragedy of History." *University of Toronto Quarterly* 55, no. 4 (summer 1986): 412–23.

Parker, Helen S. E. "Taking Traditional Plots beyond the Traditional Theatre: Some Modern Versions of *Ataka/Kanjincho.*" *Japan Forum* 8, no. 1 (May 1996).

Pearlman, E. "*Macbeth* on Film: Politics." In Davies and Wells, *Shakespeare and the Moving Image.*

Perloff, Marjorie. " 'Literature' in the Expanded Field." In Bernheimer, *Comparative Literature in the Age of Multiculturalism.*

Pickard, Roy. *The Award Movies: A Complete Guide from A to Z.* New York: Schocken Books, 1981.

Polan, Dana. "Formalism and Its Discontent." *Jump Cut* 26 (1981): 63–66.

———. *Power and Paranoia: History, Narrative, and the American Cinema, 1940–1950.* New York: Columbia University Press, 1986.

Powell, Brian. "Matsui Sumako: Actress and Woman." In *Modern Japan: Aspects of History, Literature, and Society,* ed. W. G. Beasley. London: Allen and Unwin, 1975.

Prince, Stephen. "Zen and Selfhood: Patterns of Eastern Thought in Kurosawa's Films." *Post Script* 7, no. 2 (winter 1988): 4–17. Reprinted in Goodwin, *Perspectives on Akira Kurosawa.*

———. *The Warrior's Camera: The Cinema of Akira Kurosawa.* Princeton, N.J.: Princeton University Press, 1991.

———. "Memory and Nostalgia in Kurosawa's Dream World." *Post Script* 11, no. 1 (fall 1991).

Ray, Robert B. "Film Studies/Crisis/Experimentation." *Film Criticism* 17, nos. 2–3 (winter–spring 1993).

———. *The Avant-Garde Finds Andy Hardy.* Cambridge: Harvard University Press, 1995.

Rentschler, Eric. *The Ministry of Illusion: Nazi Cinema and Its Afterlife.* Cambridge: Harvard University Press, 1996.

Review of *Rhapsody in August. Variety,* 20 May 1991.

Richardson, Robert. *Literature and Film.* Bloomington: Indiana University Press, 1969.

Richie, Donald. "The Unexceptional Japanese Films Are More Preferred in Japan than Those That Intrigue the West." *Films in Review* (June–July 1955): 273–77.

———. *Japanese Movies.* Tokyo: Japan Travel Bureau, 1961.

———. *The Japanese Movies: An Illustrated History.* Tokyo: Kodansha International, 1966.

———. *Ozu.* Berkeley: University of California Press, 1974.

———. "The Japanese Film: A Personal View—1947–1995." *Asian Cinema* 7, no. 2 (winter 1995): 3–17.

———. *The Films of Akira Kurosawa.* 3d ed. Berkeley: University of California Press, 1998.

Richie, Donald, and Joseph L. Anderson. "Traditional Theater and the Film in Japan: The Influence of the Kabuki, Noh, and Other Forms on Film Content and Style." *Film Quarterly* 12, no. 1 (1958).

Romney, Jonathan. Review of *Rhapsody in August. Sight and Sound* (January 1992).

Rosen, Phil. "History, Textuality, Nation: Kracauer, Burch, and Some Problems in the Study of National Cinemas." *Iris* 2, no. 2 (1984).

Rosenmeyer, Thomas G. "Am I a Comparatist?" In Gossman and Spariosu, *Building a Profession.*

Roud, Richard, ed. *Cinema: A Critical Dictionary.* 2 vols. New York: Viking Press, 1980.

Sakaguchi Ango. "Nihon bunka shikan." *Sakaguchi Ango zenshu.* Vol. 14. Tokyo: Chikuma Shobo, 1990.

Sakai Naoki. *Shizansareru nihongo nihonjin.* Tokyo: Shin'yosha, 1996.

Sakuramoto Tomio. *Dai Toa Senso to Nihon eiga: Tachimi no senchu eigaron.* Tokyo: Aoki Shoten, 1993.

Sarris, Andrew. "Notes on the Auteur Theory in 1962." In Mast and Cohen, *Film Theory and Criticism.*

Sato Masaru. *Oto no nai eigakan.* Tokyo: Rippu Shobo, 1986.

——. *300/40: Sono e, oto, hito.* Tokyo: Kinema Junposha, 1994.

Sato Tadao. "Kurosawa Akira to Masumura Yasuzo: *Akahige* to *Heitai yakuza* e." *Eiga geijutsu* (June 1965): 15–18.

——. *Nihon eiga shisoshi.* Tokyo: San'ichi Shobo, 1970.

——. *Hasegawa Shin ron.* Tokyo: Chuo Koronsha, 1975.

——. *Chushingura: iji no keifu.* Tokyo: Asahi Shinbunsha, 1976.

——. *Kimi wa jidaigeki eiga o mitaka.* Tokyo: Jakometei Shuppan, 1977.

——. *Kurosawa Akira no sekai.* Tokyo: Asahi Shinbunsha, 1986.

——. "Kurosawa's *Rhapsody in August:* The Spirit of Compassion." *Cineaste* 19, no. 1 (1992).

Sawachi Hisae. *Otoko arite: Shimura Takashi no sekai.* Tokyo: Bungei Shunju, 1994.

Schilling, Mark. "The Political Incorrectness of Kurosawa Akira." *Japan Quarterly* (October–December 1991): 484–89.

Schneider, Harold W. "Literature and Film: Marking Out Some Boundaries." *Literature/Film Quarterly* 3, no. 1 (winter 1975).

Schrader, Paul. *Transcendental Style in Film: Ozu, Bresson, Dreyer.* Berkeley: University of California Press, 1972.

Seltzer, Alex. "Seeing through the Eyes of the Audience." *Film Comment* 29 (May–June 1993).

Shimizu Akira. *Senso to eiga.* Tokyo: Shakai Shisosha, 1994.

Shimizu Akira et al. *Nichi-Bei eigasen: Paru Haba 50-syunen.* Tokyo: Seikyusha, 1991.

Shindo Kaneto. *Shosetsu Tanaka Kinuyo.* Tokyo: Bungei Shunju, 1986.

Shioda Nagakazu. *Nihon eiga gojunen shi: 1941–91–nen.* Tokyo: Fujiwara Shoten, 1992.

Silverstein, Norman. "Kurosawa's Detective-Story Parables." *Japan Quarterly* 12, no. 3 (July–September 1965): 351–54.

Simone, R. Thomas. "The Mythos of 'The Sickness unto Death': Kurosawa's *Ikiru* and Tolstoy's *The Death of Ivan Ilych.*" *Literature/Film Quarterly* 3, no. 1 (winter 1975): 2–12.

Smith, Henry D., II. "Tokyo as an Idea: An Exploration of Japanese Urban Thought until 1945." *Journal of Japanese Studies* 4, no. 1 (winter 1978): 45–80.

Smith, Paul. *Clint Eastwood: A Cultural Production.* Minneapolis: University of Minnesota Press, 1993.

Staiger, Janet. "The Politics of Film Canons." *Cinema Journal* 24, no. 3 (1985).

———. *Interpreting Films: Studies in the Historical Reception of American Cinema.* Princeton, N.J.: Princeton University Press, 1992.

Stam, Robert, Robert Burgoyne, and Sandy Flitterman-Lewis. *New Vocabularies in Film Semiotics: Structuralism, Poststructuralism, and Beyond.* London: Routledge, 1992.

Stephanson, Anders. *Manifest Destiny: American Expansion and the Empire of Right.* New York: Hill and Wang, 1995.

Suematsu Norizumi. "Engeki kairyo enzetsu." *Jiji shinpo,* 6–12 October 1886. Reprinted in Kurata, *Geino.*

Suzuki Akinari. *Rappa to yobareta otoko: Eiga purodyusa Nagata Masaichi.* Tokyo: Kinema Junposha, 1990.

Suzuki Sadami. *Nihon no "bungaku" o kangaeru.* Tokyo: Kadokawa Shoten, 1994.

Suzuki Tadashi. *Engeki to wa nanika.* Tokyo: Iwanami Shoten, 1988.

Tada Michitaro. *Fukusei geijutsuron.* Tokyo: Keiso Shobo, 1962.

———. "The Destiny of Samurai Films." *East-West Film Journal* 1, no. 1 (December 1986).

Takenaka Tsutomu. *Kikigaki Arakan ichidai: Kurama Tengu no ojisan wa.* Kyoto: Shirakawa Shoin, 1976.

———. *Yamagami Itaro no sekai.* Kyoto: Shirakawa Shoin, 1976.

Takeuchi Yoshimi. *Nihon to Ajia.* Tokyo: Chikuma Shobo, 1993.

Takizawa Hajime. "Jidaigeki to wa nani ka: *Chuji tabinikki* o chushin to shite." In Imamura Shohei et al., *Koza Nihon eiga,* vol. 2.

Tanaka Jun'ichiro. *Nihon eiga hattatsushi.* 5 vols. Tokyo: Chuo Koronsha, 1975–76.

Tanizaki Jun'ichiro. *In Praise of Shadows.* Trans. Thomas J. Harper and Edward G. Seidensticker. New Haven, Conn.: Leete's Island Books, 1977.

Taut, Bruno. *Nippon.* Tokyo: Kodansha, 1991.

Terdiman, Richard. *Present/Past: Modernity and the Memory Crisis.* Ithaca, N.Y.: Cornell University Press, 1993.

Thompson, Ann. "Kurosawa's *Ran:* Reception and Interpretation." *East-West Film Journal* 3, no. 2 (June 1989): 1–13.

Thornton, S. A. "The Shinkokugeki and the Zenshinza: Western Representational Realism and the Japanese Period Film." *Asian Cinema* 7, no. 2 (winter 1995): 46–57.

Todorov, Tzvetan. *On Human Diversity: Nationalism, Racism, and Exoticism in French Thought.* Cambridge: Harvard University Press, 1993.

Toei junenshi. Tokyo: Toei, 1962.

Togawa Naoki. "Hitsunaru ningenkan: *Shichinin no samurai.*" *Eiga geijutsu* (July 1954): 56–60.

———. "Kurosawa Akira no shikaku gengo." In *Kurosawa Akira shusei III.*

Toida Michizo. "Kurosawa Akira no tokushitsu." *Eiga geijutsu* (March 1957): 51–53.

———. "Jidaimono to engi no dento." *Eiga geijutsu,* no. 129 (July 1958): 46–49.

Toyoda Minoru. *Nihon eigakushi no kenkyu.* Tokyo: Iwanami Shoten, 1939.

———. *Shakespeare in Japan: An Historical Survey.* Tokyo: Iwanami Shoten, 1940.

Tsuchiya Yoshio. *Kurosawa san! Kurosawa Akira tono subarashiki hibi.* Tokyo: Shinchosha, 1999.

Tsurumi Shunsuke. "Sengo no taishu bunka." In *Koza nihon eiga.* Vol. 4. Tokyo: Iwanami Shoten, 1986.

———. *Tenko kenkyu.* Tokyo: Chikuma Shobo, 1991.

Tsuruya Hisashi. *Kauboi no Beikoku shi.* Tokyo: Asahi Shinbunsha, 1989.

Tsusho Sangyosho, ed. *Eiga sangyo hakusho: Waga kuni eiga sangyo no genjo to shomondai.* Tokyo: Shobundo, 1963.

Tsutsui Kiyotada and Kato Mikiro, eds. *Jidaigeki eiga towa nanika: Nyu firumu sutadizu.* Kyoto: Jinbun Shoin, 1997.

Tsuzuki Masaaki. *Kurosawa Akira.* 2 vols. Tokyo: Intanaru Shuppan, 1976.

Uchida Tomu. "Jidaigeki wa kawatte yuku." *Eiga geijutsu,* no. 129 (July 1958): 34–35.

Ueno Koshi. *Nikutai no jidai: Taikenteki '60-nendai bunkaron.* Tokyo: Gendai Shokan, 1989.

"University Film Teaching in the United States." *Film Quarterly* 16, no. 3 (spring 1963).

Uraoka Keiichi. *Eiga henshu to wa nanika: Uraoka Keiichi no giho.* Tokyo: Heibonsha, 1994.

Uryu Tadao. *Eigateki seishin no keifu.* Tokyo: Getsuyo Shobo, 1947.

———. "Ikimono no kiroku: Kyomi bukai hasso." *Eiga geijutsu,* no. 100 (February 1956): 43–45.

Uryu Tadao, Hanada Kiyoteru, and Hirosue Tamotsu. "Shinpojiumu Kurosawa Akira." *Eiga geijutsu* (August 1962): 26–34, 102.

Varley, Paul. *Japanese Culture,* 3d ed. Honolulu: University of Hawaii Press, 1984.

Watanabe Tamotsu. *Kabuki: Kajonaru kigo no mori.* Tokyo: Chikuma Shobo, 1993.

————. *Kanjincho: Nihonjinron no genzo.* Tokyo: Chikuma Shobo, 1995.

Wellek, René. "The Crisis of Comparative Literature." In Nichols, *Concepts of Criticism.*

Whitaker, Sheila. Review of *To the Distant Observer: Form and Meaning in the Japanese Cinema,* by Noël Burch. *Framework* 11 (autumn 1979): 47–48.

Wolf, Barbara. "Detectives and Doctors." *Japan Quarterly* 19 (January–March 1972): 83–87.

————. "On Akira Kurosawa." *Yale Review* 64, no. 2 (December 1974): 218–26.

Wollen, Peter. *Signs and Meaning in the Cinema.* Bloomington: Indiana University Press, 1972.

Wood, Robin. *Hitchcock's Films Revisited.* New York: Columbia University Press, 1989.

"Workshop Discussion: Kurosawa Kaleidoscope." In Kawamoto et al., *The Force of Vision.*

Wright, Will. *Sixguns and Society: A Structural Study of the Western.* Berkeley: University of California Press, 1975.

Yakir, Dan. "The Warrior Returns." *Film Comment* 16, no. 6 (November–December 1980): 54–57.

Yamamoto Akira. "Jugonen senso ka, Nihon no senso eiga." In *Koza Nihon eiga,* vol. 4.

Yamamoto Kajiro. *Katsudoya suiro.* Tokyo: Chikuma Shobo, 1965.

Yamamoto Kikuo. *Nihon eiga ni okeru gaikoku eiga no eikyo: Hikaku eigashi kenkyu.* Tokyo: Waseda Daigaku Shuppanbu, 1983.

Yamamoto Shugoro. *Nichinichi heian.* Tokyo: Shinchosha, 1965.

————. *Kisetsu no nai machi.* Tokyo: Shinchosha, 1970.

Yanagida Izumi. *Meiji shoki hon'yaku bungaku no kenkyu.* Tokyo: Shunjusha, 1961.

Yodagawa Nagaharu. *Yodagawa Nagaharu Kurosawa Akira o kataru.* Tokyo: Kawadeshobo Shinsha, 1999.

Yoneda Yoshikazu. *Itami Mansaku.* Tokyo: Musashino Shobo, 1985.

Yoshida Chieo. *Mo hitotsu no eigashi: Katsuben no jidai.* Tokyo: Jiji Tsushinsha, 1978.

Yoshihara Yukari. "'Hankai' Nihon: 'Venisu no shonin' Meijiki hon'an." *Gendai shiso* 24, no. 3 (March 1996): 21–33.

Yoshimoto, Mitsuhiro. "The Difficulty of Being Radical: The Discipline of Film Studies and the Postcolonial World Order." In Miyoshi and Harootunian, *Japan in the World.*

Yoshino, Kosaku. *Cultural Nationalism in Contemporary Japan.* New York: Routledge, 1992.

Yoshioka Hiroshi. "Samurai and Self-Colonization in Japan." In *The Decolo-*

nization of Imagination: Culture, Knowledge, and Power, ed. Jan Nederveen Pieterse and Bhikhu Parekh. London: Zed Books, 1995.

Zambrano, Ana Laura. "*Throne of Blood:* Kurosawa's *Macbeth.*" *Literature/ Film Quarterly* 2 (summer 1974).

Žižek, Slavoj. *The Sublime Object of Ideology.* London: Verso, 1989.

———, ed. *Everything You Always Wanted to Know about Lacan (but Were Afraid to Ask Hitchcock).* London: Verso, 1992.

INDEX

327–31; and ambivalent representation of Japanese nation, 324–25, 330–31; audiovisual technology in, 321–24

High Treason incident (Taigyaku Jiken), 221

Hijikata Toshizo, 220

Hino Tomiko, 253, 420 n.8

Hirano Kyoko, 401 n.11

Hirata Akihiko, 295

Hiroshima, 366. *See also* Atomic bomb; Nagasaki; Nuclear fallout

Hisa Yoshitake, 228

Hisaita Eijiro, 119, 344, 375, 392 n.22

Hitchcock, Alfred, 30, 55–56

Hogaku (Japanese-style music), 263–64

Hoganbiiki, 94

Hojo Masako, 253, 420 n.8

Horikawa Hiromichi, 294

Horror film (*kaidan eiga*), 290

"House in the Village" (Mura no ie), 118, 123

Humanism: Kurosawa and, 88, 425 n.3

Humanity and Paper Balloons (Ninjo kamifusen), 237–38

Humor, 291, 296–97

Huston, John, 30

Ibsen, Henrik, 104

Ichikawa Danjuro VII, 107

Ichikawa Danjuro IX, 107–8, 111

Ichikawa Kon, 317, 335, 427 n.1

Ichikawa Raizo, 100

Ichikawa Utaemon, 100, 224, 227–28

Ide Masato, 355, 392 n.22

Identification, 201–3

Idiot, The (Hakuchi), 95, 177, 190–93, 351, 411 n.1

Ii Yoho, 399 n.35

Ike no Zenni, 253, 420 n.8

Ikeda Hayato, 288

Ikiru (Ikiru), 27, 60, 77, 94, 190, 194–204, 282, 326–27, 351, 411 n.1, 431 n.1

Image, 315; as opposed to reality, 180–81, 350–51

Imagination, 67, 337, 374; as opposed to reality, 339; power of, 343

Imai Tadashi, 231, 290–91

Imamura Shohei, 35

"In a Grove" (Yabu no naka), 182–83, 410 n.2

Inagaki Hiroshi, 240, 393 n.22

Individual will vs. social circumstances, 173–74

Innami Takaichi, 411 n.1

Inoue Kaoru, 106

Inoue Masao, 210

"Interactionist self," 243

International film festivals, 267

Irie Production, 298

Irie Takako, 298, 424 n.9

Ishihara Yujiro, 228

Ishimatsu of the Forest (Mori no Ishimatsu), 230

Isn't Life Wonderful, 135

Itami Juzo, 352

Itami Mansaku, 182, 235–38, 291, 417 n.70; on war responsibility, 126–27

Ito Daisuke, 215, 219, 236–37

Ito Hirobumi, 106

Iwasaki Akira, 262

Iwata Yukichi, 219

Izawa Shuji, 264

Jameson, Fredric, 45, 207

Japan vs. the West, 20

Japanese cinema; and cryptic images of the American Occupation, 408 n.23; humanist studies of, 18, 22–23; indifference of East

Moori Motonari, 355–56
Moral Manichaeism, 311–12; ambivalence of, 313, 328
Mori Arinori, 106
Mori Iwao, 125
Mori Kazuo, 238–39
Mori Masayuki, 192
Morita Kan'ya, 105
Morning with the Osone Family, A (Osoneke no asa), 118–19
Moroguchi Tsuzuya, 219
Morris, Ivan, 94
Most Beautiful, The (Ichiban utsukushiku), 81, 87–88, 326, 424 n.9
Motogi Sojiro, 140, 205
Multicamera shooting, 246–47, 322
Muraki Yoshiro, 270, 375
Music: Kurosawa's use of, 136–37, 246
Muttsuri Umon, 231

Nabeyama Sadachika, 122
Nagai Kafu, 221
Nagasaki, 364–69. *See also* Atomic bomb; Hiroshima; Nuclear fallout
Nagata Masaichi, 65, 82, 125, 188
Najita, Tetsuo, 18
Nakadai Tatsuya, 290, 294, 296, 304, 348, 353
Nakai Asakazu, 375
Nakamura Kinnosuke, 100, 228
Nakamura Kusatao, 236
Nakamura Mitsuo, 410 n.2
Nakane Chie, 18
Nakano Shigeharu, 118, 123
Nakazato Kaizan, 213, 220–21
Name: as a rebus, 163–65
Naoki Sanjugo, 214
Naruse Mikio, 35, 140
Narutaki-gumi, 392 n.22
National character, 10, 16–18; and

cinema, 17–18; and cultural patterns, 16; Japanese, 10–11, 16–17, 403 n.24
National cinema (*kokumin eiga*), 84–85, 262
National culture, 105
Natsume Soseki, 74
Naturalism, 394 n.12
Nature: in conventional Japanese films, 75–77; in Kurosawa films, 74–75, 77, 80, 345–47, 373–74
New Tales of the Taira Clan (Shin Heike monogatari), 230–31
New Wave, 274
Niblo, Fred, 231
Nichinichi heian (Peaceful Everyday), 294
Night Drum (Yoru no tsuzumi), 231
Night of the Doll Festival, The (Hinamatsuri no yoru), 211
Nihon Roman-ha (Japanese romanticists), 264
Nihonga (Japanese-style painting), 263–65
Nihonjinron, 26, 403 n.24
Nikaten, 236, 338
Nikkatsu, 210, 214, 228, 298, 352
Ninjo, 18, 234, 312
Ninjutsu (art of the ninja) film, 208, 229
Nishimura Yuichiro, 136
No Regrets for Our Youth (Waga seishun ni kuinashi), 62, 114–22, 128, 133–34, 172, 186, 326, 351, 359, 368, 401 n.11
Noh, 99–101, 107–8, 263, 266, 273; in *Kagemusha*, 111, 352; in *The Men Who Tread on the Tiger's Tail*, 92, 267, 352; orientalist appropriation of, 267; in *Sanshiro Sugata, Part 2*, 92; in *Throne of Blood*, 111, 252–54, 261–62, 267–69

Mitsuhiro Yoshimoto is Associate Professor of Japanese, Cinema, and Comparative Literature at the University of Iowa.

Library of Congress Cataloging-in-Publication Data

Yoshimoto, Mitsuhiro
Kurosawa : film studies and Japanese cinema / Mitsuhiro Yoshimoto.
p.   cm. — (Asia-Pacific : culture, politics, and society)
Includes filmography.
Includes bibliographical references and index.
ISBN 0-8223-2483-0 (cloth : alk. paper) —
ISBN 0-8223-2519-5 (pbk. : alk. paper)
1. Kurosawa, Akira, 1910 — Criticism and interpretation.
I. Title.   II. Asia-Pacific.
PN1998.3.K87 Y67   2000
— dc21
99-056661